The Noble Flame of Katherine Philips

Medieval & Renaissance Literary Studies

Originally titled the *Duquesne Studies: Philological Series* (and later renamed the *Language & Literature Series*), the ***Medieval & Renaissance Literary Studies Series*** has been published by Duquesne University Press since 1960. This publishing endeavor seeks to promote the study of late medieval, Renaissance, and seventeenth century English literature by presenting scholarly and critical monographs, collections of essays, editions, and compilations. The series encourages a broad range of interpretation, including the relationship of literature and its cultural contexts, close textual analysis, and the use of contemporary critical methodologies.

The Noble Flame of
KATHERINE PHILIPS

A Poetics of Culture, Politics, and Friendship

Edited by David L. Orvis and Ryan Singh Paul

DUQUESNE UNIVERSITY PRESS
Pittsburgh, Pennsylvania

Published in the United States of America by
Duquesne University Press
600 Forbes Avenue
Pittsburgh, Pennsylvania 15282

Library of Congress Cataloging-in-Publication Data

The noble flame of Katherine Philips : a poetics of culture, politics, and friendship / eadited by David L. Orvis and Ryan Singh Paul.
pages cm. — (Medieval & renaissance literary studies)
Includes bibliographical references and index.
Summary: "This collection of essays devoted to Interregnum and Restoration poet Katherine Philips explores cultural poetics and the courtly coterie, innovation and influence in poetic and political form, and articulations of female friendship, homoeroticism, and retreat"— Provided by publisher.
ISBN 978-0-8207-0474-6 (hardcover : alk. paper)
1. Philips, Katherine, 1632–1664—Criticism and interpretation. I. Orvis, David L., editor. II. Paul, Ryan Singh, 1976– editor.

PR3619.P4Z85 2015
821'.4—dc23

2015010923

∞ Printed on acid-free paper.

For
Meg Lota Brown
Kari Boyd McBride
Kathryn M. Moncrief
Susan C. Staub

But since your boundless mind upon my head,
Some rays of splendour is content to shed . . .
You must endure my vows, and find the way
To entertain such Rites as I can pay.

— *Katherine Philips, "To my Lady M. Cavendish, choosing the name of Policrite"*

Contents

Acknowledgments ix

Introduction 1
David L. Orvis and Ryan Singh Paul

1. Katherine Philips and the Post-Courtly Coterie 41
Catharine Gray

2. The Failure of Royalist Heroic Virtue: Philips's "On the 3. of September, 1651" 65
Christopher Orchard

3. Biblical Poetics, Royalist Politics, and Anti-Eschatological Prophecy in Philips's Poetry 87
David L. Orvis

4. Restoring Orinda's Face: Puritan Iconoclasm and Philips's *Poems* as Royalist Remonumentalization 125
Amy Scott-Douglass

5. Inventing the English Sappho: Katherine Philips's Donnean Poetry 153
Paula Loscocco

6. Katherine Philips at the Wedding 187
Elizabeth Hodgson

7. The Conjuncture of Word, Music, and Performance Practice in Philips's Era 213
Linda Phyllis Austern

8. "Friendship so Curst": *Amor Impossibilis,* the Homoerotic Lament, and the Nature of *Lesbian* Desire 243
Valerie Traub

9. The Body of the Friend and the Woman Writer: Katherine Philips's Absence from Alan Bray's *The Friend* 267
Lorna Hutson

10. Versions of Pastoral: Philips and Women's Queer Spaces 291
Harriette Andreadis

Afterword: The Most Deservedly Admired Mrs. Katherine Philips—Her Books 311
Elizabeth H. Hageman

Notes 325

Bibliography 399

About the Contributors 439

Index 443

Acknowledgments

This volume could not have been completed without the support and encouragement of numerous parties, to which the editors owe immense gratitude. First and foremost, we would like to thank our contributors for their excellent work as well as their grace and patience during an admittedly long process of revision. It has been a pleasure to work with such a fabulous group of scholars who share our excitement for the future of Philips criticism. We are especially grateful to Elizabeth Hageman for reading the manuscript cover to cover and sharing her inimitable acumen and expertise at every stage of the process. At Duquesne University Press, we would like to thank our anonymous readers for their trenchant feedback; Susan Wadsworth-Booth and Rebecca Totaro for their enthusiasm and support for this project from its inception; and Kathy Meyer for helping to transform our sprawling manuscript into a coherent collection of essays. At Appalachian State University, we would like to thank Anthony Calamai, dean of Arts and Sciences, and Carl Eby, chair of the English Department, for generously providing subventions for some of the book's reprinted material. The cover image is taken from a copy of the 1667 *Poems* gifted to David Orvis by John and Paula Mitcherling; their unwavering support in this and all his endeavors, whether professional or personal, means more than words will allow. Finally, the editors would like to offer our heartfelt thanks to Meg Lota Brown, Kari Boyd McBride, Kathryn M. Moncrief, and Susan C. Staub—mentors who continue to inspire us and influence our work, and to whom we appreciatively dedicate this volume.

Introduction

> Let the male Poets their male Phoebus chuse,
> Thee I invoke, Orinda, for my Muse;
> He could but force a Branch, Daphne her Tree
> Most freely offers to her Sex and thee,
> And says to Verse, so unconstrain'd as yours,
> Her Laurel freely comes, your fame secures:
> And men no longer shall with ravish'd Bays
> Crown their forc'd Poems by as forc'd a praise.
>
> —Philo-Philippa, "To the Excellent Orinda"

I. *"I but knew you by report"*

Katherine Fowler was born on or around New Year's Day, 1632, to John Fowler and Katherine Oxenbridge of London, their only daughter.[1] Her family was of the middling sort, part of the growing merchant classes of London. John Fowler seems to have been quite successful as a cloth merchant in Bucklersbury; at the time of his death in 1642, he left a comfortable estate to his heirs, including a £1,000 marriage portion for Katherine in addition to her £400 inheritance. Through her mother Katherine was related to a number of prominent and radical-minded Puritans, including her great-grandfather and her uncle, both named John Oxenbridge, both Puritan radicals; the younger would become an intimate of Andrew Marvell and John Milton. Her earliest biographer, John Aubrey, notes both her intellect and her piety; whether or not his reports of her puritanical leanings as a child are strictly accurate, there is no doubt that she grew up in a familial and social environment bristling with radical sentiment.

According to Aubrey, when Katherine was eight years old she entered a boarding school in Hackney run by a Presbyterian schoolmistress named Mrs. Salmon. During her years at school, she forged friendships with Mary Aubrey and Mary Harvey, the first in a series of significant relationships that would define her personal and professional lives. Offering access to the social circles of royalists in retreat, these friendships spurred the young Katherine's interest in Cavalier ideologies and poetics at a time when England was torn by the civil wars, and when other personal ties drew Katherine closer to those counted among the king's parliamentary enemies.

Sometime around 1646, it seems, Katherine moved with her mother to Pembrokeshire in Wales. The elder Katherine had remarried, to Sir Richard Phillipps of Picton Castle. (This was, in fact, her third marriage: after the death of John Fowler, she had married a man named George Henley sometime around 1640.) Two years later, her 16-year-old daughter would marry a relative of her stepfather, James Philips, whose own family home was Cardigan Priory, in southwest Cardiganshire, Wales. In 1655, a long-awaited son, Hector, died in infancy, but a daughter, Katherine, was born the next year and lived to adulthood. Her husband's career—first as an officer in the parliamentary forces during the civil wars, and then as an official for the commonwealth—apparently kept Katherine away from London for the rest of her life. And yet, as a member of Parliament, James Philips was duty-bound to spend time in London as well, and Katherine's friendships with various Londoners suggest that she sometimes joined him there.

Scholarly consensus holds that the Society of Friendship was a virtual community existing solely in the realm of circulated manuscripts with few if any actual physical encounters between its members; the extent to which its members even considered this network as a nameable "society" is, in fact, uncertain. Still, it is clear that Philips was inspired in part by the court of Queen Henrietta Maria and the fashion in France at the time for literary salons. Philips was at the center of the society and she handpicked the predominantly royalist women and men who would gain admittance. She also conferred upon some members pseudonyms borrowed from a variety of classical and contemporary sources; hers was "Orinda." Mary Aubrey was "Rosania," while Mary Harvey's husband, Edward Dering, was known as "Silvander." Other important figures included Philips's husband ("Antenor"), her close friend Anne Owen ("Lucasia"), and the prominent courtier Charles Cotterell ("Poliarchus"); scholars have identified more than 20 in total, revealing a network of influential literary and political figures.

During the Interregnum, Philips's poetry circulated among this alternative literary coterie, gaining her admirers and growing her reputation. Her work ranged across genres, modes, and forms: she wrote epithalamia and elegies, pastorals and panegyrics, dialogues and Pindaric odes; she even tried her hand quite successfully at dramatic translation. Although Philips worked primarily in the circulatory manuscript culture of the seventeenth century coterie, her significance as a poet is attested also by her appearance in a few notable print publications. The public and published face of her career began auspiciously with a commendatory verse in the 1651 edition of William Cartwright's *Comedies, Tragi-Comedies, with Other Poems*. The 19-year-old Philips's poem is titled "To the most Ingenious and Vertuous Gentleman Mr. Wil: Cartwright, my much valued Friend" and is the only one written by a woman; many prominent royalists were among the other 53 (male) commenders, including Dering (Silvander).

Philips had a variety of other prominent literary engagements in her short career. Henry Lawes, who was also included in the Cartwright volume, set at least four of her verses to music, one of which was published in his 1655 *Second Book of Ayres and Dialogues*. In 1657, the Anglican divine Jeremy Taylor would dedicate his treatise on friendship, *A Discourse on the Nature, Offices and Measures of Friendship,* to Philips, declaring on its title page that the work was written in response to her query about the relationship between Christian ethics and the ethics of friendship. In

1663, Abraham Cowley's Pindaric ode "On *Orinda's Poems*" was published in the miscellany *Poems, by Several Persons* alongside Philips's own ode "Upon Mr. Abraham Cowley's Retirement." While in Dublin in 1662, Philips met Roger Boyle, Earl of Orrery, who encouraged her in the successful performance and publication of her *Pompey*. And in addition to those directed at Charles II and his immediate court, Philips addressed in verse other prominent cultural and political figures of the period, including Henry Vaughan, Elizabeth Boyle, Ann Boyle, and Margaret Cavendish. The relationships fostered through the society's network clearly aided Philips in overcoming her geographic isolation and spreading her name and her poetry to prominent figures in the Isles.

Unfortunately, Philips's career ended abruptly, just as it seemed poised to take off. The Restoration of Charles II offered opportunities for advancement for a skilled poet of royalist sympathies, and Philips had connections with the court, most significantly through Charles Cotterell. Through him, Philips would present to the Duchess of York a special manuscript copy of her translation of Corneille's *La mort de Pompée,* after its successful debut in Dublin and subsequent publication there and in London. At the beginning of 1664, in response to his sense of an untapped market, Richard Marriott printed an apparently unauthorized edition of Philips's poems. It was quickly suppressed by her London contacts and retracted with apologies by Marriott; both parties wished expressly for an official version from the author's hand. The scene attests both to a public demand for Philips's work as well an intense sensitivity among many interested parties regarding her public image. In any case, she would be unable to participate in plans for future publication, should there have been any. In June 1664, Katherine contracted smallpox and died. Thomas adds a poignant detail in his biography: "A note in a manuscript in the National Library of Wales records that Rosania, her first great friend, tended her during this final illness. She was buried in the church where her little son had been interred."[2] An amended and self-asserted "official" edition of her *Poems* appeared in 1667, reprinted in 1669 and 1678; Tonson would print it in 1710. W. Onley printed a volume of

Familiar Letters in 1697 (reprinted 1699), and Bernard Lintot published two editions of *Letters from Orinda to Poliarchus* in 1705 and 1729. Her poetry would not see formal publication again until the early years of the twentieth century.

With editions of her poetry going out of print within a few decades of her death, Philips seems to have fallen into relative obscurity, at least compared to the praise that attended her during her life and immediately after. Critics explain Philips's apparent demotion to minor poet in a variety of ways. Paula Loscocco attributes the poet's decline to the emergence of a neoclassical culture that radically changed the literary valuations associated with gender to the point that "literary femininity... had in fact become a potent tool of critical dispraise."[3] Penelope Anderson argues that over the course of the seventeenth century, as early manuscript readers stripped away the political meanings of her friendship poems, Philips's "innovative use of the entangled politics and passions of *amicitia* becomes illegible." Consequently, Philips is characterized as "a minor writer, the well-behaved modest poetess who wrote verse about the inconsequential subject of women's friendship."[4] This would come to be the dominant view of Philips held by early twentieth century scholars.

Still, we should remember that Orinda's reputation remained strong for a number of years after her death and that she continued to find an audience among those in the know. Gillian Wright calls our attention to the fact that "Philips was also the first English woman writer to be regularly cited, almost always with approval, by other members of her own sex." She was cited, explicitly and implicitly, by many significant women writers of the seventeenth century, serving as a model of the successful and respected woman writer. Indeed, Wright even argues that Philips more so than Aphra Behn "marks the start of a coherent and self-conscious tradition of women's writing in English."[5] But her influence was not confined solely to women authors or readers, nor can it be limited to the realm of "women's writing." Noted male authors also found in Philips much to inspire and enjoy. "You must have heard of her, and mostly likely read her Poetry," writes John Keats in a letter to John Hamilton Reynolds: "I wish you have not, that I may have the pleasure of treating you with a few stanzas—I do it at a venture.—You will not regret reading them once more."[6] The poem Keats dutifully copies out is "To Mrs. M. A. at Parting," one of several friendship poems Philips addresses to Mary Aubrey, the Rosania of Orinda's Society of Friendship. So although Philips may have faded from the mass literary consciousness, her work still drew admirers and maintained a significant, if modest, popularity.

Nearly 200 years after the publication of the 1710 edition of Philips's collected works—the last time her work had been published—George Saintsbury included her in the first volume of his *Minor Poets of the Caroline Period*.[7] Conventionally, Saintsbury's anthology has been considered as marking rediscovery of Philips and the beginning of modern scholarship on her life and works. But ironically, her renaissance went hand-in-hand with her aesthetic and intellectual marginalization. The respect accorded to her by her peers was not shared by the early twentieth century critics, who would assess Philips as unoriginal, a minor talent notable more for her personal associations with notable courtiers than her literary talents.

To speak more accurately, Katherine Philips has only experienced her restoration in the latter end of the twentieth century. Philips's return to the literary canon began with feminist, lesbian, gay, and queer critics who, in the 1980s and 1990s, marshaled her works into debates at the intersections of gender, sexuality, politics, and religion. Introducing Philips into a range of disciplinary discussions, these pathbreaking studies have shaped, and indeed continue to shape, the trajectory of contemporary Philips criticism. And just as the elusive nature of Philips's personal affections and the amenability of her works to erotic readings have made sexuality a central scholarly locus, recent works confirm a turn toward her equally slippery politics as the nature and extent of her royalism has been questioned. In both of these overlapping and mutually affecting discourses, Philips's poetry has been used to challenge old hierarchies and undermine exclusivist, identitarian divisions.

As editors of the first scholarly collection devoted to the poetry of Katherine Philips, we intend this book both to demonstrate the "state of the art" in scholarship at the present moment, and to reorient current understandings of Philips and her milieu. Some of the essays collected here address methodological and theoretical concerns posed by earlier scholarship, while others focus on developing and expanding pertinent cultural, religio-political, and philosophical contexts. Still others attend to generic and formal considerations or to the material conditions of manuscript and print. Of the foundational essays addressed, five are reprinted in this volume. One of these essays—Elizabeth Hodgson's "Katherine Philips at the Wedding"—has been revised and expanded with the aims of this collection in mind.[8] The other reprinted essays—by Catharine Gray, Lorna Hutson, Paula Loscocco, and Valerie Traub—include newly written authors' and editors' notes that resituate their arguments within Philips scholarship.[9] Collectively, the new and reprinted works that follow will, we hope, help set the course for future Philips scholarship even while enlarging its boundaries.

II. *"Teach the World a new love"*

Philips's friendship poems have played the biggest role in her restoration to the English canon. It is through these poems—passionate articulations of female intimacy and devotional friendship—that scholars first began to investigate Philips's complex articulations of affective and political subjectivity. Yet it is these same poems that seem to be responsible for her early critical dismissal as her rediscovery went hand-in-hand with her aesthetic and intellectual marginalization by literary critics of the early twentieth century. In his 1931 biography, Philip Webster Souers ultimately dismisses Philips as a poet capable of generating "little enthusiasm," obsessed to an unhealthy and almost comic degree with the fantasy of a "Platonic mingling of the souls" with her female friends.[10] Attention colored by disdain was a recurrent feature of early criticism about the poet, which often mocked her expressions of devotion as hysterical. "When her poetry was rediscovered in the nineteenth century and first made widely available," writes Elizabeth Wahl, "there was a critical tendency to dismiss her idealization of female friendship as largely banal and full of affectation."[11] Although Edmund Gosse states that Philips made an important contribution to the development of discourses of friendship, "his actual descriptions of both Philips's poetry and her relations with her female friends suggest he found her version of idealized friendship to be narcissistic, affected, and silly."[12] These early scholars then argued that the "triteness" they found in Philips's poetry explains—and hence explains away—the passionate expressions between women as mere pretense; move along, nothing to see here. In his "dogmatic introduction to the first modern edition of Philips's poems," observes Wahl, "Saintsbury attempts to negate any erotic reading of the poems; at the same time, he uses a bowdlerized version of their thematics of friendship in order to deny them any literary merit."[13] Souers concludes his biography by damning Philips with faint praise:

> Her greatest claim to attention is that she was among the few who kept alive in the teeth of Puritan scorn and persecution the old court tradition, and handed it over ready for use to the returning wits of the Restoration. On the actual merits of her writing, little enthusiasm is possible, even to one who has come to know her well. To the student of the drama her translations will always prove interesting, but they probably will never call forth more commendation than that due to a task well done. Her appeal must come from her other works. The spirited portrait that she draws of herself in the *Letters to Poliarchus,* and the few agreeable, if somewhat artificial, songs and poems that represent the luckier moments of a gift by no means contemptible, should always find admirers, even among the more particular of general readers.[14]

Philips's greatest achievement, in other words, was to preserve a masculine political tradition she inherited until male royalists, the true artists, could return from exile and resume their rightful place on top of England's literary scene. In Souers's opinion, the real measure of Philips's artistry is the extent to which she maintained these conventions without adulteration or effeminization.

These early critics enacted a double erasure, dismissing her poetry as an inferior imitation of masculine verse while also obscuring the ways in which Philips departed from or even challenged dominant traditions.

In breaking with these reactionary early judgments, modern scholars of Philips assert that she gives voice to an important subjective experience that deserves recovery from, and renewed expression after, a long history of patriarchal exclusion. Their work has challenged the epithet "minor," demonstrating Philips to be a significant and original voice in the seventeenth century. One aspect of this work has involved a critical reexamination of her relation to her male forebears and contemporaries; in turn, this has led to rethinking conventionally accepted lines of influence and recognition of Philips as an innovator. Another aspect, inextricably linked to the first, has focused on questions of desire and sexual identity, reading Philips as vocalizing an erotically transgressive female subject.

Published in 1981, Lillian Faderman's *Surpassing the Love of Men: Romantic Friendship and Love between Women from the Renaissance to the Present* is a landmark text in both Philips scholarship and lesbian literary criticism, providing one of the earliest significant critical commentaries on the poet. According to Faderman, the passionate language through which Philips's friendships find expression bears a striking resemblance to more modern articulations of lesbian desire. "Had she written in the twentieth century," Faderman surmises, "her poetry would undoubtedly have been identified as 'lesbian.'" Yet, Faderman distinguishes sharply between early modern romantic friendship and modern lesbianism on the grounds that Philips's works seem to conform to "a model of the perfect romantic friend as an expression of platonism which delighted not in physicality but in the union of souls and in philosophizing and poetizing."[15] Setting spirituality against physicality, Faderman points to Philips's emphasis on the mingling of souls rather than of bodies as evidence that her poems represent not an early modern instantiation of lesbian desire, but a platonically inspired female friendship.[16]

Like any pioneering study, *Surpassing the Love of Men* drew effusive praise as well as spirited critique, often from the same scholars. Unsurprisingly, the increasing critical attention paid to Faderman's argument correlated with a renewed interest in, and wider circulation of, Philips's works, while the context established the core methodological concerns with which early Philips criticism grappled. In a sustained critique of Faderman, Liz Stanley enumerates three controversies surrounding romantic female friendship that would also become foci of Philips scholarship:

> One controversy concerns whether the notion of romantic friendship is itself a romantic idea that denies the erotic and/or sexual element in such relationships through operating as a form of conceptual imperialism: the theory says that such friendships were not sexual, and the nature of actual friendships is then deduced from the theory. A related controversy concerns the specification of lesbianism as a late-nineteenth-century phenomenon, rather than either a form of conduct with earlier origins, or indeed origins which lie in behaviours which predate the invention of labels which gloss them. A third controversy overlaps with the concerns of predominantly, if not exclusively, gay male historians with the "essentialist v. constructionist" debate concerning "the homosexual." Proponents of romantic friendship see "the lesbian" as the invention of a group of male "sexologists," who constructed "the lesbian" as a specific and different kind of person who was, as part of her condition, "mannish," and then applied this stereotype to erstwhile romantic friends in order to discredit these relationships.[17]

Taken together, these controversies form the contours of debates over cultural and historical alterity and continuity that have scrutinized many prior assumptions about the sexual practices (and identities) of historical persons.[18] To assume, for instance, that early modern expressions of female romantic friendship represent precursors to modern articulations of lesbian desire is to collapse and confound disparate periods and cultures.[19] It is no less problematic, however, to assume that in the absence of the sexological discourse that gave rise to the homo/hetero divide, women could not have fostered meaningful erotic relations or identities among one another.[20] To negotiate these controversies, Stanley proposes "a middle way, one which does not impose a theoretical structure on the lives and experiences of historical people, but which recognizes that love between women could take many shapes and meanings, one of which was an erotic genital sexual involvement which had meaning specific to these persons and their time and social location."[21] Like Sedgwick's widely cited definition of "queer" as referring to an "open mesh of possibilities," Stanley's "middle way" aims to open up, rather than cordon off or explain away, a multiplicity of erotic, affective, and even identificatory possibilities for women-desiring women.[22]

While debates in queer studies over the costs and benefits of historicist frameworks have brought historicism *qua* historicism under scrutiny, queer Philips criticism has, by and large, remained committed to lesbian historiography.[23] Although Elaine Hobby has been criticized for identifying Philips as a "closeted" "seventeenth century lesbian poet," few scholars have found it prudent to dispense with either concept.[24] While taking Hobby and others to task for their essentialist analyses, Paula Loscocco nonetheless finds "lesbian" a productive concept for evaluating Philips's verse: "Philips's Commonwealth-era poetry, the Restoration commendatory verses, and our own critical responses turn out to occupy different points within a single (if complex) cultural narrative of (early) modern lesbianism. Only as we become critically self-conscious about our place in that story can we resist its pressure to identify texts and sexuality in literal and reductive ways, and begin to perceive Philips's actual achievement."[25] Drawing correlations between Donne's "Sappho to Philaenis" and Philips's own use of Sappho, Loscocco writes, "In the transition from Donne's to Philips's poems, Sappho evolves from a failed if fascinating conceit, Donne's ingenious poetical object, to the eponymous progenitor of a coherently Sapphic discourse—a uniquely female and libidinal rhetoric available for a variety of expressive purposes." In Philips's hands, this discourse "openly celebrate[s] its status as a homoerotic and discursively sapphic text," a gesture that reads uncannily like a lesbian coming-out narrative.[26]

The question, then, is not whether to use "lesbian" at all, but rather how best to deploy the concept without obfuscating meaningful differences between early modern and modern articulations of female homoerotic desire. Three books published within a few years of one another forcefully make the case for Philips's pivotal role in the history of lesbianism while articulating the nature of that history in different terms: Elizabeth Susan Wahl's *Invisible Relations: Representations of Female Intimacy in the Age of Enlightenment*; Harriette Andreadis's *Sappho in Early Modern England: Female Same-Sex Literary Erotics, 1500–1714*; and Valerie Traub's *The Renaissance of Lesbianism in Early Modern England*.[27] Keenly aware that the term "poses problems because it requires a disclaimer of any contemporary connotations," Wahl uses "lesbian" in its adjectival sense "to describe relations of intimacy between women, partly because women rarely refer to their own sexual experiences in explicit terms and partly because many of them were struggling to find a language with which to define their love for one another in opposition to the strongly hierarchical and phallocentric model of heterosexual relations."[28] Wahl speaks not of subjectivity but of "sensibility," one that in Philips's case renders visible "internal tensions between a platonic ethos of egalitarianism and mutuality and an underlying eroticism that she expressed through the use of a courtly language of conquest, submission, and carnal pleasure."[29] This sensibility signifies a potentially transgressive homoeroticism that punctures heterosocial fantasies of female friendship's innocence.

Although her project differs from Wahl's in fundamental ways, Andreadis shares the conviction that "a terminology that is not problematized attributes to an earlier era the relatively recent notion of 'lesbian' identity and assumes its transhistorical presence."[30] Rather than use "lesbian" to name what Wahl calls "invisible relations," Andreadis leverages the term's origins in nineteenth century sexology in order to throw into sharp relief distinctions between modern lesbian discourse and early modern Sapphic discourse. This framework enables Andreadis to map out women writers' strategies for producing a nonthreatening form of female same-sex literary erotics. Nevertheless, in tracing the emergence of Sapphic discourse, Andreadis identifies Philips's homoerotic verse as site of iconic convergence, a place where Sapphists and lesbians meet, if only in retrospect: "That these texts not only are now amenable to lesbian reading, but also spoke to contemporary female readers of their own feelings and attachments, is evidenced by the response of Philo-Philippa and by the popularity and influences of Philips's texts among the seventeenth-century woman writers who followed her."[31] Thus, whereas Wahl uses "lesbian" to designate "invisible relations," Andreadis situates both "lesbian" and "Sapphist" in their respective milieu and in a larger history of "erotic ellipsis"—that is, of either trivializing or ignoring sexual acts that do not mimic "valorized male penetrative action."[32]

Foregrounding the heuristic value of "lesbian" as a category of analysis, Traub proposes in *The Renaissance of Lesbianism* a "lesbian-affirmative analytic" that "resists the opening move of much lesbian scholarship, which begins by defining its central term: 'a lesbian is *x*.'" Instead, Traub employs "lesbian" as "a strategic anachronism as well as an ongoing question: how does it function, what investments does it carry with it, what aims does it achieve?"[33] This "strategic anachronism" allows Traub to attend simultaneously to alterity and continuity as she delineates the increasingly intertwined trajectories of the tribade and the female friend, two figures who were not always associated with each other. Like Wahl and Andreadis, Traub (in an excerpt included in this collection) considers Philips an important figure in lesbian historiography since her verse "functions as a symptomatic break: between the Renaissance discourse of chaste, innocuous insignificance, on the one hand, and the increasingly public discourse of illicit desire that carries with it the stigma of significance, on the other."[34] This "symptomatic break" provides the conditions for what Traub, following Joel Fineman, calls "a 'subjectivity effect' of and for homoerotic verse"—an "effect," in other words, that leaves open the possibility for a "lesbian" subjectivity that predates, and thus remains fundamentally detached from, those "lesbian" subjects produced by modern regimes of gender and sexuality.[35]

As Wahl, Andreadis, and Traub continue to rework and refine their approaches both to Philips and to lesbian historiography, other scholars have been building on and extending this work in a variety of ways.[36] In *Closeted Writing and Lesbian and Gay Literature: Classical, Early Modern, Eighteenth-Century,* David M. Robinson demonstrates that while the concept of "the closet" might be a distinctly modern invention, the act of hiding or veiling one's (homo)sexual desires dates back to antiquity and thus was a strategy available to Philips. In a chapter devoted in part to "Philo-Philippa," the otherwise anonymous author of the commendatory poem "To the Excellent Orinda" from the 1667 *Poems,* Robinson shows how the poet's artful revisions of Ovidian myths produce a coded lesbian writing. Folding lesbian-affirmative appropriations of Ovid's tales of Iphis and Ianthe and of Apollo and Daphnae into the standard conventions of commendatory verse, Philo-Philippa offers paean both to Philips's art and, for the knowing few, the lesbian desires it expresses.[37]

Other recent work on representations of female-female eroticism in Philips's verse focuses on their inscription in the discursive structure of early modern friendship. Influenced by Alan Bray's pioneering research on ethical (male) friendship, Andreadis and Hutson have published essays demonstrating we still have much to learn about the (homo)erotics of (female) amity.[38] Building on Bray's analysis of the signal tropes of male friendship, Andreadis argues that "Philips's use of the discourse of 'union' both to affirm her passion for her female friends in her poems and to create a sociofamilial network of intimate relations exemplifies female appropriate of masculine—and masculinist—ideology."[39] Many of Philips's friendship poems, Andreadis claims, serve as rejoinders to Jeremy Taylor's *A Discourse of the Nature, Offices, and Measures of Friendship with Rules of Conducting It* (1657)—a treatise, according to its title page, "written in answer to a Letter from the most ingenious and vertuous M. K. P. [Mrs. Katherine Philips]."[40] As Andreadis points out, Taylor's masculinist responses rely wholly on examples of friendships between men; what is more, Taylor draws the conclusion that women should only cultivate bonds of amity with their husbands. This hegemonic definition of friendship provides at least one impetus for Philips's friendship poems: to "passionately rearticulate the prose precepts of popular treatises on male friendship."[41] Turning to Philips's correspondence with Sir Charles Cotterell, Andreadis shows that this homoerotic, Sapphic rearticulation of friendship is echoed in the representation of heterosocial bonds: "The letters illustrate the complexities of her friendship with Sir Charles: her many attempts to bring him closer into her family circle and the ways in which she implicated him as a go-between in her homoerotic relationship with Owen, displacing the agency for her erotic desires into a heterosocially acceptable framework."[42]

Like Andreadis, Hutson aims to reassess Philips's versions of friendship vis-à-vis the male model espoused by Taylor and analyzed by Bray. In an essay reprinted in this collection, Hutson takes as her starting point Philips's conspicuous absence from Bray's *The Friend*. She seeks to "reopen, in the spirit of inquiry and dialogue on these issues, which Bray himself did so much to foster, the question of how his persuasive narrative of radical change in the meaning of the body as signifier of (male) friendship might prompt a rethinking of the relation of embodiment to the cultural capital of friendship in seventeenth century women's writing, as exemplified by Katherine Philips."[43] Whereas the body of the male friend became a site of contestation as signs of intimacy increasingly became signs of sodomy, female friendship faced very different obstacles. Hutson argues that "for Philips, as a woman writer, the difficulty lies not in the need to distinguish ethical bodily gestures from transgressive sexual ones but in the very claim of writings on female friendship to signify as ethical and political at all."[44] From this vantage, Philips's absence from *The Friend* illustrates not a defect on Bray's part, but rather the incommensurability of male and female models of friendship and the radical nature of Philips's outspoken assertions of female intimacy. More than a placeholder, Philips emerges from her reconsideration by these scholars as an innovative, even transgressive, poet, not simply parroting the discourse of more accomplished male poets but constructing a new language of desire.

III. *"And all our titles shuffled so"*

Early critics such as Souers and Saintsbury likely were discomfited not only by the suggestive eroticism of Philips's works, but also by the ideological challenges her poetry posed to tradition. As Hutson reminds us, complicated and subtle transactions take place between the affective and the political realms; the unsilencing of Philips raises questions not only about sexual identity but also about the role of gender in structuring political relations. In her study on the English civil wars, Ann Hughes calls attention to the importance of gender in the political scene of the mid-seventeenth century. She highlights both the gendered nature of political ideology in the period and the messy, complicated realities of men and women's roles in the wars. Bringing together social and political histories through a gendered analysis, Hughes not only shows how numerous women played an active part in the various factions competing for power but also articulates the ways in which the overlapping realms of the political and the domestic transformed cultural understandings of man- and womanhood.[45] By adopting the explicitly male and political discourse of friendship, Philips infiltrates and unsettles the masculinist, heterosocial order, prompting further examination of her female relationships vis-à-vis the demands of the state. As with scholarship addressed to questions of homoerotic desire, this work demonstrates both the importance of Philips's political engagements and the slipperiness of pinning her down with one label or another.

The range of scholarship produced to account for and redress Philips's absence from literary and historical studies of the English civil wars, the Interregnum, and the Restoration has undermined Souers's claim that Orinda was merely a placeholder for exiled royalist men. Critics have placed Philips in dialogue with the literary discourse of the ousted cavaliers and interpreted her scenes of female intimacy and pastoral retreat as implicit critiques of factionalism, intolerance, and absolutism. Reading Philips's works against these vicissitudes reveals, to quote Robert C. Evans, "a poet of contradictions who lived and wrote in highly contradictory times."[46] Critics have attended to these contradictions in a variety of ways, situating Philips's works in a range of philosophical and religio-political debates. One of the key debates has concerned Philips's monarchism, complicating assumptions about a simplistic devotion to royalist ideals and revealing the subtle challenges to absolutism embedded within her panegyrics to the Stuarts and their supporters.

Responding at least in part to the breadth of scholarship on the (homo)erotics of Philips's (female) friendships, scholarship has sought to delineate the philosophical and political dimensions of Orinda's poetry, most particularly through her role in creating her Society of Friendship. Patrick Thomas was among the first to highlight Philips's importance as an explicitly royalist poet, based first on her opening commendatory poem in the 1651 edition of Cartwright, a volume with "strong [royalist] political overtones."[47] Although critics have pointed out that Cartwright was probably not, in fact, Philips's "much valued Friend,"[48] and that the poem is more a gesture of solidarity with fellow royalists, the inclusion of her verse in the Cartwright collection indicates that the matchless Orinda experienced a meteoric rise in royalist circles despite her Puritan upbringing and middle-class background. In his edition of Philips's verse, Thomas argues that her friendship poems were implicitly political "plea[s] for harmony," noting that Philips addresses her Parliamentarian husband by the name "Antenor," the Trojan counselor who attempted to negotiate peace between Greeks and Trojans.[49]

With the execution of Charles I and the exile of Charles II, royalists were pushed out of the centers of English political power; adopting the language of pastoral retreat allowed them to disavow their situation and present their absence from politics as a form of freedom. Introduced to the English court by Queen Henrietta Maria, the French literary style of *préciosité* associated with these salons provided Philips a model for developing a royalist community that would endure despite the exile of Charles II and many of his supporters and the obliteration of the monarchy.[50] As Carol Barash demonstrates, the gynocentric, courtly tradition of *préciosité* offered Philips, in the figure of the *femme forte* or "heroic woman," a compelling model for her own Society of Friendship.[51] Although Philips's poetry privileges the society's female members—one poem, for instance, is titled "To the Excellent Mrs. Anne Owen, upon her receiving the Name of Lucasia, and Adoption into our Society, December 28, 1651"—an unpublished letter written by Sir Edward Dering a few months after Philips's death indicates that while men may have been less prominent, they were not, as Souers contended, excluded from membership.[52] Dering writes, "Orinda had conceived the most generous designe, that in my opinion ever entred into any breast, which was to unite all those of her acquaintance, which she found worthy, or desired to make so, (among which later number she was pleased to give me a place) into one societie, and by the bonds of friendship to make an alliance more firme then what nature, our country or equall education can produce: and this would in time have spread very farr, & have been improved with great and yet unimagined advantage to the world."[53] According to Thomas, the society's membership comprised two distinct groups: "One, concentrated in London, consisted of former schoolmates and members of Henry Lawes's circle of Cavalier writers and musicians, while the other was made up of members of the Pembrokeshire and Cardiganshire gentry families whom Orinda had come to know after moving to west Wales."[54] As Hero Chalmers and Catharine Gray demonstrate, Philips's use of the pastoral mode resonates with the sentiments of the defeated royalists. Philips constructs the pastoral world of her society as a space for the Platonic reconstitution of a virtuous kingdom separate from the concerns of the fallen world.[55] Untethered from any specific time or place, Philips's woman-centered yet heterogeneous society exemplified royalist resolve in the face of rebellion, civil war, and exile.

Yet just as the pastoral world draws its power and appeal from its marginal status relative to the "real" world, so too did the Society of Friendship rely on the monarch's absence in order to function as a site of royalist—and female—community. Barash argues that Charles II's return from exile marked an important shift in the significance of Philips's female friendships. Whereas during the Interregnum Orinda's homoerotic bonds with Rosania (Mary Aubrey) and Lucasia (Anne Owen) could be figured as mutual longing for the absent monarch, "this symbolic coherence crumbles when the king reappears both as monarch and as a man in *Poems* (1664)."[56] Upon the king's return, in other words, the *femme forte* ceases to be heroic and virtuous, representing instead a threat to marriage and the heterosocial order on which the monarch's authority relies.

Chalmers is similarly interested in the changes wrought upon female friendship over the course of the 1650s, as England transitioned from a commonwealth back into a monarchy. For Chalmers, Orinda's society preserved royalist ideals during the Interregnum in at least two ways: first, it established a "conception of friendship, identified with royalism, as representative of religious cohesion and social stability"; and second, it employed "depictions of feminine withdrawal... to represent the space of retirement or interiority as the actual centre of power."[57] Correlating religio-political discord and social unrest with the eradication of the monarchy, Philips masterfully relocates concord and cohesion with the exiled king and his supporters in retreat. Like Barash, Chalmers registers a change in the meaning of female friendship at the Restoration, but where Barash perceives a potentially transgressive erotics that must be contained, Chalmers sees a shift in emphasis from retreat to political reconciliation. Comparing the concerns of Philips's Interregnum poetry to those of her Restoration drama, Chalmers concludes, "The frequency with which her Restoration writings use the term friendship diminishes markedly and the political valence of friendship changes from a partisan coding of royalist community and monarchical order during the 1650s to representing a Restoration spirit in favour of reconciliation and against military conflict."[58] Of course, Philips had personal reasons for advocating reconciliation: her husband, James Philips ("Antenor"), was a Parliamentarian who served under Cromwell and later faced significant reversals in fortune upon the Protectorate's dissolution. Despite their differences, then, Barash and Chalmers concur that

Philips's conceptualization of female friendship served as a conduit for royalist ideals, preserving them through civil war and exile and reaffirming them at the triumphant return of Charles II.

These critics demonstrate that Philips worked at the intersection of the personal and the political. For Barash, intimations of difference emerge from the political and social disparity between Philips and her female addressees. By stepping into the masculine position of the courtier-poet, Philips acknowledges the difference in status between herself and her social betters through the love lyric's discourse of desire; simultaneously, she attempts to collapse this distance in the fantasy of friendship created in the textual expression of her desire.[59] Elizabeth Wahl argues that the "tensions" within the friendship poetry emerge from Philips's erotic, rather than political, desire. Although Philips "idealizes female friendship precisely as a potential embodiment of an egalitarian relationship that marriage could not offer," her poems bear witness to a struggle "between a platonic ethos of egalitarianism and mutuality and an underlying eroticism...of a courtly language of conquest, submission, and carnal pleasure."[60] For Graham Hammill, it is these very tensions that evoke in Philips an "imaginative use of society to explore a mode of life that resists integration into the state."[61] Elucidating differences between poems to Rosania and to Lucasia, Hammill argues that Philips's friendship poems of the 1650s imagine two distinct political forms that try to manage virtue and pleasure: "In the Rosania poems, Philips depicts her passionate attachment to Rosania through political terms that describe a sovereign's tyrannical control over her population in order to illuminate a pleasure in self-destruction as the erotic experience of passionate friendship, while in the Lucasia poems, Philips portrays the free choice of friendship as the basis of virtuous society through modes of self-governance and the regulation of the senses in order to imply a division between the actualization of virtue through friendship and the passions that motivate it."[62] In Hammill's analysis, the two models of friendship we find in Philips's poetry provide two different ways of exploring a notion of erotic interest that traverses public and private spheres.

In using Philips's works to construct historical and biographical narratives about her transition from Interregnum to Restoration poet, these scholars also raise important questions about the periodization of Philips's politics. For example, on the one hand, although the first unauthorized edition of Philips's *Poems* appeared in print several years after the Restoration, much of her verse was composed and circulated in manuscript during the Interregnum. On the other hand, her translation of Corneille's *Pompey*, the work that brought Philips the most acclaim during her lifetime, was among the last texts she composed, but the first to be published, roughly a year before the 1664 *Poems*. As for her letters to Sir Charles Cotterell ("Poliarchus"), they were written between 1661 and 1664, but not collected and published as *Letters from Orinda to Poliarchus* until the early eighteenth century. In an essay reprinted in this collection, Catharine Gray reminds us that "Philips emerged into the busy public sphere of the seventeenth century not as a Restoration writer or poet of private homoerotic verse, but as an Interregnum writer of public-political commendation, linked to a heterosocial coterie of Royalist men."[63] In emphasizing the heterosocial aspect of the coterie, Gray does not mean to trivialize the homoerotics of Philips's friendship poems. On the contrary, she contends that the heterosocial coterie provided the conditions for such poems to signify as royalist verse. In the context of the Interregnum, "Philips' poetry helps to create a paradoxical Royalist counterpublic, in which royalty becomes the prerogative of a politicized coterie rather than the King, a coterie that represents Caroline values poetically without engaging in the direct polemic that might compromise their elitist socio-political status."[64] Evans is also interested in the paradoxes that inhere in the poems Philips composed during the Interregnum. For Evans, such paradoxes reveal a poet who may have identified with royalist causes, but whose support was by no means unqualified. About the poem "L'accord du bien," Evans writes, "Here, as so often, Philips, hardly a naive Royalist, suggests that the specific features of the political constitution are less important than the moral constitution of a society and its leaders; she champions kingship less than virtuous rule, especially personal self-control. Her poem expresses nicely balanced skepticism, not only about the king's opponents but also about any Pollyannaish view of kings."[65] Where Gray sees a "paradoxical Royalist counterpublic," Evans observes admonitions against fawning royalism.

As other critics have shown, to suggest that Philips critiqued royalist values is not to conclude that her works repudiate royalism *in toto*. Rather, it is to understand more fully the ever-shifting positions Philips occupied as a royalist woman living and writing in a country beset by political turmoil. Andrew Shifflett writes that Philips's poems are "politically neutral in their condemnation of the world's vices" and, like Evans, submits that Orinda was more interested in promoting a virtuous, reconciled kingdom than an absolute monarchy.[66] In his reading of *Pompey*, Shifflett argues that Philips critiques Charles II's arrogation of absolute authority in clemency. Although a political virtue touted since antiquity, clemency posed significant problems because it bound monarch and recipient in a contradictory, divided relationship, a problem born out in the figure of Pompey's widow Cornelia, who must stoically accept Caesar's mercy as his subject while continuing in her personal hatred toward him.[67] Shifflett explores the significance of Philips's use of the trope of sovereignty as a model for friendship. If "friendship is a sovereign state composed, somehow, of two independent sovereigns," he argues, then enmity is a natural aspect of this union; drawing parallels to Hobbes, Shifflett writes that just as our natural independence tends toward conflict, "so there always seems to be the *potential* for recrimination and competition within Philips's friendly polity."[68]

Where Shifflett reads Philips alongside Hobbes, Penelope Anderson reads her within the classical tradition of *amicitia*. In *Friendship's Shadows*, Anderson shows that Philips appropriates the language of *amicitia* to enter into public debates about conflicting obligations and multiple allegiances.[69] Correlating friendship's failures and betrayals with acts of treason, a crime for which husbands are not held legally responsible for their wives, Philips exploits a fault-line in coverture that, paradoxically, authorizes the wife not only to engage in public debates but also to cultivate political communities. Anderson argues that Philips understands betrayal to be an inevitable aspect of friendship, but that it does not mark friendship's end. The bitter poems of recrimination "commemorate, rather than obliterate, the history of changing allegiances" and the continuance, through the kingly virtue of clemency, of friendship's bonds even after its ostensible failure.[70] Although it may seem counterintuitive to suggest that poems on friendship's failures offer generative models of governance, Anderson argues in compelling fashion that "the most important thing about Philips's imagination of political community through *amicitia* is that it is *remade,* again and again, after and through articulations of betrayal. By requiring process and resilience, betrayal strengthens friendship, making it a union of reiterated choices and clear-eyed pragmatism."[71] Anderson also notes, however, that later readers disentangled the political and passionate sides of Philips's articulation of *amicitia,* with the unfortunate effect of a "truncating of the possibilities of political community that Philips imagines through her lyrics: their complicated negotiation of multiple obligations disappears."[72]

Philips criticism has also benefited from recent studies of archipelagic literature and culture. Shifting focus from England to the wider network of nations, this scholarship has helped "to strip away modern Anglocentric and Victorian imperial paradigms to recover the long, braided histories played out across the British-Irish archipelago between three kingdoms, four countries, divided regions, variable ethnicities and religiously determined allegiances."[73] John Kerrigan shows that Philips's concept of retreat relies on a negotiation of English and Welsh identities: "It is not the least of the paradoxes that the value of a dark retreat depends on an awareness of its distance from the bright lights, and Philips's identification with Wales seems to have been heightened by her familiarity with London and Dublin. She became a Welsh poet through having an archipelagic sense of her situation."[74] Sarah Prescott also stresses the importance of seeing Philips as a Welsh poet since she wrote much of her poetry while living in Wales. However, whereas Kerrigan reads in Philips a generally negative connotation of Wales, Prescott contends "that if we avoid interpreting Philips's relation to Wales in negative terms only and instead become more alert to her sense of her Welsh retreat as a 'chosen' privacy, we gain new insights into her poetry and her significance for Wales."[75] Calling into question the assumption that Philips perceived her immigration to Wales as a kind of exile, Prescott demonstrates "that Philips's archipelagic sense of the world beyond her own allows her to refashion her retreat in discursive terms, as a chosen retirement and a moral choice, a stance which is also, of course, informed by her Royalist sympathies and her gendered sense of herself as a woman writer."[76] Although she spent considerably less time there, Ireland also holds special significance for Philips, not least because her translation of Corneille's *La mort de Pompée* was first produced and printed in Dublin in 1663. Focusing on the play and its commendatory matter, Gray shows that Philips's *Pompey* celebrates cross-cultural connections, "present[ing] an Ireland that, once graced by a shaping female figure, becomes not just mirror and hammer but also alembic: a tool for distilling or reinventing a courtly Englishness fit for an Anglo-Irish and British ruling elite, and for a restored multi-kingdom monarchy."[77]

Like Gray, Mihoko Suzuki emphasizes the significance of Philips's geopolitical location on the margins of the emerging British Empire. Extending the work of scholars who have revised our understanding of Philips's royalism to emphasize her critical attitude toward absolute monarchy, Suzuki argues that in poems such as "The Irish Greyhound" and "On the Welch Language" as well as in her translation of *Pompey,* Philips identifies herself with the marginalized subject of English colonialism, speaking empathically about the virtue and honor of these "remote" areas as the locus of a sort of ur-British identity. Both Gray and Suzuki argue that Philips leveraged her marginal position by identifying the colonial spaces of Ireland and Wales as the sources of renewed British virtue crucial to successfully fashioning a multikingdom empire in which the London court is in a dynamic, interdependent relationship with its peripheries.

IV. *"Let verse revenge the quarrel"*

Scholars focused on Philips's political engagements have demonstrated that far from being a passive vessel of masculine, royalist discourse, Philips was an active participant in the political discourse of the Interregnum and Restoration. In her poetry, Philips rewrote royalist ideologies and poetics, and attempted to construct alternate modes of ethical rulership. Similarly, the archipelagic turn encourages us to rethink the direction of influence between geopolitical center and margin. Despite spending most of her life far from the centers of government and literary culture, Philips participated in vibrant, overlapping intellectual communities that she also helped to generate and support. Alongside recognition of her political importance has come attention to Philips's contributions to poetics as a stylistic and formal innovator, recognizing the impressive breadth of her generic experiments: for example, Wright calls the 1667 *Poems* "the most varied and ambitious single-volume female-authored publication yet produced."[78] Heeding Sasha Roberts's call for a "dialogic formalism" that brings together feminist interests in recovering women's experiences and voices with questions of literary form, scholars have rejected the notion that, as a versifier, Philips merely imitated superior male poets. As Elizabeth Scott-Baumann powerfully demonstrates, "poetic form is a site for experimentation and engagement" by early modern women writers, a site in which authors like Philips transformed the materials of masculine poetic discourses in service of her singular vision.[79]

In illuminating Philips's contributions as a poet, critics looked first to the ways in which she constructs an authorial voice, itself an important act of poetic transgression, through the appropriation of conventional modes and genres. In an article on religious lyric, Elizabeth Clarke argues that Philips was one of a number of women who deployed the "private" discourse of religious verse as a means of justifying political speech: "Once a strategy to silence women, sequestration becomes in the spiritual economy a qualification to speak. The midcentury perception of the symbolic value of private writing offers a potentially public voice to women simply because the closet has been their privileged domain."[80] In terms of Philips's reception of the male-authored poetic tradition, John Donne figures as her most significant and influential predecessor. Andreadis argues that Donne's "male heterosexual poetic discourse, with its Platonism, its implicit eroticism, and its impassioned argument via conceits" gives Philips not only a culturally accepted model upon which to construct her lyric voice but also an erotic language for the "unvarnished expression of her love" toward Rosania and Lucasia.[81] Bronwen Price makes a similar argument about Philips's appropriation of the Petrarchan voice, a tradition in which the speaker's masculine subjectivity constructs itself by silencing the woman as an object of the male gaze. According to Price, Philips gives agency to the women friends in their mutual connections as fluid, intertwined partners by locating their interaction in a retired, often internal space in which the boundaries of subject and object are erased.[82]

In assessing Philips's departures from Donne, scholars have emphasized how she constructs egalitarian relationships that defy the gendered power dynamic of much male-authored poetry. For example, Elaine Hobby compares the two poets' use of the compass image in, respectively, "A Valediction: Forbidding Mourning" and "Friendship in Emblem, or the Seal. To my dearest Lucasia." In Donne, the conceit "celebrate[s] woman's immobility and fixity in 'the centre,' and man's freedom to move and still be loved"; Philips transforms it into an image of "equal freedom and equal control" between Orinda and her addressee, Lucasia.[83] Andreadis does not claim explicitly, as Hobby does, that the friends in Philips's poems are "equal," but she does prioritize Philips's "Sapphic-Platonic" desire for union with her addressees. In her germinal essay on Donnean poetics, Loscocco calls Philips "Donne's last and best heir and innovator" and argues that she adapts Donne's style to develop a "Sapphic (in the particular sense of female and libidinal) poetics expressive of (homoerotic) union." Arguing that Donne's influence on Philips has been misread, in large part due to the influence of Izaak Walton's own reductive interpretation of Donne, Loscocco shows how Philips abandons Donne's elaborate metaphysical conceits in favor of a "specular poetics" of unity "adequate to the expressive demands of (female) union."[84]

These readings rely upon the Neoplatonic model of union as the grounds of Philips's vision of friendship, whether that friendship is deemed explicitly Sapphic or not. But as Andrea Brady points out, the *précieux* tradition that influences Philips's poetic style differs from the traditional Neoplatonic model of hierarchical order in which all being desires to merge upward into a divine One. The tradition that Philips receives from the influence of the queen's court in France does not construe the Platonic union of loving souls to involve necessarily the dissolution of the individual; rather, it "allow[s] individuals to retain their particularities," transcending the barriers of the self to mix with another while simultaneously retaining independent being.[85] Within the space of the singular friendship, the multiple presences of the friends remain: the intimate partners are united and recreated outside of themselves in a union that is also a multiplication. In Mark Llewellyn's view, Philips thus should be read as a serious philosophical thinker in her own right. Placing her work in dialogue with the Cambridge Platonists and high Anglican iconography, he writes that for Philips, "Friendship...is not part of an idealized union between two souls *for its own sake* or for the sexually subversive undercurrents it can mask, but rather [is] an imagining of the spiritual possibilities of such an 'intermixing' in allowing the attainment of a higher knowledge."[86]

Building on these insights, Scott-Baumann identifies in Philips's engagements with Donne the creation of "a dramatic poetics of similarity and absorption rather than of opposition and difference."[87] Philips, she writes, adopts many of Donne's stylistic elements, including both his striking, paradoxical images as well as his penchant for inexact rhymes, but crucially modifies these aspects in her own verse. For example, Philips writes "Friendship in Emblem" in consecutive rhyming couplets (*aabb*) instead of the interlocking couplets (*abab*) of Donne's "A Valediction: Forbidding Mourning," a change, writes Scott-Baumann, that helps to transform the famous compasses from an image of erotic coupling to one of passionate friendship.[88] More significantly, Philips creates a new poetic subjectivity through her engagement with Donne, replacing his insistent and central "I" with an "explicitly plural female voice"—the "we" of the Society of Friendship.[89] This "we," however, is not unproblematized, as Philips draws on the "dissonant elements of Donne's own poetics"—the speaker's anxieties and the painful absence of his object of desire—to explore the challenges of "negotiat[ing]...power relations on both the public stage and the intimacy of personal relationships" within the figure of a pluralized poetic subjectivity.[90]

Another poet whose relationship to Philips has been rethought is Abraham Cowley. Stella Revard has written on Philips's place in the development of the seventeenth century Pindaric. A genre "largely invented" by Abraham Cowley, the English Pindaric ode served as a means for Philips to engage in a poetic dialogue with Cowley: each wrote commendatory Pindarics to the other, published first in 1663 in the collection *Poems by Several Persons,* and Cowley also contributed a funereal ode to the 1667 *Poems.* Although "he never lets us forget that we are looking at best a most curious phenomenon—a woman who writes," Cowley's poems to Orinda are motivated at least in part by anxiety over a feminine incursion into a masculine literary domain; in other words, writes Revard, they are part of "a literary contest between men poets and women poets." Philips's death ensured that Cowley had the last word in their conversation, but Aphra Behn would later take up the genre as a means of female authorization.[91]

Scott-Baumann's reading goes even further in demonstrating the significance of Philips's engagement with Cowley, arguing for a rethinking of the vectors of influence between the two. She reads the two poets together and contends that their poetic dialogue "had a central part in forging a new and influential model of retreat" in the 1650s and 1660s.[92] Like Revard, Scott-Baumann highlights the friendly rivalry between the two that emerges in their Pindaric poetry. When Cowley offers her "a curious compliment with one showy classical allusion (to manure)," Philips responds by calling Cowley's triumphant verse a "Parthian conquest," an allusion, Scott-Baumann writes, that portrays the male poet as something of underhanded combatant, as the Parthians supposedly "fired over their shoulders while retreating." Moreover, Philips's ode "Upon Mr. Abraham Cowley's Retirement" played a role in shaping Cowley's reputation and style. It was, argues Scott-Baumann, Philips's poem to Cowley that first established in a significant way his reputation as a poet of retreat, and her emphasis on the self-mastery of solitary retreat and the intellectual freedom that it brings would transform Cowley's own Pindaric style from one focused "on soaring inspiration and bold digression" to "anti-heroic, quiet, calm, and serious freedom."[93]

The arena of Philips's influence that has been least explored is that of music. Henry Lawes is said to have set four of Orinda's poems to verse, although only two are extant: a "simple triple-meter" setting of "Orinda upon Little Hector," Philips's elegy, discovered by Joan Applegate, for her son who died in infancy, and "Friendship's Mystery, to my dearest Lucasia," set under the title "Mutuall Affection between *Orinda* and *Lucatia*."[94] Applegate deems Lawes's setting a fitting accompaniment to Philips's poem of mourning, even suggesting that Philips may have had a hand in choosing the musical style: "Philips's grief at the loss of little Hector, expressed in five deceptively modest quatrains, is served with equal modesty by the musical setting her old friend devised. But, as with the verse, the song's apparent simplicity of style masks an expressive potential that was equal to its sad occasion."[95] The setting of the latter poem has engendered greater debate. Lydia Hamessley argues, on the one hand, that Lawes intentionally downplayed the homoerotic passion of Philips's work by setting it to music that simplified its metaphysical and prosodic intensity in favor of tunefulness and broad appreciation. Dianne Dugaw and Amanda Powell, on the other hand, contend that the "light catchy tune repeated for each stanza" captures in music Philips's intention to fashion a Sapphic subjectivity through the parody of Petrarchan tropes and the gender hierarchy they articulate.[96]

V. *"More Copies of it abroad than I could have imagin'd"*

This perhaps esoteric distinction raises pertinent questions of agency in the generation of poetic meaning: How much does Lawes shape, or reshape, the meaning of Philips's verse through his musical settings? To what extent can Philips or her verse control its reception? Gillian Wright's work on Philips and other women writers elegantly shows how simple notions of individual agency become problematized when we examine the material and social forces that went into the poetic production. Philips's own emergence into print demonstrates Wright's insight that "literary agency in this period is not a singular or uniform category."[97] The story is well known to those familiar with Philips: in 1664, the bookseller Richard Marriott advertised a volume entitled *Poems by the Incomparable, Mrs. K. P.*, in the London *Newes*.[98] Philips expressed shock and dismay when she learned of the unauthorized publication from John Jeffries; her London associates, led by Sir Charles Cotterell, quickly suppressed it. The exact reasons for Philips's agitation and the quick suppression of the work have been the subject of some debate. Philips complained that she had heard that the unauthorized edition contained numerous errors as well as poems written by others, a claim repeated in the posthumous, "authorized" edition of 1667.[99] But as Thomas points out, the 1664 *Poems* is often closer to the one extant manuscript identified to be in Philips's own hand than is the 1667 *Poems*, the latter having been extensively revised by its editor.[100] The theory that Philips objected to the very idea of being in print also proves unsatisfactory: besides her inclusion in the 1651 edition of Cartwright's works (discussed above), a few of Philips's poems were published, apparently without her objection, in *Poems, by Several Persons* in 1663.[101] Additionally, Philips's willingness to let her translation of *Pompey* go to press suggests, according to Elizabeth Hageman, that "she belongs among the rank of early modern women for whom the printing press was a boon."[102] A minority opinion even suggests that Philips herself was behind the pirated edition and only feigned her displeasure to keep up appearances.[103] Most scholars, though, have concluded that Philips's sense of violation was authentic, and that as a woman writer she recognized the need to carefully manage her reputation to avoid seeming either overly proud of her work or eager for attention.[104]

The question of textual authority has continued to be a subject of intense interest and debate in Philips scholarship, highlighting the elusive nature of an "authentic" and fixed Philips canon. Despite its claims to authenticity, the 1667 *Poems* (and its reprints) has proven just as problematic for modern scholars as the pirated 1664 volume, and not only because it was published posthumously and without any apparent input by Philips herself. In his anthology, Saintsbury takes Henry Herringman's "authorized" edition as the final word, dismissing the differences between it and the 1664 *Poems* as "neither many nor important."[105] Scholars since have tended to prefer manuscript sources, particularly the one known to be in Orinda's hand, to the printed editions, although within this general orientation there remain debates over the relative authority of the various texts.[106] In 1951, Paul Elmen called for a new edition of Philips's works based on then newly discovered manuscripts that, he theorized, represented "final versions" of her works, or at least versions closer to Orinda's final intentions than the either the 1664 or 1667 editions.[107] Ellen Moody argues that the ordering of the poems in the printed editions, both of which place Philips's pro-Stuart poetry first, misrepresents her as a poet.[108] Not only does it mask her more nuanced political beliefs and the "many dissonant passages of lament, dejection, and pessimism" that color her "political" verse, more importantly it "displaces Orinda's...romantic friendships with women," which, Moody argues, were Orinda's chief poetic inspiration. Moody intends to restore the "true" Philips by reorganizing her works in chronological, and thus biographical, order; she says this will counter both the "strain of antifeminism" among past critics who minimized Philips's poetic skills as well as those "contemporary feminist scholars" who treat Philips as "a whipping 'girl'.... [a] modest, politic paragon who...gave later women a stultifying model."[109]

While Moody's case against the ordering of the print editions is compelling, she also runs the risk of engaging in what Deborah Jacobs calls "critical imperialism," the tendency to "romanticize marginality" and "'find' everywhere...[modern] themes of resistance and subversion."[110] Indeed, one must recognize that Philips's feminine decorum and modesty were an essential component of her strategy of self-authorization and cannot be read or edited out of her poetry, as in Elizabeth Clarke's argument about Philips's canny deployment of the religious lyric as political expression. For example, Philips's "Upon the double murther of K. Charles," as a response to a Cromwellian poem by Vavasor Powell, establishes its authority by paradoxically invoking the cultural expectation that a woman should thus be silent on public matters.[111] Philips writes that she "thinke[s] not on the state" (1) and is concerned instead with "God's laws" (21) and Christ's kingdom; she presents herself as a dutifully pious woman while also speaking out on the defining political event of seventeenth century England without appearing to violate gender propriety. Rather than a sign of her weakness, Philips's posture of feminine humility should be read as a testament to her political savvy.

Moreover, the very nature of coterie poetic practices problematizes the attempt to construct a fixed Philips canon. In recent years, archival work has uncovered manuscripts containing not only new poems now thought to have been written by Philips but also variants of poems already accepted into her corpus; such work has been crucial in transforming our understanding of Philips and how her poetic voice was fashioned within coterie practices.[112] As Arthur Marotti demonstrates in his study of Donne, coterie literary practice was characterized by its flexibility through the circulation of loose papers, transcription of different authors into commonplace books and miscellanies, and the de- and re-contextualization of occasional poems, originally produced in a specific biographical or social setting, into new situations by readers and copyists.[113] Most importantly in Marotti's view, coterie verse was social: not the work of individuals writing in isolation but, rather, a dialogic discourse between multiple authors and readers-*cum*-collaborators.

Like the drama of the sixteenth and seventeenth centuries, coterie verse seems to have been by nature a collaborative work-in-progress; for Orinda and her interlocutors the process of alteration and improvement by others was an essential part of the production of her work, what Paul Trolander and Zeynep Tenger call "amendment criticism."[114] Manuscript circulation problematizes notions of "intentionality" because of the unstable nature of the text, and, as Hageman argues, scholars "must be aware of the material circumstances in which women's writing has been produced and reproduced"—that is, that the artifact of the textual poem may in fact not be reflective of the author's "intention." Any manuscript, then, even if in Orinda's hand, may represent not a finished project but the version *du jour,* so to speak.[115] As Wright demonstrates in her cogent analysis of Philips's autograph manuscript, no single "narrative" of the poet's development or mindset emerges from the text and its sequencing of poems.[116] In a similar vein, Germaine Greer contends that a strong sense of individual ownership of a work was discouraged by both the practical realities of circulation and the attitudes of the participants: "possessiveness" was simply unbecoming for a high-minded poet.[117] In fact, Philips was active in seeking out corrections of her work by others, Cotterell in particular. In numerous letters, she asks or thanks him for his corrections to her verse.[118] In one letter from 1662, she writes that a poem to the Duchess of York "shall not be seen at Court, till you have first put it in a better Dress, which I know you will do, if it be capable of Improvement." She also writes to him regarding her translation of *Pompey,* asking him to correct her metrics and grammar before its publication: "I am not Critick enough to resolve this Doubt, and therefore leave it wholly to your Determination" (June 1663). Philips appears to have been willing to allow her work to circulate with changes she herself had never seen or explicitly authorized, trusting others to improve her work in the act of friendly collaboration.

Cotterell's emendations to her poetry parallel his emendations to her political and social standing, and Philips seems to have seen the two as part of the ongoing fashioning of her life and reputation:

in the same sentence that she asks Cotterell to "put [her poetry] in a better Dress" before its circulation, she complains of her husband's poor fortunes in the newly restored court, a problem for which she sought aid from Cotterell.[119] Bringing together questions of publication, coterie practices, and friendship, Hilary Menges persuasively argues for understanding Philips's poetic activity and processes of textual emendation as central to the construction and maintenance of her interpersonal relationships. Contending that "Philips's interest in the friend is not driven by either sexual or platonic desire," Menges examines salient connections between Philips's languages of friendship and authorial reputation, particularly in her vitriolic attacks on disloyal friends and her expressions of horror at the unauthorized 1664 printing of her works. Friendship serves as a sacred retreat wherein one is safe from the dangers of the outside world; its betrayal casts the secrets of the friend into public exposure, even "prostitution," violating the chastity of the friendly bond. Ultimately, Menges argues, "the friend emerges as the true medium" of her verse: it is through the mediating presence of the friend as addressee and respondent that Philips attempts to construct and manage her literary reputation.[120]

While complicating our understanding of Philips, the discovery of previously unknown poems and textual variants has demonstrated, as Hageman and Sununu write, that "Philips was a social poet in ways we had not hitherto fully realized—that her writing responds directly and immediately to personal, political, social, and literary events of her time; and also that she was very much a part of both the literary and the musical life of seventeenth-century Britain." Barash notes as well that the differences in the sequencing of poems within extant manuscripts "suggest that Philips organized her poems differently for different audiences."[121] Taking this into consideration, the differences between her copybook and the 1667 printing, or even the more radically altered Rosania manuscript, can be seen to represent not corruptions but new and valid creations that emerge from and make up an equally important part of her body of work—not because they come from her hand directly but because they fulfill her larger poetic intention: that her work would be part of a shifting, changing dialogue, as much her expression as the expression of her friends. Philips's poetry, Marie-Louise Coolahan argues, emerges from the social occasion, and its (and her) amenability to recontextualization and revision "indicates participation in [the] literary culture rather than an eye to posterity."[122] Philips was clearly an active participant in a dynamic poetic culture; that her works were copied, recopied, and amended testifies to her significant impact upon the literary traditions in which she worked.

VI. *"Which all our Joys and noble thoughts inspires"*

As we have hoped to demonstrate in this introduction, the field of Philips scholarship is a rich and diverse one, despite its relative youth. Scholars have demonstrated in compelling fashion the breadth and depth of her poetry; her work resists attempts to pigeonhole it by subject matter or genre, bringing together questions of politics, sexual desire and identity, and poetic tradition in innovative and striking ways. As such, we have been mindful that attempts at strict differentiation among scholarly approaches to Philips risk oversimplification; nonetheless, we have identified three salient fields of inquiry that continue to organize Philips criticism, and which we have loosely followed in organizing the present volume: (1) cultural poetics and/or the courtly coterie; (2) innovation and influence in poetic and political form; and (3) articulations of female friendship, homoeroticism, and retreat.

Beginning with Catharine Gray's reading of Philips as the author of a "royalist counterpublic," the essays in the first section of this volume explore the ways in which the poet articulates her political vision within the context of the courtly coterie. Gray, as discussed above, brings to light the heterosocial makeup of the Society of Friendship, emphasizing it as a space to articulate and preserve the values of the Caroline court in retreat. In her prefatory note, newly written for this volume, Gray considers how this essay has influenced later scholarship, providing a basis for analyzing Philips within "expansive literary networks that crossed Cardigan,

London, and Dublin," as well as demonstrating "the fluid ambiguities and tense contradictions within Philips's ideas of public political allegiance."

Christopher Orchard's essay builds on this foundation to discover in Philips's poetry alternative models for governance. He contends that "On the 3. of September, 1651" functions as a scathing critique of a poetics that associates royalist leadership with heroic virtue. Philips deconstructs the ideology of heroic virtue—particularly as expressed by William Davenant in *Gondibert*—by exposing its violent costs. The bloody defeat of the royalists in the battle of Worcester, the occasion of her poem, reveals the insufficiency of this royalist poetics of leadership. In its place, argues Orchard, Philips produces "a friendship-based model for heroic virtue that cut across party lines and provided a successful alternative to the disastrous Royalist examples in life at Worcester and in print with the preface to *Gondibert*." Instead of seeing Philips as a single-minded royalist, Orchard presents her as one of many who remained loyal to the crown while growing progressively more disenchanted with royalist policies.

In his contribution, David Orvis looks to Orinda's use of biblical sources in the fashioning of a theory of monarchism. Orvis contends that while several Philips poems do offer a latitudinarian vision, the prophetic language through which this vision is conveyed establishes Orinda as a prophet in possession of divine truth. Like the millenarian prophets of the seventeenth century, Orinda interprets the events of the civil wars, Interregnum, and Restoration as reflections of divine will. However, whereas millenarian visionaries cited biblical passages correlating these events with the end-times, Orinda draws primarily upon the Old Testament and upon old covenant theology to espouse an *anti*-eschatological message. Yet, this prophecy should not be confused with latitudinarianism or irenicism: in her visions, Orinda prophesies a period of suffering that culminates not in the *eschaton* but in God's forgiveness and the divinely sanctioned restoration of the monarchy.

The essays in the second section turn to questions of influence and genre. Amy Scott-Douglass reads Philips's works and legacy within a long literary tradition of associating an author's works with an author's body. Demonstrating Philips's own use of this trope—for example, in her horrified reaction to the unauthorized 1664 *Poems* as a sexualized violation—Scott-Douglass shows that the prefatory materials of the 1667 *Poems* appropriate Philips's metaphors of defacement, redeploying them in commendatory verses to restore the poet and her body of work. Through a series of metonymic gestures equating defacement with Puritanism and restoration with royalism and high church Anglicanism, the prefatory poems employ Philips's *Poems* as a metaphor for the restoration of the monarchy and its values. What is more, "Philips herself functions as a symbol of the monarchy and, by connection, the Anglican church—innocent, assailed, and, for a time, defeated, but ultimately resurrected from the dead and restored to glory." Hence, while the more memorable image is of the precocious young girl who, according to her biographer John Aubrey, "read the Bible thorough before she was a full four yeares old," it is clear that Philips remained committed to the Word, even as she made the drastic conversion from Puritanism to high church Anglicanism.[123]

The essays by Paula Loscocco and Elizabeth Hodgson turn to questions of form and poetic influence. As discussed above, Loscocco's essay tackles the relationship between Philips and her poetic antecedent, Donne. Her reading uncovers an important transformation of Donnean poetics to suit the demands of a poetry of female erotic union, an early example of scholarship that investigated and asserted Philips's originality as a poetic voice. In a similar vein, Hodgson reads in Philips's epithalamia a "simultaneous deconstruction and reconstruction of the teleological" marital narrative employed by Donne and Herrick that "attempt[s] to construct an independent feminine perspective on the antibridal cast of most epithalamia while also reinvoking those same traditional strategies" to empower both bride and female speaker. More significantly, Philips's experiments with marriage verse generate some of the most diverse and interpretively rich poems of her oeuvre; the constant shifting of poetic structures within these texts problematizes any simple identification of either her attitudes toward her addressees or toward the institution itself on questions of power, female independence, and desire.

Linda Austern's contribution to this volume is the first major article on Philips and music, and it promises to set the measure for future research. In a thorough study of the intersection of seventeenth century literary and musical aesthetics, Austern argues compellingly for the importance of music to Philips's writing, both as a trope for harmonious erotic union as well as a means to heighten her poetry's affective powers. In particular, Austern draws our attention to the importance of performance to an understanding of Philips's works, both those set to music and those not. Raised in a culture keenly attuned to the power of music to affect its listeners, Orinda adopts musical metaphors in order to write performative texts in which readers and auditors participate in the movements and countermovements of harmonious accord and interaction. Austern's interdisciplinary analysis demonstrates both the importance of recognizing historical differences in aesthetic reception as well as the complexity that emerges when scholars examine early modern literature within the broader contours of its historical and cultural moment.

The three essays in the final section return to those questions of desire and eroticism that launched Philips's recovery in modernity. The reprinted essays by Valerie Traub and Lorna Hutson, each discussed above, include new introductory notes placing them within their original scholarly context and assessing their ongoing influence on the study of Philips in particular, and of sexuality more generally. As discussed above, Traub identifies Philips as a crucial figure in the emergence of a lesbian "subjectivity effect" by claiming the discourses of *amicitia* for her articulation of female relationships. In Traub's reading, Philips occupies a liminal position between a historical discourse in which the "impossibility" of female-female love marked it as innocent and a more suspicious Enlightenment understanding of sexual practice and individual identity. Through her interventions in the pastoral tradition, Philips redefines Nature so that it serves not as a barrier to but a vehicle for same-sex love, a move that simultaneously allows her to retain the notion of female relationships as innocent. In her thoughtful rejoinder to Traub, Hutson questions the usefulness of the historical narrative that Traub adopts from the work of Alan Bray, thus highlighting a perhaps more fundamental challenge facing Philips: the problem of signification as such for a woman writing about female desire. As the introductory note to her essay points out, these topics continue to be a fecund source for scholarship as critics, including many in this volume, pursue the task of understanding the nature of Philips's poetry within its many discursive and historical contexts.

In her new contribution, Harriette Andreadis takes up these issues of historical narrativizing and female erotic signification. She places Philips within a tradition of female pastoral that stretches from the seventeenth century to the present, placing her in dialogue not only with near contemporaries Aemilia Lanyer and Anne Killigrew but also with nineteenth and twentieth century poets Christina Rosetti, H. D., and Olga Broumas. As a genre always notable for its "coded" manner of expression, pastoral, in Andreadis's view, provided Philips and others a "safe haven" to speak forbidden erotic desires and political sentiments that challenged dominant discourses. Andreadis does not claim a direct lineage from Philips to the present but, rather, argues that although "coding may no longer be necessary" in the twenty-first century to express same-sex desire or nonconformist politics, Philips took advantage of the pastoral mode's inherent subversive potential and thus provided a discourse that has been taken up since her time in different ways by poets for their own libidinal expressions.

With characteristic erudition, Elizabeth Hageman concludes the collection with an afterword that points one way forward by taking us back to historical materials and showing us what our assumptions about Philips's reputation have allowed us to miss. Presenting what she describes as "additional evidence of Philips's 'staying power' from the seventeenth century to our own time," Hageman offers three examples, beginning with two quatrains by Philips inscribed in a seventeenth century hand on a windowpane in the Long Gallery at Haddon Hall. She then discusses Washington

Irving's appropriation of these inscriptions in his 1822 fiction *Bracebridge Hall*. Finally, she turns to readers' marks in printed copies of Philips's writings that now reside in libraries around the world. Collectively, Hageman's evidence demonstrates that our assumptions about the rapid decline of Philips's reputation need to be questioned; that perhaps more evidence of her "staying power" is out there waiting to be uncovered; and that, whatever methodological and theoretical debates come to the fore in future Philips criticism, the import of her life and works will continue to be self-evident not only to scholars of diverse disciplines but also to casual readers who find in Orinda's story a compelling narrative of female empowerment.

1 ❖ Katherine Philips and the Post-Courtly Coterie

Catharine Gray

Author's Note

"Katherine Philips and the Post-Courtly Coterie" attempted to couple the insights of scholars such as Margaret Ezell, who insisted on the social nature of early modern authorship, with those of critics such as Carol Barash, who revealed the political roots of royalist women's poetry. Arguing for Philips's importance to a displaced group of Oxford royalists during the turbulence of the 1650s, it aimed to illuminate the intertwined complexities of her coterie circulation and political commitments. Recent scholarship on Philips has deepened and complicated analysis of these particular aspects of Philips's work—its circulation and politics—in at least two significant ways. First, scholars are busy uncovering the archipelagic dimensions of Philips's writing. Participating in a broader scholarly move to foreground the transnational contacts and geopolitical tensions of early modern British literature, scholars argue for Philips's shaping contributions to expansive literary networks that crossed Cardigan, London, and Dublin. Some, such as Deana Rankin, Rosalinde Schut, Marie-Louise Coolahan, and myself, focus on her literary productions for an Old English and

Anglo-Irish elite in Restoration Ireland.[1] Others, notably Sarah Prescott and John Kerrigan, demonstrate her poetry's investment in Welsh localities, identities, and bardic traditions.[2]

Second, and sometimes overlapping with this geographically expanded sense of Philips's interests and reach, more recent scholarship stresses the fluid ambiguities and tense contradictions within Philips's ideas of public political allegiance. Analyzing her play translations, for example, Hero Chalmers, Anne Russell, and Mihoko Suzuki emphasize Philips's construction of female characters and dramatic interludes that work to accommodate the opposing parties of the Restoration settlement. Russell and Suzuki combine this emphasis with an attention to Philips's transcultural Anglo-Irish and English-French contexts; however, all three scholars also show Philips illustrating the complex political associations of this period.[3] In a similar vein, in this volume David Orvis shows Philips's prophetic subversions of the relations of monarch and subject, while Christopher Orchard argues that Philips critiques royalist military heroism (real and poetic) to embrace ideals of virtuous friendship that unite political enemies. Perhaps exemplary of this analysis of Philips's exploration of divided duties is Penelope Anderson's examination of the prevalence of themes of betrayal in Philips's poetry, themes that show Philips meditating on the widespread problem of the competing loyalties—domestic, erotic, and political—produced by the intimate clashes of civil war.[4] Combining detailed historicism with nuanced close readings, these scholarly works, and others like them, all illustrate the astonishing breadth and sophistication of current work on Philips, her contacts, and politics.

I

John Berkenhead, writing on the royalist divine and playwright William Cartwright, makes Cartwright's wit the "blood of verse" which, "like a German Prince's title, runs / Both to thy eldest and to all thy Sons."[5] Berkenhead's fantasy of the dissolution of primogeniture into a leveled fraternity of royalist poets would seem to exclude women, yet the collection of prefatorial poems in which his elegy appears did include one woman writer: Katherine Philips. Philips is perhaps best known for her poetry of love addressed to women, published along with her other poetry in 1664 and 1667. However, her poem to Cartwright, her first published poem, was printed not in the Restoration but in 1651. Given that the prefatory poems to Cartwright's *Comedies, Tragi-Comedies, with Other Poems* were written by royalist sympathizers, and that it was published just one month before the exiled Charles II's invasion from Scotland, the Cartwright volume was as much a political as a poetic performance.[6] Thus, contrary to modern critical characterizations of the importance of her work, Philips emerged into the busy public sphere of the seventeenth century not as a Restoration writer or poet of private homoerotic verse, but as an Interregnum writer of public-political commendation, linked to a heterosocial coterie of royalist men. Philips's published and manuscript poetry of this period helped to forge this coterie: in her writing of the revolutionary period, Philips figures herself as a proxy poet at the center of a complex, postcourtly community, born of the decentering of royal power and royalist panegyric. Paradoxically, given Philips's royalist commitments, this decentering sanctions the emergence of the nonaristocratic woman writer as a privileged member of the group.

Cartwright's *Comedies* is crucial for rethinking Philips's poetry, both historically and poetically. Historically, it forces our attention to her considerable poetic production before the Restoration. She seems to have started writing in earnest around the time of this publication to Cartwright—we can date only two or three of her poems (her juvenilia) before 1651—and well over half her poetry was written in the early to mid-1650s.[7] Like Andrew Marvell, whose *Miscellaneous Poems* was not published until 1681, but who is most often associated with the turbulence of the commonwealth period that produced much of his most famous poetry, Philips can be productively situated in the revolutionary context that impelled her to write. Poetically, the fact that Philips was the only woman to be included in the unprecedented number of commendatory poems prefaced to the Cartwright volume (54 in all), coupled with her increased poetic output at this time, shows the importance of this group of mostly male writers to her poetry at the start of her career, and her commitment to a loyalist politics that has been largely overlooked by modern critics. For while scholars of Katherine Philips chart the groups of men and women evoked by her poems, they rarely discuss the public-political aspects of this verse. Some writers have simply chosen to ignore the politics of Philips's poetry, focusing on questions of gender and sexuality to the exclusion of contemporary debates over state power and public representation. Maureen Mulvihill and Claudia Limbert, for example, provide invaluable biographical details about Philips's connections to male literary elites, while Harriette Andreadis and Arlene Stiebel give sophisticated readings of the eroticism of her love poetry to women, but none of them attempts to link either Philips's heterosocial or homoerotic verses to her royalism, or to her complicated sociopolitical position as a woman with many royalist friends married to a moderate Cromwellian.[8] Some scholars even present Philips's poetry as entirely divorced from political concerns, defining it as "apolitical" or focused on "private themes."[9]

This treatment of Philips's verse as disengaged from public-political issues is in danger of reproducing post-Renaissance notions of gendered separate spheres in a very different sociopolitical context, and it ignores the instability and flexibility of the categories of public and private during the seventeenth century.[10] In this period, categories of public and private are in dispute, as the ideal of a public power invested in the patriarchal icon of the king (embodied in courtly genres like the masque) gives way to the concept of a sphere of public discourse in which men and women of all classes may jostle to participate.[11] While this arena of public discourse is by no means gender neutral, the upheavals of the revolutionary period enabled even royalist women to participate in the creation of what Nancy Fraser calls counterpublics: discursive communities for the public formation of alternative politics and identities.[12]

The exceptions to the above critical rule of separating Philips's poetry from its revolutionary context are Patrick Thomas, Philips's editor, and Carol Barash.[13] Barash in particular mounts a complex exploration of the connections between representations of gender and political power in Philips's texts, arguing that the elegiac female community imagined in Philips's poetry emblematizes the body of the Restoration monarch, Charles II. Like Barash's essay, this study focuses on gender and politics, arguing that, especially given the changing nature of public and private during this period, we need to explore the connections between the public political and the gender political in early modern women's writing. Barash, however, underestimates the importance of Philips's many addresses to her male colleagues during the revolutionary period and her debt to the collective politics and aesthetics of the seventeenth century coterie. During this period, Philips exchanged poems and complimentary dedications with moderate royalists such as Sir John Berkenhead, Sir Edward Dering, Henry Vaughan, Henry Lawes, and Francis Finch.[14] Some of Philips's love poetry to women were imitated and circulated among these men: Sir John Berkenhead and Sir Edward Dering both wrote love plaints to Philips's beloveds "Lucasia" (Anne Owen) and "Rosania" (Mary Aubrey), and Dering even explicitly masqueraded as Philips's poetic persona "Orinda" in his verse.[15] One of Philips's poems to Lucasia, "Friendship's Mystery," was set to music and published by Henry Lawes in 1655,[16] while Lawes also wrote music for two of her other homoerotic poems, "A Dialogue between Lucasia and Orinda" and "To Mrs. M. A." All three of these songs may have been performed at the royalist gatherings at Lawes's London house that occurred during the Interregnum.[17] These publications and performances indicate that the poems of love to women on which modern critics have focused are not only private expressions of lesbian desire, but formed part of a public, poetic performance, one that circulated in a complex system of compliment, cross-gender identification, and political affiliation.

II

Cartwright's *Comedies* displays its political colors in part by foregrounding royalist Oxford as a lost ideal. Of the 53 men who wrote commendatory poems for the volume, 38 had attended Oxford University, and of the 19 still at Oxford after Charles's defeat there in 1646, 15 were either expelled or refused to submit to the parliamentary visitors sent up to purge and reform the colleges.[18] *Comedies* mourns the loss of Oxford as both a geopolitical space—it had housed the king and his army until the siege of Oxford—and as a school of royalist culture. Oxford had been the seat of royal panegyric during the Personal Rule, issuing ten volumes of commendatory verses to Charles I and Henrietta Maria between 1633 and 1643 alone, written for the most part in Latin.[19] All but one of the contributors to the Cartwright volume later associated with Philips wrote for these ornate celebrations of the public power of the royal family,[20] and Cartwright himself, a staunch royalist who had been appointed to the king's Council of War but who died an unheroic death of camp fever in 1643, contributed to nine out of the ten volumes.[21] The sheer number of commendatory poems to Cartwright recalls the collective acts of panegyric offered by Oxford before the civil war, but Cartwright's book is aimed at a broader and thus partly female London audience familiar with English rather than Latin. The connection between the Cartwright volume and royalist Oxford is made more explicit by the publisher, Humphrey Moseley, who presents Cartwright as "a late student of Christ Church," mocks the "Oxford Visitors," and in the absence of systems of court patronage that traditionally supported courtly writers, even dedicates the volume not to a great patron but to the university itself, nostalgically evoked in all its past glory: "To the most renowned and happy mother of all learning and ingenuity, the (late most flourishing) University of Oxford, these poems, as most due, are humbly dedicated."[22]

Moseley presents the *Comedies* as the performance of a coded and ideologically inflected community, or coterie. According to Arthur Marotti, during the 1640s and 1650s, royalists used manuscript collections "as a form of social and political bonding,"[23] and the Cartwright volume suggests that this bonding can extend to the public sphere of print. The opening reference to Henry Lawes as setting "The Ayres and Songs" to music two years before Lawes's first publication of his airs points to a collective poetic and musical production that happens offstage, an elitist sphere of nonprofessional activity epitomized by Cartwright's own texts: "You will do him wrong to call them his works; they were his recreation."[24] The preface then presents a text forced into publication by a series of accidents—Cartwright's death, plagiarism of his works, and the fall of Oxford—all shaped into a narrative of loss that licenses the move to print. Moseley even defends the number of commendatory poems in terms that cast the 54 prefatory poets as Cartwright's friends and force the readers either to identify with them or see themselves as alienated outsiders: "if you think He hath too many Commenders, it is a sign you knew him not."[25] In his very appeals to a broad public, therefore, Moseley constructs this text in terms of exclusivity, inscribing an elitist circle of the knowing few—or a knowing many—within the wider public sphere.[26]

The text then works to foreground a collection of displaced Oxford wits gathered to mourn the loss of the university as a royalist power base, and Cartwright comes to stand as a synecdoche not only of this geopolitical space, but of its symbolic center: Charles I. For although the king rarely appears in the poems to Cartwright, he haunts the edges of the verse as the central mourned absence of the text. Berkenhead, figuring the shame of being a survivor of the royalist defeat, says of Cartwright, "Thou liv'st after Death, We die before," turning Cartwright's inglorious death into a heroic martyrdom that outshines those unlucky enough to be left alive under parliamentary rule.[27] These lines, however, echo an anonymous elegy in *Monumentum Regale,* one of the books of poetry published after Charles's execution in 1649: "We only died, he only lived that day."[28] Francis Finch presents Cartwright himself as the central spectacle of royalist ideology, which in the absence of court and masque becomes a powerful oxymoron of dark glory drawing the gazes and creative talents of the royalist poetic community, even those (like Mildmay Fane) ordered by Parliament to stay within five miles of London:

> Thy Friends who five-mile Prisons do confine,
> And those that breathe within the larger Line,
> Will joy to see thy glorious Shadow move,
> The Object of their Wonder and their Love.[29]

Finch's poem, however, again echoes an elegy for Charles I from *Monumentum Regale,* one that presents the volume itself as a substitute for the public power of the king: it is "the living Emblem of glorious shade."[30] In the Cartwright volume, therefore, the poetic martyr, like royalist elegy itself, becomes a dark reflection of the lost royal ideal, the unspoken object of the texts and their doubled mourning for Cartwright and the former Oxford: the king.

III

It is into this series of mourned absences that Katherine Philips steps. Philips herself has a complicated ideological background: she was brought up as a Puritan in London and educated at an all-female school in Hackney run by a Mrs. Salmon, who was a Presbyterian, but most of her connections were with royalists. At Mrs. Salmon's she befriended Mary Aubrey, the daughter of a Welsh cavalier, and Mary Harvey (later married to Sir Edward Dering, also a moderate royalist), and in 1646 she moved with her mother to Wales, a center of support for the king. However, once there, she married James Philips, a considerable landowner and colonel, a member of the army committee who increased his estates as a commissioner of sequestration—a role he performed with such gusto that he apparently gained quite a reputation.[31] In 1650, when the Propagation Act was passed, Colonel Philips was appointed by the Rump Parliament as a member of the Commission for the Propagation of the Gospel in Wales, which was, according to A. H. Dodd, "the real government of Wales," not only ejecting Anglican ministers, but filling local administrative posts: "treasurers, militia commissioners, receivers of taxes and the like."[32] Thus, at 16 Katherine

Philips married a powerful member of the military middle class that ran Wales during the revolutionary period. Despite the fact that James Philips was a moderate, in conflict with local radicals and on friendly terms with local royalists,[33] Philips's contribution to Cartwright's *Comedies* publicly declares a political affiliation at odds with her husband's Parliamentarianism, particularly given the fact that during the very week that Cartwright's *Comedies* was published, Colonel Philips had helped to suppress a royalist revolt in Cardiganshire, Wales, in which 28 royalists were killed and 60 taken prisoner.[34]

Although she was too young to have known Cartwright as an adult (she was not born until 1632), Philips's poem is the first of the 54 that preface his volume, and as such it occupies a position of some prominence. In the collections of verse panegyrics dedicated to members of the royal family published in Oxford before 1646, the order of writers reflects social status: as Raymond Anselment notes, university officials and nobles "claim the privileged place at the beginning, while the lesser academic and social ranks vie to succeed them."[35] In a volume dedicated to Oxford and dominated by the contributions of Oxford men, Philips's prominence must not be ignored and may reflect an attempt by the other writers to gain the favor of a royalist woman married to an influential member of the parliamentary forces who had himself matriculated from Oxford in 1610.[36] However, we should also note that her inclusion in the volume relies on the *absence* of the very university structure that organized the earlier collections. Universities were all-male provinces in the seventeenth century, sites of homosocial competition in rhetoric and the arts, and of the preparation for careers unavailable to women, in public service and in the church. Thus, if the Cartwright volume contains many poems by the Oxford men who published in these earlier volumes, Philips herself can only emerge as the sole female member of the group after parliamentary divines began regulating the Oxford press in 1646, and many of the royalist men and their panegyric moved to London. From the start, her place in the publication was conditioned both by a displacement of the powerful royalist center of Oxford to the relative margins of defeated royalism in Wales and London and by her own contradictory position as a royalist connected by marriage to a sympathetic parliamentary leader.

Given her precarious relation to the other writers, as a woman and the wife of a Cromwellian, it is perhaps not surprising that Philips's poem presents itself as a rude interruption, the opening lines simultaneously casting Cartwright as a substitute royal and holding him at bay:

> Stay, Prince of Fancy, stay, we are not fit
> To welcome or admire thy Raptures yet;
> Such horrid ignorance benights our Times,
> That Wit and Honour are become our Crimes.[37]

The abrupt command to "Stay," and the following caesura and enjambment emphasize the verse's function as a break with, rather than a continuation of, poetic history, particularly as Philips herself usually writes in fairly regular heroic couplets. The metrical disarray mimics the startling banishment of Cartwright, a banishment that is even more indecorous due to Cartwright's role as "Prince"—it is as if Philips had suddenly stopped the inexorable descent of a powerful masque figure with the warning that the audience is not ready to receive him.

Other contributors nostalgically cast Cartwright as the end of the Caroline aesthetic line: Dering writes, "I'll only tell / The World when Wit and pleasing Fancy fell; / They died with thee."[38] In contrast, Philips makes Cartwright a symbol of future royalist possibilities that might include the loyalist wife of a moderate Cromwellian within their scope:

> But when those happy Powers that guard thy Dust,
> To us and to thy Memory shall be just,
> And by a Flame from thy blessed Genius lent,
> Shall rescue us from this dull Imprisonment,
> Unsequester our Fancies, and create
> A Worth that may upon thy Glories wait;
> Then shall we understand thee, and descry
> The Splendor of Restored Poetry.[39]

Philips's poem then becomes an exercise in prolonged deferral, a gesture toward a futurity not elaborated in a logical procession of historical events but condensed into a mythic reversal of present political relations, one as sudden and unconflicted as the court masque's banishment of the antimasque. The shift from politics to poetry, however, not only elevates Cartwright to the status of prince, but also enables Philips to identify herself with the royalist "us" who have suffered under the present regime. Many of the contributors—such as John Berkenhead, who had been the editor of the official royalist newsbook, *Mercurius Aulicus,* until 1646, or Henry Lawes, who had been a prominent court musician until the king's move to Oxford in 1642—had lost their livings as well as their king with the royalist defeat.[40] Other contributors to the Cartwright volume, however, such as Francis Finch, who came from a "moneyed family of prosperous lawyers," and Edward Dering, whose composition fee was removed in 1644, had not suffered financially under the wars.[41] Philips herself benefited, if only vicariously, from her husband's sequestrations of at least 11 estates.[42] Given the proximity of Charles II just across the border in Scotland, readying his invasion, and her husband's activities for Parliament throughout the year, Philips's presentation of herself as an ardent royalist may be politic as well as political. By claiming that Cartwright will "Unsequester" *fancies,* she situates herself as culturally, if not materially, impoverished by commonwealth policies and flattens out the differing economic hardship suffered by the group to represent a community that suffers ideologically even when its estates remain intact.

Furthermore, the prolonged deferral of Cartwright's presence enables Philips's own performance. By implication, Philips only comes into being as a poet because the *real* royalist poet is not only literally dead but politically and aesthetically beyond the understanding of "our Times." If "we," the reading public, are not yet ready for Cartwright, "we" are obviously ready for Philips, who acts as a stand-in, a poet whose public appearance depends on the vicissitudes of the very political context she disparages. The closing couplet of her poem continues both her identification of

Cartwright with standard royal images and her deferral of his presence: "Til then, let no bold hand profane thy Shrines / Tis high Wit-treason to debase thy coin."[43] Philips presents her poetic product as built around the shrine of Cartwright's poetry, a fairly standard conceit taken up by the other poets who describe his book as an "Epitaph," a "Legacy," and "thy Monument."[44] While Philips's deferral stands in contrast to the nostalgia of the other writers, the repetition of the conventional trope of the text as shrine or monument presents a royalist community bound together through mourning, structured around a series of central absences—Oxford, Cartwright, the king—that rob the male poets of place and preferment but enable them to present poetry as an ideological commitment to the royalist cause, and allow Philips in particular to become a leading proponent of that cause, a proxy poet who heads the collection despite her status and her gender.

Philips's manuscript poetry continues the work of transforming a loose group of affiliated poets into a politicized coterie of which she is a centering force, its circulation and poetic repetitions binding together a group of royalist writers as an elitist counterpublic. As Margaret Ezell warns, we should not read manuscript poetry as private but as an alternative forum for the formation of public identities: Katherine Philips, Philip Sidney, John Donne, and Anne Wharton "all had public reputations long before their verses were printed."[45] Philips reached a wide audience: in addition to the men already mentioned, her poems were read by Anne Owen, Mary Harvey, Mary Aubrey, an ex-Oxford man named Nicholas Crouch, the third Earl of Bridgewater, Jenkin Jones (a radical approver under the Propagation Act), the royalist divine Jeremy Taylor (who had also attended Oxford), John Davies, the republican Robert Overton, and Andrew Marvell.[46]

The surviving autograph manuscript from the 1650s forges links with a number of royalist writers already mentioned in connection with the Cartwright volume, most notably Berkenhead, Vaughan, Dering, and Finch. The poems to these men were all written around the time of the publication of Cartwright's *Comedies* and of a later collective publication, featuring many of the same writers alongside Philips, by Henry Lawes—his *Second Book of Ayres and Dialogues*.[47] The proximity of these poems to the two printed volumes suggests that Philips wrote them not as bids for individual economic patronage, but in order to smooth her entry into these projects of collective publication. The poems to the four male writers differ in mode of address and, to some extent, imagery, but all are praised in terms of the royalist virtues so prevalent in her poem to Cartwright. Finch, for example, from a powerful family in Kent connected to the Derings through marriage,[48] wrote a discourse on friendship that seems to have become the inspiration for Philips's many poems on the subject. Philips's manuscript verse to Finch, "To the noble Palaemon on his incomparable discourse of Friendship," commends him for a loving restoration of the "Crown" of friendship, central to the mutual ties of the coterie, which in turn allows the royalist community to unmask itself:

> We had been still undone, wrapt in disguise,
> Secure not happy; cunning, but not wise;
> War had been our design, interest our trade,
> We had not dwelt in safety, but in shade.[49] (1–4)

In another poem, "On Mr. Francis Finch," she praises him as the ideal friend and positions him at the head of the royalist community: "He's our original, by whom we see / How much we fail, and what we ought to be" (61–62).

However, as comparison between these poems and the one addressed to Cartwright suggests, there is no stable original in Philips's poetry. Instead, each writer in turn comes to occupy center stage, filling in for the absent court and king. Thus, in her poem to Henry Vaughan, "To Mr. Henry Vaughan, Silurist, on his poems," his poetry takes on the role of royal martyr. Like the death of Charles I, Vaughan's verse expiates for the present sins of the nation, but does so in the infinitely repeatable form of the poetic text, reborn at each reading: "For each birth of thy muse to after-times / Shall expiate for all this ages crimes" (7–8). In Philips's poem to Berkenhead, where she praises one of his anonymous publications,[50] the style that betrays Berkenhead's authorship to Philips is likened to the overpowering visibility of royalty that breaks through any disguise: "As when some Injured Prince assumes disguise... Yet hath a great betraying mien and air" ("To Mr. J. B., the noble Cratander," 1–3). Berkenhead's publication is thus situated within a narrative that echoes Charles I's infamous escape from Oxford disguised as a servant in 1646, publication itself rewritten as a romantic and heroic act. Dering is praised in terms of a heroics of patronage, his virtue symbolized by his discursive charity which "can enough reward" brave actions and gives honor that is "than kings more permanent / Above the reach of Acts of Parliament" ("To the truly noble Sir Edward Dering," 15–16). In this way, Philips constructs a series of almost interchangeable literary heroes, royalists who show their commitment to the cause not through the military exploits from which she would be barred as a woman but through the kind of poetic production she engages in to create them. "To the noble Palaemon" even suggests that the fall of the monarchy itself has elevated writing to new heights of loyalist heroism that paradoxically transcend even the monarch's nobility; Finch's discourse on friendship proves, she says, "Tis greater to support then be a Prince" (20).

IV

To read Philips's manuscript poems of commendation is to watch a shuffling of identities, one poet after another coming to stand at the center of the group of worshipful friends. Philips is rarely alone in her veneration: as in the poem to Cartwright, the manuscript poems emanate from the first person plural, as Philips invokes a collective audience in part created out of their emulation of each poet. This audience revolves around a constantly changing center, each poet elevated to prominence in a dizzying series of quick changes that makes the men she is addressing seem infinitely interchangeable. While she is careful to distinguish each writer in terms of his individual work, the poems themselves also frequently echo the others' imagery and form. Philips's panegyric to Vaughan, for example, draws on the Neoplatonic concept of harmony as the organizing principle of man and the universe: "All truths of use, or strength, or ornament, / Are with such harmony by thee displayed, / As the whole world was first by number made" (34–36). Her poem "To the truly noble Mr. Henry Lawes" is couched in similar terms, with Lawes's music occupying the place of Vaughan's poetry as the Platonic law stabilizing the universe:

> Nature which is the vast Creation's Soul,
> That steady curious Agent in the whole,
> The Art of Heaven, the Order of this Frame,
> Is only music in another name. (1–4)

These repetitions do not indicate Philips's lack of poetic talent but, rather, signal her attempt to rework conventional terms of royal panegyric within a new, narrowed context for royalist writers. The reiteration of conventional terms of address, like the interchangeability of each poet she addresses, marks the participation of each individual and each individual poem in a collective project. The pastoral names adopted by some members of the group are another marker of participation in the project, the inscription of a shared cultural investment and the transformation of individual writers into ideal characters from royalist plays and romances. The repetitions of tropes and romantic/heroic personas construct a community through identification, condensing each verse and each addressee into a single space of homogeneous politico-aesthetic value.

Even Philips herself takes part in the interchange of identities. Her poem to Dering, in particular, implicates her poetry and her poetic persona "Orinda" in the system of substitution that so pervades her commendatory verse. It responds to the aforementioned poem written by Dering in which he masquerades as "Orinda" to address one of her female beloveds, "Rosania." Philips's poem to Dering is self-consciously engaged in a game of poetic compliment and exchange: her verse follows a copied-out fragment of his poem and her title recalls its content.[51] This exchange of poetic compliment demonstrates the antiphonal nature of coterie poetry, the call-and-response envisioned as an act of literary cross-dressing in Philips's poem. Dering can only descend to join the poetic community once he has been disguised as Orinda: "You must descend within our reach and sight, / (For so divinity must take disguise, / Least mortals perish with the bright surprise)" (10–12). Seven lines later, however, Philips reverses this dichotomy of divine masculine interior and sartorial feminine exterior, turning her earlier trope inside out: "My thoughts with such advantage you express / I hardly know them in this charming dress" (19–20). Both versions put Philips in a position of some power as the vehicle for Dering's divine presence or as the intellectual inspiration he refashions. But the poem's confusion of inside and outside ultimately confounds poetic origin: is Dering the originator of poetic creativity or is Philips?

The poem resolves the potentially infinite reversibility of poetic identity in a closing couplet that makes Dering his own original: "For you (god-like) are so much your own fate, / That what you will accept, you must create" (35–36). Philips's poem works to transform Dering into a master of his own destiny, a gesture of compensation that puts a defeated royalist on top, even if it is only on top of his own fate. The couplet echoes Marvell's description of the Fairfaxes, written around the same time, who "make their destiny their choice."[52] However, unlike Fairfax, ex-leader of the parliamentary forces, Dering does not demonstrate active virtue through voluntarily fulfilling his divinely appointed role in prophetic history but instead must bend history to his own "will." This sense of the royalist coterie subject as involved in a powerfully egotistical self-fashioning appears in other poems, such as "On Mr. Francis Finch," written at least two years later:

> He's his own happiness and his own Law,
> Whereby he keeps Passion and fate in awe;
> Nor was this wrought in him by time or growth,
> His Genius had anticipated both. (33–36)

Cartwright's Caroline poem on Bishop Duppa praises his patron in similar terms: "Whose round and solid Mind knows to Create / And fashion your own fate,"[53] but here Philips pushes stoic self-sustenance to the limit. Finch's proleptical guiding spirit preempts his own personal history; he is both a beginning and an end in himself, a natural-born alpha and omega who, like the royalist's king, exists beyond the law.

Philips's poetry is busy filling up the empty space left by royalist defeat not with present debate and political experiment, but with the cultural and political artifacts and idealized identities of her royalist friends. The multiple royalist revolts of 1651, 1654, and 1655; parliamentary experiments with republicanism and a Parliament of Saints; even the centralized and authoritarian government of the Protectorate and Parliament's offer of the crown to Cromwell are all largely absent from her poetry, which replaces historical events with narratives of purely poetic heroism. Unlike Andrew Marvell in his panegyrics to Cromwell, Philips does not attempt to fashion a form of panegyric that can assimilate the violence of recent events into its aesthetic.[54] Instead, she constructs heroes who give birth to themselves in a void, current events appearing only intermittently in these commendatory poems, in vague references to "this sullen age," "this age's crimes," and "rude malice."[55] Each figured as what Catherine Gallagher might call a "*moi absolu*,"[56] the objects of her panegyric have only themselves and each other as referents in a poetic world that mimics the enclosed court not so much as a space of private retreat but of public and privileged subjectivity that attempts to change history from afar. She thus recasts literary production as an act of loyal chivalry both more stable and more noble than the monarchal heroes it replaces.

The interchangeability of each member of the group blurs differences of degree between them. The Finch family, for example, seems to have become Berkenhead's patrons after a political favor he did them in 1656.[57] Interchangeability also blurs differences of gender, Philips using only her initials in the volume to Cartwright, her identity and gender remaining a secret that only a select few would know.[58] Finally, interchangeability smoothes over sticky questions about political affiliations: Dering's absence on the Continent during the crucial war years of 1643–44, and the removal of the composition fee on his estate; Berkenhead's role as a royalist agent and spy, and his simultaneous family connection to the notorious royalist traitor Isaac Berkenhead, his brother; and Philips's own problematic political relations.[59] These complex and varied sociopolitical positions are suspended by the circulation of an ideal royalist identity. In Philips's panegyric the lost king is internalized as a series of cultural and political values that turn each poet into a "glorious shadow," an *eikon basilike,* in a dissemination of the spectacular public power of the royal father to the group who act as public performers for—and reformers of—the age.[60]

V

This image of an idealized community suspended in a void reaches its apex in Philips's poems to her female friends, in particular those to Anne Owen and Mary Aubrey. Embedded within the coterie, Philips constructs an even more exclusive intimate sphere, inhabited by Orinda and the objects of her poetry, Lucasia and Rosania. Critical assumptions about Philips's political neutrality stem from a misreading of her homoerotic verse as unproblematic withdrawal from the upheavals and debates of the commonwealth period. However, this poetry has a more complex relation to the political: it functions, in much the same way as the other poetry, to formalize a corporate identity for the displaced royalists, but one centered on the romantic-Platonic discourse of mutual love. Much of Philips's poetry to female friends draws on John Donne's images of an intimate sphere that repudiates at the same time that it reinscribes the public world beyond the bounds of the lovers' embrace. Arlene Stiebel and Harriette Andreadis have focused on Philips's erotic debt to Donne, but he was also useful to Philips as a model of religio-political alienation. The two poems she most clearly revises, "The Sun Rising" and "A Valediction: Forbidding Mourning," were both written after Donne's ambitions for public office were thwarted by his secret marriage to Anne More, the niece of his patron's wife, an act that caused him to be dismissed from his post of secretary.[61] Donne's subsequent "implosion of epic aspirations" into the little rooms of his songs and sonnets[62] is useful to a writer like Philips, busy inscribing politics within the narrowed sphere of the coterie.

Like him, she transforms public-political narratives of religious dispute and state power into gender-political images of love and domestic bliss. If Donne remodels his rejected Catholic faith as an iconography of secular love, Philips appropriates the godly's renewed faith in narratives of providence and millenarian wonders for her religion of friendship in her "Friendship's Mystery":

> Come, my Lucasia, since we see
> That miracles men's faith do move
> By wonder and by Prodigy,
> To the dull, angry world let's prove
> There's a religion to our Love.[63] (1–5)

In this way Philips turns religious controversy into postcourtly conceit, recasting theological debate over predestination and election, for example, as witty, erotic paradox: "But our election is as free / As Angels, who with greedy choice / Are yet determined to their joys" (8–10).

This reinscription of religious belief or controversy as a lexicon of love between women suggests that Philips's relationship to Lucasia operates as an alternative or corrective to the emphasis placed on theological reform by the godly commonwealth. The fact that she transforms Donne's stridently heterosexual language of love into a homoerotic discourse of friendship between women is perhaps, then, no accident: it allows her to reject the Puritan emphasis on chaste and fruitful marriage as godly vocation that is so central to Anglo-Calvinist ideology.[64] Philips's focus on the homoerotic also stands in contrast to the cavalier creation of a libertine anti-Puritan sexuality, one that takes Donne's incipient Ovidianism to an extreme.[65] Philips's homoeroticism allows her simultaneously to reject the role of sex object assigned to women in the homosocial world of the Interregnum *carpe diem* lyric, as she emphasizes the chaste sexuality of a love that can never bear fruit: "The hearts (like Moses bush presumed) / Warmed and enlightened, not consumed" ("Friendship in Emblem," 19–20), and to replace godly images of productive and reproductive marriage as female vocation with an alternative erotic economy of friendship. If Spenser's militant Protestant sonnets turn the golden "fetters" of Petrarchan "bondage" into the sweet "bands" of the "sacred bower" of marriage,[66] Philips transforms them into courtly ornament: "'Twere banishment to be set free, / Since we wear fetters whose intent / Not bondage is, but Ornament" ("Friendship's Mystery," 18–20). Philips's concept of female friendship does not threaten marriage but transcends or transforms it, rescuing marriage from the Puritan discourse of spiritual duty and relocating it within a homoerotic and heterosocial network of voluntary but elitist affiliation:

> Nobler then kindred or marriage band,
> Because more free; wedlock felicity
> It self doth only by this Union stand
> And turns to friendship or to misery. ("A Friend," 13–16)

Like the poetry to her male friends, Philips's homoerotic poetry works toward homogeneity and interchangeability as she rewrites the patriarchal hierarchies of Donne's secular poems to emphasize the similarity between the women. As Kathleen Swaim argues, Philips replaces the masculine persuasive force of Donne's heterosexual lyric with equality.[67] His famous conceit of lovers as the legs of a compass, in which the static center of the female half anchors her male partner's public wanderings, becomes a more equal relation of mutual support in Philips's "Friendship in Emblem," where "Each follows where the other leans, / And what each does, the other means" (27–28). The parity envisioned here contrasts not only with the gendered asymmetry of Donne's poem, but also with the absolutist rhetoric on which it is founded.[68] Donne's mimicry of political hierarchy within the intimate sphere and Philips's rejection of it can be seen most clearly in his "She's all States, and all Princes I,"[69] which Philips rewrites as "And all our titles shuffled so, / Both Princes, and both subjects too" ("Friendship's Mystery," 24–25). This is the interchangeability of the coterie poetry taken to its logical extreme, one that threatens to undo royalist hierarchy altogether. In the poems that revise Donne, Philips rewrites the intimate sphere as a space that mimics not so much the royalist logic of her commendatory poetry as the reshuffling of titles that accompanied the rise of a new political elite and class of landowners like James Philips during the sequestrations and parliamentary reconstitutions of the 1640s and 1650s. Certainly, this particular image was acceptable to another writer indebted to her poetry, the republican Robert Overton. While Overton revised other of Philips's conceits to fit his politics, he left these lines intact.[70]

Philips's revision of these two central images of Donne indicates that royalist solidarity, taken to its limit, enables a protofeminist defense of women's equality that allows them to join the coterie: "If souls no sexes have, for men t' exclude / Women from friendship's vast capacity, / Is a design injurious and rude / Only maintained by partial tyranny" ("A Friend," 19–22). Here, Philips appropriates the antityrannical rhetoric increasingly used by royalists against Cromwell and puts it to use in a war of the sexes.[71] This sense of women's equality may stem from royalist emphasis on class rather than gender as the primary marker of power, articulated in the idealizing discourse of love prevalent at the Caroline court. Philips's familiarity with this discourse can be shown by her choice of a coterie name for Anne Owen, Lucasia, which comes from William Cartwright's tragicomedy *The Lady Errant,* probably written between 1633 and 1635 but first published in the *Comedies* of 1651. Cartwright presents his heroines as philosophers and paragons of virtue: with all the men at war, the Princess Lucasia and her lady Eumelia discuss love, friendship, duty, and honor in high rhetorical mode while simultaneously saving the court from a female plot and solving the offstage international conflict through marriage (a favorite trope of Caroline drama, ever since Charles's marriage to the French Henrietta Maria). However, the very context for this female empowerment limits it. Both Lucasia and Eumelia evoke a democracy of love that licenses Eumelia to contradict her mistress, their mutual participation in an elevated discourse of ethics and sentiment temporarily erasing privilege and power. Lucasia, for example, claims: "Love's kingdom is / Founded upon a parity; Lord and subject, / Master and Servant, are names banished thence."[72] Yet this courtly leveling does nothing to alter the material and political differences between the two women and is set in contradiction to the comic subplot in which a group of women attempt to steal real political power from the absent men, a female rebellion that culminates in the kind of parliament of ladies later used by royalist writers to satirize the commonwealth parliaments.[73]

Cartwright's elevation of women to positions of erudition and moral heroism may have been part of what attracted Philips to royalism in the first place, but in *The Lady Errant* gender parity is sanctioned only insofar as it works to support state power and royal hierarchy. The circulation of the rarefied discourse of Platonic love becomes itself a marker of membership in court culture in the play, as it did in the Caroline court under Henrietta Maria. In Philips's poetry the democracy of love functions in a similar way, as a coterie game, the idealized prerogative of a like-minded cultural and political elite. The mutual support of the compass image suggests that female erotic parity enables women's forays into the coterie and even into the wider public sphere, as champions of royalist cultural ideals, "To teach the world heroic things" ("Friendship in Emblem," 40). But in Philips's verse it also operates as a trope of mutual regulation, the inscription of a closed circuit. Philips ensures that the parity of poetry and friendship—both heterosocial and homoerotic—is ostentatiously cut off from the "multitude" where their utopian equality might have more radical implications: "For vulgar souls no part of friendship share: / Poets and friends are born to what they are" ("A Friend," 65–66). If Philips's poetry mimics some of the rhetoric of political mobility imagined by republicans like Milton, it does so in order to resituate this mobility within the charmed circle of poetic production, where men and women's equality of virtue and affect becomes a sign of a decidedly elitist ideological affinity.[74]

Philips's discourse of female friendship repeats on a smaller scale the homogenizing impulse of the panegyric to her male friends, inscribing an elitist public sphere within the wider arena of debate. Her own vexed relation to this arena is dramatized by her poem "To (the truly competent judge of Honour) Lucasia, upon a scandalous libel made by J. Jones," which responds to Jones's threatened publication of a poem she wrote to Vavasor Powell about Charles I's execution. Like Powell, Jones was a radical approver on the Commission for the Propagation of the Gospel in Wales who went north to fight Charles II in 1650,[75] and he was also responsible for threatening Thomas Vaughan (Henry Vaughan's brother) and his friends, refusing to let them preach.[76] The possibility that he might publish her politically sensitive verse leads Philips to assert defensively that "honour is its own reward and end" (37). She goes on to mock those who seek public approval, "beg[ging] the suffrage of a Vulgar tongue" (39), and then to link this elitist attitude to monarchical arguments for divine right: "from a Clown / Would any Conqueror receive his Crown?" (43–44). However, she also notes that the scandal surrounding her poem has "advantage in't: for gold uncoined / Had been unusefull, nor with glory shined" (55–56). This contradictory relation to a wider public sphere presented as both a demeaning, democratic devolution of poetic power and as a minting of texts that are otherwise devoid of use value, is partially resolved by Philips's final appeal to a royalist readership, embodied by Lucasia, which will vindicate her political poem: "Yet I'll appeal unto the knowing few, / Who dare be Just, and rip my heart to you" (65–66). Philips's other poetry constructs this loose group of ideal writers and readers.

Resituating Philips in the postcourtly coterie offers us at least two insights. First, her dissemination of the public power of the royal father to a group of publishing poets marks the shift from royal to royal*ist,* from monarchy as a matter of fact to monarchy as matter of public debate—a political ideology that must be defended in print, even when the very terms of divine right deny the importance of that debate in its claim to power. Philips's poetry helps to create a paradoxical royalist counterpublic in which royalty becomes the prerogative of a politicized coterie rather than the king, a coterie that represents Caroline values poetically without engaging in the direct polemic that might compromise their elitist sociopolitical status. Second, by exploring the way in which even a royalist woman writer benefits from the vicissitudes of the revolutionary period, we can begin to appreciate the complexity and diversity of women's writing during this period. In Philips's case, in particular, this exploration allows us to chart the contradictory relation of an all-female sphere of erotic parity to the public politics of a new kind of loyalist resolve.

2 ❖ The Failure of Royalist Heroic Virtue

Philips's "On the 3. of September, 1651"

Christopher Orchard

The battle of Worcester, the occasion of Katherine Philips's poem "On the 3. of September, 1651," not only signaled a comprehensive defeat for the royalist party but also brought the third phase of the British civil wars to a decisive end. At the end of the poem, Philips praises the constancy of virtue because it does not possess the political instability symbolized by the "Crowns and Scepters" present at Worcester. This seemingly apolitical turn inward, though, is only considered by Philips after she spends most of the poem attacking an incompetent royalist leadership in general and an irresponsible Prince Charles in particular. When Philips indirectly but provocatively asks Charles whether he still wants to be king, the question is raised in the context of the battle itself, which was instructive not only in showing how "such Diadems become so cheap" but also in pointing to the ignominious sight of "hero's tumble in a common heap." The loss of rank was an inevitable facet of the leveling nature of death, of course, but the ignominious "tumble" taken by these "hero's" astutely exposes and deconstructs the rhetorical value inherent in the heroic virtue with which royalists had inscribed their campaign and cause.

Philips's perceptive reading is also, I suggest, a critique of a royalist poetics that subscribed to and advocated this association between royalist leadership and heroic virtue. The salutary lesson offered by Philips's take on Worcester applies specifically to the preface to William Davenant's *Gondibert* (1651), which centers on a royalist military and court culture. Davenant began *Gondibert* while a resident of the exiled royalist court of Henrietta Maria at the Louvre, a day after Charles was triumphantly crowned king of the Scots at Scone. As Charles was escaping into France in late October after the debacle of Worcester, Davenant was captured by Parliamentarian forces and imprisoned on the Isle of Wight, abandoning his poem while awaiting possible execution. Davenant had tumbled like those at Worcester, and the preface to *Gondibert* became the signifying text of an unrealistic royalist model of heroic virtue. This failure may explain why Philips turns away from abject royalist political and literary examples of leadership and embraces a model of virtue centered on the coterie circles of friendship that characterized her poetry and that have become the focus of much critical attention.

What I suggest, however, is that this focus on retired virtue and friendship ignores a more political and pragmatic understanding of virtue available for Philips's consideration in 1651. The literary model for this was *Parthenissa,* and the author was Roger Boyle, Lord Broghill, with whom Philips would later collaborate in Dublin in the 1660s. Unlike Davenant, Broghill was successful in both personal and literary spheres. He had seamlessly weathered the political storm by transitioning from royalist affiliations to a successful military and administrative career under a new commonwealth government, while his romance *Parthenissa* was completed and successfully published in 1651. What is most pertinent about his text is the way it offers a heroic narrative that neutralizes the divisiveness of civil war hatred. It provides Philips with intimations of the friendship-based model for heroic virtue that cut across party lines and provided a successful alternative to the disastrous royalist examples typified in life at Worcester and in print in the preface to *Gondibert*.

I

Many critical evaluations of Philips's poetry have presented her as a committed royalist. Hero Chalmers, for example, views her poetry as a vehicle for encoded royalist alliances expressed through friendship and a counternarrative of her personal life as the wife of a prominent local Parliamentarian.[1] Catharine Gray sees Philips not only as part of "an elite circle of heterosexual collectivity opposed to Parliamentary rule" but also as one of its chief spokespersons.[2] She regards the verses of contributing writers to the William Cartwright edition of 1651 as showing their "ideological commitment to the Royalist cause," in which Philips's own contribution indicates her role as "a leading proponent of that cause," a key point that is also made in the present volume by Amy Scott-Douglass, who sees Philips as the "defender of the royalist face."[3] These readings, however, downplay reading Philips's poetry as the site of dissatisfaction with, if not a disengagement from, royalist ideology. Furthermore, such viewpoints ignore her volatility of feeling and shifts in political affiliations. If Philips can be presented as a leading advocate of the royalist cause when Cartwright's poems were printed in June 1651, how might we explain her disdain toward royalist policy three months later when the battle of Worcester takes place? I take my cue then from Robert C. Evans, one of the few critics who argues for the complexity of her political thought. Evans's own reading of the Worcester poem is perhaps too cautious in concluding that Philips "seems to have been a Royalist capable of seeing even a king as a flawed, fallible man"; I argue that her dismissive tone goes far beyond this humanistic statement of vulnerability.[4] However, his reading is significant because he does see her ambivalence as existing prior to the Cartwright volume. He notes that the dark ambiguity of her poem to Mrs. Awbrey, dated April 1651, shows a possible contempt for Charles as he was about to shed blood in his conquest of England. Furthermore, Evans's observation that "L'accord du bien" is a poem in which "she champions kingship less than virtuous rule, especially personal self-control" anticipates her critique of Charles in the Worcester poem, where he conspicuously demonstrates a selfish willfulness in pursuing the military campaign into England.[5]

There is much in the body of Philips's verse that indicates her adversity to the unpalatable nature of war. A poem such as "A Country Life" typifies the Virgilian life of *otium* while "A Retir'd Friendship. To Ardelia" is redolent with images that suggest the beneficial nature of withdrawal into mutual friendship, mercifully free from "the quarreling for Crowns," "Bloud and plots," or "the noise of Wars."[6] But there are also certain images that cross over her poetic genres and suggest ways in which martial and bucolic demarcations were becoming blurred. For example, Philips's depiction in her antiheroic Worcester poem of the bodies of heroes in a heap is similar to the conception of the leveling nature of death that she had conveyed in "La grandeur d'esprit," where kings and conquerors are among those that "Are tumbled in their grave in one rude heap" (25). The shared words "tumble" and "heap" suggest that philosophical meditations about death and the brutality of war have become inseparable: war has invaded the meditative space and meditation has entered the battlefield. But the presence of these images in "On the 3. of September, 1651" is also a material fact, an accurate representation of the battle scene itself. Francis Collins reports in his newsbook an account given by Robert Stapylton as follows: "it is certified from Worcester, that what with the dead bodies of men, and the dead Horses filling the street there was such a nastinesse in the city of Worcester than a man could hardly abide in the town."[7] Both Philips's and Stapylton's descriptions of the pile of bodies recall the figure of King Death presiding over the charnel house of Worcester.

Death's proclamation warns those of Charles Stuart's generation that if they choose to jostle Death or be his competitor, then he will soon capture them, and their end will be swift: "If the first step be in the Throne, the second shall be in the Grave" (fig 2.1). It is an admonition necessarily incisive given that, as the broadsheet

Fig. 2.1. Death's proclamation. Courtesy of the British Library, © The British Library Board, 669.f.16(29).

acknowledges, Charles was still a fugitive, having evaded capture.[8] The author also includes a "List of the Family from which Charles the second King of Scotland descended, that sat in the fatall Throne of Scotland, and came to untimely ends," as well as a list of those killed or captured during the battle itself. The lists and the image suggest that Worcester both continued the royal curse and emphatically demonstrated in its own right the futility of fighting for the royalist cause.

The futility should have been obvious from the moment the campaign for Worcester began. The fact was that up until August the government knew exactly where Charles's supporters were located; it was hard not to know. Cromwell was still in Scotland, and regular packets of letters were arriving in Whitehall detailing troop movements. There were various skirmishes, but the Royal Army was tentative and made few forays. Cromwell informed Parliament in early August that he had deliberately allowed Charles to march south to save Parliament the expense of prosecuting the war and to avoid another winter in Scotland, where his troops had previously suffered from the cold and lack of food. Most accounts suggest that Charles received little support once he entered England. Furthermore, there was little support for Charles's intentions. In a letter dated from Newcastle August 7, 1651, to the Council of State describing Parliament's successes in Scotland, George Downing notes in a postscript: "The generalitie of the Scots were against the present attempt for England, but the KING told them hee would march with as such as would follow him: hee look's very despondingly, but must adventure all."[9] The support simply had never been there. A report from Carlisle on August 9, 1651, informs Parliament that "The Scots themselves confesse that 16 of their great Lords have diserted their King in his attempting to come into England, he having none for him before he marcht in."[10] More incriminating is the revelation, in the same issue, of a batch of letters seized by parliamentary scouts, one of which was a letter written by Duke Hamilton to William Crofts, Charles's ambassador to Poland. In the August 8 letter, Hamilton recalls his meeting with two noble lairds "who are all laughing at the rediculousnesse who left Scotland, being scarce able to maintain it, and yet we grasp at all, and nothing but all will satisfie us, or to loose all. . . . All the Rogues have left us, I shall not say, for feare or for disloyalty."[11] In fact, newspaper reports for the month of August say everything about the futility of this campaign. The Parliamentarian Major General Thomas Harrison reports from Bolton, Lancashire, on August 15 that "Their King we hear is discontented and cast downe, that his subjects (as he still cals them) come in no faster to him, his expectations being great therein, though answered inconsiderably either to persons or numbers; many more of their old Souldiers running away from them daily."[12] Support quickly melted away. Later in the same issue, Pecke reports that "not one county in England, notwithstanding their march so far, appeares in the least kind for them; but every County raiseth Forces against them."[13] In retrospective analyses, broadsheets depict it as "A Mad Designe," showing illustrations of Charles sitting upon a throne prior to the invasion of England "in a melancholy posture, between hope and fear."[14]

Worcester had clearly been Charles's initiative, and it reflects his fatal presumption about a widespread national commitment to the royalist cause. In the aftermath, as the royalist military command scattered and many of its leadership were captured, the young Prince of Wales fled to France. Loyal to their monarch, royalist newsbooks explained Charles's failure through the treachery of others: the Scottish nobility in general and General David Leslie in particular. Leslie was Charles's lieutenant-general but had advised against the march on England, and he held his cavalry in reserve at Worcester.

Philips, however, does not look for scapegoats elsewhere. Her response to the crushing defeat is a scathing attack on those responsible for the humiliation of an ill-planned campaign. Her focus on those responsible for the debacle reads like a political policy paper, identifying the mistakes that the royalist leadership had made in the ill-fated journey from Scotland to Worcester. What irks Philips in particular is not how the monarchy itself had been put at risk in this foolhardy venture, but the extent to which Prince Charles had endangered so many other royalists. This irresponsibility, that "Their weight sinks others" ("On the 3. of September," 23), she argues, was what Charles failed to consider prior to his rash decision to march on England.[15] Her citations of classical and biblical figures—Pompey and Samson—indicate their selfishness in taking down others with them, thereby placing Charles in their company.

Philips was not alone among loyalists critical of royalist strategy in 1651. John Ogilby, another writer who would turn up in Dublin theater circles after the Restoration, uses his version of Aesop's *Fables* (1651) to indict a strategic policy rooted in stubbornness, inflexibility, and imprudence. In the sixty-seventh fable, "the Oke and the Reed," the oak cannot be destroyed by fire, so 32 winds conspire to bring it to the ground because it cannot bend. Encountering a reed as it drifts helplessly down the river, the oak wonders why the reed was not also destroyed. The reed replies that it bends in the direction of the storm rather than using strength against strength. The strategy of survival, as the moral implied, is to accept superior oppositional forces rather than resist them using brute strength: "Though strong, resist not a too potent foe; / Madmen against a violent torrent row."[16] In other words, royalist policy at Worcester had failed because their strategies had lacked flexibility and because they had been too disdainful to listen to those who may have preached caution.

As Philips moves toward the end of her poem, she turns from a critique of policy to the consequences of the aftermath of defeat. If she had composed the poem immediately after reports of the battle had been published, it was a time of urgent anxiety for royalists who had pinned their hopes on the 21-year-old prince. No one knew where Charles was or whether he was alive. It was certain, though, that the royalist leadership faced an uncertain future, one characterized either by a life on the run or the discomforts of exile. Philips's line "Who'd trust to Greatness now, whose food is air" ("On the 3. of September," 27) invokes John Ogilby's depiction of royalists as "on hard coasts / Wedded to famine."[17] Both authors acknowledge the bitter fruits of defeat. Charles was on the lam, staying in safe houses and wearing the clothes of washerwomen and sailors to avoid capture. He and those lucky enough to escape now had to accept the material realities faced by those who had chosen exile.

II

The sharpness of Philips's analysis is caused not only by the fact that this was a critique of a young adult by a young adult, a 19-year-old writer analyzing the actions of a 21-year-old prince, but also by the outcome of local occurrences related to the disaster at Worcester. Philips would have been all too aware of how this war was coming so close to home. Although born in London, Philips had moved to Pembrokeshire in Wales when her mother had remarried. She was married to James Philips and living in Cardigan by 1648. Wales was always going to be a bull's-eye in this third stage of the war. The move south from Scotland by royalist forces in August 1651 initiated a decisively western-slanted part of the civil war campaign, oriented around Lancashire, Cheshire, and the Isle of Man in the northwest. Parliamentary intelligence indicated that royalist forces "expect assistance from *Wales*, which makes them keep on that side of the Country as much as possibly they can."[18] They had high hopes of picking up support because Wales was assumed to be royalist country. In a retrospective royalist analysis of the campaign, Wales is described as "a Countrey eminent for security and for faithfulness, where the People, and there dwellings, would have outvied each other in loyalty."[19] It was not surprising, then, that three pro-royalist events around the time of the campaign were Welsh in origin. First, there was a royalist insurrection in Cardiganshire in June 1651 that had potentially serious consequences. In that month, R. D. reported to Parliament about his skirmish with royalists 14 miles from Cardigan where he was stationed. He reports that the royalists were carrying around a declaration "which reflected much upon the Parliament, & the present Government. The people were made to believe that Charles Stuart had an army within 40 miles of them, and that all the Nation, as also these Counties would rise."[20] Second, the Earl of Derby landed in Lancashire from his base on the Isle of Man and rallied his troops around North Wales, where it was reported that he had the support of 8,000 Welshmen. Finally, the Welsh Presbyterian minister Christopher Love, originally from Cardiff, used his pulpit in London to provide explicit support to Charles's cause.

The consequences for royalists in all three events, however, would have demonstrated to Philips the foolhardy nature of royalist heroism and the pointless commitment to a losing cause. The rebellion was easily suppressed by her husband, among others. Parliamentary forces were raised in surrounding counties, and 40 royalists were killed and 60 captured. The defeat was decisive and was regarded as succeeding in "prevent[ing] any design that may be on foot in this county." After Love's arrest, his friends signed a petition in July 1651 asking for reconcilement as a gesture of healing and conciliation following the divisions of civil war; it only resulted in a brief reprieve. He was executed on August 22, the day Charles and the Scots-royalist army arrived in Worcester. A similar fate awaited Derby. On October 15, while Charles finally set sail from Gravesend to Holland disguised as a sailor, Derby was executed in Bolton, despite his efforts to get his wife to hand over the Isle of Man to the government to save his life. The local government in Wales moved quickly to punish those involved in the push toward Worcester. In the weeks after the battle, courts-martial were carried out over the Welsh border in Chester on October 1, where an act of Parliament was read concerning treason for corresponding with Charles. Prominent executions took place at Chester, Shrewsbury, and at Bolton. A week later, at least nine others suspected of treason, either colonels or ministers, were arrested. The Welsh component of the royalist cause had been decisively shattered, a reality that must have played on the mind of the young Philips in Cardigan.

III

These series of arrests, trials, and executions had signified the prosaic realities of a failed campaign and poor leadership centered around the concept of the hero. But Philips's poem is not simply about critiquing Charles's military tactics and selfish behavior: she also questions the job itself. Why *would* Charles still want to be king given what he had seen? As Philips said in another poem, absence makes love "useless as crowns to captiv'd Kings" ("A Dialogue of Absence 'twixt Lucasia and Orinda"). And Charles had almost become one. He had barely escaped with his life and was about to endure a decade of exile while England abolished the monarchy and created a republic. Was it worth making the personal sacrifice simply because of his hereditary position, whose privilege has provided him with the opportunity to "see such diadems become so cheap"? Who indeed would ever want to lead given that those who followed had clearly not been inspired by the concept of heroism and yet had met a similar fate?

Royalist poetics had to take a share in the blame for this political ethos. Philips's critical assessment could equally have been aimed at the promulgation of those leadership values contained in theories about heroic poetry current at the time she was composing her poem. The most culpable of those writers was William Davenant, whose preface to *Gondibert* (1651) encouraged an exaggerated sense of heroic virtue in military and political leaders for whom the poem was intended.

Davenant's preface is an important complement to Philips's poem. The decisive battle of Worcester can be seen as a psychological turning point for royalist attitudes in which antithetical moods are present on either side of the battle itself. If we are to understand Philips's poem as the more negative of these moods, an astute retrospective critique of royalist military and political strategies, we also need to see that she can only write it this way because the prevailing mood leading up to the defeat was the opposite of her cynicism: exuberance, self-congratulatory assuredness, but also possessing a naïveté that generated false assumptions. Davenant's preface offers a valuable insight in relation to Philips's poem for two reasons: first, it is written as a political directive. Just as Philips's poem offers a critical analysis of what went wrong, Davenant's work offers critical advice, couched as poetics, of how to conduct a military campaign to ensure that everything goes right; second, it contains a postscript published shortly after the disaster of Worcester that shows that Philips's critique was justified. For despite the realities of defeat that Philips addresses, Davenant is in denial, somber in mood, but refusing to acknowledge the implications for his party.

Davenant's preface is ostensibly a contribution to the apologia genre of poetry. The Renaissance tradition of advocating the efficacy of poetry over other disciplines and defending it from false charges of immorality and irreligion was articulated most famously by Sir Philip Sidney in his *Defense of Poesy*. Davenant reworked the same topics but refashioned them as a means of advocating poetry's crucial importance as a tool for ensuring social obedience in the masses. Davenant was writing a heroic poem whose settings of court and army were inhabited by "the most necessary men" who exhibited virtue either by "prerogative of blood" or "greatnesse of mind."[21] Davenant's equation of virtue with nobility of birth and mind necessarily meant the exclusion of virtue in those who were neither. So, whereas poetry was for a very specific social class of reader, laws were for commoners, whom this poem "deserts." Davenant justifies such dismissive hauteur by arguing that it is the responsibility of leaders to set the example: "for if the examples it presents prevails upon their Chiefs, the delight of imitation... will rectify by the rules which those Chiefs establish of their own lives, the lives of all that behold them" (*Gondibert*, 30). It follows that heroic poetry would make such men virtuous, and then they would influence those who followed: "Princes and Nobles being reform'd and made Angelicall by the Heroick, will be predominant lights, which the People cannot chose but use for direction" (100).

Thomas Hobbes concurred with this opinion when he crafted his reply to Davenant's preface. In identifying the three regions of the world in which humankind resides—courts, cities, and the country—Hobbes praises the courts because they contain "Princes, and men of conspicuous power (anciently called *Heroes*) [who cast] a lustre and influence upon the rest of men."[22] By calling such men "conspicuous," Hobbes seems to be drawing attention to those whose visible political influence should be exercised in rallying others around the royalist cause. But this could only be attained if leaders emerged from private seclusion to take on these roles, a crucial consideration given that Davenant was writing the preface just as Charles was being defined as a Scottish king and beginning to gauge the interests of local Scottish support for his English campaign. His preface is partly, then, a royalist poetics of recruitment, its own version of the Marvellian "forward youth" in "An Horatian Ode." Marvell finds his example, of course, in the vibrantly kinetic Cromwell who, ironically, is the ideal example of the leader Davenant is promoting since he emerges from his "private garden" to assert a new identity for the state. In contrast, even at this early stage of Charles's public identity as Scottish king, Davenant is already anticipating just how difficult it will be to motivate certain individuals to become the leaders the royalist cause needs. For while these men will ensure that "the Multitudes would endure that subjection which God hath decreed them," thereby ensuring class acquiescence perhaps of the large number of citizens they would need to recruit in support of Charles's southern journey, Davenant acknowledges that the virtue of public office involves "painful activenesse" (*Gondibert,* 33). This raises the question of whether emerging into public life is worth the price of sacrificing retirement for those royalists who would prefer to remain on the fence and see how the campaign plays out.

Davenant raises this issue because he sees his own work as political engagement. He offers similitudes between the work of writing and organizing a military campaign of the kind royalists were contemplating in January 1651. In referencing the time it took to organize the poet's material, Davenant's conceits apply equally to the preparations needed for a successful martial strategy: "great forces ask great labour in managing, then by an arrogant braving the world, when he enters the world with his undisciplin'd first thoughts: For a wise Poet, like a wise Generall, will not shew his strengths until they are in exact government and order; which are not the postures of chance, but proceed from Vigilance and Labour" (*Gondibert,* 53–54). The preparation needed to write a good poem, with its emphasis on discipline, hard work, and careful watching, suggests the first steps of a concerted campaign, advice, ironically, that would not be heeded in the rush to get out of Scotland. The preface also emphasizes discipline in writing and military tactics alike. For example, Davenant suggests that giving the plot of the story away too soon is akin to one "who commanding a party out...imparts openly the design ere he begins the action" (40–41).

Other imitative discursive moves follow. The preface contains so many tropes saturated with military metaphors of subterfuge and spying that it suggests that poetics is engaged in the same practice as gathering intelligence on the verge of a campaign. Hence, imitating other writers and deciding where to place their influence is as acceptable as "a forward Scout, discovering the Enemy, to save his own life at a Passe, where he then teaches his Party to escape" (*Gondibert*, 56). Inspiration is likened to verbose and incommunicative observers on the front lines. Those who write from their conscience tend to produce texts like "a fearful Scout, after he hath ill survey'd the Enemy, who then makes incongruous, long, and terrible Tales" (67). Even Hobbes is recruited for his covert activities. In thanking him for being his editor and receiving his poem in parcels, Davenant comments, "and who so guided can suspect his safety, even when he travels through the Enemy's country" (61). In this atmosphere, no one can be trusted, particularly readers, who are to be treated as hostiles. Davenant advises caution against a small but potent number of learned readers who "lie as small parties, maliciously in ambush, to destroy all new Men who look into their Quarters." And there is a suggestion that without the author's firm control over them, the reader will prove disloyal and succumb to republican inclinations: "who, though he be noble, may perhaps judge of supreme Power like a very Commoner, and rather approve Authority, when it is in many, then in one." The poet's duty, then, is to maintain the party line and ensure no disloyalty among readers and subjects to the ideology of either text or campaign. Once the reader/subject is secured, Davenant can reassure the political campaigners in Scotland that they should expect to get the support they need in England. When Davenant remarks that his Christian characters will appeal to the reader since they share the same values, Davenant suggests that this is akin to ensuring the subjects' loyalty to the king rather than the new commonwealth: "Subjects bred under the lawes of a Prince...will rather die near that Prince, defending those they have been taught, then live by taking new from another" (19).

In retrospect, though, Davenant was as deceived as Charles concerning the level of support. The end of Davenant's narrative mirrors the disaster of the campaign. In an uncanny act of political replication, Davenant himself and his text were left fighting for survival. Charles had barely escaped with his life, while other supporters had been captured and executed. Likewise, writing from incarceration on the Isle of Wight in October 1651, a month after Worcester, Davenant reports that he had only written up to the middle of the third book of *Gondibert* before being captured on his way to Virginia and charged with treason. Fellow royalist writers seemed convinced that he would not survive. Samuel Sheppard alludes to him in his third pastoral as follows:

> There is a shepheard cag'd in stone
> Destin'd unto destruction,
> Worthy of all before him were
> Apollo him doth first preferre
> *Renowned Laureate be content*
> *Thy workes are thine own Monument.*[23]

Surely, Davenant must have wondered about his survival as well. In a postscript to the third book written while he was imprisoned, the only compensation he sees for his melancholic disposition is the cold comfort of what he leaves behind; "he who writes a *heroick* POEM leaves an Estate entayl'd; and he gives a greater gift to Posteritie, than to the present age" (*Gondibert,* n.p.).

What must have irritated Philips about Davenant's postscript is the refusal to accept mistakes. In his postscript, Davenant comments on the malicious reader who is perhaps smug that Davenant will not live to enjoy the fame he had boasted about in his preface. Davenant admits the vanity of fame but sees it as a necessary form of self-preservation: "For when I observe that Writers have many Enemies, such inward assurance... resembles that forward confidence in Men of Armes, which makes them to proceed in great Enterprise; since the right examination of abilities, begins with enquiring whether we doubt our selve" (n.p.). The simile is telling since it is a defense of Davenant's decision to write *Gondibert,* and, by inference, Charles's self-assurance in deciding to march on England. Both men had never doubted that they were doing the right thing, and both felt they had the right stuff. In both cases, the results had been disastrous. They had looked foolish, and Davenant's poetics was as much a failure as the political march it paralleled. It is no wonder, then, that Philips wanted to write a poem that sought to deconstruct the lack of self-awareness and self-conceit that had caused such a disaster.

IV

It was clear, based on Davenant's self-delusional understanding of defeat, that the preface to *Gondibert* would not offer a blueprint for any pragmatic political solution for a defeated party. Nor could his poetics of leadership remain intact. Philips's poem saw to that in undermining Davenant's representation of royalist heroic poetry as a site of virtue. But there was an available model of heroic virtue that exemplified a successful praxis that could replace its explication in a theory of poetics. And it was a model proposed by an individual who worked for the new commonwealth and with whom Philips would have a working as well as a personal relationship after the Restoration.

While Davenant only hoped that his heroic poem would activate royalist virtue in England, Roger Boyle, Lord Broghill, was actively displaying such virtue in Ireland in person as a military officer of the new commonwealth administration and in writing through the characters in his romance *Parthenissa,* which first appeared in eight books in 1651, the year of Worcester and Philips's poem. What appeals to Philips is that Broghill's characters exemplify not only the kind of virtue that Philips looks to embrace—qualities of constancy and gallantry—but also a virtue of generosity that enables Broghill's characters to cross political party lines and reconcile with those against whom they fought. Broghill's text is a romance of conciliation, a means by which Philips might find a middle ground between her skeptical distrust of political examples of virtue prompted by Worcester and her inclination to locate virtue only within the coterie of friendships that she had established, largely among royalist friends. What I want to suggest here, then, is that Broghill's text acted as an ideological counterpoint to Davenant's preface to *Gondibert* and could help Philips pivot away from the pre-Worcester farce of a romanticized and impractical royalist zeal to a post-Worcester ethos of conciliation and political virtue.

Broghill's decision to write a heroic prose romance may have been prompted by the failure of Davenant's heroic poem, but it was more likely inspired by his own actions. As Philips's husband was helping to put down the royalist insurrection in Cardiganshire, Broghill was engaging in a military campaign in Ireland on behalf of Parliament, where he ensured the ongoing defeat of royalist Irish forces. He sent dispatches to Parliament in the summer of 1651 detailing his efficient and successful defeat of pro-royalist forces in Irish towns such as Limerick. One of his most exemplary moments, which closely resembled the actions of his characters, occurred with his routing of the forces of Lord Muskerry in August 1651. His defeat of Muskerry a month before Worcester was repeated frequently in newsbooks, which depicted him as a risk-taker who refused quarter after his troops had been outflanked. He was quickly picked out by the enemy "upon the refusall whereof they cryed, kill the fellow with the Gold lace coat," only to be rescued by one of his lieutenants.[24] The defeat of the royalists was comprehensive. Samuel Pecke later printed the report of Colonel John Hewson, the governor of Dublin, who stated, "Muskery was met with by my Lord Broghill, and was routed, with the loss of five hundred men upon the place, and as many wounded."[25] It is likely that Broghill orchestrated his own media release concerning this encounter as Parliament received and then published his account, which was repeated verbatim in newsbook reports.[26]

As in life, so in fiction, where Broghill envisions virtue as characteristic of the courageous individual who leads by example. In book 1 of *Parthenissa,* Artabanes is tempted to seize the enemy's standard despite the fact that is it guarded by 8,000 men. When it is initially captured, he tells his soldiers, "you have just now learn'd, that Victory is woone by Vertue not by multitudes."[27] This statement must surely have resonated with Philips, who blamed political leaders for the collateral damage that occurred whenever they participated in military encounters. In her allusion to Charles, she cites Pompey and Samson, the latter of whom "could not life conclude, / Unless attended with a Multitude." Similarly, Broghill's departure from Davenant's idea that virtue is hereditary may have signaled his anti-royalist position, but the inability of hereditary leaders and members of the nobility to successfully conduct a military campaign with dire consequences, as figure 2.1 shows, would have also resonated with Philips, whose poem demonstrates the ineffectiveness of class privilege. Kings and other "heroes" may have led the fight but they all fell in a "common heap." What war taught Philips was the emergence of class indistinction. In her poem "Friendship's Mystery: To my Dearest Lucasia," she concludes by validating the constancy of friendship because social upheaval in England had enabled them to witness "all our Titles shuffled so; / Both Princes, and both subjects too" (24–25).

Given this political card game, Broghill argues that virtue always trumps breeding or birth. When Artabanes demonstrates his risk-taking with the seizure of the standard, he does it for his love Parthenissa, whom he knows "much more esteem'd the effects of Vertue, than those of Fortune, or Birth" (75). Similarly in book 2, Artavasdes exposes a plot against the king of Armenia by one of his own subjects. Humbly accepting praise for his heroic action, he talks about the origins of his family, who had never had a crown "which succession and not Vertue commonly casts upon men" (93). This preference for nonmonarchical virtue many explain Broghill's willingness to fight for Cromwell in Ireland. In the fourth book of *Parthenissa,* Broghill seems to figure Cromwell as Hannibal, whose commitment to courage and fortune was similar to the descriptors used by Marvell to describe Cromwell in "An Horation Ode." Like Marvell's Cromwell, Hannibal assumed his leadership role through merit not inheritance. Hence, the character Oristes says that he would not be surprised if Izabella rejected her lover and gave herself over to Hannibal, "for though Hanniball be not borne a king, yet his virtue makes him the distributer of Kingdomes, which is a more glorious power than any that can be deriv'd from Succession or birth" (103). What is striking here is the implication that there is no necessary correlation between monarchy and heroic virtue. Virtue is innate, and seemingly a republican trait, but it can be neither taught nor inherited, a lesson that had been plainly revealed to Philips by the events at Worcester.

What *Parthenissa* illustrates above all else, though, and which would have appealed to Philips, are examples of heroic virtue that rise above party politics. Philips's turn inward to the virtues of constancy and friendship had been motivated by her repulsion toward the incompetency and selfishness of those whose policies had brought down everyone around them. There had been no consideration of their own party members. Likewise, Parliament had quickly sent out proclamations for the arrest of Charles and all his supporters, and those captured after Worcester had been rapidly brought to trial if they were prominent royalists or sent into slavery abroad if common soldiers.[28] All sides had demonstrated uncivil behavior.

Parthenissa offers a new model for heroic virtue, one in which clemency extends to one's enemy for displaying qualities that produce admiration rather than disdain. Broghill's philosophy is summed up by a character who observes that he "cherishes vertue where ever/ it is plac'd" (309–10). When truly heroic characters are killed, there is only remorse. For example, when Perolla finds out that he killed Hannibal's brother in battle, there is a distinct lack of gloating: "learning afterwards how great a virtue he had kill'd, deplor'd than gloried in the action" (189). Instead, characters value virtue regardless of the political affiliation of the person who espouses it. Hence, in book 1, when Artabanes thinks he has killed the king, he finds out that it is Artavades in disguise who begs for his life. Artabanes requests it of his own king, "for besides the preserving of so generous an Example for all men to imitate, 'twould be an ill president to have a Prince punish a Subject for being faithfull to his King" (80). Here the virtue of loyalty crosses party lines, and Broghill's observation implies that the same courtesy should be extended to those who had demonstrated such qualities on behalf of Charles. Virtues such as courage and gallantry characterize Broghill's heroes, whose lives are saved by those against whom they fought. In book 2, Artabanes saves the life of Phanasder, despite the fact that his superior Celindus is a traitor, because of his valor. He offers his friendship, and Phanasder accepts because he also has a generous mind and realizes Artabanes's own goodness and generosity. In book 3, Artabanes morphs into the historical figure of Spartacus. When Spartacus attacks the city of Salapia, a

Roman called Perolla persuades the citizens not to yield. The citizens listen because his gallantry is as great as his courage. Because the Salapians had told him of his character, Spartacus desires Perolla as his friend rather than his enemy.

In Broghill's narrative, friendships are formed between characters who are at ideological odds but who share reciprocal qualities of virtue. Thus, when Perolla hears of Spartacus's magnanimity, "he knew not whither the missfortune was greater in haveing so much virtue to his Enemy, or the happinesse in haveing so amply an occasion of glory" (302). Similarly, when Perolla sends a message that all wounded prisoners will be treated honorably out of respect for the high regard he has for Spartacus's gallantry, the reader is told that "this high Generosity had so powerfull an influence on [Spartacus], that had not his honor bin so deeply engag'd, he had rais'd the Seidge, and would have thought it more glorious to decline fighting against so gallant and so civill an Enemy than to have conquer'd him" (306). He continues the siege, he argues, only in order to make himself worthy of Perolla's friendship.

V

Philips highly valued friendship and disdained the selfishness and waste of life produced by war. Philips had never trusted Davenant and Hobbes's locations for virtue. In her poem "Content, To my dearest Lucasia," Philips seeks virtue in friendship and rejects the idea that you could find it in schools, courts, and camps "Where Noise and Tumult and Destruction Live." Her poem on one of those camps, Worcester, exemplified what happened to the virtue of those who were bred up in those locations. The poem was also an opportunity to provide a withering analysis of the systemic problems of a royalist leadership model committed to a futile monarchical cause. The 21-year-old heir apparent had clearly not been ready to exhibit virtue, an admission that poets made when writing verse celebrating Charles II's arrival in England in 1660. Two of those writers knew each other: Abraham Cowley and Philips herself.[29] In one stanza of his poem, "Ode, upon the blessed restoration and returne of His Sacred Majesty, Charles the Second," Cowley associates Charles with virtue on two occasions. In the first Cowley argues that Charles's experiences in European exile had gradually hardened *"his young Virtue"* (13). It was hard to disagree with Cowley's evaluation since Charles was now entering his third decade. The other example suggests that now he possesses "sufficient virtue" (13) to rebuild his country. What "sufficient" implies, though, is that he had not been ready before his exilic experiences. It was hardly flattery to imply that he just about had what it took to exhibit qualities of leadership. Similarly, in her poem, "Arion on a Dolphin, To his Majesty at his passage into England," Philips points to the "miracles" of virtue and safety that guaranteed Charles's return to England. What is noticeable, however, is that virtue lacks all descriptors. Philips is silent on exemplifying the word in relation to Charles and only details the aspects of safety that ensured his survival: uncertain of his fate and betrayed by friends, he is protected from "stabs" or assassination attempts only by heaven's intervention. What emerges is a king only kept "upright" by Providence, an image suggesting the merciless buffeting he had undertaken immediately after Worcester.

Lacking a royalist model for virtue, even after the Restoration, it is easy to see how Philips might have sought her own kind of inner stasis and own set of virtues. Her preferences, though, infer more suggestively that the concluding couplet of her poem—"Oh, give me Virtue then, which sums up all, / And firmly stands when crownes and scepters fall" ("On the 3. September, 1651," 33–34)—is her declarative rejection of an impractical political ideology founded on a risky concept of heroic virtue. Davenant had found a similar fate while engaged in royalist poetics. Davenant's postscript clearly indicates the price he paid, personally and politically, for that ideological stance. Royalist heroic poetry was foolhardy: it risked the lives of those who promoted it, like Davenant, and those who sought to embody it such as the fallen at Worcester. In contrast, Broghill's text offers a way in which heroic virtue in public life can work. His idea of heroic virtue produces friendships out of enemies and creates a set of values—generosity, gallantry, and civility—that trump ideological division. Broghill offers the romance genre as a new literary model of political conciliation. *Parthenissa*'s heroes are not bifurcated into the binaries of "them" and "us," the enemy and the loyalist, as they were in Davenant's preface. Certainly, Broghill's fiction is a replication of dissent and constant military conflict as his heroic characters interrupt their love interests to fight on behalf of their leaders. But these are heroes who often in the midst of battle acquire respect for an individual who, through reports of his or her conduct, demonstrates proof of a heroic kind of virtue. What better way of modeling the aspirations of a country fatigued by two decades of war? What better way for Philips to reconcile her own royalism with her husband's dedication to the commonwealth than to seek a post-Worcester Britain in which there was a willingness to cross party lines to create a coalition of those individuals most suited to characterizing its qualities? It is perhaps no wonder then that a unified Restoration Britain would see a collaboration between Broghill and Philips in Dublin, one that may have been initiated by her reading of a romance that offered the kind of virtue that had been noticeably absent on the streets and fields of Worcester.[30]

3 ❖ Biblical Poetics, Royalist Politics, and Anti-Eschatological Prophecy in Philips's Poetry

David L. Orvis

Among the biographies collected in John Aubrey's *Brief Lives* is an entry on Katherine Philips, close friend of the biographer's cousin, Mary Aubrey. Although critics tend to dismiss Aubrey's text as the work of a gossip, Philip Webster Souers observes that on Philips, "Aubrey is more trustworthy than usual, for he was a cousin of Orinda's own Rosania, *née* Mary Aubrey, who could tell him much about her old friend and could direct him to others who could tell him more. His life of Katherine Philips is at least one monument to his accuracy."[1] Patrick Thomas likewise claims that *Brief Lives* remains "the most important source of information about the poet's parentage and upbringing."[2] If we take Aubrey at his word, then certainly one of Philips's more impressive feats as a young girl was "that she read the Bible thorough before she was a full four yeares old; she could have sayd I know not how many places of Scripture and chapters."[3] While one suspects Aubrey is indulging in a bit of hyperbole here, Thomas suggests that "such precocious attainments may not have been very unusual in a serious little girl from a Puritan background."[4] Perhaps not. What's clear from Aubrey's portrait, even if some details have been exaggerated, is that Philips "was very religiously devoted when she was young."[5]

Aubrey's anecdote has made its way into most Philips biographies, where it has served primarily two functions: first, to demonstrate the poet's intellect and piety, both evident from a very early age; and second, to throw into relief the swiftness of her conversion from a devout Puritan who inveighed "much against the bishops, and prayed to God to take them to him," to an ardent royalist of Laudian persuasion.[6] While it is notable, although by no means unheard of, that someone raised in a Puritan household and wedded to a Parliamentarian who would serve under Cromwell would become a prominent royalist, one unfortunate consequence of the scholarly emphasis on Philips's early abandonment of Puritanism is the scant attention paid to the influence of Scripture on her literary works. That is not to say critics have neglected Philips's biblical allusions. Yet, perhaps because only a few of her poems deal explicitly with religious and doctrinal matters—indeed, she composed just one poem meditating on Scripture—critics have tended not to view Philips as a religious poet in the company of, say, John Milton or Aemilia Lanyer. Whereas Milton and Lanyer were engrossed in biblical exegesis, expounding Scripture and intervening in attendant doctrinal and religio-political debates, Philips, so the story goes, offers only the occasional scriptural allusion, usually to ponder more secular themes—friendship and apostasy, civil war and restoration, exile and triumphant return.

At least one Philips poem may, in fact, invite portrayals of the poet as loath to engage in religious disputes. "On Controversies in Religion" opens with Philips's lamenting the disastrous effects religious conflicts have had on humanity:

> Religion, which true policy befriends,
> Design'd by God to serve Man's noblest ends,
> Is by that old deceiver's subtle play
> Made the chief party in its own decay.[7] (1–4)

Drawing upon the language of Genesis, Philips attributes the "decay" of religion not to a particular Christian sect but, rather, to the machinations of the "subtle" serpent typologically associated with "that old deceiver" Satan. This characterization of sectarianism as a kind of fall does not render sectarians any less culpable than Adam and Eve, but it does recast the conflict: true religion versus false religion becomes all religions versus Satan. Of course, the question of which original parent deserves more culpability for the Fall was, and in some quarters still is, fiercely debated, with misogynist screeds against Eve far outnumbering defenses of her. Refusing to fill in the blanks and tell us which sect is Eve and which Adam, Philips implies that such "Quarrells" (18) are beside the point.

In an effort to transcend sectarian squabbles and recover "Religion.../ Design'd by God," Philips espouses an ecumenical vision of the church:

> And as i'th'Moone's Eclipse some pagans thought
> Their barb'rous clamours her deliverance wrought:
> So we suppose that Truth oppressed lyes,
> And needs a rescue from our Enmitys.
> But 'tis injustice, and the mind's disease,
> To think of gaining truth by loosing Peace.
> Knowledge and Love, if true, doe still Unite;
> God's Love and Knowledge are both infinite. (19–26)

Although Philips did not date this poem, the references to "Enmitys" and "loosing Peace" echo other works composed during and shortly after the English civil wars. In the face of these wars, Philips appeals to irenicism, chiastically linking mortal "Knowledge and Love," which, "if true, do still Unite," and "God's Love and Knowledge," which are "both infinite" and therefore able to subsume diverse Christian doctrines. This call for tolerance as a peaceful resolution resonates on at least two levels, as Philips found herself writing as both an English subject witnessing the ravages of civil war and a royalist wedded to a Parliamentarian. This dual perspective offers an important contrast: whereas England has allowed doctrinal difference to become one impetus for war, Philips's relationship with her husband, James Philips, remains intact. Indeed, Philips conferred upon James the sobriquet "Antenor," after the Trojan elder who sought (albeit unsuccessfully) a peaceful end to the Trojan War. Elsewhere in her works, Philips does, of course, bemoan the structural violence of marriage, especially when it functions as an extension of the patriarchal state, but in "On Controversies in Religion," Orinda and Antenor's marriage figures as a microcosm against which the macrocosm of the state might be usefully contrasted.[8] The solution, in other words, in marriage and in national politics, is tolerance.

On its face, "On Controversies in Religion" rejects sectarianism and the competing claims to "Truth" it engenders in favor of a religious pluralism. That pluralism is founded upon God's "infinite" love and knowledge, which exceed any individual Christian sect. However, the assertion that no doctrine has sole possession of divine truth is no less presumptuous, no less absolute, than the belief systems of those Philips chastises. Philips, like Laud or Cromwell, stakes a claim to divine truth, and she does so not as a cleric or a politician but, rather, as a prophet. "Truth doth delight to ly / At some remoteness from a Common eye," the prophet Orinda reminds us: "Yet 'tis not in a Thunder or a Noise, / But in soft whispers and the stiller voice" (27–30). The wording here recalls the Old Testament prophet Elijah, who in 1 Kings flees into the wilderness to escape the wrath of Jezebel. God instructs Elijah to emerge from his cave and "stand upon the mount before the Lord": "And he said, Come out, and stand upon the mount before the Lord. And behold, the Lord went by, and a mighty strong wind rent the mountains, and brake the rocks before the Lord: but the Lord was not in the wind: and after the wind came an earthquake: but the Lord was not in the earthquake: / And after the earthquake came fire: but the Lord was not in the fire: and after the fire came a still and soft voice."[9] Orinda draws a parallel between the elements "the Lord was not in" and the doctrinal disputes and martial conflicts dividing England: they not only lack God's presence but also distract us from receiving what Orinda calls the "soft whispers and the stiller voice" of divine truth. Although Orinda extends the possibility of divine visitation to her readers, the circumstances of Elijah's prophetic calling cast doubt upon such a premise. As Orinda and her coterie audience would have known, Elijah belongs to the Old Testament's elite class of righteous men—figures such as Noah and Moses, who obey the Lord when virtually no one else does. Elijah observes, "I have been very jealous for the Lord God of hosts: for the children of Israel have forsaken thy covenant, broken down thine altars, and slain thy Prophets with the sword, and I only am left, and they seek my life to take it away" (1 Kings 19:10). What is more, the story of Elijah and his successor, Elisha, suggests that one cannot simply choose to be a prophet. God selects Elijah, who is in turn commanded to anoint "Elisha the son of Shaphat of Abel Meholah... to be Prophet in thy room" (1 Kings 19:16). In taking up the mantle of Elijah, then, Orinda assumes the identity of a scriptural "one just (wo)man" who not only becomes the conduit for divine truth but also establishes a prophetic community. From the mouth of a prophet even the irenic plea for religious tolerance and doctrinal pluralism assumes an authoritarian edge.

In associating her poetic voice with Elijah, Philips establishes a prophetic mode that subtends her poetry. In the present essay, I want to distill that mode against the backdrop of the culture of female prophecy that flourished during the English civil wars and Interregnum. As scholars have amply demonstrated, the tumult of the 1640s and 1650s afforded visionaries compelling evidence that the eschaton was at hand, and that, in accordance with God's promise in the Acts of the Apostles, the time for prophecy had arrived: "And it shall be in the last days, saith God, I will pour out of my Spirit upon all flesh, and your sons, and your daughters shall prophesy, and your young men shall see visions, and your old men shall dream dreams. / And on my servants, and on my handmaids I will pour out of my Spirit in those days, and they shall prophesy" (Acts 2:17–18). Phyllis Mack estimates that roughly 300 women prophesied between 1640 and 1660, a period marked by a crisis of authority that upended the social order and empowered female visionaries.[10] I would add Orinda to the period's diverse cast of prophets and argue that she, no less than her contemporaries, interprets the events of her day as divinely ordained and biblically significant. However, whereas the bulk of her fellow female visionaries construe the decades of turmoil as a sign of the end-times and/or the grounds for radical political critique, Orinda develops a biblical poetic that contests eschatological hermeneutics and rejoins millenarian prophecy.[11]

Simultaneously exploiting and eschewing the biblically sanctioned link between the approach of the end-times and the appearance of prophets, Orinda delivers a series of *anti*-eschatological visions that relate contemporary political crises to the covenant theology of the Old Testament. Specifically, Orinda invokes the Davidic covenant to prophesy the endurance of the sacral monarchy in the Stuart dynasty and the Mosaic covenant to prophesy the deliverance of the monarchy's supporters, who are figured as a covenanted people. What is more, Orinda folds the Davidic covenant into the Mosaic covenant, demonstrating that even during the Interregnum, when England is without a king, the Stuarts and their supporters remain God's chosen people. Grounded in the Pentateuch and in the Deuteronomistic history of the righteous and wicked kings of Israel and Judah, old covenant theology enables Orinda to reframe the execution of Charles I and the establishment of the commonwealth not as a harbinger of the eschaton, as other prophets would have it, but as yet another episode in the longstanding history of righteous and wicked kings, a history that would continue with the return from exile and coronation of Charles II. In this way, Orinda is responding to the increasingly popular trend in radical polemics of reading Charles's reign as a sign of the end of days.[12] She is also following an exegetical tradition that has endeavored to reconcile the terms of Davidic covenant, which states unequivocally that David's line will reign forever, with the eventual conquest of Jerusalem. Like the Deuteronomist, Orinda folds the unconditional Davidic covenant into the conditional Mosaic covenant, suggesting that although the sacral monarchy is, as it was to David, eternally *available* to the Stuart line, the restoration of the English monarchy is contingent upon the English people's fidelity to their own covenant with God.[13]

At times this exegetical project might coincide with the aims of royalist propaganda, but as recent scholarship has shown, it would be a mistake to assume that Philips's works constitute a fawning endorsement of the Stuart monarchy.[14] On the contrary, in ascribing to Orinda the status of prophet, Philips places her in an antagonistic relationship with the monarch, as Old Testament narratives attest. Returning to "On Controversies in Religion," we observe that if Orinda is a contemporary Elijah, then Charles I and Henrietta Maria are Ahab and Jezebel, respectively. And as 1 Kings makes clear, "Ahab proceeded, and did provoke the Lord God of Israel more than all the kings of Israel that were before him" (16:33). When God anoints a king to succeed Ahab, He send Elijah to make the announcement: "And Jehu the son of Nimshi shalt thou anoint King over Israel" (1 Kings 19:16). For her part, Jezebel responds to news that Elijah has murdered prophets of Baal with a death threat: "Then Jezebel sent a messenger unto Elijah, saying, The gods do so to me and more also, if I make not thy life like one of their lives by tomorrow this time" (19:2). This is the pledge that sends Elijah into the wilderness, where God speaks to him in a "still and soft voice." The conflict between prophet and monarch is, as George Savran points out, central not just to 1 and 2 Kings but to the Deuteronomistic history as a whole: "The classic power struggle in Kings is that between prophet and king, and the former is always shown to be the person of greater authority, even though political and military might resides with the monarch.... Despite the imbalance of power, the prophet is usually impervious to the threats of the king, as Elijah proves victorious over Ahab and his son Ahaziah."[15] The claim to prophecy authorizes Orinda to convey divine truths about monarchs and monarchical rule, but it also subverts the dynamic between sovereign and subject, elevating the latter above the former. Or, to put it another way, Orinda defends the concept of monarchy at the expense of individual monarchs.

Another perhaps inevitable consequence of this prophetic mode is that in the process of proclaiming covenant theology and the sacral monarchy, Orinda reinforces the very typological associations between biblical and contemporary figures that mobilized antimonarchical and even regicidal rhetoric. Unsurprisingly, John Milton was particularly skilled at adapting Old Testament tales of wicked kings to make the case for regicide. Christopher Hill notes that in *Eikonoklastes* alone, "Charles I is described as worse than Ahab, Jeroboam, Rehoboam or Saul, comparable with the wilful apostate Ahaz, with Nimrod, Balak and Agog. Milton noted that 'the cowardly and idolatrous King Amaziah' was put to death by his own people, and that his own subjects drove out Nebuchadnezzar."[16] The litany of wicked kings Milton marshals against Charles is only slightly more comprehensive than the lists compiled by sundry other radicals who consulted the Deuteronomistic history in their screeds against the English crown.[17]

Comparisons of Charles and Henrietta Maria to Ahab and Jezebel are especially common. In *No King but Jesus* (1652), Henry Haggar claims that Charles's execution was condign punishment for keeping false prophets, a transgression associated with Ahab:

> These [prophets] are they which again in King *Ahab*'s time deluded him, and caused him to go up to *Ramoth-gilead* to fight, when that one Prophet of the Lord, *Micaiah,* withstood four hundred of them to their faces, and warned *Ahab* not to go up; yet he believing the four hundred false Prophets, rather then that one Prophet of the Lord, went up, and was slain. Thus we see, that through their lyes and delusions, they bring even Kings and Princes to destruction both of body and soul.
>
> These are they which in our age, and in this Nation of *England,* have done the same to *Charles* deceased, which their fore-fathers did to King *Ahab* in stirring of him up to war against his subjects, especially against those that most feared God; and so have brought him to destruction. And these are still at this present time deluding his ignorant son, calling of him *Charles the second.*[18]

In Haggar's typological reading, Ahab becomes a type of Charles, in the same way that righteous figures of the Old Testament are types of Christ. And just as Christ fulfilled the promises articulated by, and represented in, characters such as Noah and Moses, Charles fulfills God's promise to dissolve earthly monarchy in anticipation of Christ's reign at the end of days. Charles's son's "ignorance," then, is scriptural: he does not know he shall meet precisely the same fate as Ahab's son, Ahaziah, who "did evil in the sight of the Lord, and walked in the way of his father, and in the way of his mother....For he served Baal and worshipped him, and provoked the Lord God of Israel unto wrath, according unto all that his father had done" (1 Kings 22:52–53). Indeed, just as Elijah prophesies, God sends Jehu to "smite the house of Ahab [his] master....For the whole house of Ahab shall be destroyed" (2 Kings 9:7–8). Other radicals invoke the story of Ahab to show that the English monarchy has never been divinely ordained. Pointing to God's exhortation to Jehu to wipe out Ahab's house, John Audley writes, "True it is, Kings were of old *Divine,* being promised of God to *Abraham, Kings shall come out of thee,* Gen. 17. 6. And some were by Gods appointment anoynted Kings, as *Saul,* and *David;* but of all Kings since Christs death, it may be questioned, *Whose are all these?* For after the Scepter departed from *Shiloh,* what man, after Christs death, was ever Anoynted King by Gods Command?"[19] For Audley, Charles represents not an antitype but an abomination, claiming divine sanction when the Deuteronomistic history indicates that sacral monarchy ended with Christ's arrival. As radical critiques of the monarchy demonstrate, the Bible's supremacy makes it an especially volatile text, one that buttresses divergent, even contradictory political philosophies that contend not only that they are right, but also that God sanctions, indeed demands, violence to enact these philosophies.

Orinda engages debates about the sanctity of the English monarchy in "Upon the Double Murther of K. Charles, in Answer to a Libellous Rime made by V. P.," a poem that appears first in every edition of Philips's *Poems* published between 1664 and 1710.[20] "V. P." refers to Vavasor Powell, who was associated with the Fifth Monarchists, a millenarian group that celebrated the execution of Charles I as a sign of the eschaton.[21] The group's name comes from Daniel, who prophesies that four kingdoms will rise and fall before the establishment of a fifth kingdom that directly precedes the end of days. According to Powell and the Fifth Monarchists, Charles is this fifth king: "And his power shall be mighty, but not in his strength: and he shall destroy wonderfully, and shall prosper, and practice, and shall destroy the mighty, and the holy people" (Dan. 8:24). Daniel prophesies that this king "shall also stand up against the prince of princes, but he shall be broken down without hand" (8:25). Emphasizing the eschatological dimension of Daniel's prophecy, Fifth Monarchists found license to read this material into Revelation's description of Christ's interim messianic kingdom:

> And I saw an Angel come down from heaven, having the key of the bottomless pit, and a great chain in his hand.
>
> And he took the dragon that old serpent, which is the devil and Satan, and he bound him a thousand years;
>
> And cast him into the bottomless pit, and he shut him up, and sealed the door upon him, that he should deceive the people no more, till the thousand years were fulfilled; for after that he must be loosed for a little season.
>
> And I saw seats, and they sat upon them, and judgment was given unto them, and I saw the souls of them that were beheaded for the witness of Jesus, and for the word of God, and which did not worship the beast, neither his image, neither had taken his mark upon their foreheads, or on their hands; and they lived, and reigned with Christ a thousand years. But the rest of the dead men shall not live again, until the thousand years be finished. This is the first resurrection.
>
> Blessed and holy is he, that hath part in the first resurrection; for on such the second death hath no power, but they shall be the Priests of God and of Christ, and shall reign with him a thousand years. (Rev. 20:1–6)

Correlating the defeat of the fifth monarch with the arrival of Christ's millennial kingdom, Fifth Monarchists would spend the Interregnum preparing for the Second Coming.[22] "After the traumatic events of 1648–9," writes David Loewenstein, "some of the most colourful radical apocalyptic discourses on the king were written by Fifth Monarchist authors, violent revolutionaries who envisioned the destruction of earthly kings as essential to the establishment of the kingdom of Christ, which they believed was imminent."[23] Once the king had been executed, everything became a sign of the end of days.

Philips's "Upon the Double Murther of K. Charles" rejects this millenarian vision and the "height of horrour" (33) realized in its name. In her refutation of eschatological prophecy, Orinda ventriloquizes a Fifth Monarchist claim and then unpacks it, attributing it not to Scripture but to human ambition:

> Christ will be King, but I ne'er understood,
> His subjects built his kingdome up with blood,
> (Except their owne) or that he would dispence
> With his commands, though for his own defence. (29–32)

Orinda's assertion that "Christ will be King" operates simultaneously as an admission to and a denunciation of Fifth Monarchist claims. Robert C. Evans writes, "In one respect this is a swipe at Powell's views as a Fifth Monarchist, since that sect expected the Lord's imminent return and earthly reign. In another sense, however, the phrase simply states a point all Christians accepted: Christ would indeed someday be king and someday sit as judge."[24] Orinda affirms the promise of the messianic kingdom while questioning the Fifth Monarchist insistence upon its imminence. The pronouncement "Christ will be king" does not stand on its own; rather, it is fused syntactically with a series of statements that belie the assertion that the execution of Charles has fulfilled Daniel's prophecy and hence reflects God's will. Although she affirms Daniel's vision that the fifth monarch's kingdom shall be marked by extreme violence—"His subjects built his kingdome up with blood"—Orinda qualifies this vision with a parenthetical phrase—"(Except their owne)"—that undermines the very foundations of millenarian prophecy. In noting that the Fifth Monarchists who celebrate Charles's death have not suffered, Orinda reminds her readers that according to Daniel's prophecy, the violence is to be waged *against* "the people of the holy ones," not *by* them. Moreover, Daniel prophesies that the fifth monarchy "shall be broken, and not by / human hands," indicating that an execution "by / human hands" contravenes God's will. Thus, with a mere parenthetical phrase, Orinda calls into question the millenarian pronouncement that Daniel's prophecy authorizes regicide.

Orinda therefore knows precisely what Fifth Monarchists seem to have conveniently forgotten: that according to Daniel, the righteous, rather than the wicked, shall undergo a period of intense suffering: "And they that understand among the people, shall instruct many: yet they shall fall by sword, and by flame, by captivity and by spoil many days. / Now when they shall fall, they shall be holpen with a little help: but many shall cleave unto them feignedly. / And some of them of understanding shall fall to try them, and to purge, and to make them white, till the time be out: for there is a time appointed" (Dan. 11:33–35). Turning Daniel's prophecy against Fifth Monarchists and other millenarians, Orinda implies that they have defied God's will. In asking why Christ "would dispence / With his commands, though for his own defence," Orinda exposes the Fifth Monarchist interpretation of Daniel as a misreading of Scripture. Obviously Christ would not "dispence / With his commands," so who has? The answer, of course, is the millenarians, who have appropriated God's words to their own selfish ends.

Orinda's rebuke of self-serving eschatology reveals something about her own prophetic mode. The mockery that attends her treatment of the millenarian refrain "Christ will be King" indicates that Orinda does not believe that the end-times are at hand. This belief might appear more sensible than the doomsday preaching of other visionaries, but it is no less bold. As Jesus tells his disciplines, "Heaven and earth shall pass away, but my words shall not pass away. / But of that day and hour knoweth no man, no not the Angels of heaven, but my father only" (Matt. 24:35–36). Although Orinda's prophecy is intended to counter eschatological rhetoric, it is nonetheless predicated upon divine knowledge that according to Christ she does not possess. In this sense, Orinda's prophecies bespeak just as much hubris as those she would disclaim. Against potential charges of hubris, Orinda crafts a biblical poetic that underlies and authorizes her prophecies. Interestingly, Orinda's use of Scripture resembles the biblical poetics of Aemilia Lanyer and John Milton. As Kari Boyd McBride and John Ulreich show, "The ground of self-authorization in both poets [i.e., Lanyer and Milton] is the practice of Biblical interpretation—a reworking of the Bible that simultaneously affirms and radically revises crucial Biblical texts. Both Lanyer and Milton are engaged in fashioning a Biblical poetic, which then becomes the basis for a radical politics that interprets all of human history in terms of Biblical prophecy."[25] Their antipodal views of kingship make Milton and Philips very strange bedfellows indeed, but both poets develop a hermeneutic that locates divine truth in radical rereadings of Scripture. This hermeneutic becomes the foundation for authority that finds expression in prophecy. In sharp contrast to Milton, who deploys biblical poetics to defend regicide, Philips, through the figure Orinda, proclaims the continuation of the sacral monarchy despite arguments that Christ has fulfilled the Davidic covenant and abolished divinely ordained monarchs.

In "Upon the Double Murther of K. Charles," Orinda implies that the sacral monarchy shall continue until the eschaton unfolds and Christ returns to reign over the messianic kingdom. Ironically, this vision depends upon the same typological associations that have been used to legitimate Charles's capture and execution. At two points in the poem, Orinda repeats the charge that the king has "broke God's lawes" (11, 21). As Evans contends, Orinda's "attack on Charles's attackers is all the more potent because she does not dispute their charges against him."[26] For Evans, this concession enables Orinda to take the moral high ground and appeal to reason, but I would add that it also allows her to situate the king's deposition within the framework of Old Testament covenant theology. The future tense of the statement "Christ *will be* King" suggests that the Davidic covenant remains in place until the establishment of the messianic kingdom, when Christ shall return for the millennial reign. In other words, Orinda reinterprets the terms of the Davidic covenant, shifting their fulfillment from the first coming to the second coming of Christ. Thus, the English monarchy does not represent an affront to God, as it does not challenge the otherworldly kingdom Christ describes to Pontius Pilate: "Jesus answered, My kingdom is not of this world; if my kingdom were of this world, my servants would surely fight, that I should not be delivered to the Jews; but now is my kingdom not from hence"

(John 18:36). If, according to Orinda, the first Advent does not fulfill the Davidic covenant, then the covenant that governs the kings of the Deuteronomistic history shall persist until Christ's return. In drawing upon the typological associations Charles's enemies have been circulating, Orinda implies that they, too, affirm at least some version of the Davidic covenant. Why else compare Charles to kings of Judah and Israel? From this vantage, Orinda's tacit acceptance that Charles, perhaps like Ahab, "broke God's lawes" and has been punished for it, demonstrates the continuation of the covenant theology to which Old Testament kings were subjected. Assuming the identity of the Old Testament prophet Elijah, Orinda accepts the typological associations of Charles with Ahab and Henrietta Maria with Jezebel. In so doing, however, she revises the terms of the Davidic covenant and the old covenant theology it represents, insinuating that if Charles is Ahab, then he, like Ahab, corroborates sacral monarchy.

This vision and the biblical poetic that underwrites it are elucidated in the only Philips poem that takes its title from Scripture. Dated April 8, 1653, "2. Corinth. 5. 19. v. God was in Christ reconciling the world to himself" is ostensibly an occasional poem inspired by Good Friday. However, the pastiche of biblical passages Orinda incorporates into her meditation on 2 Corinthians yields a prophecy about the English monarchy, which is to endure a period of Christlike suffering that marks the monarch and his supporters as a covenanted people. In comparing the English king to Christ, Orinda reinforces the doctrine of divine right, identifying the Stuart monarchs as both heirs to and predecessors of Christ's kingship. That Orinda offers this vision in a meditation on a text attributed to Paul is especially illuminating, since he, perhaps more than any other New Testament author, insists that in Christ a new covenant has been instituted, and thus the old covenant no longer obtains. In fact, in 2 Corinthians, just a few chapters before the passage Orinda interprets, Paul writes,

> If then the ministration of death written with letters and engraven in stones, was glorious, so that the children of Israel could not behold the face of Moses, for the glory of his countenance (which glory is done away).

> How shall not the ministration of the Spirit be more glorious?
>
> For if the ministry of condemnation was glorious, much more doeth the ministration of righteousness exceed in glory.
>
> For even that which was glorified, was not glorified in this point, that is, as touching the exceeding glory.
>
> For if that which should be abolished, was glorious, much more shall that which remaineth be glorious.
>
> Seeing then that we have such trust, we use great boldness of speech.
>
> And we are not as Moses, which put a veil upon his face, that the children of Israel should not look unto the end of that which should be abolished.
>
> Therefore their minds are hardened; for until this day remaineth the same covering untaken away in the reading of the Old Testament, which veil in Christ is put away.
>
> But even unto this day, when Moses is read, the veil is laid over their hearts.
>
> Nevertheless when their heart shall be turned to the Lord, the veil shall be taken away.
>
> Now the Lord is the Spirit, and where the Spirit of the Lord is, there is liberty.
>
> But we all behold as in a mirror the glory of the Lord with open face, and are changed into the same image, from glory to glory, as by the Spirit of the Lord. (2 Cor. 3:7–18)

The "bold[ness]" that suffuses this and other passages in Paul's epistles emerges from, and is validated by, the articulation of the new covenant, which supersedes the old covenant embodied in Moses. Predictably, Moses does not fare well when compared to Christ; indeed, Paul portrays Moses as unenlightened, despite the fact that he served as a conduit for divine truth. In Christ, God "will make a new covenant with the house of Israel, and with the house of Judah" (Jer. 31:31). This covenant will, according to God, "put my Law in their inward parts, and write it in their hearts, and will be their God, and they shall be my people. / And they shall teach no more every man his neighbor and every man his brother, saying, Know the Lord: for they shall all know me from the least of them unto the greatest of them, saith the Lord: for I will forgive their iniquity, and will remember their sins no more" (Jer. 31:33–34). Because this new covenant involves the second

Advent, where Christ will return to fulfill its terms, new covenant theology is inherently eschatological: "And I saw a great white throne, and one that sat on it, from whose face fled away both the earth and heaven, and their place was no more found. / And I saw the dead, both great and small stand before God, and the books were opened, and another book was opened, which is the book of life, and the dead were judged of those things, which were written in the books, according to their works" (Rev. 20:11–12). On various counts, then, the passage Orinda has chosen to expound the plight of the monarchy threatens to work against the old covenant theology that is so crucial to her antimillenarian visions.

Yet, Orinda appropriates Paul's audacity, ascribing Christ's ministry of reconciliation specifically to the outcast English monarchy. The poem begins in the past tense, chronicling the circumstances of the Incarnation:

> When God, contracted to humanity,
> Could sigh and suffer, could be sick and dy;
> When all that heap of miracles combin'd
> To form the greatest, which was, save mankind:
> Then God took stand in Christ, studying a way
> How to repaire the ruin'd world's decay.
> His Love, pow'r, wisedome, must some means procure
> His mercy to advance, Justice secure. (1–8)

The "contract" Orinda mentions at the outset is sufficiently vague to encompass all the covenants that precede the Incarnation, while the emphasis in subsequent lines on "humanity" and "the ruin'd world's decay" invokes the Mosaic covenant made between God and the Israelites. As Moses attests, "I call heaven and earth to record this day against you, that I have set before you life and death, blessing and cursing; therefore choose life, that both thou and thy seed may live, / By loving the Lord thy God, by obeying his voice, and by cleaving unto him, for he is thy life, and the length of thy days; that thou mayest dwell in the land which the Lord sware unto thy fathers, Abraham, Isaac, and Jacob, to give them" (Deut. 30:19–20). Here and elsewhere in the Pentateuch the Mosaic covenant is described as conditional—contingent upon the obedience of the Israelites. Paul makes explicit that the new covenant eradicates the Mosaic covenant, but the language of supersessionism is notably absent from Orinda's meditation on Christ's "reconciling the world to himself":

> And since man was in so much misery hurl'd,
> It cost him more to save, then to make the world.
> O what a desperate Lump of sins had we,
> When God must plot for our felicity!
> When God must beg us that he may forgive!
> And dy himself before mankind could Live! (9–14)

Presumably, the "Lump of sins" refers to original sin, since Orinda, in stating that Christ must "dy himself before mankind could Live," echoes Paul's opinion that, "as in Adam all die, even so in Christ shall all be made alive" (1 Cor. 15:22). However, Orinda does not draw the Pauline conclusion that in Christ all earlier contracts become null and void; rather, she elides it. Although the poem's first 14 lines present a chronological narrative that begins with the Incarnation and culminates in the Passion, Orinda's originary characterization of God as "contracted to humanity" does not undergo revision, nor is it abrogated. In the absence of such supersessionist language, the phrase "contracted to humanity" functions as an appositive describing God's ongoing covenantal relationship with humankind. Thus, while Orinda does not deny the signal importance of the Passion, she resists the totalizing logic of Pauline supersessionism, which holds that new covenant theology is incompatible with, and has therefore invalidated, old covenant theology.

The stakes of Orinda's anti-supersessionist, anti-eschatological interpretation of the Passion and its relation to old and new covenant theology are brought into focus as the poem shifts from past to present, from Christ's Crucifixion to the English's monarch's exile—a shift that reveals Christ's ministry of reconciliation to be but a prelude to what becomes a meditation on the divinity of the Stuart monarchy. In a sense, Orinda is merely picking up where Charles I had left off in his *Eikon Basilike,* a work Laura Blair McKnight considers "the most successful piece of royalist propaganda to issue from the English Civil Wars."[27] Following her monarch's lead, Orinda makes the connection between Christ and Charles overt:

> And what still are we, when our king in vain
> Begs his lost Rebells to be friends again!
> What flouds of Love proceed from heaven's smile,
> At once to pardon and to reconcile! (10–13)

The ambiguity of the locution "our king" conjures up (and in so doing draws together) at least three monarchs—Christ, Charles I, and Charles II—whose reigns are defined by former and/or future sacrifice. These kings, who endeavor through "heaven's smile, / At once to pardon and to reconcile," constitute the dynasty of reconciliation signified in the more abstract concept of "our king," which subsumes all (English) monarchs. A similar ambiguity surrounds the possessive pronoun "our." The pronoun might be inclusive, encompassing even those persons who do not recognize the monarch. This reading informs Thomas's suggestion that "the fervour with which she stresses God's love and fatherhood and Christ's redemptive power would seem to imply a universalist view of salvation." This view, Thomas writes, adduces "Orinda's desire for reconciliation and harmony between man and God," which "was paralleled by her desire for political reconciliation and harmony."[28] While this vision is consonant with Orinda's irenicism, the universalism Thomas perceives is tempered by the visionary's demarcating sides in the religio-political conflict facing the nation:

> O wretched men! who dare your god confine,
> Like those who separate what he does Joine.
> Go, stop the Rivers with an infant's hand!
> Or count with your Arithmetique the Sand!
> Forbid the Light! the fertile earth perswade
> To shut her bosom from the lab'rer's spade!
> And yield your God (if these cannot be done)
> As Universall as the Sea or Sun. (19–26)

The juxtaposition of "our king" and "your god" underscores the salience of perspective: on the one hand, God is "As Universall as the Sea or Sun," his will operating irrespective of humankind's actions or beliefs; on the other hand, those who do not accept God's "Universal[ity]" are deemed "wretched." Following Orinda's dynastic vision, this authority extends to Charles I, who has already been sacrificed, and to Charles II, who remains king even to those "wretched men" responsible for or otherwise complicit in exiling him to the Continent. In addition to constructing a monarchical lineage comprising heavenly and earthly kings, Orinda's comparison sets up an intriguing typology, where Christ is simultaneously a type (in his first Advent) and an antitype (in his second Advent) of both Charles I and II.

Crucially, this sacral monarchy also includes King David, the reputed author of the Psalms and hence the source for Orinda's enjoinment to the "wretched men" to "count with [their] Arithmetique the sand."[29] In Psalm 139 (which is "of David," according to the headnote), the psalmist delivers a doxology on God's infinite powers, which far surpass human comprehension: "How dear therefore are thy thoughts unto me, O God! how great is ye sum of them! / If I should count them, they are more than the sand: when I wake, I am still with thee" (17–18). The allusion to David reinforces the distinction Orinda makes between enlightened royalists, who know and have internalized the Word, and ignorant radicals, who repudiate divine truth. More importantly, the allusion to David, the prophet-king and Christ's ancestor, reinscribes the sacral monarchy within the Davidic covenant. Appearing to the prophet Nathan, God says of King David,

> I will give thee rest from all thine enemies: also the Lord telleth thee, that he will make thee an house.
>
> And when thy days be fulfilled, thou shalt sleep with thy fathers, and I will set up thy seed after thee, which shall proceed out of thy body, and will establish his kingdom.
>
> He shall build an house for my Name, and I will establish ye throne of his kingdom forever.
>
> I will be his father, and he shall be my son: and if he sin, I will chasten him with the rod of men, and with the plagues of the children of men.
>
> But my mercy shall not depart away from him, as I took it from Saul whom I have put away before thee.

> And thine house shall be established and thy kingdom forever before thee, even thy throne shall be established forever. (2 Sam. 7:11–16)

Although Paul maintains that the first Advent fulfilled the Davidic covenant, placing Christ on the throne for eternity, Orinda pursues an anti-supersessionist, anti-eschatological alternative, delaying the fulfillment of this covenant to the millennial kingdom at the end of days. All at once, then, Orinda introduces and interweaves typological and genealogical justifications for the divinity of the Stuart monarchy. This strategy serves at least three purposes: first, it counters millenarian prophecies associating Charles I's execution with the eschaton; second, it reconceives the suspension of the English monarchy as a period of trial that shall end with Charles II's return from exile; and third, it ensures that the Stuart line will reclaim the crown, even though the monarchies of the Deuteronomistic history do not obey the system of primogeniture that makes Charles II heir apparent.[30]

If roughly the first half of Orinda's meditation on "God was in Christ reconciling the world to himself" fixates on the sacrifices that bear out the divinity of the monarchy, the second half turns inward, explicating the prophet's role during periods of persecution and exile. As in the poem on Charles I's execution, Orinda mimics and then attenuates the histrionics of millenarian prophecy:

> He [i.e., God] hath a father's, not a tyrant's Joy;
> 'Tis equall pow'r to save, as to destroy.
> Did there Ten thousand worlds to ruine fall
> One God would save, one Christ redeem them all.
> Be silenc'd then, you narrow souls; take heed
> Least you restrain the mercy you will need. (31–36)

Orinda mocks the millenarian obsession with God's capacity "to destroy," which makes the "father" out to be a "tyrant," rather in the same way that parliamentarian invective against the king has painted him as a despot. Positioning herself among the prophets, Orinda alludes to Daniel's description of the heavenly throne room: "A fiery stream issued, and came forth from before him: thousand thousands ministered unto him, and ten thousand thousands stood before him: the judgment was set, and the books opened" (Dan. 7:10). This prophecy coheres with John's vision of the throne room in Revelation: "Then I beheld, and I heard the voice of many Angels round about the throne, and about the beasts and the Elders, and there were ten thousand times ten thousand, and thousand thousands" (Rev. 5:11). Both prophets foresee the millennial kingdom, which shall begin with the judgment of many thousands of people. Whereas millenarian prophets foreground visions of the impending Judgment Day, instilling in their audiences a sense of urgency that has helped catalyze radical religio-political movements and foment rebellion and revolution, Orinda counterbalances the "ten thousand times ten thousand" with the "One God [who] would save, one Christ redeem them all." Ironically, the "narrow souls" are those who fret over the widespread destruction that accompanies the eschaton when they should take comfort in the salvation embodied in Christ. One of Orinda's roles, then, is to reinterpret biblical accounts of the end-times and offer a prophetic corrective to the eschatological visions that have inspired acts of insurrection masquerading as divine will.

Another, no less transgressive role is to assert the endurance of sacral monarchy through a careful revision of the relationship between Old and New Covenant theology. Profoundly aware of the consequences of such a view, Orinda compares herself to Christ:

> But O my soule, from these be different,
> Imitate thou a nobler president:
> As God with open arms the World does woo,
> Learn thou like him to be enlarged too;
> As he begs thy consent to pardon thee,
> Learn to submit unto thy enemy;
> As he stands ready thee to entertain,
> Be thou as forward to return again;
> As he was Crucify'd for and by thee,
> Crucify thou what caus'd his Agony;
> And like to him be mortify'd to men,
> Dy to the world, as he dy'd for it then. (37–48)

Following the example of her God and her king, Orinda strives "to submit unto [her] enemy"—that is, those "narrow souls" who have misread the political upheaval and social unrest of the English civil wars as portents of the eschaton. However, submission is not the same as renunciation, as Christ's and Charles's sacrifices show. Significantly, Orinda channels Paul to convey her determination to prophesy despite any persecution she may encounter. The poem's final lines recall a passage from Galatians: "But God forbid that I should rejoice, but in the cross of our Lord Jesus Christ, whereby the world is crucified unto me, and I unto the world" (Gal. 6:14). In its immediate context, Paul is "boast[ing]" about the promise of the new covenant, through which Christ has redeemed humanity. Orinda abstracts from Galatians Paul's boldness and applies it to her own vision—a testament to her conviction.

Other poems composed during the Interregnum figure Orinda's Society of Friendship as a covenanted people carrying the promises of the Davidic and Mosaic covenants. In a sense, these covenants sanction the royalist politics that have been the subject of much edifying Philips scholarship.[31] As Carol Barash demonstrates, "Royalist ideals of monarchy are symbolically protected by the 'Society of Friendship' created between 'Orinda' and her female friends."[32] Expanding the definition of friendship to include male authors, Hero Chalmers argues, "The ideas of Philips, [Francis] Finch, and [Jeremy] Taylor intersect specifically in the conception of friendship, identified with royalism, as representative of religious cohesion and also of social stability."[33] Throughout her poems, Orinda classifies friendship as a religion—one, paradoxically, that offers both respite from and a means to engage and critique Parliamentarian and republican ideologies. Catharine Gray writes, "Philips marks off Royalists from the wider public through the circulation of discourses of commendation and love, creating a community she refers to as 'the knowing few,' defined by its elitism in terms of political commitments, aesthetic tastes, and status. Countering radical and republican visions of political culture, these knowing few both hold themselves apart from public debate and offer themselves as an oppositional corrective to Parliamentary power, addressing and even attempting to assimilate a broader readership into their homogeneous and hierarchical vision of Royalist culture."[34] This religion—and here I follow Kamille Stone Stanton in taking seriously Orinda's designation—obtains its authority through the biblical poetics Orinda deploys to affirm the enduring presence of the Davidic and Mosaic covenants.[35] As we shall see, Orinda folds the Davidic covenant into the Mosaic covenant, reinforcing the belief that the exiled monarch and his loyal subjects bear witness not just to Charles II's status as the divinely ordained king but to the royalists' status as a covenanted people. This synthesis of covenants is simultaneously legible in and perpetuated by the typological associations Orinda makes between figures of the Mosaic and Davidic covenants. Of course, as we have already seen, typology has the capacity to unsettle as much as it confirms, and so the biblical poetics Orinda employs are always-already at risk of undermining the divine authority they aim to instill.

As I have argued, Orinda's prophetic self-fashioning positions her to speak authoritatively on the vicissitudes of the state as reflections of divine will. On the one hand, the prophetic vocation empowers Orinda to prophesy strategically, countering eschatological interpretations of Scripture and the radical politics they incite; on the other hand, the prophet, as a conduit for divine truth, occupies an antagonistic position with respect to the monarch, who is frequently compelled to obey, rather than deliver, God's Word. The subversiveness of the dynamic between king and prophet is, as I have suggested, evident in Orinda's identification with the prophet Elijah. In fact, Orinda makes reference to Elijah in several poems, indicating that his prophetic career anticipates, and therefore is a type of, the society's visions. In addition to "On Controversies in Religion," where the prophet draws inspiration from Elijah to convey her vision of irenicism and tolerance, Orinda calls upon Elijah and his successor Elisha in at least three other poems. For instance, "On Rosania's Apostacy, and Lucasia's

Friendship" relates the society to the prophetic community of Elijah and Elisha:

> Hail, Great Lucasia, thou shalt doubly shine:
> What was Rosania's own is now twice thine;
> Thou saw'st Rosania's chariot and her flight,
> And so the double portion is thy right:
> Though 'twas Rosania's spirit, be content,
> Since 'twas at first from thy Orinda sent. (19–24)

In passing the mantle from Rosania, who has turned apostate, to Lucasia, Orinda becomes the "still and soft voice" of God that, as I noted earlier, speaks to Elijah in the wilderness, instructing him to anoint Elisha as his successor. Orinda names Lucasia the Elisha to Rosania's Elijah, alluding to the spectacle recounted in 2 Kings:

> And as they went walking and talking, behold, there appeared a chariot of fire, and horses of fire, and did separate them twain. So Elijah went up by a whirlwind into heaven.
>
> And Elisha saw it, and he cried, My father, my father, the chariot of Israel, and the horsemen thereof: and he saw him no more: and he took his own clothes, and rent them in two pieces.
>
> He took up also the cloak of Elijah that fell from him, and returned, and stood by the bank of Jordan.
>
> After, he took the cloak of Elijah, that fell from him, and smote the waters, and said, Where is the Lord God of Elijah? And so he also, after he had stricken the waters, so that they were divided this way and that way, went over, even Elisha. (2 Kings 2:11–14)

Although the poem's title would suggest that Rosania has committed the sin the Old Testament God most abhors, in the final stanza she exits as Elijah does. That Orinda allows the apostate a divinely inspired departure suggests, first and foremost, that the society's prophets remain in Orinda's—and through her, God's,—favor, despite their transgressions. Even Elijah, the one just man, is admonished by God for expressing doubts about the prophetic career (1 Kings 19:9–10). Rosania's marvelous departure also leaves open the possibility that she might return to the society. Indeed, as Penelope Anderson argues, poems of betrayal put into discourse a version of *amicitia* that accommodates multiple friendships and thus reenvisions amity as a political model: "The continuance of friendship beyond—and by means of—the poems of friendship's failures demonstrates clemency, a virtue traditionally reserved for kings...but transferred, in the absence of a single monarch, to a royalist group of friends."[36] In comparing Elijah's departure to Rosania's "flight," then, Orinda casts the prophet's exit as evidence of God's enduring favor.

Unique to Elisha in the Old Testament, prophetic succession shows divine preferment for the monarchy in its absence as the Society of Friendship, prophesying for "the knowing few" (to borrow Gray's phrase), carries the promise of the Davidic and Mosaic covenants. Upon Rosania's departure, Lucasia receives "the double portion" that Orinda states "is [her] right." According to the Deuteronomistic history, Elisha requests the double portion: "Now when they were passed over, Elijah said unto Elisha, Ask what I shall do for thee before I be taken from thee. And Elisha said, I pray thee, let thy Spirit be double upon me. / And he said, Thou hast asked an hard thing: yet if thou see me when I am taken from thee, thou shalt have it so: and if not, it shall not be" (2 Kings 2:9–10). Of course, just as Elisha witnesses Elijah's exit, so Lucasia observes Rosania's apostasy. In the society, however, Orinda rewards Lucasia with the double portion, presumably to assuage her concerns about the circumstances of her succession: although Lucasia replaces Rosania, Orinda maintains that "Rosania's spirit...'twas at first from thy Orinda sent." As in Deuteronomy, where the firstborn son is entitled to a double portion of his father's wealth (Deut. 21:15–17), Orinda assumes the father's role and declares Lucasia Rosania's heir. The prophetic community cultivated within the society both prophesies and exemplifies the divine preferment that rests with the exiled monarchy and the knowing few who remain loyal to it.

One cannot overstate the aptness of Orinda's appropriation of Elijah and Elisha's ministry to declare divine favor. In the scriptural account Orinda cites, Elijah and Elisha cross the Jordan in a scene reminiscent of Moses: "Then Elijah took his cloak, and wrapped it together, and smote the waters, and they were divided hither and thither, and they twain went over on the dry land" (2 Kings 2:8). In this instance, Elijah parts the Jordan as Moses does the Red Sea in Exodus: "And Moses stretched forth his hand upon the Sea, and the LORD caused the Sea to run back by a strong East wind all the night, and made the Sea dry land, for the waters were divided" (Exod. 14:21). After Elijah's departure, Elisha repeats the actions of his predecessors in a feat that evidences his succession: "And so he also, after he had stricken the waters, so that they were divided this way and that way, went over, even Elisha" (2 Kings 2:14). But this similarity is only one of many that emphasizes the typological association between Moses and his assistant Joshua on the one hand and Elijah and Elisha on the other. As Savran writes, Moses "is portrayed as Elijah *redivivus*":

> Elijah experiences a divine revelation at Mount Sinai (Horeb) after a journey of forty days in the desert (1 Kings 19). Like Moses, he is fed in the wilderness by God (1 Kings 17:4, 19:5–7) and provides food for others as well (17:14–16). The slaughter of the priests of Baal as a response to idolatry in 1 Kings 18 is reminiscent of the aftermath of the Golden Calf incident in Exodus 33:26–29. Most striking, however, is the series of events surrounding the prophet's death in 2 Kings 2. . . . Unlike any other prophet but Moses, his death is mysterious, and his place of burial is unknown (Deut. 34:6). In an unprecedented move, he appoints his own successor in the person of Elisha, whose similarity to Joshua in this story is unmistakable: he splits the waters of the Jordan in order to cross into the land and then assumes command of his "people," the band of prophets who were formerly loyal to Elijah. That his first stop along the way is Jericho helps to round out the analogy.[37]

These consonances betoken a link between Mosaic and Deuteronomistic prophecy, where the promises of the latter emerge from, and hence are contained within, the former. That is, the Mosaic covenant God makes with the Israelites absorbs the Davidic covenant God makes with the house of David. The ministry of Elijah and Elisha represents the imbrication of these contracts, which Orinda then uses to prophesy God's unwavering support of the outcast monarch and persecuted royalists. Folding the Davidic covenant into the Mosaic covenant, Orinda avers that the Society of Friendship and its followers remain a covenanted people, their king a sacral monarch.

Although Orinda does not allude to Malachi in her poetry, it is worth noting that in this brief prophetic book Elijah serves as both type and antitype. The book's concluding words read, "Remember the law of Moses my servant, which I commanded unto him in Horeb for all Israel with the statutes and judgments. / Behold, I will send you Elijah the Prophet before the coming of the great and fearful day of the Lord. / And he shall turn the heart of the fathers to the children, and the heart of the children to their fathers, lest I come and smite the earth with cursing" (Mal. 4:4–6). At the same time that Elijah is beholden to Moses' "decrees and laws," he is installed as the messenger of the eschaton, the prophet who shall presage "that great and dreadful day . . . the Lord comes." Inhabiting Elijah, Orinda speaks an anti-eschatological message in the voice of an eschatological prophet. In so doing, she extends the duration of old covenant theology, which Elijah shall embody until the second Advent. In the interim, God will continue to allocate divine favor to covenanted people, including kings, and Elijah and Elisha will continue to act as surrogates who bear the message.

Moses' vital role in Orinda's visions helps explain various Mosaic allusions that appear in the poems composed during the Interregnum and immediately after the Restoration. During the Interregnum, Moses offers a reassuring presence, reminding the knowing few that they remain a covenanted people. In "Friendship in Emblem, or the Seal. To my dearest Lucasia," Orinda likens friendship's flame to the theophany on Mount Horeb:

> From smoak or hurt those flames are free,
> From grossness or mortality:
> The hearts (like Moses bush presum'd)
> Warm'd and enlighten'd, not consum'd. (17–20)

As in the burning bush episode, where God informs Moses, "I will send thee unto Pharaoh, that thou mayest bring my people the children of Israel out of Egypt" (Exod. 3:10), friendship as Orinda articulates it shall offer respite to the knowing few until God delivers them out of exile. Like the burning bush, then, the flaming hearts symbolize perseverance within and eventual freedom from bondage, when God has "seen the trouble of [his] people," "heard their cry," and "know[n] their sorrows" (Exod. 3:7). In this context, the titular "emblem" designates both a poetic genre, where the text gestures toward a depiction of a flaming heart similar to the one we find in George Wither's *Collection of Emblemes* (1635) (fig. 3.1), and an exemplar for others in the religion to follow.[38] Employing covenantal language, Orinda states,

> As these [i.e., heroic deeds] are found out in design
> To rule and measure every line;
> So friendship governs actions best,
> Prescribing Law to all the rest. (41–44)

The society's mode of "friendship" simultaneously "Prescrib[es]" and enacts the "Law" that governs the covenanted people. As it pertains to the society, "Law" is doubly significant: it distinguishes the knowing few from the ignorant masses and, hence, elevates the law of friendship above laws implemented during the Interregnum. Indeed, their identity as covenanted people depends upon their privileging one law over the other.

Likewise, in "On Mr. Francis Finch (the excellent Palemon)," Orinda equates enduring friendship with the Ark of the Covenant that God instructed Moses to build and that priests carried as the Israelites made their exodus from Egypt. Although Souers maintains that "sex alone would exclude" Finch (among others) from the society, Orinda's encomium to Palemon depicts him as a savior of friendship.[39] Finch's status might owe to his discourse on *Friendship:* in his dedicatory epistle, he dedicates the work "To the truly honourable Mrs. A. O." (i.e., Anne Owen) and identifies himself using his sobriquet Palemon; as for the text itself, it opens with the address "D. Noble Lucasia-Orinda" and is again signed "Palemon."[40] Perhaps in response to Palemon's discourse, Orinda credits him with revitalizing friendship during a period of uncertainty and instability:

Fig. 3.1. "Friendship, and true-love, indeed." George Wither, *A Collection of Emblemes, Ancient and Modern* (London, 1635), 237. © The British Library Board, G.11603.

> 'Twas he that rescu'd gasping friendship when
> The bell toll'd for her funerall with men.
> 'Twas he that made friends more then lovers burn,
> And then made Love to sacred friendship turn:
> 'Twas he turn'd honour inward, set her free
> From titles and from popularity. (49–54)

Interestingly, Orinda praises Palemon's unique ability to reinvigorate friendship "when / The bell toll'd for her funerall *with men*." Thus, while critics are surely right to emphasize the female homosociality that drives the bulk of Philips's friendship poems—a homosociality that incubates women from the violence inherent in patriarchal order—here, in this encomium to Palemon, the strength of "sacred friendship" derives from its ability to cut across boundaries of gender, uniting the knowing few by "turn[ing] honour inward."[41] In Orinda's vision, Palemon is the receptacle that carries the Ark of the covenanted people:

> Now fixt to virtue, she [i.e., honor] begs praise of none,
> Is witness'd and rewarded both at home;
> And in his brest this honour's so enshrined,
> As the old Law was in the Ark confin'd;
> To which posterity shall all consent,
> And less dispute then acts of Parliament. (55–60)

While scriptural accounts disagree as to the Ark's contents, they concur that it contained the two tablets of the law delineating the Ten Commandments. Orinda seems to be drawing from Exodus, where Moses, in preparation for the flight from Egypt, "took and put the Testimony in the Ark, and put the bars in the rings of the Ark, and set the Mercy seat on high upon the Ark" (Exod. 40:20). This passage would suggest that Palemon, like the Ark of the Covenant, possesses the law that the knowing few transport into the wilderness. Yet, the internalization of the law also points to its continuation even after the disappearance of the physical Ark, as when the Babylonians conquered Jerusalem and destroyed Solomon's Temple.[42] Palemon may have garnered praise for composing *Friendship,* but the "old Law" he espouses there lives on "in his brest," just as the Mosaic covenant outlives the Ark that both contains and symbolizes God's contract with the Israelites in the Old Testament.

Although Orinda does not grant Henry Vaughan a pseudonym, he too exhibits a typological connection with Moses. As in her portrayal of Palemon, in "To Mr. Henry Vaughan, Silurist, on his Poems," Orinda lauds Vaughan's commitment to the covenantal ideology of friendship that constitutes the Society's religion. About Vaughan's verse, Orinda writes,

> What savage brest would not be rapt to find
> Such Jewells in such Cabinets enshrin'd?
> Thou (fill'd with Joys too great to see or count)
> Descend'st from thence like Moses from the Mount,

> And with a candid and unquestion'd aw,
> Restor'st the golden age when verse was law. (23–28)

According to Thomas, in this passage Orinda alludes to the moment in Exodus when Moses "returned and went down from the mountain with the two Tablets of the Testimony in his hand, the Tablets were written on both their sides; even on the one side and on the other were they written. / And these Tablets were the work of God, and this writing was the writing of God graven in the Tablets" (Exod. 32:15–16).[43] If this is the case, it bears notice that a few verses later, Moses smashes the tablets when he observes the Israelites participating in idol worship: "Now, as soon as he came near unto the host, he saw the calf and the dancing; so Moses' wrath waxed hot, and he cast the Tablets out of his hands, and brake them in pieces beneath the mountain" (32:19). Within a couple chapters, the covenant is renewed when Moses returns to the Lord, copies down the law a second time, and once again descends the Mount to deliver the tablets: "So when Moses came down from mount Sinai, the two Tablets of the Testimony were in Moses' hand, as he descended from the mount, (now Moses wist not that the skin of his face shone bright, after that God had talked with him)" (34:29). Although recent biblical scholarship attributes the repetition of Moses' descent to a larger pattern of doublets that are the result of a redactor's compiling two different sources for the same events, for Orinda the separate episodes might evince the renewal of the covenant despite possible transgressions.[44] Thus, Vaughan's "Restor[ation of] the golden age" is a continual, rather than singular, event. And as with Palemon, Vaughan simultaneously articulates and embodies the law.

Predictably, the tropes Orinda develops in the anti-eschatological, anti-supersessionist prophecy of her Interregnum poetry structure her verses on Charles II's coronation. In the occasional poem "On the faire weather at the Coronacon," Orinda describes Charles as a Mosaic figure who has delivered his people out of exile. The poem begins with the antitype:

> Soe that we knew not which look'd most content,
> The King, the people, or the firmament.

But the solemnity once fully past,
The intermitted stormes return'd as fast,
And heaven and earth each other to out do,
Vyed both in Cannon and, and in fire workes too. (9–14)

One might expect the "fast" return of "intermitted stormes" to be an ominous sign, but not for Orinda. She interprets the severe weather as a kind of celebration where "heaven and earth each other to out do." This reading might seem like a stretch, but as Gerard Reedy argues, a vast body of coronation literature was dedicated specifically to favorable interpretations of all the events surrounding Charles II's accession, including the fierce storms that occurred on April 23, 1660.[45] For her part, Orinda correlates the potentially ominous weather with the biblical account of Moses parting the Red Sea:

So Israel past through the divided floud,
While in obedient heapes the Ocean stood;
But the same sea, the Hebrewes once on shore,
Came back in Torrents where it was before. (15–18)

Reading the coronation back into Exodus, Orinda parallels the "intermitted stormes" with acts of divine intervention. First, Moses "stretched forth his hand upon the Sea, and the LORD caused the Sea to run back by a strong East wind all the night, and made the Sea dry land, for the waters were divided. / Then the children of Israel went through the midst of the Sea upon the dry ground, and the waters were a wall unto them on their right hand, and on their left hand" (Exod. 14:21–22). As for the thunder and lightning, it recalls God's appearance in a "fiery and cloudy pillar" (14:24). Both acts signal God's residing first with the Israelites and then with Charles and the knowing few who accompanied him in literal or figurative exile. Yet, the acts Orinda perceives as signs of favor are also divine punishments: according to Scripture, the theophany "struck the host of the Egyptians with fear" before "Moses stretched forth his hand upon the Sea, and the Sea returned to his force early in the morning, and the Egyptians fled against it; but the LORD overthrew the Egyptians in the midst of the Sea. / So the water returned and covered the chariots and the horsemen, even all the host of Pharaoh that came into the Sea after them; there remained not one of them" (14:24, 27–28). Following Orinda's vision to its logical conclusion, one perceives in this coronation poem a threat to the new generation of Egyptians. Of course, Orinda does not specify which group (or groups) is liable to meet the Egyptians' fate, but the implied promise of divine retribution stands in stark contrast to the politics of clemency Andrew Shifflett identifies in Philips's celebrated heroic drama *Pompey*.[46]

In other poems composed around the coronation, Orinda figures Charles II as other Old Testament figures, indicating that the monarch's accession means more than the restoration of the English crown. Rather, it signifies, according to Orinda's visions, the deliverance of the knowing few out of exile and the reestablishment of the sacral monarchy, all in accordance with God's will. This divine sanction might be a source of comfort for the society, but it also subordinates Charles II to precisely the same covenantal theology used to legitimate the deposition and execution of his father. Thus, "On the numerous accesse of the English to waite upon the King in Holland" describes the English as "unmonarch'd...for want of thee [i.e., Charles II], / So till thou com'st we shall unpeopled be" (13–14). Orinda laments the "unmonarch'd" state of England, but her allusion to Jacob and Joseph reveals that the period of Interregnum was a reflection of God's will:

> So when Old Jacob could but credit give
> That his prodigious Joseph still did live,
> (Joseph that was preserved to restore
> Their lives, who would have taken his before)
> It is enough (says he) to Egypt I
> Will go, and see him once before I dye. (21–26)

Although this story precedes the covenants Orinda invokes elsewhere in her poetry, it falls firmly in line with the contractual framework that characterizes her visions. In the Genesis account, Joseph's brothers sell him into slavery out of jealousy, but when they encounter him again in Egypt, "Joseph said to his brethren,

I am Joseph! Doeth my father yet live? But his brethren could not answer him, for they were astonished at his presence. / Again, Joseph said to his brethren, Come near, I pray you, to me. And they came near. And he said, I am Joseph your brother, whom ye sold into Egypt. / Now therefore be not sad, neither grieved with yourselves, that ye sold me hither; for God did send me before you for your preservation" (Gen. 45:3–5). In her revision of the tale, Orinda proclaims that Charles II, like Joseph, was exiled "for [his] preservation." However, in the process of reinterpreting the king's exile as divine intervention, Orinda shows that the events preceding the Interregnum—among them Charles I's execution—transpired as a result of the covenanted people turning away from God. In this way, a poem of praise carries with it a note of caution for the returning king.

A similar duality structures "Arion on a Dolphin, To his Majestie at his passadge into England," where Orinda celebrates Charles II as another Solomon:

> Th'united world will you allow
> Their Cheife, to whom the English bow,
> And monarchs shall to yours resort,
> As Sheba's Queen to Judah's court,
> Returning thence constrained more
> To wonder, envy, and adore.
> Discover'd Rome will hate your crowne,
> But she shall tremble at your frowne:
> For England shall (rul'd and restor'd by you)
> The suppliant world protect, or else subdue. (65–74)

Undoubtedly, this poem serves as a paean to Charles II's triumphant return to England. In a testimony to his wisdom, Orinda prophesies monarchs from around the world visiting Charles as Sheba had Solomon: "And Solomon declared unto her all her questions: nothing was hid from the King, which he expounded not unto her. / Then the Queen of Sheba saw all Solomon's wisdom, and the house that he had built, / And the meat of his table, and the sitting of his servants, and the order of his ministers, and their apparel, and his drinking vessels, and his burnt offerings, that he offered in the house of the Lord, and she was greatly astonied" (1 Kings 10:3–5). In the marginal notes, the Geneva Bible elaborates on Sheba's astonishment, adding, "there was no more spirit in her." Like Solomon, Charles shall inspire awe, or else he shall conquer.

Yet, as Orinda and her readers knew, Solomon is remembered for two things: his wisdom and his weakness for idolatrous women. The former may have brought the likes of Sheba to court, but the latter caused God to divide the kingdom into two:

> And so did he for all his outlandish wives, which burnt incense and offered unto their gods.
>
> Therefore the Lord was angry with Solomon, because he had turned his heart from the Lord God of Israel, which had appeared unto him twice,
>
> And had given him a charge concerning this thing, that he should not follow other gods: but he kept not that, which the Lord had commanded him.
>
> Wherefore the Lord said unto Solomon, Forasmuch as this is done of thee, and thou hast not kept my covenant, and my statutes (which I commanded thee) I will surely rent the kingdom from thee, and will give it to thy servant.
>
> Notwithstanding in thy days I will not do it, because of David thy father, but I will rent it out of the hand of thy son:
>
> Howbeit I will not rent all the Kingdom, but will give one tribe to thy son, because of David my servant, and because of Jerusalem which I have chosen. (1 Kings 11:8–13)

In the context of this passage, the comparison of Charles II to Solomon is as much a warning as a song of praise. Just as Solomon inherited from his father a united kingdom, Charles II ascends the throne in "th'united world." Whether he will make the same mistakes as Solomon is up to Charles. It might seem reasonable to wager that the king will resist the temptation to take "seven hundred wives, that were princesses, and three hundred concubines" (1 Kings 11:3), but that does not mean he would not wed someone who might seduce him into idol worship. Although we cannot know how Philips felt about the king's courtship with Catherine of Braganza, Orinda's channeling Elisha, the prophet who challenged

Jezebel's worship of Baal, suggests that perhaps Charles II should not make the same mistake as his father. As in the comparison to Jacob and Joseph, then, Orinda uses an Old Testament figure to offer a hopeful vision that doubles as a cautionary tale.

Orinda's visions for the Restoration appear fairly early in Philips's published *Poems*. In both the 1664 and 1667 editions, the only verse by Philips that precedes them is "Upon the Double Murther of K. Charles, in Answer to a Libellous Rime made by V. P." Unfortunately, we have no concrete evidence that this ordering reflects Philips's wishes—except, perhaps, for the fact that, as Thomas points out, "the pirated edition contained 116 poems in the same non-chronological order as the authorised edition of 1667 which simply adds another 14 poems."[47] Nevertheless, whoever organized the *Poems* was invested in foregrounding the most overtly pro-royalist poems, a shrewd strategy in post-Interregnum England. For my purposes, it is notable that this cluster of poems features typological associations that affirm the monarch's divinity while also exhorting him to remember the transgressions of his predecessors. Orinda may not concur with Thomas Beard, who in *The Theatre of God's Judgments* "observed that of forty kings in Judah and Israel . . . only ten pleased God," but in choosing Elijah as the model for her prophetic vocation she displays a keen sense of the prophet's role in helping the monarch negotiate his covenantal relationship with God.[48]

In some instances, this role might entail operating as a conduit for God to admonish the monarch who turns to or otherwise tolerates idol worship. In 1 Kings, Elijah brings Ahab to the point of despair—"Now when Ahab heard those words, he rent his clothes, and put sackcloth upon him and fasted, and lay in sackcloth and went softly" (1 Kings 21:27)—and this state prompts God to delay punishment on the house of Ahab until his son is king: "Seest thou how Ahab is humbled before me? Because he submitteth himself before me, I will not bring that evil in his days, but in his son's days will I bring evil upon his house" (21:29). In other instances, the prophet is called upon to bypass or even contravene the monarch, as Elijah does when he slays the prophets of Baal (1 Kings 18:40).

Throughout her poems, then, Orinda wields the power of prophecy to assert that the English monarch is a sacral monarch, that the Society of Friendship and the knowing few are a covenanted people, but these relationships are no less contractual than the Davidic and Mosaic covenants on which they are modeled. In this sense, divine favor contains within it conditions for apostasy and subsequent judgment.

My aim in this essay has been to show that Philips's scriptural allusions amount to more than mere window dressing for poems that center on secular themes. Although I have focused primarily on the anti-eschatological, anti-supersessionist hermeneutics that empower Orinda to prophesy, the biblical poetics that structure Philips's poems are not limited to the trajectories I have explored. While I do not imagine Philips will ever be numbered among the great devotional poets of the seventeenth century, I do hope that future studies of what Christopher Hill termed "the Biblical Revolution" will consider the unique contribution Orinda makes.[49] Indeed, Philips's deployment of Scripture reveals not only a poet who knew the Word intimately but also an exegete whose radical revisions offered an important contrast to the millenarian prophecies and politics of her day.

4 ❖ Restoring Orinda's Face
Puritan Iconoclasm and Philips's *Poems* as Royalist Remonumentalization

Amy Scott-Douglass

On January 14, 1664, an advertisement appeared in the *London Newes* announcing the publication of "the Poems of the incomparable Madam *Catherine Philips*. Sold by *Richard Marriot* at his shop under St. Dunstan in *Fleetstreet*."[1] Katherine Philips claimed that she did not authorize the publication of the book, that her poems were printed surreptitiously, and her complaints motivated a series of events that ultimately resulted in what Margaret Ezell calls "the most celebrated incident of a woman's distress over appearing in print."[2] In the weeks immediately following the advertisement of the 1664 edition of *Poems*, Philips sent out several letters asking her friends to publicize her innocence on her behalf. In the version of her letter to Sir Charles Cotterell reprinted in the 1667 edition of *Poems*, Philips represents the piracy of her poems as a violation against her corporeal person—a "cruel" incident of "abuse" and "injury" that has left her unveiled and "expos'd to the world."[3] In another letter, Philips informs Dorothy Temple, "some most dishonest person hath got some collection of my Poems as

I heare, and . . . I have been on [the] rack ever since I heard it." Philips tells Temple that she has instructed Colonel John Jeffreys "to get [the] Printer punished, the book called in, and me some way publickly vindicated" and ends her letter to Temple by charging her to rally support among their friends at court; otherwise, she explains, "I must never show my face there or among any reasonable people again."[4] With this reference, Philips introduces the metaphor of defacement, which, I argue in this essay, becomes the central motif of the enterprise to restore both Philips and her poetry: from rape to restitution, from sickness to health, from defacement to restoration.

Philips's allies responded quickly to their friend's loss of face. On January 18, 1664, four days after he had advertised the poems, the *London Intelligencer* published Richard Marriot's confession that in unwittingly printing an incorrect, unauthorized edition of her poems, he had done Philips "a double Injury." Marriot announced that he had withdrawn the edition and concluded by expressing his "hope" that "this false Copy, may produce the true One."[5] Cotterell, too, encouraged Philips to publish an authorized edition of her poems, and, although she thought it "too airy a way of resenting such an Injury," she promised, "if you still think it proper, I will resign my Judgment and Humour to yours, and try what I can do that way."[6] Even six months later, when composing the last poem that she wrote, "To his Grace Gilbert Lord Arch-Bishop of Canterbury," she was still preoccupied with the piracy of her poems, which she dramatized as the rape and molestation of a "Hebrew Virgin":

> That private shade, wherein my Muse was bred,
> She alwaies hop'd might hide her humble head;
> Believing the retirement she had chose
> Might yield her, if not pardon, yet repose;
> Nor other repetitions did expect,
> Than what our Ecchoes from the Rocks reflect.
> But hurry'd from her Cave with wild affright,
> And dragg'd maliciously into the Light.
> (*Which makes her like the Hebrew Virgin mourn*

When from her face her Veil was rudely torn)
To you (my Lord) she now for succour calls,
And at your feet, with just confusion falls.[7]

In the rest of the poem, Philips suggests the similarities between her victimized, unveiled, defaced self and the broken condition of the Anglican church, and she concludes with a request to the archbishop to "Govern," "Restore," and "repair" the "Ruines" of both.[8]

We will never know whether or not Philips intended to publish an authorized edition of her poems; six months after the surreptitious publication, she died of smallpox. In 1667, the second edition of Katherine Philips's collected works was published. Titled *Poems By the most deservedly Admired Mrs. Katherine Philips The matchless Orinda: To which is added Monsieur Corneille's Pompey & Horace, With several other Translations out of French* (fig. 4.1), the compilation and production of the 1667 edition was probably overseen by Cotterell, the master of ceremonies to Charles II, who functioned, in effect, as Philips's literary agent during her lifetime as well as her protector following the supposed piracy in 1664.

The revised edition of *Poems* was printed by Henry Herringman, unquestionably the most important bookseller in England from 1661 to 1693, who, by 1667, had already established himself as the printer of books by the most prominent royalist writers.[9] In contrast to the 1664 edition of Philips's *Poems,* published in octavo and with only two commendatory verse prefaces and no portrait frontispiece, the 1667 edition of *Poems* is a gorgeous folio with extensive prefatory material, including (1) a portrait frontispiece; (2) a direct address to the readers titled "The Preface," probably written by either Cotterell or Herringman, detailing and reprinting in full a copy of the letter that Philips had sent to Cotterell to distribute on her behalf after the 1664 edition of *Poems* was published; (3) elegies on Philips by James Tyrrell, Thomas Flatman, and Abraham Cowley; and (4) commendatory verses in praise of Philips and her poetry and dramatic translations, written by Cowley; Roger Boyle, Earl of Orrery; Wentworth Dillon, Earl of Roscommon; and an unidentified contributor named "Philo-Philippa." As was the case

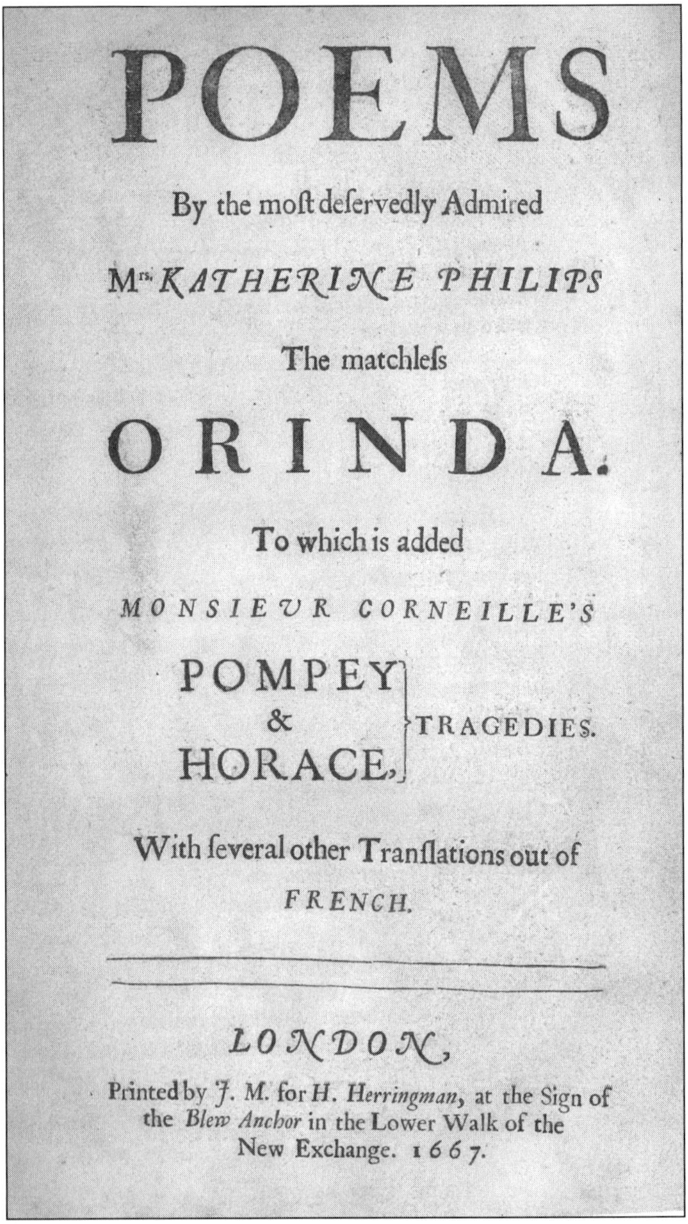

POEMS

By the moſt deſervedly Admired

M[rs.] *KATHERINE PHILIPS*

The matchleſs

ORINDA.

To which is added

MONSIEUR CORNEILLE'S

POMPEY
&
HORACE, TRAGEDIES.

With ſeveral other Tranſlations out of
FRENCH.

LONDON,

Printed by *J. M.* for *H. Herringman*, at the Sign of
the *Blew Anchor* in the Lower Walk of the
New Exchange. 1667.

Fig. 4.1. Title page to Katherine Philips's *Poems* (1667). Courtesy of David L. Orvis.

with those who supplied prefatory verses to Cartwright's volume of poetry, Philips's list of commenders are predominantly royalist sympathizers. Carol Barash points out that this collection of commendatory verses and elegies "was crucial in constructing the public image and reputation of Philips that has stood for over three hundred years."[10] What I find most interesting about the prefatory materials is the degree to which they engage in the same discourse of defacement and restoration that Philips herself employed in the presentation of her public self throughout her literary career and especially in response to the surreptitious publication. In these prefatory materials, the entire enterprise of the compilation and publication of *Poems* (1667) is portrayed as a group effort to restore the virtuous royalist poetess who had been forcibly defaced, both body and book, only to be recovered by her political allies and fellow poets, and put back together, once again, to live forever. Taken as a whole, the prefatory materials represent Philips's recovered poetry book as a metaphor for the restored face of royalism. Philips herself functions as a symbol of the monarchy and, by connection, the Anglican church — innocent, assailed, and, for a time, defeated, but ultimately, resurrected from the dead and restored to glory.

I

Each of the three terms in the title of this essay, "Restoring Orinda's Face," points to important, recurrent themes in the textual presentation of *Poems* (1667). To begin with, the book itself is offered to readers as the *recovered* text, and the restoration of its appearance and authority becomes synonymous with the restoration of Katherine Philips's potentially damaged virtue and reputation. In particular, the publisher and the editor(s) of *Poems* (1667) are preoccupied with restoring Philips's damaged textual body to good health, transforming it into the property of the spiritual, virtuous Orinda. Interestingly, they set about the task of recovering Philips by literally re-covering her body of work with layer after layer of commendatory verses and prefatory tributes to her, as if in an effort to produce an impenetrable face, the face of Orinda, posthumously restored to life.

Drawing upon Philips's representation of the piracy of her poems as the rape of a virgin, the author of "The Preface" to the 1667 edition of Philips's *Poems* represents both the unauthorized 1664 book of poems and the poet herself as despoiled bodies. He outlines the story of the piracy, referring to the 1664 book as "the false Edition" that "exposed" the author, and recalling the efforts of Philips and her "friends" to "get it suppress'd."[11] The author of "The Preface" then reprints the letter that Philips wrote to Cotterell in 1664 following the piracy of her poems. In it, Philips complains of her "unworthy usage." "Every way I have so much injury," Philips writes, "...that so few things in the power of Fortune could have given me so great a torment as this most afflictive accident." She insists upon her "innocence" and expresses her desire to "recover those fugitive Papers that have escap'd [her] hands," quoting Lord Falkland to establish her resistance to "a Press" and citing Sir Edward Dering's epilogue to her own *Pompey* as proof of her "chaste lines." In particular, Philips objects to the theft of her private property, referring to herself as "that unfortunate person that cannot so much as think in private, that must have [her] imaginations rifled and exposed." "This is," Philips claims, referring to the surreptitious publication, "a most cruel accident."[12]

After quoting Philips's letter in its entirety, the author of "The Preface" goes on to tell the story of her death and of the subsequent production of the 1667 edition of *Poems,* making a clear distinction between those who were involved in the production of the 1664 and 1667 editions. The latter group is concerned with engineering the metamorphosis of Katherine Philips's "deformed Poems" into "the beauties of [Orinda's] mind" by making the "Collection *as full and as perfect as it might be.*" "The Preface" concludes with a reference to "these once transformed, or rather deformed Poems, which, are here in some measure *restor'd* to their native Shape and Beauty."[13] "The Preface," for instance, portrays the guilty stationer as the father of Philips's first edition of poems who "possess'd himself of a false Copy, and sent those children of her Fancy into the

World, so martyred." In doing so, the stationer becomes "an injurious...Printer of her face." What the stationer has done to Philips's textual face, "The Preface" goes on to argue, the smallpox has done to Philips's physical body:

> But the small Pox, that malicious disease (as knowing how little she would have been concern'd for her handsomness, when at the best) was not satisfied to be as injurious a Printer of her face, as the other had been of her Poems, but treated her with a more fatal cruelty than the Stationer had them; for though he to her most sensible affliction surreptitiously possess'd himself of a false Copy...that murtherous Tyrant, with greater barbarity seiz'd unexpectedly upon her, the true Original, and to the much juster affliction of all the world, violently tore her out of it, and hurried her untimely to her Grave, upon the 22 of June 1664, she being then but 31 years of age.[14]

Martha Straznicky has remarked that this passage "exhibits a concerted effort to disembody the author," which she interprets as "a rhetorical strategy that morosely takes advantage of Philips's premature death of small pox." She finds this preface "sportive" and posits that "the criss-crossing between physical violence and surreptitious publication is unsettling, not least because its primary effect is to replace Philips the person (and author) with Philips the collected works."[15] Similarly, Dorothy Mermin suggests that women's "works and their selves are so often confused with each other. Their physical person—their beauty, or in the case of Philips, who died of smallpox, its despoiling—is generally the prime object of critical regard."[16] But it is Philips herself who introduces the analogy between surreptitious publication and her own physical illness. In her letter to Cotterell that is quoted in "The Preface" to *Poems* (1667), Philips writes of the 1664 publication, "[it] hath made so proportionate an impression upon me, that really it hath cost me a sharp fit of sickness since I heard it." Philips even describes the remedies for her dilemma in corporeal terms: if it becomes "absolutely necessary to the reparation of this misfortune," Philips suggests that she might consent to authorize a second edition of poems, but only "with the same reluctancy as [she] would cut off a Limb to save [her] Life."[17]

Moreover, in establishing an equation between the author's body and her body of work, Philips's printer and editor were following a well-established tradition of folio production, one example of which is Jonson's preface to Shakespeare's first folio, which, as Leah S. Marcus points out, "abolishes Shakespeare as an entity apart from his writings" to such an extent that "there is no space at all between the man and his work.... Shakespeare *is* the book."[18] According to Marcus, this trend toward the "identification of corpse and *corpus*" is well established early in the century, as evidenced in the prefatory materials to John Donne's *Poems* (1633). Indeed, Philips and her commenders borrow heavily from the language of Donne's preface writers, including the bookseller John Marriot, who, in his prefatory commendation, establishes Donne's book as, in Marcus's words, "the poet's living soul."[19] Coupled with the attention to the poet's spirit is an awareness of his physical body. In "The Printer to the Understanders," Miles Fletcher represents the 1633 edition of Donne's poetry, published without Donne's sermons and speeches, as "a scattered limbe of this Author" rather than "a whole body."[20] There was a precedent, then, for posthumously published literary collections to be presented to readers as the bodies and souls of the late poets themselves, regardless of the writer's sex.

Similarly, in many seventeenth century prefatory verses and epistles, editors and commenders present the posthumous publication of an author's collected works as having the ability to bring the author back to life. As Marcus explains, "If books diminished the living they could, like necromancy, reanimate the dead."[21] In the case of Philips's *Poems* (1667), it is both "the true Original" (the body of Philips's poems) and the author's "face" (her reputation, her beauty, and her worthiness of commendation) that the publisher and editor(s) of the 1667 edition seek to restore. They attempt to restore her poems by putting them "into the order they were written in, as she possibly her self would have done, had she consented to a second Edition" and making "this Collection as full and as perfect as might be." The author of "The Preface" is the first to draw the readers' attention to Philips's "Face" (i.e., her portrait), the very constructedness of which is meant to point out the authenticity of the poems themselves, the true representatives of Philips's spirit and mind.[22] Following that, Cowley, in his commendatory poem to Philips, makes the analogy between the beauty of Philips's poetry and that of her face, admiring her poetic meter, which he describes as being as "smooth" as her "Forehead," and her elevated "Fancies," which are as "sparkling as [her] Eye."[23] Cowley's subsequent piece, his elegiac ode, is addressed to the smallpox, the "Cruel disease" that "assaults the fairest place...even the face."[24]

On the one hand, the prefatory materials to *Poems* are drawing from the tradition that evoked the image of the innocent girl who has been deflowered and defaced as a metaphor for the surreptitiously printed text. In the preface to Thomas Norton and Thomas Sackville's second edition of *Gorboduc* (ca. 1570), John Day's "The P[rinter] to the Reader," the printer of the first edition is imagined as a rapist of the feminized text, who emerges from her first pressing barely recognizable to "her frendes," with "bescratched her face" and a "berayed and disfigured" body.[25] The image of the despoiled face restored to its former beauty also occurs as a metaphor for the posthumously revised text in the materials that preface Mary Sidney Herbert's edition of *Arcadia,* published after Philip's death.[26] Hugh Sanford's epistle "To the Reader," which introduces the 1593 edition of the *The Countess of Pembroke's Arcadia,* refers to the old *Arcadia* as "the disfigured face" that Mary took "in hand...wiping away those spots wherewith the beauties thereof were unworthely blemished."[27] Similarly, Mary's prefatory poem to *Psalms,* "To the Angell spirit of the most excellent Sir Philip Sidney," refers to the manuscript left at Sidney's death as a "half maim'd peece" that his "matchlesse Muse begunne" and she has "finish't now."[28]

Mary Sidney Herbert's language to describe the restoration of the "maimed" works of a "matchless" poet is echoed in the prefatory materials to the 1667 edition of the collected works of Katherine Philips, the "Matchless Orinda."[29] And certainly the attention to Philips's disfigured face in the prefatory materials to *Poems* (1667) is even more appropriate given the extent to which the language of faces is often used in conjunction with spirituality, morality, and propriety by Philips herself, in her own poetry. In "On Controversies in Religion," for instance, Philips refers to the soul's "open face." In "To the Honoured Lady E. G.," Philips claims that her subject's religion "shews her face" and tells her, "your glories in your face be seen." In "The World," Philips imagines the afterlife as a place where sin and "stain" are "defac'd." And finally, in Philips's poem "Submission," when divinely ordained government and order fail, the whole World is "disorder'd and defac'd."[30]

But over and above the precedent of the motif of the spotted and recovered face in the prefaces to Sidney's posthumously revised books, and over and above the prevalence of the imagery contrasting the open and the disordered face in Philips's own poetry, there is an even more appropriate context we need to consider. By the middle of the seventeenth century, the restoration of despoiled, broken faces was characteristically a royalist theme, a politically loaded discourse born out of the parliamentary legislation of defacement that authorized acts of Puritan iconoclasm as well as the literature about Charles I's own self-defacement and his subsequent seizure and decapitation. When we take this into account, we can see that the theme of defacement and restoration in the prefatory materials to *Poems* (1667) serves a larger, and yet also a more immediate, purpose than a simple literary device for marketing Philips's book: the restoration of Orinda's face and the recovery of her book function as symbols of the restoration of the monarchy, the reestablishment of the Church of England, and the reassertion of royalism.

II

The discourse of defacement was, of course, fundamental to the anti-Laudian legislation enacted by the Puritan iconoclasts who dominated Parliament in the early 1640s, legislation that resulted in the destruction of statues, currency, tombs, carvings, and relics in Anglican churches across the country. In 1641, Edmund Gurnay, a Church of England clergyman based in Norfolk, published *An*

Appendix unto the Homily against Images in Churches, in which he called for his readers "utterly to deface" the improvements and embellishments in Anglican churches that had been instituted under the supervision of Archbishop Laud, and which Gurnay and other Puritan sympathizers found idolatrous.[31] In that same year, the first ordinance against Laudian innovations was passed in the House of Commons, and London MP and future mayor Isaac Penington proposed sending officials "into all Countries, for the defacing, demolition, and quite taking away of all Images..., Pictures, Monuments, and Relicts of Idolatry."[32] In ordinances published in 1643 and 1644, Parliament ordered that "Monuments of Superstition or Idolatry" be "taken away and defaced" or, as the May 9, 1644, ordinance put it, "utterly defaced."[33] As a result of the legislation of defacement, the early 1640s saw the destruction of "the statues [and] images in the tombs and monuments" in churches and chapels across the country.[34]

What the Puritan iconoclasts of the 1640s were reacting against was the Laudian enterprise of beautifying Anglican churches by establishing the communion table as "a true and proper altar" and decorating that altar "with tapestries, sculptures of saints, crucifixes and colored glass."[35] When their fervor began to extend to royal graves, one observer wrote that the Puritan iconoclasts "strook off all the heads of all the statues, on all Monuments in the Church, [and] especially they deface the Bishops Tombs, leaving one without a head, another without a Nose, one without a hand, and another without an Arme... they pluck down and deface the Statue of an Ancient Queen, the wife of Edward the Confessor... mistaking it for the Statue of the blessed Virgin Mary."[36]

During the English civil wars, the practice of defacement extended from churches to universities and, what is especially relevant to Philips's *Poems* (1667), to royal monuments of the dead. Although from the earliest declaration in 1641, the ordinances were supposed to protect the effigies and gravestones of "any King, Prince, or Nobleman, or other dead Person which hath not been commonly reputed or taken for a Saint,"[37] the parliamentary army nevertheless defaced representations of both monarchs and courtiers. In her seminal work, *Puritan Iconoclasm during the English Civil War,* Julie Spraggon recounts that army soldiers defaced statues of James I and Charles I at Winchester Cathedral in 1641, portraits of Edward VI at Chichester Cathedral in 1642, the arms and tombs of Mary Stuart and Catherine of Aragon at Petersborough, and the tomb of King John at Worcester. The monuments of royalist subjects were attacked as well, including effigies of Robert of Normandy at Gloucester Cathedral and Sir Humphrey Orne at Lichfield Cathedral in 1643. Spraggon argues that the latter tombs were attacked because of a verse epithet carved underneath the statues that included the line "This is an Altar, not a Grave," pointing out that "the very word 'altar' gave such offence" to Puritan iconoclasts "that it led to the destruction" of royalist tombs.[38] The following year, in May 1644, Parliament passed an additional ordinance authorizing the defacement of "representations of... angels [and] saints" in churches and cathedrals.[39]

According to James Loxley, the motif of defacement is best illustrated in the royalists' anxious reactions to what is known as "the King's disguise," the series of events that took place on April 27, 1646, when Charles I fled Oxford wearing servant's clothes, his hair and beard cut short, his personage literally defaced of the markers of his royalty. Loxley argues that the *Eikon Basilike* (1649) was published in an effort to restore the image of the monarch in general and the representation of Charles's body in particular: "as a relic of the royal martyr the *Eikon* appropriates the corporeal substance of its author, fusing writer and writing in the one object."[40] Following Charles's execution, the discourse of defacement in the parliamentary legislation was extended to portraits and iconography of Charles I. A resolution passed by the House of Commons on April 9, 1650, ordered that "the Arms of the late King... be taken down, and defaced, in all Churches, Chapels, and all other publick places within England [and] Wales," and this was followed by a similar resolution on December 27, 1650, which noted that there were "still remaining the Arms and Pictures of the late King, in several Churches, Halls, upon the Gates, and in other publick Places, of the City of London" that needed to be "taken down and defaced" by Parliament-appointed officials.[41] Spraggon observes that "after the execution of the king and the establishment of a Commonwealth in 1649, Stuart symbols—in the form of arms, statues and inscriptions—were ordered removed from churches and elsewhere, and were treated in a similar way to religious images: they were not only to be removed but to be *defaced*." Spraggon argues that "in many ways the defacing of such artifacts was a stronger comment and a clearer statement of victory—it was a symbolic act, demonstrating the power of the new regime."[42]

Philips's own history is remarkably complicated in relationship to Puritan iconoclasm given that it is quite possible that in the 1640s Katherine's family—and perhaps even Katherine herself—would have been some of the most extreme offenders. To say that Philips was born into a Puritan family is an understatement. Her great-grandfather was John Oxenbridge, the "Northamptonshire Puritan radical divine" who lost his rectory due to his Presbyterian leanings and Puritan alliances.[43] Her uncle, also called John Oxenbridge, was also a radical Puritan minister, and before that he was a tutor at Magdalen Hall, Oxford, until, in 1634, he was "deprived" of his position by Archbishop Laud, then chancellor of Oxford, for refusing to sign an oath. Another uncle, by marriage, was "the prominent Parliamentarian leader Oliver St. John."[44] Scholars often note that Katherine's family's radical leanings would have influenced where she went to *school*—at Mrs. Salmon's Boarding School for Girls in Hackney, a Presbyterian school at which Katherine made friends with Mary Aubrey and Mary Harvey Dering. Curiously, however, no one has ever paid attention to where Katherine might have gone to *church*. John Aubrey records that by 1642, "when she was but 10 yeares old," Katherine "was very religiously devoted...; prayed by herself an hower together, and took Sermons verbatim," and at this same time of her life, "when a Child," Katherine was "much against the Bishops, and prayd to God to take them to him, but afterwards was reconciled to them."[45] Aubrey is admittedly not the most reliable source one would wish for, and yet, although he may not be accurate with regard to details such as her specific age and the length of her prayers, we have no reason to question his overall depiction of Katherine as having been, in her youth, a Puritan devout.

Here we have, then, a portrait of a young girl who was so zealous in her religious sectarianism that she memorized radical Puritan sermons and prayed for the deaths of Anglican priests. Aside from the fascinating mystery of when and why Katherine was reconciled to the bishops, we might also wonder: what radical Puritan violence did she witness in the meantime? Or, put more directly in relation to the topic of this article: where was Katherine, the bishop-hating little girl, when the Anglican churches were being defaced? The answer seems to be that she was smack dab in the middle of the defacement. What we find when we look at the churches with which Katherine and members of her family circle are consistently associated with—St. Mary Woolchurch and St. Stephen's Coleman—is that these are the very churches whose congregations included the most vehement Puritan iconoclasts.

Born in 1632, Katherine was only nine years old when Parliament authorized the orders of defacement, the same age that Aubrey identifies as the height of her Puritan zeal. Spraggon describes the church in which Philips was baptized and may well have continued to worship, St. Mary Woolchurch, as a "Puritan paris[h] eagerly welcoming the long-awaited opportunity for reform."[46] In 1641, it was one of the first churches to be defaced. The effort was led by churchwarden Michael Herring, who was so full of iconoclastic zeal that he overstepped the House of Common's directive that "tombs must not be touched" and went so far in his "indiscretion" as to "deface statues on tombs simply because they were in the act of kneeling at prayer."[47] Parliamentarian Simonds D'Ewes described Herring's behavior as a "great scandal" on the House of Commons, "as if we meant to deface all antiquities."[48] St. Mary Woolchurch was also the church of parishioner Captain Richard Hunt, who is characterized in *Mercurius Aulicus* as "the first that committed Sacriledge on his owne Parish Church..., pulling downe the Crosse from off the Steeple, the Crosse from off the King's Crowne over the Font, lopping off the hands and pulling out the eyes from the Tombes and Monuments, cutting off the Cherubims wings placed upon the Arches."[49] Spraggon refers to Hunt as "one of the very first church iconoclasts in London," and she describes him and his associates as "wealthy merchants, committed Parliamentarians and religious activists."[50] Yet another connection between Katherine Philips and St. Mary Woolchurch is the fact that St. Mary Woolchurch was the church in which, in 1642, her father, John Fowler, would be buried. In 1641, however, he was still alive, and there is no reason to think that Katherine's family resided anywhere other than London or worshipped anywhere other than St. Mary Woolchurch. More to the point, there is no reason to presume that John Fowler did not take part in the defacement of the church. And even if he did not, he and his family almost assuredly would have known and associated with those who did.

The second church that Spraggon targets as particularly vehement in its iconoclasm, St. Stephen's Coleman, would have been familiar to Katherine as well. Her grandfather, Daniel Oxenbridge, had left the family "lands and tenements in the most radical Puritan parish in the City, St Stephen's, Coleman Street" upon his death.[51] The vicars at St. Stephen's during Katherine's lifetime, including John Davenport and John Goodwin, either resigned or were removed from the pulpit for their anti-Anglican views. Spraggon argues that if there are no reports of iconoclasm at St. Stephen's as the 1640s progress, it is only because the parishioners had already thoroughly defaced it. Those vehement Puritan iconoclasts who worshipped at St. Stephen's—including the likes of those Parliamentarians who were impeached by Charles I: Isaac Penington, John Pym, John Hampden, Denzil Holles, Sir Arthur Haselrig, and William Strode—had already anticipated the legislation, in some cases by years, and thoroughly defaced the church in advance.[52] By the end of 1642, there were no innovations at St. Stephen's left to destroy.

In 1647, Katherine apparently moved to Wales with her mother, who married Sir Richard Phillipps, and she presumably lived with her mother and stepfather in Picton Castle, a property that was one of the most hotly contested of the civil wars, having been occupied by both royalist and parliamentary forces. In Wales, Katherine married James Philips, the widower of Sir Richard's daughter, Frances, Katherine's stepsister, who left behind a newborn daughter, also called Frances, making Katherine a stepmother overnight, at the age of 16. Like Katherine and her family members, James was a Puritan. A colonel in the parliamentary army, he eventually became high sheriff of Cardiganshire and then served as a member of the House of Commons. Katherine, meanwhile, went on to write poetry in commendation of the most ardent royalists, some of which was published less than four years into her marriage.

It is fascinating to contemplate what might have motivated Philips's conversion from one set of political alliances to the other, just as it is also fascinating to think about what might have prompted Philips to marry when she did, how she might have felt about being wedded to her late stepsister's husband, and what her relationships might have been like with all of these people—especially with her extraordinary mother, who herself married four times. Given the massive amount of material we have on Katherine Philips's life—including record after record of her letters and direct statements—it is mind-boggling that so many questions remain. Is there any seventeenth century poet about whom we know so much and yet whose true identity is more slippery than Philips? Her feelings about her family and husband, her political stances within those relationships, her core beliefs and real motivations are all still question marks for us. But if Philips was politically conflicted privately, she was not politically conflicted poetically. And what I find so interesting is that the thing that marks her poetry's politics is her stance against defacement, the very practice that she would have grown up witnessing and being encouraged to practice.

III

The iconolatry that runs throughout the poetry Philips wrote in the 1650s and 1660s cannot be defined as a veneration of images in general; rather, Philips's iconolatry must be said to be decidedly anti-Puritan. Philips's iconolatry is, first and foremost, characterized by her advocacy for the restoration of the defaced image, and her criticism and disgust are very specifically directed toward those Puritans who legislated against innovations and subsequently destroyed the beautified Anglican churches and royalist graves in the 1640s and 1650s. In her poetry, Philips celebrates a checklist of innovations and practices that she would have been encouraged to condemn when she was younger, referring to her subjects as angels and saints, setting up monuments and altars in praise of them, and engaging in purposefully heightened idolatrous reverence. She imagines her coterie to be a "Temple of Divinity" in which their "Tombs" will be visited by "Pilgrims...ten Ages hence" and refers to the "Altars, Priests, and Off'rings" made between herself and Anne Owens.[53] Philips even undercuts the changes that Puritan iconoclasts had made to the marriage service in the *Book of Common Prayer* when they removed the husband's vow to "worship" his bride.[54] In her encomiums, Philips reinstates the discourse of the uxorious suitor when she imagines that her coterie will "worship" the "Mind" of Anne Owen and when she notes that John Jeffreys "worships" Regina Collier.[55] Similarly, Philips's marriage and courtship poems refer to the "shrine[s]" of various women, such as the Countess of Thanet and Mary Carne,[56] and her elegies characterize several women as "Saint[s]," including her late stepdaughter Frances Philips, a Pembrokeshire friend named Mary Lloyd, and, of course, Philips's beloved Anne Owen.[57]

Philips's poetry also responds defiantly to the Puritan iconoclasts' practices of ruining graves, funeral statues, and effigies. Catharine Gray is correct when she identifies Philips's inclination to "turn each [royalist] poet into...an *eikon basilike*."[58] It is the same case for each of the subjects of Philips's poetry; every poem is a little monument to its namesake. Here it seems relevant to mention the many epitaphs that Philips wrote that were then carved into actual funeral monuments, in addition to Philips's construction of what she called poetic "Monument[s]" to everyone from "Mrs. Wogan" to Elizabeth of Bohemia.[59]

That Philips was invested in the politics of literary monumentalization and not just making conventional use of a common literary trope is evidenced in her construction of one such elegiac tribute: "Epitaph on my truly honoured Publius Scipio," a memorial to her late stepfather, Sir Phillip Skippon. Katherine's mother's fourth husband, Skippon served in the king's armies from a young age but defected from Charles's side during the English civil wars and was eventually appointed the major-general of the New Model Army, distributing to his troops the devotional tracts he had authored and using his parliamentary bonuses to buy up the confiscated land and property of bishops and other royalists.

What is especially relevant to my argument here, though, is that Skippon was directly involved in the defacement of an Anglican church, in this case none other than St. Paul's Cathedral. In his epistle dedication prefacing *The History of St. Paul's Cathedral in London* (1658), William Dugdale explains how he was compelled to record his memories of the cathedral's funeral monuments in order to "preserve" their "Inscriptions" even after the monuments were destroyed—not by the London Fire, which would not happen for another eight years after the publication of Dugdale's book—but by the "Presbyterian contagion" which "began violently to breake out" and "ruine" them immediately following the Long Parliament.[60] While St. Paul's had already been significantly defaced by Puritan iconoclasts earlier in the decade, Skippon's troops would do further damage. Ian J. Gentles describes Skippon, "unswerving adherent of the revolution," as the person "who kept a deeply unhappy City in Parliament's grip from the outbreak of the second civil war to the time of the king's trial."[61] Skippon did so by housing his troops in St. Paul's. Gentles reports that "they kept themselves warm by tearing down 'the carved timber, scaffolds and other materialls' and making great fires on the cathedral floor."[62] These "other materialls" included documents and charters as well as innovations.[63]

In her tribute to her stepfather, Philips totally rewrites Skippon's politics, reimagining the Parliamentarian as having been "forced" to "be a Party in [England's] Civil Wars" and representing him as having advocated for religious tolerance. But Philips's use of the larger conceit of poem-as-monument throughout her elegy is just as pointedly political. In the seemingly nondescript line in which she "commit[s]" Skippon's "Name" to "the officious Marble,"[64] Philips trumps the parliamentary army's defacement of St. Paul's Cathedral by simply counteracting their behavior: where the parliamentary army had torn down monuments, Philips raises them up; where the Puritan iconoclasts had ruined funeral inscriptions, Philips writes them.

While the poem to Skippon is instructive, it is also relatively unique in that most of Philips's monument poems are not directed to parliamentary men, family or not. Characteristically, Philips's full-out iconolatry is reserved for two subjects in particular: the first is women, as we have already seen, and the second is royalist poets. In Philips's commendatory verse to Henry Vaughan, for instance, she attests to "admir[ing]" his poetry and landscape designs "almost t' idolatry" and credits them for "Restor[ing] the Golden Age when Verse was Law." She invokes the same conceit when she tells Francis Finch that in writing the "Discourse of Friendship," he has "rais'd" to himself "a glorious Monument" that will outlive "Temples and Statues."[65]

And it is not merely in Philips's later poems that she employs the conceit of royalist poetry as a shrine. She makes the comparison from her very first publication, her commendatory poem which prefaces the posthumously published collected works of William Cartwright, the Oxford scholar and Anglican churchman who had turned soldier during the first civil war and died of camp fever in 1643 at the age of 32. Philips's poem looks forward to the day that Cartwright will rise from the dead, in print if not in person, and usher in the era that recognizes "the splendour of restored Poetry": "Till when let no bold hand profane thy shrine, / 'Tis high Wit-Treason to debase thy coin."[66] It is remarkable, as Philips's contemporary Sarah Jinner pointed out at the time, that a poem by a young woman would be included in a collection of no less than 54 commendatory verses, 53 of which were composed by men.[67] But what is even more remarkable is that a poem by a 19-year-old, connected by birth to radical Presbyterian ministers and by marriage to high-ranking parliamentary army officers and government representatives, would be placed at the head of a collection of poems written by a group that Patrick Thomas describes as "a roll-call of royalist sympathisers."[68] Commendatory verse from the midcentury, perhaps more than any other genre of the time, illustrates the royalists' endeavors to maintain a sense of prestige after the English civil wars and during the Interregnum. Richard Helgerson suggests that, "on the basis of commendatory poems alone, we can draw lines connecting, directly or indirectly, virtually all the cavalier poets."[69] In her commendatory verse to Cartwright, Philips does just that: linking herself to the cause of royalism from her very first publication. What interests me in particular is *how* Philips chooses to align herself with royalism. She does so by condemning one religio-political practice in particular—the practice of Puritan defacement—and representing herself as the opposite: the iconoclast of the Anglican church and the court party.

Gray mentions, in reference to these lines, that Philips's representation of Cartwright's poetry as a shrine is "a fairly standard conceit taken up by the other poets who describe his book as an 'Epitaph,' a 'Legacy,' and '[a] Monument.' "[70] But I would argue two points in response. First, although Robert Waring's, John Raymond's, and Robert Gardiner's commendations include references to shrines, these are simply passing references rather than sustained conceits.[71] Instead, most of the other commendatory poems in the Cartwright volume take their metaphors from academia and nature. Cartwright, who was a reader in metaphysics at Oxford, is described in imagery that references either libraries, classical theater, music, geography, or exploration. In fact, Henry Davidson goes as far as to say that Cartwright's fame will be found in "libraries" *rather than* "tombs."[72] In comparison to the imagery at work in the 53 other commendatory poems that preface the Cartwright collection, Philips's extended use of metaphor of the "text as shrine or monument" is, in fact, absolutely unique.

Second, Philips is not merely employing the conceit as a "conventional trope." Philips represents Cartwright's book of poetry very specifically as the shrine of *royalist* poetry. The reference to Cartwright's "coin" that risks being "debase[d]" by those guilty of "high Wit-treason" makes the connection clear: Philips is alluding to the parliamentary army's defacement of the king's image. Her language echoes the proposal issued to General Sir Thomas Fairfax's troops in August 1647, in which several anonymous royalists warned the Roundheads, "We hope it is not the intent of this al-conquering Army, to diminish, much less to extinguish the Glorious Lamp of Majesty," and concluded, "If Majesty be *defaced* in the Royal stamp, his Subjects will not passe for currant Coyne."[73] In representing Cartwright as the "Prince of Fancy" and imagining that his "shrine" has the potential to be destroyed by a rebel party, Philips is pointedly alluding to the destruction of Anglican church embellishments and cavalier funeral monuments.[74] Significantly, both in the Cartwright poem and throughout her poetry, Philips represents herself as the protector of these images—the defender of the royalist face. In her commendatory verses and funeral epitaphs, Philips works to recuperate the Laudian ideal of iconolatry, not by disassociating the Anglican practice of beautification from Catholic ritual but by hyper-associating the two and, seemingly, reveling in such an association—repeatedly constructing sites of funeral monuments, altars, and temples in her poems, and then staging canonizations, scenes of ritual worship, and episodes of idolatry at these sites. Stone altars, embellished shrines, royal statues, images of saints—this is the iconography of Katherine Philips. In this sense, her poetry strives to restore the beautified Church of England that, growing up, she would have seen her congregation members destroy.

IV

It would seem, then, that when the authors of the prefatory verses to *Poems* (1667) characterize Philips and her writings as worthy of being worshipped, they are, in fact, appropriating the poet's own particular language of iconolatry. Abraham Cowley's commendation characterizes Philips's poems as "Angels," Thomas Flatman's elegy compares Philips herself to the same celestial bodies, "The Preface" represents Philips's book as a "Monument which she erected for her self," and Flatman draws readers' attention "To th' Altar."[75] In the case of James Tyrrell's tribute, Tyrrell imagines the commendatory verses to Philips's collection as offerings upon the altar of the "bright Saint," Katherine. He describes himself as a "Vot[a]ry" who as one of the commenders of Philips's book has entered into the company of a "sacred . . . throng":

> Where looking round me, ev'ry one I see
> Is a sworn Priest of Phœbus, or of thee.
> Forgive this forward zeal for things divine,
> If I strange fire do offer at thy Shrine.[76]

Significantly, Abraham Cowley's elegy resonates with Tyrell's conceit, imagining Philips's body as a temple that has been destroyed by smallpox:

> Wast not enough, when thou, Profane Disease,
> Didst on this glorious Temple seize,
> Wast not enough, like a wild zealot there,
> All the rich outward ornaments to tear,
> Deface the Innocent Pride of beauteous Images?
> Wast not enough thus rudely to defile,
> But thou must quite destroy the goodly Pile?
> And thy unbounded Sacrilege commit
> On the inward Holyest Holy of her Wit?
> Cruel Disease! there thou mistook'st thy Power;
> No Mine of Death can that Devour;
> On her Embalmed Name it will abide
> An Everlasting Pyramide,
> As high as Heaven the Top, as Earth the Basis wide.[77]

Traditionally, scholars have tended to interpret these characterizations of Philips as angelic, saintly, and divine as being patronizingly gendered. Loxley, for instance, argues that Philips's commenders are "unable to consider [her] poems without an insistent emphasis on the poet's sex" and claims that Cowley's verses in particular exhibit an "unrelenting focus on Philips's biological sex."[78] But this argument ignores the ways in which the imagery of angels, saints, monuments, and shrines very decidedly harkens back to the royal rhetoric that was employed to endorse the enterprise of beautifying Anglican churches in the 1610s and 1620s, rhetoric in which "churches were likened to temples, where physical and ritual decorum was appropriate."[79] In Cowley's elegy, in particular, it could not be any more clear that the image of Philips's body as a beautiful temple is not meant as some sort of generic Petrarchan conceit; rather, Cowley is alluding to the defacement of the Church of England at the hands of the Puritans. Cowley takes his vocabulary directly from the legislation by the Long Parliament authorizing the destruction. He literally uses the word "deface," and his discourse is equally pointed when he describes the destruction of "ornaments" and "beauteous Images" at the hands of the "wild zealot." The image in the second stanza of his elegy makes explicit the politics of his iconography. "Of all the female race," Cowley writes of Katherine Philips, "This is the sovreign Face."[80]

Given all of the focus that Philips's face receives in the paratextual materials—from Cowley, the author of "The Preface," and Philips herself—it is of extraordinary significance that the editors of *Poems* (1667) chose to add, and draw attention to, an image of Philips's face in the form of a portrait frontispiece. In the seventeenth century, the selection of a frontispiece is rarely an indiscriminate act. As Wendy Wall points out, "When publishers chose to display the author's portrait in the introductory material to their books, they asked their audience to read the work not only through the rubric of a singular writer, but also according to a specified visual, often emblematic, and embodied perception of that writer."[81] To the extent that the paratextual materials ask us to read *Poems* as a response to Puritan iconoclasm, the portrait frontispiece seals the deal (see fig. 4.2). The frontispiece represents Philips *as a statue*—and not just any statue but a living statue, specifically a classical bust, the very type of statue that the Puritan iconoclasts had targeted for destruction first when they argued that "the Greeks and the Romans" had "fallen by images."[82]

Importantly, the frontispiece depicts Philips's face as though it has been fully restored after having suffered the effects of

Fig. 4.2. The Matchless Orinda: frontispiece to Katherine Philips's *Poems* (1667), by William Faithorne. Courtesy of David L. Orvis.

smallpox. This choice also has political resonances. According to David E. Shuttleton, literary representations of smallpox began to take on "overtly politicised meanings" when "within months of the Restoration" Charles II's brother and sister suddenly contracted and died of the disease: Prince Henry, Duke of Gloucester in September 1660, and Princess Mary of Orange in December 1660. Shuttleton explains that it was at this time in history that royalist writers sought to counter the "perception that smallpox was the peculiar scourge of the Stuarts" by aligning smallpox with the parliamentary army, as in Thomas Shipman's elegy to Mary in which the poet compares the disease to "the destructive, criminal activities of the Parliamentarians."[83] To present Philips in her frontispiece as having fully healed from smallpox is to present the face of royalism as having fully recovered from such destruction.

Steven Zwicker argues that during and immediately after the civil war, "the language of prefaces and defenses of poetry" reflects the writers' concern with "the restoration of the state," and Zwicker and Kevin Sharpe identify a postwar "language of healing."[84] In the prefaces to *Poems* (1667), the two languages are interrelated. In her poem to Francis Finch, Philips had characterized him as the "great Deliverer" of Friendship, who "rescu'd her" after she had been "flung down" by "rude Malice," elevated her, "unveil'd her Face, and then restor'd her Crown."[85] In their commendatory verses to the second edition of Philips's *Poems*, Finch and Philips's other friends do just that—they restore her face and then they restore her crown. *Poems* (1667) is represented as a monument recovered from the effects of defacement, a testament—to use Philips's language—to both "the splendour of restored Poetry" and the "splendor" of "England . . . rul'd and restor'd by" Charles II.[86]

V

While on the one hand, the discourse of defacement and restoration is part and parcel of the inherited convention of the posthumous text—even the preface to Shakespeare's first folio by Hemming and Condell refers to previous editions as "stolne, and surreptitious copies" that were "maimed, and deformed" and are now "cur'd, and perfect of their limbes"—when read in the context of the legislation and practices of defacement, the prefatory materials to the restored edition of *Poems* (1667) are loaded with royalist defiance and fortitude in reaction to Puritan iconoclasm.[87] It is in her own poetry that Philips herself sets the precedent for the discourse of restorative iconolatry, a stance that she marks as decidedly royalist and which she firmly grounds in a critique of the practice of Puritan defacement. We see this from the very first poem in Philips's collection on the subject of Charles's death, in which the poet's focal point is not so much the monarch's execution as the mistreatment that his grave receives afterward:

> Hath Charles so broke God's Laws, he must not have
> A quiet Crown, nor yet a quiet Grave?
> Tombs have been Sanctuaries; Thieves lie there
> Secure from all their penalty and fear.
>
> ....
>
> Oh! to what height of horrour are they come
> Who dare pull down a crown, tear up a Tomb![88]

We also see it at the end of her dramatic works that conclude *Poems,* as in *Pompey,* which ends with the directive to have "Altars...Buil[t]" in "Immortal Honou[r]" of the title character: "Then after all the Blood that's shed / Let's right the living and the dead: / Temples to Pompey raise."[89] It is correct to observe that *Poems* starts with the problem of Charles I's execution and the subsequent English civil wars and ends with the reconstruction of the Anglican church. But it is even more accurate to argue that *Poems* starts with the specific problem of Puritan defacement and ends with the equally specific answer of Anglican restoration.

And this brings us back to the poem with which we began and with which Philips ended: her poem to Archbishop Gilbert Sheldon, the last poem Philips ever composed, written just ten days before her death. I would make the argument that writing to Sheldon as her last poetic act was purposeful on Philips's part because Sheldon's commitment to repairing the damage that Puritan iconoclasts caused to the Anglican church aligned so strongly with

Philips's own poetic mission. As Spraggon notes, "the restoration of episcopacy" brought along with it "the refurbishment of often-neglected churches and the reintroduction of utensils, furnishings and vestments outlawed by the Long Parliament. Communion rails, images and windows removed and hidden away during the Interregnum were now restored."[90] According to Kenneth Fincham and Nicholas Tyacke, Sheldon was the "key figure" behind the enterprise to restore the defaced Anglican church.[91] Victor D. Sutch explains that during the Interregnum, Sheldon was almost single-handedly responsible for preserving the remnants of the Anglican church. He set to work "locat[ing] the scattered Anglican clergy," "constructing an underground correspondence net," "establish[ing] the 'Charitable Uses Fund' to provide basic necessities for displaced Anglican clergymen," maintaining the king and other royals, naming tutors, chaplains, and pastors to "expatriate" families and congregations, and contriving methods for the consecration of new bishops so that church leadership did not die out.[92] In 1660, when Charles II returned to England, Sheldon performed baptisms, funeral services, the majority of the coronation, and the marriage ceremony of Charles and Catherine, and he was appointed "dean of the Chapel Royal," which came "with the duty of providing court preachers."[93]

Out of all of his accomplishments, it is for his efforts to re-beautify the Anglican church and restore it to its Laudian ideal that Philips praises Sheldon. While her poem to commemorate his election as Archbishop might seem a safe panegyric, especially since it begins, as Philips's poems so often do, with an ample recitation of feigned humility and female innocence, in writing this poem Philips was actually making quite a bold statement in that she was siding with Sheldon against the king. Although in 1659 Edward Hyde could write that Charles II "reverence[d] nobody more" than Sheldon, by 1662 Sheldon had already clashed with Charles II on the matter of religious toleration, and Sheldon would repeatedly interfere with and thwart Charles's attempts to grant royal indulgences to dissenters to the extent that Charles would eventually break with Sheldon entirely.[94] Remarkably, in Philips's poem on the matter of religious toleration against sectarians, whom Philips calls "the sullen Schismatick[s]," Philips sides with Sheldon, assigning attributes of "Majest[y]" and "Government" to Sheldon and establishing her belief that Sheldon has been "preserv'd to Govern and *Restore*" the church. Philips represents Sheldon as having the ability to "repair" the "Ruines" of the "torn Church," and steer the "shatter'd Vessel" through the "angry reliques in the Wave and Wind." The conceit is of a warship, but the language is of Puritan defacement and Anglican restoration. Philips imagines Sheldon as the scourge of the iconoclasts, having unfurled the church's "Cross" as an "Ensign" in order to frighten away "Pagan Gods," as though the English civil wars were the equivalent of the Crusades.[95] In her vision of the monarchy and church presented in this poem, the ideal is pre–civil war. It is as if Philips wishes that Archbishop Sheldon were Archbishop Laud, the same Archbishop Laud who in the 1620s and 1630s authorized the repair and beautification of the church.

Interestingly enough, according to Sutch, in Sheldon's early career and relative youth he had been "oppos[ed]" to Laudian "innovations" and to Laud's larger enterprise of "revamping the Church of England."[96] It was the experience of having "witnessed the terrible chaos which the Calvinists visited upon both Church and State during the Civil Wars" that caused Sheldon to change his mind.[97] Fincham and Tyacke write that Sheldon eventually accepted "Laud's vision of . . . decorous public worship," and, following the Restoration, Sheldon accepted the task that Philips praises him for, that of reestablishing "the Laudian innovations in cathedral worship of the 1630s—the provision of a rail and dressed altar, and the performance of a stately ritual during divine service."[98] Sutch calls Sheldon's reversal of his stance on church iconography "the *only* change [we] can see in Sheldon's views over a lifetime."[99] Given the extreme contrast between Philips's upbringing and her stance against Puritan defacement in her poetry, I have to believe that a similar reversal on the subject of church iconography must have been one of the most significant shifts in Philips's life as well.

5 ❖ Inventing the English Sappho

Katherine Philips's Donnean Poetry

Paula Loscocco

Author's Note

Ten years ago, Philips scholars were still often preoccupied with her poetry's ostensibly autobiographical content—its supposedly reactionary royalism, radical lesbianism, and canny careerism. Resisting that trend, I situated Philips's Donnean poems of love and friendship in the context of 1650s royalist culture, English literary tradition, and the stipulative existence of an afigural and female homopoetics within prevailing Petrarchan rhetoric. In the essay reprinted below, I argue that Philips invoked Donne's love poems, particularly "A Valediction: Forbidding Mourning" and "Sapho to Philaenis," to succeed where Donne had failed—namely, in realizing the possibilities of total amorous union (versus intimate interrelationship) and of a corresponding unitary or self-contained discourse that embodies (versus signifies or points to) its own meaning. I show how Philips developed a discourse adequate to the expressive demands of an entirely private or sealed union, arguing that this discourse underlies her poems both of marriage and of homoerotic friendship. In her verses to her husband, Philips guards the ongoing marital conversation, closing it to all but the spousal reader; in poems to female friends, the amorous dialogue is entirely open to a beloved who is posited as the only reader. In both cases, the union Philips describes is homoerotic, given that union is defined as the identity of lover and beloved. In both cases, too, the discourse is homopoetic or Sapphic, given that a poetics based on an identity of sign and signifier is, within the parameters of metaphorical and masculinist Petrarchan rhetoric, necessarily afigural, erotic, and feminine.

Ten years later, substantial advances in the study of royalist culture, Sapphic poetics, and rhetorical tradition, sometimes by Philips scholars themselves, have made it possible to discern Philips's masterful deployment of complex poetic materials at a key moment in English cultural history. Building on pioneering work by Erica Veevers and Carol Barash, Catharine Gray and Hero Chalmers have located Philips in the newly reconceived royalist culture of 1650s England.[1] As the introduction elaborates, these critics show how her love poems participate in the larger royalist project of creating a reformed courtly identity based on a reconfigured (anti-Puritan and anti-cavalier) poetics of mutual love and invested in the discourses and values of female friendship, heroic women, and women's writing. As the introduction also notes, Gray's recent work has dovetailed with William Kerrigan's positioning of Philips within archipelagic English culture: she positions Philips at the forefront of Restoration efforts from around the British nation to establish a renewed monarchy rooted in earlier associations of royalism with romance and femininity.[2] Locating Philips within a royalist culture now valued for its vital and fluid complexity, these studies enable us to read Philips in the informed way we do such male peers as Henry Vaughan or Andrew Marvell.

A similar sophistication has developed in studies of Philips's Sapphic poetics, as critics have explored how she makes use of the topoi and discourses of early modern friendship. In essays included in this volume, Lorna Hutson reverses the tragic narrative underlying Valerie Traub's groundbreaking discussion of Philips's deployment of the traditions of *amor impossibilis*, the homoerotic lament, and the elegiac pastoral of Renaissance drama. Situating Philips between Jeremy Taylor's anachronistic notions of male friendship and John Locke's emerging contract theory, Hutson sees in Philips's poems a model of female bonding that sets the stage for eighteenth century contractual relations.[3] Penelope Anderson goes farther, as this volume's editors note, linking Philips's poems of excess love and rage to the classical tradition of *amicitia perfecta* and arguing that Philips's dramatic poems anticipate a contract theory designed to enable government to persist through repeated breakdowns and changes.[4]

The identification of Philips as a baroque writer whose resonant reinventions of established rhetorical traditions account for her unparalleled contemporary reputation—Marcus Nevitt notes the milestone for women writers of the 1667 folio edition of *Poems*—is perhaps the signal achievement of the last ten years of Philips scholarship.[5] Most pertinently for my own essay, Dianne Dugaw and Amanda Powell have set Philips (and other English women writers) in the proto-feministic context of the "baroque Sapphic mode" of pan-European court culture: "Women poets linked the conventionalized petrarchan stance, in which the poet contemplates a beloved, to the context of aristocratic court culture in texts that foreground female homoerotic passion and sexuality, satirize the silencing of women, and often advocate for their equality with men."[6] Similarly, Alex Davis provides a rhetorical parallel to the work done by Gray and Chalmers when she explores the continental romance traditions that Philips uses to create a broad-based community of readers and writers devoted to values associated with women, reading, and female virtue.[7] These studies do the invaluable service of empowering readers to evaluate Philips not only as a professional writer, committed monarchist, and contemporary woman but also as one of her era's most skilled literary artists.

There is still no standard edition of Philips's works, nor are there more than a handful of her poems in any anthology, as

Nigel Smith notes.[8] In terms of larger scholarly studies, moreover, Kerrigan is unusual in including Philips in his exploration of archipelagic English culture: neither Alan Bray (homoerotic friendship), as Hutson first noted, nor Paul Hammond (Restoration poetry), nor Nicholas McDowell (the common ground of friendship, patronage, and literature), nor Shannon Miller (Milton and women writers) consider Philips.[9] The current collection, exploring as it does Philips's engagement with a broad range of literary, textual, cultural, and political discourses, at last puts Philips on the big map of seventeenth century literary and cultural studies.

Katherine Philips's Donnean poems of love and friendship, which are integral to her sophisticated, innovative, and largely unrecognized poetics, have given rise to a number of critical myths.[10] Scholars claim that in those verses that invoke the love lyrics of John Donne, Philips reveals herself to be (unappealingly) royalist in her politics and conservative in her social and professional loyalties.[11] They argue that her Donnean marriage poems lack genuine feeling, and that the true content of her Donnean friendship poems is lesbian passion.[12] They assume that Philips's poetry is an authentic report of autobiographical emotion, whether political or amorous.[13] They claim that Philips manifests both internal ambivalence (in the face of competing political, social, and sexual loyalties) and external defensiveness (against imposed cultural barriers), and that her Donnean poems are correspondingly either conflicted or strategic.[14] And they insist that Philips used literary figures such as Donne not only to signal covertly her political loyalties, as many writers did in the 1650s, but also to screen her professional ambition and private sexuality.[15]

The triple focus of most critical narratives of Philips's Donnean poetry—on her presumably royalist politics, lesbian sexuality, and alternately transparent or screened poetry—has made it almost impossible to understand or appreciate her work as it deserves.

Regarding her poetry as autobiographical code, readers reduce it to its alleged political or sexual content and respond to it with perplexing ideological passion. In her 1991 study of the parallel between coded royalist writing and Philips's "'closet' lesbian verse," for example, Elaine Hobby resorts to strong language: revolted generally by "the tedious and inhuman dynamics of heterosexuality" and particularly by "the controlling, self-satisfied male figure who fills so much of John Donne's verse," Hobby sees Donne as a straw man that Philips invokes only to reject. Such rejection does not exonerate Philips in Hobby's eyes, however, and she confesses herself "repelled" by the taint of royalism that "infects" a Donnean poem like "To My excellent Lucasia, on our friendship."[16]

I would suggest that reading Philips's Donnean verses for their polemical content keeps us from perceiving not only her politics, which some studies have started to appreciate as complex,[17] but also her poetics, which is sophisticated in ways that accommodate but are not exclusively or even principally concerned with political signification. I would also suggest that Philips's marriage and friendship poems derive from a single and powerful affective source and that whatever model of sexuality we attach to these poems tells us more about their nuanced deployment of gendered Renaissance rhetoric than it does about Philips herself. Finally, I think that misplaced focus on ideological content has led critics to develop theories of discourse on the basis of a few conflicted poems, whereas a more inclusive survey of Philips's Donnean verses discovers a largely (if not entirely) untroubled poetics that alternates purposefully between mysterious privacy and radical expressiveness.

This essay begins with a meditation on the royalist model of Donnean poetry offered by Donne's first biographer, Izaak Walton. Walton's notorious and polemical simplification of Donne's richly metaphorical poetry recalls critical characterizations of Philips's friendship verses; as such, it serves as a baseline from which to measure her very different poetic project. More pertinently, comparison of Walton's work with Donne's suggests an even greater difference between Philips's project and Donne's original lyrics: Donne was for Philips an inspirational but limited forebear whom she moved beyond as she developed her own poetics.

Philips's marriage poems indicate that she uses Donne to posit an intimate relationship but drops him both when she transforms his notion of private relationship into her ideal of sealed "Union" and when she dismisses his poetry of elaborate comparison in favor of what is in these poems a mysteriously "unitary" or specular poetics. Not all of Philips's Donnean verses are devoted to union, however. In certain of her verses to female friends, she seems to find Donne's model of amorous relationship and comparative discourse expressive. The dream of union and specular discourse haunts even these verses, however, giving her allusions to Donne's powerful negative connotations: when she invokes him to describe female relationship, there is a desperate edge to her verse, and when she uses him to describe female union, there is manifest tension and strain. Philips resolves her affective and discursive dilemma, however, by pushing through to what Donne himself attempted but failed to achieve. In a second group of friendship poems, Philips develops a noncomparative discourse appropriate to union that is, given the gendering of Renaissance rhetoric, explicitly identified with female eroticism—both in Donne's "Sapho to Philaenis" and in several of Philips's friendship poems. In what might therefore be described as her Sapphic poetry, Philips picks up where Donne's "Sapho" leaves off, taking the specular discourse that his elegy vainly seeks and that her marriage poems keep mainly to themselves, and revealing it to be a fully developed Sapphic poetics brilliantly adequate to the expressive demands of (female) union.

Philips was Donne's last and best heir and innovator and a major poet in her own right. How is it, then, that her work has been so misrepresented and ignored? As I explore Philips's Donnean poems of love and friendship, I consider some answers: the occluded nature of Sapphic discourse within masculinist rhetorical tradition; the possibility that in sealing up Donne for 200 years Walton sealed up the Donnean Philips for 300; and Philips's status as "the English Sappho," a complex and fluid designation that may or may not identify her as poet, leader, wanton, or lesbian, and that was at her death undergoing a semantic shift that still colors our response to her poetry.

I. *"If we be two?"*

In his survey of royalist writing during the Cromwellian 1650s, Derek Hirst argues that defeated royalists countered republican claims of godly election and "cavalier" immorality in two principal ways. They cultivated pious attitudes that let them assert moral superiority over republican "passion" or controversy, and they produced texts whose literary and allusive nature led them to claim England's cultural traditions as their own.[18] There may be no better model of this kind of royalist writer than Izaak Walton, a man committed to appropriating literary tradition for royalist culture who almost single-handedly made John Donne England's most morally respectable and poetically forgettable lyricist. Although it took him until the fourth and final edition of his hagiographical *Life* (1675) to find a way to bring Donne's love poetry into royalist line, in the end he succeeded, largely through his contextualization and revision of a single verse, "A Valediction: Forbidding Mourning." In his version, Walton straitens the lovers' erotic and private bond into an absolutist union of wife, husband, king, and church, and he collapses Donne's conceited and suggestive poetry into correspondingly rigid rhyme.

In an episode involving Donne's supposed vision (in France) of Anne More mourning a stillbirth (in England), Walton offers "A Valediction, Forbidding to Mourn" as evidence of a "sympathy of souls" that he perceives as spiritually ideal.[19] The framing narrative—concerning Donne's participation in a diplomatic mission between James I and Henri IV and testifying to James's regard for Donne as a clerical apologist—gives political and ecclesiastical meaning to the union, and the passing tribute to the loyal wife left at home gives it a patriarchal explicitness absent in Donne's own writing.

The ideological agenda that governs Walton's portrait of Donne's marriage shapes his revision of the "Valediction." In a poem that wrestles with the painful reality that imminent departure brings into focus—namely, two lovers are and yet they are not one—Donne himself finally arrives at a suitably expressive image: "If they be two, they are two so / As stiffe twin compasses are two."[20] The consolation here is the consolation of analogy: the lovers' souls, together and apart, are like compasses; their souls are like themselves; and they, bodies and souls, are comparable to the two feet of a compass. In the end, it is the relationship between the conceit's highlighted vehicle and its affective tenor that most eloquently expresses the "inter-assured" nature of the lovers' bond. Because their souls are "two" and not one, because they are like but not the same as the compasses, because the lines refer tactfully to "they" and not "we," there is endless room for amorous interpretation. And when he uses such neutral terms as "it," "the other," and "that" to refer to his compass's feet, he draws delicious attention to his figure's suggestively described signifier:

> Thy soule the fixt *foot,* makes no show
> To move, but doth, if the'other doe.
> And though *it* in the center sit,
> Yet when *the other* far doth rome,
> *It* leanes, and hearkens after it,
> And growes erect, as *that* comes home.
> (27–32; emphasis added)

Walton's re-presentation of the final image of "Valediction," in contrast, manifests a discursive ideal—of language absorbed safely into meaning—that corresponds to his larger ideal of wife absorbed into husband and subject into king.[21] "If we be two?," he posits, "we are two so / As stiff twin-compasses are two" (25–26). Replacing "they" with "we," Walton immediately collapses the interpretive interstices Donne opens among souls and lovers and compasses. "We" are further diminished as the rhyme proceeds, as his alterations of Donne's lines move the lovers away from bodies and language and toward souls and ideas. In Walton's version, "thine," "my," and "mine" are possessive pronouns that repeatedly return the reader to the figure's signified idea of "soul":

Thy *soul,* the fixt foot, makes no show
To move, but does, if th'other do.
And, though *thine* in the Center sit,
Yet, when *my* other far does rome,
Thine leans, and hearkens after it,
And grows erect as *mine* comes home. (27–32; emphasis added)

A similar impulse to limit both Donne's poetic resonances and the reader's interpretive options governs Walton's rendering of Donne's lines 17–20, where he replaces "love" and "selves" with "Soul" and "souls," and reduces "Care lesse, eyes, lips, hands to misse" to an emphatic "Care not" (17–20).

Arising as it did from powerful polemical impulses, Walton's pietizing *Life* proved enormously influential. As students of Donne's reception have noted, the biography played a pivotal role in reducing Donne's rich and fluid identity to the crude and static binary of Jack Donne and Dr. Donne, collapsing the love poet into the loyal priest and keeping him there for over 200 years.[22]

Given this history, it should not surprise us if the Donnean Philips, writing 20 years before Walton's final shutdown, was similarly lost in the Restoration silencing of Donne's poetry. The possibility should open our eyes. Scholars troubled by the didacticism, propriety, and conservatism of "the chaste Orinda" need to give her poems the same revisionist scrutiny that brought the "Doctor" (who is so much more than "holy") from the grave. That Walton could have contributed to her obscurity, however, points to other critical issues. A Donnean writer both in her principal source of allusion and in her verbal skill and intellectual inventiveness, Philips produced a poetry of affective and discursive union that departs in substantial ways from Donne's conceited poetry of amorous relationship, even as it proves to be at odds with Waltonian rhyming.

II. *"Possest of their desire"*

In her marriage poems to "Antenor" (James Philips), Philips invokes Donne's love lyrics, both to establish an intimate relationship and to separate that relationship from the world. Despite such invocations, though, these poems are oddly non-Donnean. In celebrating a marriage she describes not as Donnean relationship but as her own union, Philips dismisses the experience of parting when there is no separation. And in transforming Donne's separation between lovers and world into an impenetrable marital seal, she describes a union she does not actually reveal, making that union private, even mysterious.

Philips's marriage poems are particularly mysterious when they hint at an innovative discourse appropriate to union. This "unitary" or specular discourse starts as Donnean conceit but emerges as an afigural way of using language in which words do not refer to but reflect or embody their own meaning. The result is literally magical: under the positive conditions of ideal marriage, specular discourse works like a charm, silently marking the enlivening circle of union itself. Under the negative conditions of contemporary life, in which reductive models of union and speech abound, it works like a curse whose words effect blight.

If Donne's "Valediction" can be read as the lover's effort to arrive at an image of separation adequate to the painful fact of (inter)relationship, Philips's "To my dearest Antenor on his parting,"[23] can be understood as the response of a beloved who is as self-possessed as she is devoted to a lover with whom she perceives herself entirely "combin'd" (6). "Though it be Just to grieve when I must part / With him that is the Guardian of my heart," she begins, between title and first line reversing the poem's agency while conceding the "Just[ness]" of a "grief" her subordinating "Though" has already dismissed, "Yet...Absence can doe no hurt to souls combin'd" (3–6). Philips disposes of valedictory grief here not because she lacks feeling but because she denies parting: if separation in Donne is the problem to which the compass image is the solution, separation in Philips is a murmur she prevents before the poem begins.

This is no small difference. Anthony Low hails the relationship implied by Donne's love poetry as a well-nigh perfect union, arguing that the poet transforms a "social and feudal" model of love into a "private and modern" one: "What Donne proposes in his most idealized love-lyrics is a union between lovers that is essentially communal, sacred, and religious."[24] But even Low admits that the "ideals and rewards" of the world "lie... oddly and somewhat uneasily" within the lovers' relationship and that Donne's "transformation" of love contains within itself "the seeds of its own contradiction."[25] Paula Blank insists on such contradiction. Though "the union of two lovers" in Donne's works "seems to promise a way of eluding change and mortality," she argues, such union inevitably founders: "difference emerges as the only inviolable, invariable feature of erotic experience with an other," ensuring "the failure of a characteristic Donnean homoerotics, in which a subject attempts to possess its object by blurring the distinction between them."[26]

In "To my dearest Antenor," however, Philips lightly assumes what Low claims for Donne and Blank denies him—the "posses[sion] of... desire" (12). Having freed herself from the exigencies of valediction before her poem begins, Philips asserts a surprisingly credible "combin[ation]" of persons. Even as she asserts the ongoing "grow[th]" of marital "Union" or "One"-ness, portraying her and Antenor's relationship as a progressive discovery of preexisting identity, for example, she describes that union as a minuet in which multiple dancers of diverse "inclinations," "interests," and "persons" forever join, divide, and rejoin: the husband first masked as "Antenor" and later described as "him," "thine [heart]," and "deare Guest," is "brought to agree" with the speaking "I" (possibly both Philips and Orinda) and her happy "heart" (1–16).

Philips creates the sense of "possest... desire" not only by referring to marriage as the ongoing discovery of rich union, but by refusing to anatomize that union for her readers' benefit. Whatever her motives—and they may be as deceptively simple as modesty, discretion, tact, or pleasure—she refrains from revealing the nature of marital union. This restraint is particularly notable in the poem's single reference to the "flame" of "desire":

> when united nearer we became,
> It did not weaken, but increase our flame.
> Unlike to those who distant joys admire,
> But slight them when possest of their desire. (9–12)

While it is possible to read these lines as distinguishing between platonic love and carnal passion—with Philips playing the role of prim lover or dutiful wife—to do so would be to mistake taciturnity for coldness. For their "flame" does not "weaken" but "increase," and they are unlike other lovers not in "posses[sing]" desire but in not "slight[ing]" it. Entirely possessed of unanimous desire as they are, they might even revel in it, though this is just the kind of erotic possibility that the poem gives us no help in imagining.

A brief comparison of "To my dearest Antenor" with a poem to a female friend clarifies the passionate privacy of Philips's marriage poem. "L'amitié: To Mrs. M. Awbrey" parallels "To my dearest Antenor" in several ways: Philips addresses her friend ("my Joy, my crown, my friend!" [1]) as she does her husband ("My guide, life, object, friend, and destiny" [36]); both poems speak of "souls" and "minds" "grown" into "divine" or "sacred" "union" ("L'amitié," 3–5, 21; "To my dearest Antenor," 8–12); both refer to shared "thought" and "desire" as a "flame" ("L'amitié," 7–8; "To my dearest Antenor," 10–12). The difference between the poems lies in their erotic explicitness. Where "To my dearest Antenor" refers to a desire that the poem does not bring to life, "L'amitié" does just the opposite:

> I have no thought but what's to thee reveal'd,
> Nor thou desire that is from me conceal'd.
>
> ....
>
> Thou shedst no teare but what my moisture lent,
> And if I sigh, it is thy breath is spent. (7–8, 11–12)

"L'amitié" is in these lines a Donnean poem, not only in its invocation of "Song: Sweetest love"—"When thou sigh'st, thou sigh'st not winde, / But sigh'st my soule away" (25–26)—but in its poetic rendering of a desire between two lovers that we are invited to share. The eroticism signaled in "To my dearest Antenor," in contrast, is not for us: it exists apart from the poem, and though it generates Philips's amorous and poetic confidence, it is not offered for our delectation. In this sense, "Antenor" is the more intimate poem: it describes a union of thought and desire so perfect that the lovers neither experience themselves as separate from one another nor require (or allow) external witness to their unitary truth.[27]

The doubled intimacy of Philips's poem—in which Donnean relationship is transformed into passionate union and Donnean separation between lovers and world into private seal—resists a critical scrutiny it nevertheless requires. In this context, it helps to compare "To my dearest Antenor" to yet another poem, though this time it is the explicitness of definition, not eroticism, that pertains. Like "To my dearest Antenor," "A Friend" defines marriage as passionate union: "wedlock felicity / It self doth only... stand" by the "Union" of "Friendship," which Philips describes as a "flame" of "Love" "Stronger than passion is" (1–15). More pertinently to a discussion of inscrutability, "A Friend" identifies union both with "Innocence" (23)—of division between friends as well as of attachment to the ways of the world—and with "secre[cy]" (26). Like innocence, secrecy has internal and external meaning. On the one hand, "it is not known" within union where friends' separate selves reside, "ally'd" as they are by "secret... Sympathy" (25–30). On the other, friends ensure that "none should know" of their bond: they "conceale" "Secrets" which, "Guarded" by "Discretion," lie safely in "one Chest" of which "none can pick the lock" (34–55). The poem's image for its own exclusivity is appropriately paradoxical: "Friends are each other's Mirrours" (62), fully reflecting only themselves and so revealing nothing of or to the occluded world.

Sealed union is the sum and substance of "To my dearest Antenor," but because "Antenor" enacts what "A Friend" defines, that union is less perceptible though more resonant. Because the "sympathy" at the poem's heart is indeed "secret" (21), moreover, and because Philips's ultimate concern in "Antenor" is with language itself, the image of a "Glasse" that she offers at her poem's end (31) functions not as a metaphor whose parallels with union are revealing, but rather as an example of a specular discourse as obscuring as union itself.

As Philips dismisses Donne's model of merely private relationship, so she dismisses his conceited poetics, though she begins by paying teasing tribute to his compass-image:

> Now as in watches, though we doe not know
> When the hand moves, we find it still doth go:
> So I, by secret sympathy inclin'd,
> Will absent meet, and understand thy mind;
> And thou, at thy return, shalt find thy heart
> Still safe, with all the Love thou didst impart. (19–24)

"We doe not know" much, but we do know that the poet who wrote the first 18 lines of "To my dearest Antenor"—and who here vows to await his "return" even as she creates the fleeting illusion that she is the one who will be "absent"—is dallying with false surmise. Deftly parodying the roles of weeping beloved (here an "understand[ing]" household saint) and of flamboyant poet-lover (here a "safe" simile-maker), she gives Donne—and perhaps (prophetically) his reductive executor[28]—a knowing nod and moves on.

What she moves on to is her own invocation of a "Glasse," an invocation radically different from Donne's compass. For where Donne's compass constitutes a conceit, a multifaceted image of the lovers' bond which it both does and does not resemble, Philips's "Glasse" functions as the verbal embodiment or realization of a union from which it is ultimately indistinguishable, or so Philips claims when she divides the image-making of others (possibly including her most "forward" forebear) from her own union-embodying "art":

> For what some forward arts do undertake,
> The images of absent friends to make,
> And represent their actions in a Glasse,
> Friendship it self can onely bring to passe. (29–32)

Philips claims that union or "Friendship"—within which the two lovers are "combin'd," "innocent," "secret," indistinguishable, identical—possesses the "magique" power (33) to "bring to passe" or realize itself verbally, so that the resulting poem is as inseparable from "Friendship" as lover is from beloved.

On its face, Philips's claim here is absurd. Insofar as her final lines enact this claim, however, it is not only credible but suggests that Philips succeeds in developing the specular poetics that Donne himself only posits. Blank argues that Donne's frustrated pursuit of amatory union (or "homoerotics") parallels his pursuit of verbally embodied desire (or "homopoetics"), so that he "fail[s] to write his (or her) desire into consummation, to persuade by means of a homopoetics that rewrites two terms as one."[29] When she combines speaker and spouse into a union that is also her poem, however, Philips does "write... consummation"—though it is in keeping with her poem's marital exclusivity that she only gives notice of a discursive achievement that she does not reveal.

In the "magique... Glasse" that is "To my dearest Antenor," Philips suggests, reflections realize themselves:

> thou shalt in me survey
> Thy self reflected while thou art away.
>
> ....
>
> So in my brest thy Picture drawn shall be,
> My guide, life, object, friend, and destiny:
> And none shall know, though they employ their wit,
> Which is the right Antenor, thou, or it. (27–28, 35–38)

Appropriately for a "Glasse," these lines set up a hall of mirrors. "Thou" is presumably the same as "Thy self," and yet in the context of that self being "in" the speaker, that self becomes a "Picture" in her breast—though it may also be the verbal picture of Philips's poem in our hands. By the time we reach "Picture," we start to get dizzy: the picture she has drawn is of a man who is (delightfully) both her "guide" and "object," and also (more seriously) her "life" and "destiny." Which is to say: his "self," which is his "Picture," is also her own "life" and "destiny," which is of course herself, so that what is in her "brest" is not only him but her, who is the other's "friend." The multiple mirroring here enables the poem to close with an enactment of Philips's claim that she and Antenor constitute a union indistinguishable from its self-reflecting, self-embodying poetic "Picture."

The poem's final triumph lies in this indistinguishability. "None"—neither the spouses who are unable to distinguish between themselves or between their union and its verbal reflection, nor those of us who receive scant notice of a bond and discourse we are not asked to experience—"shall [ever] know, though they employ their wit," the difference between Antenor and "it," where "it" includes the knowing speaker, the pair's sealed union, and that union's poetic "Glasse." In this context, the poem is indeed the "magique" charm that the speaker says it is: "beguil[ing]" the laws of "both fate and time" (33), it "bring[s] to passe" or conjures up enlivening union even as it makes that union imperceptible to unknowing readers.

If specular discourse can function as a charm, simultaneously embodying and shielding union, however, it can also function as a curse, dooming the disaffected to utter darkness. In "To Antenor, on a paper of mine wch J. Jones threatens to publish to his prejudice," Philips sets herself (and Antenor) against a man whose reductive notions of union and speech seek to enforce social and political conformity.

"To Antenor on a paper of mine" responds to an attack on Philips's husband by Jenkin Jones, a Fifth Monarchist sympathizer who evidently charged James with Cromwellian disloyalty to the republican cause and Katherine with marital disloyalty to a husband whose politics do not correspond to those of a particular Philipsian "paper."[30] Despite his radical republican credentials, that is, the hostile Jones rather closely resembles the hagiographical Walton, as both attempt to equate wife with husband and poetry with political position.

Philips responds to Jones's coercively narrow ideas of appropriate union and speech with a bravura performance of her marital poetics. She begins by describing a marriage so serene that it accommodates wifely independence to a literal, oft-repeated, and clearly unrepentant fault: "My love and life I must confesse are thine, / But not my errours, they are only mine" (7–8). The distinction Philips claims here is characteristically collapsible: the perfectly rhyming iambic pentameter couplet folds the asserted division into a single whole, and her claim of being "Alone" with errors she insists are "only" hers (21) sets up a pairing that mirrors marital union itself. In a poem that thus enacts its own ideal of freedom within marriage, it is no surprise that what Philips first refers to as "crimes" (1) and later calls only "follies" (18) becomes in the end the tools of her trade—"lines," "inke," "staine," "verse," "poet[ry]," and "wit" (19–29).

Orinda is Antenor, her crimes are her own, her poems are her crimes, and her poems manifest their marriage. It is surely no wonder, then, that her tone finally shifts from wickedly charming to companionably malign. Though "'Tis possible" that Jones "May yet enjoy a...wife" as Philips does a husband (13–16), the poem's taunting enactment of mutual marital freedom, responding as it does to Jones's call for patriarchal identity of husband and wife, makes such a possibility remote. And though she could let "verse revenge the quarrel" (27)—pitting her potent "verse" against a "rime...so dull" (26) that it can only "spell" political or patriarchal union (14)—she desists: "hee's...below a poet's curse" (27–28). Or so she says. In fact, it is hard to imagine a malediction darker than the speaker's closing wish for the antagonist she leaves unnamed, immobilized, silenced, single, and sterile: "Let him be still himselfe, and let him live" (30).

III. *"They are, and yet they are not, two"*

Not all of Philips's poems are marital, of course, and not all are as powerful or invulnerable as "To my dearest Antenor" or "To Antenor on a paper of mine." In her poems that address relationships other than perfect union, including several of her poems to female friends, the curse she visits upon Jones comes back to haunt her in the form of emotional and poetic isolation and impotence. More puzzlingly, this curse also haunts some of the friendship poems devoted to union, shattering the poise and privacy of Philips's specular poetics and replacing them with the textual and sexual display that her marriage poems so easily assign to Donne. If "To my dearest Antenor" bespeaks union in elliptical ways that preserve it from scrutiny, that is, "Friendship in Emblem, or the Seal. To my dearest Lucasia," considered here, spells union with a hyper-Donnean explicitness that destroys it. Only in the final group of poems I explore, poems to friends that are neither sealed in marriage nor strained to breaking by anxious revelation, does Philips find a way to posit the reader as her beloved and so speak (of) union freely.

Brief examination of a pair of verses in which Philips relinquishes her claims to union suggests the anxieties and even terrors that disunion holds for her. These in turn not only make sense of what we see in her poems to Antenor, where she invariably transforms Donne's notions of relationship and conceited poetics into her own ideals of union and specular discourse, but they may explain what happens in "Friendship in Emblem," where she spectacularly and inexplicably misapplies Donnean rhetoric to non-Donnean union.

"Orinda to Lucasia parting," a poem in which the collapse of friendship utterly dispossesses the speaker of the pleasures and powers that union provides, comes as a shock after Philips's self-contained marriage poems. As she had once been united with her beloved friend (Anne Owen), so now she finds herself at one with the world external to union: "[I] ruine am without, passion within," she tells Lucasia, and "would'st thou for thy old *Orinda* call, / Thou hardly could'st unravel her at all" (10, 15–16). Having lost her only self (the "Orinda" who is the Lucasia with whom she no longer is one), she feels herself "so entangl'd and so lost a thing" (13) as to be "unravel[able]"—as devastatingly imperceptible within chaotic disunion as she had been happily imperceptible within crystalline union. Worse than being "lost," though, is being heard: stripped of the innocent and secret veil of specular discourse, she finds her potent verse reduced to naked rhyme: "Oh, pardon me for pow'ring out my woes / In Rhime, now that I dare not do't in Prose [prosody?]."

"Parting with a Friend" offers an alternative image of discursive hell. Even as it posits "unions" that neither time nor chance "divide[s]" (20), the poem withdraws this possibility from the speaker herself. Midway into the poem, Philips reveals that the union she had first presented as "ours" (24) is in fact only "Yours" (27), the exclusive possession of her friends, Lucasia and Rosania (Mary Aubrey). And while "each to other is combin'd" (31), she herself is excommunicated, one of the living dead whose voice echoes off their sealed union to sound in no one's ear but her own:

> Wherein may you that Rapture find,
> That sister *Cherals* [cherubs?] have,
> When I am in my Rocks confin'd,
> Or seal'd up in my Grave. (45–48)

"Friendship in Emblem" is a poem of union so unsettled by this specter of discursive disunion—verse reduced to a bare rhyme that sounds only in its speaker's ear—that it ultimately founders. The poem founders, moreover, at the precise moment when, like "To my dearest Antenor," it would invoke and thereby dismiss Donne's conceited poetics. Unlike "Antenor," though, the poem apparently hears in that poetics supra-Donnean echoes of a disunion threatening enough to disable it entirely.

"Friendship in Emblem" opens with two familiar motifs: the two hearts are so "intermixed" that " 'Joyn'd and growing, both in one, / Neither can be disturb'd alone" (1–4); and they are "flames" that, "like Moses bush presum'd," are "Warm'd and enlighten'd, not consum'd" (17–20). Unlike in "To my dearest Antenor," however, when Philips then turns to Donne's compass, she neither teases nor takes off on her own, but stalls for nine painful stanzas. She begins:

> 6
>
> The compasses that stand above
> Express this great immortall Love;
> For friends, like them, can prove this true,
> They are, and yet they are not, two.
>
> 7
>
> And in their posture is express'd
> Friendship's exalted interest:

Each follows where the other Leanes,
And what each does, the other meanes.

8

And as when one foot does stand fast,
And t'other circles seeks to cast,
The steddy part does regulate
And make the wanderer's motion streight:

9

So friends are onely Two in this,
T'reclaime each other when they misse:
For whose're will grossely fall,
Can never be a friend at all. (21–36)

Everything is wrong with these lines, starting with their insistence not on Philipsian union but Donnean relationship—"They are, and yet they are not, two"; "friends are onely two"—and ending with their performance not of Philips's specular discourse but of Donne's conceited poetics: "The compasses.../ Express...Love"; "friends, like them"; "in their posture is express'd"; "as one foot.../ And t'other.../ So friends."

What is most striking about these lines, however, is how comprehensively they dismantle Philips's specular poetics. Where "To my dearest Antenor" enacts its own innocent secrecy, for example, the stated goal of "Friendship in Emblem, or the Seal" is to emblematize, to make friendship visible, public, understandable. In this context, the title's "Seale" suggests not a mirror, barring access, but rather a coat of arms whose meaning is obvious enough to reduce language to barest sign:

There needs no motto to the Seale,
But that we may the Mine reveale
To the dull ey, it was thought fit
That *friendship* onely should be writ. (57–60; emphasis mine)

Where "To my dearest Antenor" only intimates the nature of "possest...desire," similarly "Friendship in Emblem" blazons intimacy, rendering it disconcertingly graphic. Hearts described as "panting centinell[s]" (7) "flame" in rather different ways than

Philips's reference to "Moses bush" suggests, as does her description of friends for whom "each part so well is knitt, / That their embraces ever fitt," and between whom "no Third can the place supply" (53–56). Philips is clearly aware of and increasingly anxious about her poem's textual and sexual explicitness,[31] which may be why she struggles with her conceit as long as she does, and why she finally shifts from idealizing description to autocratic prescription in order to end it:

> As these [compasses] are found out in design
> To rule and measure every line;
> So friendship governs actions best,
> Prescribing Law to all the rest. (41–44)

It would be hard to imagine a stanza further in spirit from the authorial free agency manifest in Philips's poems to Antenor, or the affective liberty suggested by the easy coexistence of Philips's verses of marriage and of friendship.

It is by no means clear why "Friendship in Emblem" fails when "To my dearest Antenor" succeeds. But it is possible that the poem fails because its invocation of Donne's conceited poetics, an invocation designed to replace that poetics with specular discourse, gets overwhelmed by post-Donnean fears of discursive disunion. If so, we may be in a position to make general sense of Philips's Donnean poetry: Philips's sealed marriage poems free her from fears of disunion, but they also deny us insight into union and its specular discourse; poems like "Friendship in Emblem" reveal union to our "dull ey," but they thereby expose her to fears of disunion; the friendship poems that imagine a single, beloved, but nonspousal reader, and so assure an identity of ideal revelation and reception, serenely open union to our perception.

IV. *"I can no likeness find"*

When we pass through the looking glass of specular poetics that seals Philips's marriage poems from our view, we discover a discourse that is, given the gendering of both Renaissance and

Donnean rhetoric, peculiarly associated with the feminine, formal, embodied, and erotic. In several friendship poems, most notably "To My excellent Lucasia, on our friendship," Philips takes what Blank describes as the failed "homopoetics" of Donne's love-poetry in general and his "Sapho to Philaenis" in particular and shows it to be brilliantly adequate to the "homoerotic" demands of Philipsian union. Blank's terms remind us that Philipsian union can be either marital or female: lesbian love is to Philips's specular poetics what marriage is to Donne's conceited writing—namely, the affective and social equivalent of a poetic discourse that tells us relatively little about that discourse's sexual content or its author's life.

In the pages that follow, I detail how Philips makes manifest the Sapphic nature of her specular poetry. I begin with "Friendship," a poem that abandons the conceited project of "Friendship in Emblem" and instead uses Donne's "Sapho to Philaenis" to point the way from comparativist to Sapphic discourse. But it is in "To My excellent Lucasia" that we see Philips developing Donne's hint into a fully developed poetics happily expressive of the female love that is the subject of her poem.

Like "To my dearest Antenor," "Friendship" begins by establishing the sealed nature of ideal union: "love" is a "noble flame" that is "abstracted" into friendship "when two soules are chang'd and mixed" into one (1–36). Unlike either "Antenor" or "Friendship in Emblem," however, "Friendship" ends neither by mystifying nor by exposing union. Rather, what begins as a poem of negative public definition ("Let the dull brutish world... know not") finally moves inward to union itself, and to the paradoxical project of expressing private union.

In a gesture that corrects "Friendship in Emblem" even as it returns "Friendship" to the solid ground of "To my dearest Antenor," Philips begins her final paean to union by claiming that friendship is like the undetectable and self-contained "fiery element" that produces "neither hurt, nor smoke, nor noise" and is "with its own heat and nourishment content, / ... Scorn[ing] the assistance of a forreign ayde" (43–46). She then runs through eight different similes, in search of a figure adequate to union:

Calme as a Virgin, and more inocent
Then sleeping Doves are, and as much content
As saints in visions; quiet as the night,
But cleare and open as the summers' light;
United more then spirits facultys,
Higher in thoughts then are the Eagle's eys;
Free as first agents. (49–55)

In the end, though, she abandons her quest as futile, confessing that friends are "kind, / As but themselves[;] I can no likeness find" (55–56).[32] Her parting admission is crucial: in describing herself as a writer at a loss for words, literally at the limits of discourse, she makes an oblique allusion to Donne's "Sapho to Philaenis," an allusion that quietly but powerfully informs her poem with female eroticism.

Briefly described, Donne's (currently lionized) "Sapho" begins with a meditation on the "fires" of poetry and desire (1–6). It then highlights the undetectability and self-sufficiency of female love:

But of our dallyance no more signes there are,
    Then *fishes* leave in streames, or *Birds* in aire.
And betweene us all sweetnesse may be had;
    All, all that *Nature* yields, or *Art* can adde. (41–44)

It rejects in list form the descriptive possibilities of simile:

Thou are not soft, and cleare, and strait, and faire,
As *Down*, as *Stars*, *Cedars*, and *Lillies* are,
But thy right hand, and cheek, and eye, only
Are like thy other hand, and cheek, and eye. (21–24)

Finally, the poem brings its insistence on self-likeness to bear on its passionate plea for homoerotic union:

My two lips, eyes, thighs, differ from thy two,
But so, as thine from one another doe;
And, oh, no more; the likenesse being such,
Why should they not alike in all parts touch? (45–48)

Sappho's plea is, of course, the one aspect of Donne's elegy not textually present in Philips's verse: this discrepancy lets Philips bring

Donne's generally erotic and specifically homoerotic burden into her poem; it also lets her do so without having to speak that burden. Indeed, the fact that his homoerotic meaning surfaces at the (final) moment when traditional poetic language fails her—"I can no likeness find"—suggests that the particular "likeness" she has in mind (of female-female union) is literally unspeakable, without verbal "likeness" or equivalency.

In this context, the fact that Philips's "silent" poem of female union has a kind of holographic existence, shimmering as it does between her and Donne's verses within the gesture of allusion, is significant. First—and in ways that recall Philips's poems of marital union—she uses her actual, written poem both to occlude and reveal her more elusive lyric of female homoeroticism. Also, by invoking a poem whose explicit concern is lesbian "likeness," she homoerotically charges not only the verbal parallels or "likenesses" between the two poems, but the very notion of allusion itself—a charge she reinforces when she makes her invocation as (un)detectable as the passion Donne describes between Sappho and Philaenis. As ever, Philips's ultimate interest in "Friendship" is less in the lesbian content of Donne's "Sapho" than in the poem as a discursive model for a Sapphic (in the particular sense of female and libidinal) poetics expressive of (homoerotic) union. It is to this poetics that we now turn.

The critical commentary on "Sapho" that predated Blank's essay on Donne proves to be an oddly useful source of information about the potential structure and function of seventeenth century Sapphic poetics. For to the extent that Philips succeeded in developing the specular discourse (homopoetics) expressive of union (homoerotics) that Blank argued always eluded Donne, his discredited critics anticipate her actual achievement.

Like Blank, James Holstun argues that lesbian love and especially language necessarily fail, though unlike her he believes that Donne's goal in "Sapho" is to dramatize this failure.[33] "Sappho begins with a stock Petrarchan rejection of stock Petrarchan similes," he notes: "But she does not move beyond them to a positive description of Philaenis through some rejuvenated language.

Instead, she attempts to generate a selfcontained signifying system that rejects analogies to anything outside itself. . . . But when all distance disappears between signifier and signified . . . she melts back into a prelinguistic immediacy: without difference, no signification."[34] If Holstun alerts us to critical skepticism about the signifying potential of a nonmetaphorical and self-referential Sapphic poetics, William West's outline of how lesbian discourse functions within the gendered context of Renaissance rhetoric provides us with valuable tools for perceiving and appreciating Philips's Sapphic achievement.[35]

While agreeing that Donne's Sappho rejects analogy, simile, and metaphor—indeed, the entire "comparative rhetoric" of Petrarchan poetics—West rebuts Holstun's argument about the insignificance of her lesbian rhetoric: "what leaves no sign is not necessarily unimportant." More importantly, West grounds his recuperative argument in Renaissance rhetorical theory.[36] Like Ben Jonson, he claims, Donne accepted the Aristotelian split between ideal speech as both metaphorical (with its deep meaning lying beneath its surface construction) and masculine, and failed speech as both afigural (without metaphoric depth and so consisting only of its own verbal surface or body) and feminine. Unlike Jonson, however, West argues, Donne explored the possibility that afigural, superficial, feminine language might be positively expressive: "Language that by its stillness reveals the absence of an interior Jonson characterizes as feminine, and devalorizes. [Donne's] Sappho embraces it."[37]

West's understanding of the rhetorical traditions underlying Donne's poem and his confidence in the poem as successful Sapphic utterance enable him to perceive and value key aspects of Sapphic speech—aspects that Holstun disregards or dismisses and that Blank denies Donne was able to achieve. For example, by arguing that Sappho eschews a poetics based on masculine meaning in favor of one founded on feminine form (as Renaissance rhetoric would have imagined the extremes of gendered discourse to present themselves), West anticipates the essentially erotic nature of Sapphic utterance: "Because [in Donne's poem] a woman's speech is not the male metaphoric speech of interiority and depth, a glass *can* render her likeness exactly as well as her speech—because her speech, as Sappho shows, is non-metaphorical; it lies on the surface and is in fact... *literally* her body." By granting significance to the poem's refusal to signify (or render meaning to the reader), West also appreciates its achievement of a non-Petrarchan exclusivity and privacy: "Sappho's poem to Philaenis does not allow the reader to come between the lover and the beloved.... She does not attempt to make Philaenis present for us through metaphor or any similar means, but her continual use of adjectives that express relation and have a referential force ('thy,' 'my,' 'thy other') implies a presence to Sappho of Philaenis on another stage, even if that presence is never realized for the reader." Finally, West argues that Sapphic speech is contained but not canceled by Donne's ultimately masculinist—in other words, figurative and Petrarchan—language. Sappho is for Donne a "metaphor for the lack of metaphor," he asserts, a sign for a discourse that signifies without the use of signs: "Having read the poem once as a dismissal of Sappho's voice as narcissistic and as inferior because incapable of producing signs—as 'insignificant,'... we can read it again to see the compensations and refigurings through which it establishes a space for an alien, non-metaphorical language within the larger, culturally validated, masculine discourse of metaphor." Donne's elegy consists of two mutually incompatible poems that occur "*simultaneously*... and in the same space," West notes, and the female poem "that to one reading would seem either misguided or utopian—'noplace'—... would have its own reality alongside and within [the poem's] male language."[38]

I have lingered over West's reading of Donne's "Sapho" because what he describes as lesbian discourse pertains so directly to both Philips's specular poems of marital union and her Sapphic poems of female union. Because he does not presume Donne's hostility to the signifying potential of a rigorously feminine and therefore erotic discourse and instead believes that Donne succeeded in developing a Sapphic poetics, West makes it easy to imagine that Philips might have regarded his "Sapho" as an inviting rhetorical resource. My own claim, however, is that while Donne aimed for but never achieved the rhetorical ideal that West ascribes to "Sapho," Philips developed just this kind of Sapphic discourse in her own poems. "Friendship," for example, adheres to the same poetical principles—a passionate, afigural, and female lyric hovering elusively within an apparently incompatible comparativist text—that West argues are at work in "Sapho."

In identifying and recovering Donne's lesbian speaker, however, Philips transforms her far beyond West's imaginings. For in the transition from Donne's to Philips's poems, Sappho evolves from a failed if fascinating conceit, Donne's ingenious poetical object, to the eponymous progenitor of a coherently Sapphic discourse—a uniquely female and libidinal rhetoric available for a variety of expressive purposes. The radical potential of this transformation is realized in the final Philips poem I consider, "To My excellent Lucasia, on our friendship," which might be described as a kind of uncloseted version of "Friendship." Or, rather, the poem speaks as if there were no world but the closet, which is, in this context, everywhere. In addition, "Lucasia" invokes Donne to do what his "Sapho" (and her "To my dearest Antenor") did not—namely, openly celebrate its status as a homoerotic and discursively Sapphic text.

At first glance, the most striking feature of "To My excellent Lucasia" is its easy embrace of a generalized Donnean amorousness. The poem's very form is rendered passionate by being modeled (in meter, stanzaic pattern, and rhyme) on Donne's "Song: Sweetest love":

> I did not live untill this time
>   Crown'd my felicity,
> When I could say without a crime,
>   I am not Thine, but Thee. (1–4)

The effect of the echo here is emotionally precise: like "To my dearest Antenor," the poem recovers the lyric sweetness of Donne's song even as it releases, as unnecessary to Philips's celebration of achieved and present union, the earlier poem's poignancy. Her recall of the compass image from "Valediction" is similarly exact.

Freed from the anxiety that in "Friendship in Emblem" compels her to struggle with Donne's conceit, in "Lucasia," Philips incorporates the conceit as only one of many such invocations, and, as in "To my dearest Antenor," she does so briefly and without anti-erotic explanation:

> For as a watch by art is wound
> To motion, such was mine:
> But never had Orinda found
> A Soule till she found thine. (9–12)

Quite unlike her modest marriage poems, however, "To My excellent Lucasia" is frankly physical. Lucasia's "Soule" actually redeems Orinda's body, enlivening her "Carkasse" (5) and "inspir[ing]" her "darken'd brest" (13–14). The speaker's quiet confidence in the interassured connections binding body and soul, moreover, frees her to parallel the shift in "Valediction" from spiritual to embodied love. Where Donne distinguishes between the dull "world" and the lovers' transcendent sphere but returns the amorous pair to their bodies in his final stanzas, Philips opposes an ignorant "world" to herself and Lucasia (6), invests that world with the erotic and public "mirth" of "Bridegroomes" and "crown'd conqu'rour's" (17), and then embraces it in its entirety: "I've all the world in thee" (20).

If Philips uses Donne's "Song" and "Valediction" to amplify her poem's erotic possibilities, however, she relies on his "Sapho" and "Elegie to the Lady Bedford" (on the death of the countess's female friend) to bring its homoerotic burden into clarifying focus. In so doing, she also effectively rejects the comparativist implications of her own allusions to the "Valediction," replacing them with more Sapphic formulations of ideal union. When she tells Lucasia, "I've all the world in thee," for example, she implicitly repudiates the conceit put forward in "Valediction" of the lovers' experiential sphere as a realm set against the "dull world."

Instead, she opts for the representation in "Sapho" of the amorous bond as a universally inclusive one, literally "all the world": "betweene us all sweetnesse may be had," Sappho insists, "All, all that *Nature* yields, or *Art* can adde" (43–44). Philips, in fact, opens her poem with a dramatic turn away from "Valediction" and toward "Sapho," countering the two-in-one implications of Donne's compass image with a Sapphic insistence on (female) union. "I am not Thine, but Thee" (4), she tells Lucasia, adding, "thou art all that I can prize, / My Joy, my Life, my rest" (15–16). "Restore / Me to mee," Sappho begs Philaenis in parallel fashion, "thee, my *halfe,* my *all,* my *more*" (57–58). And, similarly: "You that are she and you, that's double shee" (1), Donne addresses the countess in his "Elegie to the Lady Bedford." The overlap among the three poems here is significantly exact: given the slippage between poetics and erotics in a poem that uses allusion (i.e., verbal likeness or near-identity) to express homoerotic passion (i.e., passion based not on sexual difference but sexual likeness or near-identity), the point at which the poems intersect in Philips's verse—"I am . . . Thee," "mee; thee," "double shee"—is rendered intensely homoerotic.

Crucially, however, the ways in which Philips's and Donne's poems diverge are also charged with homoerotic meaning, signaling as they do Philips's independent departures from the model of lesbian erotics that Donne provides in "Sapho." As she did in her reworking of the "Song," for example, Philips recovers from "Sapho" and the "Elegie" Donne's homoerotic meaning even as she dismisses as irrelevant his elegiac mode. "Lucasia" neither begs (like "Sapho") nor mourns (like the countess in the "Elegie"), but simply states: "I am . . . Thee." The achievement this simplicity of statement represents is considerable, as comparison with the "Elegie" makes luminously clear. Donne suggests that Bedford experiences her friend's death as self-loss, a devastating decline from joint identity, "she and you," to a mere "Carkasse" whose "Soule is gone" (11–13). Philips reverses this tragic narrative by describing her progression from a state of animated mortality before Lucasia ("This Carkasse breath'd, and walk'd, and slept" [5]) to present union ("I am . . . Thee") and life (Lucasia's "Soule . . . inspires . . . my darken'd brest" [12–14]).

The most significant instance of the poem's simultaneous indebtedness to and independence from "Sapho," however, is at the level of discourse. The poetics implied by "Lucasia" derives from the afigural, female, erotic poetics that Donne develops in "Sapho," but this Sapphic poetics dominates in her poem in ways it does not in his. Simply put, everything in "Lucasia" conspires against metaphor, despite first appearances to the contrary. For example, though two metaphors and a simile appear in the first 12 lines, Philips consigns these (Donnean) figures to her past: "This Carkasse *breath'd,* and *walk'd,* and *slept*" (5); "For as a watch by art is wound / To motion such *was* mine" (9–10; emphases added). Even more forcefully, in lines that initially appear to deploy a Petrarchan incomparability topos, Philips rejects figuration altogether:

> Nor Bridegroomes nor crown'd conqu'rour's mirth
> To mine compar'd can be:
> They have but pieces of this Earth,
> I've all the world in thee. (17–20)

Tempting as it may be to read these lines as assertions of the priority of female friendship over marriage and politics, it is truer to Philips's poem to recognize them as articulations of Sapphic discursive principles. Analogy works when "pieces of this Earth" are compared one to another, but in the erotic/poetic world of Philips's lyric, where Orinda and Lucasia are self-identical ("I am... Thee") and all-inclusive ("I've all the world in thee"), the possibility for analogy does not exist: nothing "can" be compared to their love because, in a truer way than we ever see in Donne, nothing else is.

In this context, the poem's final sequence—"As innocent as our design, / Immortal as our Soule" (23–24)—represents not so much ambiguous comparison as open-ended apposition that points to the final inadequacy of comparative aesthetics. If we recall that "Friendship" ended by abandoning the comparative quest ("I can no likeness find") and that it was this very abandonment that brought "Sapho," with its parallel rejection of analogy, into Philips's poem, we can discern the rhetorically radical implications of the last lines of "Lucasia." Extrapolating from the lyric to an eroticized poetics based on identity and apposition (versus difference and comparison), we might read these lines back into the poem as a whole to arrive at this approximate translation: "I am / as Thee am / as our brest am / as innocent am / as our design am / as immortal am / as our Soule."

Philips's "Lucasia," then, radically rewrites Donne's "Sapho." Insofar as it contains its own (Donnean) figures and metaphorical poetics, setting them within an afigural and female discourse, it inverts the rhetorical model (of a lesbian lyric enabled and controlled by a Petrarchan text) provided by West's Donne. What makes this innovation so dramatic, however, and so different from "To my dearest Antenor," is the poet's remarkable openness about her discursive project. For "Lucasia" is, above all, a poem about speaking (female) union freely: she begins by observing that "this" is a "time" when she can finally "say without a crime" (1–3); and she ends by insisting that "no bold feare" will keep her from letting the "flame" of their love "light and shine" for all to see (21–22).

The effect of this framing frankness about the poem's rhetorical project is profound. First, it points to Philips's awareness of the enabling opportunity that Sapphic discourse represents for her. She knows she can speak Sapphically in "Lucasia" because the poetic world in which she locates herself is a thoroughly homoerotic one: in her poem's discursive universe, where "I" is "Thee" and "I-Thee" constitute "all the world," she has absolute expressive freedom because she has absolute receptive privacy. In poems like "Friendship's Mystery" and "A Retir'd Friendship," Philips represents friendship as a spatial and temporal retreat from a hostile world. In so doing, she at best contains Sapphic eroticism and rhetoric within the larger universe of comparative poetics (as Donne does in "Sapho" and as she may do in "Friendship"); at worst, she colludes with comparativist poetics in ways that distort and destroy the nature of ideal union and specular discourse, as she does in "Friendship in Emblem." In "Lucasia," however, where there is no one and no world but "Thee," she can literally "say without a crime."

In addition, her representation of "Lucasia" as a poem about Sapphic "say[ing]" reflects back upon Philips in suggestive ways, begging the unanswerable question of just how much the poet (who never mentions Sappho herself) might have thought of her true forebear not as Donne, but as Sappho herself—woman, lover, lesbian, and originary Sapphic speaker.[39]

V. *"The English Sappho"*

"She has call'd herself ORINDA, a name that deserves to be added to the number of the muses," Philips's editor observes in his preface to the 1667 posthumous edition of her *Poems,* but

> we might well have call'd her the English Sappho, she of all the female poets of former Ages, being for her verses and her virtues both, the most highly to be valued.... Were our language as generally known to the world as the Greek and Latin were anciently, or as the French is now, her verses could not be confin'd within the narrow limits of our islands.... And for her virtues, they as much surpass'd those of Sappho as the Theological do the Moral, (wherein yet Orinda was not her inferior) or as the fading immortality of an earthly laurel, which the justice of men cannot deny to her excellent poetry, is transcended by that incorruptible and eternal Crown of Glory.[40]

Philips's critics tend to paraphrase this passage roughly as follows: "we might call her the English Sappho for her verses, but then we would have to insist on her unique sexual virtues." This reading requires some syntactical gymnastics, however, since it involves taking the term "but" from the actual phrase, "but she has call'd herself ORINDA," and inserting it between "verses" and "virtues," as the 1667 editor does not, in order to separate the Sappho famous as poet and lover/lesbian from the Orinda celebrated for her poetry and sexual purity. Thus, for example, Lydia Hamessley argues that "while Philips is meant to gain by comparison to the ancient Sappho (equal in skill, superior in virtue), the lesbian character of her poetry is virtually erased."[41] And Harriette Andreadis suggests that "writers of contemporary encomia to Orinda understood the nature of the allusions to Sappho but were eager to dispel any suggestions of unnatural sexuality. They wished to pay her the high compliment of comparing her to the great classical lyricist not only for her poetical voice, but also for the uniqueness of her subject matter, at the same time that they wished to reconfirm her platonic purity. The encomium was appropriate and perhaps inevitable, if somewhat uncomfortable."[42]

Contrary to such readings, I would suggest that it is possible to read the epithet "the English Sappho" as a fairly narrow assertion of Philips's status as a major English poet. In a passage that bows to Philips's own self-designation, identifies her as the tenth muse, and imagines for her the same classical status that Walton does for Donne,[43] the editor describes her as a poetic and specifically moral Sappho—"Orinda was not her inferior" in "Moral... virtues"—whose principal distinction was her Christian (versus pagan) status.[44]

In positing the relative purity of the editor's motives, I do not mean to ignore contemporary sources that certainly did identify Sappho as a wanton from whom Philips needed distinguishing. "They talk of Sappho, but, alas the shame! / Ill manners soil the lustre of her fame," Abraham Cowley writes in his 1664 "Upon Mrs. Philips her Poems": "Orinda's inward virtue is so bright... / It through the paper shines where she doth write."[45] But Cowley's double vision of Sappho, like the editor's single one, is conventional and tells us little or nothing about Philips, her poetry's content, her poetics, or her contemporaries' perceptions of these issues. As scholars have noted, several "Sapphos," springing from multiple sources, circulated in Renaissance culture, the most common being Sappho as poet, wanton, lesbian, and Amazon, and it being just as likely before 1650 for the term to be applied to a woman writer or leader, by others or herself, in positive as well as negative ways.[46]

Things started to change in the 1650s, moreover, vexing any assessment of Philips's status as "the English Sappho." A major transition in cultural perceptions of Sappho and lesbianism seems to have occurred sometime between Madeleine de Scudery's 1649–53 *Artemene,* in which Scudery identified herself as a pure Sappho, and the 1660s–1680s, when "lesbianism as we know it, with Sappho as its chief exemplar,...entered vernacular discourse in England,"[47] and when an "influx of French pornographic materials...entered English bookstalls" along with an emergent "medico-legal discourse for sexual relations between women."[48]

Andreadis's phrase "lesbianism as we know it" raises a final complication: Philips's commonwealth-era poetry, the Restoration commendatory verses, and our own critical responses turn out to occupy different points within a single (if complex) cultural narrative of (early) modern lesbianism. Only as we become critically self-conscious about our place in that story can we resist its pressure to identify texts and sexuality in literal and reductive ways and begin to perceive Philips's actual achievement. Our emerging perception is its own reward, however, for in recognizing her work we do her a justice that has not been easily possiblc to do since the publication of her (unauthorized) *Poems* in 1664 and (posthumous) *Poems* in 1667. We may never know how to read the panegyrics that appear in these two volumes: we have little sense of which traditions her admirers were touching upon when they responded to her poetry, and even less of whether or not those responses reflect genuine awareness of her innovative achievement of a Sapphic poetry expressive of both marital and female union. The extraordinary nature of her contemporary reputation suggests a knowing appreciation of her artistic accomplishment; the self-occluding structure of a Sapphic poetics, itself likely obscured by a Waltonian shutdown of Donne's poetry, leaves open the possibility of perfect ignorance of her achievement. Mercifully, that achievement remains, however, and we may now be in a position to recognize it. "I did not live untill this time," we remember Philips writing, "Crown'd my felicity."

6 ❖ Katherine Philips at the Wedding

Elizabeth Hodgson

Katherine Philips's wedding poems form an oddly stylized but recursive theme in her collected verse. Given the preference in recent criticism for viewing Philips as a gynocentric or queer author,[1] this interest in heterosexual matchmaking might seem somewhat unexpected, especially if such celebrations of marriage are seen as more than a sublimated comment on her real feelings for women. In fact, the poems offered as gifts in honor of marriages—her epithalamia—are particularly key sites for discovering how Philips imagines the roles and meanings of wives in her social networks; they stand awkwardly but informatively beside her friendship poems to complicate our readings of her sexual politics. Far more significant, however, are the ways in which Philips's epithalamia demonstrate how opaque and variable are her social and literary manipulations of the poetic marriage scene. When Philips shows up at a wedding, she becomes a very complicated poet indeed.

Philips's poetic comments on marriage have sometimes been read by critics interested in her friendship practices (erotic or otherwise) as forms of complex displacement. If she writes of marriage at all, in this view, she is sublimating her erotic same-sex interests or her desire for female friendship through a more conventionally acceptable heteronormative discourse. Arlene Stiebel argues that Philips masks the homoerotic energy of her poems precisely through that disingenuous air of placid respectability that would seem to suggest a highly conventional sexuality.[2] Harriette Andreadis argues that in the pro-marriage letters, Philips "displaces and reroutes through Sir Charles her own longings for proximity to female friends and patrons" and "her ambivalent relation to her own conflicted feelings of duty toward her husband."[3] Certainly the female addressees of many of Philips's epithalamia, their gestures of feminine solidarity, their rejection of masculinist conventions, seem to suggest that a certain gynocentric or potentially homoerotic mode colors these heterodox (in every sense) poems. What is difficult to prove, though, is that any or all of Philips's marriage poems are doing this same psychic work, especially given how responsive they are to the conventions of epithalamic verse and how much they vary in tone, argument, and mode. It seems more defensible to conclude that Philips's marriage poems mirror her friendship poems in their profound ambivalence and their complex intertwining of literary contextualization and apparent topicality. As Andrew Shifflett notes in a discussion of Philips's friendship poems, her marriage poems move "through several moods or phases" in which though they imitate "a higher nature," "competitive and even coercive" perspectives coexist. According to Andrea Brady, the assertion that "Orinda desires to define her friendships in exclusively female terms obscures Philips's adoption of concepts and diction associated with a masculine intellectual tradition." Elaine Hobby argues that the letters are likewise complex performances responding to "specific conventions" of literary culture. Susannah Mintz and Paula Loscocco both show how Philips invokes and then very specifically reinvents the topoi in Donne's "Songs and Sonnets."[4] These critics are all suggesting two things: that the patterns in Philips's lyrics are far less unified, psychologically or ideologically, than arguments about her true preferences sometimes imply, and secondly, that Philips is overtly artful in her uses of forms and genres, just as likely to respond to a literary line as to an emotional history. As Elizabeth Scott-Baumann argues, "in order to understand women's place in literary history, we need to excavate and analyse their dialogue with existing traditions."[5] Engaging in this process reveals clearly how the voice of Philips at a wedding is full of just such poetic engagement and literary artifice.

If Philips's epithalamia are doing the cultural work of genre, they are less antagonistic to the friendship poems than their differing erotic topoi might imply. In fact, the most sophisticated readings of friendship in Philips's work recognize that marriage and friendship poems are closely connected in terms of the kinds of cultural work they do and the kinds of artifice they employ. Harriette Andreadis juxtaposes Philips's friendship letters to Charles Cotterell with her poems to female friends, noting the ease with which Philips shifts registers in her affective relationships. James Loxley reads the eroticism of Philips's friendship poems against the polemics of sexual potency of the royalist writers with whom she was associated. Valerie Traub reads Philips's "production of a compelling homoerotic subjectivity" not as "'self-expression'... but rather as a 'subjectivity effect,'"[6] a mask like the other literary personas she adopts in her coterie alliances. Hutson points to Alan Bray's argument about the history of shared work between friendship and marriage (kinship, patronage, loyalty, discursive communities); Bray argues that marriage was increasingly appropriating friendship's force, which is certainly clear in Milton's divorce tracts and Jeremy Taylor's discourses on wives as friends.[7] According to these various analyses, reading the friendship and marriage poems as positive and negative versions of Philips's own erotic desires explains very little about Philips's actual poetic objects or their explicitly social and literary contexts. Considering how and why Philips writes her marriage poems the way she does, understanding the rich local literary contexts for her verses on marriage, and uncovering the atypical, asymmetrical, contradictory tactics of these poems, allow Philips's marriage poems to do more than warm a lonely bed.

Philips's *oeuvre* is certainly far from silent on the subject of marriage more broadly. She does indeed write several poems satirizing (male and female) interest in marriage. She also, however, writes several poems addressed to or referencing her own husband in positive terms; likewise, in her many elegies for men and women, she cites approvingly their marital affections and roles. In those posthumously published letters to Charles Cotterell, Philips functions as an enthusiastic and cunning (though ultimately unsuccessful) matchmaker in order to participate in a social exchange of favors and favorites with a man to whom she and especially her husband are politically indebted. In her poetic works, this focus on a similar ceremonial gift exchange appears to be in play in Philips's epithalamia or marriage poems, which are presented as gifts to her friends and relations, some more enthusiastically than others. Reading these gestures in all of their complexity is the art of wedding Philips to her poetic and social milieux, understanding more particularly how and why Philips puts in a poetic appearance at weddings.

Looking at the epithalamia with an eye to discovering Philips's views on gender in particular, sexually or otherwise, rapidly becomes itself a highly problematic enterprise, and this is, in fact, the virtue of such a project. For the problems raised by a search for "Philips on marriage and women" are, in fact, fundamental to the epithalamic form and to the writer herself. Philips's epithalamic poems respond in many different ways to the forms of marriage verse common to her male predecessors, and they each respond differently to the questions of the power of women in marriage. This variety of voices, strategies, and arguments is a significant factor in Philips's verse, and her personas and their stereotypes cannot be (should not be) easily assimilated to each other.

Philips's marriage poems in particular contain a far more opaque discourse on brides and marriage than they seem at first to possess. They are, in the first instance, not as immediately biographical as has been assumed sometimes; her epithalamia are, of course, occasional poems, but Philips's subject position, voice, and intertextual dialogues with other epithalamic texts also make these poems less localizable than their triangulation in biographical space and time might suggest. Philips's epithalamic poems are also particularly labile, containing a persistent negotiation with the very idea of a narrator or poetic speaker, an insistence on certain kinds of disguise and ambiguity, and varying degrees of resistance to masculine generic traditions. The prophetic female voice for which Philips is famous is, in the epithalamia, strikingly visible and invisible at the same time. Philips is using this very literary and formally social medium of exchange, of kinship and patronage, and engaging specifically with the questions of agency, the conventions of interdependence and domination raised by the genre, some of which have to do with her real or performative gender roles. Her poems on marriage illustrate in new ways the difficult relationship to authority and identity that is endemic in the epithalamic texts of this period.

I. *Epithalamia*

When Philips writes her epithalamia, she is speaking into an ancient but flexible tradition. Poems celebrating marriage as a source of fertility, political union, social order, and sexual pleasures have a history dating back to Sappho, Aristophanes, Theocritus, and Catullus.[8] The lyric epithalamium has an extensive history of subversion, ambiguity, tension, and conflict, however, even though (or perhaps it would be more accurate to say because) it is so often used to support hegemonic oligarchies, hierarchies of class and gender, and patronage systems. Such conflicting narratives include bawdy "fescennine" verses that remember the epithalamium's origins in wedding charivari ("epithalamium" is literally a song sung "on the threshold" of the bedroom). These ribald bacchanalia coexist with and within more socially and sexually decorous marriage poems. The "chiasmus of epithalamium and elegy" in pastoral texts as early as Bion's "Lament for Adonis" creates another central dynamic of the epithalamic genre,[9] as pastoral loss and pastoral fantasy infuse each other. The antisexual mysticism of the late medieval period spawned an extensive tradition of marriage poems that either celebrate human marriages as analogies to the divine (Song of Songs) or denigrate fleshly unions in comparison with mystical marriages of the soul with Christ.[10] Secular satires of marriage's financial machinery, its hypocrisies and artifices, likewise appear within the epithalamic form, from Catullus's earliest poems forward.[11]

This is clearly true of the epithalamia of seventeenth century England. Flourishing as lyric poems in honor of court marriages like the Somerset wedding of 1613 or as part of wedding masques, the marriage poems of this period come from the pens of most major authors (Spenser, Chapman, Donne, Jonson, Herrick) and range wildly in style, tone, and methodology. As Dubrow argues in *A Happier Eden,* the Stuart epithalamia in their early celebratory mode not only pick up on the new Stuart emphasis on marriage (a married king with marriageable sons and daughters) but also nostalgically (if diversely) "emphasiz[e] or reinterpret" Edmund Spenser's famous sixteenth century epithalamium, the benchmark of the form for English poets.[12]

As varied as seventeenth century English epithalamia are, they are variations on a set of well-known themes. For the most part, until Philips, as Dubrow and others note, this genre appears to have been exclusive to male poets.[13] It seems evident that the "men who wrote these poems, like those who composed the conduct books on marriage, are concerned at once to celebrate and to circumscribe the power of the women they evoke."[14] The limited agency of the bride and the dependent position of the patronage-seeking speaker suggest an alliance that the epithalamic form in its English versions both resists and acknowledges.[15] This often manifests itself in a self-consciously poetic convention that develops "an anti-bridal cast in which a relation of dependency brings death—to the virgin, to the creative imagination, to the 'expectation vayne' of both."[16] The limited power of the Stuart poet and the gendered function of the bride, according to many of the scholars of the form, are often then connected and articulated in complex ways through self-authorizing and antagonistic moments of satire and elegy within the epithalamic form.

II. *Stuart Epithalamia: John Donne and Robert Herrick*

This schema does in part help to define examples of the male-authored epithalamic poems to which Philips's poems respond. Two particularly striking examples, to which Philips's poems are almost direct replies, are John Donne's "Epithalamion made at Lincolnes Inne," and Robert Herrick's "Nuptiall Song." These two marriage poems contain different balances of celebration, satirical critique, and "anti-bridal... death[s],"[17] but in each the negotiations between the nuptial couple and the authority of the speaker as host, pander, critic, and priest are emphatically central. Philips clearly "explores the cultural coding of the forms she uses,"[18] here very specifically in the precursors by both Donne and Herrick.

John Donne's "Epithalamion made at Lincolnes Inne" develops the same arguments as his later epithalamia in demonstrating the annihilation of the bride so apparently necessary to the masculinist project of marital consummation. Donne's poem is, however, not primarily designed to win a patron, and so in some ways (though not for gender) it declines to articulate the often conservative ambitions or ideologies that scholars of the form so often find within this genre. The poem has therefore a powerful satirical edge while it is still entangled in the artificial destruction of the bride so common to the genre. Donne is extremely explicit here in his critiques of the economics of the marriage market; his graphic display of the sexual aggression underlying the sweet romance of Spenser's famous wedding poem is, however, more problematic. His epithalamium's confusion of ecclesiastical, monetary, and anatomical terms create the strange blend of feminized sacred profanity that Donne in other contexts attributes to the institution of marriage itself.[19]

Donne's careful use of the lyric epithalamium's classical and Spenserian conventions—a chronological narrative of the marriage day beginning with the rising of bride and groom and including descriptions of the bride's beauty, the floral procession, the feast, and the delays before the bedding of the bride—certainly reveals his debt to earlier poets, but the tone of the Lincoln's Inn epithalamium is alternately laudatory and mocking, which has fueled the critical debate over its circumstances. David Novarr argues that the work is early, written in the 1590s as a parody for a mock wedding staged by the students at the Inns at Court.[20] Wesley Milgate argues more forcefully for the literary occasion of the epithalamium: "the satirist in Donne... was especially stimulated by Spenser's poem; for Donne could not fail to note the discrepancy between the perfect paradigm of marriage and what weddings were really like in the City."[21] Heather Dubrow, conversely, argues that Donne is not satirizing Spenser but genuinely imitating him, writing an admittedly unsuccessful poem in his younger years for the wedding of a friend or colleague.[22]

More interesting than the situation of the poem or the intentions of its author, though, is the complex web of gendered eroticism and parody in the poem. The epithalamium is particularly and graphically concerned with sex: the speaker collaborates with the event enough to describe the bride's "warme balme-breathing thigh" that "must meet another, / Which never was, but must be, oft, more nigh" (7, 9–10); women are "golden mines" and the church doors are compared to the bride's "two-leav'd" labia.[23] Donne explains that "in their beds commenc'd / Are other labours, and more dainty feasts," where the bride is "best in nakednesse." The goddess of the feast is Flora, whose festival in Rome was, as Milgate remarks, "celebrated with much licentiousness."[24]

All of these sexual images are tightly connected, though, to the more object-oriented satires of wealth and class:

> Daughters of London, you which bee
> our Golden Mines, and furnish'd Treasurie,
> You which are Angels, yet still bring with you
> Thousands of Angels on your mariage daies.
>
> ....
>
> And you frolique Patricians,
> Sonnes of these Senators wealths deep oceans,
> Ye painted courtiers, barrels of others wits,
> Yee country men, who but your beasts love none. (13–16, 25–28)

The currency of sex and the economics of marriage merge in the erotic bodies of the "daughters of London," as the speaker develops his poetic voice by mocking this easy sale of bodies. His is the work of art in the age of mercantile reproduction.[25]

The poem's speaker moves closer to the groom and acquires his agency again at the end of the poem, however, as he insists, in even more grotesque and mocking imagery, on the correlation of the bridal bed with the death of the bride. Her body marks the bed as "like to a grave, the yielding downe doth dint" (5), and that same bed will "smother" her when she returns after the ceremony. The third stanza develops a more graphic and monstrous version of this:

> Thy two-leav'd gates, faire Temple, 'unfold,
> And these two in thy sacred bosome hold,
> Till, mystically joyn'd, but one they bee;
> Then may thy leane and hunger-starved wombe
> Long time expect their bodies and their tombe,
> Long after their owne parents fatten thee. (37–42)

The juxtaposition of the "hunger-starved wombe" of the church's crypt with the bride's genitalia is one of the more perverse metaphors in the Donnean canon. The most striking image of this imagery in the poem, though, comes in the final stanzas where the bride, a "pleasing sacrifice," "at the Bridegroomes wish'd approach doth lye, / Like an appointed lambe, when tenderly / The priest comes on his knees t'embowell her" (88–90).[26]

Such a juxtaposition of bridal sexuality with mockery, parody, and grotesque violence invites comparison with the fescennine epithalamic tradition in which lechery and licentiousness of all sorts are advocated by the narrator. But if "Lincolnes Inne" is a mock epithalamium, or a satire of Spenser's decorous harmonies, it also voices the same ideology as Donne's other more conventionally celebratory epithalamia, and the alliance of groom and speaker in figuring the sacrificial bride appears in many other epithalamia of the period.

Donne does suggest in the poem the generative possibilities available to the bridal victim as she accepts "perfection, and a womans name." He says that "this bed is onely to virginitie / A grave, but, to a better state, a cradle" (79–80), and he declares that "shee a mothers rich stile doth preferre" (87). "No more be said, I may bee, but, I am" (83) is his admonition to this new wife. The bride and groom empower one another when "mystically joyn'd, but one they bee" (39), banishing "all elder claimes, and all cold barrennesse" (43). This advice to the bride chooses to valorize and celebrate the bride's potential maternality, her "mothers rich stile." Such praise sits uneasily beside the broadly parodic lechery of the rest of the epithalamium. As Schenk claims for Spenser's "Prothalamion," "Lincolns Inne" is ambiguous in its views of the wife, her role in marriage, and indeed the functions of marriage itself. Donne's poem's inherent instability, then, lies in the speaker's shifting relationship to the event itself, sometimes resisting and sometimes claiming its power, especially as designated by the sexual and economic power of the groom over the bride.

Robert Herrick's "A Nuptiall Song, or Epithalamie, on Sir Clipseby Crew and His Lady" celebrates the marriage of Crew and Jane Pulteney in 1625.[27] Herrick's poem repeats the traditional Spenserian (Catullan) narrative structure for epithalamia, beginning with the procession of the bride and ending with her bedding. Herrick's "Nuptiall Song" is far less satirical than Donne's, as Herrick embraces the powerful agency of the narrator to create an alliance with the groom. Herrick takes on the persona of a lover, celebrating in dramatic and cathected fashion an extravagant series of intensely erotic and sensual images of desire:

> See where she comes; and smell how all the street
> Breathes Vine-yards and Pomgranats: O how sweet!
> As a fir'd Altar, is each stone,
> Perspiring pounded Cynamon.
> The Phenix nest,
> Built up of odours, burneth in her breast.
> Who therein wo'd not consume
> His soule to Ash-heaps in that rich perfume?
> Bestroaking Fate the while
> He burnes to Embers on the Pile. (21–30)

Herrick compels the lovers forward into the sexual act through this intense language of scent, flame, and texture, repeating the "nest" image in more urgent terms as the bridal bed becomes an enormous swan: "throw, throw / Your selves into the mighty overflow / Of that white Pride, and Drowne / The night, with you, in floods of Downe" (117–20). Though the language is often as strenuous as Donne's, then, its tendency is to construct intimacy with the culture of marriage and sex rather than distance from it.[28]

Herrick's poem also constructs its sense of agency through violence. The speaker emphasizes, celebrates, and imaginatively initiates the annihilating effects of sexual consummation. The groom "burnes to Embers" in the first passage above; the couple "drown...in floods of Downe," the groom suffers sexual tortures while waiting. "Frie / And consume, and grow again to die" (136–37) is the advice Herrick gives to them.[29]

In this violent universe, sexual domination, annihilating force, belongs in the end to the speaker-groom alliance. Sir Clipsby Crew is a "bold bolt of thunder" (148) who is "in his desires / More towring, more disparkling then thy fires" (35–36). The speaker proves himself an ally/proxy/pander as he commands the bridesmaids to "strip [the bride] of Spring-time" (91) so that the groom may "undo her" (100).[30] She may walk slowly to the wedding to increase the "price / Set on [herself] by being nice" (153–54), but the speaker reiterates the command she operates under: "On, then, and though you slow- / ly go, yet, howsoever, go" (59–60). As Marjorie Swann argues, "women in Herrick's poetry display great reluctance to marry: Herrick's virgins must be cajoled—or coerced—into fulfilling their social duty."[31]

The tension in Herrick's epithalamium, then, is slightly different from that in Donne's. "Lincolnes Inne" sits ambiguously between social satire, the separateness of the speaker from the event, and a kind of antagonistic celebration of the bride's loss of power. In "A Nuptiall Song" the speaker adopts the sexually aggressive mode of the groom to compel the bride into compliance with social necessity in an enactment of the gendered dependence within the cultural event. Both poems do illustrate the powerful dynamics of the narrative epithalamium in its conventional forms, especially the literarily functional teleology of the bride's loss of agency. Philips negotiates with this particular energy in her own marriage poems.

III. *Philips's Epithalamia*

Philips's marriage poems as a group (there are five of them) do use some of the conventional tropes of the epithalamic form, especially invocations of the muses (in "To the Lady Mary Butler," the muses are the bridesmaids), compliments on the family lineage of the couple, prayers for fertility, and the granting of cosmic powers to the marriage (in "To My Lord and Lady Dungannon" time and fate are subject to the couple). Philips's epithalamia are not noticeably provoked by patronage demands, though the issues of poetic voice and alliance are explicitly central in these poems. Philips also chooses for all of her epithalamia a far less narrative structure than the Spenserian model used by Herrick and Donne in the same period.[32] The particularly potent dynamic in Philips's epithalamia, though, is her simultaneous deconstruction and reconstruction of the teleological relationship between the bride and the speaker-observer. In unexpected and inconsistent ways, Philips's epithalamia reenact this central element of the epithalamic narrative speech-act, with all of its conventional subversions, while also resisting it. This particular expression of alliance, resistance, and elegy within the epithalamic form manifests itself particularly clearly, but very differently, in four of Philips's marriage poems: "To my dear Sister Mrs. C. P. on her nuptialls," "To my Lord and Lady Dungannon on their Marriage 11. May 1662," "To the Lady Mary Butler at her marriage with the Lord Cavendish, Octobr. 1662," and "To the Countess of Thanet, upon her Marriage." Though Philips uses the topoi of the epithalamium form sparingly (very few of her marriage poems provide a guide to the day itself), perhaps the longest of Philips's epithalamia is the one most consistent with the epithalamic tradition. "To the Countess of Thanet, upon her Marriage" compliments the bride and groom, imagines the community gathered around, and provides a series of wishes for the bride and groom that imagine the marriage's future happiness and fertility. The poem particularly adopts the "Lincolnes Inne" images of the bride as a sun, with its resplendent, overwhelming power; Philips's poem limits to some extent the obverse process by which the bride's light is overpowered by the groom's. Only partly so, however: Philips's compliments keep implying the same model of ownership that Donne's and Herrick's poems assume. In this poem, the groom's and the poet's power in naming and bestowing are, as in the epithalamic tradition writ large, quite closely aligned—despite Philips's ostensible focus on the countess herself.

The ironic central image of the poem is revealed early:

> [You] Whose matchless worth transmits such Splendid rayes
> As those that envy it are forc'd to prayse;
> Since you have found such an Illustrious Spheare,
> And are resolv'd to fix your Gloryes there;
> A Heart whose bravery to his Sex secures
> As much renown as you have done to yours;
> And whose perfections, in obtaining you,
> Are both discover'd and rewarded too. (7–14)

The bride is the addressee here, as she is in other epithalamia. She is portrayed as a celestial sun shedding "Splendid rayes" on the court and the world, also as she is in other epithalamia. In Philips's poem, however, she is a stationary object fixed in the "Illustrious Spheare" of the groom, set "in this bright Constellation" (31), gradually diminishing to a point of light in the night sky. She becomes a thing "obtained" by her husband, for which he becomes the new object of praise. He is "discover'd" to be "perfection" when he discovers her, in every sense. The public face of the bride, her renown, the public envy that attends her, she who brings "Credit to all wonders" (1), is gradually overshadowed by the groom himself.

The poem attempts to reconstruct the bride's splendid power through the obeisance both of the speaker herself, "whose ruder off'rings dare approach your Shrine" (23) and through Fortune and Virtue, who are both repeatedly portrayed as the bride's friends, those who owe her their "officious vowes" (20). The poem's final wishes, though, do not turn that abject worship into bridal authority:

> And may the happy Owner of your breast,
> Still find his Passion with his Joyes encreas'd;
> Whilst every Moment your Concern makes known,
> And gives him too, fresh reason for his own:
> And from their Parents may your Ofspring have
> All that is wise and lovely, soft and brave:
> Or if all wishes we in one would give,
> For him, and for the world, long may you live. (41–48)

The final blessings are all deflected from (or provided by) the bride to the groom, to their children, and to the broader "world." While the bride is hailed with the royal salutation ("long may you live"), her apparent function is to ensure that her children are beautiful, that her husband continues to desire her, and that he continues to be aware of her concern for him. Even her long life is not for her own sake but for the sake of others. The bride may be the primary recipient of the poem's "off'ring," but in many respects she herself is still, as in the Lincoln's Inn epithalamium, the last best offering of the wedding day.

Another epithalamium that echoes but reverses this epithalamic offering and its competitive, usurping rhetoric of praise is one of Philips's last, "To the Lady Mary Butler at her marriage with the Lord Cavendish, Octobr. 1662." Here, it is the groom who atrophies; he is replaced not by the bride but by the speaker's poetic powers, in a complex variant on the notion of marital supremacy.

In this poem, the bride is imagined as being attended by her bridesmaids and celebrated in a series of toasts to the couple. The path to the wedding (courtship, familial lineage) is charted as well, and the couple adorned with compliments in that narrative of praise that marks the epithalamic genre. This narrative frame does not really describe the wedding day, however, but is reinvented indirectly as the poem itself:

> The muses, Madam, will not be deny'd
> To be the bride maides where you are the bride.
>
> ....

> Admit them, beauteous Madam, then to be
> Attendants on this great solemnitie,
> And every muse will in a charming straine
> Your honour and their owne pretence maintaine. (3–4, 17–20)

Philips's poem speaks her praise by proxy, through the invented bridal entourage of the muses who take turns complimenting the bride's "Auncestors" and "fortune," (22, 25), her "mother's glories" (31), her "great lover" (37), and their mutual courtship. They conclude their catalogue of praise by declaring that the marital couple has proven "that love and fortune are no longer blind," granting them both the miraculous powers so often bestowed upon the bride.

Philips's speaker introduces the muses not as the bride's friends, however, but as her competitors:

> They know...
> What bright opposers they are like to find,
> Whose birth and beauty never will give way
> To such obscure competitours as they. (5–8)

The muses, like the sun in Donne's epithalamia, know that the bride surpasses their power. The poem, then, through its inventive avatars, claims the inadequacy trope as a sign of bridal power. She is the better maker; she is the ruler.

As a ruler the bride can be petitioned, though, whether by right or by humility, exercise of power or acknowledgment of loss:

> But yet, as injur'd princes still do strive
> To keep their title and their claime alive,
> So they affirme they do but aske their due,
> Having hereditary right in you. (9–12)

The parsing of power transfer from subject to object is complex in Philips's poem, as the muses must beg but also claim their "due" from the bride. They rule but do not rule; they have authority but cannot own it. The bride becomes the patron of her own poem, then, in Philips's extended play with these self-authorizing gestures of the complimenting poet. A competitive community of female speakers makes the wedding poem. While in Donne's and

Herrick's poems power ultimately returns to the groom, only temporarily visiting the bride with consumptive force, Philips makes the bride a conqueror not of the men in the poem but of the poetic impulse itself. This ambivalent alliance of bride with poem and poetic speaker with the defeated muses repeats the competitive violence of Donne's and Herrick's epithalamia, with a different destructive vector.

Philips's earliest epithalamium, "To my dear Sister Mrs. C. P. on her nuptialls," reads least like a classical epithalamium but is ironically the most literarily self-conscious of the lot. Here the speaker explicitly and with a flourish resists the conventions of the lyric epithalamia as Spenser, Donne, or Herrick use them, pointedly refusing to describe the bride's or the day's progress and concentrating instead on a mix of literary satire and blessing, which attempts to forge a speaker-bride alliance. Philips clearly strives in this poem to grant to herself, whom she specifically names as "Orinda," a new sacramental power over epithalamic language and the cultural act it represents. She does so using a deliberately plain and deceptively direct language, as if to suggest that the evocations of the poem come entirely from herself as prophetic narrator and bridal ally.

The poem follows Donne's Lincoln's Inn epithalamium in satirizing the Spenserian romantic mode, but despite Philips's clear imitation of Donne's poetic style in other works, in every other respect this poem is far more openly critical of her literary forebears than Donne is of his. "To my dear Sister Mrs. C. P." abandons virtually all of the elements of the epithalamic tradition: the poem has no mythical figures, no Christian imagery, no nature allegories, no elaborate compliments of families, no Catullan discussions of the value of marriage as an institution. The poem describes neither bride nor groom nor wedding day nor marriage itself. Her stripped-down version of the marriage poem may be partly a nod to the new codes for civil marriage,[33] but the poem more interestingly enacts as well a self-authorizing critique of masculinist epithalamia, a critique that also encodes a strong ambivalence about marriage and its effects on female autonomy. Philips's use of names and naming in the poem, and the ambiguous tensions between the poet-narrator and the figure of the groom, demonstrate resistance to the conventions of marriage in her culture, both literary and social, even as its celebration facilitates her voice.

The formal elements of the conventional epithalamium are precisely those that lend authoritative weight to the speaker: the dramatic address to the bride, elements of social satire, and a poet-speaker who acts as a kind of "master of ceremonies."[34] Philips's poem uses these conventions to distinguish her own voice from the male poets' voices of the epithalamic tradition:

> We will not like those men our offerings pay
> Who crown the cup, then think they crown the day.
> Wee'l make no garlands, nor an Altar build,
> Which help not Joy, but ostentation yield.
> Where mirth is justly grounded, these wild toys
> Do but disturb, and not adorn our Joys. (1–6)

Philips employs the epithalamium's generic tendency toward satire to construct her own agency. She positions herself in an alliance with the bride against "those men" who "think they crown the day" with either their festivities or their poetic praise of the same: "wee'l make no garlands, nor an Altar build" critiques both the bacchanalian elements of poems like Spenser's and the idolatrous sacrifices to and of women in epithalamic verse and marriage rites. She imagines, and then denies, Donne's sacrificial altars upon which the bridal bed is mapped.

Philips emphasizes a power struggle between male and female poets as well as grooms and brides: the men are full of "ostentation" and "wild toys," while the women ("wee") are concerned with more modest poetic and erotic pleasures. But her tone of self-deprecation is a strategy in her authorizing criticism of the masculine institutions of marriage poetry.

Philips also sees women-poets'/brides' agency existing in some clear tension with these institutions. She emphasizes competitive offerings, payment, crowning and yielding in the poem to articulate this tension. The poem's images likewise contrast height and depth: the male writers build up (as in Horace's "monumentum" and Herbert's "altar"), and the women are "grounded." The male poets seek crowns (as in Donne's "La Corona"), and the bride seeks "bands" like a swaddled infant. These ambiguous contrasts manifest themselves in her use of the traditional elm-and-ivy image of the classical epithalamium:[35] "May his and her pleasure and Love be so / Involv'd and growing, that we may not know / Who most affection or most peace engross'd" (15–17). Philips enjambs the first two lines to emphasize the entwining of the vine, while a faint sexual undertone ("pleasure...involv'd and growing," "affection...engross'd") heightens the echoes of epithalamia past. But these, she argues, are "my great solemnitys," an assertion of ownership of and independence from the triumphalist "wild toys" of Spenserian epithalamia.

Philips, in her poetic persona of "Orinda," attempts to offer a substitute for the conventional epithalamium, one governed instead by the values of feminine friendship, spiritual decorum, "gratitude and Love" (24). In a direct challenge to the ribald male collegium of Donne's "Lincolne's Inne" epithalamium, Philips posits her

> great solemnitys,
> Orinda's wishes for Cassandra's bliss.
> May her content be as unmix'd and pure
> As my affection, and like that endure;
> And that strong happiness may she still find
> Not owing to her fortune, but her mind. (7–12)

Philips here signals several significant shifts from the self-authorizing strategies of existing epithalamic models. As in "To the Lady Mary Butler," the narrator/poet claims a direct and exemplary relationship with the bride rather than with the bridegroom and insists that that relationship continue in the future, unlike the isolation and transfiguration of the bride figure in male-authored epithalamia. Philips further implies that the bride must remain intellectually distinct from her role as wife: "Cassandra" can depend, she argues, only on "her mind." So while the hazards of marriage for women are enacted in Philips's poem as they are in Herrick's and Donne's, "To my dear Sister Mrs. C. P." urges the bride to maintain a kind of symbolic independence and fortitude.

Philips's epithalamium is still negotiating, however, with the ideology of marriage implied in the literary tradition. Her speaker attempts to appropriate and reconstruct the female voice within the marriage rite, but as in other epithalamia the capacity of the institution to overwhelm the bride's individuality is nonetheless present. This tension is clearest when Philips prays that Mrs. C. P. "know no grief but in the name." Philips echoes the refrain from Donne's "Lincolnes Inne" poem, where the bride, in assuming her husband's name, also "puts on a woman's name." Here Philips ironically implies both that the bride will be protected from suffering and that the "name" she is acquiring may also be itself a source of grief. The poet reinforces this suggestion with the name she bestows on the bride: "Cassandra." A more unhappy association for a new bride it would be hard to imagine, and the classical Cassandra's own inability to affect the world around her is only too appropriate for Philips's arguments about the power and dangers of male poets and husbands.

Indeed, the name fits the narrator herself, who clearly claims a prophetic but also powerless role on the subject of marriages. This is clear in the second stanza, where the speaker uses herself as the floating point of comparison: "May her content be as unmix'd and pure / As my affection, and like that endure" (9–10). Philips implies, but does not attempt to confirm, that her own affection is pure and long lived, but her use of the optative makes both sides of the equation less a promise than a wish. As in Milton's frequent double negatives, the enigmatic "unmix'd" suggests its opposite as well.

The speaker's own ambiguous relationship to the marriage is also clear in the final lines: "every day like this may sacred prove / To Friendship, duty, gratitude and Love."

The list itself is full of unanswered questions: Duty to whom? Gratitude for what? Is Philips here reassigning her "dear sister" the role of humble, submissive wife, making her an object (as throughout the poem, where Mrs. C. P. is "she" rather than "you")? Or is this a deliberate challenge: friendship rather than love is the most important bond, and the speaker's construction of this "sacred" day again defies and implicitly critiques the male revelers of the opening stanza? Philips appropriates the bride's name as a speaker function throughout the poem, but as these two lines emphasize, that appropriation is both potentially deconstructive of the bride (in line with the epithalamic tradition) and deconstructive of the tradition that would silence both the bride and her poet ally.

The complex connections between sex and satire are everywhere evident in Philips's poem, then, as her ironic commentary on male poets' and grooms' celebrations of marriage is inflected by her own awareness of their power over the ambiguous "sisterhood" she here attempts to inscribe on these nuptials. Her mockery of male poets and masculine triumphs in marriage is offset by her own ambiguous relationship to the bride and the marriage itself, as her poetic narrator's allegiances are both clearer and more fraught than that of male epithalamic speakers. The difficulties of making herself a prophet for matchlessness, in every sense of that phrase, are everywhere apparent in "To Mrs. C. P."

The epithalamium "To my Lord and Lady Dungannon on their marriage 11. May 1662" is more complex still. It is in many respects a return to epithalamic conventionality, for one thing. Philips here engages the muses; invokes Spenser's suggestion that the sun should wait upon the couple; repeats Donne's image from the Somerset epithalamium of a picture of the bride on the groom's heart; and includes the blessings for children, prosperity, and happiness of most epithalamic verse. All of these revived conventions, however, serve only to emphasize the denatured agency that so strongly marks this epithalamium.

In "To my Lord and Lady Dungannon," Philips surrenders the assertive Orinda persona, remaining almost invisible as a speaker. Even when the speaker seems to point to herself, it is to emphasize her own dislocation of authority. The one moment where the poetic speaker seems to break into self-referentiality comes late in the poem and is itself indirect: "the shafts of Chance as vain will prove, / As all things else did that oppos'd your Love" (37–38), perhaps a (rare) allusion to Philips's own opposition to the marriage. Likewise, the next wish seems to suggest that the poetic persona is slipping into autobiography: "And may you never other sorrow know, / But what your pity feels for others woe" (49–50). Philips reports in a letter that she wept in misery at their wedding.[36] But the point of both allusions, if that is what they are, is only to reinforce the speaker's displaced, untenable agency and authority. Philips herself, the poem suggests, has been powerless to effect her own will on the bride or groom.

This ideology of agentlessness extends, notably, to the bride. While "To my dear Sister Mrs. C. P." uses "we" to suggest a collaboration between bride and speaker, "To my Lord and Lady Dungannon" frequently addresses the groom exclusively:

> Her Pencil (Sir) within your brest did draw
> The Picture of a Face you never saw,
> With touches, which so sweet were and so true,
> By them alone th'original you knew. (15–18)

In addition to the passivity of the bride expressed in these lines, Philips's speaker declines to address Lady Dungannon directly in any fashion—no "we," only a "she" or a collective "you." This despite the fact that Lady Dungannon was "Lucasia," one of Philips's most frequent addressees in her friendship poems. In all of these respects, this poem reiterates the distance between disembodied speaker and disenfranchised bride of the epithalamic tradition.

The poem's symbolic iconography does play with a series of alternate sources of authority to replace the uneasy speaker-bride alliance of "To my dear Sister Mrs. C. P." The speaker avoids self-authorization, dismissing likewise the muses as a source of empowerment, calling them "useless" (4). Instead, the speaker flatters the couple by allowing them, as an entity, a certain indistinct magical authority: "you, who, in your selves, do comprehend / All you can wish, and all we can commend; / Whom worth does guide, and destiny obey" (1–3). But this power gradually dissipates as their love becomes a creation of "providence" and "fate," the ultimate agents of all human endeavor, who are the female divinities creating and governing the marriage.

The functions of these divinities in the poem are extremely complex and more than a little ambiguous. Providence, first, is allied in the poem with heaven itself, as the force that destines and itself deifies the couple:

> Well may they wonder to observe a Knot,
> So curiously by Love and Fortune wrought,
> To which propitious Heaven did decree,
> All things on earth should tributary be;
> By gentle, sure, but unperceiv'd degrees,
> As the Sun's motion, or the growth of Trees,
> Does Providence our wills to hers incline,
> And makes all accidents serve her design. (7–14)

The married couple disappears here in a complex dance of causes and effects. The "knot" is made by "love" and "fortune"; heaven decrees that the bond made by love and fortune should master the earth. The couple is therefore both supreme agent of domination and an abstract entity constructed by arbitrary external forces. It is Providence that controls the wills of the lovers in making that knot, which is implied to be an "accident" brought about by heaven. The couple's own agency vanishes now in this ambiguous, contradictory statement over the divine agency governing the marriage. Heaven causes "accidents"; Providence influences not events but human wills. Philips implies, then, that the marriage is a kind of natural force destined by heaven, one that is ruled by Providence and one that rules in turn over Nature. But the complex ideology of arbitrary destiny makes the couple's own authority disappear in that of divine Providence.

Providence thus becomes a kind of feminine deity, manipulating and manufacturing desire through divine artifice:

Her Pencil (Sir) within your brest did draw
The Picture of a Face you never saw,

....

'Twas by the same mysterious power too,
That she has been so long reserv'd for you. (15–16, 21–22)

Providence is both artist and imitator, with a power that supersedes that of the lovers themselves. But Providence itself becomes a participant in a battle over jurisdictions, as becomes clear in the shifting pronouns. "She" is at first Providence; "she" then becomes the bride herself. The conflation of poetic speaker and bride of the epithalamic tradition is echoed in this linguistic overlap between Providence, the engineer of the marriage, and the bride who has withheld herself for it (or rather been withheld for it).

The poem likewise enacts the conflation of artistic energy with sexual conquest of Herrick's epithalamium. The "artist" of both nature and love is at first Providence; then the groom becomes the one possessed of art, as the poem's language becomes militaristic:

And at that sight with satisfaction yield
Your freedom, which till then maintain'd the field.
'Twas by the same mysterious power too,
That she has been so long reserv'd for you;
Whose noble passion, with submissive art,
Disarmed her scruples, and subdu'd her heart. (19–24)

The groom yields his territory, but the bride (who has been "reserved" for him in some kind of stasis) is in turn "subdued" and "disarmed" by his art. He is ruled by divine will, but he is also given similar powers of domination in return.

The agencies of Love and Fortune or Fate are equally problematic when they resurface later in the poem:

O! may it so, and may the wheel of Fate,
In you no more change than she feels, create;
And may you still your happinesses find,
Not on your Fortune growing, but your mind. (33–36)

The repeated images of circling and cycling ("the Sun's motion, or the growth of Trees," line 12) in the poem are here exploited to create ambiguous symbols of agentlessness. The rolling wheel of fate suggests not so much transcendence as the inevitability of suffering. The couple's happiness must not depend "on their Fortune growing," for Fortune does not grow upwards, like a tree, but rather circles and cycles like the sun, from day to night. The requirement for self-construction comes, then, from the impossibility of controlling the external environment. Likewise, Fate, Philips prays, should not create "more change than she feels," but this implies no guarantee of stability. Certainly it repeats the poem's pattern of blurring and disarming any predictable agency, masculine or feminine, creating or overseeing the marriage.

The poem's description of the couple's future as Lord and Lady Dungannon is likewise two-edged. The epithalamium uses many terms suggestive of political power: "great degree" (39), "so rever'd a President" (41),[37] "all things do your vertues court" (46). But the ambivalent power of wishing blessings likewise grants and removes agency: the speaker offers prayers that the couple will be "like [the] Divine" (51) in their capacity to grant comfort, but her dismissal of Time's "sythe" (48) also reinvokes the cycle of fortune and human decay which will ultimately control them. To negate is still to say, and to wish is to remain powerless: this is the paradox underlying the blessings at the end of the poem.

"To my Lord and Lady Dungannon on their Marriage" has a complex relationship to the epithalamic form and to Philips's other exercises in that form, then. It sits uneasily between the frustrated advocacy of "To my dear Sister Mrs. C. P." and the masculinist violence of Herrick's or Donne's poems, both rejecting a female speaker-bride alliance and resisting the groom's triumph so common in the tradition. The speaker's agency is uncertain and obscure, but there is no one authority (divine or human) to displace or replace it, as the speaker's self-authorizing gestures on her own, the couple's, or heaven's behalf seem to deconstruct themselves as quickly as they form. Though the poem seems celebratory, it is without the anticonventional voice for which Philips is so famous.

In combination, these four marriage poems establish just how Philips's epithalamic poems utilize speakers whose strategies for empowerment are multiple and frequently ambivalent. Philips's marriage poems are frequently agile in negotiating with the question of authority, gender, and difference, but the nature of their flexibility is variable. Both of these epithalamia certainly do demonstrate, though, the ways in which epithalamic forms, because they are instruments of social constraint and coherence, tend to make manifest the limits of that coherence. Philips both invokes and confronts the form's conventions, attempting to construct an independent feminine perspective on the antibridal cast of most epithalamia while also reinvoking those same traditional strategies. The epithalamic precedents in Philips's cultural bank ironically invite just such working and reworking, which may be why Philips's marriage poems are so symptomatic of the diverse voices she employs in all of her verse.

Philips makes use of the marriage poem's investment in gendered alliances and the blending of gender identities, and she makes use of its satiric modes, but in endlessly varied patterns. Poetic preoccupations with gender, with woman-woman alliances, with a new or prophetic mode confronting the masculinist past, seem to create an endless kaleidoscope in which neither Philips herself nor her subject position holds steady. Her speaker's stances are in constant negotiation with convention and invention, and the variations in her epithalamia alone confirm the ambiguities expressly written into her toasts at these weddings.

7 ❖ The Conjuncture of Word, Music, and Performance Practice in Philips's Era

Linda Phyllis Austern

A number of scholars in musicology and English literature have remarked on the fact that four poems by Katherine Philips are known to have been set to music during her lifetime by her older contemporary Henry Lawes (1596–1662). Two of these settings have been lost, one remains extant in a printed anthology of music from 1655, and the other has survived in a slightly later manuscript collection of vocal songs. There is no evidence that Philips and Lawes collaborated on these works, nor, in fact, that the poet and composer were personally acquainted, although they clearly moved in overlapping social-artistic circles and she probably attended concerts that he sponsored.[1] Both of his extant settings of her poems are typical of midcentury English song for accompanied solo voice, able to be performed by any person with moderate vocal skill, a reasonable ear, and/or beginning-to-intermediate ability on lute, viol, or virginals. Neither is musically remarkable; they have attracted scholarly attention primarily because they set Philips's words. Neither is available on a commercial recording, nor in regular concert repertory even among performers who specialize in seventeenth century English song.[2] Both pieces are tuneful airs that follow the form of the poetry and would have a charming simplicity when performed by a singer with a pleasant voice, crisp diction, and even a little technical training in vocal production. They are the product of an era in which music was largely a domestic affair, not only by political necessity but also by historical antecedent. The educated culture of mid-seventeenth-century England was still influenced by the older concept of the courtier whose musical skills helped to define his or her class standing and status as a learned person. At the same time, it had begun to metamorphose into a polite society in which music served as a finishing tool for marriageable women and an agreeable pastime for all members of the leisured classes. Both compositions perfectly exemplify what it means for poems to have become songs and circulated as such in mid-seventeenth-century England. As complete works—poem conjoined to music, intended for performance by and for bodies and their senses, and circulating in prescriptive form as part of two distinct consumer objects—they provide quite a bit of information about the position of song and music in Philips's world.

Nothing is known of any musical training the young Katherine Fowler may have had, nor of her direct involvement with the art after her marriage to Colonel James Philips. Her earliest biographer emphasizes her youthful religious devotion and aptitude for the verbal arts as one might expect of a future poet and young girl reputed to have "loved poetry at schoole, and made verses there."[3] Members of the social, economic, and educational class into which Katherine was born—children of successful merchants whose religious convictions led them to emphasize access to the written word and whose extended families valued learning—were often trained to sing and/or to play lute, viols, or the plucked-string keyboard instruments known generically in England as the virginals. The Puritan culture to which Katherine's family belonged had emphasized for generations the need to be able to sing the psalms at home and in church, and quite a range of musical psalm settings were available for domestic use.[4] The same printers and booksellers that purveyed mass-market psalms of David to devout consumers also proffered secular songs of the sort for which Katherine's poetry was later used, sometimes in the same volume. Domestic music manuscripts of the mid-seventeenth century, including those owned by young women of similar background to Katherine's, most often mixed the sacred with the secular, English-language psalms with songs of love and other worldly concerns in a variety of narrative voices.[5]

Whether the very young Katherine learned music from her mother, nurse, or a tutor as was often the practice in her era, the art was a vital part of the school curriculum for young ladies before the civil war and during the commonwealth period.[6] As Robert Burton observes, many genteel parents believed that early training in music and dance would help their daughters on the marriage market.[7] Mrs. Salmon's boarding school in Hackney, to which Katherine was sent in 1640, most likely taught music as well as Latin, French, dancing, and other skills deemed necessary for the daughters of prosperous London merchants and country gentry.[8] Music stood among these skills not only for the social graces it conferred through performance, but also the potential for more advanced training, informed judgment of new works, and future arts patronage. Katherine's school friend Mary Harvey later became the first English woman whose compositions were published under her own name as well as being a staunch supporter of Henry Lawes and his music.[9] In further keeping with the conventions of mid-seventeenth-century English girls' schools, Katherine and her colleagues probably performed plays, an activity from which music and dance were considered inseparable; other schools of the era featured masques and similar musical theatrical entertainments.[10]

Whatever her involvement with music at school, the adult Philips was a professed connoisseur of the art according to several of her poems, most notably her dedicatory verse "To the much honoured Mr. Henry Lawes, On his Excellent Compositions in Musick" at the beginning of the composer's *Second Booke of Ayres, and Dialogues*.[11] She also "ventur'd to lengthen" her translation of

Corneille's *La mort de Pompée* "by adding Songs in the Intervals of each Act" to "make it fitter for the Stage" where it was performed in 1663.[12] These songs were "set [to music] by several Hands," ranging from an old friend to an Irish Parliamentarian to Frenchmen retained by Lord Orrery and the Duchess of Ormond.[13] As we shall see, Katherine was much moved by a performance of one of them by her good friend Lady Elizabeth Boyle. In the grand tradition of both the oral balladeer and the most celebrated poets of her nation, Philips also wrote at least one "song" and another poem to preexisting melodies: her lyrical and passionate two-stanza "How Prodigious Is My Fate" to the tune of "Sommes nous pas trop heureux," and one simply headed "To my Lord Biron's tune of—Adieu Phillis."[14] Philips clearly inherited the notion that Sir Philip Sidney had expressed for an earlier generation: the art of the poet included "words set in delightful proportion, either accompanied with or prepared for the well enchanting skills of *Musicke*."[15]

Early modern English poets shared with musicians the notion that theirs was an art of aurality, of pleasing congruence of sounds, irrespective of inspiration by, preparation for, or performance with, the other. At the end of the sixteenth century, "poesie" had been defined as "a skill to speak or write harmonically, and verses or rhyme [to] be a kind of musical utterance, by reason of a certain congruity in sounds pleasing to the ear."[16] Throughout Philips's era, music and poetry remained sibling arts, sharing overlapping concepts of accent, rhythm, and meter within a temporal and at least potentially oral framework. Both were further linked to the arts of rhetorical persuasion and memory, and, during the first half of the seventeenth century, were subject to mutual experimentation, particularly with respect to the enhanced passionate and persuasive qualities each could lend the other in performance. Many thinkers of the era remind us that language and music formed an inseparable continuity of communication in which the former provided rational content and the latter bestowed an extrarational conduit for memory or affect. Music theorist and composer Thomas Ravenscroft, for example, explains that music gives "both a *relish* and a *beauty*" to poetry, and that music makes "*Poems* both willinglier heard, and better remembered."[17]

Song is the quintessential merger between "words set in delightful proportion" and "the well enchanting skille of *Musicke.*" It is indeed a form of "musical utterance" that, during Philips's era, almost invariably incorporated poetry that by itself had "a certain congruity in sounds pleasing to the ear." At its most basic, song consists of a certain quantity of suitable verse combined with a relatively short stretch of music that includes a distinct closure and which may be strophically repeated. Some poems are too complex or intellectually dense to be rendered easily into song. The ways in which song lyrics interact with their music can be quite subtle, as they are shaped into new form, blurred, reinforced, or rendered literal or ironic in a continual interplay between sound and meaning. Music may alter the duration of words from their conventional spoken patterns, add new emphases, and potentially compete with them for attention in performance. Therefore, the poems most suitable for song tend to be relatively simple and direct. Musical settings usually formalize poetic structure and may alter the balance between a poem's formal, semantic, and thematic elements.[18]

More than poetry, which can be read silently, song belongs to the realm of oral communication. Listeners cannot return for clarification to a word or phrase already delivered, whereas readers may do as they please with written text. They can put a work aside for any length of time and alter it by personal inscription without affecting its fundamental essence. Literary voices are silent phantoms, called to mind by the sense of sight and purged of the irregularities of spoken voices.[19] Song, music, and all forms of oral communication emanate from the bodies producing them, leaving their material and concentrated localization to enter the body of the hearer. Sound surrounds and invades. Where seeing may be analogized to touching, hearing is like being touched, except that the sensation does not stop at the skin.[20] Music, the element that renders poetry into song, is as insubstantial as thought or the souls of animate beings. In early modern terms, it was likened to vivified air, capable of penetration and circulation into and through solid bodies and spiritual entities. Unlike objects processed by the other senses, music enters the human body through the one apparatus that cannot be closed or withdrawn on its own. It lacks substance but alters the hearer's psycho-physical state. Says Philips's older contemporary and fellow lyricist George Sandys, "Musicke in it selfe most strangely works upon our humane affections.... because the Spirits which agitate in the heart, receave a warbling and dancing aire into the bosome, and are made one with... the rest of the Spirits dispersed through the body, raising or suppressing the instrumental parts according to the measures of the Musick: sometimes inflaming and againe composing the affections the sence of hearing stricking the Spirits more immediately, then the rest of the sences."[21] This invasive quality, involuntary affective response, and immediacy have, since antiquity, rendered music into an object of both power and suspicion in Western thought. "To some [music] seems offensive," summarizes the late sixteenth century schoolmaster Richard Mulcaster, "bycause it carrieth away the eare, with the sweetnesse of the melodie, and bewitcheth the mind with a *syrens* sound, pulling it from that delite, wherin of duetie it ought to dwell, unto harmonicall fantasies, and withdrawing it, from the best meditations, and most virtuous thoughts to forreigne conceites and wandring devises."[22]

This admixture of power, pleasure, and desire, plus the capacity to cross between the physical and the psychological, have rendered music proximate to sexuality. Both have been subject to strong social regulation to keep them where duty dictates they ought to dwell. And, especially since the emergence of modern tonality in Philips's era, Western music has often mapped patterns of erotic desire through sound.[23] At the level of direct bodily involvement—at its most potentially sexual—music, like other forms of performance, becomes "nested, trapped, contained, distilled, held, restrained, metaphorized" as a special form of communication to limit its affecting power.[24] The rituals of Western musical performance (as opposed to music that is part of a larger ritual) feature independently identifiable musical works executed by designated performers for an audience whose principle interest is to listen to the music made.[25] This presumes willing surrender of an aspect of the listener's selfhood to the performer in the designated performance venue and for the entire duration. Like Odysseus, an audience may be drawn in by a performance but is also distanced from bodily proximity.

Song is more powerful than instrumental music in performance not only because it marries the rationality of word to the elemental sensuality of music, but because its very vocality captures the attention and fosters identification by the listener with the singer. As a 1651 English translation of Henry Cornelius Agrippa von Nettesheim's *Three Books of Occult Philosophy* explains,

> Singing can do more then the sound of an Instrument, in as much as it arising by an Harmonical consent, from the conceit of the minde, and imperious affection of the phantasie and heart, easily penetrateth by motion, with the refracted and well tempered Air, the aerous spirit of the hearer, which is the bond of soul and body; and transferring the affection and minde of the Singer with it, It moveth the affection of the hearer by his affection, and the hearers phantasie by his phantasie, and minde by his minde, and striketh the minde, and striketh the heart, and pierceth even to the inwards of the soul, and by little and little, infuseth even dispositions: moreover it moveth and stoppeth the members and the humours of the body.[26]

The singer's musical voice and persona are not mediated through an artificial and specially designed object like the instrumentalist's. The voice communicates directly from the seat of the body's affections, from interior to interior, fantasy to fantasy. As an embodied or "natural" instrument of performance, the singing voice conveys the emotive and symbolic over the rational. It carries the singer's corporeality through its sound and renders the uniqueness of the singing body into an object of desire. To listen to a song—to give it ear awhile as a number of early modern ballads say—is to participate in a willing fusion between self and singer, to be drawn into the emotional state, the posture, the attitude, and the persona offered by the song through its performer—to willingly surrender mind, affection, fantasy, heart, and soul to the performer as Agrippa would have it. Listening initiates a relationship with another and carries an image in sound of that individual's physical and psychological state.[27]

The Western elite cultural privileging of composition and criticism above performance not only reinforces the idea that written forms are true and enduring. It also emphasizes the cleanness of intellectual products above the immediacy of bodily gesture and desire. Especially since the seventeenth century, composition has been subject to strict regulations that control and rationalize every aspect of prescribed sound. Musical scholarship and criticism are relatively young endeavors that render sound into sight, raw affect into controlled verbal analysis. Perhaps, as musicologist Suzanne Cusick suggests, a focus on textual aspects of music tends to trick us into remaining in a paradigm of power-over that is close to the regime of compulsory heterosexuality.[28] Certainly in patriarchal cultures, with or without the expectation of heterosexuality, a female (or boy) singer reverses the usual gender power polarity for a male listener, who must, like Odysseus, remain vigilant and conscious of the potential consequence of full surrender. The early modern era did indeed ascribe to music the potential for "power-over," likened repeatedly to feminine beauty and charm that threatened the manly rationality and self-restraint of all persons. Robert Burton reports that "many [men] are undone by" the "great allurement" of a young gentlewoman performing music, and William Prynne suggests that the way to prevent the moral dangers from female participation in song, dance, and masque is for women to only sing psalms and only in private.[29]

Philips, steeped in love of words from childhood, contributed to song and music by inscription of the linguistic signifier. Her words preceded not only musical setting, but also performance, by others. Even when inspired by the sound of a tune, she added the rational specificity of language and left to others the choice of whether and how to perform. For her era, as more widely in Western cultural history, this placed her firmly in the Platonic and arguably masculine position of privileging the rational, enduring aspect of language above the abstract, ephemeral, and potentially effeminating sound of music.[30]

However, as a connoisseur of both music and womanly attractions, she was ripe to participate in the ancient poetic topos of the listener undone by the alluring female musician, in which her inscribed voice takes the role usually assigned to a male auditor.[31] Also distinct from the convention, she makes clear that it was she who had written the words sung by the object of her affection, giving her a more active role in her own (acoustic) seduction. On hearing and seeing her friend Lady Elizabeth Boyle sing a setting of one of the songs whose text she wrote for her translation of *Pompey,* she was inspired to pen:

1

Subduing Fayre! What will you win
    To use a needless dart?
Why then so many to take in
    One undefended heart?

2

I came expos'd to all your charms,
    And for the first half hours
I had no will to take up arms,
    And in the next no power.

3

How can you choose but win the day?
    Who can resist your siege?
That in one action knows the way
    To vanquish and oblige?

4

Your voice, which can in moving strains
    Teach beauty to the blind,
Confines me yet in Stronger chains
    By being soft and kind.

5

Whilst you my triviall Fancy sing,
    You it to wit refine,
As leather once stamp'd by a King,
    Became a currant coyne.

6
By this my verse is sure to gain
Eternity with Men,
Which by your voice it may obtain,
Though never by my Pen

7
But in your favour I would live,
Rather then by a name,
And a much greater rate would give
For happiness then Fame.[32] (1–28)

By participation as an auditor, Philips opened herself to conquest by Lady Boyle, whose weapon was her voice. Philips had arrived exposed to all of the singer's charms—a willing participant in her own undoing. Even so, her listening persona has been subdued and vanquished by a multitude of darts in a campaign through which that "warbling and dancing aire" of music had invaded her defenseless body to penetrate her heart, pierce inward to her soul, and leave her powerless. The phallic and militaristic metaphors are striking among Philips's oeuvre but had become discursive commonplaces in reference to music by the mid-seventeenth century.[33] Lady Boyle's voice alone is both beauty and strength, charming, enchanting, and leaving the listener-poet ensnared in chains by its paradoxical softness and kindness. The singer thus retains her distinct femininity even while also ascribed critical descriptors of masculinity.[34] By raising Philips's "trivial fancy" to the level of musical performance, Boyle increases its value like precious metal to the mold for a coin. As in that metaphor, the singer has provided unique physical substance to the form that was the poet's text. According to the poet, the singer certainly bestowed on it "both a *relish* and a *beauty*" and renders it "both willinglier heard, and better remembered" as music was believed to do for poetry in song. In so doing the singer has also conquered the listener's heart. Intriguingly, Philips claims that Boyle's performance is what will bring renown to her verse, whereas she fails to name, or even acknowledge, the existence of, the composer who set the song. Also absent is any reference to instrumental accompaniment, a necessary and conventional element of the mid-seventeenth-century performance of composed music. It is Lady Boyle who, through her embodied voice, becomes a unique and immediate object of desire. It is Philips, the listening poet, who is stricken by Boyle's charm and beauty. She is left wishing not for fame through the words she'd written, but for the singer's favor. However, by providing verse, she had contributed to her own undoing. As mid-seventeenth-century music theorist and composer Charles Butler explained of the voice, "which is the work of Nature," "Good Voices alone, sounding onely the Notes, ar sufficient, by their Melodi and Harmoni, to delight the ear: but being furnished with soom laudable *Ditti,* they becoom yet more excellent."[35] In Philips's account, the singer had eroticized, through her person and performance, the material penned by the poet. It was the latter's ditty that had ultimately raised Lady Boyle's delightful voice, a gift of nature, to the level of excellence.

Like other learned persons in seventeenth century England, poets such as Philips inherited the notion that music consisted of two aspects, only one of which was this vibrant, ravishing, and counter-rational element of performance that sometimes worked like bewitchment or a love charm. Since antiquity, music had also served as a polyvalent metaphor for things known but unseen, including the erotic, the divine, and all forms of order. In this verbal form, it had become rendered into an object of rational contemplation, "contained, distilled, held, restrained, metaphorized" and stripped of its physical urgency while still being ascribed the highest and most universal elemental power. As Thomas Morley puts it in a treatise that remained in use from 1597 until after 1771, "Musicke is either *speculative* or *practicall. Speculative is that kinde of musicke* which by Mathematical helps, seeketh out causes, properties, and natures of soundes by themselves, and compared with others[,] proceeding no further, but content with onlie contemplation of the Art. *Practical* is that which teacheth al that may be knowne in songs, eyther for the understanding of other mens or making of ones owne."[36] Where Philips's poem about Boyle's performance is a tribute to the powers of practical music, references to speculative music—to unheard harmony and proportion—also appear in several of her works. Two of the central themes of her poetry—friendship and the need for harmony, unity, order, and peace during the Interregnum—lent themselves especially well to musical metaphor since music was the art of harmony. It was literally concord made out of diverse elements working together, whether capable of apprehension by the human ear or operating silently on some other level.

From antiquity onward, especially codified in the Middle Ages, music had been said to exist at three concentric levels: the sort that can be heard and performed by human beings (*musica instrumentalis*), the unheard symmetries of soul and body (*musica humana*), and the harmony of the universe or heavenly spheres (*musica mundana*). Each of these had its basis in the abstract mathematics of number and proportion and thus bound all things together, either "*Musick* to the *Ear,* or to the *Intellect,*" as Philips puts it.[37] *Musica instrumentalis,* the form capable of being listened to or performed by human voice or instrument, was generally accounted the least powerful, a poor imitation of the eternal sorts. But it could still act on body and soul and suggest the music of higher realms. Countless literary works had drawn on the reflections and contrasts between these forms of music, perhaps most famously in Lorenzo's speech to Jessica in act 5, scene 1 of William Shakespeare's *Merchant of Venice.*[38] By the mid-seventeenth century, the tripartite topos of music and its universal signification and effect had mostly moved from the domains of mathematics and natural philosophy into that of literary metaphor. At the same time, writing on musical aesthetics and praxis began to eclipse philosophical speculation.

As musical performance skills became more accessible to members of the leisured classes through formal programs of education and the plethora of treatises that followed Morley's, musicianship became less and less content with contemplation as an end. Speculation was either incorporated into experimental science, transformed into critical theory, or referenced in a new generation of poetry.[39] During the seventeenth century, reflections among the three domains of musical action were especially used as metaphors for government of self, household, and nation-state; contemplation of the divine; and powerful, inspired love.

Philips was well acquainted with her era's conventions of musical metaphor and made use of them in several ways. Her 27-stanza strophic poem for peace and civic order, "L'accord du bien" ("The agreement of the good") especially calls upon the tradition of the concord between disparate factions as a form of harmony. With its metrical four-line stanzas and strong rhythmic pulse, the work also has that "congruity in sounds pleasing to the ear" that suggests song even when not associated with a musical rendition. The text begins by working its way from *musica mundana* through *musica instrumentalis* to *musica humana,* and returns at the end to the blissful harmony of the heavens. It is significant that sensual music here comes between the more abstract kinds that govern the heavens, the body, and the body politic. Philips links the silent mathematical underpinnings of music both heard and unheard to the controlled art that worked with varied sound, including dissonance; by her era, the most acclaimed compositions were the most internally varied and concluded with dissonance dissolving into strong cadential consonance. Even with its conventional metaphors of harmony as numerical proportion, congruity of sound, and the echo of divine creation in the human being, Philips's poem retains a sense of the audibility of music:

1

Order, by which all things were made,
And this great world's foundation laid,
Is nothing else but Harmony,
Where different parts are brought t'agree.

2

As Empires are still best maintain'd
Those ways which first their greatnes gain'd
So in this Universall frame
What made and keeps it is the same.

3

Thus all things unto peace do tend;
Even discords have it for their end.

The cause why Elements do fight,
Is but their instinct to Unite.

4

Musique could never please the sence
But by united excellence:
The sweetest note which numbers know,
If onely struck, would tedious grow.

5

Man, the whole world's epitomy
Is by creation harmony.
'Twas sin first quarrell'd in his brest,
Then made him angry with the rest.

The work concludes with a reference to heaven and its glory as "one harmonious constant blisse."[40] Stanzas three and four in particular draw on the intersection between the acoustic practice of music and contemplation of sound for its hidden meanings. Francis Bacon points out that in seventeenth century musical practice, "the *Falling* from a *Discord* to a *Concord,* which maketh great Sweetnesse in *Musicke,* hath an Agreement with the *Affections,* which are reintegrated to the better, after some dislikes." He also explains that "the sweetest and best *harmony* is, when every *Part,* or Instrument, is not heard by it selfe, but a Conflation of them all."[41]

These ideas of the metaphysical nature of musical harmony and its application to the self, the divine, and hidden sympathy between human beings are applied with greater personal immediacy in several of Philips's poems addressed to Lucasia (Anne Owen). Here we see the stock commonplaces applied to the friendship between Orinda and Lucasia, or to Lucasia herself. The through-composed poem entitled "Lucasia" praises its object as the proportionate original of *musica mundana* among its list of her spiritual virtues. Here again, the capacity for the rational judgment of music by the human senses merges with the numerical basis of the art and its extension into a metaphor for perfection. The knowing reader would understand the basis of the reflection between Lucasia's soul, the celestial spheres (here with their attendant muses), and the body that displays these virtues as elements of an entire composition in which "every chord's examin'd and found good." The poet follows Lucasia's harmony from soul and body to the spheres and thence to her entirety in music in a variation on the conventional Platonic ascent to the divine through the beloved:[42]

> That souls were made of number could not be
> An observation but a prophesy.
> It meant Lucasia, whose harmonious state
> The spheares and muses faintly imitate.
> But as then Musique is best understood
> When every chord's examin'd and found good:
> So what in others Judgement is, and will,
> In her is the same even reason still.[43] (21–28)

"To my Lucasia" builds on the idea that "Such harmony is in immortal souls, / But whilst this muddy vesture of decay / Doth grossly close it in, we cannot hear it"[44] while mocking the crudely physical investigative methods of the first phase of the scientific revolution. In this case the hidden entirety is not an individual who reflects cosmic order but blissful union between souls. The poem begins with a reference to harmony as an object of both nature and natural philosophical inquiry—in this case, a hyperfeminine Nature with a womb whose secrets aspiring "dull philosophers" should not probe with "low experiments" if they wish to learn the source of the harmonies between aspects of the whole. Here, Philips links nature and harmony to the soul (all three are gendered feminine in Latin) against the prying methods of the hypermasculine empirical philosophy of her era.[45] Instead, she returns the inquiry to a metaphysical plane reflecting erotic passion:

> Let dull Philosophers enquire no more
> In nature's womb, nor causes strive t'explore,
> By what strange harmony and course of things
> Each body to the whole a tribute brings;
> What secret Unions neighbouring agents make,
> And of each other how they doe partake.
> These are but low experiments; but he
> That nature's harmony entire would see,

Must search agreeing soules, sit down and view
How sweet the mixture is! How full! How true!
By what soft touches spirits greet and kiss,
And in each other can compleat their bliss:
A wonder so sublime it will admit
No rude spectator to contemplate it.[46] (1–14)

Philips presents nature's harmony as unheard and incomprehensible by the current analytic methods of philosophy, grounded in what was later considered scientific investigation. Instead, it is the cause of secret agreement between souls and the spirits that greet and kiss and softly merge with each other through the most feminine of senses, touch. This inaudible harmony is the sensory opposite of the piercing darts of Lady Boyle's voice in song, though both have a soothing softness and extraordinary affective power over sense or intellect.

In contrast, the 20-stanza "To my Lucasia, in defense of declared friendship" includes noteworthy use of a commonplace borrowed from scientific empiricism, which builds on reflection between physical and metaphysical music:

But when that look is dress'd in words, 'tis like
    The mystique power of musick's Unison;
Which when the finger does one Violl strike,
    The other's string heaves to reflection.[47] (69–72)

Francis Bacon, in his seminal natural history *Sylva sylvarum,* describes an experiment using the stringed instruments favored by the privileged classes, not for aesthetic purpose but as laboratory sounding bodies: "There is a Common Observation, that if a *Lute* or *Vial* [viol], be laid upon the Back with a small straw upon one side of the *strings;* and another *Lute* or *Vial* be laid by it; And in the other *Lute* or *Viall* the *Unison* to that *string* be stricken, it will make the *string* move; Which will appear both to the Eie, and by the *straws* falling off. The like will be if the *Diapason* or *Eight* [octave] to that *string* be stricken, either in the same *Lute* or *Viall,* or in others lying by; But in none of these there is any report of *Sound,* that can be discerned but onely Motion."[48] Henry Peacham's courtesy manual *The Compleat Gentleman,* first published in 1622, had made a similar observation about "two Lutes of equall size being laid upon a Table, and tuned Unison, or alike," and asks why "the one stricken, the other untouched shall answer it?"[49] In Philips's verse, pragmatic probing into the secrets between two like instruments makes manifest their similitude while also suggesting the age-old metaphors of the body as an instrument, heartstrings that can be struck or tuned, and the unheard sympathy between quavering lover and the beloved's identical response.[50] Her specific evocation of the viol, with its slender waist between symmetrically rounded curves and the upright embrace required by the performer to give it sound, further underscores the intensely feminine quality of the professed friendship. As in the other two Lucasia poems, true music is that of speculation, the mystical sympathy between similitudes, in this case so strong that they are one and the same (see fig. 7.1).

The manifest dimensions of music heard and music contemplated are brought together in Philips's address "To the much honoured Mr. Henry Lawes, On his Excellent Compositions in Musick," which is given pride of place as the first commendatory poem in the composer's *Second Booke of Ayres and Dialogues* of 1655. The poet's 40-line praise of Lawes and his music is full of widely resonant references touching on both speculation and practice, some of which appear in others of her poems. Steeped in the Platonic doctrines of her era, Philips begins with an invocation of the hidden music that unifies all ordered, constructive things, beginning with raw Nature:

> Nature which is the vast Creation's Soule,
> That steady curious Agent in the whole
> The Art of Heav'n the Order of this Frame
> Is only *Musick* in another Name. (1–4)

Having identified music as the bond between heaven and earth, she follows it through social and personal accord to the faculties of perception and wit by which it can be judged:

> And as some *King* conqu'ring what was his own
> Hath choice of severall Titles to his Crown;

Fig. 7.1. The reflection between physical and metaphysical music in which the string of an untouched lute vibrates in sympathy to the same string struck on another. National Gallery of Art Library, David K. E. Bruce Fund.

So *Harmony* on this Score now, that, then,
Yet still is all that takes and governs Men.
Beauty is but *Composure;* and we find
Content is but the *Concord* of the mind;
Friendship the *Unison* of well tun'd Hearts;
Honour's the *Chorus* of the noblest parts:
And all the world on which we can reflect,
Musick to the *Ear,* or to the *Intellect.* (5–14)

Even before she introduces Lawes or his compositions, she has reminded the reader that his art reflects the realm of the divine, friendship, honor, the "little world" of the human soul and body, the body politic, and, above all, nature as the *spiritus mundi* or soul of all creation.

The poet next turns to the composer. Borrowing from the literary conventions of the *Laus musicae* and from current commendatory practice, she endows the man himself and his body of work with the positive, celestial capacities of music in general.[51] As she addresses him in the second person, she again emphasizes Nature and reflection between realms as well as the interplay between sensory apprehension and intellectual comprehension:

> If then each Man a little world must be,
> How many Worlds are coppy'd out in thee?
> Who art so richly furnish'd, so compleat,
> T'Epitomize all that is Good or Great;
> Whose Starrs this brave advantage did impart,
> Thy *Nature's* as *Harmonious* as thy *Art:*
> Thou dost above the *Poets* Prayses live,
> Who fetch from Thee th'Eternity they give;
> And as true *Reason* triumph's over Sense,
> Yet is subjected to *Intelligence;*
> So *Poets* on the lower World look down,
> But *Lawes* on them, his height is all his own:
> For (like Divinity it selfe) his Lyre
> Reward's the wit it did at first inspire:
> And thus by double right Poets allow
> Their and His Lawrells to adorn his brow (15–30)

Ever the poet, Philips grants Lawes the power to elevate her art by his music and to render words eternal, much as she does to a lesser extent with Lady Boyle's voice. The composer is adorned not only by poet's laurels as well as music's, but is raised even beyond poets (reminding us of the capacity of music to refine poetic wit, as Philips herself put it in her description of Lady Boyle's singing). Finally, the poem returns to a more general praise of music, unifying its power for dull and sullen moderns as well as those ancients who had witnessed musical miracles:

> Live then (Great Soul of Nature) to asswage
> The savage dullness of this sullen Age;
> Charm us to sense; and though Experience fail,
> And Reason too, thy Numbers may prevail.
> Then (like those Ancients) strike, and so command
> All Nature to obey thy generous hand:
> None can resist, but such who needs will be
> More stupid than a *Fish*, a *Stone*, a *Tree:*
> Be it thy care our Age new to create,
> What built a world, may sure repair a State.[52] (31–40)

Throughout the entire commendation, the nature imagery that features prominently in Philips's poetry not only suggests Lawes's place and perfection with universal Nature reflected in his own harmonious nature. It also evokes the vital seventeenth century connection between music and the natural world, links literature to music as well as speculation to practice within musical discourse. In this case it is not the ditty that raises the voice beyond the realm of nature, but the composer who gives notes to the words. Philips likens Lawes's control over Nature to that of Arion, Amphion, and Orpheus, for whom, respectively, fish, stones, and trees—animals, minerals, and plants—had done as commanded. In her era, this notion extended well beyond the fictions of the ancients. Quite a number of seventeenth century treatises on the theory and practice of composed music, as well as works of natural philosophy, were concerned with musical styles and practices that regulated unruly elements of Nature.[53] Absent from the poem is the sense of raw sensuality that pervades the Western tradition of musical performance. Lawes not only inhabits the world above the poets who are already beyond the lower (corruptible, sensate) one. Sense and reason, ear and intellect, are repeatedly tied together. Even when Lawes makes music, it is to strike his mythic lyre (likened to divinity), by which his powers become those of the most ordered, positive musicians of lost antiquity. Thus is the composer, the ordered inscriber of musical text, connected further to the poet and distanced from the embodied performer. It is worth noting that the next commendatory verse in the collection, written by singer and Lawes student Mary Knight, relies on some of the same commonplaces about the eternal, hidden powers of music. Where Philips's praise sets Lawes above the poet's art, Knight's does so above the singer's. However, the vocalist particularly emphasizes the music's therapeutic power and its ability to ravish the listening ear. For her, it is not Nature but the God of love that has most prominently tuned the composer's soul.[54]

Henry Lawes was the most prolific mid-seventeenth-century English composer of songs, praised by a number of poets whose works he set, including Milton, Herrick, and Waller as well as Philips. He was a staunch patron of other contemporary English poets, and at least two printers confirmed Philips's assertion that he conferred distinction on the verses he set to music.[55] He had risen to prominence as a court musician under Charles I and is best known to literary scholars as the composer for Milton's *Comus*. By the early 1650s he had gained renown among socially elite connoisseurs both as a private teacher and for the concerts that he sponsored in his London house. The exclusive and likely royalist audience for the latter seems to have been a mix of aristocrats, literati, and personal friends, some of whom found others as delightful an attraction as the featured entertainment. Says Edward Phillips (nephew of John Milton) of these occasions,

> 'Twere in me rudeness, not to blazon forth
> (Father in *Musick*) thy deserved praise,
> Who oft have been, to witness thy rare worth,
> A ravish't hearer of thy skilfull Lay's.
> Thy Lay's that wont to lend a soaring wing,
> And to my tardy Muse fresh ardour bring.
>
> While brightest *Dames*, the splendor of the Court,
> Themselves a silent *Musick* to the Eye,
> Would oft to hear they solemn *Ayres* resort,
> Making thereby a double Harmony:
> 'Tis hard to judge which adds the most delight,
> To th'Eare thy Charms, or theirs unto the Sight.[56]

Katherine Philips may have been among those who "resorted" to these musical occasions, as were certainly her old school friend Lady Mary [Harvey] Dering and her husband, Sir Edward Dering (the worthy "Silvander" of Orinda's coterie, who later wrote the epilogue to her translation of *Pompey*). Other distinguished participants included Margaret Cavendish and Sir Charles Cavendish, the Duchess and Earl of Newcastle; Lady Mary Herbert; and Alice, Countess of Carbery. Lawes's "solemn ayres" circulated during the era in manuscript and in print. Plans for the print editions may have come in parallel to his domestic music meetings, and his *Second Booke,* to which Philips contributed her commendatory verse, includes multiple intersections with her work and her circle.[57] This book is also an important document of the history of women and music in early modern England not only because it includes prefatory poetry by Philips and Knight under their own names or because it includes a setting of a poem by the former. It also showcases songs by England's premier published woman composer and states most unusually, in Lawes's address to the reader, that its contents are intended for use by "Musitians of both sexes."[58]

At the center of the collection stands its dedicatee, "the Honourable, the Lady Dering, Wife to Sir Edward Dering of Surenden Dering, Baronet," schoolmate and friend of Philips, student of Lawes, and the first English woman whose musical compositions were made public under her own name.[59] It is clear from Lawes's dedication that Lady Dering, who had been his student since not long after her marriage in 1648,[60] had, in the course of her lessons, performed the entire contents of the collection, certainly with voice and perhaps her own accompaniment on lute or keyboard. She had "resolv'd to keep it private," presumably in the form of a manuscript used for study, practice, and possibly domestic performance for family members. Her husband had provided both the payment for lessons and, perhaps somewhat unusually, the three poems she set as accompanied songs: "When First I Saw Fair Doris' Eyes," "And Is This All? What One Poor Kisse," and "A False Design to Be Cruell (In Vain Fair Chloris, You Designe)."[61] She had either read or sung to her late mother as an aid to the latter's meditation, perhaps from Lawes's or his brother William's exquisite psalm settings.[62] In the complicated economy of exchange between student and teacher, patron and musician, wife of a baronet and professional from the artisan class, Lawes was prescripted to praise Lady Dering's talent as well as the inward harmony evident in both her and her husband.[63]

Nonetheless, evidence is beginning to suggest that some extremely talented English gentlewomen of the mid-seventeenth century, who, by virtue of both class and gender could not aspire to public careers in music, were trained to professional or near professional levels in performance and composition.[64] Lady Dering may have been among these. Financial, artistic, and presumably moral support by her husband, and perhaps his presence as a chaperone at lessons, lent necessary propriety to Lady Dering's musical endeavors in an era in which women's musical performance had the potential to enflame auditors. No institution more sanctioned controlled erotic conflagration in the early modern era than marriage. Dering's compositional style is much like her teacher's, typical of English songwriting in an era that strove to privilege the meaning of the text over arcane complexities of sound. Most interestingly and as may be typical for women learners of the mid-seventeenth century, the "Songs which fill this Book" require the singer to assume multiple genders and what would today be considered sexualities. The songs of "The Lady *Deerings* Composing" would have required her to play the part in performance of three persons in love with women, one an Arcadian shepherd and the other two an individual who uses the literary language of the spurned male lover, passionate for the alternately cruel and kind Cloris. In "And Is This All? What, One Poor Kisse?" the singer must call for pleasures well beyond kisses, "all, that Lovers love," and suffer the double entendre of orgasmic death.[65]

Immediately following Lady Dering's three pieces in the collection is Lawes's setting for accompanied solo voice of Philips's "Friendship's Mystery, to my dearest Lucasia," here entitled "Mutuall Affection between *Orinda* and *Lucatia*." The poet is credited as "Mrs. *Catherine Philips*."[66] The poem consists of six stanzas of five-line verse whose congruity in sounds is pleasing to the ear in ways that both do and do not easily loan themselves to music. The first stanza is given between staves of the score in Lawes's *Second Booke,* with the other five as poetry on the same page.[67] Lydia Hamessley argues persuasively that, according to the styles of song composition of his era, his setting is a musical misreading of the poet's intense and highly personal passion for the very real object of her love. Lawes, she contends, has both trivialized and missed the intensity of the affection between the female poet-narrator and her same-sex beloved and has blurred Philips's authorial voice by setting it to music that fails to evoke real erotic power or strength. In short, the composer participates in the dominant discourse of the era that downplays female friendship and assigns true erotic passion only to relationships that involve men.[68] Ian Spink, however, counters that Lawes's failure to emphasize the lesbian implications of the poem might also be seen as his compliment to Philips's intent by treating the text no differently from the way he treats many "men-to-women" love lyrics.[69] The situation becomes even more complicated through consideration of the work not as compositional alteration of an authorial voice, but as a script for the male or female singer who will add yet another level of ownership to what is ultimately a collaborative product—a product presented as a script in a mass-market collection designed to reach as wide a consumership as possible. The creation of a character through song is substantially governed by the music itself. However, in performance, the narrative personhood is most immediately and powerfully the singer.[70] Lawes, as composer, mediates between the poet who wrote the words and the performer who delivers the message.

In his process for setting songs, Lawes considered himself to be governed by the poetry. "The way of *composition* I chiefly profess," he says, "is to shape *Notes* to the *Words* and *Sense.*" As to the former and the peculiarities of English diction for the singer, he places responsibility on both composer and performer by stating that "if *English* words which are fitted for *Song* do not run smooth enough, tis the fault either of the *Composer* or *Singer.*" He says little of the sense, beyond the fact that approbatory music, whether English or foreign, necessarily includes "*Passions, Spirits, Majesty,* and *Humours*."[71] The unknown author of the 1680 elementary song performance treatise, *Synopsis of Vocal Musick*, concurs by stating with equal lack of specificity that "Vocal Musick is an Art of expressing rightly things by Voice, for the sweet moving of the affections and the mind....For exhilarating the animal spirits, it moderateth gratefully the affections, and this penetrateth the interiours of the mind, which it most pleasantly doth affect."[72] Again, we see the affective capacities of performed music as the goal in each of these cases but nothing of the necessary compositional tools. Charles Butler is a little bit more specific, explaining that the composer

> must have a special care that the Note[s] agree to the nature of the Ditti [poem]. Plain and slow Musik is fit for grave and sad matter: qik Notes or Triple time, for Mirth and rejoicing. A manly, hard, angry, or cruel matter is to bee exprest by hard and harsh short tones...but words of effeminate lamentations, sorrowful passions and complaints, ar fitly exprest by...notes which change the direct order of the Scale. Also words importing the circumstances of Time and Place, ar to bee fited with Notes agreeable: as those that signifie running or speedy motions, also short syllables of any words, with short Notes.[73]

Modern scholars have divided seventeenth century English solo song into tuneful and declamatory types. The former is related stylistically to dance and balladry with their clear rhythms and memorable melodic contours. The latter emphasizes the rhetorical aspects of the text as it might be spoken. Declamatory song also bears a closer evident relationship to the experimental vocal music of seventeenth century France and especially Italy and found its way fairly early into the English theater. As is often the case with categories imposed retrospectively, there is a great deal of overlap between these types. However, the contrast between them is more striking in Lawes's work than that of his contemporaries. His tuneful airs tend to be light, quite dancelike, usually in triple meter, often strophic, and "sometimes almost frivolous in their simplicity" in the words of Elise Bickford Jorgens, whereas his declamatory songs are usually in duple meter and more closely oriented toward their texts.[74] "Come, my Lucasia, since we see" belongs to the former category.

Set strophically in triple time in the bright key of G major, Lawes's song is dancelike and charming, with new music for each phrase of the stanza. Lawes does indeed fit short syllables with short notes and the contrary with contrary as Butler recommends; his treatment of the "*English* words which are fitted for *Song*" are certainly clear enough to guide the performer of the first stanza to avoid linguistic barbarisms.[75] As Butler further reminds us, mid-seventeenth-century composers were expected to make their notes agree with the nature of the text, the first stanza—the one always most closely set by composers in strophic songs—of which is

> Come, my Lucasia, since we see
> That miracles men's faith do move
> By wonder and by Prodigy
> To the dull, angry world let's prove
> There's a religion in our love.[76]

Lawes gives Philips's poem the musical meter that Butler says is fit for "Mirth and rejoicing," which favors the narrator's desire to show her mutual affection with Lucasia to the world. This is, according to Lawes, no "grave or sad" matter, nor does it include anything "manly, hard, angry, or cruel." Where insightful readers of the poem might find emotive complexities and passing sorrowful passions (most notably the "divided joys" and "griefs" of the fourth stanza), Lawes's overriding emotion is one of joy. The only very controlled "alterations to the scale" help to propel the motion of the second and third lines upward and to illustrate the words "wonder" and "angry" (which receives passing clashing dissonance) in the first stanza and those that occupy analogous positions in later ones. Text-setting is mostly one note per syllable to allow the shape and meaning of each word and line to come through clearly in performance; from the first stanza, only "wonder," "prodigy," and "angry" are singled out for more extravagant melismatic settings. And, as is conventional in the era's music, the penultimate word of each stanza passes from dissonance to the central tonal consonance of the work. This is gentle affection, not painfully powerful attraction.

Metaphysical poetry generally provided quite a challenge to composers, whose art often adds inventive dimensionality to straightforward broadly interpretable text. The five-line construction of Philips's poetic stanzas in particular prohibits a conventional mid-seventeenth-century musical phrase structure. Furthermore, the formal configuration and rhyme scheme of each five-line stanza of Philips's poem varies between 3 + 2 and 2 + 3 according to its semantic structure, for which a strophic musical setting necessarily does injustice to some. The internal musical cadences of Lawes's setting primarily propel one poetic line gently forward to the next without strong goal orientation until the end of the third and fifth lines of each stanza, eliding multiple possibilities for clear musical-textual climax before the closing cadence. The song is an example of what has been called "Lawes's suave urbanity," favoring a flowing, tuneful setting over the emotional depth suggested by its poetry.[77] In this case, Lawes privileges tunefulness and musical unity above Philips's metaphysical complexity and careful phrase structure, leading both Hamessley and Spink to wonder why he did not set it in a more free-flowing declamatory style. Perhaps, as Spink suggests, the composer may have considered tunefulness to be more "feminine," or as Hamessley suggests, he may have deliberately misread the poem's female homoeroticism.[78] Or perhaps the dancelike rhythms, sung in close quarters at an appropriately sprightly tempo, would invite the listener to join with the singer in imagined mutual motion. In any case, Philips herself praised Lawes for elevating her words with his music in the book in which the song circulated. In performance, any singer, male or female, would become a new Orinda, expressing mutual affection for her Lucasia, even if at a lower level of intensity than the poet originally intended. According to the era's attitudes toward music, the very act of singing words enhanced them and rendered them more immediately affective to the listener, tuning heart to heart, soul to soul, in mutual sympathy. Considering Philips's attitude toward Lady Boyle singing far less personal lyrics, with the mysterious absence of mention of any composer or strictly musical aesthetic, Lawes's notes in this case may have mattered less than the performing body and disposition of its listener.

Lawes's other extant setting of a poem by Philips circulated in a manuscript collection mostly consisting of love songs, political ballads, and drinking songs by a number of mid-seventeenth-century English composers, in the hand of the same John Playford who dominated the era's music printing industry and brought out Lawes's *Ayres and Dialogues*.[79] It is more introspective than sweetly celebratory and is another piece that has baffled modern critics: an elegant and lyrical setting of the first stanza of Philips's poem "On the death of my first and dearest childe, Hector Philips, borne the 23rd of Aprill, and dy'd the 2nd of May 1655."[80] In the manuscript it is entitled "On the Death of an Infant," an incongruous addition to an anthology of music mostly celebrating manly delights:

> Twice forty months of wedlock did I stay
> Then had my vows crown'd with a lovely boy
> And yet in forty days he drop't away
> O swift vicissitude of humane Joye.

The poem's four-line stanzaic structure loans itself easily to a balladlike musical setting, even if its subject matter might make it more fit for an anguished lament. Lawes sets it tunefully as "a sarabande of the utmost delicacy," perfectly respecting the structure of the poem and subtly augmenting the natural spoken syllabification of each line.[81] It is "plain and slow," yet in triple time, although its text is unfit for either mirth or rejoicing. The song has none of the conventional markers of "effeminate lamentations, sorrowful passions and complaints" as it might have done in a more declamatory style. But, as Joan Applegate points out, that would have elevated Philips's poem into a miniature dramatic *scena*.[82] As is, it is a deceptively simple underpinning for Philips's unassuming quatrain with the sweetness of a lullaby, set in the somber key of g minor to a tune that could be sung by even a modestly trained singer. This is poetry become therapeutic, raised through the art of harmony to an

"Art of expressing rightly things by Voice, for the sweet moving of the affections and the mind.... For exhilarating the animal spirits, it moderateth gratefully the affections, and this penetrateth the interiours of the mind, which it most pleasantly doth affect." With Lawes's music, Philips's poem becomes a vehicle to retune the suffering soul, not to enflame it or express its felicity.

Although not known as a musician, Philips inhabited a world in which music was a sister to poetry, the unheard harmony that bound together all of Nature and remained resonant in souls, as well as an art capable of moving the affections more powerfully than the read or even spoken word. According to Philips's writings, and borrowing from stock conventions of her era, one can conclude that music had the power to elevate poetry to a sublime level in composition and especially in performance. Philips was enough of a connoisseur to have praised composer Henry Lawes for his ability to set English poetry and, in all probability, had attended concerts he sponsored at a time when there was no public venue for musical performance. And she was ready to adapt poetic commonplaces of music to her own ends, including as a means to enhance metaphors of accord and amity, and to respond to her emotional transport on hearing a female friend sing one of her songs. As collaborative products, her two extant poems that were set by Lawes have a lot to tell us about literary-musical relations in mid-seventeenth-century England, including the possibility that the era's basis for the aesthetic judgment of a work, on paper or in performance, may have been somewhat different from our own.

8 ❖ "Friendship so Curst"

Amor Impossibilis, the Homoerotic Lament, and the Nature of *Lesbian* Desire

Valerie Traub

Editors' Note

In her magisterial book *The Renaissance of Lesbianism in Early Modern England,* Valerie Traub traces an epistemic shift in understandings of female homoeroticism. Leveraging historical difference and diachronic change, Traub offers not a prehistory of the modern lesbian but, rather, a "genealogy of *lesbianism*" attentive to "the conditions of intelligibility whereby female-female intimacies gain, or fail to gain, cultural signification."[1] Throughout the book, therefore, she italicizes the terms "lesbian" and "lesbianism" in the hope that "the persistent typographical strangeness... will remind readers of their epistemological inadequacy, psychological coarseness, and historical contingency."[2] Traub's genealogy unfolds over the course of the seventeenth century, during which, she argues, a presumption of the impossibility, and thus "insignificance," of female-female eroticism gradually gives way to a logic of suspicion that reads the signs of dangerous desire where they had previously been excluded. Examining representations of love and desire between women in a range of discourses, she demonstrates how the figures of the innocent, chaste female friend and the dangerous, exotic tribade converge, suturing erotic acts and desires to gender and to identity.

In the chapter from which the following is excerpted, Traub explores the trope of female-female love as an *amor impossibilis,* excluded by Nature from the realm of possibility and marked by an elegiac feeling of loss. In texts that range from Ariosto's *Orlando Furioso* and Sandys's translation of *Metamorphoses,* to dramas by Lyly and Cavendish, Nature bars women from loving other women by imposing social and bodily imperatives toward companionate, heterosexual marriage. Relief only comes, if at all, in the form of utopian fantasies of sexual transformation, such as occurs in the climax of Lyly's *Galatea.* By laying claim to the discourse of friendship and aligning its values with those of Nature, Philips brings female same-sex desire within the realm of the natural, even the exalted, although it is still painfully excluded from possibility by the crudity and violence of the "rough, rude world." But while Philips is able to maintain that such female bonds are chaste, after her the woman-desiring-woman is figured ambivalently as hermaphroditic, even though an author like Aphra Behn could employ it with a certain transgressive boldness and pride.

Because Philips is a pivotal figure in Traub's narrative, the reverse is also true—*The Renaissance of Lesbianism* set new vistas for scholars working on sexuality in Orinda's verse. In addition to situating Philips's corpus within a rich cultural history, Traub provides conceptual tools for historicizing early modern representations of female homoeroticism. Influenced by Alan Bray's germinal book, *Homosexuality in Renaissance England,*[3] Traub's methodological approach to the discursive structure of female friendship has paved the way for subsequent work on Philips's friendship poems.Whereas Traub adapts Bray's historical trajectory to chart transformations in understandings of female friendships that *exclude* men, Harriette Andreadis builds on his insights about the masculinist ideology of male friendship to show how Philips appropriates the discourse "both to affirm her passion for her female friends in her poems and to create a sociofamilial network of intimate relations" that *includes* men.[4] Lorna Hutson, in contrast, disputes the utility of the interpretative mode Bray delineates in *The Friend*.[5] In an essay reprinted in this collection, Hutson argues that because women were denied access to the bodily gestures through which (male) ethical friendship signified publicly, it becomes more significant that "in Philips's poems we have a male tradition of ethical friendship being appropriated for women, and for royalist politics, but in ways which, above all, appeal to the passions and interests as capable of bringing about the erotic and political subjection of one woman to another."[6] Penelope Anderson likewise challenges the exclusive focus on bodily signs of love and desire, instead claiming that Philips and her contemporary Lucy Hutchinson "insist upon the textual basis of humanist friendship's generativity."[7] Examining the conflicting obligations of female friendship, Anderson shows that textually generative same-sex alliances offer a political model that, in de-emphasizing the body and bodily reproductivity, elevates women to civic subjects. With a similar focus on discursive structures over embodied signification, Graham Hammill contends that Philips's passionate language of erotic experience shapes the political models that she envisions in her works.[8] The range of this research reveals an increasingly complex notion of female friendship that draws upon and revises diverse discursive traditions.

Given the centrality of friendship to Philips's poetry, it is perhaps unsurprising that much queer work continues to investigate its erotic and affective lineaments. Yet, as Susan Lanser's work on Sapphism demonstrates, Traub's analysis of Orinda and her Society of Friendship lays the groundwork for other kinds of queer historicist projects. As Lanser points out, Traub's analysis of Philips's homoerotic verse as "subjectivity effect" rather than "self-expression," as "erotic similitude" rather than "deeply interiorized desire," represents an important break from two trends in previous scholarship: the linking of poetry and identity, and the opposition between erotics and politics.[9] This universalizing perspective informs Lanser's recent work on the connection between the Sapphic and the modern, where "sapphic subjects function as both cause and effect of a cataclysmic shift into (an always incoherent) modern order, a slate upon which modernity wrote and rewrote itself."[10] With this connection, Lanser demonstrates that Sapphic subjectivity is a political subjectivity claimed by women who, whatever their erotic interests, produce homoerotic literary works in an act of solidarity with other women, against the masculinist heterosocial order.[11] This reconceptualization of Sapphism and Sapphic literary production, finding its fullest expression in Lanser's *The Sexuality of History,* brings into focus Philips's participation in female alliances beyond her Society of Friendship.[12]

While *The Renaissance of Lesbianism* continues to inspire and inform queer Philips scholarship and histories of sexuality more generally, it bears notice that Traub's work on the historiography of sexual identities and desires opens up further avenues of inquiry for a more capacious understanding of Philips's oeuvre. In particular, Traub attends to the problematics of methodology, responding to recent challenges to historicism's dominance in early modern studies with a call to transform notions of chronology and the epistemological grounds upon which scholars interpret the past. The central thrust of her approach has been a renewed focus on the *longue durée* in order to extend our perspective beyond the established disciplinary periods that currently organize the study of sexuality. She argues that such an approach will give us a richer understanding of sexuality precisely by framing it "*as an epistemological problem.*"[13] In "The Present Future of Lesbian Historiography," Traub uses Philips as an example of how such a perspectival shift would benefit queer historicist work: "From one set of concerns, the all-female 'Society of Friendship' formed by seventeenth-century poet Katherine Philips looks a lot like an avatar of late nineteenth-century Boston marriage; both social forms spiritualize female emotional bonds; both derive sustenance from women's intellectual capacities; both arise from within the confines of feminine domesticity; both defer to class decorum in matters of the desiring body. But from another angle—say, the freedom to advocate for female intimacy as a political alternative to patriarchal marriage—the gulf between them is profound."[14] Rather than take sex as a given object that can readily be identified and analyzed, Traub highlights the need to question how sex signifies: What counts as sex, and for whom? When do acts cross the threshold of eroticism, and who decides? This insight into "the epistemological opacity of sex"[15] offers important direction for the study of women's writing in general, and for the study of Philips more particularly.

Given the historical context within which Philips writes—a tumultuous period of political and religious upheaval—a shift in perspective that reads her as a participant in a much larger history of sexuality not only generates a richer understanding of the genealogies of lesbianism and sexual identity but also provides an opportunity for a more complex reading of the interpenetration of sexuality with other categories of historical analysis. Lanser's work on Sapphism represents one promising future trend for queer historicism. Indeed, of Lanser's trenchant essay "Mapping Sapphic Modernity," Traub writes, "Lanser offers a temporally focused synchronic analysis in the service of a diachronic one, along the way pointing to how the history of sapphism (and not just historiography) is inextricably bound up with narrative.... The effect is a careful balancing act: chronological and sequential, but neither progressive nor teleological—and about as far from hetero-reproductive as it is possible to be."[16] Andreadis's essay in this volume represents another promising trend. Deploying a transhistorical focus on the pastoral, Andreadis develops a new history of the Sapphic genre that includes not only Philips but also Aemelia Lanyer, Anne Killigrew, Christina Rosetti, H. D. (Hilda Doolittle), and Olga Broumas. Such work reveals more complex and richer interactions among marginalized voices and demonstrates their significance to cultural constructions of sexual identities and their political and historical valences.

"We may generally conclude the Marriage of a Friend to be the Funeral of a Friendship; for then all former Endearments run naturally into the Gulf of that new and strict Relation, and there, like Rivers in the Sea, they lose themselves for ever."[17] So wrote Katherine Philips in a letter to her literary friend, Sir Charles Cotterell, rejecting precisely the compromise between friendship and marriage that Cavendish's *Assaulted and Pursued Chastity* so miraculously achieved.[18] Wed at age 16 to a man of 54, Philips not only sets up an opposition between these two forms of relatedness, but does so in terms that emotionally privilege friendship (the flowing River of an Endearment) while admitting ruefully the superior social power of that strict relation, the marital gulf or sea.

Philips's radical expression of the opposed claims of friendship and marriage registers, from the vantage of historical hindsight, a huge ripple in the waters of female love and friendship. Lauded posthumously as "the Matchless Orinda" (the subtitle of the 1667 edition of her poems as well as the title of Webster Souers's biography),[19] Philips authored over 50 poems addressed to a succession of women, many of them passionate lyrics of love. Long relegated to an obscurity unknown in her lifetime, Philips has been reclaimed by feminist literary critics as an icon of seventeenth century women's writing.[20] This status is based partly on Philips's masterful appropriation and revision of masculine poetic conventions and partly on the communitarian impulse of her aesthetic practice. In the 1650s, she instituted a Society of Friendship in order to foster political, literary, aesthetic, and affective bonds among women (as well as select men). This circle of friendship (some aspects of which may have begun during her boarding school years) continued until her death in 1664. Self-consciously appropriating the imaginative resources of pastoralism, she and her coterie adopted pastoral names, wrote and circulated among themselves poetry extolling the virtues of friendship, and, in Philips's case, explored a range of intense emotions toward women.

Many scholars have attempted to define the precise nature of Philips's attachments to the various women with whom she was intimately involved, both during her adolescence and after her marriage, by analyzing the homoerotic content of her verse.[21] Although biographical criticism has predominated, critics also have demonstrated Philips's indebtedness to a discourse of classical male *amicitia,* to the genre of pastoral, and to the conventions of heterosexual love poetry, particularly the metaphysical conceits of John Donne. What is striking about all of this scholarship is that it seems to assume that no prior literary traditions of female homoeroticism existed. But Philips clearly was working within and through the tradition of *amor impossibilis* and homoerotic lament. Her attraction to pastoral was not simply a measure of her indebtedness to neoclassicism, as many critics contend, nor was it merely the means by which she merged concepts of Platonic love with heteroerotic conventions to ennoble female friendship. Rather, her appropriation of pastoral conventions interrupts and reconfigures the tradition of the *amor impossibilis,* which, from Iphis and Ianthe to *The Convent of Pleasure,* had confronted the claims of Nature while remaining caught within a marital resolution. Philips's *Poems,* published four years before *The Convent of Pleasure,* breaks the *amor impossibilis* apart into a diverse set of themes, including emotional longing, ecstasy, heartbreak, anger, bitterness, and betrayal. Central to her lyric repertoire is a homoerotic lament that focuses not on the self-evident unnaturalness of female-female desire but on the physical absence of the beloved and the inadequacies of what she calls the "rough, rude world."

Philips's translation of the *amor impossibilis* from a cry of pain about the body, desire, and Nature into a mournful negotiation of the lover's absence marks an alteration in aesthetic sensibility, strategy, and subjectivity. Cavendish's characters, for instance, are cardboard spokespersons for abstract concepts: Amity, Amour, and Sensuality (1656) operate like figures on a chessboard, and even Lady Happy (1668) functions more as an allegorical personification than a character possessing interiority. In contrast, despite her often allegorical language, Philips's lyrics of female love cut much closer to the bone. Part of the reason is her choice of genre. Like Shakespeare, Sidney, and Spenser, Philips contributed to the construction of a lyric tradition that, at least since the Romantics, has been read under the auspices of the subject: as the exemplary expression of a subject's interiority, as the authentic revelation of inward thought, and as the immediate outpouring of intimate desire. Read within these terms, the lyric tends to be viewed as a fictionalized private utterance, as soliloquy or dramatic monologue or, in the words of Virginia Jackson's critique of this concept, "privacy gone public."[22] The result is that poetic voice, persona, and author tend to be conflated at the same time that all three are sundered from history (and, thus, the "individual voice" is rendered timeless and universal).[23]

Philips's production of a compelling homoerotic subjectivity, however, is not best understood as "self-expression" at all but rather as a "subjectivity effect." I appropriate this phrase from Joel Fineman's account of Shakespearean literary subjectivity to force a wedge between Philips as author and "Philips" as lyric voice and persona.[24] Such a dissociation Philips herself would have resisted, as she was passionately invested in her literary subjectivity ("Orinda" functions within her pastoral coterie as a proper name, a passionate identification, not a pseudonym or cover). Nonetheless, this disarticulation is crucial if we are to apprehend the extent to which Philips participates in a series of conventions that precede and define the terms within which, and against which, she writes. According to Fineman's analysis of Renaissance poetry, the literary formation of the self occurs in the slippage between self-presence and representation; it is only through such slippages that the voicings of the lyric subject are interpretable as expressing a deeply interiorized desire. Although this fiction of self-presence is, in fact, predicated on loss and self-distance, it is no less powerful or constitutive for that. My appropriation of Fineman's argument is both homage and critique. For, in Fineman's relentlessly masculine and heterosexualizing account of Shakespeare, eroticism and subjectivity are always that of the male subject, whose desire is achieved only by misogynistically erecting a distance between himself and "woman," the figure who thematizes the deceptiveness of literary language. Fineman's rigid geometry of gender and sexuality, which apprehends the presence of sexuality only within the articulation of (gender) difference, necessarily elides *as sexual* Shakespeare's poems to the young man, which are judged instead as "ascetic."[25] By suggesting that Philips manipulates in her epideictic poetry the terms of similitude that Fineman sees governing Shakespeare's sonnets to the young man, I insist on the erotic power of what Paula Blank has called in another context "homopoetics."[26] Philips's love poetry attempts to articulate a homoerotic subject through the fictions and temporalities of lyric expression, deploying the lyric voice to disrupt those relations between ideology, causality, and sequence that, in the drama and prose narrative, propel the plot teleologically toward a marital conclusion. Philips bypasses the tradition of miraculous transformation (or the fortuitous replacement of a woman by her brother), crafting instead a strategy of legitimation that is at once profoundly confrontational and conventional: in addition to the idealizing similitude which she ascribes to her loving relationships, over and over again she insists that her love for other women is "innocent."

Assertions of innocence in Philips's poetry generally have been read by critics as an elevation of *lesbian* love into the spiritually lofty realm of Platonic friendship; proof positive that she did not carnally desire her friends; a phobic disavowal of the fact that she *did* desire her friends; or a strategic cover for a *lesbian* not yet ready to come out of the closet. None of these interpretations, I believe, adequately accounts for Philips's appropriation of innocence as the proper term for passion among women.

We can gain some purchase on Philips's deployment of a rhetoric of innocence by noting the way certain discriminations are negotiated in those masculine discourses of *amicitia* which Philips so deliberately regenders. The *locus classicus* for the uneasy if productive proximity of masculine friendship to eroticism in the early modern era is Michel de Montaigne's "De l'amitié."[27] Eulogizing with a keen sense of loss his intense friendship with Étienne de La Boëtie, Montaigne idealizes the bonds of sympathy and equality among men. But while drawing on a web of classical allusion, Montaigne nonetheless distinguishes his concept of *amitié* from "that alternative licence of the Greeks" which "is rightly abhorrent to our manners; [C] moreover since as they practised it it required a great disparity of age and divergence of favours between the lovers, it did not correspond either to that perfect union and congruity which we are seeking here" (210). The distance Montaigne would erect between his own pure, equal love and that of the licentious and hierarchical Greeks, however, does little to dispel the erotic force animating those passages articulated through somatic metaphors, as when Montaigne describes how "the same affection [was] revealed each to each other right down to the very entrails," or through the use of penetrative tropes:

> This friendship has had no ideal to follow other than itself; no comparison but with itself. [A] There is no one particular consideration—nor two nor three nor four nor a thousand of them—but rather some inexplicable quintessence of them all mixed up together which, having captured my will, brought it to plunge into his and lose itself [C] and which, having captured his will, brought it to plunge and lose itself in mine with an equal hunger and emulation. [A] I say "lose myself" in very truth; we kept nothing back for ourselves: nothing was his or mine. (212–13)

Despite Montaigne's own effort to delineate between the passion of men for women (which he describes as "active, sharp and keen"; "rash...fickle, fluctuating and variable") and the love of men for men (a "general universal warmth, temperate moreover and smooth, a warmth which is constant and at rest, all gentleness and evenness, having nothing sharp nor keen"), the salient difference seems to be less the gender of the beloved object than the relative state of ease experienced by the desiring subject (209). For as soon as "sexual love," which is but "a mad craving for something which escapes us," "enters the territory of friendship (where wills work together, that is) it languishes and grows faint. To enjoy it is to lose it; its end is in the body and therefore subject to satiety. Friendship, on the contrary, is enjoyed in proportion to our desire: since it is a matter of the mind, with our souls being purified by practising it, it can spring forth, be nourished and grow only when enjoyed" (209). In Montaigne's ecology of desire, it is less that male-male love is not of the body than that male-female love is not of the mind. Linking friendship to a desire that can never be sated, that is nourished and grows through its enjoyment, Montaigne's metaphors for male friendship thoroughly eroticize it.

Such eroticized friendship is, as Alan Bray's *The Friend* (2003) makes clear, one aspect of a widespread network of affects and obligations among men. Tracing the rituals of sworn brotherhood through a variety of medieval and early modern documents and artifacts, Bray provides an archaeology of masculine friendship that demonstrates its utility to other social institutions, including the family. Indeed, Bray's research suggests that the early modern family, rather than providing the only basis of social cohesion, subsists within larger structures of relation, including the "voluntary kinship" of intimate male friends.

Both the discourse of *amicitia* and the practices of voluntary kinship were predominantly masculine prerogatives. Montaigne provides one of the most potent ideological expressions of female insufficiency in this regard:

> women are in truth not normally capable of responding to such familiarity and mutual confidence as sustain that holy bond of friendship, nor do their souls seem firm enough to withstand the clasp of a knot so lasting and so tightly drawn. And indeed if it were not for that, if it were possible to fashion such a relationship, willing and free, in which not only the souls had this full enjoyment but in which the bodies too shared in the union—[C] where the whole human being was involved—it is certain [A] that the loving-friendship would be more full and more abundant. But there is no example yet of woman attaining to it [C] and by the common agreement of the Ancient schools of philosophy she is excluded from it. (210)

But women could be friends—not least of which among themselves. They formed their own alliances among kinswomen, regularly visited with neighbors, and pursued long-distance epistolary correspondences.[28] Yet, there was little public discourse about the virtues and possibilities of friendship between women, and what discourse did exist had none of the elevated social standing accorded to Montaigne's essays.[29] Nor did female friendship function as effectively as did men's to create and maintain legal, economic, and familial advantages. In this context, women's friendships were unmarked, naturalized, as little subject to scrutiny as to celebration.

It is of no little import, then, that Katherine Philips laid explicit claim, in life as in poetry, to both *amicitia* and voluntary kinship in the mid-seventeenth century. Indeed, her life expresses the tension between submission to dynastic marriage (undertaken for the sake of kinship, politics, religion, wealth) and the quest for personal happiness which men were licensed to find outside of the nuclear family. In this sense, Philips's Society of Friendship functioned as an alternative form of voluntary kinship.[30] There is no question that Philips felt herself to be kin to Anne Owen (the "Lucasia" of her poetry): she commemorated the deaths of Owen family members in eulogies; she spent a full year away from her husband while accompanying the newly married Anne Owen, Lady Dungannon, to Ireland; and when she wrote a poem about the burial place of her husband's ancestors, "Wiston Vault," it is not her anticipated inclusion in her husband's patrimony that she versifies, but the more lasting "monument" provided by Lucasia's love:

> But after death too I would be alive,
> And shall, if my *Lucasia* do, survive.
> I quit these pomps of Death, and am content,
> Having her heart to be my Monument:
> Though ne'er Stone to me, 'twill Stone for me prove,
> By the peculiar miracles of Love.
> There I'll Inscription have which no Tomb gives,
> Not, *Here Orinda lies,* but, *Here she lives.*[31] (15–22)

Just as the desire that friendship could be on equal par with marriage is demonstrated throughout her life, so too Montaigne's trope of souls "mingled and confounded in so universal a blending that they efface the seam which joins them together" (211–12) is adopted by Philips as her signature *cri de coeur*. By deploying an idiom of idealized *amicitia* heretofore reserved for men, Philips not only usurps some of that tradition's symbolic capital but also makes manifest the homoerotic potential lodged within other representations of chaste female friendship from the late sixteenth through the late seventeenth century.[32]

When literary critics move beyond the issue of whether Philips's oeuvre is legitimately viewed as homoerotic, they tend to focus on the emotional affects expressed in her poems. Harriette Andreadis, for instance, defines Philips's "Sapphic platonics" via poems that celebrate the ecstatic merger of the beloved with the self. Focused on the issue of power relations, Elaine Hobby interprets certain poems as expressing sadomasochistic desire. Carol Barash and Elizabeth Wahl implicitly mediate between these views when they argue that a tension emerges in Philips's poetry between, in the words of Wahl, an "abstract or 'programmatic' rhetoric of friendship that Philips uses to describe an egalitarian relationship of mutual sympathy and a mystic transformation of two selves into one soul and a more 'courtly' rhetorical strain in which she adopts the hierarchical relation between a male suitor addressing his female beloved to woo a particular woman in the name of friendship."[33] Rather than focus on the two poetic modes—Platonism and courtly love—within which Philips worked, or the two erotic stances—merger and aggression—authorized by these modes, my strategy is to read Philips's thematizations of Nature from a *lesbian*-affirmative perspective. How does Nature look, even in those poems not addressed to the female beloved, when viewed from the perspective of someone whose desires have been, in the prior literary tradition, defined as outside or against it?

Philips typically invokes Nature via pastoral associations, as in her meditation on the moment of separation, "Lucasia, Rosania, and Orinda parting at a Fountain, July 1663":

> Here, here are our enjoyments done,
> And since the Love and Grief we wear
> Forbids us either word or tear,
> And Art wants here expression,
> See Nature furnish us with one. (1–5)

Forbidden by love and grief to cry or speak their sorrow, the women appropriate the image of the pastoral fountain nymph whom Nature has kindly provided to mimetically enact their grief:

> The kind and mournful Nimph which here
> Inhabits in her humble Cells,
> No longer her own sorrow tells,
> Nor for it now concern'd appears,
> But for our parting sheds these tears. (6–10)

Her own concerns forgotten, the fountain nymph sheds watery tears *for them;* her sorrow articulates and authorizes their grief. With this conceit of mutual identification, "Orinda" mediates the pain of parting by forging a link between the pastoral victims of classical tales—Iphis, Calisto, Diana's nymphs—and the losses felt within her own loving circle.

Whereas here Orinda authorizes her emotional affects by placing them comfortably within a homoerotic pastoral tradition, in "To my Lucasia," a poem that repudiates the new empirical philosophy for its mechanistic understanding of the universe, she more directly contests the putative priority of Nature:

> he
> That Nature's harmony intire would see,
> Must search agreeing Souls, sit down and view
> How sweet the mixture is, how full, how true;
> By what soft touches Spirits greet and kiss,
> And in each other can complete their bliss. (7–12)

Invited to witness "Nature's harmony intire," the male reader is instructed to search "agreeing Souls." He should "sit down and view" female spirits greeting and kissing, touching softly and mixing sweetly. Mildly voyeuristic, this poem echoes the sensual intimacies enjoyed in Cavendish's convent of pleasure as it transports the loving couple to a *locus amoenus;* but with complete "bliss" offered as the epitome of Nature's "harmony intire," the distance could not be greater from Lady Happy's resigned tautology, "Nature is Nature."

Indeed, in other poems Philips makes clear that Nature is something to be manipulated. In "To Mr. Henry Lawes," Philips ends her encomium to the man who set her and other poets' verses to music by invoking his power over Nature:

> Live then, great Soul of Nature, to asswage
> The savage dulness of this sullen Age.
> Charm us to Sense; for though Experience fail,
> And Reason too, thy Numbers may prevail.
> Then, like those Ancients, strike, and so command
> All Nature to obey thy gen'rous hand.

None will resist, but such who needs will be
More stupid than a Stone, a Fish, a Tree.
Be it thy care our Age to new-create:
What built a World, may sure repair a State. (31–40)

Philips's reformulation of Nature, I want to suggest, is an integral part of a poetic stance that, at least in these poems, conflates rather than separates the spiritual and the bodily. Although some of Philips's poems assume and work within the opposition between the Platonic and the courtly, the spiritual and the fleshly, other poems rhetorically merge these affective registers. In these latter poems, the aim is not to elevate the spiritual in a transcendence of the body, but to reject the opposition. Orinda, for instance, mediates both the meaning of her desire and the anguish of parting from her beloved through the willful assertion of spiritual merger. Often elegiac, these poems seek to overcome the absence and loss of the beloved's presence through a determined negation of difference and distance. "To Mrs. M. A. at Parting," for instance, begins with the disclosure:

I have examin'd and do find,
Of all that favour me,
There's none I grieve to leave behind
But only only thee.
To part with thee I needs must die,
Could parting sep'rate thee and I. (1–6)

The point, of course, is that parting cannot separate her from Mary Aubrey (Rosania), for their "mingled Souls are grown / To such acquaintance... That each is in the Union lost" (13–14, 18), a spiritual unification so extraordinary that it will "teach the World new Love" and "Redeem the Age and Sex" (50–51). Anyone who thinks that women are inferior to men in performing the rites of friendship will be proved wrong.

Nonetheless, "the tedious smart / Of absent Friendship" is, in "Parting with Lucasia: A Song," a rather more physical pang (9–10). What's more, "absent Friendship" is the victim, not of Nature but necessity:

Yet I must go: we will submit,
    And so our own Disposers be;
For while we nobly suffer it,
    We triumph o're Necessity. (13–16)

Having dutifully performed the rites of separation—"that rigid thing / Which makes Spectators think we part" (1–2)—but in reality having triumphed over physical absence through the mingling of souls, these beloved friends look forward to a future meeting:

Nay then to meet we may conclude,
    And all Obstructions overthrow,
Since we our Passion have subdu'd,
    Which is the strongest thing I know. (21–24)

Structured by an enabling paradox, this poem implies that even as their passion is suppressed, it overcomes all obstacles. Yet sometimes Orinda's passion cannot be subdued, and we gain a glimpse of the effort expended in the attempt. As she says in "To my Lucasia,"

But Bodies move in time, and so must Minds;
And though th'attempt no easie progress finds,
Yet quit me not, lest I should desp'rate grow,
And to such Friendship adde some Patience now. (23–26)

Asking for Lucasia's patience as she attempts to control her feelings, Orinda places herself in the position of supplicant, Lucasia in the position of power. Indeed, the absence of Lucasia calls forth a lament that draws all its mournful force from Orinda's utter dependence on the love object. In "Orinda to Lucasia parting October 1661. at London," she bids her love good-bye: "Adieu, dear object of my Love's excess, / And with thee all my hopes of happiness" (1–2). Just as unrestrained and despairing is the epideictic "Orinda to Lucasia," which, after a stanza based on the conventional conceit of the sun's necessity to the natural world, ventures a hyperbolic comparison:

Thou my *Lucasia* art far more to me,
Than he to all the under-world can be;
    From thee I've heat and light,
    Thy absence makes my night.

But ah! my Friend, it now grows very long,
The sadness weighty, and the darkness strong:
    My tears (its dew) dwell on my cheeks,
    And still my heart thy dawning seeks,
And to thee mournfully it cries,
    That if too long I wait,
    Ev'n thou may'st come too late,
And not restore my life, but close my eyes. (13–24)

Becoming the sorrowful nymph of the fountain, Orinda tearfully grieves that the "heat and light" she derives from Lucasia's presence are the Nature she needs: the "dawning" that her "heart" "seeks" in a love melancholy that threatens her very life.

By the use of such conceits, Orinda appropriates and reconstitutes the image of Nature bequeathed to her by the tradition of homoerotic lament: no longer the taboo forbidding female love or the ground against which perversion is defined, Nature becomes the *means* of homoerotic expression. Inverting the terms of this tradition, Orinda positions Nature as fully *continuous* with female desire, a continuity intensified by Philips's use of images of pastoral retreat as the proper home for passionate women. What women alone together possess, she makes clear in "To Mrs. M. Awbrey," is precisely what the "factious World" has "lost":

Let the dull World alone to talk and fight,
And with their vast Ambitions Nature fright;
Let them despise so Innocent a flame,
While Envy, Pride and Faction play their game:
But we by Love sublim'd so high shall rise,
To pity Kings, and Conquerours despise,
Since we that Sacred Union have engrost,
Which they and all the factious World have lost. (15–22)

Proceeding by a series of oppositions—the dull, factious World versus frightened Nature; vast Ambitions versus innocent Flame; Envy, Pride, and Faction versus Love—Orinda aligns female-female love with a frightened but innocent Nature while aggressively elevating the "Sacred Union" of women above the kings she pities and the conquerors she despises. Blaming men for the loss of her royalist World, she evinces a tone of condescension and denial that is amplified in "A Retir'd Friendship. To Ardelia," a lyric that disdains "the boisterous World" (34), confident that the pleasures enjoyed in the all-female seclusion of a "Bower" is "what Princes wish in vain" (1, 36). As the salvific antidote to what she repeatedly calls the "rough, rude world" and the "dull angry world,"[34] Philips's pastoralism echoes the sentiments of those cavalier poets who, as Warren Chernaik remarks, were "constantly drawing magic circles that will shut the world out, seeking to find an autonomous realm of love and art, a court immune to change."[35] But unlike that of the cavaliers', Philips's retreat is exclusively female; and like the representations of Diana's virgin circle, the pleasures of Orinda's conclave are repeatedly contrasted to the violent, intemperate, and phallic world of men. Indeed, in her "Articles of Friendship," Philips appropriates from a "Goddesse" (6) the power to "perform the rite" (5) of friendship, which is explicitly compared to the "knitting together" or "conjugiam" of marriage:

> The Soules which vertu hath made fitt
> Do of themselves incline to knitt;
> Yet wedlock having priests, allow
> That I be friendships Flamen now. (1–4)

The rite which she performs is not only "a simulacrum of holy wedlock,"[36] but a repetition of Diana's injunction to her coupled nymphs: "If you these terms do disapprove, / Ye cannot, or ye will not love. But if ye like these lovely bands, / With them join hearts, & lips, & hands!" (37–40).

As Carol Barash argues, Philips's love poetry, especially her poetry of retreat, is embedded in the political turmoil of mid-century England: "Orinda's Society of Friendship is not merely about community among women, but also about how, through the 'mutual love' of friends, one can soar into heaven with one's political allies, leaving one's opponents in the dust."[37] Barash provides a fascinating account of the changes in Philips's love poetry as the political climate altered. Prior to the Restoration, Charles I functions as "the absent third party in these poems, making them not only about the relationship between Orinda and Lucasia, but also about their mutual longing for the material presence of the king."[38] After the Restoration, "the relationship between Orinda and Lucasia comes to be situated more specifically in relation to literal marriage. Lacking a referent outside the women themselves, friendship, as symbol, loses its mystical potential. In this context, the two women's friendship proves a real—indeed, a sexual—threat."[39] Without a masculine and royalist third term to mediate their intimacy, the meaning of their love is made newly subject to suspicion and condemnation.

For Barash, the restored monarch contextualizes this change. But as I have argued, other midcentury phenomena had a significant impact on female-female eroticism as well, particularly the ideology of domestic heterosexuality.[40] Changes at the level of patriarchal alliance directly and recursively pressured the terms of female homoeroticism. Once friendship becomes a goal of marriage for men and women, female friendship begins to look a lot like companionate marriage. At the same time, when female-female love becomes, as I've argued, increasingly available as an imaginative and social reality, the burden on women *to choose* to bond with men increases.[41] It is in the context of this amplified discourse on female choices that I suggest we read Orinda's repeated assertions of innocence. For instance, in "Friendship in Emblem, or the Seal. To my dearest Lucasia," Orinda dissociates the heart from the pull of "lower ends":

> The Hearts are free from lower ends,
> For each point to the other tends.
>
> They flame, 'tis true, and several wayes,
> But still those Flames do so much raise,
> That while to either they incline
> They yet are noble and divine. (11–16)

Self-consciously acknowledging the presence of erotic heat, admitting that their hearts are aflame and that these flames move in "*several* wayes," this poem nonetheless refutes the notion that such flames are anything but "noble and divine." Their nobility depends, I believe, not on their dissociation from erotic passion, but from a studied awareness of passion's proper end: as in companionate marriage, erotic love should be selfless, directed toward the other, and hence ultimately inclined heavenward.

Such sentiments are reiterated in "To my Lucasia, in defense of declared friendship," wherein Orinda figures the body as the necessary site of merger she desires. "O My *Lucasia,* let us speak our Love" (1) the poem exultantly begins, moving through a description of a friendship that would fail to claim enough of its due:

> If this be all our Friendship does design,
> We covet not enjoyment then, but power:
> To our Opinion we our Bliss confine,
> And love to have, but not to smell, the flower. (17–20)

The wish to inhale rather than simply hold the flower, to experience its full promise of "enjoyment" and break out of that which would "confine" "our Bliss" is followed by an extended simile that rewrites, in the name of pleasure, Philips's imagery of the victory of marriage over friendship:

> And as a River, when it once hath paid
> The tribute which it to the Ocean owes
> stops not but turns, and having curl'd and play'd
> On its own waves, the shore it overflows. (41–44)

Materializing female passion as an ever-swirling wave, curling and playing on and around itself, Orinda then appropriates this physical image of self-reflexive pleasure to describe the amorous soul:

> So the Soul's motion does not end in bliss,
> But on her self she scatters and dilates,
> And on the Object doubles till by this
> She finds new joys which that reflux creates. (45–48)

The soul's motion does not, and has no, end; rather, "she" continually scatters and dilates, both on herself and on the "Object." This process of "reflux creates" "new joys," which the loving soul then "finds." Such joys cannot be "contained" by the Soul, however, and the poem returns to the metaphors of ear and speech that it has worked throughout:

But then because it cannot all contain,
 It seeks a vent by telling the glad news,
First to the Heart which did its joys obtain,
 Then to the Heart which did those joys produce. (49–52)

Speaking first to oneself and then to the beloved, the Soul must use a "vent"—or, as she says in the eighth stanza, since the Soul is imprisoned by the Flesh, "There's no way left that bondage to controul, / But to convey transactions through the Ear" (31–32).

The erotic imagery of this poem is simultaneously atemporal and spatially incontinent. Able to overflow boundaries, desire is figured in the humoral terms of female orgasm: a dilation, swirling, and scattering of fluids. Yet such erotic imagery is not always without ambivalence for Philips. As Wahl argues, "As much as Philips tries to limit or deny any connection between her love for Lucasia and the bodies through which that attraction is mediated, her recourse to a rhetoric of transcendence continually finds its spiritual images contaminated by erotic, carnal resonances that reinforce the reader's sense that Philips cannot exclude the physical world from her desire to create a union of hearts and minds, and on some level may not even wish to."[42] Barash, likewise, reminds us that the terms of female friendship were socially contested, that Philips felt the need to reassert the innocence of her passion, and that "Against Pleasure" (set to music and appearing in many manuscript miscellanies) is "an indictment of Orinda's desire for Lucasia as part of what she calls the 'fruit of *Sodom*' ":

For by our Pleasures we are cloy'd,
 And so Desire is done;
Or else, like Rivers, they make wide
 The Channel where they run. (13–16)

Suggesting that " 'Rivers' enlarging the 'Channel where they run' enact female ejaculation, as if desire, whether admitted or not, becomes overpowering liquid, like semen," Barash notes Philips's use of similar images in many other poems.[43]

How, given the repeated use of such erotic imagery, do we interpret Philips's assertions of innocence? Wahl argues that "the very overdetermination of these qualities of 'innocence' and 'transparency' paradoxically contributes to the reader's sense that Philips does feel that she has something to hide and betrays her anxiety that such relations might be viewed as morally or sexually suspect despite all her protestations to the contrary."[44] Barash, while suggesting that the language of politics makes "possible the innocently expressive language of heroic women," also acknowledges that there is an ongoing struggle here: "Philips resolves her relationship with [Anne] Owen by making the terms of its 'Innocence' explicit—it is friendship not idolatry, religious duty not pagan sensuality. But the 'funeral of Friendship' happens no more permanently in *Poems* (1664) than it did in fact. As in the manuscript version of the relationship, Lucasia returns, and the 'Innocence' of the love between the two women must be 'declared' yet again." "Why," Barash asks, "does Philips insist upon this repetition of elegies for friendship—elegies which refuse to be elegies because their object will not die or disappear?"[45]

The answer, it seems to me, is that Philips's professions of innocence draw from and manipulate prior conventions of chaste female intimacy even as they reformulate Nature to newly authorize such bonds. It thus is a mistake to read Philips's expressions of innocence solely in terms of her own struggle to overcome erotic feelings or as part of a strategy of coding, masking, or disguising a desire that is not yet ready to "come out of the closet."[46] Read in the context of the literary traditions and historical discourses of eroticism analyzed throughout *The Renaissance of Lesbianism in Early Modern England,* Philips's recourse to innocence is apprehensible neither as the "truth" of her closeted desire nor as proof of her disinterest in genital contact. Rather, innocence is the historically accurate word that Philips appropriates from the literary heritage of chaste femme love. It is the same innocence that had been conferred regularly onto such Shakespearean characters as Helena and Hermia (*A Midsummer Night's Dream*), Rosalind and Celia (*As You Like It*), Emilia and Flavina (*The Two Noble Kinsmen*). The difference, however, is that Philips attributes this innocence not to adolescent "maids," but to mature, even married, women. In addition, having silently absented men (and in large part patriarchal marriage) from her representation of loving friendship, Philips's consistent imagery of the "rough, rude world" suggests that the world of men is one of intrusion, intemperance, and conflict, both political and sexual. In contrast, the vision of intimacy in her verse is one in which relationships are governed—indeed, "governed" is precisely the word, as we can see the careful effort involved in formalizing female relations through ritual—by the desire (whether it is fulfilled or not) for an eroticized merger of body and soul. Philips's poetry, indebted as it is to a prior tradition of chaste female friendship—including the *amor impossibilis,* the homoerotic lament, and the elegiac pastoralism of Renaissance drama—simultaneously registers, as Wahl and Barash suggest, changed social conditions. As such, the verse of Philips functions as a symptomatic break: between the Renaissance discourse of chaste, innocuous insignificance, on the one hand, and the increasingly public discourse of illicit desire that carries with it the stigma of significance, on the other.[47]

9 ❖ The Body of the Friend and the Woman Writer

Katherine Philips's Absence from Alan Bray's *The Friend*

Lorna Hutson

Editors' Note

One of the hallmarks of feminist scholarship—and of the various modes of cultural studies more generally—is a concern with the construction of historical narrative. Recognizing the ideological nature of history, such scholarship intervenes in the hegemonic narratives that have shaped our cultural identities by exposing gaps and uncovering traces of marginalized, suppressed, and obscured voices. Such is the case with Lorna Hutson's "The Body of the Friend and the Woman Writer: Katherine Philips's Absence from Alan Bray's *The Friend* (2003)," an essay that re-examines the significance of the gendered and sexed body in early modern discourses of friendship.

Emerging from the Perdita-sponsored "Still Kissing the Rod?" conference held at St. Hilda's College, Oxford, in 2005, Hutson's essay was first published in a special 2007 issue of *Women's Writing,* edited by conference organizers Elizabeth Clarke and Lynn

Robson.[1] In her work, Hutson intervenes in critical debates about the cultural significance of ethical (male) friendship by articulating the disruptive effects of its appropriation by women writers. She begins from the fact of Philips's omission from Alan Bray's posthumously published *The Friend,* a gendered aporia that Bray himself acknowledges by explicitly noting the absence of women as such from the history he was attempting to articulate.[2] In the space of this absence, Hutson asks "how [Bray's] persuasive narrative of radical change in the meaning of the body as signifier of (male) friendship might prompt a rethinking of the relation of embodiment to the cultural capital of friendship in seventeenth-century women's writing, as exemplified by Katherine Philips." In other words, did embodied signs of friendship—the kiss, the embrace, the sharing of intimate spaces—carry cultural capital for women, as Bray's work shows they did for men?

Hutson's answer, in brief, is that they did not. The bold subversion of Philips's poetry lies not in its appropriation of the body as a signifier for women's intimacy, but in its witty and erotic play with the language of *amicitia,* the language that for centuries endowed male intimacy with political prestige. In making this argument, Hutson also engages with Valerie Traub, whose pioneering book, *The Renaissance of Lesbianism in Early Modern England,* acknowledges "a structural affinity to the work of Alan Bray."[3] Whereas Traub, in her review of *The Friend,* maintains that Bray's methodology has useful applications for studies of female friendship, Hutson asserts that Philips cannot be assimilated uncritically into Bray's thesis. Simply adapting his analysis of the changing significance of the body as a site of intimacy between men to the experiences of women takes for granted that the body of the female friend could, in fact, signify publicly or ethically.[4] In actuality, as Hutson observes, "women's friendships tended to lack a 'formal and objective character,' or a publicly acknowledged ethical dimension and social and familial efficacy." The scandal of Philips's poems, then, derives primarily not from a paradigmatic shift in the meanings of bodily intimacy, as argued by Traub in a chapter of *The Renaissance of Lesbianism* excerpted in the present volume. Rather, her "very appropriation in writing of the ethical discourse, the witty casuistry of friendship," serves notice both of a transformation in the nature of friendship as such and the ethical and political work of friendship within early modern culture.[5] Answering Kate Lilley's call "to take seriously the erotics of *writing*," Hutson's essay proposes a history of female friendship and female-female intimacy that does not belong in, except perhaps to unsettle, the history of male embodiment advanced in Bray's *The Friend*; in effect, Hutson "question[s] whether Bray's history of the embodiment of male friendship is at all relevant to a history of female-female intimacy."[6]

The languages of friendship in early modernity possessed a long and distinguished pedigree, underwriting ideas of individual and civic virtue. So within the historical contexts of the English revolution and seventeenth century contract theory, the disruptive effects of Philips's appropriation become all the more visible and significant: in laying claim to female friendship's ethical dimension, Philips's poems also posit a libidinal economy of erotic and political obligation between women, bringing women into the political sphere as active participants. Hutson's work, then, serves as an important touchstone within current scholarship on friendship and its cultural-political meanings, and not least for its powerful demonstration of the importance of Philips herself to seventeenth century understandings of friendship. One such work is *Discourses and Representations of Friendship in Early Modern Europe, 1500–1700*, a volume edited by Hutson, Daniel T. Lochman, and Maritere López, which "lay[s] the groundwork for a taxonomy of the transformations of friendship discourse in Western Europe and its overlap with emergent views of the relationship of the self to individuals, classes, social institutions, and the state."[7] In her contribution to this volume, Penelope Anderson demonstrates how Philips's divergence from the traditional model of *amicitia* provides a salient political model for the monarchy that includes women as civic subjects.[8] For Philips, Anderson argues, the incorporation of an ethics of clemency offers the possibility to reconcile the conflicting obligations that arise in turbulent times, precisely such as those of the civil wars, Interregnum, and Restoration. Expanding this argument in her 2012 volume, *Friendship's Shadows: Women's Friendship and the Politics of Betrayal in England, 1640–1705,* Anderson crystalizes Philips's investment in what Melissa Sanchez refers to as "the sexual dimension of politics."[9] Indeed, the same-sex affective model we find in Philips's poetry serves as an alternative to the "operative tropes of late sixteenth-century discourse—Foxean martyrdom and Petrarchan courtship—[that] continued to shape the concepts of sovereignty and obedience in the seventeenth century."[10]

Other studies of the intersection of erotics and politics in Philips's friendship poems indicate a decisive break from the heretofore standard critical practice of bifurcating erotics and politics, examining one at the expense of the other. For example, Catharine Gray argues that Philips's love poems to women are at once "private expressions of homoerotic desire" and "public performance[s] of cross-gender identification...that helped create an elite culture of heterosocial collectivity opposed to Parliamentary rule."[11] Harriette Andreadis similarly addresses the ways in which Philips's appropriation of friendship forges heterosocial sociofamilial networks with men such as Sir Charles Cotterell, whereas Graham Hammill submits that Philips's use of political models in her homoerotic verse "replac[es] the model of erotic friendship based on the monarch's rights over life and death...with a model of erotic self-governance whose norms are embodied by a natural order of harmony and unity."[12] Hence, while certain critics continue to assert the importance of prising apart erotic and political discourse, especially when considering the philosophical traditions informing Philips's corpus, this critical tendency has been counterbalanced by scholarly work attentive to intersections and consonances.[13]

Notably, Philips figures prominently in five of the nine essays appearing in "Still Kissing the Rod?"—in discussions of female friendship, the literary canon, women's literary capital, women and classical philosophy, and ideas of "public" and "private."[14] If not an official organizing principle of the volume, Philips and her milieu nonetheless emerge as a rich cultural field, enabling contacts and convergences that have only begun to be excavated. These interventions, therefore, demonstrate that while the recovery and inclusion of diverse female voices remains a crucial task for future studies of early modern women's writing, further research on canonical women writers, including Philips, promises to yield other insights.

The question I want to explore here is not a new one. Central to the work of recovering early modern women's writing, and to our reflections on the effects of that work over the past 20 years, has always been the question of whether its results can be absorbed into existing narratives of literary and cultural history, or whether the attempt to include women's writing is more disruptive, requiring us to rethink not only the more orthodox narratives and periodizations of history, but their "oppositional" variants as well. The woman writer I want to consider as perhaps having this disruptive potential is Katherine Philips (1632–64). Philips is not, of course, obscure to those interested in women's writing of the early modern period. By comparison with some of the seventeenth century writings in manuscript now more widely known as a result of the Perdita Project, Philips's work can be considered to be part of a "canon" of early modern writing by women in English. Scholars of the period eagerly await the appearance of Philips's work in an authoritative edition by Elizabeth Hageman, the progress of which was the subject of Hageman's inspiring opening plenary at the "Still Kissing the Rod?" conference in July 2005.[15] Excellent articles and chapters on questions of politics and sexuality in Philips's poetry by Carol Barash, Elizabeth Wahl, James Loxley, Kate Lilley, and Valerie Traub have appeared, adding to and frequently transforming earlier exploratory feminist work, and immeasurably enriching the experience of teaching Philips at graduate or undergraduate level.[16]

What I want to do in this essay is not to offer a new reading of Philips, but to point to the meaning of her omission from a recent and important intervention in the histories of friendship and sexuality by the late Alan Bray. The omission is a significant one because it arguably calls into question the periodization and narrative coherence—at least for women—of the story of friendship Bray sought to tell. Nevertheless, Bray's narrative has been absorbed into recent and illuminating criticism of Philips herself, a fact that again raises further interesting questions. I should say at the outset that I emphatically don't want, in drawing attention to the omission of Philips from Bray's book, to seem to be berating Alan Bray himself, who was nothing if not conscious of the gender asymmetry of the history of friendship he was writing. ("There is no more revealing question," he wrote, "about the friendship of traditional society than to ask how it encompassed women.")[17] Rather, I want to reopen, in the spirit of inquiry and dialogue on these issues, which Bray himself did so much to foster, the question of how his persuasive narrative of radical change in the meaning of the body as signifier of (male) friendship might prompt a rethinking of the relation of embodiment to the cultural capital of friendship in seventeenth century women's writing, as exemplified by Katherine Philips.

Historical narratives have had exceptional explanatory force in gay and lesbian studies, where so much has been, and continues to be, at stake in the question of understanding the conditions under which forms of behavior are legitimized or proscribed, rendered intelligible or anathematized, codified as sins or crimes or conceived as "case histories" in medical and psychoanalytic discourse. Alan Bray's contribution to the question of periodization in the history of male homosexuality has been enormously influential. In *Homosexuality in Renaissance England,* Bray argues that the uncompromising and anathematic language of sodomy officially applied to same-sex desire in the sixteenth century did not easily align with people's perception of their own ordinary relations and acts.[18] The first signs of a change, a move toward a more systematic and secular legal persecution of something like a modern "homosexual identity" took place in the last quarter of the seventeenth century with the emergence of a visible sexual subculture in the form of the so-called molly-houses. Bray's articulation of this shift proved influential, both for social histories of sexuality and for literary criticism: Eve Sedgwick has based two books on the argument, indebted to Bray, that post-Romantic homosociality is homophobically structured, and Jonathan Goldberg acknowledges in the introduction to *Queering the Renaissance* that Bray's *Homosexuality in Renaissance England* remained "the groundbreaking and unsurpassed historical investigation" for any history of sexuality in the period.[19]

In a review of Bray's posthumous *The Friend,* however, Valerie Traub suggests that we risk missing what is most analytically generative about Bray's methodology and his approach if we focus only on his reconfiguring of the narrative of the emergence of a homosexual identity.[20] She has, rather, identified as the most unsettling and productive characteristic of Bray's work his "determined ambivalence regarding the disciplinary field of sexual studies," which prompts him to reject "the very idea of an autonomous field of erotic relations" in the premodern period.[21] Bray's alertness to the hermeneutic possibilities of traces of intimacy in the past has always gone with an immense caution about assigning sexual meanings to that intimacy. In his work since *Homosexuality in Renaissance England,* the emphasis has indeed been arguably less concerned with a narrative than with exploring an interpretative *tension* of the early modern period: the tension between the body as public and prestigious signifier of the most idealized, even sacred meanings of friendship between men and the openness of the very same signifier to the interpretation of the forbidden intimacy damned in Christian discourse as sodomy. Bray outlines this tension in his 1990 "Homosexuality and the Signs of Male Friendship in Elizabethan England."[22] His posthumously published book-length study *The Friend,* moreover, shows that his research since 1990 involved expanding the implications of this interpretative tension into the historical account of a "seismic change" in meanings attached to bodily intimacy between friends.[23]

The Friend traces a narrative of the gradual disarticulation of spiritual and social meanings attaching to the body's participation in medieval and early modern rituals of friendship and voluntary kinship. The book opens by considering the sworn, or "wedded," brotherhood prominent in the funeral monuments, chronicles, and romances of the fourteenth and fifteenth centuries in England, arguing that it carried a "formal and objective character" that made its bodily intimacy as socially visible and important as that other form of voluntary kinship, marriage, with which it was perfectly compatible.[24] Bray's study then goes on to show that recognition once accorded to such physical intimacy as a sign of oath-bound, voluntary kinship gradually became unintelligible and even scandalous as friendship was increasingly, in modern civil society, relegated to the private world of the affections. The ritual contexts in which public expression of same-sex intimacy signified as both ethical and culturally prestigious themselves fell into disuse: these had included Christian rites of peacemaking, reconciliation and kinship formation, the ritual or conventional language of intimacy and desire in familiar correspondence, and the architectural topography which made intimacy a public sign of status and favor in the commensality and shared beds of the great households of the medieval and early modern periods. Where hierarchical rituals of kinship had worked, within the structure of the traditional household and its affinity, to "embed the family, in the more narrow sense of a group of parents, within a wider and overlapping network of *friendship,*" social developments in the late seventeenth and early eighteenth century isolated the relation between husband and wife as a kind of affective monopoly within a world of contractual relations. The consequence, Bray argues, was that bodily intimacy between friends lost its capacity to signify socially and ethically, and placed "on the sexual bond between husband and wife a burden of social meaning that before it had not been required to carry alone."[25]

There is, however, continuity between Bray's *Homosexuality in Renaissance England* and the narrative of *The Friend* insofar as each identifies the same historical moment—the turn of the seventeenth century—as a paradigm shift. In *The Friend,* Bray identifies John Locke's abstraction of the notion of "society" with the historical moment specified in his earlier work, at which "the images of the masculine 'sodomite' lost the alien associations that had kept it at such a distance from an image that might normally apply to oneself, to one's neighbour or one's friend."[26] Public signs of friendship and kinship—the kiss, for example, which in ecclesiastical and other ritual settings symbolized peace and being in charity with neighbors and allies—became open to scandalous interpretation. Bray cites an instance in 1749 of an Englishman expressing distaste at the thought of two men kissing one another. Examples could be multiplied: "I never knew any good coming of one Fellow's beslavering another," comments a gentleman rake on seeing his male friends embrace in Benjamin Hoadly's mid-eighteenth century play *The Suspicious Husband.*[27]

The question of how Bray's history of the disembodiment of the cultural prestige accorded to male friendship might relate to women is complicated. The general trajectory of Bray's narrative, emphasized by his reliance on historians who encourage a nostalgia for the sociability of "traditional" Catholicism such as John Bossy and Eamon Duffy, suggests that things got worse as the religious significance of bodily presence—in the Eucharist, in the kiss of peace, in purgatorial time-space beyond the grave—came to be etiolated. However, he can offer little evidence of a female counterpart to the culturally prestigious sworn, or "wedded," brotherhood of the medieval period.[28] Bray later identifies same-sex "weddings" between women in the seventeenth and nineteenth centuries—the celebrated cases of Amy Poulter marrying Arbella Hunt in 1680, and Anne Lister's intention to settle her property on Anne Walker, as if they were married—but these are clearly not the heirs of "wedded" brotherhood, since, as Bray himself says, "wedded" brotherhood was perfectly compatible with heterosexual marriage and was not about property and inheritance.[29]

The first wave of feminist criticism of the early modern period saw in the humanist rhetoric of "companionate marriage" (a rhetoric that helped discredit the bachelor households of the late medieval period) a positive development for the representation of women.[30] Later feminist criticism challenged this sanguine view, pointing out the inaccessibility of humanist education to women and the new ideological constraints imposed by the identification of ideals of domesticity less with an active role in the family than with chastity and obedience.[31] The idea that lesbianism as a category of female sexuality might have a history or prehistory in this period further complicates the relationship of these contested narratives, not least because of the long history of lesbianism's rhetorical figuration as invisibility, or unrepresentability.[32] By far the most sophisticated and comprehensive historicization of the modern category of the lesbian in the representational terms of the early modern period has been Valerie Traub's *The Renaissance of Lesbianism in Early Modern England*. What seems uncanny, though, is the way in which Traub's account of the historical emergence into visibility of something like the modern category of the "lesbian" mirrors so exactly, in spite of men's and women's very different historical relationships to property and prestige, the emergence into scandalous visibility of the male "molly." Traub's earlier articles have already indicated how a complex convergence of discourses contributed to the marking, at the turn of the seventeenth century, of intimacy between women as "suspicious" and possibly "unnatural." She showed how later sixteenth century Europe saw a poetic revival of interest in the classical satirical discourse of the sexually predatory "tribade," alongside a medical "rediscovery" of the clitoris.[33] At the same time, vernacular literary productions—stage plays, masques, operas, pastoral romances—offered various representations of chaste female love.

Traub's account of the historical emergence of the *lesbian,* then (the italics mark the inadequacy and historical contingency of the term), resembles Bray's of the emergence of the demonization of the molly, or effeminate man: in both cases, the signs associated with an ideal and unthreatening same-sex friendship become susceptible to being read as the encoding of secret, unnatural vice. In Traub's magisterial *The Renaissance of Lesbianism,* the same contours of argument are followed, but the account is considerably enriched, and differs in that Katherine Philips has become a pivotal figure in Traub's tracing of the transition from chaste female friendship to *lesbian*, and that Bray's book, *The Friend*, has enabled this reading of Philips.

Traub's argument is brilliantly persuasive. The sixteenth century poetic representation of chaste female friendship is, as she shows, grounded in the Ovidian topos of the impossibility of love between women because it is "against nature"—a lament which, voiced by the female Iphis in agony over her feelings for Ianthe, seems incontrovertibly proved by Iphis's subsequent sex change. Philips, argues Traub, transforms the topos, refusing its apparent finality and reimagining a feminized "Nature" as wholly sympathetic to love and friendship between women, lamenting with them when they part from each other. Thus, though Philips's poems of friendships are frequently elegiac, they both affirm the spirituality of female friendship and suggest its homoerotic potential in that they *lament the physical absence of friends*, not the impossibility of love and friendship between women (a prime example is Philips's "Lucasia, Rosania and Orinda parting at a Fountain, July 1663").[34] They are able to do this because, as Traub notes, they challenge the male monopoly on the notion that only men's souls are capable of elevated friendships, friendships that transcend distance and partings by means of shared writing. "Orinda," as Traub puts it, "mediates both the meaning of her desire and the anguish of parting from her beloved through the wilful assertion of spiritual merger."[35]

Philips, Traub says, appropriates and "regenders" the eroticized rituals and discourses of the elevated ethical and spiritual character of friendship between men. Traub points out: "Such eroticized friendship is, as Alan Bray's *The Friend* makes clear, one aspect of a widespread network of affects and obligations among men. Tracing the rituals of brotherhood through a variety of medieval and early modern documents and artifacts, Bray provides an archaeology of masculine friendship that demonstrates its utility to other social institutions, including the family."[36] Traub thus concludes her chapter by emphasizing that Katherine Philips's writing inadvertently marks the transition between the early presumption of innocence in depictions of female intimacy and the later tendency for such depictions to be regarded with suspicion: "In her strategic revisions of the terms of Nature, we can catch a glimpse of how female friendship would become, *despite Philips's own intentions,* less innocent, less obviously chaste, more suspect, more in need of defense. Before Philips, intense female intimacy was rarely in danger of social condemnation; after Philips, such intimacy was rarely completely free from it."[37] In this powerful account, Philips's poetry both appropriates for women *for the first time* (in English) the concept of friendship as spiritually elevated, as "a mingling of souls,"[38] and simultaneously infuses that spiritual ideal with erotic passion. The account is presented as if it aligned smoothly with Bray's history of the gradual demonization of the bodily and erotic dimensions of male homosocial relations. As Traub says, drawing on recent work on early modern women's alliances with other women, it is not as if women didn't have socially significant friendships, but "there was little public discourse about the virtues and possibilities of friendship between women, and what discourse did exist had none of the elevated social standing accorded to Montaigne's essays."[39]

Yet if there was so little discourse on the virtue of female friendship and so much on the virtue of male friendship, it seems possible to question whether Bray's history of the embodiment of male friendship is at all relevant to a history of female-female intimacy. For, as Traub herself noted in her review, Bray's emphasis on the significance of male bodily intimacy as a sign of legitimate and prestigious social relation in "traditional society" itself has the effect of "minimizing the importance of sexuality in the bonds being described."[40] The body is present for Bray as a sign of the "formal and objective character" of friendship; if women's friendships tended to lack a "formal and objective character," or a publicly acknowledged ethical dimension and social and familial efficacy, signs and gestures of bodily intimacy between women would tend only in very exceptional cases to have the gift-giving and fidelity-pledging significance that Bray ascribes to the socially and institutionally pervasive "gift of the friend's body" between men.[41]

The importance of all-male institutions (Oxbridge colleges and bachelor households) to Bray's account would seem to underscore this point. Insofar as traces of the socially and materially significant practices of male friendship involve gesture and the body, Bray seeks them not in letters and poems, but in a historical reconstruction of the living spaces of the traditional open household, whether aristocratic home or Oxbridge college. These signifying household spaces are treated in detail in chapter 4, "The Body of the Friend," under a series of subheadings: "Embrace," "Table," "Bed," "Body and Society," "Letter" (the section on the "letter" is included to refute the idea that humanism wrought any kind of textualizing change in the exchange of signs of friendship, arguing that the letter does not displace the body), "Laughter," and "Desire." Finally, at the end of the chapter, we have a section entitled "The Silence between the Lines." Traub took this phrase, in her review, to characterize Bray's hermeneutic method, his alertness to gaps, silences, and omissions in the evidence he is looking at. In this instance, however, Bray meant "silence between the lines" to refer to the lack of evidence, in the traces he had found, of women's friendships. He writes: "the public embraces, the common tables, and the shared beds of this chapter seem to signify largely if not entirely in a world of men.... The guide to the place of such gestures, I have argued, was in the nature of the signs themselves."[42] So Bray appears here to be saying that while women undoubtedly shared in the world of embodiment, their embodiment does not signify publicly as friendship—this is largely, he suggests, "because they often lacked the property and influence of which such records are often the trace."[43]

However, if women shared in a world of embodiment, but one which did not signify publicly, can this then be considered a world of gift-giving or ethically and socially significant friendship in Bray's sense? If the erotic embodiment of friendship is an effect of the capacity to signify friendship publicly, then this suggests that what Bray recognizes as the embodiment of friendship in the past is crucially affected by the medium and wider intelligibility of its public signification. The erotic presence of the body, in this sense, can only come into being (and so redeem its own eroticism for Bray) as a *sign*—whether that sign is the scripting of a ritual kiss or the presence of a Ciceronian rhetoric of *amicitia* in letters. Recognizing this would indicate not that traditional society lacked embodied female intimacy but that we have mistaken the capacity of aristocratic male friendship to signify publicly in traditional society as referencing the anterior embodiment of that friendship, when that embodiment can only exist as part of a system of publicly intelligible signs. The bodily intimacy of friendship, then, is *produced* as part of its capacity to signify ethically, and women will not have access to the means to signify this bodily intimacy until they effectively appropriate the ethical discourse. If this hypothesis is true, it would go some way toward explaining the conspicuous absence from Bray's consideration of the early modern same-sex friendship poetry of Katherine Philips.

Chapter 4, the chapter from which Katherine Philips's absence is so marked, is clearly the center of Bray's book and marks the turning point of his historical argument. Its title, "The Body of the Friend," recalls the title of the essay Bray wrote in 1999 with Michel Rey.[44] The chapter begins with the monument that 20 years ago, as Bray tells us in his introduction, provided the inception of the book, when he was invited to Christ's College, Cambridge, to give a lecture and his host, Jonathan Walters, showed him "the seventeenth-century monument by the communion table that marks the burial in the same tomb of John Finch and Thomas Baines." Bray was asked what he made of the monument, and his book, he says, "is a long-delayed reply to that question."[45]

Thomas Baines and John Finch met as students in the 1640s and remained inseparable throughout their lives; Baines died in Constantinople in 1681, and Finch, who was ambassador there, brought his remains to England where he himself would die the following year. The monument Bray saw in Christ's College features the image of a knotted cloth, "a visual pun on the marriage or love knot," as Bray describes it, and he notes that the terminology of marriage had been employed by Finch in an inscription he left to the memory of Baines in Constantinople, where he described their friendship as an "Animorum Connubium," a marriage of souls.[46] The historical trajectory that Bray has traced thus far has led from the shared tombstone of Sir William Neville and Sir John Clanvowe in Constantinople in 1391, with its imagery of kissing helmets and titled shields, all the way to the end of the seventeenth century. Bray plausibly argues that the Finch and Baines monument partakes of the traditional imagery of "wedded" brotherhood, but he wants, as well, to identify its historical moment more precisely, at the very end of the period of this tradition's centrality. In order to do this, he invokes a contemporary discourse on friendship by the Anglican divine Jeremy Taylor. "What is certain," Bray writes, is that the terms Finch used here were no eccentricity at the end of the seventeenth century:

> at this point... there is an explicit intellectual context for the terms of this monument. In describing their friendship as a "marriage of souls," Finch used the same terms employed by Jeremy Taylor, the Caroline divine (later bishop) in his *Discourse on Friendship,* a work that was reprinted some seven times between 1657, when it first appeared, and 1684, when the monument in Christ's College was completed. The closing lines of the inscription on the Christ's College monument also look back to Taylor's work.
>
> "So that they who while living had mingled their interests,
> fortunes, counsels, nay rather souls, might in the same manner,
> in death, at last mingle their sacred ashes."

Both inscriptions draw on the same passage in Jeremy Taylor's *Discourse,* in which he describes friendships as "marriages of the soul, and of fortunes, interests and counsels" and friendship is, as he puts it, "all the bands this world hath."[47] Taylor's *Discourse* is important for Bray's argument because Taylor, while articulating some of the familiar Ciceronian arguments about friendship, also puts a remarkable emphasis throughout on the comfort of the friend's bodily presence.[48] Thus, even as Taylor expresses the principle that a friend is defined by his ability to give counsel as well as pleasure, the stress falls on the pleasure: "He is only fit to be chosen for a friend who... can and will, when I need it, do me good: only this I adde: into the heaps of doing good, I will reckon [loving me], for it is a pleasure to be beloved."[49] In another place, Taylor anticipates his interlocutor, "if you yet enquire further, whether fancy may be an ingredient in your choice?," and he answers in the affirmative: Jesus loved John, he says, and glosses: "that is, he fancied the man."[50] Finally, Taylor concludes his discourse with the injunction, which Bray quotes, that friends should exchange gifts and embraces: "give him gifts and upbraid him not," writes Taylor, "a gift fastneth friendships...so must the love of friends sometimes be refreshed with material and low Caresses, lest by striving to be *too divine* it become *less humane*."[51]

So we can see why Bray thought it important to represent the central paradigm shift described by his book—the shift from a traditional, Christian ethics of voluntary kinship to a rational, contracting society—in terms of the opposition he discerned between the worldviews of Jeremy Taylor and John Locke: "if the voice of this older world was Jeremy Taylor's claim that friendship is 'all the bands this world hath,' then the most cogent voice of the confident new world replacing it was unquestionably the 'civil society' of John Locke in his *Essay concerning the True Original, Extent and End of Civil Government*."[52] In Locke's work, Bray argues, "society" is no longer embodied friendship but an abstraction. However, if Taylor's *Discourse* is so important, and important because it gives evidence of an "older world" in which the "body of the friend" was still thought of as significant, then surely it is important, too, that Taylor's *Discourse* was called into being by a woman, who was also a poet of friendship.

Jeremy Taylor's *Discourse,* which plays such a pivotal role in Bray's history of the body in friendship, would never have come into existence if it had not been for Katherine Philips writing to Taylor with a question about the extent to which exclusive, intimate friendship is compatible with Christian ethics. Taylor's warm affirmation of this compatibility in the world of men, then, may be read as a casuistical response to Philips's question.[53] The treatise's title page explains that the *Discourse* is a response to a letter: "A Discourse on the Nature, Offices and Measures of Friendship, with Rules of conducting it. Written in answer to a Letter from the most ingenious and vertuous *M. K. P.*" It opens with reference to the question: "you first inquire," the author begins, "how far a Dear and perfect friendship is authoriz'd by the principles of Christianity?" The question of the compatibility of intimacy with one special friend—the Ciceronian "other self"—with the principle of universal Christian charity is then rehearsed. Christianity declared that "our friendship should be as universal as our conversation; that is, *actual* to all those with whom we converse, and *potentially extended* unto those with whom we did not."[54] Although Christianity's imperative is that friendship should be universal, in practice it is limited because people are. So, rules in choosing friends follow. Predictably enough, Taylor scoffs at the idea of choosing friends simply because one is physically attracted to them, though attraction is an element: "the *good man* is a profitable, useful person, and that's the band of an effective friendship." He writes:

> He is only fit to be chosen for a friend who can give me counsel, defend my cause, or guide me right, or relieve my need, or can and will, when I need it, do me good: only this I adde: into the heaps of doing good, I will reckon [*loving me*], for it is a pleasure to be beloved; but when his love signifies nothing but Kissing my Cheek or talking kindly, and can go no further, it is the prostitution of the bravery of a friendship to spend it upon impertinent people who are (it may be) loads to their families, but can never ease my loads.[55]

Here we have a perfect exemplification of Bray's argument that in early modern Europe the pleasures of same-sex intimacy—two men kissing and talking "kindly" or lovingly—were perfectly intelligible as the signs of a friendship beneficial to the families of the two friends involved. Indeed, Taylor's argument goes further and insists that *unless* intimacy signifies thus, it is a "prostitution" of the "bravery" or ostentatious signifying practices of friendship.

Does it matter that neither Taylor in 1657 nor Bray in the twenty-first century acknowledged that the bodies in question here were women's, that the *friendships* in question, or about whom the question was asked, were women's? For while Taylor does concede women to be sometimes capable of the "useful" qualities that define the most perfect friendships, his examples are not of women as friends to other women, but as friends, counselors, and assistants to men, usually husbands. So while Warren Chernaik sees Philips's friendship poetry as "making a similar point" to Taylor's about women being capable of friendship, only "more forcefully," it seems, rather, that Philips is reacting against Taylor's confinement of female friendship to relations between wife and husband. Taylor acknowledges Philips as addressee only to admit the old humanist commonplace of the wife as friend to the husband: "But by the way (Madam) you may see how much I differ from the morosity of those Cynics who would not admit your sex into the communities of noble friendship. I believe some Wives have been the best friends in the world."[56] Philips, by contrast, writes:

> If soules no sexes have, for men t'exclude
> Women from friendship's vast capacity,
> Is a design imperious and rude,
> Onely maintained by partial tyranny.[57] (19–22)

Kate Lilley, indeed, argues that Taylor's *Discourse,* with its remarkably pointed omission of examples of friendship between women (the only glimpse it gives of female-female relations is a lurid image of sexual rivalry: "a pretty bride murdered in her bride-chamber by an ambitious... Rival"), was, in fact, "a veiled chastisement, a corrective of her excessive attention to women and her critique of men as credulous in such poems as 'Content, to my dearest Lucasia': they 'think they have it, when they have it not.' "[58] Lilley's contention that Philips's friendship poetry was seen as threatening and disorderly from very early in the poet's writing career—and she adduces in support of this claim Peter Beal's publication of John Taylor's abusive invective against Philips's poetry, which must have been written earlier than 1653—should prompt us to rethink some of the claims of Alan Bray's narrative of the loss of an "older world" in which bodily intimacy could signify the ethical bonds of friendship and voluntary kinship, an "older world" whose "voice... was Jeremy Taylor's claim that friendship is 'all the bands this world hath.' "[59] For Jeremy Taylor's implicit denial of an ethical dimension to women's friendships and John Taylor's abuse of Philips as "a second Sapho" both point clearly to a sense of scandal generated by Philips's writing. However, this scandal was not the result of a new illegibility of the bodily intimacy within a traditional social encoding of ethical friendship. Rather, it was the result of a woman's very appropriation in writing of the ethical discourse, the witty casuistry of friendship.

When we find, then, that an erotic quality suffuses Philips's feminization of the poetry of patronage, this is not because, as Bray's model would have it, the conventional language of patronage as friendship works as one of the "remaining traces left by the practices of friendship, of commendation and countenance that once employed them."[60] Philips can write poems that recreate the erotic charge of social prestige in itself—the eros, that is to say, not in the embodiedness of the body-as-sign, but in the *significance* of the body-as-sign. Such a poem is "To my Lady Ann Boyle's saying that I look'd angrily on her." In this witty comment on the opacity of gesture and expression, Philips first asks how "Valeria" (the daughter of the Earl of Cork and Burlington, wife to the Earl of Sandwich) could "so misspell the language of my Face, / When in my heart you have so great a place?" (1, 3–4). The poem concludes by turning a compliment so neat as to risk obsequiousness. Philips acknowledges that Ann Boyle's exhibition of "Jealousy" in attempting such a close reading of her expression is, in itself, "obliging": "For at that quarrel I can ne're repine / Which *shews your Kindness,* though it questions mine" (14–16; my italics).[61] The very fact that this poem is not as swooningly enthralled as those addressed to Ann Boyle's sister, Lady Elizabeth Boyle, or "Celimena" (from whose "charms," Philips elsewhere says, "neither Sexe can flie"), helps us to recognize that it is not bodily intimacy as such but the risks and thrills of interpreting signs of affection that charge its comic narrative with passion.[62] Sensitivity to the pain of misunderstanding is, too, what prevents the poet's gratification at Ann Boyle's inadvertent revelation of feelings of "Kindness" toward her from seeming merely opportunistic, or devoid of warmth. At the same time, Philips's insistence on our awareness that it is Boyle's

"Jealousy" that has forced her to reveal her "Kindness" is flirtatiously triumphant: the poem revels in the eros of civilized friendship's power games.

Bray's narrative suggests that the advent of civil society brought about a loss of the integration of networks of friendship and intimate same-sex relations into the recognized ethical and material well-being of the "family." The architectural changes of the great house, he argues, "chart that bodily intimacy was ceasing to be intelligible as it had once been."[63] Although poems and letters may be mimetic recreations of the spaces and scenes in which bodily intimacy carried such emotional and ethical significance, they are more than traces of ritual or gestural practices. We need, as Kate Lilley writes in relation to Philips, "to take seriously the erotics of *writing*."[64] To do so means being aware, too, of how the *literary* representation of male intimacy changed over the course of the seventeenth century in ways that were not only indicative of a loss in homoerotic forms of expression. Early in the seventeenth century, Ben Jonson had begun to fashion a new "virile" style of erudite masculine intimacy based on men's tacit, unacknowledged pleasure in a shared understanding of allusions to risqué, libertine meanings and double entendres.[65] *Epicoene* (1609) defined this new style of virile, allusive masculine intimacy by contrasting the sexual libertinism and extreme discretion of the gentlemen hero, Dauphine, with the readiness of garrulous would-be male and female libertines and wits to expose themselves sexually even when they had, in fact, done nothing physical.[66] Jonson satirizes with especially marked savagery the pretensions of women to rival men in constituting themselves as a salon—a group of learned and witty friends, "ladies that call themselves the Collegiates, an order between courtiers and country madams" (1.1.71–72). It is these women's claims to have mastered the civilized and erotic pleasures of implicit meaning that Jonson subjects to ridicule. One of these collegiates, Mavis, professes to have composed a literary "riddle," which she asks Dauphine to "solve," but it turns out to be a very blatant sexual assignation. Dauphine's scornful comment sounds the keynote of the play: "By my faith, a subtle one! Call you this a riddle? What's their plain dealing, trow?" (5.2.60–61). It is the inability to express erotic feeling subtly that damns both the would-be male libertines, Sir Jack Daw and Sir Amorous La-Foole, and the female collegiates.

Philips, who knew Jonson's play, responded to its satirizing of the Amazonian *femme forte* as lamentably easy to read both in her literary and sexual aspirations in her poem "To Sir Amorous La Foole." Here, Philips denies that the garrulous, banal exchanging of "Amorous ware" (9) that passes for courtship between men and women is motivated by women's sexual needs, or women's desire to be courted. Philips's opening exclamation, "Bless us! here's a doe indeed / That she must so much Courtship need" (1–2) reveals the feminine pronoun as a construction of the imputed "need" for courtship. In a startling reversal, Philips then redefines the traditional poetic construction of feminine "cruelty" as the precondition for such courtship by introducing her own fantasy of sexual response to a genuine feminine indifference to male courtship:

> Scorn sits so handsome on this face,
> With such an unaffected grace,
> That I could wish my sex were changed to be
> A Lover onely of your cruelty.[67] (3–6)

Where Jonson's play associated the opacity of desire with a glamorous, homoerotic virility (the enigmatic Dauphine berates his friend, Clerimont, for being "a strange, open man, to tell everything thus" [1.3.1]), Philips enjoys a homoerotic fantasy of sexual seduction by the glamorous power of indifference, the handsome grace of a woman's unresponsiveness to a man. As she does so, she appropriates the seductive impunity of indirect homoeroticism for femininity, in defiance of Jonson.

Valerie Traub reads Philips's "production of a compelling homoerotic subjectivity" not as "'self-expression'... but rather as a 'subjectivity effect,'" participating in a more widespread cultural shift from predominantly innocent to predominantly suspicious ways of reading female friendship.[68] However, this formulation perhaps discourages awareness of the extent to which erotic feeling in Philips's poetry is inseparable from a conscious taking of pleasure in the intensely civilized conjunction of tact and passion, compliment, warmth, and fantasy. Also, perhaps Traub's reading, brilliant as it is, relies too heavily on Bray's narrative of the displacement of a traditional world of significant and embodied friendships by a "civil" society of rational contracting and homophobic subjects. Victoria Kahn argues that it is a deficiency of our readings of seventeenth century contract theory that we assume that the emergence of the subject of contract was the emergence of a subject imagined to be rational. We need to see that what the English revolution brought about, for royalists and Parliamentarians alike, was a heightened awareness that bonds of association were not given or natural, and that voluntarily consenting to them, or contracting them, was not a rational but a passionate and interested act.

This awareness gave rise to concerns about motivation and psychology—why do people bind themselves to each other? What guarantees the bond? Is it love or fear? And these questions were in turn resolved by analyses of the passions and interests of the contracting subject. Kahn describes this as "a shift in the libidinal economy of political obligation" in the period.[69] In this context, it becomes more interesting that in Philips's poems we have a male tradition of ethical friendship being appropriated for women (and for royalist politics), but in ways that, above all, appeal to the passions and interests as capable of bringing about the erotic and political subjection of one woman to another. Bray himself noticed that Taylor calls friendships "marriages of the soul, and of fortunes, interests and counsels," so that the materialist calculus of passions and interests has already, even in his *Discourse,* overtaken a traditional appeal to God as the cause of bonds of peace between men. Philips, in one of many idealizing moves, speaks of "Friendship's exalted Interest" ("Friendship in Emblem," 26).[70] This suggests that for Philips, as a woman writer, the difficulty lies not in the need to distinguish ethical bodily gestures from transgressive sexual ones but in the very claim of writings on female friendship to signify as ethical and political at all. So, for the history of female friendship and its poetry, the recovery of "the gift of the friend's body" may not be as important as the revolutionary upheaval that made it thinkable to deploy materialistic discourses of the passions and the interests in articulating a kind of libidinal economy of passionate obligation between women.

10 ❖ Versions of Pastoral
Philips and Women's Queer Spaces

Harriette Andreadis

"Poet[s] devised the eclogue...not of purpose to counterfeit or represent the rustical manner of loves and communication, but under the veil of homely persons and in rude speeches to insinuate and glance at greater matters, and such as perchance had not been safe to have been disclosed in any other sort, which may be perceived by the *Eclogues* of Vergil, in which are treated by figure matters of greater importance than the loves of Tityrus and Corydon."[1] The coded nature of the Renaissance pastoral here suggested by Puttenham has been explored by a number of scholars such as Louis Adrian Montrose and Josephine Roberts, among others.[2] While pastoralism has long been seen as a vehicle for a complex and coded court politics, we have only relatively recently begun to examine the ways in which this coding works to express transgressive eroticisms. Bruce Smith, Frederick Greene, and Stephen Wayne Whitworth began the work of opening up the pastoral for queer reading, specifically for male-male queer reading in pre-Restoration literature.[3] But, as is often the case, these male-authored critical studies neglect the possibilities for a female erotics.[4] In an analysis of the pastoral erotics employed by Aphra Behn, Elizabeth Young remarks on the number of female poets who write pastoral during the Restoration and eighteenth century: "Pastoral is, perhaps, a 'ladylike' form, one categorically disempowered by the critical generic hierarchy. But it is also a particularly subversive form that... challenges conventions of both genre and gender."[5] In Behn's skillful hands, the pastoral does just that in poems such as "On a Juniper-Tree, cut down to make Busks," "The Willing Mistress," "The Disappointment," "On Her Loving Two Equally," and "To the Fair Clarinda, Who Made Love to Me, Imagined More Than Woman," in which she deploys traditional pastoral conventions to explore the complexities of female desire as it struggles against social constraints. But even before Behn's excursions into the pastoral, the forms and conventions of pastoralism had opened up a space for a female same-sex coded erotics that was shaping a tradition in women's poetry that was to extend into the twentieth and twenty-first centuries. I propose here to suggest the ways in which the pastoral in English before Behn—that is, from at least the work of Katherine Philips and Aemilia Lanyer—provided an important vehicle for the coded expression of a female eroticism, serving both personal erotic and politically charged, class-conscious purposes.[6]

The well-known story of the pastoral and its cultural work begins with the third century BCE *Idylls* of Theocritus and his "The Passion of Daphnis" as its *locus classicus*. The elegaic features with which we have become so familiar as characterizing the pastoral are seen in their performative/dramatic quality, in their trajectory from grief and darkness to renewal and consolation, in the presence of flowers, in Nature's mourning (pathetic fallacy), and in other familiar characteristics such as the convention of "the shepherd [as] a type of the first artist." In identifying two different traditions of Renaissance pastoralism, Bruce Smith describes the Theocritan pastoral as "soft," as "essentially escapist in spirit," and as "celebrat[ing] the *locus amoenus*" of bodily pleasure. In contrast, he categorizes the pastoral modeled on the later eclogues of Virgil as "hard" and as performing a different kind of cultural work insofar as "the social order of the world beyond the shepherd's fields casts shadows on the landscape of desire."[7] In women's writing as well as in men's, these two models of pastoralism often merge, so that the escapist posture of the Theocritan idyll is shadowed by the Virgilian sense of a social order beyond the *locus amoenus;* such a fusion of these two pastoral modes is particularly suitable for the coding of female eroticism since it is always already complicated by social constraints.

Women writers of the seventeenth century make frequent use of such pastoral places as gardens, country houses, and wilderness settings in which to situate a queer female erotics that emphasizes the *frisson* of same-sex longings, desire frustrated by separation, and romantic nostalgia for same-sex emotional union. Katherine Philips is perhaps the most notable exemplar of such bucolic metaphors for eroticism in the seventeenth century, and her deployment of a female pastoralism was widely emulated by a number of the women writers who followed her. It is easy to recognize the "soft" Theocritan pastoral in Philips's poems of escape to friendship, or longing for the presence of the beloved friend, and the fusion of that softness with the hard shadowing of that escape by the grim realities of a disrupted social order. Friendship in a pastoral landscape is for her solace against the painful realities of regicide and the long night of the Interregnum. It also becomes a vehicle for the oblique, coded expression of intimate passions that might not have had other acceptably "respectable" outlets.[8]

"A Retir'd Friendship. To Ardelia" is a good example of Philips's escapist pastoralism. The speaker urges her beloved to join her in fleeing the perils of an urban court for a pastoral "bowre":

1

Come, my Ardelia, to this bowre,
    Where kindly mingling Souls a while,
Let's innocently spend an houre,
    And at all serious follys smile.

2

Here is no quarrelling for Crowns,
    Nor fear of changes in our fate;

No trembling at the great ones frowns,
    Nor any Slavery of State.

3

Here's no disguise nor treachery,
    Nor any deep conceal'd design;
From blood and plots this place is free,
    And calm as are those looks of thine.

The pastoral escape is defined largely by its negation of the values of a corrupt social world. Philips evokes the pastoral as subtext when she uses a pastoral name for her beloved friend and situates the poem in a "bowre." In calling up the "Come live with me and be my love" lyricism of earlier heteroerotic pastoralism, Philips both codes erotic desire for her (female) friend and inflects its escapism, and the idealism of friendship's two fused souls, with the elements of the Virgilian hard pastoral.

After six stanzas, Philips makes explicit the submerged pastoral setting that describes the psychic landscape of the beloved friends:

7

Let's mark how soon Apollo's beams
    Command the flocks to quit their meat,
And not entreat the neighbour-streams
    To quench their thirst, but coole their heat.

8

In such a scorching Age as this,
    Whoever would not seek a shade
Deserve their happiness to misse,
    As having their own peace betray'd.

9

But we (of one another's mind
    Assur'd,) the boisterous world disdain;
With quiet souls, and unconfin'd,
    Enjoy what princes wish in vain. (25–36)

The speaker's evocation of a bucolic setting conjures up the hot sun and cool water of a summer's day whose imagery becomes the metaphor for a "scorching Age" from which "shade" must be sought. She reaffirms the "Assur'd" intimacy of the poem's "we" and underlines the quiet freedom of their souls in disdaining the "boisterous world." The pastoral escape, then, provides all the comforts and solace that worldlings will never attain, and "friendship" secures a permanent psychic peacefulness.

Another clear example of Philips's exploration of these ideas is "Invitation to the Countrey," again addressed to one of her most intimate friends:

> Be kind, my deare Rosania, though 'tis true
> Thy friendship will become thy penance too;
>
> ....
>
> For a retirement from the noise of Towns,
> Is that for which some Kings have left their Crowns:
> And Conquerours, whose Laurells prest their Brow,
> Have chang'd it for the quiet Mirtle bough.
> For titles, honours, and the world's address,
> Are things too cheap to make up happiness;
>
> ....
>
> Kings may be slaves by their own passions hurl'd,
> But who commands himself commands the World.
> A countrey=life assists this study best,
> When no distractions do the soule arrest:
> There heav'n and earth ly open to our view,
> There we search nature and its authour too;
>
> ....
>
> There (my Rosania) will we, mingling souls,
> Pitty the folly which the world controuls;
> And all those Grandeurs which the most do prize
> We either can enjoy, or will despise. (1–2, 11–16, 39–44, 47–50)

The language of a bustling, unrewarding political economy which even "some Kings" and "Conquerours" have rejected is counterpoised against a country life where self-command is possible and where "no distractions do the soule arrest" or curtail spiritual quest. "Mingling souls" with the beloved friend—"(*my* Rosania)" suggests an impassioned fusion—they can look down on worldly folly. The elements of pastoral escape are all here: the pastoral name of the "friend," the invitation to leave the noise and corruption of city places, the description of the pleasures of peace, and the "mingling" of souls made possible by the refusal of worldly temptations.

Philips's use of pastoral to envision safe communal space as escape from the court and worldly corruption is shaped by the frustrations of the civil war and Interregnum and appropriates in many ways the assumptions of the country-house poems of male cavalier poets; Thomas Carew's *To Saxham* and Richard Lovelace's *Amyntor's Grove,* for instance, reject the Jonsonian pastoral world in *To Penshurst* as a *locus amoenus* that preserves a traditionally balanced social and cosmic order and focus instead on the preservation of the aristocracy through isolation from the vagaries of nature and a politically hostile public sphere.[9] But Philips might also have been extending the complex perspective of Aemelia Lanyer's 1611 *A Description of Cooke-ham,* which preceded *To Penshurst* by five years as the first country-house poem. Lanyer also codes a female same-sex ardor within an eroticized pastoral setting as well as expressing a conflicted and sometimes bitter sense of class difference that was also integral to Philips's poetic address to her female patrons and aristocratic "friends."

Much has been made of the peculiar episode[10] in the poem in which Lanyer, having throughout the poem imbued the natural world of Cooke-ham with a kind of animism, appropriates as her own totem the tree that Anne Clifford kissed in parting from the country house to which she had retreated with her mother—Margaret Clifford, Countess of Cumberland—and Lanyer:

> But specially the love of that faire tree,
> That first and last you did vouchsafe to see:
>
> . . . .
>
> Where many a learned Booke was read and skand
> To this faire tree, taking me by the hand,
> You did repeat the pleasures which had past,
> Seeming to grieve they could no longer last.
> And with a chaste, yet loving kisse tooke leave,
> Of which sweet kisse I did it soone bereave:
> Scorning a sencelesse creature should possesse
> So rare a favour, so great happinesse.
> No other kisse it could receive from me,

> For feare to give backe what it tooke of thee:
> So I ingratefull Creature did deceive it,
> Of that which you vouchsaft in love to leave it.[11] (157–58, 161–72)

This passage is odd not only in describing Clifford's unusual, and quasi-erotic, embrace of the tree, but in the oddly misleading grammar of the passage that initially directs us to believe that Clifford has embraced, and kissed, Lanyer rather than the tree: "taking me by the hand,... with a chaste, yet loving kisse tooke leave." But then the poet rapidly twists the apparent meaning of the previous lines to clarify that it is the tree—the inanimate, senseless "it"—that has been kissed: "Of which sweet kisse I did it soone bereave." The sudden turn from the possible intimacies suggested by Clifford's having kissed Lanyer drains the lines that follow the hand-holding of their ambiguities: "You did repeat the pleasures which had past, / Seeming to grieve they could no longer last." Should we have wondered about the nature of those pleasures, they have now been relegated to the innocence of reading in the shade of the beloved tree.

In this "poem of loss" in which "the poet figure [is] left behind in a ruptured Eden to memorialize paradise lost,"[12] Lanyer's conflicted and intermittently bitter struggle with her class position leads her from encomia to the Cliffords to grieving at her loss of status in losing them and back again:

> Unconstant Fortune, thou art most too blame,
> Who casts us downe into so lowe a frame:
> Where our great friends we cannot dayly see,
> So great a diffrence is there in degree.
> Many are placed in those Orbes of state,
> Parters in honour, so ordain'd by Fate;
> Neerer in show, yet farther off in love,
> In which, the lowest alwayes are above. (103–10)

Inveighing against Fortune and Fate for her now lowly, subjected "degree," Lanyer grieves the separation enforced by a sociopolitical system—"those Orbes of state"—that keeps close those "farther off in love" as it severs her and her deeper feelings from her "great friends." She enjoins "sweet Memorie" to "retaine / Those pleasures past, which will not turne againe": "Whereof depriv'd, I evermore must grieve, / Hating blind Fortune, carelesse to relieve" (117–18, 125–26) Thus, grieving and resentment at her status and unrequited devotion proceed in counterpoint throughout the poem. Finally, she concludes on a Shakespearean note, asserting the longevity of her tribute to Cooke-ham ("When I am dead thy name in this may live" [206]), the Cliffords, and the fulfillment of her promise to memorialize their time there. But the very last line of the poem evokes for the last time her conflicted relation to her patron, to patronage, and her need to secure them for her own survival: "Tying my heart to her by those rich chaines" (210). While Philips might be said to appropriate Lanyer's tremulously eroticized version of escapist pastoralism, she tends to keep it separate from the poems and letters in which she expresses class resentment. Her poetic pastoralism focuses, instead, on the corruption of external, urbanized society.[13]

Philips's coding of a female erotics in the language of friendship ("mingling Souls") and in a pastoralism shadowed by a refusal of urban corruption became a model for a number of the female poets who succeeded her in the later seventeenth and eighteenth centuries. Of these later poets—among them the pseudonymous "Ephelia"; Lady Mary Chudleigh; Anne Finch, Countess of Winchelsea; and Jane Barker—Anne Killigrew (1660–85) is perhaps most interesting for the ways in which she exploits the possibilities of pastoral themes. Heir to Philips's poetic legacy, Killigrew reframes the pastoralism in which Philips had situated her female friends; she uses pastoral names and settings but emphasizes the inverted conventions of her own gloomily barren landscapes, the failures of human reason confronted with sexual passion, and the futility of erotic relations between men and women. Killigrew articulates the ideals of friendship on a number of occasions, but her stance in relation to these ideals is complex and ambivalent.

The three odes that conclude her small 1686 volume of poetry, and that are its most distinctive poems, gesture toward a probably transgressive experience that may have overstepped the bounds of what was more acceptably idealized in the oblique discourses of so many other female poets. In these odes, Killigrew develops her use of what I have called an inverted pastoralism in which the traditional elements of the classical pastoral are eroticized and turned topsy-turvy to suggest their opposites.[14] Killigrew's pastoral landscapes and their trappings (e.g., the pseudoclassical names of shepherds and shepherdesses) do not conventionally offer escape and solace from the world of the court or from the larger world of human folly and viciousness; rather, her inverted pastoral world is a grim landscape from which to rail bitterly against human corruption. The pastoralism of these odes is a space within which Killigrew explores the underside of eroticism: it is a familiar but at times distorted and surreal landscape; this inverted pastoralism, in other words, acts as a vehicle for a coded eroticism by elaborating the shadowed elements of the Virgilian hard pastoral.

In the first of the three odes, "Cloris Charmes Dissolved by Eudora,"[15] the speaker's journey of despair through an allegorical, Dantesque, and Stygian landscape is concluded only with the approach of Eudora to dispel the darkness of the speaker's grief, caused by Cloris's "Wandring Fire." The landscape, which suggests a psychic rather than literal space, has become increasingly macabre as the speaker passes "a Murderers Walk" and a place where "Witches...Nightly Dance"; she finds solace only in "a Cave, / Dreadful as Hell, still as the Grave" that echoes the tumultuous passions she endures. Eudora appears as "A Form Divine and bright," disperses the monsters and "The Terrors of the Cursed Wood," and enjoins the speaker to send Cloris word of the dissolution of the spell that has bound her to grief. Like a (male) courtly lover, the speaker has been bewitched by the "Charmes" of Cloris and is released by "The Gentle Power" of another woman's love: "Dissolv'd is Cloris spell, / from whence thy Evils fell." The speaker's relation to Cloris is explicitly passionate and erotic in the tumultuous emotions it has unleashed, particularly in its parallels with the postures of courtly love.

The second ode, "Upon a Little Lady under the Discipline of an Excellent Person,"[16] describes a "Scene from whence Loves grief arose, / And Heaven and Nature both did discompose"[17] in which a young woman is dominated and disciplined by an older and more powerful personage, Eudora. The narrative provides a frequently ambiguous account of the speaker's coming to terms with Eudora's apparent cruelty as a disciplinarian. An erotic "discipline" by an "other" excites through suggestions of bodily containment and release.

The poem's concluding stanza turns toward reconciliation and harmony. The speaker not only comes to terms with what appeared to be a disturbingly transgressive erotic behavior but also now finds it desirable. The last lines of the poem are unmistakable in their erotic suggestiveness:

> Eudora also shew'd as heretofore,
> When her soft Graces I did first adore.
> I saw, what one did Nobly Will,
> The other sweetly did fulfil;
> Their Actions all harmoniously did sute,
> And she had only tun'd the Lady like her Lute.[18]

A well-worn symbol for female sexuality, the lute appears here in the familiar metaphor of tuning "the Lady like her Lute": Killigrew leaves little doubt about the kinds of behaviors explored by Eudora and the Lady. The poem tempts us to read it as an account of the poet/speaker's reconciliation with her own resistance to an erotics that seemed to her to be transgressive and painful. Instead, this erotics reveals itself as not only "no Sacriledge" but "sweetly" fulfilling. The poet inverts the bucolic peacefulness of pastoral convention to explore the ambiguities of her coded desires.

The third and last ode, "On the Soft and Gentle Motions of Eudora," picks up the image of the lute and compares the gentleness of Eudora's motions to music; the poet pays tribute to Eudora's exquisite movement: "How downie, how smooth, / Eudora doth Move, / How Silken her Actions appear."[19] The final couplet describes Eudora's motions as more musical than music because they are "so soft, so Noyseless a Thing": "O This to express from thy Hand must fall, / Then Musicks self, something more Musical."[20] This poem is a tribute to the pleasure given by Eudora's motions. We are led to conclude, given the position of this poem following the two previous odes, that the speaker/poet now enjoys those erotic pleasures herself. From the perspective of these last odes, other poems in which Killigrew ventriloquizes a male speaker, rather than inhabiting a female poetic voice, can begin to be reread with more certainty as coded discourses that cross-dress her desires.

Less than two centuries later, Christina Rosetti's *Goblin Market* (1862) in many ways echoes Killigrew's earlier inverted pastoralism; like Killigrew's "Eudora" odes, it offers its readers a dank and dangerously erotic psychic landscape that threatens to overwhelm all innocence and destroy any faith in the goodness of a social order dominated by (goblin) men. The many and varying readings of Rosetti's poem—from one critic's certainties that the poem describes Laura's experience with absinthe (i.e., wormwood) to another's that locates the meaning of the poem in the abuses of a capitalist market economy[21]—have failed to provide a single definitive reading of this multilayered pastoral extravaganza in which two young "sisters" find themselves lost in a maze where temptation threatens to overwhelm them and they are driven by a fear of succumbing to forbidden (sexual) enticements:

> "We must not look at goblin men,
> We must not buy their fruits:
> Who knows upon what soil they fed
> Their hungry thirsty roots?"
> "Come buy," call the goblins
> Hobbling down the glen.
> "Oh," cried Lizzie, "Laura, Laura,
> You should not peep at goblin men."
> Lizzie covered up her eyes,
> Covered close lest they should look.[22]

The contaminating possibilities of the gaze are evoked to suggest transgressiveness and the forbidden realm of "peeping." Lizzie's sacrifice for Laura takes the form of a kind of self-immolation in the woods followed by a curatively erotic gift-giving to her "sister":

> She cried, "Laura," up the garden,
> "Did you miss me?
> Come and kiss me.
> Never mind my bruises,
> Hug me, kiss me, suck my juices
> Squeezed from goblin fruits for you,

> Goblin pulp and goblin dew.
> Eat me, drink me, love me;
> Laura, make much of me:
> For your sake I have braved the glen
> And had to do with goblin merchant men."[23]

Laura "clung about her sister, / Kissed and kissed and kissed her.../ She kissed and kissed her with a hungry mouth."[24] These lines give permission for the acting out of a transgressive erotic connection between the "sisters" at the same time that they repress its possibility by providing an apparently rational narrative about the curative powers of self-sacrifice. The pastoralism of the setting and subject—fruits, the glen, the garden, juices—here evokes not escape and bucolic pleasures but rather a treacherously erotic subtext that pressures the apparently rational narrative by "insinuat[ing] and glaunc[ing] at greater matters," dark matters from a social world beyond the environs of the poem where women are fair game for goblin men. This tale of two young women and their encounters with the dangers of the heterosexual goblin men ends with their hunger for each other; it is a hunger assuaged by an erotic intimacy facilitated by the encounter with the goblin men. Like Killigrew's vision of inverted pastoral, the psychic landscape created by Rosetti here is a dark version of pastoral, inflected by treacherous seduction rather than bucolic escape, and suffused by the coded eroticism of female same-sex desire.

Later still, H. D. (Hilda Doolittle, 1886–1961) is known for the hermetic modernism of her complexly realized poetic experiments. Her poems bring together the influences of a classical literary education, her relationship with Ezra Pound, her analysis with Sigmund Freud, both world wars, and the circulation in the West not only of Japanese haiku but also of Japanese graphic arts. H. D.'s sexual relationships with men and her lifelong partnership with Bryher (Annie Winifred Ellerman, 1894–1983) are coded in the richly inflected female eroticism of her poetry. Her conscious emulation of (and translations from) Sappho ensure that her articulation of a female same-sex erotics is not misread by those able to understand it. The traditional pastoralism that was reshaped in earlier periods to code a female erotics is transformed by H. D.

into the incantatory pastoral lyricism of a Sapphic voice. Fields and streams and shepherds and woods become fruit and sea plants, wind and storms and sensuous landscapes shimmering with a tactile sensuousness that leaves no doubt about its eroticism.

"Oread" is from her early collection of imagist poems, *The God:*

> Whirl up, sea—
> whirl your pointed pines,
> splash your great pines
> on our rocks,
> hurl your green over us,
> cover us with your pools of fir.[25]

Susan Stanford Friedman comments on this poem that " 'Oread' and most of H. D.'s imagist poems... are poems about consciousness, not the world of objects external to consciousness. The center of 'Oread,' as the title indicates, is... the perceptions and emotions of an oread, a nymph of the mountains, as she regards the sea aroused in a whirling passion of intensity.... The experiential reality of the poem illustrates that externally opposite qualities such as active/passive or masculine/feminine coexist within single individual."[26] Indeed, we might well read in the imagism of the poem a modernist transformation of the pastoral elements that were earlier used to code female eroticism. The passion of sea, pointed pines, rocks, pools of fir, and the color green evoke those earlier pastoral landscapes at the same time that they allude to Japanese graphic art and express an interior landscape of whirling intensity.

Again, H. D. elaborates a slightly longer account of the "Sea Rose" from *Sea Garden*:

> Rose, harsh rose,
> marred and with stint of petals,
> meagre flower, thin,
> sparse of leaf,
>
> ....
>
> Stunted, with small leaf,
> you are flung on the sand,
> you are lifted
> in the crisp sand
> that drives in the wind.[27] (1–4, 9–13)

The quiet, female escapist pastoral spaces made familiar by Katherine Philips and her followers are instead turned inside-out to focus on the erotic details of a "wet rose / single on a stem—," (6–7) on "crisp sand / that drives in the wind," on "the spice rose [that] drip[s] such acrid fragrance" (14–15). Eileen Gregory notes that "the title of the collection points to the governing experience in all its poems. The *garden* is traditionally the place of consummation of love. In H. D.'s poems the garden is still the place of love, but love washed with salt. It is a *sea* garden, inimical to all but the most enduring."[28] The rose, traditional love emblem, becomes here a spice rose dripping an acrid fragrance, enduring in a brutal environment, pointing up the shadowed nature of the passions of transgressive love. Like Killigrew and Rosetti, H. D. complicates pastoral landscape, emphasizing its interiority, its sensuousness and sensuality, and its multifaceted ambiguities; unlike them, however, she reserves the social matter of the Virgilian hard pastoral for her poems about the war in *Trilogy*'s "The Walls Do Not Fall." But she also deliberately invokes the spare lyricism of Sappho's fragments and their passionate same-sex erotics.

As well known, and as frequently anthologized as "Oread," is "Heat" (or part 2 of "Garden" from *Sea Garden*):

> O wind, rend open the heat,
> cut apart the heat,
> rend it to tatters.
>
> Fruit cannot drop
> through this thick air—
>
> . . . .
>
> Cut the heat—
> plough through it,
> turning it on either side
> of your path.[29] (1–5, 10–13)

The breathless hothouse atmosphere here depends for its effect on a female and erotic imagery of a heat so thick it "blunts / the points of pears / and rounds the grapes" that stand in for breasts and bellies and the fullness of female parts (7–9). Thus, the poem indulges and conveys pure sensation, a purely fleshly pleasure.

In "The Shepherd," H. D. comes closest to deploying the elements of traditional pastoral, including an added flourish using the classic homoerotic myth of the boy Hyacinth, lover of Apollo and desired by Zephyr: flowers, bees, marshes, and swamp-lands, Hyacinth, a shepherd who offers his/her beloved "golden crocuses," a speaker's lament of rejection by Hyacinth, and a distant city that diminishes Hyacinth's beauty are the elements of its narrative:

> I'll shake the bees
> from the thyme-heads for you,
> and gather mint,
> bound with coarse strands of grasses,
> I'll tempt the marshes for the mirrored iris,
> and break the thorn-bough's blossom. (1–6)

The myth of Hyacinth was a classical metaphor of the death and rebirth of nature, and here H. D. plays with the ambiguities of his transformation in death from boy lover to flower. As a presumably male speaker, she cross-dresses a same-sex desire that is fused with Hyacinth's dual role as boy/flower. The tenderness with which s/he gathers gifts from nature for the beloved soon turns to bitter grief when her/his gifts are mocked and scorned:

> O Hyacinth of the swamp-lands,
> Blue lily of the marshes,
> How could I know,
> Being but a silly shepherd,
> That you would mock at me?
>
> . . . .
>
> the day comes and the
> white stars dim
> and lessen
> and the lights fade in the city:
> so in the city do they dim your beauty;
> only the fields have kept it and the singing
> of goat-boys who must follow
> to my piping.[30] (14–18, 26–37)

As in the traditional pastoral, the urban landscape corrupts and destroys, so the poem concludes with a gesture toward the preservation of (Hyacinth's) beauty by the "fields" and "goat-boys," remnants of pastoral innocence and purity.

In "Pursuit," H. D. employs the trope of present absence and the marks left behind by the lover's past presence to explore—as did Katherine Philips before her—the nuances of longing for the beloved:

> What do I care
> that the stream is trampled,
> the sand on the stream-bank
> still holds the print of your foot:
> the heel is cut deep.
> I see another mark
> on the grass ridge of the bank—
> it points toward the wood-path.
> I have lost the third
> in the packed earth.
>
> ....
>
> But here
> a wild hyacinth stalk is snapped:
> the purple buds—half ripe —
> show deep purple
> where your heel pressed.
> A patch of flowering grass,
> low, trailing—
> you brushed this.[31] (1–10, 16–18)

The poem recounts with enormous delicacy, and sorrow, the speaker's following the footsteps of the absent beloved. And again, hyacinth—this time the flower with its erotically charged "purple buds"—is used as an emblem of sexual love departed, serving as a physical marker for the passage of the beloved. Throughout the poem, the speaker pursues the subtle ways in which the beloved has left an imprint in nature. But while the focus of the lover's pursuit is on loss and longing for the beloved, the marks made on nature by the beloved—the "trampled" stream, the "snapped" stalk, the "pressed" heel, the "brushed" grass—suggest the destructiveness of the beloved's passage. Longing is fraught with ambiguity: are the speaker's longing for and pursuit of the beloved perhaps tinged with a sense of his/her cruelty, disregard of the fragility of nature, of the speaker's feelings? Nature offers solace as well as evidence of the beloved's heedless plunge through a pristine landscape.

More recently, from the late twentieth century and into the present, Olga Broumas shares with H. D. a classicist background, a use of Greek mythology, and a self-conscious placing of herself in the tradition of female poets claiming Sappho as poetic and erotic foremother. Now, there is no longer any need for the coding of lesbian eroticism: female same-sex sexuality is overt and explicit; there is no holding back. Broumas uses translations from the Greek of Sappho to underline her lesbian erotics and the landscapes she paints are objective correlatives of sensual desire. Of all our modern lesbian poets—Adrienne Rich, Audre Lorde, Judy Grahn foremost among them—Broumas most often "achieves a complexly articulate eroticism without vagueness or reticence."[32] The titles of her books themselves gesture toward the traditions that inform her work: *Pastoral Jazz* and *Sappho's Gymnasium*.[33] And, for example, "Emblem" from *Pastoral Jazz* manages to echo both the impassioned rhythms of H. D. and the wondrous lyricism of Sappho:

> A woman whose existence is indifferent to yours
> attracts you
> No music comes of this
>
> no love
> orgasms of the earth oneiric
> deja-vus for you these healthy portions
>
> field hillock and field
> Inside the mind small mirrors and wool
> Frames of some wisdom
>
> miniatured there
> All the wells open to rain
> deep-throated praising spouts there

too Someone in awe who feels
it ministers out of some greater body
If someone else is hubristic

keen lemon yellow hurts that eye In time
a familiar word like *hair* passing between you
enters a desert of camels' bones.

For Broumas, nature—and, often, the sea—is the ground against which life evolves, both externally, in the world outside the self, and in the mind. Landscape, even when mentioned only suggestively in passing, is powerfully present in almost all her poems.[34] As in "Emblem," she gives us the constant, persistent presence of the natural world, whether green, lush, sensual, and life-affirming ("field hillock and field / Inside the mind") or brown and reminding us of mortality ("a desert of camels' bones").

Broumas very deliberately patterns her words on the page so that they create, or follow, expressive vocal rhythms; they are meant to be spoken aloud, capturing incantatory, erotic vocal rhythms: "I learned to want to capture the rhythm in which one speaks in one's soul."[35] Her rhythms are those of a passionate embodiment that sometimes evokes H. D. and Philips, as in "Aubade":

She wakes having flown
half a dozen illegal ones

The truth is erotic and shiny
language it breaks

what's small and can't contain
its sigh It leaves a wisdom that bleeds

metallic
segues idioms red flags in Kansas

She wakes up singing I have three cunts
red yellow brown

copper pennies in the skulls
of Americans

We turn the air is full of sound
golden enclave of hair and blood

sweet perineum
between the two crossed fingers and the thumb

Here we are
breathing together like dolphins

soaked calmed bespattered with the sun
atop the Rockies snow-capped and the whales

they resemble in a mind
snow-lined by pleasure

whole
pastures new like bare feet in the sun

green so young it squints of yellow
true cobalt summer blue of noon.[36]

Here Broumas brings together an explicitly articulated lesbian eroticism embedded in a swirlingly lyrical embrace of the movements of dolphins and whales and the intense colors of sea, sun, and sky. All this follows the veiled suggestion of humanitarian, albeit politically illegal, activity. But there is not a narrative to be understood here, only the overflowing of feeling and the power of words to give it expression, and of nature to embody female erotic passion.

From its beginnings in the seventeenth century, we can pursue the female queer pastoral in women's poetry into the twenty-first century.[37] That the pastoral offered a sustained and sustaining safe haven for the expression of coded desire as well as for the articulation of social and political sentiment becomes apparent once we take a longer historical perspective on women's poetry. In the twenty-first century, while coding may no longer be necessary, the pastoral—or at least its descendent in the uses of an eroticized and eroticizing nature—continues as a powerful expressive vehicle for female same-sex erotics and politics and implicitly pays homage to Katherine Philips, who stands at the head of this tradition and initiated a conscious, self-aware female pastoralism.

Afterword
The Most Deservedly Admired Mrs. Katherine Philips— Her Books

Elizabeth H. Hageman

As the title page of Henry Herringman's 1667 folio edition of her poems and plays says, and as the essays in this volume attest, Katherine Philips was in her own time, as she is today, "Most deservedly Admired." From Amy Scott-Douglass's treatment of the 1667 folio of Philips's poetry as "a metaphor for the restored face of royalism" (chapter 4) and Elizabeth Hodgson's observation that "when Philips shows up at a wedding, she becomes a very complicated poet indeed" (chapter 6) to Harriette Andreadis's account of Philips (and also Aemelia Lanier) opening up a tradition of pastoral "as a vehicle for the coded expression of a female eroticism, serving both personal erotic and politically charged, class conscious purposes" (chapter 10), these essays demonstrate once and for all that Philips was an active participant in a series of overlapping seventeenth century social, political, and literary movements. She was a vital figure in British literary history, a history that we now understand as more complicated and interesting than we knew before Philips and a host of other early modern women writers—Mary Sidney, Isabella Whitney, Anna Trapnell, Anne Bradstreet, and Margaret Cavendish, for example—were "rediscovered" in the 1970s and 1980s.

As the essays in this volume affirm, Katherine Philips incorporated, commented upon, and/or transmuted a multitude of political, religious, and philosophical ideas current in her time. She used a wide variety of verse forms as she expanded and developed many literary genres—from Petrarchan wooing poems and elegiac poems of parting to philosophical verse letters. Her two plays, both translated from her French contemporary Pierre Corneille, were the first plays by a woman to be presented on the public stages of Dublin (her *Pompey*) and London (*Horace*); they were also among the first rhymed neoclassical heroic dramas on the British stage. Printed more than 40 years after her death, Philips's *Letters from Orinda to Poliarchus* provide an engaging view of a seventeenth century writer in conversation with her friends and her culture. Answered, emulated, sometimes consciously rejected by later British writers, Philips is a writer whose works reward our close attention.

Pleased to have been invited to write the afterword to this volume, I soon realized that rather than rehearse arguments so clearly made in its introduction and in the essays themselves, I could complement and extend their analyses by discussing some additional evidence of Philips's "staying power" from the seventeenth century to our own time. In what follows, then, I will discuss a newly recognized material record of the circulation of Philips's writing—this in Derbyshire in the English midlands, where two quatrains from her poems are inscribed in a seventeenth century hand on a windowpane in the Long Gallery at Haddon Hall. Second, I will note what the American writer Washington Irving did with Katherine Philips and the Derbyshire windows in his 1822 fictional *Bracebridge Hall.* I will then close with a brief survey of readers' marks in some of the numerous printed copies of her writings now in libraries in England, Wales, Scotland, and Ireland; the United States and Canada; France, Germany, Japan, Australia, New Zealand, and South Africa. As David Pearson writes in his *Books as History,* "Books develop their own individual histories which become part of our wider heritage and evidence base."[1] As readers of this volume of essays on "the Matchless Orinda" will, I trust, agree, any analysis of the seventeenth century is incomplete unless it includes the histories of women writers and their readers.

I. *Mottos in Windows*

Among notes on Philips by her contemporary John Aubrey is the information that Aubrey's "cozen" Mary (Aubrey) Montagu told him that Philips "wrote out verses in innes, or mottos in windowes, in her table-booke."[2] With the word "table-booke," Montagu (Philips's Rosania) may have meant an album of blank paper like the one in which Philips transcribed her own poems, the volume now called the Tutin manuscript,[3] though she may have been thinking of the kind of book described in two essays published in 2004—one in *Electronic British Library Journal;* the other in *Shakespeare Quarterly:* a small book comprising erasable leaves upon which one could write with a metal stylus, the latter often called a "pin." These erasable books were handy, as the authors of the *Shakespeare Quarterly* essay say, for "collecting pieces of poetry, noteworthy epigrams, and new words; recording sermons, legal proceedings, or parliamentary debates; jotting down conversations, recipes, cures, and jokes; keeping financial records; recalling addresses and meetings; and collecting notes on foreign customs while traveling."[4] If we do one day find such a table-book containing Philips's now well-known handwriting, it will of course show only her latest jottings, for the longer she used the book, the more early layers of notes would have been erased. Even without seeing the actual book, though, the idea of reading Philips's records of "verses in innes, or mottos in windowes" raises interesting questions about the circulation of poetry in early modern England—the same sorts of questions that are raised by Philips's early poem beginning "A married state affords but little ease," which includes lines that later reappear in other writers' manuscript and printed antimarriage poems—lines, one might suspect, that were not "original" to Philips.[5]

As most readers of this afterword will know, stories of early modern verses written on windows are legion. According to John Foxe, both Elizabeth Tudor and Lady Jane Grey wrote mottos (short, generally epigrammatic poems) on windows: Elizabeth wrote with a diamond at Woodstock, "Much suspected by me / Nothing proved can be. Quoth ELIZABETH, Prisoner," and Lady Jane wrote in the Tower of London, "Do never think it strange, / Though now I have misfortune; / For if that fortune change, / The same to thee may happen / Jane Dudley."[6] Mary, Queen of Scots, is said to have inscribed verses in windows in the spa town of Buxton, in Derbyshire, where she was taken by George Talbot, sixth Earl of Shewsbury each spring from 1572 to 1584. Her now famous "Farewell to Buxton" was recorded in Latin by William Camden in the third edition of his *Britannia* (1590) and then in 1610 accompanied by an English translation by Philemon Holland, who enlarged upon Camden's description of Buxton to say,

> George Earle of *Shrewsbury* lately beatified [Buxton] with buildings.... At which time that most unfortunate Lady, Mary Queene of *Scots* bad farewell unto *Buxton* with this *Distichon,* by a little change of *Cæsars* verses concerning *Feltria,* in this wise.
>
> Buxtona *quæ calidæ celebrabere nomine lymphæ*
> *Fortè mihi posthac non adeunda, vale.*
> *Buxton,* that of great name shalt be, for hote and holsome baine,
> Farewell, for I perhaps shall not thee ever see againe.[7]

Currently on display in what is now the Old Hall Hotel in Buxton is a recently engraved glass panel replicating a sixteenth century manuscript record of 29 items engraved in Buxton by Mary, Queen of Scots, and contemporaries who visited her there—among them the Earls of Leicester and Pembroke; Anne Talbot, daughter-in-law of the Earl of Shrewsbury; and Edward Manners, third Earl of Rutland, of Haddon Hall in nearby Bakewell.[8]

Early in the seventeenth century, John Donne in "A Valediction: Of my Name in the Window" treated his own signature engraved in a window as a sign of "love's magic," and George Herbert famously alluded to window poems in "The Posie" and "Dulnesse." Closer to

Philips's own time is Martha, Lady Gifford's account of her brother Sir William Temple's love for Philips's future friend Dorothy Osborne, which includes two stories of poems written with diamonds on windows. On the occasion of William and Dorothy's first meeting in 1648 on the Isle of Wight, Dorothy's brother Robin engraved on a window pane an insult against Temple's cousin, the Parliamentarian Colonel Robert Hammond: "And Hammon was hanged upon the gallows he had prepared for Mordecai." When Robin was apprehended by the authorities, Dorothy saved the day and attracted William's admiration by taking responsibility for the verses.[9] Later, while he was pining for Dorothy, William (apparently not thinking about the implications of the swan having raped Leda) wrote on a window near a garden statue of her, "Tell me Leda, which is best, / n'ear to move, or n'ere to rest? / Speak that I may know there by, / Who is happier, you or I."[10]

As far as I know, however, the only surviving early modern English window poems are in Haddon Hall, still owned—as it was in Philip's lifetime—by the Manners family. One, written on a diamond-shaped windowpane in the hall's state bedroom, is a translation of an oft-repeated distich by the third or fourth century Roman writer Dionysius Cato: "That man nere Lived / nor never Shall / that did all well / & had no fault att all."[11] In the nearby Long Gallery on a small rectangular windowpane are two quatrains identified by Antony Cox as excerpts from poems by Katherine Philips. About five inches tall and four inches wide, the Elizabethan glass pane looks to a modern eye very much like a glass analogue of a paper page in an early modern octavo book. As Claire Byrony Williams observed when she and I visited the hall in 2012, the forms of the neatly written letters, including the engraver's use of a long *s*, together with spellings and punctuation marks throughout both quatrains indicate that they were transcribed in the late 1600s or possibly in the early 1700s—perhaps, but not certainly, by the person who transcribed the distich from Cato.[12]

Although it is impossible to say whether Philips's quatrains were engraved from a printed or manuscript copy of her poems, it is worth noting that, as often happened when extracts of Philips's poems or plays were copied into poetical miscellanies or commonplace books, these two quatrains have been given new titles. Their new headings place them within a real or imagined literary coterie whose members include an Orinda and also a Cornelea and a Leonora, neither of whose names appear elsewhere among known members of Philips's coterie—though, of course, Cornelia is the name of a character in her *Pompey.* The first quatrain inscribed on the Haddon Hall windowpane comprises the second stanza of Philips's "Lucasia and Orinda parting with Pastora and Phillis at Ipswich": The second engraved stanza is a slightly rewritten version of the final quatrain of "To my Lady Elizabeth Boyle, Singing—Since affairs of the State &c.":

Cornelea parting with Leonora

How perifhed is the Joy thats paft
the present how unfteady
What comfort can be great and laft
When this is gone already.

Orinda to Leonora

I'd rather in your favour Live
then in a lafting name
And much a greater rate would give
for hapynefse then fame.

Although none of the other extant windows in Haddon Hall is inscribed by the same hand(s) that wrote out Philips's poems or the Cato distich, the names Cornelea and Orinda—but not Leonora—are engraved alongside other names in several diamond-shaped panes in the state bedroom. Apparently written out by inexperienced engravers on glass, not all of the names in the following list of seven can be transcribed with complete certainty—they are (approximately) "Corneilia / Armeda / Cammella / Urania / Corynda / Harold / Arthur."[13] On a nearby pane are two names separated by a squiggle and followed by a date: "Theodosius / orinda [*sic*] / 1706." In a third pane is inscribed, "Theodosius / Orinda / Gertrude." A fourth pane shows one name only, this name surrounded by squiggles: "orinda [*sic*]."

The digit "6" in the year 1706 in the Theodosius/orinda window could possibly be read, as it was by Washington Irving in 1816, as a zero.[14] If, in fact, the engraver meant to write "1700" rather than "1706," we might conclude that all of the windows mentioned here were engraved by members and/or acquaintances of the family of John Manners, ninth Earl of Rutland, before the year 1703 when he was created first Duke of Rutland and the family moved from Haddon Hall to Belvoir Castle in Wiltshire.[15] If, however, some or all of these windows were actually engraved in 1706, they may have been the work of strangers to the Manners family, for in the two centuries when the house was uninhabited, visitors often toured the premises, sometimes with a housekeeper or other local person, other times on their own.[16] Although no other dated eighteenth century inscriptions are presently found on Haddon Hall windows, there are a number of undated signatures perhaps from that time—and also a few records of nineteenth century visitors: in the state bedroom, for example, "Mary Blodget / 20th July 1821" and "C. J. Booth Leeds 1846."[17]

II. *The Fair Mrs. Philips in Bracebridge Hall*

Washington Irving's handwritten notes from his visit to Haddon Hall in 1816 include transcripts of not two but four quatrains by Philips that he saw engraved in the Long Gallery. The first quatrain in Irving's notes is based on lines 5–8 of Philips's "Song, to the Tune of *Sommes nous pas trop heureux*":

Camilla and her Cassander 1700

Leonora if you with Kindness bless me
    Since from you I soon must part
Fortune will so dispossess me
    That your love will break my heart.
                        Camilla

The second and third quatrains Irving transcribed are the two stanzas that remain today in the Long Gallery, though Irving changes them slightly, perhaps because he had some difficulty reading the seventeenth century script in which they are written. Irving's fourth transcription is a version of lines 1–4 of Philips's "Parting with a Friend," again with a new heading:

Orinda parting with Ariana

Whoever thinks that joys below
Can lasting be and great
Let him behold this parting blow
And cure his own deceit.[18]

How it happened that the first and fourth quatrains Irving recorded are no longer in Haddon Hall is not clear, though one might guess that the pane(s) on which they were inscribed were broken or lost in the process of the twentieth century restoration of the Hall by John Henry Manners, ninth Duke of Rutland, grandfather of its current occupant, Lord Edward John Francis Manners.

Although Irving's notebooks include no mention of Katherine Philips, Geoffrey Crayon, the narrator of his fictional *Bracebridge Hall* (1822), describes windows on which "scraps of poetry [are] engraved...with diamonds, taken from the writings of the fair Mrs. Philips, the once celebrated Orinda." Crayon imagines connections between the window poems and nearby portraits of "four sisters of nearly the same age, who flourished about a century since" and also "old romances in the library [that] have marginal notes expressing sympathy and approbation [for the lovers described in the books]." Under the misapprehension that one can easily tell the gender of early modern handwriting, Crayon says,

> Some of these seem to have been inscribed by lovers; and others, in a delicate and unsteady hand, and a little inaccurate in the spelling, have evidently been written by the young ladies themselves, or by female friends, who have been on visits to the Hall. Mrs. Philips seems to have been their favourite author, and they have distributed the names of her heroes and heroines among their circle of intimacy.[19] Sometimes, in a male hand, the verse bewails the cruelty of beauty, and the sufferings of constant love; while in a female hand it prudishly confines itself to lamenting the parting of female friends.[20]

In Crayon's bedroom is a "bow-window...[which] has several of these inscriptions. I have," he says, "one at this moment before my eyes, called 'Camilla parting with Leonora.'" After quoting the poem inscribed at Haddon as "Cornelea to Leonora," Crayon goes on to say, "close by it is another, written, perhaps, by some adventurous lover, who had stolen into the lady's chamber during her absence." Using Theodosius and the date 1700, Irving transforms the Haddon Hall "Orinda to Leonora" into an early eighteenth century wooing poem by a young man to a beloved lady:

Theodosius to Camilla

I'd rather in your favour live,
Than in a lasting name;
And much a greater rate would give
For happiness than fame.
Theodosius. 1700

All of this, Crayon says, incites "a cloud of melancholy stealing over the present gaieties around me," for it reminds him of the passing of time and the inevitable deaths of even the truest loves.[21] Irving writes here in what is by 1822 a well-established tradition of transforming bits and pieces of what Christina Lupton calls "abandoned writing" into affecting narratives; in the eighteenth century, Lupton writes, "sentimental novels and essays are filled with forgotten manuscripts found moldering in drawers, handwritten notes discovered in the form of wastepaper, and poems and initials scratched into glass, trees, or pathos-inducing gravestones."[22] Bracebridge Hall itself is an amalgam of various stately homes Irving had visited—Aston Hall in Birmingham, Brereton Hall in Cheshire, Sir Walter Scott's Abbotsford in Scotland, and of course Haddon Hall;[23] so too, the material objects Crayon finds there are from a fictionalized past, rewritten and cobbled together to create a romantically melancholy place visited by a sensitive visitor who can "read" it properly.

III. *Marking Readers of Philips's Writing*

In a chapter entitled "Noting Readers of the *Arcadia* in Marginalia and Commonplace Books" in her *Reading Material in Early Modern England*, Heidi Brayman Hackel observes that about 70 percent of 151 copies of Sir Philip Sidney's *Arcadia* she has examined contain handwritten readers' marks "ranging from signatures to a few stray scribbles to elaborate polyglot marginalia and indices." Among the kinds of handwritten marks found by Brayman Hackel are many that appear as well in extant printed copies of Philips's writings: fragments of verse; mathematical calculations, drawings of stick figures, doodled letters or numbers, emendations, underlinings, check marks, x's, and penciled lines beside titles on contents pages and beside the writing itself. As she points out, Brayman Hackel's study of readers' marks in the *Arcadia* is one of many "microhistories" that together can create a collective view of early modern books and their readers.[24] In suggesting here a microhistory of extant copies of Katherine Philips's writing, I aim, in part, to complement Brayman Hackel's history of the *Arcadia*. For while Sidney's sixteenth century prose romance is directed, as Brayman Hackel notes, to women readers,[25] the seventeenth century Katherine Philips is a woman writer whose poems are addressed to both men and women and whose plays, both named for heroic men, include remarkably interesting female characters.[26]

Many, though by no means all, of more than 100 copies of Philips's writing I have surveyed exhibit handwritten marks of ownership, typically written on books' front pastedowns, flyleaves, or title pages, several owners in fact signing the 1664 octavo published by Richard Marriot within the laurel wreath adorning its title page. Early owners sometimes insert their names in margins within the books themselves, even on occasion signing them more than once. As undoubtedly is also true with the *Arcadia,* many surviving copies of Philips's writing also convey ownership information by way of heraldic bindings or, more often, printed bookplates. Taken together (and seen alongside evidence such as sale catalogues from the period), these bits and pieces of information show that early modern owners of Philips's books included both men and women; scholars and clergymen; members of merchant, landed gentry, and aristocratic families; and residents of Ireland, Wales, Scotland, England, even colonial America.

More recent owners include the nineteenth century Welsh poet Andrew Jones Brereton (Andreas ô Fon), whose 1664 octavo is now at the University of Syracuse in New York; the English writer Robert Southey, who owned at least two copies of Philips's writing (one now in the Beineke Library at Yale University, the other at the University of Edinburgh); and the American Sarah Orne Jewett, who owned a 1664 octavo (now at Harvard), a 1669 folio (the New York Public Library), and a copy of the 1904 selected edition of Philips's poems edited by Louise Guiney and published by J. R. Tutin (also now at Harvard). Copies once owned by twentieth century literary scholars include exemplars of the 1667 folio owned by Cleanth Brooks, Don Cameron Allen, and W. W. Gregg at the University of Southern Mississippi, San Diego State University, and the Massachusetts Center for Renaissance Studies, respectively.

Among copies of Philips's books that have been enhanced by additional information about their author are exemplars of the 1664 octavo in which the letters "hilips" are written after "Mrs. K. P." to create the name "Mrs. K. Philips" or in which "Katherine Philips" is written below her initials. Some copies of the *Letters* identify *Orinda* and *Poliarchus* on their title pages, and a copy of her writing now at Monash University in Australia contains a list of Philips's friends and their sobriquets (as does the well-known manuscript copy of some of Philips's poems by Nicholas Crouch of Balliol College, Oxford). An exemplar of the 1667 folio at Trinity College, Dublin, includes a handwritten cast list for the 1668 court production of *Horace* and a prologue and epilogue for the same play,[27] and a 1669 folio at the Folger Shakespeare Library includes a handwritten note by Charles Cottrell indicating that Philips's letter about the publication of the 1664 octavo of her poems imbedded in the book's preface was written to "my paternal Great Great Grandfather."

As Brayman Hackel notes, and these volumes verify, handwritten marks in books often offer glimpses into the lives of readers, when, for example, a recipe or a mathematical calculation or (in a volume to be discussed below) a poem by another author "reveal[s] something of the interests and circumstances of the reader."[28] As several scholars of early modern annotations have noted, although marks such as stray words or stick figures in margins or on flyleaves sometimes look strange to us, they, together with corrections of obviously misprinted words or lines, pointing manicules, check marks, crosses, and lines or crosses beside titles in contents pages or in margins beside the writing itself provide evidence about the process of early modern reading—often, in fact, showing that in many ways it resembles our own. Seventeenth and eighteenth century readers sometimes wrote out individual lines from Philips's poems or plays in their books' margins and sometimes recorded longer passages on flyleaves. Although it is often said that such writings are examples of readers practicing their handwriting, it is worth noting here that these lines are often the kind of moral passages that one finds copied out in contemporary commonplace books: lines such as "Ther is no such thing as plesur hear It is all a parfict Cheat" written twice (with variants) on a front flyleaf of a folio volume bearing the name of one Ann Knight and now at the University of California at Berkeley seem more like entries in commonplace books than handwriting exercises.

A few copies contain corrections of errors within prefatory poems or in Philips's writing itself, and one of two copies of the 1664 octavo now at the University of Texas has on its page 236 a small piece of paper neatly pasted over the word "Finis" printed below the book's seventy-fourth poem before a last-minute decision was made to add to the book Philips's ode "Upon Mr. Cowley's Retirement." Signed on its title page by one "Ann Littleton," this copy has added to it an engraving after Faithhorne's 1667 frontispiece by Michael Van der Gucht used in Bernard Lintot's 1705 edition of the *Letters,* as does a copy of the 1664 octavo at the University of Alberta. Copies of the 1667 folio edition at the University of Alberta and at the Folger Shakespeare Library now bear as their frontispieces not the Faithhorne engraving we would expect to see, but a smaller anonymous portrait (also engraved after Faithhorne's) with the inscription "Mrs. Catherine Philips" rather than "Orinda" on its pedestal—this image from Jacob Tonson's 1710 octavo edition of Philips's writings. Occasionally a second portrait—in one folio a copy of Isaac Beckett's seventeenth century mezzotint portrait of Philips and in another William Finden's nineteenth century image of her modeled after the painted portrait now at Knole House in Kent—creates an "extra-illustrated" or "Grangerized" volume of writing by "The Matchless Orinda."

Among books whose owners inscribe materials with no obvious relationship to Philips is a copy of the 1669 folio listed in Sotheby's 1931 sale catalogue of George Thorn-Drury's library and donated in 1940 to the National Library of Art at the Victoria and Albert Museum in London by the renowned expert on armorial bindings, Henry J. B. Clements of Killadoon, County Kildare, Ireland. Bound in handsome red morocco with the cypher of Anne Tighe on its spine, the Thorn-Drury/Clements volume was owned in the seventeenth century by the eldest daughter of Christopher Lovett, alderman in Dublin and then lord mayor from 1676 to 1677. Anne Lovett's first husband, William Tighe of Rutland, County Carlow, died in 1679, and in the next year Anne Tighe wrote on her book's first back flyleaf, "Ann : Tighe : / August ye 26th 1680." Above that signature, in the same hand, is a 24-line pastoral lament headed, "The Teares of the Consort for Mr Tighe Writt by / My Lord Blessington 1679."[29] On February 7, 1681, the widowed Anne Tighe married Thomas Coote, later judge of the Irish King's Bench, and 19 years later she, or someone else, wrote beside the poem an intriguing complaint: "Coppyd by ye never Enough Valued / Mrs Ann Coote / July ye 25th 1700 / Saturday."

Another kind of evidence of women's use of an exemplar of Philips's writing is in a copy of the 1678 folio now at Duke University and available online through EEBO. This book contains at the top of its title page the inscription "Penelope Winniatt my Booke Presented by / Mr John Winniatt." Under the word "Poems," she writes, "Given by me to my Daught^r^"; then on either side of "The Matchless" is "Elizabeth" and "Winniatt." That this Penelope Winniatt is the Penelope Pindar who was born ca. 1668, who married into the Winniatt family of Dymock, Gloucester, and who died in 1732 is confirmed by a book I now have in my possession: a copy of the 1670 ninth impression of Owen Feltham's *Resolves.* This folio is prefaced by two title pages, the first of which presents an engraved image contrasting *Sapientiæ* and *Veritatis* with *Opinio[n]* and *Ignorantia.* At the top of that page is Penelope Winniatt's signature. At the top of the second title page, she has written her birth name, "Penelope Pindar"; in the center of that page, "Given by Me to my Son / Thomas Winniatt"; and on either side of the printer's ornament, "Penelope" and "Winniatt." Here, and also with Anne Tighe's volume, one wishes for more details. On what occasion(s) did Winniatt present these books to her children? Did she give similar folios to other family members? Why did she choose Philips for her daughter and Feltham for her son? Was Anne Tighe's complaint playful or serious? But even without further information, our glimpses of Winniatt and Tighe's writings in books provide data for book historians and for scholars of woman's history who seek anecdotal evidence of actual women's lives to balance—even correct—impressions about early modern life derived from sources such as strictures in conduct books, encomia of saintly women in funeral sermons, or characters such as Cordelia, Goneril, and Regan in *King Lear.*[30]

As I have written this afterword, I have thought about copies of Philips's writing now on my own bookshelf, especially about a 1667 folio formerly owned by the Gell family of Hopton Hall near Wirksworth in Derbyshire, not far from Haddon Hall. In the spirit of Irving's Geoffrey Crayon, I am tempted to suggest that Temperance Gell (d. 1730), who owned Hopton Hall after the death of her brother Philip in 1719, who in 1722 endowed a school for 20 local girls and boys in the nearby village of Carsington, and whose signature is in my 1667 folio, was present when the quatrains from Philips's poems were engraved in the windows of Haddon Hall. Scholarly restraint, however, reminds me to simply remark the coincidence of the survival of three pieces of material evidence—a windowpane, a journal kept by a visiting American, and a signature in a printed book—demonstrating that Katherine Philips's writing traveled, not long after her early death in 1664, to a part of England that she herself never visited.

Notes

Notes to Introduction

1. This brief biographical narrative is based upon a synthesis of the work of the most significant biographers of Katherine Philips, including John Aubrey, Edmund Gosse, Philip Webster Souers, Patrick Thomas, Claudia Limbert, Elizabeth H. Hageman, and Warren Chernaik. See Aubrey, *"Brief Lives," chiefly of Contemporaries, set down by John Aubrey, between the Years 1669 and 1696,* vol. 2, ed. Andrew Clark (Oxford: Clarendon Press, 1898); Gosse, *Seventeenth-Century Studies: A Contribution to the History of English Poetry* (London: K. Paul Trench, 1883), 229–58; Souers, *The Matchless Orinda* (Cambridge, MA: Harvard University Press, 1931), Thomas, *Katherine Philips ("Orinda")* (Cardiff: University of Wales Press, 1988); Limbert, "Katherine Philips: Controlling a Life and Reputation," *South Atlantic Review* 56, no. 2 (1991): 27–42; Hageman, "Katherine Philips (1632–1664)," in *Dictionary of Literary Biography: Seventeenth-Century British Nondramatic Poets,* vol. 131, ed. M. Thomas Hester (Detroit: Gale Research, 1993), 202–14; and Chernaik, "Philips [nee Fowler] Katherine (1632–1664)," in *Oxford Dictionary of National Biography* (Oxford University Press, 2006), www.oxforddnb.com (accessed Sept. 13, 2014).

2. Thomas, *Katherine Philips,* 49.

3. Paula Loscocco, "'Manly Sweetness': Katherine Philips among the Neoclassicals," *Huntington Library Quarterly* 56, no. 3 (Summer 1993): 266.

4. Penelope Anderson, *Friendship's Shadows: Women's Friendship and the Politics of Betrayal in England, 1640–1705* (Edinburgh: Edinburgh University Press, 2012), 154.

5. Gillian Wright, *Producing Women's Poetry, 1600–1730: Text and Paratext, Manuscript and Print* (Cambridge: Cambridge University Press, 2013), 21, 22.

6. John Keats to John Hamilton Reynolds, Sept. 21, 1817, in *The Letters of John Keats,* 3rd ed., ed. Maurice Buxton Forman (London: Oxford University Press, 1947), 45–46.

7. George Saintsbury, *Minor Poets of the Caroline Period,* vol. 1 (Oxford: Clarendon Press, 1905). On early editions of Philips's poems, see Patrick Thomas, ed., introduction to*The Collected Works of Katherine Philips: The Matchless Orinda,* vol. 1, *The Poems* (Stump Cross, Essex: Stump Cross Books, 1990), 50–55.

8. For the earlier version of her essay, see Elizabeth M. A. Hodgson, "Katherine Philips: Agent of Matchlessness," *Women's Writing* 10, no. 1 (2003): 119–36.

9. Catharine Gray, "Katherine Philips and the Post-Courtly Coterie," *English Literary Renaissance* 32, no. 3 (Autumn 2002): 426–51; Lorna Hutson, "The Body of the Friend and the Woman Writer: Katherine Philips's Absence from Alan Bray's *The Friend* (2003)," *Women's Writing* 14, no. 2 (2007): 196–214; Paula Loscocco "Inventing the English Sappho: Katherine Philips's Donnean Poetry," *Journal of English and Germanic Philology* 102, no. 1 (2003): 59–87; Valerie Traub, *The Renaissance of Lesbianism in Early Modern England* (Cambridge: Cambridge University Press, 2002), 295–325.

10. Souers, *Matchless Orinda,* 41, 277.

11. Elizabeth Susan Wahl, *Invisible Relations: Representations of Female Intimacy in the Age of Enlightenment* (Stanford, CA: Stanford University Press, 1999), 131–36.

12. Ibid., 132.

13. Ibid., 134.

14. Souers, *The Matchless Orinda,* 276–77.

15. Lillian Faderman, *Surpassing the Love of Men: Romantic Friendship and Love between Women from the Renaissance to the Present* (New York: Quill, 1981), 68, 71.

16. In *Odd Girls and Twilight Lovers: A History of Lesbian Life in Twentieth-Century America* (New York: Columbia University Press, 1991), Faderman makes the case more emphatically: "The sexologists were certainly the first to construct the conception of the lesbian, to call her into being as a member of a special category. As the century progressed, however, women who agreed to identify themselves as lesbian felt more and more free to alter the sexologists' definitions to suit themselves, so that for many women 'lesbianism' has become something vastly broader than what the sexologists could possibly have conceived of—having to do with lifestyle, ideology, the establishment of subcultures and institutions" (4). Terry Castle questions what she calls, in reference to Faderman, "the no-lesbians-before-1900 school" in *The Apparitional Lesbian: Female Homosexuality and Modern Culture* (New York: Columbia University Press, 1995), 104–05.

17. Liz Stanley, "Epistemological Issues in Researching Lesbian History: The Case of Romantic Friendship," in *Working Out: New Directions for Women's Studies,* ed. Hilary Hinds, Ann Phoenix, and Jackie Stacey, 161–72 (New York: Routledge, 1992), 161. See also Stanley, *The Auto/Biographical I: The Theory and Practice of Feminist Auto/Biography* (Manchester: Manchester University Press, 1992), 214–37.

18. The terms of the alteritist/continuitist debate were set by Louise Fradenburg and Carla Freccero in their introductory essay, "Caxton, Foucault, and the Pleasures of History," in *Premodern Sexualities,* ed. Fradenburg and Freccero (New York: Routledge, 1996), xiii–xxiv. In that essay, Fradenburg and Freccero question the critical tendency to privilege historical and cultural difference (i.e., alterity) over historical and cultural consonance (i.e., continuity). Cf. David Robinson, *Closeted Writing and Lesbian and Gay Literature: Classical, Early Modern, Eighteenth-Century* (Aldershot: Ashgate, 2006), vii–viii; and Traub, *Renaissance of Lesbianism,* 331–34, and "The Present Future of Lesbian Historiography," in *The Blackwell Companion to Lesbian, Gay, Bisexual, Transgender, and Queer Studies,* ed. George Haggerty and Molly McGarry (London: Blackwell, 2007), 124–45.

19. The Ur-text for this constructionist perspective is, of course, Michel Foucault, *The History of Sexuality,* vol. 1, *An Introduction,* trans. Robert Hurley (New York: Vintage, 1990). See also David M. Halperin, *How to Do the History of Homosexuality* (Chicago: University of Chicago Press, 2004); *One Hundred Years of Homosexuality: And Other Essays on Greek Love* (New York: Routledge, 1989); and *Saint Foucault: Towards a Gay Hagiography* (Oxford: Oxford University Press, 1997).

20. In addition to Fradenburg and Freccero, "Caxton, Foucault," see also Kenneth Borris, general introduction, *Same-Sex Desire in the English Renaissance: A Sourcebook of Texts, 1470–1650* (New York: Routledge, 2003), 1–16; John Boswell, "Categories, Experience and Sexuality," in *Forms of Desire: Sexual Orientation and the Social Constructionist Controversy,* ed. Edward Stein, 133–73 (New York: Routledge, 1992); Claude J. Summers, "Homosexuality and Renaissance Literature, or the Anxieties of Anachronism," *South Central Review* 9, no. 1 (1992): 2–23; and Robinson, *Closeted Writing,* 3–17. Although Boswell is often dismissed as an essentialist, Mathew Kuefler reminds us that Foucault cited approvingly Boswell's *Christianity, Social Tolerance, and Homosexuality: Gay People in Western Europe from the Beginning of the Christian Era to the Fourteenth Century* (Chicago: University of Chicago Press, 1980). According to Foucault, Boswell's book is "a truly groundbreaking work. Boswell reveals unexplored phenomena with an unfailing erudition" (qtd. in Mathew Kuefler, ed., "The Boswell Thesis," in *The Boswell Thesis: Essays on "Christianity, Social Tolerance, and Homosexuality,"* 1–31 [Chicago: University of Chicago Press, 2006], 10).

21. Stanley, "Epistemological Issues," 169.

22. Eve Kosofsky Sedgwick, *Tendencies* (Durham, NC: Duke University Press, 1993), 8.

23. For a notable exception to this trend, see Kate Lilley, "Fruits of Sodom: The Critical Erotics of Early Modern Women's Writing," *Parergon* 29, no. 2 (2012): 175–92. For Lilley, the fruit of Sodom is an apt metaphor for the critical erotics that subtends the field of early modern women's writing, since "Sodom-apples, the fruits of conscious feminine disobedience and fair-seeming impersonation, signify the abortive issue of Eve's perverse desire and her criminal intent. They raise the spectre of a pleasure that is original and originating, aspiring but also terminal, located at the intersection of the shameful and the shameless, the fruitful and the fruitless, the auto and alloerotic. Sodom-apples, then, as well as being carnal and sodomitical, are also paradoxically genealogical: of the line of 'Eve's distained nature' (in Southwell's phrase)" (186). In her brief discussion of Philips, Lilley argues that "the fruit of Sodom" we find in line 9 of "Against Pleasure" refers not to lesbian desire per se, but to "the problematic of unauthorized feminine knowledge and incorrigible desire" (191). This problematic, Lilley maintains, represents a powerful link between modern and early modern critical erotics.

On the un/historicist divide in queer studies, see Valerie Traub, "The New Unhistoricism in Queer Studies," *PMLA* 128, no. 1 (2013): 21–39. In defense of queer historicism, Traub critiques the unhistoricist, antiteleological methodologies exemplified in the scholarship of Carla Freccero, Jonathan Goldberg, and Madhavi Menon, among others. See Carla Freccero, *Queer/Early/ Modern* (Durham, NC: Duke University Press, 2006); Freccero, "Queer Spectrality: Haunting the Past," in *A Companion to Lesbian, Gay, Bisexual, Transgender, and Queer Studies,* ed. George E. Haggerty and Molly McGarry (Malden, MA: Blackwell, 2007), 194–213; Freccero, "The Queer Time of the Lesbian Premodern," in *The Lesbian Premodern,* ed. Noreen Giffney, Michelle M. Sauer, and Diane Watt, 61–73 (New York: Palgrave, 2011); Freccero, "Queer Times," *South Atlantic Quarterly* 106, no. 3 (2007): 485–94; Jonathan Goldberg and Madhavi Menon, "Queering History," *PMLA* 120, no. 5 (2005): 1608–17; Menon, "Afterword: Period Cramps," in *Queer Renaissance Historiography: Backward Gaze,* ed. Vin Nardizzi, Stephen Guy-Bray, and Will Stockton, 229–34 (Farnham: Ashgate, 2009); Menon, *Unhistorical Shakespeare: Queer Theory in Shakespearean Literature and Film* (New York: Palgrave Macmillan, 2008).

24. Elaine Hobby, "Katherine Philips: Seventeenth-Century Lesbian Poet," in *What Lesbians Do in Books: Lesbians as Writers, Readers and Characters in Literature,* ed. Elaine Hobby and Chris White, 183–204 (London: Women's Press, 1991); *Virtue of Necessity: English Women's Writing, 1649–88* (London: Virago, 1988).

25. Loscocco, "English Sappho," 86. See her chapter 5 in the present volume.

26. Ibid., 80.

27. In addition to the monographs by Wahl, Andreadis, and Traub, see the following essays: Harriette Andreadis, "The Erotics of Female Friendship in Early Modern England," in *Maids and Mistresses, Cousins and Queens: Women's Alliances in Early Modern England,* ed. Karen Robertson and Susan Frye, 241–58 (Oxford: Oxford University Press, 1999); Celia A. Easton, "Excusing the Breach of Nature's Laws: The Discourse of Denial and Disguise in Katherine Philips," *Restoration: Studies in English Literary Culture, 1660–1700* 14, no. 1 (Spring 1990): 1–14; Mary Libterin, "Female Friendship in Women's Verse: Towards a New Theory of Female Poetics," *Women's Studies* 9, no. 3 (Feb. 1982): 291–308; Kate Lilley, "'Dear Object': Katherine Philips's Love Elegies and Their Readers," in *Women Writing, 1550–1750,* ed. Jo Wallwork and Paul Salzman, 179–90 (Bundoora, Australia: Meridian, 2001); Susannah B. Mintz, "Katherine Philips and the Space of Friendship," *Restoration: Studies in English Literary Culture, 1660–1700* 22, no. 2 (Fall 1998): 62–78; Arlene Stiebel, "Not Since Sappho: The Erotic in Poems of Katherine Philips and Aphra Behn," in *Homosexuality in Renaissance and Enlightenment England: Literary Representations in Historical Context,* ed. Claude Summers, 153–71 (New York: Haworth Press, 1992).

For relevant dissertations completed during the same period, see Susan Hardbeck, "'If Soules No Sexes Have...': Women, Convention and Negotiation in the Poetry of Katherine Philips" (Ph.D. diss., Northwestern University, 1996); Jennifer Lange, "'Hearts Thus Intermixed Speak': Erotic 'Friendship' in the Poems of Katherine Philips" (Ph.D. diss., Bowling Green State University, 1995); David M. Robinson, "To Boldly Go Where No Man Has Gone Before: The Representation of Lesbianism in Mid-Seventeenth- and Early Eighteenth-Century British and French Literature" (Ph.D. diss., University of California–Berkeley, 1998).

28. Wahl, *Invisible Relations,* 6.

29. Ibid., 130.

30. Harriette Andreadis, *Sappho in Early Modern England: Female Same-Sex Literary Erotics, 1550–1714* (Chicago: University of Chicago Press, 2001), 20.

31. Ibid., 98.

32. Ibid., 104–05.

33. Traub, *Renaissance of Lesbianism,* 13, 16.

34. Ibid., 308. See chapter 8 in the present volume.

35. Ibid., 341.

36. See Harriette Andreadis, "Re-Configuring Early Modern Friendship: Katherine Philips and Homoerotic Desire," *SEL: Studies in English Literature, 1500–1900* 46, no. 3 (Summer 2006): 523–42; "Versions of

Pastoral: Philips and Women's Queer Spaces," chapter 10 in the present volume; Valerie Traub, "Present Future."

37. Robinson, *Closeted Writing,* 19.

38. Alan Bray, *The Friend* (Chicago: University of Chicago Press, 2003).

39. Andreadis, "Re-Configuring," 524–25.

40. Jeremy Taylor, *A Discourse of the Nature, Offices, and Measures of Friendship with Rules of Conducting It* (London, 1657).

41. Andreadis, "Re-Configuring," 529.

42. Ibid., 532.

43. Hutson, "The Body of the Friend," 197. See chapter 9 in the present volume.

44. Ibid., 210.

45. Ann Hughes, *Gender and the English Revolution* (Abingdon: Routledge, 2012).

46. Robert C. Evans, "Paradox in Poetry and Politics: Katherine Philips in the Interregnum," in *The English Civil Wars in the Literary Imagination,* ed. Claude J. Summers and Ted-Larry Pebworth, 174–85 (Columbia: University of Missouri Press, 1999), 174.

47. Patrick Thomas, "Orinda, Vaughan, and Watkyns: Anglo-Welsh Literary Relationships during the Interregnum," *Anglo-Welsh Review* 26, no. 57 (1976): 96.

48. Carol Barash, *English Women's Poetry, 1649–1714: Politics, Community, and Linguistic Authority* (Oxford: Clarendon Press, 1996), observes, "Philips was only 12 years old when Cartwright died. " She goes on: "it is unlikely that [Philips] knew [Cartwright] well, or that she was implying emotional intimacy in calling him a 'friend'" (63).

49. Thomas, introduction to *Collected Works,* 13.

50. On Henrietta Maria's role in the importation of the *précieuses* tradition, see Barash, *English Women's Poetry,* 32–40; and Erica Veevers, *Images of Love and Religion: Queen Henrietta Maria and Court Entertainments* (Cambridge: Cambridge University Press, 1989).

51. Barash, *English Women's Poetry,* 66.

52. Souers, *The Matchless Orinda,* 44. On Philips's deployment of pseudonyms, see Margaret J. M. Ezell, "Reading Pseudonyms in Seventeenth-Century English Coterie Literature," *Essays in Literature* 21, no. 1 (Spring 1994): 14–25; and Martha Rainbolt, "Women Naming Women: The Use of Sobriquets by Aphra Behn, Anne Finch, and Katherine Philips," *Names: A Journal of Onomastics* 50, no. 2 (June 2002): 133–53.

53. Qtd. in Thomas, *Katherine Philips,* 13–14.

54. Ibid., 14.

55. Hero Chalmers, *Royalist Women Writers, 1650–1689* (Oxford: Clarendon Press, 2004), 105–13.

56. Barash, *English Women's Poetry,* 92.

57. Chalmers, *Royalist Women Writers,* 65, 105.

58. Ibid., 104.

59. Barash, *English Women's Poetry,* 75–81.

60. Wahl, *Invisible Relations,* 130.

61. Graham Hammill, "Sexuality and Society in the Poetry of Katherine Philips," in *Queer Renaissance Historiography: Backward Gaze,* ed. Vin Nardizzi, Stephen Guy-Bray, and Will Stockton, 185–205 (Farnham: Ashgate, 2009), 185.

62. Ibid., 202.

63. Gray, "Post-Courtly Coterie," 427. See chapter 1 in the present volume.

64. Ibid., 450–51.

65. Evans, "Paradox," 179.

66. Andrew Shifflett, "'Subdu'd by You': States of Friendship and Friends of the State in Katherine Philips's Poetry," in *Write or Be Written: Early Modern Women Poets and Cultural Constraints,* ed. Barbara Smith and Ursula Appelt, 177–95 (Burlington, VT: Ashgate, 2001), 183.

67. Andrew Shifflett, *Stoicism, Politics, and Literature in the Age of Milton: War and Peace Reconciled* (Cambridge: Cambridge University Press, 1998), 75–106.

68. Shifflett, "States of Friendship," 85–89.

69. Penelope Anderson, *Friendship's Shadows: Women's Friendship and the Politics of Betrayal in England, 1640–1705* (Edinburgh: Edinburgh University Press, 2012), 69–113, 153–88.

70. Penelope Anderson, "'Friendship Multiplyed': Royalist and Republican Friendship in Katherine Philips's Coterie," in *Discourses and Representations of Friendship in Early Modern Europe, 1500–1700,* ed. Daniel T. Lochman, Maritere López, and Lorna Hutson, 131–45 (Burlington, VT: Ashgate, 2010), 141.

71. Anderson, *Friendship's Shadows,* 103. See also Anderson, "Friendship Multiplyed."

72. Anderson, *Friendship's Shadows,* 154.

73. John Kerrigan, *Archipelagic English: Literature, History, and Politics, 1603–1707* (Oxford: Oxford University Press, 2008), 2.

74. Ibid., 213.

75. Sarah Prescott, "'That Private Shade, wherein My Muse Was Bred': Katherine Philips and the Poetic Spaces of Welsh Retirement," *Philological Quarterly* 88, no. 4 (Fall 2009): 347.

76. Ibid., 359.

77. Catharine Gray, "Katherine Philips in Ireland," *English Literary Renaissance* 39, no. 3 (Autumn 2009): 561. See also Gray, *Women Writers and Public Debate in Seventeenth-Century Britain* (New York: Palgrave Macmillan, 2007), 105–42.

78. Wright, *Producing Women's Poetry,* 98.

79. Sasha Roberts, "Feminist Criticism and the New Formalism: Early Modern Women and Literary Engagement," in *The Impact of Feminism in English Renaissance Studies,* ed. Dympna Callaghan, 67–92 (Basingstoke: Palgrave, 2007), 89. Elizabeth Scott-Baumann, *Forms of Engagement: Women, Poetry, and Culture, 1640–1680* (Oxford: Oxford University Press, 2013), 3.

80. Elizabeth Clarke, "The Garrisoned Muse: Women's Use of the Religious Lyric in the Civil War Period," in *The English Civil Wars in the Literary Imagination,* ed. Claude J. Summers and Ted-Larry Pebworth, 130–43 (Columbia: University of Missouri Press, 1999), 132–33.

81. Andreadis, *Sappho,* 42.

82. Bronwen Price, "A Rhetoric of Innocence: The Poetry of Katherine Philips, 'The Matchless Orinda,'" in *Write or Be Written: Early Modern Women Poets and Cultural Constraints,* ed. Barbara Smith and Ursula Appelt, 223–46 (Burlington, VT: Ashgate, 2001).

83. Hobby, *Virtue of Necessity,* 139.

84. Loscocco, "English Sappho," 62, 77–78, 76.

85. Andrea Brady, "The Platonic Poems of Katherine Philips," *Seventeenth Century* 25, no. 2 (2010): 308.

86. Mark Llewellyn, "Katherine Philips: Friendship, Poetry and Neo-Platonic Thought in Seventeenth Century England," *Philological Quarterly* 81, no. 4 (Fall 2002): 462–63.

87. Scott-Baumann, *Forms of Engagement,* 122.

88. Ibid., 117–18.

89. Ibid., 120–22.

90. Ibid., 115, 124–25.

91. Stella P. Revard, "Katherine Philips, Aphra Behn, and the Female Pindaric," in *Representing Women in Renaissance England,* ed. Claude J. Summers and Ted-Larry Pebworth, 227–41 (Columbia: University of Missouri Press, 1997), 228, 230–31, 236–40.

92. Scott-Baumann, *Forms of Engagement,* 81.

93. Ibid., 103–04, 109.

94. Joan Applegate, "Katherine Philips's 'Orinda upon Little Hector': An Unrecorded Musical Setting by Henry Lawes," *English Manuscript Studies 1100–1700* 4 (1993): 272–80.

95. Ibid., 278. As the phrase "old friend" indicates, Applegate thinks it likely that Lawes and Philips were personally acquainted and that it is "very possible that Lawes even had his own sobriquet within the circle—that of 'Thrysis,' referring to the role he played in Milton's *Comus*" (275). However, as Linda Austern points out in chapter 7 in the present volume, "There is no evidence that Philips and Lawes collaborated on these works, nor, in fact, that the poet and composer were personally acquainted, although they clearly moved in overlapping social-artistic circles, and she probably attended concerts that he sponsored."

96. Lydia Hamessley, "Henry Lawes's Setting of Katherine Philips's Friendship Poetry in His Second Book of Ayres and Dialogues, 1655: A Musical Misreading?," in *Queering the Pitch: The New Gay and Lesbian Musicology,* ed. Philip Brett, Elizabeth Wood, and Gary C. Thomas, 116–38 (New York: Routledge, 1994). Dianne Dugaw and Amanda Powell, "Sapphic Self-Fashioning in the Baroque Era: Women's Petrarchan Parody in English and Spanish," *Studies in Eighteenth-Century Culture* 35 (2006): 137.

97. Wright, *Producing Women's Poetry,* 17.

98. For one version of the story, see Thomas, *Katherine Philips,* 46–47. Nathan P. Tinker identifies John Grismond as the printer of the 1664 edition. See his "John Grismond: Printer of the Unauthorized Edition of Katherine Philips's Poems (1664)," *English Language Notes* 34 (1996): 30–35.

99. Elizabeth H. Hageman, "Making a Good Impression: Early Texts of Poems and Letters by Katherine Philips, the 'Matchless Orinda,'" *South Central Review* 11, no. 2 (1994): 54.

100. Thomas, introduction to *Collected Works,* 19.

101. Hageman, "Katherine Philips (1632–1664)," 210.

102. Hageman, "Making a Good Impression," 47.

103. See Lucy Brashear, "The Forgotten Legacy of the 'Matchless Orinda,'" *Anglo-Welsh Review* 65 (1979): 68–76; and Germaine Greer, *Slip-Shod Sibyls: Recognition, Rejection and the Woman Poet* (New York: Penguin, 1995), 147–72. Peter Beal argues that Philips was unlikely to have authorized the edition because of her careful sense of self-promotion, while Hageman's extensive textual comparisons have led her to conclude that it was based on a "false copy" or somewhat defectively copied manuscript. See Peter Beal, *In Praise of Scribes: Manuscripts and Their Makers in Seventeenth-Century England* (Oxford: Clarendon Press, 1998), 147–91. Elizabeth H. Hageman, "Treacherous Accidents and the Abominable Printing of Katherine Philips's *1664 Poems,*" in *New Ways of Looking at Old Texts, III,* ed. W. Speed Hill, 85–96 (Tempe: Arizona Center for Medieval and Renaissance Studies, 2004).

104. See Hageman, "Making a Good Impression," 49–55; Travis Dupriest, introduction to *Poems (1667) by Katherine Philips* (Delmar, NY: Scholars' Facsimiles and Reprints, 1992), 3–25; Claudia A. Limbert, "Katherine Philips: Controlling a Life and Reputation," *South Atlantic Review* 56, no. 2 (1991): 27–42; and Price, "A Rhetoric of Innocence."

105. Saintsbury, *Minor Poets,* 486n1. While Saintsbury does use the spelling of the Herringman edition, his employs the 1678 rather than the 1667 printing as his copy-text.

106. See, for example, Thomas, introduction to *Collected Works;* Claudia A. Limbert, "The Poetry of Katherine Philips: Holographs, Manuscripts and Early Printed Texts," *Philological Quarterly* 70, no. 2 (1991): 181–98; and Catherine Cole Mambretti, "'Fugitive Papers': A New Orinda Poem and Problems in Her Canon," *Papers of the Bibliographical Society of America* 71 (1977): 443–52.

107. Paul Elmen, "Some Manuscript Poems by the Matchless Orinda," *Philological Quarterly* 30 (1951): 53–57.

108. Ellen Moody, "Orinda, Rosania, Lucasia *et aliae:* Towards a New Edition of the Works of Katherine Philips," *Philological Quarterly* 66, no. 3 (1987): 325–54.

109. Ibid., 328, 330, 333, 335–36.

110. Deborah Jacobs, "Critical Imperialism and Renaissance Drama: The Case of *The Roaring Girl,*" in *Feminism, Bakhtin, and the Dialogic,* ed. Dale M. Bauer and Susan Jaret McKinstry (Albany: State University of New York Press, 1991), 73–74.

111. Elizabeth H. Hageman and Andrea Sununu, "'More Copies of it abroad than I could have imagin'd': Further Manuscript Texts of Katherine Philips, 'the Matchless Orinda,'" *English Manuscript Studies, 1100–1700* 5 (1995): 128–31.

112. Elizabeth H. Hageman and Andrea Sununu, "New Manuscript Texts of Katherine Philips, the 'Matchless Orinda,'" *English Manuscript Studies, 1100–1700* 4 (1993): 174–219; Hageman and Sununu, "'More Copies'"; Hageman, "The 'false printed' Broadside of Katherine Philips's 'To the Queens Majesty on her Happy Arrival,'" *The Library: The Transactions of the Bibliographical Society* 17, no. 4 (1995): 321–26; and Patricia M. Sant and James N. Brown, "Two Unpublished Poems by Katherine Philips (text)," *English Literary Renaissance* 24, no. 1 (1994): 211–28.

113. Arthur F. Marotti, *John Donne, Coterie Poet* (Madison: University of Wisconsin Press, 1986), 3–24.

114. Paul Trolander and Zeynep Tenger, "Katherine Philips and Coterie Critical Practices," *Eighteenth-Century Studies* 37, no. 3 (Spring 2004): 367–87.

115. Hageman, "Making a Good Impression," 40.

116. Wright, *Producing Women's Poetry,* 105–07.

117. Germaine Greer, "Editorial Conundra in the Texts of Katherine Philips," in *Editing Women,* ed. Ann M. Hutchison (Cardiff: University of Wales Press, 1998).

118. For example, letters 9 and 13 in *Letters from Orinda to Poliarchus* (London: 1705). The following quotations appear from these letters, respectively.

119. Trolander and Tenger, "Coterie Critical Practices," 374.

120. Hilary Menges, "Authorship, Friendship, and Forms of Publication in Katherine Philips," *SEL* 52, no. 3 (2012): 517–41.

121. Hageman and Sununu, "New Manuscript Texts," 175; Barash, *English Women's Poetry,* 62.

122. Marie-Louise Coolahan, "'We live by chance, and slip into Events': Occasionality and the Manuscript Verse of Katherine Philips," *Eighteenth-Century Ireland* 18 (2003): 13.

123. Aubrey, *Brief Lives,* 154.

Notes to Chapter 1 / Gray

"Katherine Philips and the Post-Courtly Coterie," by Catharine Gray, was previously published in *English Literary Renaissance* 32, no. 3 (Autumn 2002): 426–51. Copyright © 2002, John Wiley & Sons. Reprinted with permission of John Wiley and Sons.

1. Deana Rankin, *Between Spenser and Swift: English Writing in Seventeenth-Century Ireland* (Cambridge: Cambridge University Press, 2005); Rosalinde Schut, "'La Femme Forte': Katherine Philips and the Politics of Her Dublin Writings, 1662–3," in *Early Modern Englishwomen Testing Ideas,* ed. Jo Wallwork and Paul Salzman, 107–19 (Aldershot: Ashgate, 2011); Marie-Louise Coolahan, *Women, Writing, and Language in Early Modern Ireland* (Oxford: Oxford University Press, 2010); Gray, "Katherine Philips in Ireland," *English Literary Renaissance* 39, no. 3 (2009): 557–85. For a discussion of the literary criticism circulated in Philips's coterie that includes a useful analysis of Anglo-Irish relations, see also Paul Trolander and Zeynep Tenger, "Katherine Philips and Coterie Critical Practices," *Eighteenth-Century Studies* 37, no. 3 (2004): 367–87.

2. Sarah Prescott, "'That private shade wherein my Muse was bred': Katherine Philips and the Poetic Spaces of Welsh Retirement," *Philological Quarterly* 88, no. 4 (2009): 345–64, and "Katherine Philips, Welsh Women's Writing, and Archipelagic Coterie Space," *Tulsa Studies in Women's Literature* 33, no. 2 (2014): 51–76; John Kerrigan, *Archipelagic English: Literature, History, and Politics, 1603–1707* (Oxford: Oxford University Press, 2008).

3. Hero Chalmers, *Royalist Women Writers, 1650–1689* (Oxford: Oxford University Press, 2004); Anne Russell, "Katherine Philips as Political Playwright: 'The Songs between the Acts' in Pompey," *Comparative Drama* 44, no. 3 (2010): 299–323; Mihoko Suzuki, "Women, Civil War, and Empire: The Politics of Translation in Katherine Philips's *Pompey* and *Horace,*" in *The History of British Women's Writing, 1610–1690,* ed. Mihoko Suzuki, 270–86 (London: Palgrave, 2011). See also Lorna Hutson's fascinating discussion of Philips's appeal to discourses of the passions and interest and their complication of both erotic and political obligations in her poetry of friendship in chapter 9 of the present volume.

4. Penelope Anderson, *Friendship's Shadows: Women's Friendship and the Politics of Betrayal in England, 1640–1705* (Edinburgh: Edinburgh University Press, 2012).

5. John Berkenhead, "In Memory of Mr. William Cartwright," *Comedies, Tragi-Comedies, with Other Poems,* by William Cartwright (London, 1651), sig. 9. I have modernized spelling where this does not interfere with the sense of the text. All the poems addressed to Cartwright, including the one by Philips, are taken from the prefatory material to his *Comedies.* The rest of Philips's poetry is taken from Patrick Thomas, Germaine Greer, and Ruth Little's modern edition of her work, *The Collected Works of Katherine*

Philips, the Matchless Orinda, 3 vols. (Stump Cross, Essex: Stump Cross Books, 1990). Peter Beal, in vol. 2 of *Index of English Literary Manuscripts* (New York: Bowker, 1993), and Elizabeth H. Hageman and Andrea Sununu, "New Manuscript Texts of Katherine Philips, the 'Matchless Orinda,'" *English Manuscript Studies* 4 (1993): 174–219, provide invaluable information regarding Philips's manuscripts and publications.

6. Other critics who note the political nature of Cartwright's volume include Carol Barash, "Women's Community and the Exiled King," in *English Women's Poetry, 1649–1714: Politics, Community, and Linguistic Authority* (Oxford: Clarendon Press, 1996), 63; Lois Potter, *Secret Rites and Secret Writing: Royalist Literature, 1641–1660* (Cambridge: Cambridge University Press, 1989), 21; Thomas, *Collected Works,* 1:6; and Derek Hirst and Steven Zwicker, "High Summer at Nun Appleton, 1651: Andrew Marvell and Lord Fairfax's Occasions," *Historical Journal* 36 (1993): 250.

7. Of the 101 poems given tentative dates by Thomas (*Collected Works,* vol. 1), 59 date from before 1660. The only two of Philips's poems for which we have dates that were clearly written before 1651 are her juvenilia, "No blooming youth" and "A married state." Thomas speculates that "To Rosania and Lucasia" may also have been written before 1651 and the title added at a later date, after Philips met Anne Owen or "Lucasia" (see Thomas, *Collected Works,* 1:398).

8. Maureen Mulvihill, "A Feminist Link in the Old Boys' Network: The Cosseting of Katherine Philips," in *Curtain Calls: British and American Women and the Theater, 1660–1820,* ed. Mary Anne Schofield and Cecilia Macheski, 71–104 (Athens: Ohio University Press, 1991); Claudia Limbert, "The Unison of Well-Tuned Hearts: Katherine Philips's Friendships with Male Writers," *English Language Notes* 29 (1991): 25–37; Harriette Andreadis, "The Sapphic-Platonics of Katherine Philips, 1632–1664," *Signs* 15 (1989): 34–60; Arlene Stiebel, "Subversive Sexuality: Masking the Erotic in Poems by Katherine Philips and Aphra Behn," in *Renaissance Discourses of Desire,* ed. Claude J. Summers and Ted-Larry Pebworth, 223–36 (Columbia: University of Missouri Press, 1993).

9. Ellen Moody, "Orinda, Rosania, Lucasia *et aliae:* Towards a New Edition of the Works of Katherine Philips," *Philological Quarterly* 66 (1987): 329; Dorothy Mermin, "Women Becoming Poets: Katherine Philips, Aphra Behn, Anne Finch," *English Literary History* 57 (1990): 336. Cecilia Easton also underestimates Philips's political commitments, describing her poetry as couched in a "discourse of denial and disguise" that "represses" dangerous "political commitments" in her essay, "Excusing the Breach of Nature's Laws: The Discourse of Denial and Disguise in Katherine Philips's Friendship Poetry," *Restoration: Studies in English Literary Culture, 1660–1700* 14 (1990): 1. Other critics who largely ignore or minimize Philips's complex engagement of public politics in the revolutionary period include Lucy Brashear, who charts Philips's literary debts;

Elaine Hobby, who claims "almost all her explicitly Royalist poems were written after the Restoration"; and Kate Lilley, whose sophisticated exploration of elegy concentrates on her more domestic writings while downplaying the importance of Philips's elegy to Cartwright. See Lucy Brashear, "The Forgotten Legacy of the 'Matchless Orinda,'" *Anglo-Welsh Review* 65 (1979): 68–79; Elaine Hobby, *Virtue of Necessity: English Women's Writing, 1649–88* (Ann Arbor: University of Michigan Press, 1989), 134; and Kate Lilley, "True State Within: Women's Elegy, 1640–1740," in *Women, Writing, History, 1640–1740,* ed. Isobel Grundy and Susan Wiseman, 72–92 (Athens: University of Georgia Press, 1992). Robert C. Evans briefly characterizes Philips's political writing of this period, while Kathleen Swaim makes an interesting comparison of Philips to Milton that does not deal with her homoerotic verse or her debt to a seventeenth century coterie. See Swaim, "Matching the 'Matchless Orinda' to Her Times," in *1650–1850: Ideas, Aesthetics and Inquiries in the Early Modern Era III,* ed. Kevin Cope and Laura Morrow, 77–108 (New York: AMS Press, 1997); and Robert Evans, "Paradox in Poetry and Politics," in *The English Civil Wars in the Literary Imagination,* ed. Claude J. Summers and Ted-Larry Pebworth, 174–85 (Columbia: University of Missouri Press, 1999).

10. Amanda Vickery, "Golden Age to Separate Spheres? A Review of the Categories and Chronology of English Women's History," *Historical Journal* 36 (1993): 383–414, questions the usefulness of the theory of separate spheres for explaining gender oppression.

11. For Jürgen Habermas's model of the transformation of the public from a status attribute, belonging most properly to the king and court, to a sphere of rational-critical discussion, see his *The Structural Transformation of the Public Sphere,* trans. Thomas Burger (Cambridge, MA: MIT Press, 1991), 1–26. For critics who have applied Habermas's model to publication and political debate in the seventeenth century, see David Norbrook, *Writing the English Republic: Poetry, Rhetoric and Politics, 1627–1660* (Cambridge: Cambridge University Press, 1999); David Zaret, "Religion, Science, and Printing in the Public Spheres in Seventeenth-Century England," in *Habermas and the Public Sphere,* ed. Craig Calhoun, 212–35 (Cambridge, MA: MIT Press, 1992); Joad Raymond, "The Newspaper, Public Opinion, and the Public Sphere in the Seventeenth Century," *Prose Studies* 21 (1998): 109–40; and Sharon Achinstein, *Milton and the Revolutionary Reader* (Princeton, NJ: Princeton University Press, 1994).

12. See Nancy Fraser, "Rethinking the Public Sphere: A Contribution to the Critique of Actually Existing Democracy," in Calhoun, *Habermas and the Public Sphere.* Fraser notes that these counterpublics, while oppositional, need not be "virtuous" but, rather, can be both "antidemocratic and antiegalitarian" (124).

13. Since this essay was written, James Loxley has also published an essay detailing the relationship between gender and royalist polemic in

Philips's verse. His cogent analysis, however, isolates Philips from the royalist coterie she helped form. See James Loxley, "Unfettered Organs: The Polemical Voices of Katherine Philips," in *The Double Voice: Gendered Writing in Early Modern England,* ed. Danielle Clarke and Elizabeth Clarke, 230–48 (New York: St. Martin's, 2000).

14. For Philips's poems on these men, see Philips, *Collected Works,* 1:100, 86, 96, 87, 83, and 143, respectively. For Vaughan's two responses, see *Collected Works,* 3:182–84. Finch dedicated his *Friendship* (1654) to "D. Noble Lucasia-Orinda." See Philip Webster Souers, *The Matchless Orinda* (Cambridge, MA: Harvard University Press, 1931), 28.

15. Thomas (*Collected Works,* 1:332) quotes the surviving fragment of this verse that appends Philips's poem. Berkenhead's poem to Lucasia, "No Reprieve," is in Henry Lawes's *Second Book of Ayres and Dialogues* (1655), 3. Lawes set this song to music.

16. Lawes, *Second Book of Ayres,* 26.

17. For the other songs Lawes set to music, see Philips, *Collected Works,* 1:337, 356. Berkenhead's biographer, P. W. Thomas, notes the interregnum gatherings that occurred at Lawes's house in *Sir John Berkenhead, 1617–1679: A Royalist Career in Politics and Polemics* (Oxford: Oxford University Press, 1969), 143–44.

18. In 1647 the House of Commons appointed a commission to restore the university that expelled 350–400 members of the colleges. See John Marriott, *Oxford: Its Place in National History* (Oxford: Oxford University Press, 1933), 135; and *The Register of the Visitors of the University of Oxford, from AD 1658,* ed. Montagu Burrows (Westminster: Camden Society, 1881), 571. Records of the visitation and college attendance are incomplete and, of the men writing poems for *Comedies* that signed their poems using only initials, three have not been identified. It is impossible to ascertain *exactly* which of these writers went to Oxford. However, 19 of the names in Cartwright match those called before the visitors during the 1640s, 5 contributors identify themselves as Oxford men in *Comedies,* and 12 more can be found in volume 2 of Joseph Foster's *Alumni Oxonienses: The Members of the University of Oxford, 1500–1714,* 3 vols. (Nendeln, Liechtenstein: Kraus Reprint, 1968). Vaughan's biographer, F. E. Hutchinson, *Henry Vaughan: A Life and Interpretation* (Oxford: Clarendon Press, 1962), notes that Vaughan attended Oxford (32–33). Thomas (*Collected Works,* 1:330) states that Francis Finch went to Balliol.

19. Raymond Anselment, "The Oxford University Poets and Caroline Panegyric," *John Donne Journal: Studies in the Age of Donne* 3 (1984): 181; and James Loxley, *Royalism and Poetry in the English Civil Wars: The Drawn Sword* (New York: Macmillan, 1997), 21.

20. John Berkenhead and Francis Finch both wrote for an Oxford collection on Henrietta Maria, *Musarum Oxoniensium Epibathpia Serenissimae*

(Oxford, 1643), and Berkenhead also contributed to a similar collection on the royalist hero Bevill Grenville, *Verses on the Death of... Sir Bevill Grenville* (Oxford, 1643). Lawes's biographer notes that Lawes set some of the poems to Henrietta Maria to music: see Willa McClung Evans, *Henry Lawes: Musician and Friend of Poets* (New York: Modern Language Association, 1941), 160. Lawes may also be the "H. L." in the Grenville volume. Henry Vaughan contributed to an Oxford collection celebrating Charles's return from Scotland in 1641 (see Hutchinson, *Henry Vaughan,* 34). The other writer strongly connected to Philips, Sir Edward Dering, does not seem to have written for any of these three volumes, but he did contribute to a Cambridge equivalent, *Irenodia Cantabrigiensis* (1641). Other contributors to the Cartwright volume also wrote for earlier collections of panegyric: Joseph Howe, Martin Lluellin, Richard Hill, and Christopher Ware contributed to *Eucharistica Oxoniensia* (Oxford, 1641), and Ralph Bathhurst, Thomas Severne, John Fell, John Finch, and Cartwright himself contributed to *Musarum Oxoniensium.* The authors of the Grenville volume sign their poems with their initials, but James Loxley identifies Jasper Mayne and Martin Lluellin as two of them, and both of these wrote for Cartwright (see Loxley, *Royalism and Poetry,* 80). In addition, two sets of the initials match the names of contributors to Cartwright's *Comedies:* "WB" may be William Bell, while "R. G." may be Robert Gardiner.

21. On Cartwright's poetic contributions, see Anselment, "Oxford University Poets," 184. For more on Cartwright's life, works, and death, see G. Blakemore Evans, introduction to *The Plays and Poems of William Cartwright* (Madison: University of Wisconsin Press, 1951), i–xxxi.

22. Humphrey Moseley, preface, *Comedies, Tragi-Comedies, with other Poems* by William Cartwright (London, 1651), title page, sig. A4, and frontispiece.

23. Arthur F. Marotti, *Manuscript, Print and the English Renaissance Lyric* (Ithaca, NY: Cornell University Press, 1995), 126.

24. Moseley, *Comedies, Tragi-Comedies,* sig. A1.

25. Ibid., sig. A2.

26. In addition, Moseley claims that the book was not published in the lavish folio version it deserves for the sake of the readers: "'tis for your own sakes; we see it is such weather that the most *ingenious* have least money," an allusion to parliamentary sequestration or perhaps to the expelled sons of that very "mother of all... ingenuity," Oxford itself (ibid., sig. A2; my italics).

27. Berkenhead, *Comedies, Tragi-Comedies,* sig. 2.

28. *Monumentum Regale; or, A Tomb Erected for that Incomparable and Glorious Monarch, Charles the First* (London, 1649), 45.

29. Francis Finch, "On Mr. Will: Cartwright's Excellent Poems," in Cartwright, *Comedies, Tragi-Comedies,* 2. The edict that released Fane from the Tower in 1643 required him to stay within five miles of London.

See *Ben Jonson and the Cavalier Poets,* ed. Hugh Maclean (New York: W.W. Norton, 1974), 197.

30. *Monumentum Regale,* 1.

31. Souers, *The Matchless Orinda,* 27.

32. A. H. Dodd, *Studies in Stuart Wales* (Cardiff: University of Wales Press, 1952), 148. He was also high sheriff for Cardiganshire, was later elected its MP, and sat on the High Court of Justice (Souers, *The Matchless Orinda,* 28).

33. He was apparently acquainted with Thomas Vaughan, Henry Vaughan's brother, and he knew Colonel John Jeffreys, who fought for the king (Thomas, *Collected Works,* 3:158–60). Both men were connected to Philips's wife through her poetry.

34. Copies of *The Faithful Scout* (June 20 and 27, 1651) and *A perfect diurnal...in relation to the armies* (June 23 and 30, 1651) carry news of the uprising and its defeat.

35. Anselment, "Oxford University Poets," 183.

36. For more on James Philips, see *The Dictionary of Welsh Biography, Down to 1940* (Oxford: Blackwell, 1959), 754. Oxford forms a geographic link between Cardigan, Wales, where the Philipses lived, and London, where James Philips conducted much of his business, and we know that he stayed there at least once in 1654 on the way back from the city (Thomas, *Collected Works,* 3:159). He may still have had contacts with Oxford graduates and scholars.

37. Katherine Philips, "To the Memory of the most Ingenious and Virtuous Gentleman Mr. Will: Cartwright, my much valued Friend," in Cartwright, *Comedies, Tragi-Comedies,* sig. A4v.

38. Edward Dering, "On the Incomparable Poems," in Cartwright, *Comedies, Tragi-Comedies,* sig. B2.

39. Philips, "To the Memory," sig. A4v.

40. The Commission for the Propagation of the Gospel in Wales, of which James Philips was a member, was the body that deprived Henry Vaughan's brother of his living as minister to St. Bridget's (Hutchinson, *Henry Vaughan,* 94).

41. For Finch, see P. W. Thomas, *Sir John Berkenhead,* 196. The fee on Sir Edward Dering's estate was removed in August 1644, after Dering's father died. It may have been dropped because although his father fought for the king, there are no records of any overtly royalist activity on Dering's part. See *Calendar of the Proceedings of the Committee for Compounding, 1643–1660,* ed. Mary Anne Everitt Green (Nendeln, Liechtenstein: Kraus Reprint, 1967), 832.

42. Philips sequestered at least 11 estates from Welsh "Papists and Recusants" in 1655 and bought David Jenkins's sequestered lands from the Treason Trustees in 1650, presumably at a reduced rate (Green, *Calendar,* 2180, 3239). James Turner, *The Politics of Landscape: Rural Scenery and Society in English Poetry, 1630–1660* (Oxford: Oxford University Press,

1979), notes that James Philips also stripped the roof of St. David's cathedral of lead for use on his own house.

43. Cartwright, *Comedies, Tragi-Comedies,* sig. A4v.

44. Ibid., sig. B2v, 4, 11.

45. Margaret Ezell, *The Patriarch's Wife: Literary Evidence and the History of the Family* (Chapel Hill: University of North Carolina Press, 1987), 70.

46. The two manuscript collections of Philips's poems dating from the 1650s are the Tutin manuscript, an autograph of 55 poems (National Library of Wales, MS 775B), and a miscellany (Cardiff City Library, MS 1073), which includes 14 of Philips's poems from 1650 to 1651 (Beal, *Index,* 128–29). Other manuscript miscellanies including Philips's poetry from the 1650s through 1662 are Worcester College, MSS 6.13 (which features a collection of 73 of Philips's poems), the Texas manuscript, and University of London MS Ogden 42 (formerly Phillips MS 4001). For these manuscripts, see Beal, *Index,* 130–36, and *In Praise of Scribes: Manuscripts and Their Makers in Seventeenth-Century England* (Oxford: Clarendon, 1998), 148. For the poems held by Crouch—expelled by the parliamentary visitors from Oxford—and Bridgewater, see Hageman and Sununu, "New Manuscript Texts," 180–81. Jenkin Jones threatened to publish Philips's poem defending the king from a poetic attack by Vavasor Powell. See below and Philips's poems, "To (the truly competent Judge of Honour) Lucasia" and "To Antenor, on a paper of mine which J. Jones threatens to publish." Jeremy Taylor addressed his *A Discourse of the Nature and Office of Friendship* (1657) to Philips, while Davies dedicated his translation of the romance *Cleopatra* (1659) to her. For arguments that Philips influenced Overton and Marvell, see, respectively, David Norbrook, "'This blushing tribute of a borrowed muse': Robert Overton and His Overturning of the Poetic Canon," *English Manuscript Studies, 1100–1700* 4 (1993): 220–67; and Allan Pritchard, "Marvell's 'The Garden': A Restoration Poem," *Studies in English Literature* 23 (1983): 371–88. After the Restoration, manuscript collections of Philips's work included one in Dering's hand and another made by a professional scribe to be given to Philips's friend, Mary Aubrey (Beal, *Index,* 129–30).

47. In 1651 (the year of the Cartwright collection), Philips wrote verse epistles and panegyrics to Dering, who adopted the coterie name "Silvander"; Sir John Berkenhead or "Cratander"; and Henry Vaughan. In 1653–54, just before the 1655 publication of Lawes's volume, she wrote two verses on Finch, whom she addressed as "the noble Palaemon," and who had himself dedicated a book to her and another friend, Anne Owen, in 1653. Finch dedicated his 1653 manuscript *Friendship* to the "noble Lucasia-Orinda," a combination of names that perhaps recalls Aurelian Townsend's "Hymen's twin," "Mary-Charles" of the 1631 masque, *Albion's Triumph,* while recasting it as a homoerotic relation. For Finch's dedication, see Souers, *The Matchless Orinda,* 28; Townsend's masque is reproduced

in *Inigo Jones: The Theater of the Stuart Court,* 2 vols., ed. Stephen Orgel and Roy Strong (Berkeley and Los Angeles: University of California Press, 1973), 2:458.

48. Finch's nephew married the sister of Mary Harvey, Philips's school friend and Dering's wife, in 1646. Alan Everitt, *The Community of Kent and the Great Rebellion, 1640–1660* (Leicester: Prometheus Books, 1966), 35, notes Finch's connections. According to Thomas (*Collected Works,* 1:267), Finch knew Dr. William Harvey well enough to witness Harvey's will.

49. Philips, *Collected Works,* 1:18. The remainder of Philips's poetry is taken from Thomas and will henceforth be cited parenthetically by line number in the text.

50. Thomas (*Collected Works,* 1:341) thinks that the poem probably refers to *Amoris Effigies,* published in 1651, a book actually written by Robert Waring, but edited by Berkenhead. However, Berkenhead's anonymous 1649 elegy on Charles I's execution, *Loyalties Tears,* was republished with the initials "J. B." in London, 1650. Philips may refer to this poem.

51. The title is "To the noble Silvander on his dream and navy, personating Orinda preferring Rosania before Salomon's traffic to Ophir in these verses," quoted in Thomas, *Collected Works,* 1:332–33. According to Souers (*The Matchless Orinda,* 70), the fragment that accompanies Philips's poem is all that survives of Dering's poem.

52. Andrew Marvell, "Upon Appleton House," *Andrew Marvell: The Complete Poems,* ed. Elizabeth Story Donno (London: Penguin, 1972), 745.

53. William Cartwright, "To Mrs. Duppa, sent with the picture of the Bishop of Chichester (her husband) in a small piece of Glass," *The Plays and Poems of William Cartwright,* ed. G. Blakemore Evans (Madison: University of Wisconsin Press, 1951), ll. 63–64.

54. Marvell's poems to Cromwell are full of figures of forceful violence, constructing Cromwell in terms of a classical militarism. This violence occurs most obviously in Marvell's image of the republic as founded upon "A bleeding head" that "Did fright the architects to run" (Marvell, "An Horatian Ode," 69–70, in Donno, *Marvell: Complete Poems*).

55. Philips, "To the truly noble Mr. Henry Lawes," 32; "To Mr. Henry Vaughan," 8; "To the noble Palaemon," 17.

56. Catherine Gallagher coins this phrase for Margaret Cavendish, another royalist poet of the Interregnum, to describe the way Cavendish models her own authorial presence on the figure of the absolute monarch. Gallagher genders this move, claiming that only women use the exiled king as a figure for authority, and adding that it renders Cavendish "eccentric because outside of anyone else's circle." See Gallagher, "Embracing the Absolute: The Politics of the Female Subject in Seventeenth-Century England," *Genders* 1 (1998): 26. However, Philips indicates not only that this model of royal autonomy can operate for men but also that its repetition creates the very circle of which Philips is a member.

57. Berkenhead helped Anne Finch when her husband was arrested by the Dutch, and her half-brother, another Francis Finch, later left seven acres of land in trust for him (P. W. Thomas, *Sir John Berkenhead,* 194–96).

58. Even in her poem to Lawes, in which Philips's full name is disclosed, she does not articulate the anxiety that her poetry transgresses gender roles. In contrast, Mary Knight (the only other female contributor) fears that in writing verse, "I by this forget my sex." See Knight's "To Her Most honored Master, Mr. Henry Lawes, On his Second Book of Ayres" (Lawes, *Second Book of Ayres,* sig. B1v).

59. On the composition fee, see Souers, *The Matchless Orinda,* 67. For Berkenhead's role as a possible spy, see P. W. Thomas, *Sir John Berkenhead,* 165. David Underdown, *Royalist Conspiracy in England, 1649–1660* (New Haven, CT: Yale University Press, 1960), describes Isaac Berkenhead's capture (along with another royalist conspirator, Thomas Coke) by parliamentary forces, his confessions, and his consequent role in scuppering the English royalists' preparations for Worcester (44–47).

60. On the day of Charles I's execution, royalists issued a commemorative text, ostensibly written by Charles himself, vindicating the king and his policies. Philip A. Knachel has edited a modern edition of this work—*Eikon Basilike: The Portraiture of His Sacred Majesty in His Solitudes and Sufferings* (Ithaca, NY: Cornell University Press, 1966).

61. Although "A Valediction: Forbidding Mourning" is often traced to Donne's departure to the Continent in 1611, Arthur Marotti dates it as written in 1605. He situates both poems in the early years of Donne's 1601 marriage. For the poems and their context, see Arthur Marotti, *John Donne, Coterie Poet* (Madison: University of Wisconsin Press, 1986), 137, 156–57, 169, 178.

62. David Norbrook, "The Monarchy of Wit and the Republic of Letters: Donne's Politics," in *Soliciting Interpretation: Literary Theory and Seventeenth-Century English Poetry,* ed. Elizabeth D. Harvey and Katherine Eisaman Maus (Chicago: University of Chicago Press, 1990), 13.

63. Henry Jessey's 1647 account of the Independent Sarah Wight's prophecies includes Philips's mother as one of the visitors; see Henry Jessey and Sarah Wight, *The Exceeding Riches of God's Grace* (London, 1647), 9. Thus, Philips may have had a close experience of the very kind of radical, providential rhetoric she displaces here.

64. Thus, Spenser's *Epithalamion,* for instance, presents marriage as procreational Protestant evangelism, its purpose "Of blessed Saints for to increase the count"; see Edmund Spenser, *Epithalamion,* in *English Sixteenth-Century Verses: An Anthology,* ed. Richard S. Sylvester (New York: W.W. Norton, 1984), l. 423.

65. Abraham Cowley's poetry, for example, fantasizes on the enjoyment, as well as the titillating withholding, of sex in terms that oppose Philips's later Platonisms: "Ye talk of fires which shine, but never burn; /

In this cold world they'll hardly serve our turn" (19–20). See "Answer to the Platonicks," *The Collected Works of Abraham Cowley,* 2 vols., ed. Thomas A. Calhoun, Laurence Heyworth, and J. Robert King (Newark: University of Delaware Press, 1989).

66. Spenser, *Epithalamion,* 4, 5, 14.

67. Swaim, "Matching the 'Matchless Orinda,'" 95.

68. Jonathan Goldberg argues in *James I and the Politics of Literature: Jonson, Shakespeare, Donne and Their Contemporaries* (Baltimore: Johns Hopkins University Press, 1983), 107–11, that Donne appropriates the language of absolutism for the private sphere.

69. John Donne, "The Sun Rising," *The Complete English Poetry,* ed. C. A. Patrides (London, 1985), l. 21.

70. After the Restoration, as Norbrook demonstrates, Overton substantially rewrites many of Philips's poems in order to reverse their religio-political significance. He thus changes the beginning of Philips's poem to Dering, for example, getting rid of the addressee and rewriting her line, "Sir, to be noble, when 'twas voted down" to become, "To live religious, when 'twas voted down" (Norbrook, "'This blushing tribute,'" 244).

71. For example, *The Famous Tragedy of Charles I* (London, 1649), likens Cromwell's ambitions to those of Richard III, while Quarles's *Regale lectum miseriae* glosses Charles's execution thus: "the worst of Tyrants killed the best of Kings." Nancy Klein Maguire discusses Quarles and other royalist depictions of Cromwell the tyrant in her *Regicide and Restoration: English Tragicomedy, 1660–1671* (Cambridge: Cambridge University Press, 1992), 6. For the *Famous Tragedy,* see Potter, *Secret Rites,* 118.

72. William Cartwright, *The Lady Errant, a Tragi-Comedy,* 3.4.1150–52, in Evans, *The Plays and Poems.*

73. For example, see *Hey Hoe for a Husband, or the Parliament of Maids* (1647) and *New News from the Old Exchange; or, The Commonwealth of Virtuous Ladies* (1649). Susan Wiseman analyzes this kind of scandalous polemic and its relation to the spectrum of royalist political writings in "'Adam the Father of all Flesh,' Porno-Political Rhetoric and Political Theory in and after the Civil War," *Prose Studies: History, Theory and Criticism* 14 (1991): 135–57.

74. This is not to suggest that homoerotic friendship is necessarily conservative: Quaker women traveled in intimate pairs of friends while preaching a radical and more widespread leveling of class and gender distinctions. See Katherine Evans and Sarah Cheevers, *Short Relation of Some of the Cruel Sufferings* (London, 1662), for an example of seventeenth century women "yoke-fellows" whose homoerotic commitment also enabled radical political activism.

75. On Jones's role in helping Major-General Harrison against the Scots, see B. S. Capp, *The Fifth Monarchy Men: A Study in Seventeenth-*

Century English Millenarianism (Totowa, NJ: Rowman and Littlefield, 1972), 54–55.

76. Hutchinson, *Henry Vaughan,* 111–19.

Notes to Chapter 2 / Orchard

1. Hero Chalmers, *Royalist Women Writers, 1650–1689* (Oxford: Oxford University Press, 2004).

2. Catharine Gray, *Women Writers and Public Debate in Seventeenth Century Britain* (New York: Palgrave Macmillan, 2007), 108. See chapter 1 in this volume.

3. Ibid., 116. See also chapter 4 in this volume, Amy Scott-Douglass, "Restoring Orinda's Face."

4. Robert C. Evans, "Paradox in Politics and Poetry: Katherine Philips in the Interregnum," in *The English Civil Wars in the Literary Imagination,* ed. Claude J. Summers and Ted-Larry Pebworth, 174–85 (Columbia: University of Missouri Press, 1999), 184.

5. Ibid., 179.

6. Katherine Philips, "A retir'd friendship. To Ardelia," *Poems* (1664), lines 5, 11, 15. Poems from this volume are hereafter cited by line numbers in the text.

7. Richard Collings, ed., *Weekly Intelligencer* 36 (Sept. 2–9, 1651): 278.

8. The government acted quickly to exact pressure on those loyal to Charles before and after the battle. On August 12, a week after the march into England began, they issued an act to deter any assistance. Not only did they warn against correspondence but also warned supporters not to deliver "any victuals, provisions, arms, ammunitions, horses plate, money, men or any other relief whatsoever, under pain of High Treason"; see Samuel Pecke, ed., *A perfect diurnall of some passages and proceedings of, and in relation to, the armies in England and Ireland, no. 88 (Aug 11–18, 1651), 1234.* The act was to be in force until December 1, 1651, presumably because they assumed he would have been stopped by then. A week later, on August 20, Charles issued his own declaration from Aberdeen as a recruitment exercise, and he requested to feed the Scottish army in return for indemnity with the exception of high profile offenders such as Cromwell and Henry Ireton. Ten days later, Parliament called in all copies to be burned. On September 10, a week after Worcester, Parliament issued a proclamation for apprehending Charles Stuart and his adherents with a £1,000 reward for bringing him in (*Severall Proceedings in Parliament,* no. 102 [Sept. 4–11, 1651], 1579–80). The anxiety to find Charles was palpable. Bodies were dug out of fresh graves at Worcester on the premise "that because he is not known among the living he might be known amongst the dead" (*A Perfect Account* 38 [Sept. 24–Oct. 1, 1651]: 304).

9. Pecke, *A perfect diurnall,* no. 88, 1215.
10. Ibid., 1217.
11. Ibid., 1218.
12. Pecke, *A perfect diurnall,* no. 89 (Aug. 18–25, 1651), 1223.
13. Ibid., 1228.
14. See Anonymous, *A Mad Designe; or, A Description of the King of Scots marching in his Disguise, after the rout at Worcester, With the Particulers where He was, and what He and his Company did, every day and night after he fled from Worcester* (London, 1651), n.p.
15. Historians concur that only Charles and his closest advisors were confident about the success of the decision to march into England. See Trevor Royle, *Civil War: The War of the Three Kingdoms, 1638–1660* (London: Little, Brown, 2004), 596.
16. John Ogilby, *The Fables of Aesop paraphras'd in verse* (London, 1651), 22. Only after the Restoration would the oak come to represent the romance of the picaresque monarch, the languid royal figure resting on the oak's boughs, eating apples while at repose.
17. Ibid., sig. 2G3v.
18. Richard Collings, ed. *Weekly Intelligencer of the Commonwealth* 33 (Aug. 12–19, 1651), 256.
19. *White-Ladies; or, His Sacred Majesties most miraculous preservation, after the battle of Worcester, September 3. 1651* (London, 1660), 15.
20. Pecke, *A perfect diurnall,* no. 82 (June 30–July 7, 1651), 1136–37.
21. William Davenant, *Gondibert: An Heroick Poem* (London, 1651), 29; hereafter cited parenthetically in the text by page number.
22. Thomas Hobbes, "Answer to Davenant's Preface to *Gondibert,*" in ibid., 121.
23. Samuel Sheppard, *Epigrams: Theological, Philosophical, and Romantick. Six Books. Also the Socratick Session; or, The Arraignment and Conviction, of Julius Scaliger with other Select Poems* (London, 1651), sig. S4v–S5r.
24. Pecke, *A perfect diurnall,* no. 88 (Aug. 11–18, 1651), 1232.
25. Ibid., no. 90 (Aug. 25–Sept. 1, 1651), 1265.
26. Roger Boyle, Lord Broghill, *A letter from the Lord Broghill to the honourable William Lenthall Esq; speaker of the Parliament of England. Containing a relation of the great successe it hath pleased God to give the Parliament forces under the command of the Lord Broghill, in defeating the army of the rebels in Ireland, under the command of the Lord Muskerry. Together with another letter touching the said defeat* (London, 1651).
27. Roger Boyle, Lord Broghill, *Parthenissa* (London, 1651), 72; hereafter cited parenthetically in the text by page number.
28. Among the ramifications of defeat were the rapid trials of the most prominent royalists, particularly the Earls of Cleveland and Lauderdale,

and the transportation of Scottish prisoners to the mines in Guinea (Royle, *Civil War*, 602).

29. Cowley had written verses praising Philips ("On Orinda's Poems," in *Verses, lately written upon several occasions*, 1663). Interestingly, the one that appeared afterward in this edition was a praise poem on Broghill.

30. For more details on their relationship in Ireland, see Anne Russell, "Katherine Philips as Political Playwright: The Songs between the Acts in Pompey," *Comparative Drama* 44, no. 3 (2010): 299–323. For Philips and Broghill's involvement in the coterie circle that focused on critical evaluations of each other's work, see Paul Trolander and Zeynep Tenger, "Katherine Philips and Coterie Critical Practices," *Eighteenth-Century Studies* 37, no. 3 (2004): 367–87. It should be noted that Broghill also collaborated with Davenant after the Restoration. Davenant staged Broghill's plays *Henry V* and *Mustapha* in 1664 and 1665, respectively. He wrote a long encomium poem to Broghill, who on September 5, 1660, became the First Earl of Orrery, which was included in Davenant's collected works, published by Henry Herringman in 1672.

Notes to Chapter 3 / Orvis

1. Philip Webster Souers, *The Matchless Orinda* (Cambridge: Cambridge University Press, 1931), 5.

2. Patrick Thomas, ed., introduction to *The Collected Works of Katherine Philips: The Matchless Orinda*, vol. 1, *The Poems* (Stump Cross, Essex: Stump Cross Books, 1990), 1.

3. John Aubrey, *"Brief Lives," chiefly of Contemporaries, set down by John Aubrey, between the Years 1669 & 1696*, vol. 2, ed. Andrew Clark (Oxford: Clarendon Press, 1898), 154. The title is a nineteenth century invention; we have no evidence Aubrey intended to publish the diary.

4. Thomas, *Collected Works*, 1:2.

5. Aubrey, *"Brief Lives,"* 153.

6. Ibid., 153.

7. I have used Thomas's *Collected Works* for citation and reference; poems are hereafter cited in the text by line number.

8. The clearest indictment of marriage appears in "A Married State," which Orinda states "affords but little ease" (1). After delineating the perils of matrimony, the poem concludes with an exhortation to "Turn, turn apostate to love's Levity, / Suppress wild nature if she dare rebell, / There's no such thing as leading Apes in hell" (13–15). This poem is not found in either the 1664 or 1667 editions of Philips's *Poems*, and probably belongs to the poet's juvenilia. On the poem's dating, see Claudia Limbert, "Two Poems and a Prose Receipt: The Unpublished Juvenalia [*sic*] of Katherine Philips," *English Literary Renaissance* 16 (1986): 383–90; and Claudia A.

Limbert and John H. O'Neill, "Composite Authorship: Katherine Philips and an Antimarital Satire," *Papers of the Bibliographical Society of America* 87, no. 4 (1993): 487–502.

9. 1 Kings 19:11–12. Because of Philips's Puritan background, I have used the 1560 Geneva Bible for citation and reference. I have modernized the spelling. Citations hereafter appear in the text.

10. Phyllis Mack, *Visionary Women: Ecstatic Prophecy in Seventeenth-Century England* (Berkeley and Los Angeles: University of California Press, 1992), 1. In three appendices, Mack provides biographical information for many of the women who prophesied during the seventeenth century.

11. On the unique agency afforded radical female visionaries during the English civil war and Interregnum, see Patricia Crawford, *Women and Religion in England, 1500–1720* (London: Routledge, 1997), 98–115; Stevie Davies, *Unbridled Spirits: Women of the English Revolution: 1640–1660* (London: The Women's Press, 1998); Hilary Hinds, *God's Englishwomen: Seventeenth-Century Radical Sectarian Writing and Feminist Criticism* (Manchester: Manchester University Press, 1996); Elaine Hobby, "The Politics of Women's Prophecy in the English Revolution," in *Sacred and Profane: Secular and Devotional Interplay in Early Modern British Literature,* ed. Helen Wilcox, Richard Todd, and Alasdair MacDonald, 295–306 (Amsterdam: VU University Press, 1996); Elaine Hobby, "Prophecy," in *A Companion to Early Modern Women's Writing,* ed. Anita Pacheco, 264–81 (Malden, MA: Blackwell, 2008); Mack, *Visionary Women;* Diane Purkiss, "'Producing the Voice, Consuming the Body': Women Prophets of the Seventeenth Century," in *Women, Writing, History, 1640–1740,* ed. Isobel Grundy and Susan Wiseman, 139–58 (Athens: University of Georgia Press, 1992); Barry Reay, *The Quakers and the English Revolution* (London: Temple Smith, 1985); Esther Gilman Richey, *The Politics of Revelation in the English Renaissance* (Columbia: University of Missouri Press, 1998); Jane Shaw, "Fasting Women: The Significance of Gender and Bodies in Radical Religion and Politics, 1650–1813," in *Radicalism in British Literary Culture, 1650–1830: From Revolution to Revolution,* ed. Timothy Morton and Nigel Smith, 101–15 (Cambridge: Cambridge University Press, 2002); Nigel Smith, *Perfection Proclaimed: Language and Literature in English Radical Religion, 1640–1660* (Oxford: Clarendon Press, 1989); Christine Trevett, *Women and Quakerism in the Seventeenth Century* (York: Ebor Press, 1991); Susan Wiseman, "Unsilent Instruments and the Devil's Cushions: Authority in Seventeenth-Century Prophetic Discourse," in *New Feminist Discourses: Critical Essays on Theories and Texts,* ed. Isobel Armstrong, 176–96 (London: Routledge, 1992).

12. For an incisive reading of the various exegetical strategies employed by radicals to figure Charles I as Antichrist, see Laura Blair McKnight, "Crucifixion or Apocalypse? Refiguring the *Eikon Basilike,*" in *Religion, Literature, and Politics in Post-Reformation England, 1540–1688,* ed.

Donna B. Hamilton and Richard Strier, 138–60 (Cambridge: Cambridge University Press, 1996).

13. On the Deuteronomist's folding the unconditional Davidic covenant into the conditional Mosaic covenant, see Richard Elliott Friedman, *Who Wrote the Bible?* (New York: HarperCollins, 1987), 141–43.

14. For studies that show Philips's ideological investments as complex and conflicted, see Robert Evans, "Paradox in Poetry and Politics: Katherine Philips in the Interregnum," in *The English Civil Wars in the Literary Imagination,* ed. Claude J. Summers and Ted-Larry Pebworth, 174–85 (Columbia: University of Missouri Press, 1999); Catharine Gray, "Katherine Philips and the Post-Courtly Coterie," *English Literary Renaissance* 32, no. 3 (2002): 426–51; Catharine Gray, *Women Writers and Public Debate in Seventeenth-Century Britain* (New York: Palgrave Macmillan, 2007), 105–42; Paula Loscocco, "Inventing the English Sappho: Katherine Philips's Donnean Poetry," *Journal of English and Germanic Philology* 102, no. 1 (2003): 59–87; James Loxley, "Unfettered Organs: The Polemical Voices of Katherine Philips," in *"This Double Voice": Gendered Writing in Early Modern England,* ed. Danielle Clarke and Elizabeth Clarke, 230–48 (New York: St. Martin's Press, 2000); Susannah B. Mintz, "Katherine Philips and the Space of Friendship," *Restoration* 22 (1998): 62–78; Andrew Shifflett, *Stoicism, Politics, and Literature in the Age of Milton: War and Peace Reconciled* (Cambridge: Cambridge University Press, 1998), 75–106; Andrew Shifflett, "'Subdu'd by You': States of Friendship and Friends of the State in Katherine Philips's Poetry," in *Write or Be Written: Early Modern Women Poets and Cultural Constraints,* ed. Barbara Smith and Ursula Appelt, 177–95 (Aldershot: Ashgate, 2001).

15. George Savran, "1 and 2 Kings," in *The Literary Guide to the Bible,* ed. Robert Alter and Frank Kermode, 146–64 (Cambridge, MA: The Belknap Press of Harvard University Press, 1987), 161–62.

16. Christopher Hill, *The English Bible and the Seventeenth-Century Revolution* (London: Penguin, 1993), 378.

17. Ibid., 47–78, and throughout.

18. Henry Haggar, *No King but Jesus; or, The Walls of tyrannie razed and the foundations of unjust monarchy discovered to the view of all that desire to see it wherein is undeniably proved that no king is the Lords anointed but Jesus* (London, 1652), 9.

19. John Audley, *Englands common-wealth shewing the liberties of the people, the priviledges of Parliament, and the rights of souldiery: with epistles to the persons mentioned* (London, 1652), 34.

20. On the dating and ordering of editions, see Thomas, *Collected Works,* 1:41–68.

21. The "libellous rime made by V. P." was discovered by Elizabeth Hageman and Andrea Sununu, "'More Copies of It Abroad than I Could Have Imagin'd': Further Manuscript Texts of Katherine Philips, 'The

Matchless Orinda,'" in *English Manuscript Studies, 1100–1700,* vol. 5, ed. Peter Beal and Jeremy Griffiths, 127–69 (London: British Library and University of Toronto Press, 1995).

22. On the influence of Daniel and Revelation on Fifth Monarchists, see David Loewenstein, "The King among the Radicals," in *The Royal Image: Representations of Charles I,* ed. Thomas N. Corns, 96–121 (Cambridge: Cambridge University Press, 2009); and Leo F. Solt, "The Fifth Monarchy Men: Politics and the Millennium," *Church History* 30, no. 3 (Sept. 1961): 314–24. On the status of Fifth Monarchism after the Restoration, see Bernard Capp, "*A Door of Hope* Re-opened: The Fifth Monarchy, King Charles and King Jesus," *Journal of Religious History* 32, no. 1 (Mar. 2008): 16–30; and Bernard Capp, *The Fifth Monarchy Men: A Study in Seventeenth-Century English Millenarianism* (Totowa, NJ: Rowman and Littlefield, 1972), 195–227.

23. Loewenstein, "King among the Radicals," 114.

24. Evans, "Paradox in Poetry," 182.

25. Kari Boyd McBride and John C. Ulreich, "Answerable Styles: Biblical Poetics and Biblical Politics in the Poetry of Lanyer and Milton," *Journal of English and Germanic Philology* 100, no. 3 (July 2001): 334.

26. Evans, "Paradox in Poetry," 181.

27. McKnight, "Crucifixion or Apocalypse?," 138.

28. Thomas, *Collected Works,* 1:370.

29. Hannibal Hamlin, *Psalm Culture and Early Modern English Literature* (Cambridge: Cambridge University Press, 2004), writes, "Although more critical readers recognized that these texts might have been written at different times by different authors, . . . the popular idea persisted throughout the Renaissance that all of them had been composed by King David" (3).

30. Hill, *The English Bible,* notes, "Succession to the thrones of Israel and Judah by no means always went by heredity in the line of David. Jehu killed Jehoram King of Israel, son of Ahab and Jezebel, as well as Ahaziah King of Judah. Jehu demanded the heads of 70 sons of Ahab; to make quite sure he 'slew all that remained in the house of Ahab in Israel.' In addition, he slew all Baal's priests; God praised his diligence. He also slew all Ahaziah's brothers. Athaliah, Ahaziah's mother, destroyed all his seed (2 Kings 9–11)" (212). On the ambiguities surrounding David's succession, see Anne Lake Prescott, "The 2011 Josephine Waters Bennett Lecture: From the Sheephook to the Scepter: The Ambiguities of David's Rise to the Throne," *Renaissance Quarterly* 65, no. 1 (2012): 1–30.

31. See Penelope Anderson, "'Friendship Multiplyed': Royalist and Republican Friendship in Katherine Philips's Coterie," in *Discourses and Representations of Friendship in Early Modern Europe, 1500–1700,* ed. Daniel T. Lochman, Maritere López, and Lorna Hutson, 131–45 (Burlington, VT: Ashgate, 2011); Carol Barash, *English Women's Poetry, 1649–1714: Politics, Community, and Linguistic Authority* (Oxford:

Clarendon Press, 1996), 55–100; Hero Chalmers, *Royalist Women Writers, 1650–1689* (Oxford: Clarendon Press, 2004), 56–128; Evans, "Paradox in Poetry"; Gray, *Women Writers;* Loxley, "Unfettered Organs"; Mintz, "The Space of Friendship"; Shifflett, *Stoicism, Politics, and Literature,* 75–106; Kamille Stone Stanton, "'Capable of Being Kings': The Influence of the Cult of King Charles I on the Early Modern Women's Literary Canon," *New Perspectives on the Eighteenth Century* 5, no. 1 (2008): 20–29.

32. Barash, *English Women's Poetry,* 61–62.

33. Chalmers, *Royalist Women Writers,* 65.

34. Gray, *Women Writers,* 106.

35. Kamille Stone Stanton, "Painting Sentinels: Erotics, Politics, and Redemption in the Friendship Poetry of Katherine Philips (1631–1664)," *Comitatus: A Journal of Medieval and Renaissance Studies* 38 (2007): 155–72.

36. Anderson, "Friendship Multiplyed," 141.

37. Savran, "1 and 2 Kings," 162.

38. George Wither, *A collection of emblemes, ancient and modern* (London, 1635), 237.

39. Souers, *The Matchless Orinda,* 44.

40. Qtd. in W. G. Hiscock, "*Friendship:* Francis Finch's Discourse and the Circle of the Matchless Orinda," *Review of English Studies: A Quarterly Review of English Literature and the English Language* 15 (1939): 466.

41. For studies that emphasize the homoerotics of the Society of Friendship, see Harriette Andreadis, *Sappho in Early Modern England: Female Same-Sex Literary Erotics, 1550–1714* (Chicago: University of Chicago Press, 2001), 55–82; Elaine Hobby, *Virtue of Necessity: English Women's Writing, 1649–88* (London: Virago, 1988), 128–42; Kate Lilley, "True State Within: Women's Elegy 1640–1740," in *Women, Writing, History, 1640–1740,* ed. Isobel Grundy and Susan Wiseman, 72–92 (Athens: University of Georgia Press, 1992); Dorothy Merwin, "Women Becoming Poets: Katherine Philips, Aphra Behn, Anne Finch," *English Literary History* 57, no. 2 (1990): 335–55; David M. Robinson, *Closeted Writing and Lesbian and Gay Literature: Classical, Early Modern, Eighteenth-Century* (Aldershot: Ashgate, 2006), 19–36; Kamille Stone Stanton, "'Panting Sentinels': Erotics, Politics and Redemption in the Friendship Poetry of Katherine Philips," *Comitatus: A Journal of Medieval and Renaissance Studies* 38 (Fall 2007): 71–86; Valerie Traub, *The Renaissance of Lesbianism in Early Modern England* (Cambridge: Cambridge University Press, 2002), 295–308; and Elizabeth Wahl, *Invisible Relations: Representations of Female Intimacy in the Age of Enlightenment* (Stanford, CA: Stanford University Press, 1999), 130–71.

42. The location of the Ark after the Babylonian destruction of Solomon's Temple is unknown. The last reference in the Old Testament occurs in 2 Chronicles, where Josiah "said unto the Levites that taught

all Israel and were sanctified unto the Lord, Put the holy Ark in the house which Solomon the son of David King of Israel did build: it shall be no more a burden upon your shoulders: serve now the Lord your God and his people Israel" (2 Chron. 35:3).

43. Thomas, *Collected Works,* 1:339.

44. According to Richard Elliott Freedman, the first version of the story belongs to E, the Elohist source written in the northern Kingdom of Israel around 850 BC, the second version to J, the Yahwist source written in the southern kingdom of Judah around 950 BC. See Richard Elliott Friedman, *The Bible with Sources Revealed: A New View into the Five Books of Moses* (New York: HarperOne, 2005); and Friedman, *Who Wrote the Bible?*

45. Gerard Reedy, "Mystical Politics: The Imagery of Charles II's Coronation," in *Studies in Change and Revolution: Aspects of English Intellectual History, 1640–1800,* ed. P. J. Korshin, 19–42 (Menston: Scolar Press, 1972).

46. Shifflett, *Stoicism, Politics, and Literature,* 75–106.

47. Thomas, *Collected Works,* 1:19. On the debates surrounding the circumstances and cultural significance of the 1664 publication of Philips's *Poems,* see Barash, *English Women's Poetry,* 81–92; Peter Beal, *In Praise of Scribes: Manuscripts and Their Makers in Seventeenth-Century England* (Oxford: Clarendon Press, 1998), 147–90; and Elizabeth H. Hageman, "Treacherous Accidents and the Abominable Printing of Katherine Philips's 1664 Poems," in *New Ways of Looking at Old Texts,* vol. 3, ed. W. Speed Hill (Tempe: Renaissance English Text Society, with Arizona Center for Medieval and Renaissance Studies, 2004), 85–95.

48. Hill, *The English Bible,* 66.

49. Ibid., 39.

Notes to Chapter 4 / Scott-Douglass

1. "Advertisements of Books," [*London*] *Newes Published for Satisfaction and Information of the People* 4 (Jan. 14, 1664): 28. Philip Webster Souers, *The Matchless Orinda* (Cambridge, MA: Harvard University Press, 1931), 234, incorrectly identified the newspaper as the *Whitehall Evening Post, or London Intelligencer;* however, Elizabeth H. Hageman, "Treacherous Accidents and the Abominable Printing of Katherine Philips's 1664 *Poems,*" in *New Ways of Looking at Old Texts,* vol. 3, *Papers of the Renaissance English Text Society, 1997–2001,* ed. W. Speed Hill, 85–95 (Tempe: Arizona Center for Medieval and Renaissance Studies, 2004), 85, later clarified that the announcement appeared in the *London Newes,* not the *Intelligencer.*

2. Margaret Ezell, *The Patriarch's Wife: Literary Evidence and the History of the Family* (Chapel Hill: University of North Carolina Press, 1987), 85.

3. Katherine Philips, *Poems by the most deservedly admired Mrs. Katherine Philips, the matchless Orinda* (London, 1667), sig. Av–A2r; Germaine Greer, Ruth Little, and Patrick Thomas, eds., *The Collected Works of Katherine Philips: The Matchless Orinda,* 3 vols. (Stump Cross, Essex: Stump Cross Books, 1993), 2:147–49. Citations from Philips are taken from these two sources. When the text of a particular poem or letter is available in both sources, I include the page numbers for both, referring to the former as *Poems* and the latter as *Works.*

4. Letter from Katherine Philips to Dorothy Temple, qtd. in Souers, *The Matchless Orinda,* 222–23. The author of the preface to *Poems* (1667), presumed to be Cotterell, explains, "She writ divers Letters to many of her other friends full of the like" (sig. [ar]).

5. Richard Marriot, "Advertisements of Books," [London] *Intelligencer Published for the Satisfaction and Information of the People* 5 (Jan. 18, 1664): 47; qtd. in Souers, *The Matchless Orinda,* 234. The reference to "double Injury" in and of itself aligns Philips with Charles I in that it alludes to her own language in her royalist complaint against Parliamentarian abuses against the king, which she terms "double murder" and "double misery." See her "Upon the Double Murder of King Charles: In Answer to a Libelous Rhyme made by Vavasor Powell" (*Poems* 1; *Works* 1:69, line 15).

6. *Works* 2:125.

7. Philips, "To his Grace Gilbert Lord Arch-Bishop of Canterbury," *Poems* 166–67; *Works* 1:239–40, lines 1–12; italics mine.

8. Ibid., lines 20–21, 41.

9. Herringman published the works of John Denham, Sir Walter Davenant, Sir Kenelm Digby, James Howell, John Dryden, and Abraham Cowley, and he was unquestionably the most important bookseller in England from 1661 (after Humphrey Mosley's death) to 1693. Indeed, he had published Philips's 1663 edition of *Pompey,* a circumstance that must have added to the perception that his 1667 edition of Philips's poems was the only true one. Henry Robert Plomer calls Herringman "the first wholesale publisher in the modern sense of the words," and explains that "his shop was the chief literary lounging place in London." See Plomer, *A Dictionary of the Booksellers and Printers Who Were at Work in England, Scotland and Ireland from 1641 to 1667* (London: The Bibliographical Society, 1907), 96–97.

10. Carol Barash, *English Women's Poetry, 1649–1714: Politics, Community, and Linguistic Authority* (Oxford: Clarendon Press, 1996), 58n12.

11. *Poems* sig. Ar. Ros Ballaster, "Restoring the Renaissance: Margaret Cavendish and Katherine Philips," in *Renaissance Configuration: Voices/ Bodies/Spaces, 1580–1690,* ed. Gordon McMullan, 324–52 (London: Macmillan, 1998), remarks that Philips's recorded compulsion to control her relationship to print complicates her protestation that she was solely interested in the manuscript circulation of her works within her coterie. In a letter to Cotterell, Philips writes, "Let me know what they say of me at Court

and every where else, upon this last Accident, and whether the exposing all my follies in this dreadful Shape has not frighted *the whole World* out of all their Esteem for me" (*Works* 2.224–25; italics mine). Philips's interest in "the whole world" suggests that she desired to reach a wider reading audience than she herself might have been willing to admit in public.

12. *Poems* sig. Av–[A2r]; *Works* 2:147–51.

13. *Poems* sig. av–[a2v]; italics mine.

14. Ibid., sig. ar.

15. Martha Straznicky, "Restoration Women Playwrights and the Limits of Professionalism," *English Literary History* 64, no. 3 (1997): 717.

16. Dorothy Mermin, "Women Becoming Poets," *English Literary History* 57, no. 2 (1990): 338.

17. *Poems* sig. Av–[A2r]; *Works* 2:148–50. This attention to body parts exists in Philips's literary works as well, particularly in her poems on female friendship. "Rosania shadowed whilest Mrs. Mary Awbrey" contains multiple references to the subject's "face," "smile," and "eyes" (*Poems* 48–49; *Works* 1:117–20). In "To Mrs. M. A. upon Absence," the poet complains of being "[k]ept from [her] face, link'd to [her] heart" (*Poems* 70; *Works* 1:141, line 16). And in "To my Lady M. Cavendish, choseing the name of Policrite," Philips remarks on the subject's "Face," "Eyes," "shape," and "form" (*Poems* 142; *Works* 2:213, line 6). In contrast to Claudia A. Limbert's assertion in "Katherine Philips: Controlling a Life and Reputation," *South Atlantic Review* 56, no. 2 (1991): 27–42, that Philips's poetry is characterized by a *lack* of attention to bodies and physical appearance (32), I would argue that Philips's poetry is preoccupied with corporeality—bodies of friends, bodies of monarchs, bodies of authors, bodies of work.

18. Leah S. Marcus, *Puzzling Shakespeare: Local Reading and Its Discontents* (Berkeley and Los Angeles: University of California Press, 1988), 19.

19. Leah S. Marcus, *Unediting the Renaissance: Shakespeare, Marlowe, Milton* (London: Routledge, 1996), 194. See John Marriot, "Hexastichon Bibliopoae," in *Poems, by J. D. With elegies on the authors death* (London, 1633), sig. A2v. Interestingly enough, John Marriot was the father of Richard Marriot, bookseller of the unauthorized 1664 edition of *Poems*.

20. M[iles] F[lesher],"The Printer to the Understanders," in *Poems, by J. D.* (London, 1633), sig. Av, qtd. in Marcus, *Unediting the Renaissance,* 193–94. Philips herself employed this metaphor in her own commendatory verse, as in, for example, "To Mr. J. B. the noble Cratander, upon a Composition of his which he was not willing to own publiquely," in which Philips writes, in reference to John Birkenhead's poetry, "We must grant thy Soul transmitted here" (*Poems* 31; *Works* 1:100, line 14).

21. Marcus, *Unediting the Renaissance,* 200.

22. *Poems* sigs. ar–v, [a2r].

23. Cowley, "Upon Mrs. K. Philips her Poems," in Philips, *Poems* sig. cr; *Works* 3"190.

24. Abraham Cowley, "On the Death of Mrs. Katherine Philips" (*Poems* sig. [f2r]; *Works* 3:215).

25. Thomas Norton and Thomas Sackville, [*Gorboduc*:] *The tragidie of Ferrex and Porrex* (London, 1570), sig. a1r.

26. Philips's letter to Cotterell regarding the dedication of her book to the Duchess of York also illustrates Philips's attention to the textual presentation of the romances by the Sidneys, specifically Philip's *The Countess of Pembroke's Arcadia* (London, 1590), his sister Mary's revision of the same (London, 1593), and Lady Mary Wroth's *The Countess of Montgomery's Urania* (London, 1621), which characteristically indicate the dedicatee by making her name part of the title rather than part of a separate dedication.

27. Hugh Sanford, "To the Reader," in *The Countess of Pembroke's Arcadia* (London, 1593), sig. 4r–v.

28. Mary Sidney Herbert, "To the Angell spirit of the most excellent Sir Philip Sidney," in *The Psalms of Sir Philip Sidney and the Countess of Pembroke,* ed. J. C. A. Rathmell (New York: New York University Press, 1963), xxxv–vi.

29. The term "matchless" is also used in reference to Renaissance manuscript scribe Esther Inglis. She and her husband Bartholomew Kello were "in charge of passports, testimonials, and *letters of commendation*"; see Jonathan Goldberg, *Writing Matter: From the Hands of the English Renaissance* (Stanford, CA: Stanford University Press, 1990), 146; italics mine. Inglis established her reputation by making devotional books, which she distributed to royalty. In Inglis's gift book transcription of *Octonaries upon the Vanitie and Inconstancie of the World* (London, 1607), which she offered to William Jeffrey, a person indentified as G. D. wrote of her as the "matchles Mistresse of the golden Pen" (qtd. in Goldberg, 150). G. D. goes on to characterize her as the "glorie of her sex, and mirakill to men" who "dost purchase to [her] selfe immortell prayse and fame / By draughts inimitable, of [her] unmatched Pen" (qtd. in Goldberg, 148). This language is so similar to that used in the recreation of Philips as the "matchless" Orinda as to suggest that Inglis might have been deliberately chosen as a model.

30. Philips, "On Controversies in Religion" (*Poems* 61; *Works* 1:132, line 73); "To the Honoured Lady E. G." (*Poems* 62; *Works* 1:133, line 47); "The World" (*Poems* 113; *Works* 1:182–85, line 95); "Submission" (*Poems* 108; *Works* 1:178–81, line 20).

31. Edmund Gurnay, *An Appendix unto the Homily Against Images in Churches* (London, 1641), 2.

32. Julie Spraggon, *Puritan Iconoclasm during the English Civil War* (Woodbridge: Boydell, 2003), 39; *House of Commons Journals,* 2:72, qtd. in Spraggon, 63.

33. *An Ordinance for the utter demolishing, removing and taking away of all Monuments of Superstition or Idolatry,* Aug. 26, 1643, in *Acts and Ordinances of the Interregnum, 1642–60,* vol. 1, ed. C. H. Firth and R. S. Rait (London: HMSO, 1911), 265; *An Ordinance for the further*

demolishing of Monuments of Idolatry and Superstition, May 9, 1644, in *Acts and Ordinances of the Interregnum, 1642–60,* 1:425; qtd. in Spraggon, *Puritan Iconoclasm,* 259, 261.

34. *Mercurius Aulicus* (Oxford, Apr. 30–May 6, 1643), 228, qtd. in Spraggon, *Puritan Iconoclasm,* 85.

35. Qtd. in John Phillips, *The Reformation of Images: Destruction of Art in England, 1535–1660* (Berkeley and Los Angeles: University of California Press, 1974), 160.

36. *Mercurius Rusticus* (1646), 220; qtd. in ibid., 193.

37. *An Ordinance for the utter demolishing,* 1:266; qtd. in Spraggon, *Puritan Iconoclasm,* 260.

38. Spraggon, *Puritan Iconoclasm,* 210, 207.

39. *Ordinance for the further demolishing;* qtd. in ibid., 78–79.

40. James Loxley, *Royalism and Poetry in the English Civil Wars: The Drawn Sword* (London: Macmillan, 1997), 139, 152, 182.

41. *The House of Commons Journals,* 6:394, 516; qtd. in Spraggon, *Puritan Iconoclasm,* 262–63.

42. Spraggon, *Puritan Iconoclasm,* 81.

43. Michael P. Winship, "Oxenbridge, John (1608–1674)," *Oxford Dictionary of National Biography* (Oxford University Press, online edition, 2006), www.oxforddnb.com/index/101021048/John-Oxenbridge.

44. William Birken, "Daniel Oxenbridge," *Oxford Dictionary of National Biography* (online edition, 2006), www.oxforddnb.com/index/101047342/Daniel-Oxenbridge.

45. John Aubrey, *Brief Lives,* ed. Oliver Lawson Dick (Ann Arbor: University of Michigan Press, 1957), 242.

46. Spraggon, *Puritan Iconoclasm,* 145.

47. Ibid., 77.

48. Simonds D'Ewes, *The Journal of Sir Simonds D'Ewes from the Beginning of the Long Parliament to the Opening of the Trial of the Earl of Strafford,* ed. W. Notestein (New Haven, CT: Yale University Press, 1923), 6; qtd. in ibid., 77.

49. *Oxford Royalist Newsbooks,* vol. 2, ed. Peter William Thomas (London: Cornmarket, 1971), 96; qtd. in Spraggon, *Puritan Iconoclasm,* 149, but editor miscited as P. Thompson.

50. Spraggon, *Puritan Iconoclasm,* 150.

51. Birken, "Daniel Oxenbridge."

52. Spraggon, *Puritan Iconoclasm,* 169.

53. Philips, "To the Excellent Mrs. Anne Owen, upon her receiving the name of Lucasia, and adoption into our Society, December 28. 1651" (*Poems* 32; *Works* 1:102, lines 20–22); "Friendship's Mystery, to my dearest Lucasia" (*Poems* 21; *Works* 1:91, line 82).

54. See Margaret Aston, "Puritans and Iconoclasm, 1560–1660," in *The Culture of English Puritanism, 1560–1700,* ed. C. Durston and J. Eales, 92–121 (London: Macmillan, 1996), 92.

55. Philips, "To the Excellent Mrs. Anne Owen" (*Poems* 32–33; *Works* 1:102, lines 6, 13); "To Regina Collier, on her cruelty to Philaster" (*Poems* 55; *Works* 1:125, line 8). In the latter poem, iconoclasm is, in fact, the predominant conceit: "To breake his heart, you breake your image too; / And by a tiranny that's strange and new, / You murther him because he worships you" (lines 6–8).

56. Philips, "To the Countess of Thanet, upon her marriage" (*Poems* 132; *Works*1:204, line 23); "To Mrs. Mary Carne, when Philaster courted her" (*Poems* 30; *Works* 1:100, line 37). See also "To the Right Honourable Alice Countess of Carbury, at her coming into Wales" (*Poems* 16; *Works* 1:84, lines 17–18): "'Tis our Confidence you are Divine / Makes us at distance thus approach your Shrine."

57. Philips, "In Memory of F. P. who died at Acton the 24. May 1660. at 12 and 12 of Age" (*Poems* 39; *Works* 1:109, line 2); "In memory of that excellent person Mrs. Mary Lloyd of Bodidrist in Denbigh-shire, who died Nov. 13. 1656. after she came thither from Pembroke-shire" (*Poems* 44; *Works* 1:114, line 106).

58. Catharine Gray, "Katherine Philips and the Post-Courtly Coterie," *English Literary Renaissance* 32, no. 3 (Autumn 2002): 444. See chapter 1 in this volume.

59. Philips, "Engraven on Mr. John Collier's Tomb-stone at Bedlington" (*Poems* 77; *Works* 1:149); "On the little Regina Collier, on the same Tombstone" (*Poems* 78; *Works* 1:149); "Epitaph of Mr John Lloyd" (*Works* 1:111–13); "To Mrs. Wogan, my Honoured Friend, on the Death of her Husband" (*Poems* 91; *Works* 1:248–49); "On the Death of the Queen of Bohemia" (*Poems* 12; *Works* 1:81–82).

60. William Dugdale, *The History of St. Paul's Cathedral in London* (London, 1658), A3v.

61. Ian J. Gentles, "Philip Skippon," *Oxford Dictionary of National Biography* (online edition, Jan. 2008), www.oxforddnb.com/index/101025693/Philip-Skippon.

62. Ibid.; quotes are from *CLRO: Repertories of the Court of Aldermen,* vol. 59, fols. 322–23.

63. Ibid.; Gentles references *Charters of St Paul's, London,* ed. S. E. Kelly (Oxford: Oxford University Press, 2004).

64. Philips, "Epitaph on my truly honoured Publius Scipio" (*Poems* 157; *Works* 1:229, lines 1–2, 13–14).

65. Philips, "To Mr. Henry Vaughan, Silurist, on his Poems" (*Poems* 28; *Works* 1:96–97, lines 22, 28); "To the noble Palaemon, on his incomparable Discourse of Friendship" (*Poems* 15; *Works* 1:84, line 34).

66. Philips, "In Memory of Mr. Cartwright" (*Poems* 71; *Works* 1:143, lines 13–14).

67. Sarah Jinner, *An almanack or prognostication for the year of our Lord 1658*... (London, 1658), sig. [B1r]; reprinted in An almanack or prognostication for the year of our Lord 1658 (London, 1658), in *The Early*

Modern Englishwoman: A Facsimile Library of Essential Works: Series II: Printed Writings, 1641–1700, part 1, vol. 6, *Almanacs*, selected and introduced by Alan S. Weber, gen ed. Betty S. Travitsky and Patrick Cullen (London: Ashgate, 2003), 17.

68. Thomas, introduction to *Works* 1:6.

69. Richard Helgerson, *Self-Crowned Laureates: Spenser, Jonson, Milton and the Literary System* (Berkeley and Los Angeles: University of California Press, 1983), 233.

70. Gray, "Philips and Post-Courtly Coterie," 437.

71. Robert Waring, "To the Memory of His Deceased Friend Mr. William Cartwright," [A]6r; John Raymond, "On Mr. William Cartwright's Excellent Poems: Collected and Published Since His Death," [B]2v; Robert Gardiner, "To the Memory of Mr. William Cartwright," verso page following [B]2v; all commendatory poems in William Cartwright, *Comedies, Tragi-comedies, with Other Poems* (London, 1651).

72. Henry Davidson, "On Mr. Cartwright and His Poems," in Cartwright, *Comedies, Tragi-Comedies*, third recto page after **4.

73. *Certain uncertain Proposals from Freeborn Subjects of England, to his Excellency Sir Thomas Fairfax; as they were presented, Aug. 9, 1647. at Croydon in Surrey* (London, 1647), 5 (qtd. in Loxley, *Royalism and Poetry*, 152; italics mine). Philips echoes this royalist rhetoric in her commendatory verse to the Cartwright collection in which she proclaims that it would be treasonous for anyone to "profane," rather than commend, Cartwright's book and concludes with the line, "'Tis High Wit-Treason to debase thy Coyn" (Philips, "To the Memory of the most Ingenious and Vertuous Gentleman Mr. Wil: Cartwright, my much valued Friend," in Cartwright, *Comedies, Tragi-comedies*, n.p.).

74. Philips, "In Memory of Mr. Cartwright" (*Poems* 71; *Works* 1:143, lines 1, 13–14).

75. Thomas Flatman, "To the Memory of the Incomparable Orinda" (*Poems* sig. e2v; *Works* 3:212–14, lines 91, 6).

76. James Tyrell, "To the Memory of the Excellent Orinda" (*Poems* sig. er–v; *Works* 3:219, lines 1, 5–9).

77. Cowley, "On the Death of Mrs. Katherine Philips" (*Poems* sig. [f2r]; *Works* 3:215, lines 11–24.

78. James Loxley, "Unfettered Organs: The Polemical Voices of Katherine Philips," in *"This Double Voice": Gendered Writing in Early Modern England*, ed. Danielle Clarke and Elizabeth Clarke, 230–48 (New York: St. Martin's Press, 2000), 231.

79. Spraggon, *Puritan Iconoclasm*, 27.

80. Cowley, "On the Death of Mrs. Katherine Philips" (*Poems* sig. f2r; *Works* 3:215–16, lines 13, 15, 31–32).

81. Wendy Wall, *The Imprint of Gender: Authorship and Publication in the English Renaissance* (Ithaca, NY: Cornell University Press, 1993), 83.

82. Edmund Gurnay, *Towards the Vindication of the Second Commandment* (Cambridge, 1639), 6, 21, 30–31, 42–44; qtd. in Spraggon, *Puritan Iconoclasm*, 36.

83. David E. Shuttleton, *Smallpox and the Literary Imagination, 1660–1820* (Cambridge: Cambridge University Press, 2007), 70, 73–74. I am very grateful to my anonymous reader at Duquesne University Press for informing me of Shuttleton's fascinating study. Although his focus is on Philips's sex rather than her politics, the observation that Shuttleton makes in passing in reference to Cowley's elegy to Philips—that "the extended image of smallpox as an enthusiastic fanatic is surely yet another barely coded reminder of puritan depredations on church monuments during the Civil War and Commonwealth" (88)—aligns with the premise of my argument in this essay.

84. Stephen N. Zwicker, *Lines of Authority: Politics and English Literary Culture, 1649–1689* (Ithaca, NY: Cornell University Press, 1993), 25; Kevin Sharpe and Steven N. Zwicker, eds., "Politics of Discourse: Introduction," in *Politics of Discourse: The Literature of History of Seventeenth-Century England*, 1–20 (Berkeley and Los Angeles: University of California Press, 1987), 16.

85. "To the noble Palaemon, on his incomparable Discourse of Friendship" (*Poems* 15; *Works* 1:83–84, lines 15–18).

86. "To Mr. Henry Vaughan" (*Poems* 28; *Works* 1:96); "In Memory of Mr. Cartwright" (*Poems* 71; *Works* 1:143); "On the Death of the Illustrious Duke of Gloucester" (*Poems* 10; *Works* 1:79, lines 53–54); "Arion on a Dolphin, to his Majesty at his passage into England" (*Works* 1:73, line 83).

87. John Heminge and Henry Condell, "To the Great Variety of Readers," in *Mr. William Shakespeare's Comedies, Histories and Tragedies* (London: 1623), A3r.

88. "Upon the Double Murder of King Charles: In Answer to a Libelous Rhyme made by Vavasor Powell" (*Poems* 1; *Works* 1:69–70, lines 33–34). Elizabeth Hageman and Andrea Sununu recovered Powell's poem, which is included in their "'More Copies of It Abroad than I Could Have Imagin'd': Further Manuscript Texts of Katherine Philips, 'The Matchless Orinda,'" in *English Manuscript Studies 1100–1700*, vol. 5, ed. Peter Beal and Jeremy Griffiths, 127–69 (London: British Library and University of Toronto Press, 1995).

89. Philips, *Pompey* (*Poems* 63–64; *Works* 3:88–89, act 5, scene 5, lines 57–58, 83–86).

90. Spraggon, *Puritan Iconoclasm*, 131.

91. Kenneth Fincham and Nicholas Tyacke, *Altars Restored: The Changing Face of English Religious Worship, 1547–c. 1700* (Oxford University Press, 2007), 326.

92. Victor D. Sutch, *Gilbert Sheldon: Architect of Anglican Survival, 1640–1675* (The Hague: Nijhoff, 1973), 37–38, 41, 43–44, 54.

93. Ibid., 65–66.

94. Letter from Edward Hyde to Gilbert Sheldon, add. mss. 4162 (Jan. 21, 1658/9); qtd. in Sutch, *Gilbert Sheldon,* 64.

95. "To his Grace Gilbert Lord Arch-Bishop of Canterbury, July 10. 1664" (*Poems* 166–67; *Works* 1:239–40, 45, 39, 49, 21, 41, 32, 36, 34, 50, 51; italics mine).

96. Sutch, *Gilbert Sheldon,* 8.

97. Ibid., 8.

98. Fincham and Tyacke, *Altars Restored,* 287, 316.

99. Sutch, *Gilbert Sheldon,* 8; italics mine.

Notes to Chapter 5 / Loscocco

"Inventing the English Sappho: Katherine Philips's Donnean Poetry," by Paula Loscocco, was previously published in *Journal of English and Germanic Philology* 102, no. 1 (2003): 59–87. © 2003 by the Board of Trustees of the University of Illinois. Used by permission of the University of Illinois Press.

1. Hero Chalmers, *Royalist Women Writers, 1650–1689* (New York: Clarendon Press, 2004); Catharine Gray, "Katherine Philips and the Post-Courtly Coterie," *English Literary Renaissance* 32 (2002): 426–51.

2. William Kerrigan, "God in Wales: Morgan Llwyd, Henry Vaughan, Katherine Philips," in *Archipelagic English: Literature, History, and Politics, 1603–1707* (New York: Oxford University Press, 2008), 195–219; Catharine Gray, "Katherine Philips in Ireland," *English Literary Renaissance* 39 (2009): 557–85.

3. Lorna Hutson, "The Body of the Friend and the Woman Writer: Katherine Philips's Absence from Alan Bray's *The Friend* (2003)," *Women's Writing* 14 (2007): 196–214 (chapter 9 in the present volume); Valerie Traub, "'Friendship so curst': *Amor impossibilis,* the Homoerotic Lament, and the Nature of *Lesbian* Desire," *The Renaissance of Lesbianism in Early Modern England* (Cambridge: Cambridge University Press, 2002), 277–325 (chapter 8 in the present volume).

4. Penelope Anderson, "'Friendship Multiplyed': Royalist and Republican Friendship in Katherine Philips's Coterie," in *Discourses and Representations of Friendship in Early Modern Europe, 1500–1700,* ed. Daniel T. Lochman, Maritere López, and Lorna Hutson (Burlington, VT: Ashgate, 2011), 131–45.

5. Marcus Nevitt, "Katherine Philips," in *The Encyclopedia of English Renaissance Literature,* vol. 1, ed. Garrett A. Sullivan Jr., Alan Stewart, Rebecca Lemon, Nicholas McDowell, and Jennifer Richards (New York: Wiley-Blackwell, 2012), 782–85.

6. Dianne Dugaw and Amanda Powell, "Sapphic Self-Fashioning in the Baroque Era: Women's Petrarchan Parody in English and Spanish," *Studies in Eighteenth-Century Culture* 35 (2006): 127.

7. Alex Davis, "'The Lady Errant': Katherine Philips as Reader of Romance," in *Chivalry and Romance in the English Renaissance* (Rochester, NY: D. S. Brewer, 2003), 169–201. Elizabeth Scott-Baumann, *Forms of Engagement Women, Poetry and Culture, 1640–1680* (Oxford: Oxford University Press, 2013), also explores Philips and influence. She builds on the present essay to argue that "as well as replacing Donne's masculine 'I' with her feminine 'we,' Philips in fact exploits the ambivalence of Donne's own poems" and "challenge[s] the distinction between speaker and beloved" (122).

8. Nigel Smith, "The Rod and the Canon," *Women's Writing* 14 (2007): 232–45.

9. Alan Bray, *The Friend* (Chicago: University of Chicago Press, 2003); Paul Hammond, *The Making of Restoration Poetry* (Rochester, NY: D. S. Brewer, 2006); Nicholas McDowell, *Poetry and Allegiance in the English Civil Wars: Marvell and the Cause of Wit* (Oxford: Oxford University Press, 2008); Shannon Miller, *Engendering the Fall: John Milton and Seventeenth-Century Women Writers* (Philadelphia: University of Pennsylvania Press, 2008).

10. Elizabeth Wahl surveys (and participates in) many critical commonplaces in "Female Intimacy and the Question of 'Lesbian' Identity: Rereading the Female Friendship Poems of Katherine Philips," in her *Invisible Relations: Representations of Female Intimacy in the Age of Enlightenment* (Stanford, CA: Stanford University Press, 1999), 130–70. Other studies of Philips's Donnean poems of friendship include Susannah B. Mintz, "Katherine Philips and the Space of Friendship," *Restoration* 22, no. 2 (1998): 62–78; Kathleen M. Swaim, "Matching the 'Matchless Orinda' to Her Times," *1650–1850: Ideas, Aesthetics, and Inquiries in the Early Modern Era* 3 (1997): 77–108; Carol Barash, "Women's Community and the Exiled King: Katherine Philips's Society of Friendship," *English Women's Poetry, 1649–1714: Politics, Community, and Linguistic Authority* (Oxford: Clarendon Press, 1996), 55–100; Lydia Hamessley, "Henry Lawes's Setting of Katherine Philips's Friendship Poetry in His *Second Book of Ayres and Dialogues,* 1655: A Musical Misreading?," in *Queering the Pitch: The New Gay and Lesbian Musicology,* ed. Philip Brett, Elizabeth Wood, and Gary C. Thomas (New York: Routledge, 1994), 115–38; Arlene Stiebel, "Subversive Sexuality: Masking the Erotic in Poems by Katherine Philips and Aphra Behn," in *Renaissance Discourses of Desire,* ed. Claude J. Summers and Ted-Larry Pebworth, 223–36 (Columbia: University of Missouri Press, 1993); Kate Lilley, "True State Within: Women's Elegy 1640–1700," in *Women, Writing, History: 1640–1740,* ed. Isobel Grundy and Susan Wiseman, 72–92 (London: B. T. Batsford, 1992); Elaine Hobby, "Katherine Philips: Seventeenth-Century Lesbian Poet," in *What Lesbians Do in Books,* ed. Elaine Hobby and Chris White, 183–204 (London: Women's Press, 1991); Elaine Hobby, "Orinda and Female Intimacy," in her *Virtue of Necessity: English Women's Writing, 1649–88* (London: Virago,

1988), 128–42; Celia A. Easton, "Excusing the Breach in Nature's Laws: The Discourse of Denial and Disguise in Katherine Philips's Friendship Poetry," *Restoration: Studies in English Literary Culture, 1660–1700* 14, no. 1 (1990): 1–14; Harriette Andreadis, "The Sapphic-Platonics of Katherine Philips, 1632–1664," *Signs* 15, no. 1 (1989): 34–60.

11. Discussions of Philips's Donnean verses as royalist texts include Wahl, "Female Intimacy"; Barash, "Women's Community"; Hobby, "Orinda and Female Intimacy"; and Easton, "Excusing the Breach." Other discussions of Philips's presumed royalism include Patrick Thomas, "Biographical Note," in *The Collected Works of Katherine Philips, The Matchless Orinda,* 3 vols., ed. Patrick Thomas, Germaine Greer, and Ruth Little (Stump Cross,Essex: Stump Cross Books, 1990–93), 1:1–39; Maureen E. Mulvihill, "A Feminist Link in the Old Boys' Network: The Cosseting of Katherine Philips," in *Curtain Calls: British and American Women and the Theater, 1660–1820,* ed. Mary Anne Schofield and Cecelia Macheski, 71–104 (Athens: Ohio University Press, 1991); and Philip Webster Souers, *The Matchless Orinda* (New York: Johnson Reprint, 1968). For Philips's social and professional loyalties, see Mulvihill, "A Feminist Link," and esp. Hobby, "Seventeenth-Century Lesbian Poet."

12. Barash is not atypical when she asserts that Philips "empties her poetic universe of the burdens of marriage and domesticity to make room for an alternative community" of female friendship ("Women's Community," 69). See Wahl, "Female Intimacy"; Easton, "Excusing the Breach"; and Hobby, "Seventeenth-Century Lesbian Poet." Wahl, Barash, Hamessley ("Henry Lawes's Setting"), Easton, Stiebel ("Subversive Sexuality"), Andreadis ("The Sapphic-Platonics"), and Hobby focus on the "lesbian" content of Philips's Donnean poems.

13. Though she provides the valuable service of bringing Philips into current discussion of Donne's "Sapho to Philaenis," for example, Hamessley argues that while Donne devalues lesbianism and (mis)uses ventriloquism (in speaking as a woman), Philips celebrates female love and "speak[s] in her own voice," writing "realistically" with an "emotional goal" ("Henry Lawes's Setting," 128).

14. Easton argues that Philips used a "discourse of denial and disguise" to hide her lesbian (and royalist) loyalties ("Excusing the Breach," 1), but is unclear about Philips's control over this discourse: while she identifies "Orinda" as the side of Philips that "circumvent[ed] the censor" of patriarchal poetics (2), Easton also refers to Orinda as "the return of the repressed," a part of her psyche that Philips neither welcomed nor mastered (5). Wahl ("Female Intimacy"), Barash ("Women's Community"), Stiebel ("Subversive Sexuality"), Hobby ("Seventeenth-Century Lesbian Poet"), and Andreadis ("The Sapphic-Platonics") argue that Philips used Donnean conventions to mask homoerotic desires not from herself but from the world.

15. Wahl ("Female Intimacy"), Barash ("Women's Community"), Swaim ("Matching"), Stiebel ("Subversive Sexuality"), Easton ("Excusing the Breach"), and Andreadis ("The Sapphic-Platonics") argue that Philips uses Donne to hide and reveal her lesbian passion.

16. Hobby, "Seventeenth-Century Lesbian Poet," 201–02.

17. Some studies challenge claims about Philips's royalist politics by pointing to the ideological complexity of her verses, though only Andrew Shifflett brings this complexity to bear on her (Donnean) friendship poetry in '"Subdu'd by You': States of Friendship and Friends of the State in Katherine Philips's Poetry," in *Write or Be Written: Early Modern Women Poets and Cultural Constraints,* ed. Barbara Smith and Ursula Appelt, 177–95 (Burlington, VT: Ashgate, 2001). See also Mintz, "The Space of Friendship"; James Loxley, "Unfettered Organs: The Polemical Voices of Katherine Philips," in *"This Double Voice": Gendered Writing in Early Modem England,* ed. Danielle Clarke and Elizabeth Clarke, 230–48 (New York: St. Martin's Press, 2000); Robert Evans, "Paradox in Poetry and Politics: Katherine Philips in the Interregnum," in *The English Civil Wars in the Literary Imagination,* ed. Claude J. Summers and Ted-Larry Pebworth, 174–85 (Columbia: University of Missouri Press, 1999); and Andrew Shifflett, '"How Many Virtues Must I Hate': Katherine Philips and the Politics of Clemency," *Studies in Philology* 94, no. 1 (1997): 103–35.

Both Evans and Shifflett argue that Philips's political poetry is moral or stoic in a way that accommodates but also departs from the more narrowly defined royalist Stoicism familiar to students of seventeenth century English letters; Shifflett even suggests that the stoic underpinnings of Philips's poetry are "providential" ('"How Many Virtues,'" 134). Nigel Smith's study of Commonwealth-era literature, *Literature and Revolution in England, 1640–1660* (New Haven, CT: Yale University Press, 1994), indirectly supports Shifflett by claiming that many categories ceded by critics to royalists—including the literary and stoic—were used by writers of all political camps.

18. Derek Hirst, "The Politics of Literature in the English Republic," *Seventeenth Century* 5 (1990): 133–55. See also Trevor Ross, "The Uses of the Dead," in his *The Making of the English Literary Canon from the Middle Ages to the Late Eighteenth Century* (Montreal: McGill-Queen's University Press, 1998), 124–43. In *Literature and Revolution,* Smith challenges Hirst's assertion of actual or total royalist appropriation of English poetry but does not discredit his claims about the nature and ambition of royalist poetics (250–94). Other studies of royalist (as well as relevant republican) poetry and politics include Robert Wilcher, *The Writing of Royalism, 1628–1660* (Cambridge: Cambridge University Press, 2001); *Writing and Political Engagement in Seventeenth-Century England,* ed. Derek Hirst and Richard Strier (Cambridge: Cambridge University Press, 1999); David Norbrook, *Writing the English Republic: Poetry, Rhetoric*

and Politics, 1627–1660 (Cambridge: Cambridge University Press, 1999); Summers and Pebworth, *The English Civil Wars;* Achsah Guibbory, *Ceremony and Community from Herbert to Milton: Literature, Religion, and Cultural Conflict in Seventeenth-Century England* (Cambridge: Cambridge University Press, 1998); James Loxley, *Royalism and Poetry in the English Civil Wars: The Drawn Sword* (New York: St. Martin's Press, 1997); Steven N. Zwicker, *Lines of Authority: Politics and English Literary Culture, 1649–1689* (Ithaca, NY: Cornell University Press, 1993); Thomas N. Corns, *Uncloistered Virtue: English Political Literature, 1640–1660* (Oxford: Oxford University Press, 1992); *Literature and the English Civil War,* ed. Thomas F. Healy and Jonathan Sawday (Cambridge: Cambridge University Press, 1990); Lois Potter, *Secret Rites and Secret Writings: Royalist Literature, 1640–1660* (Cambridge: Cambridge University Press, 1989); Erica Veevers, *Images of Love and Religion: Queen Henrietta Maria and Court Entertainments* (Cambridge: Cambridge University Press, 1989); Jonquil Bevan, *Izaak Walton's The Compleat Angler: The Art of Recreation* (New York: St. Martin's Press, 1988); Kevin Sharpe, *Criticism and Compliment: The Politics of Literature in the England of Charles I* (Cambridge: Cambridge University Press, 1987); Leah S. Marcus, *The Politics of Mirth: Jonson, Herrick, Milton, Marvel, and the Defense of Old Holiday Pastimes* (Chicago: University of Chicago Press, 1986); Annabel Patterson, *Censorship and Interpretation: The Conditions of Writing and Reading in Early Modern England* (Madison: University of Wisconsin Press, 1984); Earl Roy Miner, *The Cavalier Mode from Jonson to Cotton* (Princeton, NJ: Princeton University Press, 1971); and Maren-Sofie Røstvig, *The Happy Man: Studies in the Metamorphosis of a Classical Ideal, 1600–1700* (Oxford: Basil Blackwell, 1954).

19. Izaak Walton, *The Lives of John Donne, Sir Henry Wotton, Richard Hooker, George Herbert & Robert Sanderson,* ed. S. B. Carter (London: Falcon Educational Books, 1951), 23–25.

20. "A Valediction: Forbidding Mourning," lines 25–26, in John Donne, *The Complete English Poems of John Donne,* ed. C. A. Patrides (London: Everyman's Library, 1985), 98. All references to Donne's poetry, hereafter cited parenthetically in the text by line number, are from this edition.

21. In contrasting Walton's 1675 "Valediction, Forbidding to Mourn" with the "A Valediction: Forbidding Mourning" from the 1633/1635 *Poems* that Patrides uses in his edition (2), I skirt the related but separate issue of which text(s) Walton may have departed from (consciously or not) in his *Life.* By 1675, there were myriad variant texts at his disposal—post-1633 editions of Donne's poetry, miscellanies, songbooks, and commonplace versions, plus Walton's possible memorization of Donne's poem. Complicating the picture, Dayton Haskin, "A History of Donne's 'Canonization' from Izaak Walton to Cleanth Brooks," *Journal of English and Germanic Philology* 92 (1993): 17–36, sees Walton's hand

not only in the *Lives* but in the *Poems* themselves, observing that the 1633 edition was the only one free from editorial and probably Waltonian efforts to censor Donne's life and writings (23–24).

22. Haskin ("History") convincingly argues that Dean Donne replaced Jack Donne by the time (and through the services) of Walton's 1640–1675 *Lives*. For a complementary discussion of the royalist/Anglican motivations behind Walton's hagiography, see Judith Maltby, *Prayer Book and People in Elizabethan and Early Stuart England* (Cambridge: Cambridge University Press, 1998), 237. For other studies on Donne's seventeenth century reception, see Kevin Pask, "'Libertine in Wit': Dr. Donne in Literary Culture," in his *The Emergence of the English Author: Scripting the Life of the Poet in Early Modern England* (Cambridge: Cambridge University Press, 1996), 113–40; Ernest W. Sullivan II, *The Influence of John Donne: His Uncollected Seventeenth-Century Printed Verse* (Columbia: University of Missouri Press, 1993); Ernest W. Sullivan II, "Who Was Reading/Writing Donne Verse in the Seventeenth Century?" *John Donne Journal* 8 (1989): 1–16; Arthur F. Marotti, *John Donne, Coterie Poet* (Madison: University of Wisconsin Press, 1986); *John Donne: The Critical Heritage,* ed. A. J. Smith (Boston: Routledge and Kegan Paul, 1975); and A. J. Smith, "Donne's Reputation," in his *John Donne: Essays in Celebration* (London: Methuen, 1972), 1–27.

23. Katherine Philips, *The Collected Works of Katherine Philips, The Matchless Orinda,* vol. 1, *The Poems,* ed. Patrick Thomas (Stump Cross, Essex: Stump Cross Books, 1990), 148–49. All references to Philips's poetry in the text are from this edition and volume, hereafter cited in the text by line number. Elizabeth Hodgson's exploration of epithalamia, chapter 6 in this volume, also complicates autobiographical readings by tracing Philips's reenactment and resistance to literary convention; see especially her discussion of "To my Lord and Lady Dungannon on Their Marriage."

24. Anthony Low, *The Reinvention of Love: Poetry, Politics, and Culture from Sidney to Milton* (Cambridge: Cambridge University Press, 1993), 33, 63.

25. Ibid., 57–59.

26. Paula Blank, "Comparing Sappho to Philaenis: John Donne's 'Homopoetics,'" *PMLA* 110, no. 3 (1995): 364, 359. See also C. Annette Grise, "Depicting Lesbian Desire: Contexts for John Donne's 'Sapho to Philaenis,'" *Mosaic* 9 (1996): 41–57.

27. See Mintz, "The Space of Friendship," 64, on mutual self-sealing in Philips's poems as a defense against political and patriarchal pressure.

28. Walton may have (mis)taken Philips's parody seriously, finding in it the marital propriety and poetic simplification he required to render the "Valediction" safe for posterity. Chronology (Philips's poem was printed in 1664 and Walton's fourth *Life* in 1675), as well as Philips's contemporary reputation, make this possibility more likely than not.

29. Blank, "Comparing Sappho to Philaenis," 358–59, 366.

30. Thomas, *Collected Works,* 1:346–48.

31. Barash attributes the tension she hears in certain Donnean poems to Philips's shifting political circumstances in the 1650s–60s ("Women's Community," 56, 67, 70–81, 92–100).

32. Germaine Greer notes differences between the 1664 and 1667 endings in "Editorial Conundra in the Texts of Katherine Philips," in *Editing Women,* ed. Ann M. Hutchinson, 79–100 (Toronto: University of Toronto Press, 1998).

33. James Holstun, "'Will you rent our ancient love asunder?': Lesbian Elegy in Donne, Marvell, and Milton," *English Literary History* 54 (1987): 835–67. See also Elizabeth Harvey, "Ventriloquizing Sappho: Ovid, Donne, and the Erotics of the Feminine Voice," *Criticism* 31 (1989): 115–38; and Hamessley, "Henry Lawes's Setting," on Philips and "Sapho to Philaenis".

34. Holstun, "'Will you rent,'" 840.

35. William N. West, "Thinking with the Body: Donne's 'Sappho to Philaenis,'" *Renaissance Papers* (1994): 67–83. See also Janel Mueller, "Lesbian Erotics: The Utopian Trope of Donne's 'Sapho to Philaenis,'" in *Homosexuality in Renaissance and Enlightenment England: Literary Representations in Historical Context,* ed. Claude J. Summers, 103–34 (New York: Haworth Press, 1992); and Stella Revard, "The Sapphic Voice in Donne's 'Sapho to Philaenis,'" in Summers, *Homosexuality,* 63–76. For contemporary analyses of lesbian poetics that correspond to West's and my own descriptions of Sapphic discourse in Donne and Philips, see Toni A. H. McNaron, "Mirrors and Likeness: A Lesbian Aesthetic in the Making," in *Sexual Practice, Textual Theory: Lesbian Cultural Criticism,* ed. Susan J. Wolfe and Julia Penelope, 291–306 (Cambridge, MA: Blackwell, 1993); and Teresa de Lauretis, "Sexual Indifference and Lesbian Representation," in *Performing Feminisms: Feminist Critical Theory and Theatre,* ed. Sue-Ellen Case, 17–39 (Baltimore: Johns Hopkins University Press, 1990).

36. West, "Thinking with the Body," 70, 74. See also Wayne A. Rebhorn, "Circe's Garden, Mercury's Rod," in his *The Emperor of Men's Minds: Literature and the Renaissance Discourse of Rhetoric* (Ithaca, NY: Cornell University Press, 1995), 133–96; and Patricia Parker, "On the Tongue: Cross Gendering, Effeminacy, and the Art of Words," *Style* 23 (1989): 445–65.

37. West, "Thinking with the Body," 76.

38. Ibid., 74–75, 77, 79, 80.

39. Philips may have learned of Sappho from several sources. Joan DeJean, "Female Desire and the Foundation of the Novelistic Order [1612–1694]," in her *Fictions of Sappho, 1546–1937* (Chicago: University of Chicago Press, 1989), 43–115, notes that Madeleine de Scudery produced two works—*Les femmes illustres* (1642) and the tenth volume

of *Artemene* (1653)—both of which feature Sappho as writer, female friend, and (heterosexual) lover. Philips translated one Scudery text—"A Pastoral of Mons. de Scudery's In ye first volume of Almahide-Englished" (*Collected Works,* 3:102–16)—and probably knew *Artemene.* See Souers, *The Matchless Orinda,* 275.

40. *Minor Poets of the Caroline Period,* 3 vols., ed. George Saintsbury (Oxford: Clarendon Press, 1905), 1:492–93. In *Collected Works,* 2:193, Patrick Thomas challenges the traditional assumption that Charles Cotterell was Philips's 1667 editor, as does Elizabeth H. Hageman, "Making a Good Impression: Early Texts of Poems and Letters by Katherine Philips, the 'Matchless Orinda,'" *South Central Review* 11 (1994): 34–65.

41. Hamessley, "Henry Lawes's Setting," 127.

42. Andreadis, "The Sapphic-Platonics," 55.

43. Walton identifies Donne's verses as a national linguistic treasure: "I beg leave to tell, that I have heard some Criticks, learned, both in Languages and Poetry, say, that none of the Greek or Latine Poets did ever equal them" (*Life,* 25).

44. Hageman points this out ("Making a Good Impression," 57).

45. Saintsbury, *Minor Poets,* 496. Cowley's poem is noted in Harriette Andreadis, "Sappho in Early Modern England: A Study in Sexual Reputation," in *Re-Reading Sappho: Reception and Transmission,* ed. Ellen Greene, 105–21 (Berkeley and Los Angeles: University of California Press, 1996); and Martha Rainbolt, "Their Ancient Claim: Sappho and Seventeenth- and Eighteenth-Century British Women's Poetry," *Seventeenth Century* 12 (1997): 111–34. See also Andreadis, *Sappho in Early Modern England: Female Same-Sex Literary Erotics, 1550–1714* (Chicago: University of Chicago Press, 2001).

46. See Andreadis, *Re-Reading Sappho; Sappho in Early Modern;* Grise, "Depicting Lesbian Desire"; Rainbolt, "Their Ancient Claim"; Lawrence I. Lipking, "Sappho Descending: Abandonment through the Ages," in his *Abandoned Women and Poetic Tradition* (Chicago: University of Chicago Press, 1988), 57–96; and Anne Lake Prescott, "Male Lesbian Voices: Ronsard, Tyard, and Donne Play Sappho," in *Reading the Renaissance: Ideas and Idioms from Shakespeare to Milton,* ed. Marc Berley, 109–29 (Pittsburgh: Duquesne University Press, 2003). My thanks to the generous members of the WWP-L and FICINO listservs for providing copious examples of women identified as "Sapphos," often positively, by others and themselves. By 1650, such women include Louise Labé, Isabella Whitney, Elizabeth I, Mary Sidney Herbert, Countess of Pembroke, Madeleine de Scudery, and Anne Bradstreet. See also *The Latin Odes of Jean Dorat,* trans. David R. Slavitt (Alexandria, VA: Orchises Press, 2000), which includes Dorat's poem on his infant daughter, who he hopes will become a poet: "Sappho of Lesbos had that gift. / She is, I know, to have been depraved; / my child, I trust, will be better behaved." My thanks here to

Prescott, who quotes this poem in her review of Slavitt in *Sidney Journal* 18 (2000): 89.

47. Andreadis, "Sappho in Early Modern England," 117.

48. Wahl, "Female Intimacy," 168.

Notes to Chapter 6 / Hodgson

Parts of this chapter, "Katherine Philips at the Wedding," by Elizabeth Hodgson, (now revised) were previously published as "Katherine Philips: Agent of Matchlessness," *Women's Writing* 10, no. 1 (2003): 119–36, reprinted by permission of the publisher Taylor & Francis Ltd., www.tandfonline.com.

1. Some examples of the readings of Philips's homoeroticism: Arlene Stiebel, "Subversive Sexuality: Masking the Erotic in Poems by Katherine Philips and Aphra Behn," *Renaissance Discourses of Desire,* ed. Claude J. Summers and Ted-Larry Pebworth, 223–36 (Columbia: University of Missouri Press, 1993); Harriette Andreadis, "Re-Configuring Early Modern Friendship: Katherine Philips and Homoerotic Desire," *SEL: Studies in English Literature, 1500–1900* 46, no. 3 (2006): 523–42; Celia A. Easton, "Excusing the Breach of Nature's Laws: The Discourse of Denial and Disguise in Katherine Philips's Friendship Poetry," in *Early Women Writers: 1600–1720,* ed. Anita Pacheco, 89–107 (London: Longman, 1998); Elizabeth Susan Wahl, "Female Intimacy and the Question of Lesbian Identity: Rereading the Female Friendship Poems of Katherine Philips," in her *Invisible Relations: Representations of Female Intimacy in the Age of Enlightenment* (Stanford, CA: Stanford University Press, 1999), 130–70; Valerie Traub, " 'Friendship so curst': *Amor impossibilis,* the Homoerotic Lament, and the Nature of *Lesbian* Desire," in her *The Renaissance of Lesbianism in Early Modern England* (Cambridge: Cambridge University Press, 2002), 276–325 (chapter 8 in the present volume).

2. Arlene Stiebel, "Not since Sappho: The Erotic in Poems of Katherine Philips and Aphra Behn," in *Homosexuality in Renaissance and Enlightenment England,* ed. Claude J. Summers, 153–71 (Harrington Park, NY: Harrington Park Press, 1992).

3. Andreadis, "Re-Configuring Early Modern Friendship," 531.

4. Andrew Shifflett, " 'Subdu'd by You': States of Friendship and Friends of the State in Katherine Philips's Poetry," in *Write or Be Written: Early Modern Women Poets and Cultural Constraints,* ed. Barbara Smith and Ursula Appelt, 177–95 (Aldershot: Ashgate, 2001), 178, 177; Andrea Brady, "The Platonic Poems of Katherine Philips," *Seventeenth Century* 25, no. 2 (2010): 305; Elaine Hobby, "Orinda and Female Intimacy," *Early Women Writers: 1600–1720,* ed. Anita Pacheco (London: Longman, 1998), 75–76; Susannah B. Mintz, "Katherine Philips and the Space of Friendship,"

Restoration 22, no. 2 (1998): 62–78; Paula Loscocco, "Inventing the English Sappho: Katherine Philips's Donnean Poetry," *Journal of English and Germanic Philology* 102, no. 1 (2003): 59–87 (chapter 5 in the present volume).

5. Elizabeth Scott-Baumann, *Forms of Engagement: Women, Poetry, and Culture, 1640–1680* (Oxford: Oxford University Press, 2013), 9.

6. Valerie Traub, "Friendship so Curst," cited in Lorna Hutson, "The Body of the Friend and the Woman Writer: Katherine Philips's Absence from Alan Bray's *The Friend* (2003)," *Women's Writing* 14, no. 2 (2007): 209 (chapter 9 in the present volume).

7. "Where hierarchical rituals of kinship had worked, within the structure of the traditional household and its affinity, to 'embed the family, in the more narrow sense of a group of parents, within a wider and overlapping network of *friendship*,' social developments in the late seventeenth and early eighteenth century isolated the relation between husband and wife as a kind of affective monopoly within a world of contractual relations. The consequence, Bray argues, was that bodily intimacy between friends lost its capacity to signify socially and ethically, and placed 'on the sexual bond between husband and wife a burden of social meaning that before it had not been required to carry alone'" (Hutson, "Body of the Friend," 199).

8. The Catullus epithalamia are the most influential; see poems 61 and 62 for the paradigms of celebration and satire, and in particular the theme of bridal reluctance, on which many English poets based their work. *Catullus, Tibullus, Pervigilium Veneri*, 2nd ed., ed. G. P. Goold (Cambridge, MA: Harvard University Press, 1988), 68–91. On the history of the genre, see Heather Dubrow, *A Happier Eden: The Politics of Marriage in the Stuart Epithalamium* (Ithaca, NY: Cornell University Press, 1990); Celeste Marguerite Schenck, *Mourning and Panegyric: The Poetics of Pastoral Ceremony* (University Park: Pennsylvania State University Press, 1988); Virgina Tufte, *The Poetry of Marriage: The Epithalamium in Europe and Its Development in England* (Los Angeles: Tinnon-Brown, 1970).

9. Schenck, *Mourning and Panegyric*, 73.

10. For a brief introduction to this very large topic, see Tufte, *The Poetry of Marriage*, 77; Christopher N. L. Brooke, *The Medieval Idea of Marriage* (Oxford: Oxford University Press, 1989); and Caroline Walker Bynum, *Jesus as Mother: Studies in the Spirituality of the High Middle Ages* (Berkeley and Los Angeles: University of California Press, 1982).

11. Catullus 62 includes the voices of the reluctant virgins who see clearly how disadvantageous marriage can be for them: "sic virgo, dum intacta manet, dum cara suis est; / cum castum amisit polluto corpore florem, / nec pueris iucunda manet, nec cara puellis" (45–47). Francis Warre Cornish's prose translation of this passage reads, "So a maiden, while she remains untouched, the while is she dear to her own; when she has lost her chaste flower with sullied body, she remains neither lovely to boys

nor dear to girls" (Goold, *Catullus*, 88–89). Subsequent references are to Goold's edition, with prose translations by Cornish.

12. Dubrow, *A Happier Eden*, xii.

13. Ibid., x.

14. Ibid., x.

15. Nina Geerdink notes this same tendency in her study of another early woman writer of epithalamic poems, the Dutch poet Katharina Lescailje (1649–1711): "The Appropriation of the Genre of Nuptial Poetry by Katharina Lescailje," in *Intersections*, vol. 16, *Women Writing Back / Writing Women Back: Transnational Perspectives from the Late Middle Ages to the Dawn of the Modern Era*, ed. Anke Gilleir, Alicia C. Montoya, and Suzan van Dijk, 163–90 (Leiden: Brill Academic, 2010), 185.

16. Schenk, *Mourning and Panegyric*, 69.

17. Ibid., 69.

18. Scott-Baumann, *Forms of Engagement*, 12.

19. See Elizabeth M. A. Hodgson, *Gender and the Sacred Self in John Donne* (Newark: University of Delaware Press, 1999), 71–113.

20. David Novarr, *The Disinterred Muse: Donne's Texts and Contexts* (Ithaca, NY: Cornell University Press, 1980), 113.

21. Wesley Milgate, ed., *John Donne: The Epithalamions, Anniversaries, and Epicedes* (Oxford: Clarendon Press, 1978), xxii. All citations are to this edition. For full textual notes on the poem's provenance and manuscript history, see Ted-Larry Pebworth, Gary A. Stringer, Ernest W. Sullivan II, William A. McClung, and Jeffrey Johnson, eds., *The Variorum Edition of the Poetry of John Donne*, vol. 8, *The Epigrams, Epithalamions, Epitaphs, Inscriptions, and Miscellaneous Poems* (Bloomington: Indiana University Press, 1995), 90–92.

22. Dubrow, *A Happier Eden*, 157.

23. John Shawcross also notes this image in "The Arrangement and Order of John Donne's Poems," in *Poems in Their Place: The Intertextuality and Order of Poetic Collections*, ed. Neil Fraistat, 119–63 (Durham: University of North Carolina Press, 1985), 122.

24. Milgate, *John Donne*, 111.

25. Celeste Schenk discusses the satirical elements of this poem in *Mourning and Panegyric*, 75–79.

26. Adrienne Eastwood, "Between Wedding and Bedding: The Epithalamic Sub-Genre in Shakespeare's Comedies," *Exemplaria: A Journal of Theory in Medieval and Renaissance Studies* 22, no. 3 (2010): 240–62, notes a similar trend in Preston's play *Cambises*, in which "the bride is led to her death instead of to the bridal chamber" (244). Eastwood points out that the sadistic groom also died (appropriately enough) by falling on his own sword (245).

27. *The Poems of Robert Herrick*, ed. L. C. Martin (London: Oxford University Press, 1965), 112–16. All subsequent citations of the poem are from this edition.

28. This relationship between groom and speaker might challenge the often argued interpretation of Herrick's verse as "pretty, useless, non-genital, infantile"—or it might reinforce it, as the speaker's relationship to sexual activity is only proximal. See William Kerrigan, "Kiss Fancies in Robert Herrick," *George Herbert Journal* 14, nos. 1 and 2 (Fall 1990–Spring 1991): 159.

29. See on this mock-serious dynamic Roger B. Rollin, *Robert Herrick* (New York: Twayne, 1966), 111–20.

30. Marjorie Swann, "Marriage, Celibacy, and Ritual in Robert Herrick's *Hesperides*," *Philological Quarterly* 76, no. 1 (1997), notes that Herrick "often stands on the sidelines at weddings to prompt his protégées until they are finally bedded" (22); I would argue that the groom, rather than the bride, is Herrick's real protégé.

31. Ibid., 22. For more on Herrick's relationship to the waning epithalamic tradition, see Katharine Wallingford, "'Corinna,' Carlomaria, the *Book of Sports* and the Death of Epithalamium on the Field of Genre," *George Herbert Journal* 14, nos. 1 and 2 (Fall 1990–Spring 1991): 97–112.

32. Katherine Philips, *The Collected Works of Katherine Philips: The Matchless Orinda*, 3 vols., ed. Patrick Thomas, Germaine Greer, and Ruth Little (Stump Cross, Essex: Stump Cross Books, 1990), 1:337. All subsequent citations to the poems are to this edition. See also Tufte, *The Poetry of Marriage*, 251–53 for a discussion of seventeenth century variations on the Spenserian form.

33. Thomas, *Collected Works*, 1:337, notes that this marriage was the first in Wales performed after the implementation of the 1553 "Act touching Marriages and the Registering Thereof," a law making marriage only legal when performed "before some justice of peace within and of the same county, city, or town." See C. H. Firth and R. S. Raith, eds., *Acts and Ordinances of the Interregnum*, 3 vols. (London: N.p., 1911), 2:715. It may be that Philips is arguing for a simpler, less "heathenish" (to use a favorite anticeremonialist term) version of marriage in line with the policy voted on by her husband, but if so, she is also taking advantage of this opportunity to make several literary points as well, in which case each disguises the other.

34. Tufte, *The Poetry of Marriage*, 161.

35. See Catullus 61: "lenta sed velut assitas / vitis implicat arbores, / implicabitur in tuum / complexum" (102–05) ("but as the pliant vine entwines the trees planted near it, so will he be entwined in your embrace") (Goold *Catullus*, 75). See also Catullus 62: "ut vida in nudo vitis uae nascitur arvo, / numquam se extollit... at si forte eademst ulmo conjuncta marita, / multi illam agricolae, multi coluere juvenci, / sic virgo dum intacta manet, dum inculta senescit" (49–56) ("As an unwedded vine which grows up in a bare field never raises itself aloft, never brings forth a mellow grape, but bending its tender form with downward weight, even now touches the root with topmost shoot; no farmers, no oxen tend it: but

if it chance to be joined in marriage to the elm, many farmers, many oxen tend it: so a maiden, while she remains untouched, the while is she ageing untended") (Goold, *Catullus*, 89).

36. Philips writes: "on *Sunday* last the Ceremony was perform'd... *I was vex'd to that degree, that I could not disguise by Concern.... I have wept so much, that my Eyes almost refuse me this present Service*" (Philips, *Collected Works*, vol 2, *The Letters*, letter 10).

37. With its multiple meanings of "precedent" and "president."

Notes to Chapter 7 / Austern

1. See Willa McClung Evans, *Henry Lawes: Musician and Friend of Poets* (New York: Modern Language Association of America, 1941), 202; Lydia Hamessley, "Henry Lawes's Setting of Katherine Philips's Friendship Poetry in His *Second Book of Ayres and Dialogues*, 1655: A Musical Misreading?," in *Queering the Pitch: The New Gay and Lesbian Musicology*, ed. Philip Brett, Elizabeth Wood, and Gary C. Thomas, 115–38 (New York: Routledge, 1994), 116, 134–35n4; Ian Spink, *Henry Lawes: Cavalier Songwriter* (Oxford: Oxford University Press, 2000), 95; Patrick Thomas, ed., *The Collected Works of Katherine Philips: The Matchless Orinda*, vol. 1, *The Poems* (Stump Cross, Essex: Stump Cross Books, 1990), 6.

2. Useful audio introductions to Henry Lawes's song style can be found on the audio compact discs "Henry Lawes: Sitting by the Streams—Psalms, Ayres and Dialogues," performed by Anthony Rooley and the Consort of Musicke (Hyperion, 1994); and "Songs by Henry and William Lawes," performed by Robin Blaze (countertenor) and Elizabeth Kenny (lute) (Hyperion, 2007). Track 16 of the latter is a performance of Lawes's setting of John Berkenhead's "No Reprieve: Now, Now Lucasia, Now Make Haste," which Hamessley ("A Musical Misreading?," 121–23) contrasts with the same composer's setting of Philips's "Friendship's Mystery: To My Dearest Lucasia."

3. John Aubrey, *"Brief Lives," Chiefly of Contemporaries*, vol. 2, ed. Andrew Clark (Oxford: Clarendon Press, 1898), 153–54.

4. See Hannibal Hamlin, *Psalm Culture and Early Modern English Literature* (Cambridge: Cambridge University Press, 2004), 37–39, 51–76; Robin A. Leaver, *"Goostly Psalmes" and "Spirituall Songes": English and Dutch Metrical Psalms from Coverdale to Utenhove* (Oxford: Clarendon Press, 1991), 246, 272; Peter LeHuray, *Music and the Reformation in England, 1549–1660* (London: Herbert Jenkins, 1967), 370–79; David C. Price, *Patrons and Musicians of the English Renaissance* (Cambridge: Cambridge University Press, 1981), 59–65; Nicholas Temperley, "'If Any of You Be Mery Let Hym Synge Psalmes': The Culture of Psalms in Church and Home," in his *Studies in English Church Music, 1550–1900* (Aldershot: Ashgate, 2009), 1–9; Nicholas Temperley, *The Music of the*

English Parish Church, vol. 1 (Cambridge: Cambridge University Press, 1979), 53–66, 71–76; and Tessa Watt, *Cheap Print and Popular Piety, 1550–1640* (Cambridge: Cambridge University Press, 1991), 33–34.

5. See, for example, *Ann Cromwell's Virginal Book, 1638,* trans. and ed. Howard Ferguson (London: Oxford University Press, 1974); and *Elizabeth Rogers Hir Virginall Booke,* ed. Charles J. F. Cofone (New York: Dover Publications, 1982).

6. Linda Phyllis Austern, "'My Mother Musicke': Music and Early Modern Fantasies of Embodiment," in *Maternal Measures: Figuring Caregivers in the Early Modern Period,* ed. Naomi J. Miller and Naomi Yavneh, 239–81 (Aldershot: Ashgate, 2000), 243–44; Jessica M. Kerr, "Mary Harvey—The Lady Dering," *Music & Letters* 25, no. 1 (1944): 27; and Amanda Eubanks Winkler, "Dangerous Performance: Cupid in Early Modern Pedagogical Masques," in *Gender and Song in Early Modern England,* ed. Leslie C. Dunn and Katherine R. Larson, 78–91 (Farnham, Surrey: Ashgate, 2014), 78–80.

7. Robert Burton, *The Anatomy of Melancholy* (Oxford: John Lichfield and James Short for Henry Cripps, 1621), 586.

8. Kerr, "Mary Harvey," 27; Thomas, *Collected Works,* 1:2–3.

9. Aubrey, *Brief Lives,* 54; Kerr, "Mary Harvey," 23–27.

10. Thomas, *Collected Works,* 1:4; and Winkler, "Dangerous Performance," 78–80; and Winkler, "High School Musicals: Understanding Seventeenth-Century English Pedagogical Masques" (paper presented at the American Musicological Society Annual Meeting, San Francisco, Nov. 2011).

11. Henry Lawes, *The Second Booke of Ayres and Dialogues, for One, Two, and Three Voyces* (London, 1655), sig. b.

12. "The Printer to the Reader," in Katherine Philips, *Pompey. A Tragoedy* (Dublin, 1663). See also Elizabeth H. Hageman and Andrea Sununu, "New Manuscript Texts of Katherine Philips, the 'Matchless Orinda,'" in *English Manuscript Studies, 1100–1700,* vol. 4, ed. Peter Beal and Jeremy Griffiths (London: The British Library, 1993), 188–89.

13. Thomas, *Collected Works,* 1:393–94. See also Michel Adam, "Katherine Philips, traductrice du theater de Pierre Corneille," *Revue d'Histoire Littéraire de la France* 85, no. 5 (1985): 847.

14. Thomas, *Collected Works,* 1:196–97, 198. Four eighteenth century manuscripts preserve Philips's "Song, to the tune of Sommes nous pas trop heureux" with its music; see Hageman and Sununu, "New Manuscript Texts," 196–200.

15. Sir Philip Sidney, *The Defence of Poesie* (London, 1595), sigs. Ev–E2.

16. George Puttenham, *The Art of English Poesy: A Critical Edition,* ed. Frank Whigham and Wayne E. Rebhorn (Ithaca, NY: Cornell University Press, 2007), 154.

17. Thomas Ravenscroft, *A Briefe Discourse of the true (but neglected) use of Charact'ring the Degrees* (London, 1614), sig. A3v. See also Elise

Bickford Jorgens, *The Well-Tun'd Word: Musical Interpretations of English Poetry, 1597–1651* (Minneapolis: University of Minnesota Press, 1982), 18–23; Diane Kelsey McColley, *Poetry and Music in Seventeenth-Century England* (Cambridge: Cambridge University Press, 1997), 1–8, 34–40; and James Anderson Winn, *Unsuspected Eloquence: A History of the Relations between Poetry and Music* (New Haven, CT: Yale University Press, 1981), 163 93.

18. See Mark W. Booth, *The Experience of Songs* (New Haven, CT: Yale University Press, 1981), 5–10; David Burrows, *Sound, Speech, and Music* (Amherst: University of Massachusetts Press, 1990), 59–62; Edward Doughtie, "Words for Music: Simplicity and Complexity in the Elizabethan Air," *Rice University Studies* 51 (1965): 2, 11; and Jorgens, *The Well-Tun'd Word*, 54–61.

19. Booth, *The Experience of Songs*, 7; Burrows, *Sound, Speech, and Music*, 58.

20. Burrows, *Sound, Speech, and Music*, 20–21.

21. George Sandys, *Ovids Metamorphosis Englished, Mythologiz'd and Represented in Figures* (Oxford, 1632), 356. See also Burrows, *Sound, Speech and Music*, 20–26; McColley, *Poetry and Music*, 7–9; and Bruce R. Smith, *The Acoustic World of Early Modern England: Attending to the O-Factor* (Chicago: University of Chicago Press, 1999), 98–106.

22. Richard Mulcaster, *Positions* (London, 1581), 38. See also James Anderson Winn, *The Pale of Words: Reflections on the Humanities and Performance* (New Haven, CT: Yale University Press, 1998), 2–8.

23. Suzanne G. Cusick, "On a Lesbian Relationship with Music: A Serious Effort Not to Think Straight," in *Queering the Pitch: The New Gay and Lesbian Musicology*, ed. Philips Brett, Elizabeth Wood, and Gary C. Thomas (New York: Routledge, 1994), 70–73; Susan McClary, *Feminine Endings: Music, Gender and Sexuality* (Minneapolis: University of Minnesota Press, 1991), 7–10; and Winn, *The Pale of Words*, 1–5.

24. Richard Schechner, "Performers and Spectators Transported and Transformed," *Kenyon Review* 3, no. 4 (1981): 83.

25. Stan Godlovitch, "The Integrity of Musical Performance," *Journal of Aesthetics and Art Criticism* 51, no. 4 (1993): 573.

26. Henry Cornelius Agrippa von Nettesheim, *Three Books of Occult Philosophy*, trans. J. F. (London, 1651), 257. See also Booth, *The Experience of Songs*, 14–15.

27. See Roland Barthes, "The Grain of Voice," in *The Responsibility of Forms*, trans. Richard Howard (Berkeley and Los Angeles: University of California Press, 1991), 269–77; Barthes, "Listening," in ibid., 254–55; and Booth, *The Experience of Songs*, 14–16.

28. Cusick, "On a Lesbian Relationship," 80.

29. Burton, *The Anatomy of Melancholy*, 586; and William Prynne, *Histrio-Mastix* (London, 1633), 273–90.

30. See Theodor W. Adorno, "Music, Language, and Composition," trans. Susan Gillespie, *Musical Quarterly* 77, no. 3 (1993): 401–02; Linda Phyllis Austern, "'Alluring the Auditorie to Effeminacie': Music and the Idea of the Feminine in Early Modern England," *Music and Letters* 74, no. 3 (1993): 350–52; Roland Barthes, *The Pleasure of the Text,* trans. Richard Miller (New York: Farrar, Straus and Giroux, 1975), 66–67; and Winn, *The Pale of Words,* 12–14.

31. For a few examples of works of this sort from Philips's era, all by male poets and addressed in their voices to female musicians, see John Hollander, *The Untuning of the Sky: Ideas of Music in English Poetry, 1500–1700* (New York: W. W. Norton, 1970), 333–36. For more information about Philips's manipulation of other conventions of male poetic discourse, see Harriette Andreadis, "The Sapphic-Platonics of Katherine Philips, 1632–1664," *Signs: Journal of Women in Culture and Society* 15, no. 1 (1989): 39–44.

32. Philips, *Collected Works,* poem 69, "To my Lady Elizabeth Boyle, Singing—Since affairs of the State & co," 1:177–78.

33. See Edward Philips, *The Mysteries of Love and Eloquence* (London, 1658).

34. For more information about the gendering of the positive descriptors "sweet" and "strong" among mid-seventeenth-century English poets, see Paula Loscocco, "'Manly Sweetness': Katherine Philips among the Neoclassicals," *Huntington Library Quarterly* 56, no. 3 (1993): 259, 262–63, 266.

35. Charles Butler, *The Principles of Musik in Singing and Setting* (London, 1636), 95.

36. Thomas Morley, *A Plaine and Easie Introduction to Practicall Musicke* (London, 1597), 195–96. See also Thomas Morley, *A Plain and Easy Introduction to Practical Music* (London, 1771); and *A Plaine & Easy Introduction to Practical Music,* 2nd ed., ed. Alec Harman (New York: Norton, 1973), 101.

37. "To the much honoured Mr. Henry Lawes, On his Excellent Compositions in Musick," in Lawes, *Second Booke of Ayres,* sig. b.

38. Hollander, *Untuning of the Sky,* 20–31; McColley, *Poetry and Music,* 8–11; William Shakespeare, *The Merchant of Venice,* 5.1.53–88, *The Complete Works,* gen. ed. Stephen Orgel and A. R. Braunmuller (New York: Penguin, 2002); Thomas, *Collected Works,* 1:366; and Winn, *Unsuspected Eloquence,* 32–34.

39. Penelope Gouk, *Music, Science and Natural Magic in Seventeenth-Century England* (New Haven, CT: Yale University Press, 1999), 261–76; and Hollander, *Untuning of the Sky,* 379–80.

40. Philips, *Collected Works,* poem 65, 1:169–73.

41. Francis Bacon, *Sylva sylvarum; or, A Natural History* (London, 1664) 31, 53.

42. For further information about Philips's adaptation of seventeenth century Platonic literary conventions to female homoerotic love, see Andreadis, "Sapphic-Platonics," 37–42.

43. Philips, *Collected Works,* poem 27, 1:104.

44. Shakespeare, *Merchant of Venice,* 5.1.63–65.

45. Seventeenth century experimental science, which gradually replaced the classical inheritance of a natural philosophy that included the musical science of harmonics and hidden sympathy, used metaphors of male domination and probing of the hidden realms of a feminine Nature, which seems to be what Philips here rebels against. For further information about the gendered aspects of these "low experiments," see Carolyn Merchant, *The Death of Nature: Women, Ecology and the Scientific Revolution* (San Francisco: Harper and Row, 1980), 164–71.

46. Philips, *Collected Works,* poem 43, 1:128–29.

47. Ibid., poem 59, 1:156.

48. Bacon, *Sylva sylvarum,* 62.

49. Henry Peacham, *The Compleat Gentleman* (London, 1622), 104. For further information about this sort of experiment in seventeenth century England, see Gouk, *Music, Science,* 166–70.

50. For further information about the early modern English poetic conceit of correspondence between instruments and their parts and portions of the universe or human body, see Hollander, *Untuning of the Sky,* 132–37.

51. For more about these conventions in early modern England, see Morrison Comegys Boyd, *Elizabethan Music and Musical Criticism,* 2nd ed. (Philadelphia: University of Pennsylvania Press, 1962), 13–36; Hollander, *Untuning of the Sky,* 346–58; and McColley, *Poetry and Music,* 218–37.

52. Lawes, *Second Booke of Ayres,* sig. b. This earliest extant version of this text may not be entirely accurate, although it is the one that circulated with Lawes's book; see Philips, *Collected Works,* 1:269. The version from Philips's autograph manuscript is edited on 87–88.

53. See Linda Phyllis Austern, "'Tis Nature's Voice': Music, Natural Philosophy and the Hidden World in Seventeenth-Century England," in *Music Theory and Natural Order from the Renaissance to the Early Twentieth Century,* ed. Suzannah Clark and Alexander Rehding, 30–67 (Cambridge: Cambridge University Press, 2001), 42–45.

54. Lawes, *Second Booke of Ayres,* sig. bv.

55. Willa McClung Evans, *Henry Lawes, Musician and Friend of Poets* (New York: The Modern Language Association of America, 1941), ix–x, 200–01; Eric Ford, "Introduction to Henry Lawes," *Music and Letters* 32, no. 3 (1951): 217; Ian Spink, *English Song, Dowland to Purcell* (New York: Charles Scribner's Sons, 1974), 76, 94–96; and Spink, *Henry Lawes,* xv–xvii.

56. Henry Lawes, *Ayres and Dialogues for One, Two, and Three Voyces* (London, 1653), sig. Av. See also Spink, *Henry Lawes,* 94–95; and Evans, *Henry Lawes,* 212–13.

57. See Evans, *Henry Lawes,* 212–14; Kerr, "Mary Harvey," 30–31; Spink, *Henry Lawes,* 94–96; and Thomas, *Collected Works,* 6.

58. Lawes, "To all Understanders or Lovers of Musick," in *Second Booke of Ayres,* opp. sig. b.

59. Lawes, dedication, in *Second Booke of Ayres.*

60. Kerr, "Mary Harvey," 29–30.

61. Lawes, *Second Booke of Ayres,* 24–25. For information about payment for her lessons from "The Household Book of Sir Edward Dering, 1648–1652," see Kerr, "Mary Harvey," 29.

62. At least some of these circulated in manuscript and were printed in their entirety as Henry Lawes and William Lawes, *Choice Psalmes put into Musick* (London, 1648).

63. For more information about the social complexities of the private music lesson in the seventeenth century, especially between male masters and their well-to-do female students, see Christopher Marsh, *Music and Society in Early Modern England* (Cambridge: Cambridge University Press, 2010), 198–208.

64. See Candace Bailey, "Blurring the Lines: 'Elizabeth Rogers hir Virginall Book' in Context," *Music and Letters* 89, no. 4 (2008): 510–43.

65. Lawes, *Second Booke of Ayres,* 24–25. In performing from her lesson book dated 1656 (early 1657 by modern accounting), Elizabeth Rogers would have also had to assume multiple genders, from a woman singing a lullaby to a lovesick boy literally burning with desire, as well as many kinds of lovers of women, men, and persons whose gender is never suggested. See Cofone, *Elizabeth Rogers Her Virginall Booke,* 93–117.

66. Lawes, *Second Booke of Ayres,* table of contents and 26.

67. Hamessley erroneously claims that only five verses were set and Joan Applegate presents a facsimile of the six in "Katherine Philips's 'Orinda upon Little Hector': An Unrecorded Setting by Henry Lawes," *English Manuscript Studies, 1100–1700,* vol. 4, ed. Peter Beal and Jeremy Griffiths (New York: Basil Blackwell, 1989).

68. Hamessley, "A Musical Misreading?," 124–30.

69. Spink, *Henry Lawes,* 97.

70. See Simon Frith, *Performing Rites: Evaluating Popular Music* (Oxford: Oxford University Press, 1996), 183–91.

71. Lawes, preface "To all Understanders or Lovers of Musick," in *Second Booke of Ayres.*

72. A. B. Philo-Mus, *Synopsis of Vocal Musick,* ed. Rebecca Herissone (Aldershot: Ashgate, 2006), 67.

73. Butler, *The Principles of Musik,* 96.

74. Jorgens, *The Well-Tun'd Word,* 131; see also 127–213; Spink, *English Song,* 75–76, 90–93; Spink, *Henry Lawes,* 6–8; and Pamela J. Willetts, *The Henry Lawes Manuscript* (London: Trustees of the British Museum, 1969), 4.

75. As Lawes himself implies, a skillful performer was expected to improvise necessary changes in multistanza works; see Applegate, "Katherine Philips's 'Orinda,'" 277.

76. For a modern transcription of the song, see Hamessley, "A Musical Misreading?," 119. A facsimile is found in Applegate, "Katherine Philips's 'Orinda,'" 276.

77. "Lawes's suave urbanity" is from Peter Walls, review of *Henry Lawes: Cavalier Songwriter* by Ian Spink, *Music and Letters* 82 (2001): 299.

78. Hamessley, "A Musical Misreading?," 121; Spink, *Henry Lawes,* 97.

79. John P. Cutts suggests Playford as the possible scribe in "Seventeenth-Century Songs and Lyrics in Paris Conservatoire MS Res. 2489," *Musica Disciplina* 23 (1969): 118; and Mary Chan confirms this with certainty in "A Mid-Seventeenth-Century Music Meeting and Playford's Publishing," in *The Well Enchanting Skill: Music Poetry, and Drama in the Culture of the Renaissance: Essays in Honour of F. W. Sternfeld,* ed. John Caldwell, Edward Olleson, and Susan Wollenberg, 231–44 (Oxford: Clarendon Press, 1990), 243n26.

80. The complete poem is printed in Philips, *Collected Works,* 1:220.

81. Spink, *Henry Lawes,* 98–99; a modern transcription is found on 98. A facsimile of the manuscript original is given in Applegate, "Katherine Philips's 'Orinda,'" 274.

82. Applegate, "Katherine Philips's 'Orinda,'" 277.

Notes to Chapter 8 / Traub

"'Friendship So Curst': *Amor Impossibilis,* the Homoerotic Lament, and the Nature of *Lesbian* Desire," by Valerie Traub, was originally published in *The Renaissance of Lesbianism in Early Modern England* (Cambridge: Cambridge University Press, 2002), 276–325. Copyright © 2002 Cambridge University Press. Reprinted with the permission of Cambridge University Press.

1. Valerie Traub, *The Renaissance of Lesbianism in Early Modern England* (Cambridge: Cambridge University Press, 2002), 28.

2. Ibid., 16.

3. Ibid., 18–19. See also Valerie Traub, "Friendship's Loss: Alan Bray's Making of History," *GLQ: A Journal of Lesbian and Gay Studies* 10, no. 3 (2004): 339–65.

4. Harriette Andreadis, "Re-Configuring Early Modern Friendship: Katherine Philips and Homoerotic Desire," *SEL: Studies in English Literature, 1500–1900* 46, no. 3 (2006): 524–25.

5. See Alan Bray, *The Friend* (Chicago: University of Chicago Press, 2003).

6. Lorna Hutson "The Body of the Friend and the Woman Writer: Katherine Philips's Absence from Alan Bray's *The Friend* (2003)," *Women's Writing* 14, no. 2 (2007): 210. See chapter 9 in the present volume.

7. Penelope Anderson, *Friendship's Shadows: Women's Friendship and the Politics of Betrayal in England, 1640–1705* (Edinburgh: Edinburgh University Press, 2012), 12.

8. Graham Hammill, "Sexuality and Society in the Poetry of Katherine Philips," in *Queer Renaissance Historiography: Backward Gaze,* ed. Vin Nardizzi, Stephen Guy-Bray, and Will Stockton, 186–205 (Farnham: Ashgate, 2009).

9. Susan Lanser, "The Political Economy of Same-Sex Desire," in *Structures and Subjectivities: Attending to Early Modern Women,* ed. Joan E. Hartman and Adele Seeff (Newark: University of Delaware Press, 2007), 162–63. See also Traub, *The Renaissance of Lesbianism,* 297–98.

10. Susan Lanser, "Mapping Sapphic Modernity," in *Comparatively Queer: Interrogating Identities across Time and Cultures,* ed. Jarrod Hayes, Margaret R. Higonnet, and William J. Spurlin, 69–89 (New York: Palgrave Macmillan, 2010), 72.

11. Lanser, "The Political Economy," 168–69.

12. Susan Lanser, *The Sexuality of History: Modernity and the Sapphic, 1565–1830* (Chicago: University of Chicago Press, 2014.

13. Valerie Traub, "Making Sexual Knowledge," *Early Modern Women: An Interdisciplinary Journal* 5 (2010): 252.

14. Valerie Traub, "The Present Future of Lesbian Historiography," in *A Companion to Lesbian, Gay, Bisexual, Transgender, and Queer Studies,* ed. George E. Haggerty and Molly McGarry, 124–45 (Malden, MA: Blackwell, 2007), 130.

15. Ibid., 255.

16. Valerie Traub, "Afterword: Comparisons Worth Making," in *Comparatively Queer: Interrogating Identities across Time and Cultures,* ed. Jarrod Hayes, Margaret R. Higonnet, and William J. Spurlin, 215–23 (New York: Palgrave Macmillan, 2010), 221.

17. Katherine Philips, *Letters from Orinda to Poliarchus,* letter 13, July 30, 1662 (London, 1705), 58. Charles Cotterell, master of ceremonies to Charles II, was Philips's closest friend at court whom he tried to marry to Anne Owen after Anne was widowed at age 21. His pastoral name in Philips's circle was Poliarchus.

18. See Traub, *The Renaissance of Lesbianism,* 292–95.

19. Souers, *The Matchless Orinda* (Cambridge, MA: Harvard University Press, 1931).

20. For treatments of Philips as seventeenth century poet and cultural figure, see Elizabeth Hageman, "The Matchless Orinda," in *Women Writers of the Renaissance and Reformation,* ed. Katharina Wilson, 566–608 (Athens: University of Georgia Press, 1987); Dorothy Mermin, "Women Becoming Poets: Katherine Philips, Aphra Behn, Anne Finch," *English Literary History* 57, no. 2 (1990): 335–55; Kate Lilley, "True State Within: Women's Elegy, 1640–1740," in *Women, Writing, History, 1640–1740,* ed. Isobel Grundy and Susan Wiseman, 73–92 (London: Batsford, 1992); Paula McDowell, "Consuming Women: The Life of the 'Literary Lady' as Popular Culture in Eighteenth-Century England," *Genre* 26, nos. 2 and 3 (1993): 219–52.

21. For readings of Philips and female homoeroticism, see Elizabeth Wahl, *Invisible Relations: Representations of Female Intimacy in the Age of Enlightenment* (Stanford, CA: Stanford University Press, 1999), chap. 3; Harriette Andreadis. "The Sapphic-Platonics of Katherine Philips, 1632–1664," *Signs* 15, no. 1 (1989): 36–60; Elaine Hobby, "Katherine Philips: Seventeenth-Century Lesbian Poet," in *What Lesbians Do in Books,* ed. Elaine Hobby and Chris White, 183–204 (London: The Women's Press, 1991); Elaine Hobby, *Virtue of Necessity: English Women's Writing, 1646–1688* (London: Virago Press, 1988), 128–42; Celia Easton, "Excusing the Breach of Nature's Laws: The Discourse of Denial and Disguise in Katherine Philips's Friendship Poetry," *Restoration: Studies in English Literary Culture, 1660–1700* 14, no. 1 (1990): 1–14; Mary Libertin, "Female Friendship in Women's Verse: Towards a New Theory of Female Politics," *Women's Studies* 9, no. 3 (1982): 291–308; Ellen Moody, "Orinda, Rosiana, Lucasia *et aliae:* Towards a New Edition of the Works of Katherine Philips," *Philological Quarterly* 66, no. 3 (1987): 325–54; Arlene Stiebel, "Not Since Sappho: The Erotic in Poems of Katherine Philips and Aphra Behn," in *Homosexuality in Renaissance and Enlightenment England,* ed. Claude J. Summers, 153–71 (Harrington Park, NY: Harrington Park Press, 1992); and Arlene Stiebel, "Subversive Sexuality: Masking the Erotic in Poems by Katherine Philips and Aphra Behn," in *Renaissance Discourses of Desire,* ed. Summers and Pebworth, 223–36 (Columbia, MO: University of Missouri Press, 1993). Dissertations by Susan Hardebeck, "If Soules No Sexes Have...': Women, Convention and Negotiation in the Poetry of Katherine Philips" (Ph.D. diss., Northern Illinois University, 1996), and Jennifer Lange, "Hearts Thus Intermixed Speak': Erotic 'Friendship' in the Poems of Katherine Philips (Ph.D. diss., Bowling Green State University, 1995), focus almost exclusively on the homoeroticism of Philips's poetry.

22. Virginia Jackson, "Dickinson's Figure of Address," in *Dickinson and Audience,* ed. Martin Orzech and Robert Weisbuch, 77–103 (Ann

Arbor: University of Michigan Press, 1996), contests "the definition of lyric poetry as privacy gone public" (78) by examining the structure of address in Emily Dickinson's poetry, "in which saying 'I' can stand for saying 'you,' in which the poet's solitude stands in for the solitude of the individual reader—a self-address so absolute that every self can identify it as his own" (79). She argues that the logic of address, which "converts the isolated 'I' into the universal 'we' by bypassing the mediation of any particular 'you'" (80) is, in fact, a product of "post-Romantic theories of the lyric" (81).

23. See, for instance, Susan Stewart, "Preface to a Lyric History," in *The Uses of Literary History,* ed. Marshall Brown, 199–218 (Durham, NC: Duke University Press, 1995), who attempts to "think dialectically regarding relations between lyric and history by paying attention to lyric as a structure of thought mediating the particular and the general" (200). Virginia Jackson and Yopie Prins, "Lyrical Studies," *Victorian Literature and Culture* 27, no. 2 (1999): 521–30, suggest that cultural studies has avoided the lyric because "lyrics have been misunderstood as the personal subjective utterances of historical subjects," which are instead "performative effect(s)" (529). See also Yopie Prins, *Victorian Sappho* (Princeton, NJ: Princeton University Press, 1999); I thank Prins for discussing with me the critical tradition of the lyric subject, voice, personification, and identification. For previous work that deconstructs the conflations between voice, persona, and author as formal, linguistic properties of the lyric, see Jonathan Culler, "The Modern Lyric: Generic Continuity and Critical Practice," in *The Comparative Perspective on Literature: Approaches to Theory and Practice,* ed. Clayton Koelb and Susan Noakes (Ithaca, NY: Cornell University Press, 1988), 284–99; Barbara Johnson, *The Critical Difference: Essays in the Contemporary Rhetoric of Reading* (Baltimore: Johns Hopkins University Press, 1980); and essays by Herbert F. Tucker, Jonathan Culler, and Paul de Man in *Lyric Poetry: Beyond New Criticism,* ed. Chaviva Hošek and Patricia Parker (Ithaca, NY: Cornell University Press, 1985).

24. Joel Fineman, *Shakespeare's Perjured Eye: The Invention of Poetic Subjectivity in the Sonnets* (Berkeley and Los Angeles: University of California Press, 1986); and *The Subjectivity Effect in Western Literary Tradition: Essays toward the Release of Shakespeare's Will* (Cambridge, MA: The MIT Press, 1991). In Fineman's account of poetic subjectivity, insofar as it is "built up on or out of the loss of itself, its identity defined as its difference from itself, a hole opens up within the whole of poetic first-person self-presence. This 'hole' within the 'whole'...inserts into the poet a space of personal interiority, a palpable syncope, that justifies and warrants poetic introspection. This accounts for the strong personal affect of Shakespeare's lyric persona, what is called its 'depth'" (*The Subjectivity Effect,* 111).

25. Fineman argues that Shakespeare's sonnets progress from visionary idealization and homologous attraction in the epideictic poems to the young man to linguistic doubleness and heterogeneous desire in the poems addressed to the "dark lady." This movement from an admiring sameness to a denigrated difference is read as a developmental transition, with the dark lady poems installing not only a novel Shakespearean subjectivity, but "the dominant and canonical version in our literary tradition of literary subjectivity per se" (*The Subjectivity Effect,* 105).

26. Paula Blank, "Comparing Sappho to Philaenis: John Donne's 'Homopoetics,'" *PMLA* 110 (1995): 358–68. The specular similitude of Philips would thus seem more akin to the homogenizing visual imagery that pervades the "ascetic" homosexual desire which Fineman reads in Shakespeare's sonnets to the young man; but Fineman would, I think, argue that such homopoetic desire, caught, as it is, in the terms of specularity, is debarred from enacting a novel subjectivity. My argument here counters Fineman's dismissal of eroticism from the purview of Shakespeare's homoerotic poetry, an issue I have addressed in more detail in "Sex without Issue: Sodomy, Reproduction and Signification in Shakespeare's Sonnets," in *Shakespeare's Sonnets: Critical Essays,* ed. James Schiffer, 431–54 (New York: Garland, 1999).

27. Michel de Montaigne, *The Complete Essays,* ed. M. A. Screech (New York: Penguin Classics, 1997), 205–19. Usually translated as "On Friendship," the Penguin edition of *The Complete Essays* translates "De l'amitié" as "On affectionate relationships," 205–19. The inserted [A] and [C] refer to the original editions of 1580 and 1592/5. Quotations from Montaigne are hereafter cited by page number in the text. My understanding of the erotic energies animating the texts of Montaigne is much indebted to Jeffrey Masten's analysis of what he calls their "language of equitable jouissance" in *Textual Intercourse: Collaboration, Authorship, and Sexualities in Renaissance Drama* (Cambridge: Cambridge University Press, 1997), 35.

28. Feminist scholarship is just beginning to excavate these alliances; see Susan Frye and Karen Robertson, eds., *Maids and Mistresses, Cousins and Queens: Women's Alliances in Early Modern England* (Collingdale, PA: Diane Publishing, 1999); Patricia Crawford and Laura Gowing, eds., *Women's Worlds in Seventeenth-Century England* (London: Routledge, 2000); and Sara Heller Mendelson and Patricia M. Crawford, eds., *Women in Early Modern England, 1550–1720* (London: Clarendon Press, 1998).

29. The chapter "Of Amity, and the love of Inclination, and Election" in Jacques Du Bosc, *The Compleat Woman* (London, 1639) diagnoses the dangers of amity in remarkably ungendered terms. *A Discourse of Friendship* (London, 1667), composed by the portrait painter Mary Beale for her friend Elizabeth Tillotson, explores the possibility of turning one's husband into one's friend.

30. As Souers, *The Matchless Orinda,* explains,

> Her family and her friends were two different parts of her life; they represented two irreconcilable points of view, and, what is even worse, two political parties. With a husband who was one of Cromwell's tools, an uncle who was a zealous dissenting minister, an aunt who was the wife of Oliver St. John, and a mother who was the wife of Philip Skippon, she was joined indissolubly to the Parliamentarians. Yet her friends were all Royalists. Lucasia was allied to the Owens, who suffered much in the early years of the war; Rosania was the wife of a man whose honors after the Restoration were too numerous to have been bestowed on a supporter of the Commonwealth; Cartwright was an out-and-out Cavalier, and so were Lawes and Birkenhead, Vaughn and Taylor. (79)

31. Katherine Philips, *Poems (1667) by Katherine Philips,* ed. Travis Dupriest (Delmar, NY: Scholars' Facsimiles, 1992); all subsequent citations in the text are from this edition. The 1664 unauthorized edition included 74 poems; the 1667 edition, which includes 116 poems and five translations, was entitled *Poems By the most deservedly Admired Mrs. Katherine Philips The Matchless Orinda. To which is added Monsieur Corneille's Pompey & Horace, Tragedies. With several other Translations out of French.*

32. This idea is developed throughout Traub, *The Renaissance of Lesbianism.*

33. Wahl, *Invisible Relations,* 147.

34. Philips, "Friendship's Mystery: To My Dearest Lucasia," 4.

35. Warren L. Chernaik, *The Poetry of Limitation: A Study of Edmund Waller* (New Haven, CT: Yale University Press, 1968), 61.

36. Wahl, *Invisible Relations,* 156.

37. Carol Barash, *English Women's Poetry, 1649–1714: Politics, Community, and Linguistic Authority* (Oxford: Clarendon Press, 1996), 73. Comparing manuscript versions to published lyrics, Barash attempts to place some distance between Philips and her poetic persona, and she traces changes in the poet's conception of friendship over the course of her career, as the friend-as-political-ally becomes the confidante who becomes the woman-with-whom-one-is-in-love. Her reading reveals less a trajectory of "the love affair" than an astute articulation of the differences between the poems addressed to Lucasia and Rosania: "The relationship with Lucasia evolves more ritualistically than the relationship to Rosania, and is contrasted with rather than mapped onto heterosexual conventions of courtly love" (70–71). As this final clause suggests, however, one problem with Barash's otherwise insightful analysis is that she views Orinda under the guise of the male courtier, reading all of the poems as if they are addressed

from a male poet to female beloved—unless and until something in the poem, like a female pronoun, gives the homoeroticism away. Assuming that male impersonation is the only available poetic stance, Barash reinscribes female-female eroticism as pseudoheterosexual. Caught between respect for historical alterity and an undertheorized notion of *lesbian* possibility, Barash says, "[this] is not to say that Katherine Philips was not in love with Anne Owen, or that that is not a question that matters. But it is important to situate relationships between women in terms of the social codes within which they would have had meaning to the participants" (78). Barash implies that "in love with" a woman would not have been intelligible to Philips, forgetting that Orinda treats her friendships as love affairs that surpass marriage in their intensity. The homoerotic readings of both Barash and Wahl rely on the narrative implicit in the manuscript versions of the poems.

38. Ibid., 92.

39. Ibid., 93.

40. Traub, *The Renaissance of Lesbianism,* 258–70.

41. This pressure to choose heterosexuality is analyzed in Theresa Braunschneider's chapter on the "reformed coquette" of eighteenth century fiction in her "Maidenly Amusements: Narrating Female Sexuality in Eighteenth-Century England" (Ph.D. diss., University of Michigan, 2002).

42. Wahl, *Invisible Relations,* 152.

43. Barash, *English Women's Poetry,* 98–99.

44. Wahl, *Invisible Relations,* 158.

45. Barash, *English Women's Poetry,* 99.

46. The concepts of coding, masking, and disguise are present in many of the essays cited above; see, in particular, Hobby, "Katherine Philips"; Stiebel, "Not Since Sappho" and "Subversive Sexuality"; and Easton, "Excusing the Breach."

47. Although our positions are very similar, there is an important difference between my reading of Philips's verse as a "hinge" and Wahl's construction of Philips as occupying "a peculiarly liminal position" (*Invisible Relations,* 168). Because she views the importation of French pornography and medical texts after the Restoration as decisive in changing the discourse about sexual relations among women, Wahl views Philips's poetry as less of an agent in that change than I do.

Notes to Chapter 9 / Hutson

"The Body of the Friend and the Woman Writer: Katherine Philips's Absence from Alan Bray's *The Friend* (2003)," by Lorna Hutson, was previously published in *Women's Writing* 14, no. 2 (2007): 196–214, reprinted by permission of the publisher Taylor & Francis Ltd., www.tandfonline.com.

1. For some background on the planning and execution of the "Still Kissing the Rod?" conference, see Elizabeth Clarke and Lynn Robson, "Why Are We 'Still Kissing the Rod'?: The Future for the Study of Early Modern Women's Writing," *Women's Writing* 14, no. 2 (2007): 177–93. The original call for papers is preserved at *CFPs in Renaissance Intellectual History:* www.phil-hum-ren.uni-muenchen.de/CFPs/cfp200409071.htm.

2. Alan Bray, *The Friend* (Chicago: University of Chicago Press, 2003).

3. Valerie Traub, *The Renaissance of Lesbianism in Early Modern England* (Cambridge: Cambridge University Press, 2002), 18. Because *The Friend* would not appear in print until a year after *The Renaissance of Lesbianism in Early Modern England,* Traub is citing Bray's earlier work: *Homosexuality in Renaissance England* (London: Gay Men's Press, 1982); and "Homosexuality and the Signs of Male Friendship in Elizabethan England," *History Workshop Journal* 29, no. 1 (1990): 1–19. *The Friend* incorporates "Homosexuality and the Signs of Male Friendship in Elizabethan England" into its chapter on "Friends and Enemies" (177–204).

4. Valerie Traub, "Friendship's Loss: Alan Bray's Making of History," *GLQ: A Journal of Lesbian and Gay Studies* 10, no. 3 (2003): 352–57.

5. Hutson, "Body of the Friend," 207.

6. Ibid., 202, 208. See also Kate Lilley, "'Dear Object': Katherine Philips's Love Elegies and Their Readers," in *Women Writing, 1550–1750,* ed. Jo Wallwork and Paul Salzman, 163–78 (Bundoora, Australia: Meridian, 2001), 168.

7. Daniel T. Lochman and Maritere López, "Introduction: The Emergence of Discourses: Early Modern Friendship," in *Discourses and Representations of Friendship in Early Modern Europe, 1500–1700,* ed. Daniel T. Lochman, Maritere López, and Lorna Hutson, 1–26 (Farnham: Ashgate, 2011), 1–2. See also Amanda E. Herbert, *Female Alliances: Gender, Identity, and Friendship in Early Modern Britain* (New Haven, CT: Yale University Press, 2014), and John S. Garrison, *Friendship and Queer Theory in the Renaissance* (New York: Routledge, 2014); neither book mentions Philips.

8. Penelope Anderson, "'Friendship Multiplyed': Royalist and Republican Friendship in Katherine Philips's Coterie," in *Discourses and Representations of Friendship in Early Modern Europe, 1500–1700,* ed. Daniel T. Lochman, Maritere López, and Lorna Hutson (Farnham: Ashgate, 2011), 131–45.

9. Melissa Sanchez, *Erotic Subjects: The Sexuality of Politics in Early Modern English Literature* (Oxford: Oxford University Press, 2011), 3.

10. Sanchez, *Erotic Subjects,* 25. In a chapter on Margaret Cavendish's romances, Sanchez observes a trend that pertains as much to the poems of fellow royalist Philips: "In embracing . . . a dialectical vision of gender and power, Cavendish challenges the misogyny of both absolute and

republican polemic, each of which imagines an infectious femininity at the roots of their respective bodies, anarchy and tyranny" (179). While Philips adopts a homoerotic model to pose such a challenge, Cavendish chooses heteroerotic courtship.

11. Catharine Gray, *Women Writers and Public Debate in Seventeeth-Century Britain* (New York: Palgrave Macmillan, 2007), 105, 108.

12. Harriette Andreadis, "Re-Configuring Early Modern Friendship: Katherine Philips and Homoerotic Desire," *SEL: Studies in English Literature, 1500–1900* 46, no. 3 (2006): 523–42. Graham Hammill, "Sexuality and Society in the Poetry of Katherine Philips," in *Queer Renaissance Historiography: Backward Gaze,* ed. Vin Nardizzi, Stephen Guy-Bray, and Will Stockton, 185–205 (Farnham: Ashgate, 2007), 197.

13. For an example of a more recent study that insists upon the separation of the erotic and the Platonic, see Andrea Brady, "The Platonic Poems of Katherine Philips," *Seventeenth Century* 25, no. 2 (2010): 300–22.

14. Listed in order of appearance, see the following essays in *Women's Writing* 14, no. 2 (2007): Hutson, "The Body of the Friend"; Nigel Smith, "The Rod and the Canon," 232–45; Sasha Roberts, "Women's Literary Capital in Early Modern England: Formal Composition and Rhetorical Display in Manuscript and Print," 246–69; Gillian Wright, "Women Reading Epictetus," 321–37; Susan Wiseman, "'Public,' 'Private,' 'Politics': Elizabeth Poole, the Duke of Monmouth, 'Political Thought' and 'Literary Evidence,'" 338–62.

15. See Elizabeth Hageman and Andrea Sununu, "New Manuscript Texts of Katherine Philips, 'The Matchless Orinda,'" *English Manuscript Studies, 1100–1700* 4 (1993): 174–216; Elizabeth Hageman and Andrea Sununu, "'More Copies of it abroad than I could have imagin'd': Further Manuscript Texts of Katherine Philips, 'the Matchless Orinda,'" *English Manuscript Studies, 1100–1700* 5 (1995): 127–69.

16. Carol Barash, "Women's Community and the Exiled King: Katherine Philips's Society of Friendship," in *English Women's Poetry, 1649–1714: Politics, Community and Linguistic Authority* (Oxford: Clarendon Press, 1996), 55–100; Elizabeth Susan Wahl, "Female Intimacy and the Question of Lesbian Identity: Rereading the Female Friendship Poems of Katherine Philips," in her *Invisible Relations: Representations of Female Intimacy in the Age of Enlightenment* (Stanford, CA: Stanford University Press, 1999), 130–70; James Loxley, "Unfettered Organs: The Polemical Voices of Katherine Philips," in *"This Double Voice": Gendered Writing in Early Modern England,* ed. Danielle Clarke and Elizabeth Clarke (London: Macmillan, 2000), 230–49; Kate Lilley, "'Dear Object': Katherine Philips's Love Elegies and Their Readers," in *Women Writing, 1550–1750,* ed. Jo Wallwork and Paul Salzman, special issue of *Meridian* 18, no. 1 (2001): 163–78; Valerie Traub, *The Renaissance of Lesbianism in Early Modern England* (Cambridge: Cambridge University Press, 2002), 276–325.

17. Alan Bray, *The Friend* (Chicago: University of Chicago Press, 2003), 10.

18. Jonathan Goldberg, introduction to *Queering the Renaissance,* ed. Jonathan Goldberg (Durham, NC: Duke University Press, 1994), 4–5. See Eve Kosofsky Sedgwick, *Between Men: English Literature and Male Homosocial Desire* (New York: Columbia University Press, 1985), and *Epistemology of the Closet* (Berkeley and Los Angeles: University of California Press, 1990), 182–92.

19. Alan Bray, *Homosexuality in Renaissance England* (London: Gay Men's Press, 1982).

20. Valerie Traub, "Friendship's Loss: Alan Bray's Making of History," *GLQ* 10, no. 3 (2004): 339–65.

21. Ibid., 342.

22. Alan Bray, "Homosexuality and the Signs of Male Friendship in Elizabethan England," *History Workshop Journal* 29, no. 1 (1990): 1–19.

23. Bray, *The Friend,* 219.

23. Ibid., 25, 82.

25. Ibid., 214, 218.

26. Ibid., 218.

27. Benjamin Hoadly, *The Suspicious Husband. A Comedy. As it is Acted at the Theatre Royal in Covent Garden* (London, 1747), 48. See also Bray, *The Friend,* 212.

28. Bray, *The Friend,* 175.

29. See ibid., 219–26; on Poulter and Hunt, see Patricia Crawford and Sara Mendelson, "Sexual Identities in Early Modern England: The Marriage of Two Women in 1680," *Gender and History* 7, no. 3 (1995): 363–77.

30. Juliet Dusinberre, *Shakespeare and the Nature of Women* (London: Macmillan, 1975).

31. For example, Lisa Jardine, *Still Harping on Daughters: Women and Drama in the Age of Shakespeare* (Hassocks: Harvester, 1983).

32. For an excellent discussion of the relationship between the metaphor of historical "invisibility" and the contemporary "unrepresentability" of lesbianism, see Annamarie Jagose, *Inconsequence: Lesbian Representation and the Logic of Sexual Sequence* (Ithaca, NY: Cornell University Press, 2002), 1–36.

33. Valerie Traub, "The (In)Significance of 'Lesbian' Desire in Early Modern England," in *Queering the Renaissance,* ed. Jonathan Goldberg (Durham, NC: Duke University Press, 1994), 62–83; Traub, "The Perversion of 'Lesbian' Desire," *History Workshop Journal* 41, no. 1 (1996): 23–49.

34. Traub, *Renaissance of Lesbianism,* 301 (chapter 8 in the present volume); Patrick Thomas, ed., *The Collected Works of Katherine Philips: The Matchless Orinda,* vol. 1, *The Poems* (Stump Cross, Essex: Stump Cross Books, 1990), 200–01.

35. Traub, *Renaissance of Lesbianism,* 302.

36. Ibid., 299.

37. Ibid., 325; my italics.

38. The idea of friendship as a mingling of souls was commonplace in the Renaissance reception of Cicero's *De amicitia*. See, for example, John Donne, "Sir, more than kisses, letters mingle soules; For thus friends absent speake," in *John Donne: Complete English Poems*, ed. C. A. Patrides (London: J. M. Dent, 1994), 187.

39. Traub, *Renaissance of Lesbianism*, 299.

40. Ibid., 345.

41. Bray, *The Friend*, 157.

42. Ibid., 175.

43. Ibid., 175.

44. Alan Bray and Michel Rey, "The Body of the Friend: Continuity and Change in Masculine Friendship in the Seventeenth Century," in *English Masculinities, 1660–1800*, ed. Tim Hitchcock and Michele Cohen, 65–84 (London: Longman, 1999).

45. Bray, *The Friend*, 1.

46. Ibid., 141.

47. Ibid., 142.

48. "Namque hoc praestat amicitia propinquitati" (Friendship is more potent than kinship); "Quocirca et absentes adsunt et egentes abundant" (Wherefore, friends though absent, are at hand, though in need, yet abound); from Cicero, *Laelius: De amicitia*, trans. W. Falconer (London: Heinemann, 1929), 128–33 (5.19, 6.22, 7.23).

49. Jeremy Taylor, *A Discourse on the Nature, Offices and Measures of Friendship* (London, 1657), 25–26.

50. Taylor explains that bodily attraction is not to be disdained: "sometimes," he writes, "the meanest persons in a house have a festival; even sympathies and natural inclinations... and a conformity of humors... and the beauty of the face, and a witty answer may first strike the flint and kindle a spark" (ibid., 36).

51. Ibid., 100–01.

52. Bray, *The Friend*, 212.

53. I use the term "casuistry" to mean the practical resolution of moral perplexities, as opposed to the elaboration of general principles, or rules. See Albert R. Jonsen and Stephen Toulmin, *The Abuse of Casuistry: A History of Moral Reasoning* (Berkeley and Los Angeles: University of California Press, 1988). On Taylor and Locke as casuists, see Barbara Shapiro, *Beyond Reasonable Doubt and Probable Cause* (Berkeley and Los Angeles: University of California Press, 1991), 14, 16–17.

54. Taylor, *A Discourse*, 8.

55. Ibid., 25–26.

56. Warren Chernaik, "Philips [née Fowler], Katherine (1632–1664)," *Oxford Dictionary of National Biography* (Oxford: Oxford University

Press, 2004); online edition, 2006, www.oxforddnb.com/index/101022124/Katherine-Philips (accessed Apr. 15, 2015). Taylor, *A Discourse,* 86, 88.

57. Philips, "A Friend," in *Collected Works,* 1:165–68.

58. Kate Lilley, "'Dear Object': Katherine Philips's Love Elegies and Their Readers," in *Women Writing, 1550–1750,* ed. Jo Wallwork and Paul Salzman (Bundoora, Australia: Meridian, 2001), 170.

59. Ibid., 169; for John Taylor's attack, see Peter Beal, *In Praise of Scribes: Manuscripts and Their Makers in Seventeenth-Century England* (Oxford: Clarendon Press, 1998), 150–53; Bray, *The Friend,* 212.

60. Bray, *The Friend,* 55.

61. Philips, "To my Lady Ann Boyle's saying that I look'd angrily on her," in *Collected Works,* 1:201–02.

62. Ibid., 221.

63. Bray, *The Friend,* 210.

64. Lilley, "'Dear Object,'" 168.

65. See Lorna Hutson, "Liking Men: Ben Jonson's Closet Opened," *ELH: English Literary History* 71, no. 4 (2004): 1065–96.

66. For example, the closely guarded secret of Dauphine's intimacy with the transvestite boy, who spends most of the play known as Mistress Epicoene, earns the couple nothing but a virile social triumph, while the would-be heterosexual and unguardedly loquacious Sir Jack Daw and Sir Amorous La-Foole are "effeminized" and exposed by their incautious boasting that they have both slept with Mistress Epicoene—before, of course, they realize that "she" is a man. See Ben Jonson, *Epicoene,* ed. R. V. Holdsworth (London: Benn, 1979), 5.1.50–85; further references in the text are to this edition. On the play's sexual libertinism, see James Grantham Turner, *Schooling Sex: Libertine Education and Erotic Education in Italy, France and England, 1534–1685* (Oxford: Oxford University Press, 2003), 58–71.

67. Philips, *Collected Works,* 1:251.

68. Traub, *Renaissance of Lesbianism,* 297.

69. Victoria Kahn, *Wayward Contracts: The Crisis of Political Obligation in England, 1640–1674* (Princeton, NJ: Princeton University Press, 2004), 21.

70. Philips, "Friendship in Emblem, or the Seale, to my dearest Lucasia," in *Collected Works,* 1:106–08.

Notes to Chapter 10 / Andreadis

1. George Puttenham, *The Art of English Poesy,* ed. Frank Whigham and Wayne A. Rebhorn (Ithaca, NY: Cornell University Press, 2007), 127–28. Chapter 18, from which this quotation is taken, "Of the shepherd's or

pastoral poesy, called eclogue, and to what purpose it was first invented and used" opens this way:

> Some be of opinion . . . that the pastoral poesy, which we commonly call by the name of eclogue and bucolic . . . should be the first of any other, and before the satire, comedy, or tragedy, because, say they, the shepherds' and haywards' assemblies and meetings . . . was the first familiar conversation, and their babble and talk under bushes and shady trees, the first disputation and contentious reasoning, and their fleshly heats growing of ease, the first idle wooings, and their songs made to their mates or paramours either upon sorrow or jollity of courage, the first amorous musics. (127)

2. See Louis Adrian Montrose, "Of Gentlemen and Shepherds: The Politics of Elizabethan Pastoral Form," *English Literary History* 50, no. 3 (1983): 415–59; and Josephine A. Roberts, "Deciphering Women's Pastoral: Coded Language in Wroth's *Love's Victory*," in *Representing Women in Renaissance England*, 163–74 (Columbia: University of Missouri Press, 1997).

3. See Bruce R. Smith, *Homosexual Desire in Shakespeare's England: A Cultural Poetics* (Chicago: University of Chicago Press, 1991); Frederick Greene, "Subversions of Pastoral: Queer Theory and the Politics and Poetics of Elegy" (Ph.D. diss., University of California, Santa Barbara, 1997); and Stephen Whitworth, "The Name of the Ancients: Humanist Homoerotics and the Signs of Pastoral" (Ph.D. diss., University of Michigan, 1997).

4. The more recent work of Stephen Guy-Bray in *Homoerotic Space: The Poetics Of Loss in Renaissance Literature* (Toronto: University of Toronto Press, 2002) also takes up the ways in which Renaissance writers inflect their debt to classical, and particularly pastoral, sources but omit any consideration of a possibly female homoerotic space. As will become evident, however, the association of pastoral with loss as well as what Guy-Bray calls its "inherently elegiac" tenor may also be seen in female poetic spaces.

5. Elizabeth Young, "Aphra Behn, Gender, and Pastoral," *SEL: Studies in English Literature, 1500–1900* 33, no. 3 (1993): 523. Young remarks further that "By the 1670s, [following Spenser, Sidney and Milton], when Aphra Behn was writing, pastoral was not simply an exercise in applying convention, but the much more difficult exercise of employing convention in order to break it. With that development in the genre came the emphasis on gender politics that characterizes so much of Behn's poetry" (525). Karoline Szatek, "Engendering Spaces: A Study of Sexuality in Pastoral Borderlands," *Classical and Modern Literature* 18, no. 4 (1998): 345–59, attempts a more extensive characterization of the ways in which the Renaissance pastorals of Richard Barnfield, Michael Drayton, Alexander Barclay, and others, challenge received gender conventions.

6. As should become evident, the female pastoral tradition I propose here is not intended to suggest a notion of opposing masculine and feminine traditions in early modern verse but rather to call attention to what we might see as complementary and often interpenetrating traditions, particularly insofar as women writers appropriated male traditions and conventions to their own uses. See Harriette Andreadis, "The Sapphic-Platonics of Katherine Philips (1631–1664)," *Signs: A Journal of Women in Culture and Society* 15, no. 1 (Autumn 1989): 34–60; Andreadis, *Sappho in Early Modern England: Female Same-Sex Literary Erotics, 1550–1714* (Chicago: University of Chicago Press, 2001); and Elizabeth Scott-Baumann, *Forms of Engagement: Women, Poetry, and Culture, 1640–1680* (Oxford: Oxford University Press, 2013), esp. chapters 3 and 4, on Katherine Philips's use of the work of, for instance, Abraham Cowley and John Donne.

7. Smith, *Homosexual Desire,* 90.

8. With the pressures of the times, mid-seventeenth-century English writers turned increasingly inward. The turmoil of dissension, the chaos of rebellion, and the catastrophe of regicide freed loyal monarchists to desert the public scene. It was this escapism, particularly its use of pastoralism, that Philips infused with her more passionate intimacy. In her attempt to create an ideal "society" of friends, in her use of pastoral nicknames for her intimates, in her reading of Italian and French romances, and in her attraction to the idea of Platonic love, Philips embraced current literary and courtly fashions for, among others, pastoralism, the ideology of friendship, quasi-philosophical meditation, and encomia to royal and aristocratic personages. In this context, critics generally note the ways in which Philips echoes the pastoralism of the cavalier poets. Valerie Traub, in offering a different perspective on Philips's use of the pastoral, draws our attention to Warren Chernaik's remark that the cavaliers were "constantly drawing magic circles that will shut the world out, seeking to find an autonomous realm of love and art, a court immune to change" (chapter 8 in this volume). See also Patrick Thomas, ed., *The Collected Works of Katherine Philips: The Matchless Orinda,* vol. 1, *The Poems* (Stump Cross, Essex: Stump Cross Books, 1990), 173–75. Philips's poems are from this edition, hereafter cited in the text by line number.

9. See esp. Mary Ann C. McGuire, "The Cavalier Country-House Poem: Mutations on a Jonsonian Tradition," *SEL: Studies in English Literature, 1500–1900* 19, no. 1 (1979): 93–108. "My own readings... suggest that the country-house poem was a fairly sensitive barometer of social change. More specifically, the country-house poems of Carew and Lovelace alter Jonsonian tradition in very specific ways that reflect the hopes and anxieties of an increasingly beleaguered propertied class" (94n4).

10. See Amy Greenstadt, "Aemilia Lanyer's Pathetic Phallacy," *Journal for Early Modern Cultural Studies* 8, no. 1 (2008): 67–97, for a detailed exploration of the erotic complexities and larger implications of this episode.

11. Aemilia Lanyer, *The Poems of Aemilia Lanyer,* ed. Susanne Woods (Oxford: Oxford University Press, 1993); cited parenthetically by line number in the text.

12. Ann Baynes Coiro, "Writing in Service: Sexual Politics and Class Position in the Poetry of Aemilia Lanyer and Ben Jonson," in *Ashgate Critical Essays on Women Writers in England, 1550–1700,* vol. 3, *Anne Lock, Isabella Whitney and Aemilia Lanyer,* ed. Micheline White, 333–52 (London: Ashgate, 2009), 347.

13. It may be that this different emphasis is a result of addressing women of her own class—her former schoolmates—in so many of her friendship poems, while often reserving occasional and commemorative works for her aristocratic patrons, though of course this dichotomy breaks down in many ways when the object of her affection is an aristocrat, e.g., Berenice. Lorna Hutson, "The Body of the Friend and the Woman Writer: Philips's Absence from Alan Bray's *The Friend*" (chapter 9 in this volume), addresses "Philips's feminization of the poetry of patronage."

14. See Harriette Andreadis, *Sappho in Early Modern England: Female Same-Sex Literary Erotics, 1550–1714* (Chicago: University of Chicago Press, 2001), 117, 119–24.

15. Anne Killigrew, *Poems* (London, 1686), sig. M2–N.

16. Ibid., sig. M2–N.

17. Ibid., sig. N2[v].

18. Ibid., sig. N4[v].

19. Ibid., sig. O.

20. Ibid., sig. O1[v].

21. See, for example, Shelley O'Reilly, "Absinthe Makes the Tart Grow Fonder: A Note on 'Wormwood' in Christina Rossetti's *Goblin Market,*" *Victorian Poetry* 34, no. 1 (1996): 108–14; and Elizabeth Campbell, "Of Mothers and Merchants: Female Economics in Christina Rosetti's 'Goblin Market,'" *Victorian Studies* 33, no. 3 (1990): 393–410. Among other approaches are Lona Mosk Packer, "Symbol and Reality in Christina Rossetti's *Goblin Market,*" *PMLA* 73, no. 4 (1958): 375–85, and Simon Humphries, "The Uncertainty of *Goblin Market,*" *Victorian Poetry* 45, no. 4 (2007): 391–413, on Christian symbolism and allegory; David F. Morrill, "'Twilight Is Not Good for Maidens': Uncle Polidori and the Psychodynamics of Vampirism in *Goblin Market,*" *Victorian Poetry* 28, no. 1 (1990): 1–16, on vampirism; Ellen Golub, "Untying Goblin Apron Strings: A Psychoanalytic Reading of 'Goblin Market,'" *Literature and Psychology* 25 (1975): 158–65, on psychoanalysis; and Linda E. Marshall, "'Transfigured to His Likeness': Sensible Transcendentalism in Christina Rossetti's 'Goblin Market,'" *University of Toronto Quarterly* 63, no. 3 (1994): 429–50, on transcendentalism.

22. Christina Rossetti, *Goblin Market: A Tale of Two Sisters,* afterword by Joyce Carol Oates (San Francisco, CA: Chronicle Books, 1997), 4–6.

23. Ibid., 48–49.

24. Ibid., 50–51.

25. Hilda Doolittle, *H. D.: Collected Poems, 1912–1944,* ed. Louis Martz (New York, NY: New Directions, 1983), 55. See also "Sea Poppies" (1916, p. 21), which is similarly expressive and takes up similar ideas.

26. Susan Stanford Friedman, *Psyche Reborn: The Emergence of H. D.* (Bloomington: Indiana University Press, 1981), 56–58. Friedman goes on to note that

> Norman Holmes Pearson warned that H. D.'s use of Greek masks as a distancing device has all too often been ignored by her critics. He [remarked that].... "She has been so praised as a kind of Greek publicity girl that people have forgotten that she writes the most intensely personal poems using Greek myth as a metaphor." The oread may be Greek, but the setting for "Oread" comes from a past not more remote than her visits to the Cornwall seacoast and her childhood summers on the shores of the Atlantic Ocean. The ultimate subject of the poem is the consciousness of the poet herself, the intellectual and emotional complex of perception that finds its clearest expression in the picture-making mode of imagist epistemology. (58–59)

27. Doolittle, *Collected Poems,* 5.

28. Eileen Gregory, "Rose Cut in Rock: Sappho and H. D.'s 'Sea Garden,'" *Contemporary Literature* 27, no. 4 (1986): 538. Gregory goes on to remark that "The sea represents here the harsh power of elemental life, to which the soul must open itself, and by which it must be transformed or die. H. D. need not have known, but probably did, that sea/salt is the arcane alchemical substance linked to the mysterious bitterness and wisdom essential to spiritual life....More importantly, the psychological experience of salt *specifies* and *clarifies* pain: No salt, no experiencing—merely a running on and running through of events without psychic body" (538).

29. Doolittle, *Collected Poems,* 25.

30. Ibid., 335.

31. Ibid., 11.

32. Mary J. Carruthers, "The Re-Vision of the Muse: Adrienne Rich, Audre Lorde, Judy Grahn, Olga Broumas," *Hudson Review* 36, no. 2 (1983): 308.

33. Olga Broumas, *Pastoral Jazz* (Port Townsend, WA: Copper Canyon Press, 1983); Olga Broumas and T. Begley, *Sappho's Gymnasium* (Port Townsend, WA: Copper Canyon Press, 1994).

34. Broumas's second book, *Soie Sauvage* (1979), is made up of 20 meditations on the Oregon landscape and its internal correlatives.

35. In Karla Hammond, "An Interview with Olga Broumas," *Northwest Review* 18, no. 3 (1980): 37. Broumas has also remarked that "I see the poem on the page really as notation for the voice" (41). See also Diane

Horton, "'Scarlet Liturgies': The Poetry of Olga Broumas," *North Dakota Quarterly* 55, no. 4 (1987): 323.

36. Broumas, *Pastoral Jazz,* 43.

37. I make a clear distinction between the female queer pastoral as examined here and nature poetry, whose primary concerns are ecological or in some other way metaphorical, even though its concerns might have their roots in the conventions of the traditional pastoral. I think here of the poems of Maxine Kumin and, perhaps more pertinently, of those of Mary Oliver who, as a lesbian, writes about nature but without embracing its possibilities for a clear same-sex eroticism. Other modern lesbian poets, such as Elizabeth Bishop and May Swenson, remained closeted even into the very late twentieth century, while Mary Oliver continues an extraordinary, and perhaps an extraordinarily unnecessary, discretion.

Notes to Afterword / Hageman

1. David Pearson, *Books as History: The Importance of Books Beyond Their Texts* (London: British Library, 2011), 23.

2. John Aubrey, *"Brief Lives," chiefly of Contemporaries,* vol. 2, ed. Andrew Clark (Oxford: Clarendon Press, 1898), 154.

3. Tutin manuscript, National Library of Wales, MS 775B.

4. Peter Stallybrass, Roger Chartier, J. Franklin Mowery, and Heather Wolfe, "Hamlet's Tables and the Technologies of Writing in Renaissance England," *Shakespeare Quarterly* 55 (2004): 381, 399, 403; H. R. Woudhuysen, "Writing-Tables and Table-Books," *Electronic British Library Journal* (2004), article 3. While treating the distinction between paper books and reusable writing tables, Woudhuysen notes that the latter were handy "for making random notes and observations, which could then be copied and perhaps written up, in a fuller and more permanent form" (5), after which time the tables' surfaces could "be wiped clean and reused" (7).

5. As Andrea Sununu and I suggest in "'More copies of it abroad than I could have imagin'd': Further Manuscript Texts of Katherine Philips, 'the Matchless Orinda,'" *English Manuscript Studies, 1100–1700* 5 (1995): 135, Philips's poem may be "one in a series of women's poems in which proverbial lines...lead toward a triumphant contradiction of the image of a virgin leading apes in hell." See also Claudia A. Limbert and John H. O'Neill, "Composite Authorship: Katherine Philips and an Antimarital Satire," *Papers of the Bibliographical Society of America* 87 (1993): 487–502.

6. Cited by Juliet Fleming, *Graffiti and the Writing Arts of Early Modern England* (Philadelphia: University of Pennsylvania Press, 2001), 55–56. For other references to poems inscribed by diamond pens or rings, see 55–57 and 180.

7. William Camden, *Britannia,* 3rd ed. (London: G. Bishop, 1590), 443–44, and *Britain,* trans. Philemon Holland (London: Eliot's Court Press, 1610), 557. Thomas Fuller, *The Church History of Britain* (London: John Williams, 1655), 9:181, refers to Camden but quotes the glass itself, which he has "had in my hand," and gives a different English translation: "*Buxton,* who dost with waters warme excell; / By me, perchance, never more seen, Farewell." The distich on which Mary's couplet is based, "Feltria, perpetuo nivium damnata rigore, / Terra mihi posthac non habitanda, vale" is said to have been inscribed by Julius Caesar on a marble post near the town of Feltre in Northern Italy and to have been destroyed during the sack of Feltre in 1509; see Robert Pierpoint, "Latin Lines on Buxton," *Notes and Queries* 10 S. viii, issue 200 (1907): 332–33.

8. For a description of the new glass, with a photographic image and a transcription of the manuscript on which it is based, see Patrick Chapman's excellent *Things Written in the Glasse Windowes at Buxtons* (Chesterfield: Whittington Moor, 2012).

9. Cited by Jane Dunn, *Read My Heart: Dorothy Osborne and Sir William Temple, a Love Story in the Age of Revolution* (London: Harper Press, 2008), 8–9. As Dunn notes, this well-known passage from Esther 7:10 is followed in the Bible by the verse, "Then was the King's wrath pacified." Here I owe thanks to Alice Eardley, who called my attention to the stories of the Temple windows.

10. Ibid., 114.

11. This is number 5 of book 1 of Cato's distiches, which circulated in both Latin and English throughout sixteenth and seventeenth century England. In a 1560 copy of *Sage and Prudent saynges of the seven wyse men* (STC 4857), the distich is translated as "If thou consyder well in thy mynde, / The fashyon of men thou shalte treuly fynde, / Howe every manne, other dothe defame, / For there is no man that lyveth without blame" (F1v). A manuscript version now in Yale University's Osborn Collection is closer to the Haddon Hall quatrain: "No man e'er lived (on earth) nor ever shall / That did all well, and had no fault at all" (MS b227, 167). For a photograph of the Haddon Hall version, see Bryan Cleary, *Haddon Hall: The Home of Lord Edward Manners* (Wymondham: Heritage House Group, 2009), 56.

12. In 2010, Anthony Cox worked with Heather Mayo and Polly Morton to transcribe and identify the inscriptions. In 2011 he told me about the windows and about *Bracebridge Hall,* whose use of Philips's poems he had found along the way, and he noted that Temperance Gell, whose copy of the 1667 folio of Philips's poems discussed in the last paragraph of this afterword, lived at Hopton Hall, not far from Haddon Hall. In September 2012, Cox and Amanda Coates kindly showed the hall and its windows to me and to Claire Byrony Williams, on whose conversation and photographs taken that day I have relied for my description and approximate dating of the handwriting within the windows.

13. The letter forms in these seven names differ enough from one another that one could suggest that they were signed by seven different people, possibly on the same day that the Philips poems were inscribed. Conversely, the names "Theodosius," "Orinda," and "Gertrude" in the other windows appear to have been written by a single person—a person whose handwriting is almost certainly later than the engraver of the Philips quatrains.

14. For Washington Irving's transcription of Philips's quatrains in Haddon Hall, see his *Journals and Notebooks,* vol. 2, *1807–1822,* ed. Walter A. Reichart and Lillian Schlissel (Boston: Twayne, 1981), 74–76; although Irving subsequently associated these poems with Philips, he does not name her in the *Journals.*

15. For a history of Haddon Hall and its owners, see Cleary, *Haddon Hall,* esp. 8–11 and 65.

16. Irving's *Journals* (2:74–77) provide an engaging account of his visit to the hall with his brother Peter in August 1816; further details of the hall from a visit with the artist Charles Leslie in September 1821 are on 2:336–41.

17. For eighteenth century workmen's inscriptions on windows, see, for example, the book jacket and page 122 of Christina Lupton, *Knowing Books: The Consciousness of Mediation in Eighteenth-Century Britain* (Philadelphia: University of Pennsylvania Press, 2012).

18. Irving, *Journals,* 2:74–75.

19. In fact, "Orinda" is the only coterie name that appears in both *Bracebridge Hall* and Philips's known writings, though Cornelia (as noted above) is a character in *Pompey,* and Camilla is in her *Horace.*

20. Washington Irving, "Family Reliques," in *Bracebridge Hall, Tales of a Traveller, The Alhambra* (New York: Literary Classics of the United States, 1991), 34–38.

21. Irving, *Bracebridge Hall,* 37–38.

22. Lupton, *Knowing Books,* 125.

23. Brian Jay Jones, *Washington Irving* (New York: Arcade, 2008), 204.

24. Heidi Brayman Hackel, *Reading Material in Early Modern England: Print, Gender, and Literacy* (Cambridge: Cambridge University Press, 2005), 137–95, esp. 158–59. For the concept of microhistories of readers, see 58 and 141. The phrase "Marking Readers" in my heading is from the subtitle of William H. Sherman's *Used Books: Marking Readers in Renaissance England* (Philadelphia: University of Philadelphia Press, 2008). See also his earlier essay, "What Did Renaissance Readers Write in Their Books?," in *Books and Readers in Early Modern England: Material Studies,* ed. Jennifer Anderson and Elizabeth Sauer, 119–38 (Philadelphia: University of Pennsylvania Press, 2002), esp. 135n16, where he observes that early modern literary texts typically show far fewer annotations than other kinds of writing.

25. Brayman Hackel, *Reading Material,* 150; she also notes that to many of his male contemporaries, the *Arcadia* "[came] to represent all that is dangerous to female readers" (155).

26. Although my microhistory focuses on early modern readers, it also includes attention to the more recent history of books by Philips as they have moved from private hands into collections where they are now housed. Another kind of microhistory important to students of women's history is, of course, the study of women's libraries such as Brayman Hackel's "The Countess of Bridgewater's London Library," in Anderson and Sauer, *Books and Readers,* 139–59; and Paul Morgan, "Frances Wolfreston and 'Hor Bouks': A Seventeenth-Century Woman Book-Collector," *The Library* 11 (1989): 197–219. For women's reading practices, see, for example, Edith Snook, *Women, Reading, and the Cultural Politics of Early Modern England* (Aldershot: Ashgate, 2006).

27. Peter Beal, *In Praise of Scribes: Manuscripts and Their Makers in Seventeenth-Century England* (Oxford: Clarendon Press, 1998), 183, presents images of "The Actors" in both the Trinity College folio and in the 1667 folio once owned by the second Earl of Bridgewater and now at Harvard University. On page 186 Beal prints an image of the prologue in the Trinity folio, and on page 189 images of the epilogue from the Trinity copy and from a folio at the Victoria and Albert Museum.

28. Brayman Hackel, *Reading Material,* 138–39.

29. This Lord Blessington was Murrough Boyle (1648–1718), first created Viscount Blessington in the peerage of Ireland in 1673.

30. For a powerful argument of the value of anecdotal evidence of women's experience, see Lena Cowen Orlin, "A Case for Anecdotalism in Women's History: The Witness Who Spoke When the Cock Crowed," *English Literary Renaissance* 31 (2001): 52–77.

Bibliography

Printed Works by Katherine Philips

The Collected Works of Katherine Philips: The Matchless Orinda. Vols. 1–2, edited by Patrick Thomas. Vol. 3, edited by Germaine Greer and Ruth Little. Stump Cross, Essex: Stump Cross Books, 1990–93.

Familiar Letters. Vol. 1, *Written by the Right Honourable, John, late Earl of Rochester, to the honourable Henry Savile, Esq; and other Letters by Persons of Honour and Quality. With Letters written by the most Ingenious Mr. Tho. Otway, and Mrs. K. Philips. Publish'd from their Original Copies. With Modern Letters By Tho. Cheek, Esq; Mr. Dennis, and Mr. Brown.* London: Printed by W. Onley, for S. Briscoe, 1697. Reprinted 1699.

Katherine Philips (1631/2–1664). Edited by Paula Loscocco. Series 2, *Printed Writings 1641–1700,* part 3, vols. 1–3. Aldershot: Ashgate, 2007.

Letters from Orinda to Poliarchus. London: Printed by W. B. for Bernard Lintot, 1705. Reprinted 1729.

Letters from Orinda to Poliarchus, The Second Edition, with Additions. London: Printed for Bernard Lintot, 1729.

Minor Poets of the Caroline Period. Vol. 1, *Containing Chamberlayne's "Pharonnida" and "England's Jubilee," Benlowe's "Theophila," and the Poems of Katherine Philips and Patrick Hannay.* Edited by George Saintsbury. Oxford: Clarendon Press, 1905. Reprinted 1968.

Poems (1667) by Katherine Philips. Edited by Travis Dupriest. Delmar: Scholars' Facsimiles and Reprints, 1992.

Poems. By the Incomparable, Mrs. K. P. London: Printed by J. G. for Rich. Marriott, 1664.

Poems By the most deservedly Admired Mrs. Katherine Philips, The matchless Orinda. To which is added Monsieur Corneille's Pompey & Horace, Tragedies. With several other Translations out of French. London: Printed by J. M. for H. Herringman, 1667. Reprinted 1669 and 1678.

Poems By the most deservedly Admired Mrs. Katherine Philips, The matchless Orinda. To which is added Monsieur Corneille's Pompey & Horace, Tragedies. With several other Translations out of French. Tonson, 1710.

Pompey. A Tragœdy. Acted with Great Applause. Dublin and London: Printed for John Crooke, 1663.

Primary Sources

Acts and Ordinances of the Interregnum, 1642–60. 2 vols. Edited by C. H. First and R. S. Rait. London: Her Majesty's Stationery Office, 1911. "Advertisements of Books." [*London*] *Newes Published for Satisfaction and Information of the People.* January 14, 1664. London: Printed by Richard Hodgkinson, 1663–65.

Agrippa von Nettesheim, Henry Cornelius. *Three Books of Occult Philosophy.* Translated by Richard Howard. Berkeley and Los Angeles: University of California Press, 1991.

Ann Cromwell's Virginal Book, 1638. Translated and edited by Howard Ferguson. London: Oxford University Press, 1974.

Aubrey, John. *Brief Lives.* Edited by Oliver Lawson Dick. Ann Arbor: University of Michigan Press, 1957.

———. *"Brief Lives," chiefly of Contemporaries, set down by John Aubrey, between the Years 1669 & 1696.* 2 vols. Edited by Andrew Clarks. Oxford: Clarendon Press, 1898.

Audley, John. *Englands common-wealth shewing the liberties of the people, the priviledges of Parliament, and the rights of souldiery: with epistles to the persons mentioned.* London, 1652.

Bacon, Francis. *Sylva sylvarum; or, A Natural History.* London, 1664.

Beale, Mary. *A Discourse of Friendship.* London, 1667.

Boyle, Roger, Lord Broghill. *A letter from the Lord Broghill to the honourable William Lenthall Esq; speaker of the Parliament of England. Containing a relation of the great successe it hath pleased God to give the Parliament forces under the command of the Lord*

Broghill, in defeating the army of the rebels in Ireland, under the command of the Lord Muskerry. Together with another letter touch the said defeat. London, 1651.

———. *Parthenissa.* London, 1651.

Broumas, Olga. *Pastoral Jazz.* Port Townsend, WA: Copper Canyon Press, 1983.

———. *Soie Sauvage.* Port Townsend, WA: Copper Canyon Press, 1979.

Broumas, Olga, and T. Begley. *Sappho's Gymnasium.* Port Townsend, WA: Copper Canyon Press, 1994.

Butler, Charles. *The Principles of Musik in Singing and Setting.* London, 1636.

Burton, Robert. *The Anatomy of Melancholy.* Oxford, 1621.

Calendar of the Proceedings of the Committee for Compounding, 1643–1660. Edited by Mary Anne Everitt Green. Nendeln, Liechtenstein: Kraus Reprint, 1967.

Camden, William. *Britain.* Translated by Philemon Holland. London, 1610.

———. *Britannia.* 3rd ed. London, 1590.

Cartwright, William. *Comedies, tragi-comedies, with other poems, by Mr William Cartwright, late student of Christ-Church in Oxford, and proctor of the university. The ayres and songs set by Mr Henry Lawes, servant to His late Majesty in his publick and private musick.* London, 1651.

———. *The Plays and Poems of William Cartwright.* Edited by G. Blakemore Evans. Madison: University of Wisconsin Press, 1951.

Catullus, Tibullus, Pervigilium Veneris. 2nd ed. Edited by G. P. Goold. Cambridge, MA: Harvard University Press, 1988.

Chapman, Patrick. *Things Written in the Glasse Windowes at Buxtons.* Chesterfield: Whittington Moor, 2012.

Charters of St. Paul's, London. Edited by S. E. Kelly. Oxford: Oxford University Press, 2004.

Cicero. *Laelius: De Amicitia.* Translated by W. Falconer. London: Heinemann, 1929.

Corporation of London Record Office (CLRO). *The Repertories of the Court of Aldermen.* Vol. 59. Oct. 1647–Oct. 1649. London, 1495–1835.

Cowley, Abraham. *The Collected Works of Abraham Cowley.* 2 vols. Edited by Thomas A. Calhoun, Laurence Heyworth, and J. Robert King. Newark, DE: University of Delaware Press, 1989.

Davenant, William. *Gondibert: A Heroick Poem.* London, 1651.

Donne, John. *Poems, by J. D. With elegies on the authors death.* London, 1633.

———. *The Complete English Poems of John Donne.* Edited by C. A. Patrides. London: J. M. Dent, 1985. Reprinted 1994.

———. *John Donne: The Epithalamions, Anniversaries, and Epicedes.* Edited by Wesley Milgate. Oxford: Clarendon Press, 1978.

———. *The Variorum Edition of the Poetry of John Donne.* Vol. 8, *The Epigrams, Epithalamions, Epitaphs, Inscriptions, and Miscellaneous Poems.* Edited by Ted-Larry Pebworth, Gary A. Stringer, Ernest W. Sullivan II, William A. McClung, and Jeffrey Johnson. Bloomington: Indiana University Press, 1995.

Doolittle, Hilda. *H. D.: Collected Poems, 1912–1914.* Edited by Louis Martz. New York: New Directions, 1983.

Dorat, Jean. *The Latin Odes of Jean Dorat.* Translated by David R. Slavitt. Alexandria, VA: Orchises Press, 2000.

Du Bosc, Jacques. *The Compleat Woman.* London, 1639.

Dugdale, William. *The History of St. Paul's Cathedral in London.* London, 1658.

Eikon Basilike: The Portraiture of His Sacred Majesty in His Solitudes and Sufferings. Edited by Philip A. Knachel. Ithaca, NY: Cornell University Press, 1966.

Elizabeth Rogers Hir Virginall Booke. Edited by Charles J. F. Cofone. New York: Dover, 1975. Rev. ed., 1982.

Eucharistica Oxoniensia. Oxford, 1641.

Fuller, Thomas. *The Church History of Britain.* London, 1655.

Grenville, Bevill. *Verses on the Death of...Sir Bevill Grenville.* Oxford, 1643.

Gurnay, Edmund. *An Appendix unto the Homily against Images in Churches.* London, 1641.

Haggar, Henry. *No King but Jesus; or, The Walls of tyrannie razed and the foundations of unjust monarchy discovered to the view of all that desire to see it wherein is undeniably proved that no king is the Lords anointed but Jesus*. London: Printed for Giles Calvert, 1652.

Herrick, Robert. *The Poems of Robert Herrick*. Edited by L. C. Martin. London: Oxford University Press, 1965.

Hoadly, Benjamin. *The Suspicious Husband. A Comedy*. London: J. and R. Tonson and S. Draper, 1747.

Irenodia Cantabrigiensis. Cambridge, 1641.

Irving, Washington. *Bracebridge Hall, Tales of a Traveller, The Alhambra*. New York: Literary Classics of the United States, 1991.

———. *Journals and Notebooks*. Vol. 2, *1807–1822*. Edited by Walter A. Reichart and Lillian Schlissel. Boston: Twayne, 1981.

Jessey, Henry, and Sarah Wight. *The Exceeding Riches of God's Grace*. London, 1647.

Jinner, Sarah. *An almanack or prognostication for the year of our Lord 1658*. London, 1658. Reprinted in *The Early Modern Englishwoman: A Facsimile Library of Essential Works*. General editors, Betty S. Travitsky and Patrick Cullen. Series 2, *Printed Writings, 1641–1700*, part 1, vol. 6, *Almanacs*. Selected and introduced by Alan S. Weber. Aldershot: Ashgate, 2002.

Jonson, Ben. *Epicoene*. Edited by R. V. Holdsworth. London: Benn, 1979.

Keats, John. *The Letters of John Keats, 1814–1821*. 2 vols. Edited by Hyder Edward Rollins. Cambridge, MA: Harvard University Press, 1958.

Killigrew, Anne. *Poems*. London, 1686.

Lanyer, Aemilia. *The Poems of Aemilia Lanyer*. Edited by Susanne Woods. Oxford: Oxford University Press, 1993.

Lawes, Henry. *Ayres and Dialogues for One, Two, and Three Voyces*. London, 1653.

———. *The Second Booke of Ayres and Dialogues*. London, 1655.

Lawes, Henry, and William Lawes. *Choice Psalmes put into Musick*. London, 1648.

Maclean, Hugh, ed. *Ben Jonson and the Cavalier Poets*. New York: W. W. Norton, 1975.

A Mad Designe; or, A Description of the King of Scots marching in his Disguise, after the rout at Worcester, With the Particulers where

He was, and what He and his Company did, every day and night after he fled from Worcester. London, 1651.

Marvell, Andrew. *Andrew Marvell: The Complete Poems*. Edited by Elizabeth Story Donno. London: Penguin, 1972.

Montaigne, Michel de. *The Complete Essays*. Edited by M. A. Screech. New York: Penguin Classics, 1997.

Monumentum Regale; or, A Tomb Erected for that Incomparable and Glorious Monarch, Charles the First. London, 1649.

Morley, Thomas. *A Plaine and Easie Introduction to Practicall Musicke*. London, 1597.

Mulcaster, Richard. *Positions*. London, 1581.

Musarum Oxoniensium Epibathpia Serenissimae. Oxford, 1643.

Norton, Thomas, and Thomas Sackville. [*Gorboduc:*] *The tragedie of Ferrex and Porrex*. London, 1570.

Ogilby, John. *The Fables of Aesop paraphras'd in verse*. London, 1651.

Peacham, Henry. *The Compleat Gentleman*. London, 1622.

A perfect diurnall of some passages and proceedings of, and in relation to, the armies in England and Ireland. London: Printed by Edw. Griffin, 1649–55.

Philips, Edward. *The Mysteries of Love and Eloquence*. London, 1658.

Plomer, Henry Robert. *A Dictionary of the Booksellers and Printers Who Were at Work in England, Scotland and Ireland from 1641 to 1667*. London: The Bibliographical Society, 1907.

Prynne, William. *Histrio-Mastix*. London, 1633.

Puttenham, George. *The Art of English Poesy*. Edited by Frank Whigham and Wayne A. Rebhorn. Ithaca, NY: Cornell University Press, 2007.

Ravenscroft, Thomas. *A Briefe Discourse of the true (but neglected) use of Charact'ring the Degrees*. London, 1614.

The Register of the Visitors of the University of Oxford, from AD 1658. Edited by Montagu Burrows. Westminster: Camden Society, 1881.

Rossetti, Christina. *Goblin Market: A Tale of Two Sisters*. Afterword by Joyce Carol Oates. San Francisco, CA: Chronicle Books, 1997.

Sandys, George. *Ovids Metamorphosis Englished, Mythologiz'd and Represented in Figures*. Oxford, 1632.

Severall Proceedings in Parliament. No. 102 (Sept. 4–11, 1651).

Shakespeare, William. *Mr. William Shakespeare's Comedies, Histories and Tragedies.* Edited by John Heminge and Henry Condell. London, 1623.

Shepphard, Samuel. *Epigrams, Theological, Philosophical, and Romantick. Six Books. Also the Socratick Session; or, The Arraignment and Conviction of Julius Scaliger with other Select Poems.* London, 1651.

Sidney, Philip. *The Countess of Pembroke's Arcadia.* London, 1590.

———. *The Defence of Poesie.* London, 1595.

———. *The Psalms of Sir Philip Sidney and the Countess of Pembroke.* Edited by J. C. A. Rathmell. New York: New York University Press, 1963.

Sidney, Philip, and Mary Sidney Herbert. *The Countess of Pembroke's Arcadia.* London, 1593.

Synopsis of Vocal Musick by A. B. Philo-Mus. Edited by Rebecca Herissone. Aldershot: Ashgate, 2006.

Taylor, Jeremy. *A Discourse on the Nature, Offices and Measures of Friendship.* London, 1657.

Walton, Izaak. *The Lives of John Donne, Sir Henry Wotton, Richard Hooker, George Herbert and Robert Sanderson.* Edited by S. B. Carter. London: Falcon Educational Books, 1951.

Weekly Intelligencer. Vol. 36. Sept. 2–9, 1651. London, 1650–55.

White-Ladies; or, His Second Majesties most miraculous preservation, after the battle of Worcester, September 3. 1651. London, 1660.

Wither, George. *A collection of emblems, ancient and modern.* London, 1635.

Wroth, Mary. *The Countesse of Montgomeries Urania.* London, 1621.

Secondary Sources

Achinstein, Sharon. *Milton and the Revolutionary Reader.* Princeton, NJ: Princeton University Press, 1994.

Adam, Michel. "Katherine Philips, traductrice du theater de Pierre Corneille." *Revue d'Histoire Littéraire de la France* 85, no. 5 (1985): 841–51.

Adorno, Theodor W. "Music, Language, and Composition." Translated by Susan Gillespie. *Musical Quarterly* 77, no. 3 (1993): 401–14.

Anderson, Penelope. "'Friendship Multiplyed': Royalist and Republican Friendship in Katherine Philips's Coterie." In *Discourses and Representations of Friendship in Early Modern Europe, 1500–1700,* edited by Daniel T. Lochman, Maritere López, and Lorna Hutson, 131–45. Farnham: Ashgate, 2011.

———. *Friendship's Shadows: Women's Friendship and the Politics of Betrayal in England, 1640–1705.* Edinburgh: Edinburgh University Press, 2012.

Andreadis, Harriette. "The Erotics of Female Friendship in Early Modern England." In *Maids and Mistresses, Cousins and Queens: Women's Alliances in Early Modern England,* edited by Karen Robertson and Susan Frye, 241–58. Oxford: Oxford University Press, 1999.

———. "Philips, Katherine (1632–64)." In *Lesbian Histories and Cultures: An Encyclopedia,* edited by Bonnie Zimmerman, 585–86. New York: Garland, 2000.

———. "Re-Configuring Early Modern Friendship: Katherine Philips and Homoerotic Desire." *SEL: Studies in English Literature, 1500–1900* 46, no. 3 (2006): 523–42.

———. *Sappho in Early Modern England: Female Same-Sex Literary Erotics, 1550–1714.* Chicago: University of Chicago Press, 2001.

———. "Sappho in Early Modern England: A Study in Sexual Reputation." In *Re-Reading Sappho: Reception and Transmission,* edited by Ellen Greene, 105–21. Berkeley and Los Angeles: University of California Press, 1996.

———. "The Sapphic-Platonics of Katherine Philips, 1632–1664." *Signs: A Journal of Women in Culture and Society* 15, no. 1 (1989): 34–60.

Anselment, Raymond. "The Oxford University Poets and Caroline Panegyric." *John Donne Journal: Studies in the Age of Donne* 3 (1984): 181–201.

Applegate, Joan. "Katherine Philips's 'Orinda upon Little Hector': An Unrecorded Musical Setting by Henry Lawes." In *English Manuscript Studies, 1100–1700,* vol. 4, edited by Peter Beal and Jeremy Griffiths, 272–80. London: British Library and University of Toronto Press, 1993.

Aston, Margaret. "Puritans and Iconoclasm, 1560–1660." In *The Culture of English Puritanism, 1560–1700*, edited by C. Durston and J. Eales, 92–121. London: Macmillan, 1996.

Austen, Linda Phyllis. "'Alluring the Auditorie to Effeminacie': Music and the Idea of the Feminine in Early Modern England." *Music and Letters* 74, no. 3 (1993): 343–54.

———. "'My Mother Musicke': Music and Early Modern Fantasies of Embodiment." In *Maternal Measures: Figuring Caregivers in the Early Modern Period*, edited by Naomi J. Miller and Naomi Yavneh, 239–81. Aldershot: Ashgate, 2000.

———. "'Tis Nature's Voice': Voice, Natural Philosophy and the Hidden World in Seventeenth-Century England." In *Music Theory and Natural Order from the Renaissance to the Early Twentieth Century*, edited by Suzannah Clark and Alexander Rehding, 30–67. Cambridge: Cambridge University Press, 2001.

Bailey, Candace. "Blurring the Lines: 'Elizabeth Rogers hir Virginall Book' in Conext." *Music and Letters* 89, no. 4 (2008): 510–46.

Ballaster, Ros. "Restoring the Renaissance: Margaret Cavendish and Katherine Philips." In *Renaissance Configuration: Voices/Bodies/ Spaces, 1580–1690*, edited by Gordon McMullan, 324–52. London: Macmillan, 1998.

Barash, Carol. *English Women's Poetry, 1649–1714: Politics, Community, and Linguistic Authority*. Oxford: Clarendon Press, 1996.

Barthes, Roland. *The Pleasure of the Text*. Translated by Richard Miller. New York: Farrar, Strauss and Giroux, 1975.

———. *The Responsibility of Forms*. Translated by Richard Howard. Berkeley and Los Angeles: University of California Press, 1991.

Beal, Peter. *In Praise of Scribes: Manuscripts and Their Makers in Seventeenth-Century England*. Oxford: Clarendon Press, 1998.

Beal, Peter, ed. *Index of English Literary Manuscripts*. Vol. 2, 1625–1700, part 2, *Lee Wycherley*. New York: Mansell, 1993.

———. "Orinda to Silvander: A New Letter by Katherine Philips." In *English Manuscript Studies, 1100–1700*, vol. 4, edited by Peter Beal and Jeremy Griffiths, 281–86. London: British Library and University of Toronto Press, 1993.

Bevan, Jonquil. *Izaak Walton's The Compleat Angler: The Art of Recreation*. New York: St. Martin's Press, 1988.

Birken, William. "Daniel Oxenbridge." *Oxford Dictionary of National Biography.* Oxford University Press, 2004. Online edition, 2006. www.oxforddnb.com/index/101047342/Daniel-Oxenbridge. Accessed Apr. 28, 2015.

Blank, Paula. "Comparing Sappho to Philaenis: John Donne's 'Homopoetics.'" *PMLA* 110, no. 3 (1995): 358–68.

Booth, Mark W. *The Experience of Songs.* New Haven, CT: Yale University Press, 1981.

Borris, Kenneth, ed. *Same-Sex Desire in the English Renaissance: A Sourcebook of Texts, 1470–1650.* New York: Routledge, 2003.

Boswell, John. "Categories, Experience and Sexuality." In *Forms of Desire: Sexual Orientation and the Social Constructionist Controversy,* edited by Edward Stein, 133–73. New York: Routledge, 1992.

———. *Christianity, Social Tolerance, and Homosexuality: Gay People in Western Europe from the Beginning of the Christian Era to the Fourteenth Century.* Chicago: University of Chicago Press, 1980.

Boyd, Morrison Comegys. *Elizabethan Music and Musical Criticism.* 2nd ed. Philadelphia: University of Pennsylvania Press, 1962.

Brady, Andrea. "The Platonic Poems of Katherine Philips." *Seventeenth Century* 25, no. 2 (2010): 300–22.

Brashear, Lucy. "The Forgotten Legacy of the 'Matchless Orinda.'" *Anglo-Welsh Review* 65 (1979): 68–76.

Braunschneider, Theresa. "Maidenly Amusements: Narrating Female Sexuality in Eighteenth-Century England." Ph.D. diss., University of Michigan, 2002.

Bray, Alan. *The Friend.* Chicago: University of Chicago Press, 2003.

———. *Homosexuality in Renaissance England.* London: Gay Men's Press, 1982.

———. "Homosexuality and the Signs of Male Friendship in Elizabethan England." *History Workshop Journal* 29, no. 1 (1990): 1–19.

Bray, Alan, and Michel Rey. "The Body of the Friend: Continuity and Change in Masculine Friendship in the Seventeenth Century." In *English Masculinities, 1660–1800,* edited by Tim Hitchcock and Michele Cohen, 65–84. London: Longman, 1999.

Brayman Hackel, Heidi. "The Countess of Bridgewater's London Library." In *Books and Readers in Early Modern England: Material Studies,* edited by Jennifer Anderson and Elizabeth Sauer, 139–59. Philadelphia: University of Pennsylvania Press, 2002.

———. *Reading Material in Early Modern England: Print, Gender, and Literacy.* Cambridge: Cambridge University Press, 2005.

Brooke, Christopher N. L. *The Medieval Idea of Marriage.* Oxford: Oxford University Press, 1989.

Burrows, David. *Sound, Speech, and Music.* Amherst: University of Massachusetts Press, 1990.

Bynum, Caroline Walker. *Jesus as Mother: Studies in the Spirituality of the High Middle Ages.* Berkeley and Los Angeles: University of California Press, 1982.

Byrne, Tracy J. "Katherine Philips and the Discourse of Virtue." Ph.D. thesis, University of Glasgow, 2002.

Campbell, Elizabeth. "Of Mothers and Merchants: Female Economics in Christina Rossetti's 'Goblin Market.'" *Victorian Studies* 33, no. 3 (1990): 393–410.

Capp, B. S. "*A Door of Hope* Re-opened: The Fifth Monarchy, King Charles and King Jesus." *Journal of Religious History* 32, no. 1 (Mar. 2008): 16–30.

———. *The Fifth Monarchy Men: A Study in Seventeenth-Century English Millenarianism.* Totowa, NJ: Rowman and Littlefield, 1972.

Carruthers, Mary J. "The Re-Vision of the Muse: Adrienne Rich, Audré Lorde, Judy Grahn, Olga Broumas." *Hudson Review* 36, no. 2 (1983): 293–322.

Castle, Terry. *The Apparitional Lesbian: Female Homosexuality and Modern Culture.* New York: Columbia University Press, 1995.

Chalmers, Hero. *Royalist Women Writers, 1650–1689.* Oxford: Clarendon Press, 2004.

Chan, Mary. "A Mid-Seventeenth-Century Music Meeting and Playford's Publishing." In *The Well-Enchanting Skill: Music, Poetry, and Drama in the Culture of the Renaissance: Essays in Honour of F. W. Sternfeld,* edited by John Caldwell, Edward Olleson, and Susan Wollenberg, 231–44. Oxford: Clarendon Press, 1990.

Chapman, Patrick. *Things Written in the Glasse Windowes at Buxtons.* Chesterfield: Whittington Moor, 2012.

Chernaik, Warren. "Philips [nee Fowler], Katherine (1632–1664)." *Oxford Dictionary of National Biography.* Oxford University Press, 2004. Online edition, 2006. www.oxforddnb.com/index/101022124/Katherine-Philips. Accessed Apr. 28, 2015.

———. *The Poetry of Limitation: A Study of Edmund Waller.* New Haven, CT: Yale University Press, 1968.

Clarke, Elizabeth. "The Garrisoned Muse: Women's Use of the Religious Lyric in the Civil War Period." In *The English Civil Wars in the Literary Imagination,* edited by Claude J. Summers and Ted-Larry Pebworth, 130–43. Columbia: University of Missouri Press, 1999.

Clarke, Elizabeth, and Lynn Robson. "Why Are We 'Still Kissing the Rod'?: The Future for the Study of Early Modern Women's Writing." *Women's Writing* 14, no. 2 (2007): 177–93.

Cleary, Brian. *Haddon Hall: The Home of Lord Edward Manners.* Wymondham: Heritage House Group, 2009.

Coiro, Ann Baynes. "Writing in Service: Sexual Politics and Class Position in the Poetry of Aemilia Lanyer and Ben Jonson." In *Ashgate Critical Essays on Women Writers in England, 1550–1700,* vol. 3, *Anne Lock, Isabella Whitney and Aemilia Lanyer,* edited by Micheline White, 333–52. London: Ashgate, 2009.

Coolahan, Marie-Louise. "'We Live by Chance, and Slip into Events': Occasionality and the Manuscript Verse of Katherine Philips." *Eighteenth-Century Ireland / Iris an Da Chultur* 18 (2003): 9–23.

———. *Women, Writing, and Language in Early Modern Ireland.* Oxford: Oxford University Press, 2010.

Corns, Thomas. *Uncloistered Virtue: English Political Literature, 1640–1660.* Oxford: Clarendon Press, 1992.

Corporaal, Marguerite. "Katherine (Fowler) Philips, *Pompey, a Tragedy* (1663)." In *Reading Early Modern Women: An Anthology of Texts in Manuscript and Print, 1550–1700,* edited by Helen Ostovich and Elizabeth Sauer, 247–49. New York: Routledge, 2004.

Crawford, Patricia. *Women and Religion in England, 1500–1720.* London: Routledge, 1997.

Crawford, Patricia, and Laura Gowing, eds. *Women's Worlds in Seventeenth-Century England.* London: Routledge, 2000.

Crawford, Patricia, and Sara Mendelson. "Sexual Identities in Early Modern England: The Marriage of Two Women in 1680." *Gender and History* 7, no. 3 (1995): 363–77.

Culler, Jonathan. "The Modern Lyric: Generic Continuity and Critical Practice." In *The Comparative Perspective on Literature: Approaches to Theory and Practice,* edited by Clayton Koelb and Susan Noakes, 284–99. Ithaca, NY: Cornell University Press, 1988.

Cusick, Suzanne G. "On a Lesbian Relationship with Music: A Serious Effort Not to Think Straight." In *Queering the Pitch: The New Gay and Lesbian Musicology,* edited by Philips Brett, Elizabeth Wood, and Gary C. Thomas, 67–84. New York: Routledge, 1994.

Cutts, John P. "Seventeenth-Century Songs and Lyrics in Paris Conservatoire MS Res. 2489." *Musica Disciplina* 23 (1969): 117–39.

Davies, Stevie. *Unbridled Spirits: Women of the English Revolution, 1640–1660.* London: The Women's Press, 1998.

Davis, Alex. *Chivalry and Romance in the English Renaissance.* Cambridge: Brewer, 2003.

DeJean, Joan. *Fictions of Sappho, 1546–1937.* Chicago: University of Chicago Press, 1989.

De Laurentis, Teresa. "Sexual Indifference and Lesbian Representation." In *Performing Feminisms: Feminist Critical Theory and Theatre,* edited by Sue-Ellen Case, 17–39. Baltimore: The Johns Hopkins University Press, 1990.

Dictionary of Welsh Biography, Down to 1940, The. Oxford: Blackwell, 1959.

Dodd, A. H. *Studies in Stuart Wales.* Cardiff: University of Wales Press, 1952.

Doughtie, Edward. "Words for Music: Simplicity and Complexity in the Elizabethan Air." *Rice University Studies* 51 (1965): 1–12.

Dubrow, Heather. *A Happier Eden: The Politics of Marriage in the Stuart Epithalamium.* Ithaca, NY: Cornell University Press, 1990.

Dugaw, Dianne, and Amanda Powell. "Sapphic Self-Fashioning in the Baroque Era: Women's Petrarchan Parody in English and Spanish." *Studies in Eighteenth-Century Culture* 35 (2006): 127–60.

Dunn, Jane. *Read My Heart: Dorothy Osborne and Sir William Temple, a Love Story in the Age of Revolution.* London: Harper Press, 2008.

Dusinberre, Juliet. *Shakespeare and the Nature of Women.* London: Macmillan, 1975.

Easton, Celia A. "Excusing the Breach of Nature's Laws: The Discourse of Denial and Disguise in Katherine Philips's Friendship Poetry." In *Early Women Writers: 1600–1720,* edited by Anita Pacheco, 1–14. London: Longman, 1998. Originally published in *Restoration: Studies in English Literary Culture, 1660–1700* 14, no. 1 (1990): 1–14.

Eastwood, Adrienne. "Between Bedding and Wedding: The Epithalamic Sub-Genre in Shakespeare's Comedies." *Exemplaria: A Journal of Theory in Medieval and Renaissance Studies* 22, no. 3 (2010): 240–62.

Elmen, Paul. "Some Manuscript Poems by the Matchless Orinda." *Philological Quarterly* 30 (1951): 53–57.

Evans, Robert C. "Katherine (Fowler) Philips, Epitaph on Her Mother-in-Law (1667)." In *Reading Early Modern Women: An Anthology of Texts in Manuscript and Print, 1550–1700,* edited by Helen Ostovich and Elizabeth Sauer, 395–97. New York: Routledge, 2004.

———. "Paradox in Poetry and Politics: Katherine Philips in the Interregnum." In *The English Civil Wars in the Literary Imagination,* edited by Claude J. Summers and Ted-Larry Pebworth, 174–85. Columbia: University of Missouri Press, 1999.

Evans, Willa McClung. *Henry Lawes: Musician and Friend of Poets.* New York: Modern Language Association, 1941.

Everitt, Alan. *The Community of Kent and the Great Rebellion, 1640–1660.* Leicester: Prometheus Books, 1966.

Ezell, Margaret. *The Patriarch's Wife: Literary Evidence and the History of the Family.* Chapel Hill: University of North Carolina Press, 1987.

———. "Reading Pseudonyms in Seventeenth-Century English Coterie Literature." *Essays in Literature* 21, no. 1 (Spring 1994): 14–25.

Faderman, Lillian. *Odd Girls and Twilight Lovers: A History of Lesbian Life in Twentieth-Century America.* New York: Columbia University Press, 1991.

———. *Surpassing the Love of Men: Romantic Friendship and Love between Women from the Renaissance to the Present.* New York: Quill, 1981.

Fincham, Kenneth, and Nicholas Tyacke. *Altars Restored: The Changing Face of English Religious Worship, 1547–c. 1700.* Oxford: Oxford University Press, 2007.

Fineman, Joel. *Shakespeare's Perjured Eye: The Invention of Poetic Subjectivity in the Sonnets.* Berkeley and Los Angeles: University of California Press, 1986.

———. *The Subjectivity Effect in Western Literary Tradition: Essays toward the Release of Shakespeare's Will.* Cambridge, MA: The MIT Press, 1991.

Fleming, Juliet. *Graffiti and the Writing Arts in Early Modern England.* Philadelphia: University of Pennsylvania Press, 2001.

Ford, Eric. "Introduction to Henry Lawes." *Music and Letters* 32, no. 3 (1951): 217–25.

Foster, Joseph. *Alumni Oxonienses: The Members of the University of Oxford, 1500–1714.* 3 vols. Nendeln, Liechtenstein: Kraus Reprint, 1968.

Foucault, Michel. *The History of Sexuality,* vol. 1: *An Introduction.* Translated by Robert Hurley. New York: Vintage, 1990.

Fradenburg, Louise, and Carla Freccero. "Caxton, Foucault, and the Pleasures of History." In *Premodern Sexualities,* edited by Louise Fradenburg and Carla Freccero, xiii–xxiv. New York: Routledge, 1996.

Fraser, Nancy. "Rethinking the Public Sphere: A Contribution to the Critique of Actually Existing Democracy." In *Habermas and the Public Sphere,* edited by Craig Calhoun, 109–42. Cambridge, MA: MIT Press, 1992.

Freccero, Carla. *Queer/Early/ Modern.* Durham, NC: Duke University Press, 2006.

———. "Queer Spectrality: Haunting the Past." In *A Companion to Lesbian, Gay, Bisexual, Transgender, and Queer Studies,* edited by George E. Haggerty and Molly McGarry, 194–213. Malden, MA: Blackwell, 2007.

———. "The Queer Time of the Lesbian Premodern." In *The Lesbian Premodern,* edited by Noreen Giffney, Michelle M. Sauer, and Diane Watt, 61–73. New York: Palgrave, 2011.

———. "Queer Times." *South Atlantic Quarterly* 106, no. 3 (2007): 485–94.

Friedman, Richard Elliott. *The Bible with Sources Revealed: A New View into the Five Books of Moses*. New York: HarperOne, 2005.

———. *Who Wrote the Bible?* New York: HarperCollins, 1987.

Friedman, Susan Stanford. *Psyche Reborn: The Emergence of H. D.* Bloomington: Indiana University Press, 1981.

Frith, Simon. *Performing Rites: Evaluating Popular Music*. Oxford: Oxford University Press, 1996.

Frye, Susan, and Karen Robertson, eds. *Maids and Mistresses, Cousins and Queens: Women's Alliances in Early Modern England*. Collingdale, PA: Diane Publishing Company, 1999.

Gallagher, Catherine "Embracing the Absolute: The Politics of the Female Subject in Seventeenth-Century England." *Genders* 1 (1988): 24–39.

Garrison, John S. *Friendship and Queer Theory in the Renaissance*. New York: Routledge, 2014.

Gentles, Ian J. "Philip Skippon." *Oxford Dictionary of National Biography*. Oxford University Press, 2004. Online edition, Jan. 2008. www.oxforddnb.com/index/101025693/Philip-Skippon. Accessed Apr. 28, 2015.

Geerdink, Nina. "The Appropriation of the Genre of Nuptial Poetry by Katharina Lescailje." In *Intersections*, vol. 16, *Women Writing Back/Writing Women Back: Transnational Perspectives from the Late Middle Ages to the Dawn of the Modern Era*, edited by Anke Gilleir, Alicia C. Montoya, and Suzan van Dijk, 163–90. Leiden: Brill Academic, 2010.

Godlovitch, Stan. "The Integrity of Musical Performance." *Journal of Aesthetics and Art Criticism* 51, no. 4 (1993): 573–87.

Goldberg, Jonathan. *James I and the Politics of Literature: Jonson, Shakespeare, Donne and Their Contemporaries*. Baltimore: Johns Hopkins University Press, 1983.

———. *Writing Matter: From the Hands of the English Renaissance*. Stanford, CA: Stanford University Press, 1990.

Goldberg, Jonathan, ed. *Queering the Renaissance*. Durham, NC: Duke University Press, 1994.

Goldberg, Jonathan, and Madhavi Menon. "Queering History." *PMLA* 120, no. 5 (2005): 1608–17.

Golub, Ellen. "Untying Goblin Apron Strings: A Psychoanalytic Reading of 'Goblin Market.'" *Literature and Psychology* 25 (1975): 158–65.

Gosse, Edmund. *Seventeenth-Century Studies: A Contribution to the History of English Poetry*. London: K. Paul Trench, 1883.

Gouk, Penelope. *Music, Science and Natural Magic in Seventeenth-Century England*. New Haven, CT: Yale University Press, 1999.

Gray, Catharine. "Katherine Philips in Ireland." *English Literary Renaissance* 39, no. 3 (2009): 557–85.

———. "Katherine Philips and the Post-Courtly Coterie." *English Literary Renaissance* 32, no. 3 (Autumn 2002): 426–51.

———. *Women Writers and Public Debate in Seventeenth-Century Britain*. New York: Palgrave Macmillan, 2007.

Greene, Frederick. "Subversions of Pastoral: Queer Theory and the Politics and Poetics of Elegy." Ph.D. diss., University of California, Santa Barbara, 1997.

Greenstadt, Amy. "Aemilia Lanyer's Pathetic Phallacy." *Journal for Early Modern Cultural Studies* 8, no. 1 (2008): 67–97.

Greer, Germaine. "Editorial Conundra in the Texts of Katherine Philips." In *Editing Women: Papers Given at the Thirty-First Annual Conference on Editorial Problems, University of Toronto, 3–4 November 1995*, edited by Ann M. Hutchison, 79–98. Toronto: University of Toronto Press, 1998.

———. *Slip-Shod Sibyls: Recognition, Rejection and the Woman Poet*. London: Penguin, 1996.

Gregory, Eileen. "Rose Cut in Rock: Sappho and H. D.'s 'Sea Garden.'" *Contemporary Literature* 27, no. 4 (1986): 525–52.

Grise, C. Annette. "Depicting Lesbian Desire: Contexts for John Donne's 'Sapho to Philaenis.'" *Mosaic* 9 (1996): 41–57.

Guibbory, Achsah. *Ceremony and Community from Herbert to Milton: Literature, Religion, and Cultural Conflict in Seventeenth-Century England*. New York: Cambridge University Press, 1998.

Guy-Bray, Stephen. *Homoerotic Space: The Poetics of Loss in Renaissance Literature*. Toronto: University of Toronto Press, 2002.

Habermas, Jürgen. *The Structural Transformation of the Public Sphere*. Translated by Thomas Burger. Cambridge, MA: MIT Press, 1991.

Hageman, Elizabeth H. "'Dearest Antenor': James Philips in the Archives." In *English Manuscript Studies, 1100–1700*. Forthcoming.

———. "The 'false printed' Broadside of Katherine Philips's 'To the Queens Majesty on Her Happy Arrival.'" *The Library: The Transactions of the Bibliographical Society* 17, no. 4 (1995): 321–26.

———. "Katherine Phillips." In *Teaching Tudor and Stuart Women Writers,* edited by Susanne Woods and Margaret P. Hannay, 185–94. New York: Modern Language Association, 2000.

———. "Katherine Philips: The Matchless Orinda." In *Women Writers of the Renaissance and Reformation,* edited by Katharina M. Wilson, 566–608. Athens: University of Georgia Press, 1987.

———. "Katherine Philips, Poems." In *A Companion to Early Modern Women's Writing,* edited by Anita Pacheco, 189–202. Oxford: Blackwell, 2002.

———. "Katherine Philips (1632–1664)." In *Dictionary of Literary Biography: Seventeenth-Century British Nondramatic Poets,* vol. 131, edited by M. Thomas Hester, 202–14. Detroit: Gale Research, 1993.

———. "Making a Good Impression: Early Texts of Poems and Letters by Katherine Philips, the 'Matchless Orinda.'" *South Central Review* 11, no. 2 (1994): 39–65.

———. "Treacherous Accidents and the Abominable Printing of Katherine Philips's 1664 Poems." In *New Ways of Looking at Old Texts,* vol. 3, edited by W. Speed Hill, 85–95. Tempe, AZ: Renaissance English Text Society, with Arizona Center for Medieval and Renaissance Studies, 2004.

Hageman, Elizabeth H., and Bruce Hindmarsh. "Readers' Queries." *Notes & Queries* 40, no. 4 (Dec. 1993): 506–08.

Hageman, Elizabeth H., and Andrea Sununu. "'More Copies of It Abroad than I Could Have Imagin'd': Further Manuscript Texts of Katherine Philips, 'The Matchless Orinda.'" In *English Manuscript Studies, 1100–1700,* vol. 5, edited by Peter Beal and Jeremy Griffiths, 127–69. London: British Library and University of Toronto Press, 1995.

———. "New Manuscript Texts of Katherine Philips, the 'Matchless Orinda.'" In *English Manuscript Studies, 1100–1700,* vol. 4, edited by Peter Beal and Jeremy Griffiths, 174–216. London: British Library and University of Toronto Press, 1993.

Halperin, David M. *How to Do the History of Homosexuality*. Chicago: University of Chicago Press, 2004.

———. *One Hundred Years of Homosexuality: And Other Essays on Greek Love*. New York: Routledge, 1989.

———. *Saint Foucault: Towards a Gay Hagiography*. Oxford: Oxford University Press, 1997.

Hamessley, Lydia. "Henry Lawes's Setting of Katherine Philips's Friendship Poetry in His *Second Book of Ayres and Dialogues*, 1655: A Musical Misreading?" In *Queering the Pitch: The New Gay and Lesbian Musicology*, edited by Philip Brett, Elizabeth Wood, and Gary C. Thomas, 116–38. New York: Routledge, 1994.

Hamlin, Hannibal. *Psalm Culture and Early Modern English Literature*. Cambridge: Cambridge University Press, 2004.

Hammill, Graham. "Sexuality and Society in the Poetry of Katherine Philips." In *Queer Renaissance Historiography: Backward Gaze*, edited by Vin Nardizzi, Stephen Guy-Bray, and Will Stockton, 186–205. Farnham: Ashgate, 2009.

Hammond, Karla. "An Interview with Olga Broumas." *Northwest Review* 18, no. 3 (1980): 33–44.

Hammond, Paul. *The Making of Restoration of Poetry*. Rochester, NY: D. S. Brewer, 2006.

Hardebeck, Susan Arlene. "'If Soules No Sexes Have': Women, Convention, and Negotiation in the Poetry of Katherine Philips." Ph.D. diss., Northern Illinois University, 1997.

Harvey, Elizabeth. "Ventriloquizing Sappho: Ovid, Donne, and the Erotics of Feminine Voice." *Criticism* 31 (1989): 115–38.

Haskin, Dayton. "A History of Donne's 'Canonization' from Izaak Walton to Cleanth Brooks." *Journal of English and Germanic Philology* 92, no. 1 (1993): 17–36.

Healy, Thomas, and Jonathan Sawday, eds. *Literature and the English Civil War*. Cambridge: Cambridge University Press, 1990.

Helgerson, Richard. *Self-Crowned Laureates: Spenser, Jonson, Milton and the Literary System*. Berkeley and Los Angeles: University of California Press, 1983.

Herbert, Amanda E. *Female Alliances: Gender, Identity, and Friendship in Early Modern Britain*. New Haven, CT: Yale University Press, 2014.

Hill, Christopher. *The English Bible and the Seventeenth-Century Revolution*. London: Penguin, 1993.

Hinds, Hilary. *God's Englishwomen: Seventeenth-Century Radical Sectarian Writing and Feminist Criticism*. Manchester: Manchester University Press, 1996.

Hirst, Derek. "The Politics of Literature in the English Republic." *Seventeenth Century* 5 (1990): 133–55.

Hirst, Derek, and Richard Strier, eds. *Writing and Political Engagement in Seventeenth-Century England*. Cambridge: Cambridge University Press, 1999.

Hirst, Derek, and Steven Zwicker. "High Summer at Nun Appleton, 1651: Andrew Marvell and Lord Fairfax's Occasions." *Historical Journal* 36 (1993): 247–69.

Hiscock, W. G. "*Friendship:* Francis Finch's Discourse and the Circle of the Matchless Orinda." *Review of English Studies: A Quarterly Journal of English Literature and the English Language* 15, no. 60 (1939): 466–68.

Hobby, Elaine. "Orinda and Female Intimacy." In *Early Women Writers, 1600–1720,* edited by Anita Pacheco, 73–88. London: Longman, 1998.

———. "Katherine Philips: Seventeenth-Century Lesbian Poet." In *What Lesbians Do in Books: Lesbians as Writers, Readers and Characters in Literature,* edited by Elaine Hobby and Chris White, 183–204. London: Women's Press, 1991.

———. "The Politics of Women's Prophecy in the English Revolution." In *Sacred and Profane: Secular and Devotional Interplay in Early Modern British Literature,* edited by Helen Wilcox, Richard Todd, and Alasdair MacDonald, 296–306. Amsterdam: VU University Press, 1996.

———. "Prophecy." In *A Companion to Early Modern Women's Writing,* edited by Anita Pacheco, 264–81. Malden, MA: Blackwell, 2008.

———. *Virtue of Necessity: English Women's Writing, 1649–88.* London: Virago, 1988.

Hodgson, Elizabeth M. A. *Gender and the Sacred Self in John Donne.* Newark: University of Delaware Press, 1999.

———. "Katherine Philips: Agent of Matchlessness." *Women's Writing* 10, no. 1 (2003): 119–36.

Hollander, John. *The Untuning of the Sky: Ideas of Music in English Poetry, 1500–1700*. New York: W. W. Norton, 1970.

Holstun, James. "'Will you rent our ancient love asunder?': Lesbian Elegy in Donne, Marvell, and Milton." *English Literary History* 54 (1987): 835–67.

Horton, Diana. "'Scarlet Liturgies': The Poetry of Olga Broumas." *North Dakota Quarterly* 55, no. 4 (1987): 322–47.

Hosek, Chaviva, and Patricia Parker, eds. *Lyric Poetry: Beyond New Criticism*. Ithaca, NY: Cornell University Press, 1985.

Hughes, Ann. *Gender and the English Revolution*. New York: Routledge, 2012.

Humphries, Simon. "The Uncertainty of *Goblin Market*." *Victorian Poetry* 45, no. 4 (2007): 391–413.

Hutchinson, F. E. *Henry Vaughan: A Life and Interpretation*. Oxford: Clarendon Press, 1947.

Hutson, Lorna. "The Body of the Friend and the Woman Writer: Katherine Philips's Absence from Alan Bray's *The Friend* (2003)." *Women's Writing* 14, no. 2 (2007): 196–214.

———. "Liking Men: Ben Jonson's Closet Opened." *English Literary History* 71, no. 4 (2004): 1065–96.

Jackson, Virginia. "Dickinson's Figure of Address." In *Dickinson and Audience*, edited by Martin Orzech and Robert Weisbuch, 77–103. Ann Arbor: University of Michigan Press, 1996.

Jackson, Virginia, and Yopie Prins. "Lyrical Studies." *Victorian Literature and Culture* 27, no. 2 (1999): 521–30.

Jacobs, Deborah. "Critical Imperialism and Renaissance Drama: The Case of *The Roaring Girl*." In *Feminism, Bakhtin, and the Dialogic*, edited by Dale M. Bauer and Susan Jaret McKinstry, 73–84. Albany: State University of New York Press, 1991.

Jagose, Annamarie. *Inconsequence: Lesbian Representation and the Logic of Sexual Sequence*. Ithaca, NY: Cornell University Press, 2002.

Jardine, Lisa. *Still Harping on Daughters: Women and Drama in the Age of Shakespeare*. Hassocks: Harvester, 1983.

Johnson, Barbara. *The Critical Difference: Essays in the Contemporary Rhetoric of Reading*. Baltimore: The Johns Hopkins University Press, 1980.

Jones, Brian Jay. *Washington Irving*. New York: Arcade, 2008.

Jonsen, Albert R., and Stephen Toulmin. *The Abuse of Casuistry: A History of Moral Reasoning*. Berkeley and Los Angeles: University of California Press, 1988.

Jorgens, Elise Bickford. *The Well-Tun'd Word: Musical Interpretations of English Poetry, 1597–1651*. Minneapolis: University of Minnesota Press, 1982.

Kahn, Victoria. *Wayward Contracts: The Crisis of Political Obligation in England, 1640–1674*. Princeton, NJ: Princeton University Press, 2004.

Kelliher, Hilton. "Cowley and 'Orinda': Autograph Fair Copies." *British Library Journal* 2, no. 2 (1976): 102–08.

Kerr, Jessica M. "Mary Harvey—The Lady Dering." *Music & Letters* 25, no. 1 (1944): 23–33.

Kerrigan, John. *Archipelagic English: Literature, History, and Politics, 1603–1707*. Oxford: Oxford University Press, 2008.

Kerrigan, William. "Kiss Fancies in Robert Herrick." *George Herbert Journal* 14, nos. 1 and 2 (1990–91): 155–71.

Kuefler, Mathew. "The Boswell Thesis." In *The Boswell Thesis: Essays on "Christianity, Social Tolerance, and Homosexuality,"* edited by Mathew Kuefler, 1–31. Chicago: University of Chicago Press, 2006.

Lange, Jennifer. "'Hearts Thus Intermixed Speak': Erotic 'Friendship' in the Poems of Katherine Philips." Ph.D. diss., Bowling Green State University, 1995.

Lanser, Susan S. "Mapping Sapphic Modernity." In *Comparatively Queer: Interrogating Identities across Time and Cultures*, edited by Jarrod Hayes, Margaret R. Higonnet, and William J. Spurlin, 69–89. New York: Palgrave Macmillan, 2010.

———. "The Political Economy of Same-Sex Desire." In *Structures and Subjectivities: Attending to Early Modern Women*, edited by Joan E. Hartman and Adele Seeff, 157–75. Newark: University of Delaware Press, 2007.

———. *The Sexuality of History: Modernity and the Sapphic, 1565–1830*. Chicago: University of Chicago Press, 2014.

Leaver, Robin A. *"Goostly Psalmes and Spirituall Songes": English and Dutch Metrical Psalms from Coverdale to Utenhove*. Oxford: Clarendon Press, 1991.

LeHuray, Peter. *Music and the Reformation in England, 1549–1660.* London: Herbert Jenkins, 1967.

Libertin, Mary. "Female Friendship in Women's Verse: Towards a New Theory of Female Poetics." *Women's Studies* 9, no. 3 (Feb. 1982): 291–308.

Lilley, Kate. "'Dear Object': Katherine Philips's Love Elegies and Their Readers." In *Women Writing, 1550–1750,* edited by Jo Wallwork and Paul Salzman, 163–78. Bundoora, Australia: Meridian, 2001.

———. "Fruits of Sodom: The Critical Erotics of Early Modern Women's Writing." *Parergon* 29, no. 2 (2012): 175–92.

———. "True State Within: Women's Elegy 1640–1740." In *Women, Writing, History 1640–1740,* edited by Isobel Grundy and Susan Wiseman, 72–92. Athens: University of Georgia Press, 1992.

Limbert, Claudia A. "Katherine Philips: Controlling a Life and Reputation." *South Atlantic Review* 56, no. 2 (1991): 27–42.

———. "The Poetry of Katherine Philips: Holographs, Manuscripts, and Early Printed Texts." *Philological Quarterly* 70, no. 2 (1991): 181–98.

———. "Two Poems and a Prose Receipt: The Unpublished Juvenalia of Katherine Philips." *English Literary Renaissance* 16 (1986): 383–90.

———. "'The Unison of Well-Tun'd Hearts': Katherine Philips's Friendships with Male Writers." *English Language Notes* 29, no. 1 (1991): 25–37.

Limbert, Claudia A., and John H. O'Neill. "Composite Authorship: Katherine Philips and an Antimarital Satire." *Papers of the Bibliographical Society of America* 87, no. 4 (1993): 487–502.

Lipking, Lawrence I. *Abandoned Women and Poetic Tradition.* Chicago: University of Chicago Press, 1988.

Llewellyn, Mark. "Katherine Philips: Friendship, Poetry and Neo-Platonic Thought in Seventeenth Century England." *Philological Quarterly* 81, no. 4 (2002): 441–68.

———. "Minor Poets and the Game of Authorship: The Poetry of Thomas Randolph, Katherine Philips, and Edmund Waller." Ph.D. thesis, University of Wales, 2005.

Lobban, Paul. "Inhabited Space: Writing as a Practice in Early Modern England; Margaret Hoby, Eleanor Davies, Katherine Philips." Ph.D. thesis, University of Adelaide, 2001.

Lochman, Daniel T., and Maritere López. "Introduction: The Emergence of Discourses: Early Modern Friendship." In *Discourses and Representations of Friendship in Early Modern Europe, 1500–1700,* edited by Daniel T. Lochman, Maritere López, and Lorna Hutson, 1–26. Farnham: Ashgate, 2011.

Loewenstein, David. "The King among the Radicals." In *The Royal Image: Representations of Charles I,* edited by Thomas N. Corns, 96–121. Cambridge: Cambridge University Press, 2009.

Loscocco, Paula. "Inventing the English Sappho: Katherine Philips's Donnean Poetry." *Journal of English and Germanic Philology* 102, no. 1 (2003): 59–87.

———. "'Manly Sweetness': Katherine Philips among the Neoclassicals." *Huntington Library Quarterly: A Journal for the History and Interpretation of English and American Civilization* 56, no. 3 (1993): 259–79.

Low, Anthony. *The Reinvention of Love: Poetry, Politics, and Culture from Sidney to Milton.* New York: Cambridge University Press, 1993.

Loxley, James. *Royalism and Poetry in the English Civil Wars: The Drawn Sword.* London: Macmillan, 1997.

———. "Unfettered Organs: The Polemical Voices of Katherine Phillips." In *This Double Voice: Gendered Writing in Early Modern England,* edited by Danielle Clarke and Elizabeth Clarke, 230–48. New York: St. Martin's Press, 2000.

Lupton, Christina. *Knowing Books: The Consciousness of Mediation in Eighteenth-Century Britain.* Philadelphia: University of Pennsylvania Press, 2012.

Mack, Phyllis. *Visionary Women: Ecstatic Prophecy in Seventeenth-Century England.* Berkeley and Los Angeles: University of California Press, 1992.

Maguire, Nancy Klein. *Regicide and Restoration: English Tragicomedy, 1660–1671.* Cambridge: Cambridge University Press, 1992.

Maltby, Judith. *Prayer Book and People in Elizabethan and Early Stuart England.* New York: Cambridge University Press, 1998.

Mambretti, Catherine Cole. "'Fugitive Papers': A New Orinda Poem and Problems in her Canon." *Papers of the Bibliographical Society of America* 71 (1977): 443–52.

———. "Orinda on the Restoration Stage." *Comparative Literature* 37, no. 3 (1985): 233–51.

Marcus, Leah S. *The Politics of Mirth: Jonson, Herrick, Milton, Marvell, and the Defense of Old Holiday Pastimes.* Chicago: University of Chicago Press, 1986.

———. *Puzzling Shakespeare: Local Reading and Its Discontents.* Berkeley and Los Angeles: University of California Press, 1988.

———. *Unediting the Renaissance: Shakespeare, Marlowe, Milton.* London: Routledge, 1996.

Marotti, Arthur F. *John Donne, Coterie Poet.* Madison: University of Wisconsin Press, 1986.

———. *Manuscript, Print and the English Renaissance Lyric.* Ithaca, NY: Cornell University Press, 1995.

Marriott, John. *Oxford: Its Place in National History.* Oxford: Oxford University Press, 1933.

Marsh, Christopher. *Music and Society in Early Modern England.* Cambridge: Cambridge University Press, 2010.

Marshall, Linda E. "'Transfigured to His Likeness': Sensible Transcendentalism in Christina Rossetti's 'Goblin Market.'" *University of Toronto Quarterly* 63, no. 3 (1994): 429–50.

Marshall, Michele Lea Goley. "'The Soule That Sees Things in Their Native Frame': Katherine Philips and the Poetics of Cultural Engagement." Ph.D. diss., University of Texas, Dallas, 2003.

Masten, Jeffrey. *Textual Intercourse: Collaboration, Authorship, and Sexualities in Renaissance Drama.* Cambridge: Cambridge University Press, 1997.

Matsuzaki, Takeshi. "Orinda no 'kusari': Kyasarin Firippusu shikiron." *Ochanomizu Joshi Daigaku Jimbun Kagaku Kiyo* 54 (2001): 49–60.

McBride, Kari Boyd, and John C. Ulreich. "Answerable Styles: Biblical Poetics and Biblical Politics in the Poetry of Lanyer and Milton." *Journal of English and Germanic Philology* 100, no. 3 (July 2001): 333–54.

McClary, Susan. *Feminine Endings: Music, Gender and Sexuality.* Minneapolis: University of Minnesota Press, 1991.

McColley, Diane Kelsey. *Poetry and Music in Seventeenth-Century England.* Cambridge: Cambridge University Press, 1997.

McDowell, Nicholas. *Poetry and Allegiance in the English Civil Wars: Marvell and the Cause of Wit*. New York: Oxford University Press, 2008.

McDowell, Paula. "Consuming Women: The Life of the 'Literary Lady' as Popular Culture in Eighteenth-Century England." *Genre* 26, nos. 2 and 3 (1993): 219–52

McGuire, Mary Ann C. "The Cavalier Country-House Poem: Mutations on a Jonsonian Tradition." *SEL: Studies in English Literature 1500–1900* 19, no. 1 (1979): 93–108.

McKnight, Laura Blair. "Crucifixion or Apocalypse? Refiguring the *Eikon Basilike*." In *Religion, Literature, and Politics in Post-Reformation England, 1540–1688,* edited by Donna B. Hamilton and Richard Strier, 138–60. Cambridge: Cambridge University Press, 1996.

McNaron, Toni A. H. "Mirrors and Likeness: A Lesbian Aesthetic in the Making." In *Sexual Practice, Textual Theory: Lesbian Cultural Criticism,* edited by Susan J. Wolfe and Julia Penelope, 291–306. Cambridge, MA: Blackwell, 1993.

Mendelson, Sara Heller, and Patricia M. Crawford, eds. *Women in Early Modern England, 1550–1720*. London: Clarendon Press, 1998.

Menges, Hilary. "Authorship, Friendship, and Forms of Publication in Katherine Philips." *SEL: Studies in English Literature, 1500–1900* 52, no. 3 (2012): 517–41.

Menon, Madhavi. "Afterword: Period Cramps." In *Queer Renaissance Historiography: Backward Gaze,* edited by Vin Nardizzi, Stephen Guy-Bray, and Will Stockton, 229–34. Farnham: Ashgate, 2009.

———. *Unhistorical Shakespeare: Queer Theory in Shakespearean Literature and Film*. New York: Palgrave Macmillan, 2008.

Merchant, Carolyn. *The Death of Nature: Women, Ecology and the Scientific Revolution.* San Francisco: Harper and Row, 1980.

Mermin, Dorothy. "Women Becoming Poets: Katherine Philips, Aphra Behn, Anne Finch." *English Literary History* 57, no. 2 (1990): 335–55.

Meyer, Sheree L. "The Public Statements and Private Losses of Ben Jonson and Katherine Philips: The Poet as Bereaved Parent." *Explorations in Renaissance Culture* 19 (1993): 173–82.

Miller, Shannon. *Engendering the Fall: John Milton and Seventeenth-Century Women Writers*. Philadelphia: University of Pennsylvania Press, 2008.

Millman, Jill Seal, and Gillian Wright, ed. *Early Modern Women's Manuscript Poetry*. New York: Palgrave Macmillan, 2005.

Miner, Earl. *The Cavalier Mode from Jonson to Cotton*. Princeton, NJ: Princeton University Press, 1971.

Mintz, Susannah B. "Katherine Philips and the Space of Friendship." *Restoration: Studies in English Literary Culture, 1660–1700* 22, no. 2 (1998): 62–78.

Montrose, Louis Adrian. "Of Gentlemen and Shepherds: The Politics of Elizabethan Pastoral Form." *English Literary History* 50, no. 3 (1983): 415–59.

Moody, Ellen. "Orinda, Rosania, Lucasia *et aliae:* Towards a New Edition of the Works of Katherine Philips." *Philological Quarterly* 66, no. 3 (1987): 325–54.

Morgan, Paul. "Frances Wolfreston and 'Hor Bouks': A Seventeenth-Century Woman Book-Collector." *Library* 11 (1989): 197–219.

Morrill, David F. "'Twilight Is Not Good for Maidens': Uncle Polidori and the Psychodynamics of Vampirism in *Goblin Market*." *Victorian Poetry* 28, no. 1 (1990): 1–16.

Mueller, Janel. "Lesbian Erotics: The Utopian Trope of Donne's 'Sapho to Philaenis.'" In *Homosexuality in Renaissance and Enlightenment England: Literary Representations in Historical Context,* edited by Claude J. Summers, 103–34. New York: Haworth Press, 1992.

Mulvihill, Maureen E. "A Feminist Link in the Old Boys' Network: The Cosseting of Katherine Philips." In *Curtain Calls: British and American Women and the Theater, 1660–1820,* edited by Mary Anne Schofield and Cecilia Macheski, 71–104. Athens: Ohio University Press, 1991.

Nauman, Jonathan. "The Publication of Thalia Rediviva and the Literary Reputation of Katherine Philips." *Huntington Library Quarterly: Studies in English and American History and Literature* 61, no. 1 (1998): 81–91.

Nevitt, Marcus. "Katherine Philips." In *The Encyclopedia of English Renaissance Literature,* vol. 1, edited by Garrett A. Sullivan Jr.,

Alan Stewart, Rebecca Lemon, Nicholas McDowell, and Jennifer Richards, 782–85. New York: Wiley-Blackwell, 2012.

Norbrook, David. "'This blushing tribute of a borrowed muse': Robert Overton and His Overturning of the Poetic Canon." *Early Manuscript Studies 1100–1700* 4 (1993): 220–67.

———. "The Monarchy of Wit and the Republic of Letters: Donne's Politics." In *Soliciting Interpretation: Literary Theory and Seventeenth-Century English Poetry*, edited by Elizabeth D. Harvey and Katherine Eisaman Maus, 3–36. Chicago: University of Chicago Press, 1990.

———. *Writing the English Republic: Poetry, Rhetoric and Politics, 1627–1660.* Cambridge: Cambridge University Press, 1999.

Novarr, David. *The Disinterred Muse: Donne's Texts and Contexts.* Ithaca, NY: Cornell University Press, 1980.

O'Reilly, Shelley. "Absinthe Makes the Tart Grow Fonder: A Note on 'Wormwood' in Christina Rossetti's Goblin Market." *Victorian Poetry* 34, no. 1 (1996): 108–14.

Orgel, Stephen, and Roy Strong, eds. *Inigo Jones: The Theater of the Stuart Court.* 2 vols. Berkeley and Los Angeles: University of California Press, 1973.

Orlin, Lena Cowen. "A Case for Anecdotalism in Women's History: The Witness Who Spoke When the Cock Crowed." *English Literary Renaissance* 31 (2001): 52–77.

Packer, Lona Mosk. "Symbol and Reality in Christina Rossetti's *Goblin Market*." *PMLA* 73, no. 4 (1958): 375–85.

Parker, Patricia. "On the Tongue: Cross Gendering, Effeminacy, and the Art of Words." *Style* 23 (1989): 445–65.

Pask, Kevin. *The Emergence of the English Author: Scripting the Life of the Poet in Early Modern England.* New York: Cambridge University Press, 1996.

Patterson, Annabel. *Censorship and Interpretation: The Conditions of Writing and Reading in Early Modern England.* Madison: University of Wisconsin Press, 1984.

Pearson, David. *Books as History.* London and Newcastle, DE: British Library and Oak Knoll Press, 2008.

Phillips, John. *The Reformation of Images: Destruction of Art in England, 1535–1660.* Berkeley and Los Angeles: University of California Press, 1974.

Pierpoint, Robert. "Latin Lines on Buxton." *Notes & Queries* 10 S. viii, issue 200 (Oct. 26, 1907): 332–33.

Potter, Lois. *Secret Rites and Secret Writing: Royalist Literature, 1641–1660.* Cambridge: Cambridge University Press, 1989.

Prescott, Anne Lake. "The 2011 Josephine Waters Bennett Lecture: From the Sheephook to the Scepter: The Ambiguities of David's Rise to the Throne." *Renaissance Quarterly* 65, no. 1 (Spring 2012): 1–30.

———. "Male Lesbian Voices: Ronsard, Tyard, and Donne Play Sappho." In *Reading the Renaissance: Ideas and Idioms from Shakespeare to Milton,* edited by Marc Berley, 109–29. Pittsburgh: Duquesne University Press, 2003.

Prescott, Sarah. "Archipelagic Orinda? Katherine Philips and the Writing of Welsh Women's Literary History." *Literature Compass* 6, no. 6 (2009): 1167–76.

———. "Katharine Philips, Welsh Women's Writing, and Archipelagic Coterie Space." *Tulsa Studies in Women's Literature* 33, no. 2 (2014): 51–76.

———. "'That private shade, wherein my Muse was bred': Katherine Philips and the Poetic Spaces of Welsh Retirement." *Philological Quarterly* 88, no. 4 (Fall 2009): 345–64.

Price, Bronwen. "A Rhetoric of Innocence: The Poetry of Katherine Philips, 'The Matchless Orinda.'" In *Write or Be Written: Early Modern Women Poets and Cultural Constraints,* edited by Barbara Smith and Ursula Appelt, 223–46. Aldershot: Ashgate, 2001.

Price, David C. *Patrons and Musicians of the English Renaissance.* Cambridge: Cambridge University Press, 1981.

Prins, Yopie. *Victorian Sappho.* Princeton, NJ: Princeton University Press, 1999.

Pritchard, Allan. "Marvell's 'The Garden': A Restoration Poem." *SEL: Studies in English Literature, 1500–1900* 23 (1983): 371–88.

Purkiss, Diane. "'Producing the Voice, Consuming the Body': Women Prophets of the Seventeenth Century." In *Women, Writing, History, 1640–1740,* edited by Isobel Grundy and Susan Wiseman, 139–58. Athens: University of Georgia Press, 1992.

Radzinowicz, Mary Ann. "Reading Paired Poems Nowadays." *Lit: Literature Interpretation Theory* 1, no. 4 (1990): 275–90.

Rainbolt, Martha. "Their Ancient Claim: Sappho and Seventeenth- and Eighteenth-Century British Women's Poetry." *Seventeenth Century* 12 (1997): 111–34.

———. "Women Naming Women: The Use of Sobriquets by Aphra Behn, Anne Finch, and Katherine Philips." *Names: A Journal of Onomastics* 50, no. 2 (2002): 133–53.

Rankin, Deana. *Between Spenser and Swift: English Writing in Seventeenth-Century Ireland.* Cambridge: Cambridge University Press, 2005.

Raymond, Joad. "The Newspaper, Public Opinion, and the Public Sphere in the Seventeenth Century." *Prose Studies* 21 (1998): 109–40.

Reay, Barry. *The Quakers and the English Revolution.* London: Temple Smith, 1985.

Rebhorn, Wayne A. *The Emperor of Men's Minds: Literature and the Renaissance Discourse of Rhetoric.* Ithaca, NY: Cornell University Press, 1995.

Reedy, Gerard. "Mystical Politics: The Imagery Charles II's Coronation." In *Studies in Change and Revolution: Aspects of English Intellectual History, 1640–1800,* edited by P. J. Korshin, 19–42. Menstone: Scolar Press, 1972.

Revard, Stella P. "Katherine Philips, Aphra Behn, and the Female Pindaric." In *Representing Women in Renaissance England,* edited by Claude J. Summers and Ted-Larry Pebworth, 227–41. Columbia: University of Missouri Press, 1997.

———. "The Sapphic Voice in Donne's 'Sapho to Philaenis.'" In *Homosexuality in Renaissance and Enlightenment England: Literary Representations in Historical Context,* edited by Claude J. Summers, 63–76. New York: Haworth Press, 1992.

Richey, Esther Gilman. *The Politics of Revelation in the English Renaissance.* Columbia: University of Missouri Press, 1998.

Roberts, Josephine A. "Deciphering Women's Pastoral: Coded Language in Wroth's *Love's Victory.*" In *Representing Women in Renaissance England,* edited by Claude J. Summers and Ted-Larry Pebworth, 163–74. Columbia: University of Missouri Press, 1997.

Roberts, Sasha. "Feminist Criticism and the New Formalism: Early Modern Women and Literary Engagement." In *The Impact of Feminism in English Renaissance Studies,* edited by Dympna Callaghan, 67–92. Basingstoke: Palgrave, 2007.

———. "Women's Literary Capital in Early Modern England: Formal Composition and Rhetorical Display in Manuscript and Print." *Women's Writing* 4, no. 2 (2007): 246–69.

Roberts, William. "The Dating of Orinda's French Translations." *Philological Quarterly* 49 (1970): 56–67.

———. "Saint-Amant, Orinda, and Dryden's Miscellany." *English Language Notes* 1 (1964): 191–96.

———. "Sir William Temple on Orinda: Neglected Publications." *Papers of the Bibliographical Society of America* 57 (1963): 328–36.

Robinson, David M. *Closeted Writing and Lesbian and Gay Literature: Classical, Early Modern, and Eighteenth-Century*. Aldershot: Ashgate, 2006.

———. "To Boldly Go Where No Man Has Gone Before: The Representation of Lesbianism in Mid-Seventeenth- and Early Eighteenth-Century British and French Literature." Ph.D. diss., University of California-Berkeley, 1998.

Rollin, Roger B. *Robert Herrick*. New York: Twayne, 1966.

Ross, Trevor. *The Making of the English Literary Canon from the Middle Ages to the Late Eighteenth Century*. Montreal: McGill-Queen's University Press, 1998.

Røstvig, Maren-Sofie. *The Happy Man: Studies in the Metamorphosis of a Classical Ideal, 1600–1700*. Oxford: Basil Blackwell, 1954.

Royle, Trevor. *Civil War: The War of the Three Kingdoms, 1638–1660*. London: Little, Brown, 2004.

Russell, Anne. "Katharine Philips as Political Playwright: 'The Songs between the Acts' in *Pompey*." *Comparative Drama* 44, no. 3 (2010): 299–323.

Salzman, Paul. *Reading Early Modern Women's Writing*. Oxford: Oxford University Press, 2006.

Sanchez, Melissa. *Erotic Subjects: The Sexuality of Politics in Early Modern English Literature*. Oxford: Oxford University Press, 2011.

Sant, Patricia M., and James N. Brown. "Two Unpublished Poems by Katherine Philips." *English Literary Renaissance* 24, no. 1 (1994): 211–28.

Savran, George. "1 and 2 Kings." In *The Literary Guide to the Bible*, edited by Robert Alter and Frank Kermode, 146–64. Cambridge, MA: The Belknap Press of Harvard University Press, 1987.

Schechner, Richard. "Performers and Spectators Transported and Transformed." *Kenyon Review* 3, no. 4 (1981): 83–113.

Schenck, Celeste Marguerite. *Mourning and Panegyric: The Poetics of Pastoral Ceremony.* University Park: Pennsylvania State University Press, 1988.

Schut, Rosalinde. "'La Femme Forte': Katherine Philips and the Politics of Her Dublin Writings." In *Early Modern Englishwomen Testing Ideas,* edited by Jo Wallwork and Paul Salzman, 107–19. Aldershot: Ashgate, 2011.

Scott-Baumann, Elizabeth. *Forms of Engagement: Women, Poetry and Culture, 1640–1680.* Oxford: Oxford University Press, 2013.

Sedgwick, Eve Kosofsky. *Between Men: English Literature and Male Homosocial Desire.* New York: Columbia University Press, 1985.

———. *Epistemology of the Closet.* Berkeley and Los Angeles: University of California Press, 1990.

———. *Tendencies.* Durham, NC: Duke University Press, 1993.

Shapiro, Barbara. *Beyond Reasonable Doubt and Probable Cause.* Berkeley and Los Angeles: University of California Press, 1991.

Sharpe, Kevin. *Criticism and Compliment: The Politics of Literature in the England of Charles I.* New York: Cambridge University Press, 1987.

Sharpe, Kevin, and Steven N. Zwicker. "Politics of Discourse: Introduction." In *Politics of Discourse: The Literature of History of Seventeenth-Century England,* edited by Kevin Sharpe and Steven N. Zwicker, 1–20. Berkeley and Los Angeles: University of California Press, 1987.

Shaw, Jane. "Fasting Women: The Significance of Gender and Bodies in Radical Religion and Politics, 1650–1813." In *Radicalism in British Literary Culture, 1650–1830: From Revolution to Revolution,* edited by Timothy Morton and Nigel Smith, 101–15. Cambridge: Cambridge University Press, 2002.

Shawcross, John. "The Arrangement and Order of John Donne's Poems." In *Poems in Their Place: The Intertextuality and Order of Poetic Collections,* edited by Neil Fraistat, 119–63. Chapel Hill: University of North Carolina Press, 1985.

Sherman, William H. *Used Books: Marking Readers in Renaissance England.* Philadelphia: University of Pennsylvania Press, 2008.

———. "What Did Renaissance Readers Write in Their Books?" In *Books and Readers in Early Modern England: Material Studies,* edited by Jennifer Anderson and Elizabeth Sauer, 119–38. Philadelphia: University of Pennsylvania Press, 2002.

Shifflett, Andrew. "'How Many Virtues Must I Hate': Katherine Philips and the Politics of Clemency." *Studies in Philology* 94, no. 1 (1997): 103–35.

———. *Stoicism, Politics, and Literature in the Age of Milton: War and Peace Reconciled.* Cambridge: Cambridge University Press, 1998.

———. "'Subdu'd by You': States of Friendship and Friends of the State in Katherine Philips's Poetry." In *Write or Be Written: Early Modern Women Poets and Cultural Constraints,* edited by Barbara Smith and Ursula Appelt, 177–95. Aldershot: Ashgate, 2001.

Shuttleton, David E. *Smallpox and the Literary Imagination, 1660–1820.* Cambridge: Cambridge University Press, 2007.

Smith, A. J., ed. *John Donne: The Critical Heritage.* Boston: Routledge and Kegan Paul, 1975.

———. *John Donne: Essays in Celebration.* London: Methuen, 1972.

Smith, Bruce R. *The Acoustic World of Early Modern England: Attending to the O-Factor.* Chicago: University of Chicago Press, 1999.

———. *Homosexual Desire in Shakespeare's England: A Cultural Poetics.* Chicago: University of Chicago Press, 1991.

Smith, Nigel. *Literature and Revolution in England, 1640–1660.* New Haven, CT: Yale University Press, 1994.

———. *Perfection Proclaimed: Language and Literature in English Radical Religion 1640–1660.* Oxford: Clarendon Press, 1989.

———. "The Rod and the Canon." *Women's Writing* 14, no. 2 (2007): 232–45.

Snook, Edith. *Women, Reading, and the Cultural Poetics of Early Modern England.* Aldershot: Ashgate, 2006.

Solt, Leo F. "The Fifth Monarchy Men: Politics and the Millennium." *Church History* 30, no. 3 (Sept. 1961): 314–24.

Souers, Philip Webster. *The Matchless Orinda.* Cambridge, MA: Harvard University Press, 1931.

Spraggon, Julie. *Puritan Iconoclasm during the English Civil War.* Woodbridge: Boydell, 2003.

Spencer, Jane. "Katherine Philips, *Poems.*" In *A Companion to Literature from Milton to Blake,* edited by David Womersley, 175–81. London: Blackwell, 2000.

Spink, Ian. *English Song Dowland to Purcell.* New York: Charles Scribner's Sons, 1974.

———. *Henry Lawes: Cavalier Songwriter.* Oxford: Oxford University Press, 2000.

Stafinbil, Susan L. "Woman in Emblem: Locating Authority in the Work and Identity of Katherine Philips (1632–1664)." Ph.D. diss., Marquette University, 2007.

Stallybrass, Peter, Roger Chartier, J. Franklin Mowery, and Heather Wolfe. "Hamlet's Tables and the Technologies of Writing in Renaissance England." *Shakespeare Quarterly* 55 (2004): 379–419.

Stanley, Liz. *The Auto/Biographical I: The Theory and Practice of Feminist Auto/Biography.* Manchester: Manchester University Press, 1992.

———. "Epistemological Issues in Reaching Lesbian History: The Case of Romantic Friendship." In *Working Out: New Directions for Women's Studies,* edited by Hilary Hinds, Ann Phoenix, and Jackie Stacey, 161–72. New York: Routledge, 1992.

Stanton, Kamille Stone. "'Capable of Being Kings': The Influence of the Cult of King Charles I on the Early Modern Women's Literary Canon." *New Perspectives on the Eighteenth Century* 5, no. 1 (2008): 20–29.

———. "Painting Sentinels: Erotics, Politics, and Redemption in the Friendship Poetry of Katherine Philips (1631–1664)." *Comitatus: A Journal of Medieval and Renaissance Studies* 38 (2007): 155–72.

Stewart, Susan. "Preface to a Lyric History." In *The Uses of Literary History,* edited by Marshall Brown, 199–218. Durham, NC: Duke University Press, 1995.

Stiebel, Arlene. "Not since Sappho: The Erotic in Poems of Katherine Philips and Aphra Behn." In *Homosexuality in Renaissance and Enlightenment England,* edited by Claude J. Summers, 153–71. Harrington Park, NY: Harrington Park Press, 1992.

———. "Subversive Sexuality: Masking the Erotic in Poems by Katherine Philips and Aphra Behn." In *Renaissance Discourses of Desire,* edited by Claude J. Summers and Ted-Larry Pebworth, 223–36. Columbia: University of Missouri Press, 1993.

Straznicky, Martha. "Restoration Women Playwrights and the Limits of Professionalism." *English Literary History* 64, no. 3 (Fall 1997): 703–26.

Sullivan, Ernest W. *The Influence of John Donne: His Uncollected Seventeenth-Century Printed Verse.* Columbia: University of Missouri Press, 1993.

———. "Who Was Reading/Writing Donne Verse in the Seventeenth Century?" *John Donne Journal* 8 (1989): 1–16.

Summers, Claude J. "Homosexuality and Renaissance Literature, or the Anxieties of Anachronism." *South Central Review* 9, no. 1 (1992): 2–23.

Summers, Claude J., and Ted-Larry Pebworth, eds. *The English Civil Wars in the Literary Imagination.* Columbia: University of Missouri Press, 1999.

Sutch, Victor D. *Gilbert Sheldon: Architect of Anglican Survival, 1640–1675.* The Hague: Nijhoff, 1973.

Suzuki, Mihoko. "Women, Civil War, and Empire: The Politics of Translation in Katherine Philips's *Pompey* and *Horace*." In *The History of British Women's Writing, 1610–1690,* vol. 3, edited by Mihoko Suzuki, 270–86. New York: Palgrave Macmillan, 2011.

Swaim, Kathleen M. "Matching the 'Matchless Orinda' to Her Times." *1650–1850: Ideas, Aesthetics, and Inquiries in the Early Modern Era* 3 (1997): 77–108.

Swann, Marjorie. "Marriage, Celibacy, and Ritual in Robert Herrick's *Hesperides*." *Philological Quarterly* 76, no. 1 (1997): 19–45.

Szatek, Karoline. "Engendering Spaces: A Study of Sexuality in Pastoral Borderlands." *Classical and Modern Literature* 18, no. 4 (1998): 345–59.

Tate, Rebecca Lynn. "Katherine Philips: A Critical Edition of the Poetry, I & II." Ph.D. diss., Texas Tech University, 1992.

Temperley, Nicholas. *The Music of the English Parish Church.* Vol. 1. Cambridge: Cambridge University Press, 1979.

———. *Studies in English Church Music, 1550–1900.* Aldershot: Ashgate Farnham, 2009.

Thomas, P. W. *Sir John Berkenhead, 1617–1679: A Royalist Career in Politics and Polemics.* Oxford: Oxford University Press, 1969.

Thomas, Patrick. *Katherine Philips ("Orinda")*. Cardiff: University of Wales Press, 1988.

———. "Orinda, Vaughan, and Watkyns: Anglo-Welsh Literary Relationships during the Interregnum." *Anglo-Welsh Review* 26, no. 57 (1976): 96–102.

Tinker, Nathan P. "John Grismond: Printer of the Unauthorized Edition of Katherine Philips's Poems (1664)." *English Language Notes* 34, no. 1 (1996): 30–35.

———. "'The Meetings of Agreeing Souls': Katherine Philips and the Sexual/Textual Politics of the Coterie." Ph.D. diss., Fordham University, 2002.

Tomlinson, Sophie. "Harking Back to Henrietta: The Sources of Female Greatness in Katherine Philips's *Pompey*." In *Women Writing, 1550–1750,* edited by Jo Wallwork, and Paul Salzman, 179–90. Bundoora, Australia: Meridian, 2001.

Traub, Valerie. "Afterword: Comparisons Worth Making." In *Comparatively Queer: Interrogating Identities across Time and Cultures,* edited by Jarrod Hayes, Margaret R. Higonnet, and William J. Spurlin, 215–23. New York: Palgrave Macmillan, 2010.

———. "Friendship's Loss: Alan Bray's Making of History." *GLQ: A Journal of Lesbian and Gay Studies* 10, no. 3 (2004): 339–65.

———. "The (In)significance of 'Lesbian' Desire in Early Modern England." In *Queering the Renaissance,* edited by Jonathan Goldberg, 62–83. Durham: Duke University Press, 1994. Originally published in *Erotic Politics: Desire on the Renaissance Stage,* edited by Susan Zimmerman, 150–69. London: Routledge, 1992.

———. "Making Sexual Knowledge." *Early Modern Women: An Interdiscplinary Journal* 5 (2010): 251–59.

———. "The New Unhistoricism in Queer Studies." *PMLA* 128, no. 1 (2013): 21–39.

———. "The Perversion of 'Lesbian' Desire." *History Workshop Journal* 41 (Spring 1996): 23–49.

———. "The Present Future of Lesbian Historiography." In *A Companion to Lesbian, Gay, Bisexual, Transgender, and Queer Studies,* edited by George E. Haggerty and Molly McGarry, 124–45. Malden, MA: Blackwell, 2007.

———. *The Renaissance of Lesbianism in Early Modern England.* Cambridge: Cambridge University Press, 2002.

———. "Sex without Issue: Sodomy, Reproduction and Signification in Shakespeare's Sonnets." In *Shakespeare's Sonnets: Critical Essays,* edited by James Schiffer, 431–54. New York: Garland, 1999.

Trefousse, Rashelle F. "The Reputation of Katherine Philips." Ph.D. diss., City University of New York, 1990.

Trevett, Christine. *Women and Quakerism in the Seventeenth Century.* York: Ebor Press, 1991.

Trolander, Paul, and Tenger Zeynep. "Katherine Philips and Coterie Critical Practices." *Eighteenth-Century Studies* 37, no. 3 (2004): 367–87.

Tufte, Virginia. *The Poetry of Marriage: The Epithalamium in Europe and Its Development in England.* Los Angeles: Tinnon-Brown, 1970.

Turner, James Grantham. *The Politics of Landscape: Rural Scenery and Society in English Poetry, 1630–1660.* Oxford: Oxford University Press, 1979.

———. *Schooling Sex: Libertine Literature and Erotic Education in Italy, France and England, 1534–1685.* Oxford: Oxford University Press, 2003.

Underdown, David. *Royalist Conspiracy in England, 1649–1660.* New Haven, CT: Yale University Press, 1960.

Veevers, Erica. *Images of Love and Religion: Queen Henrietta Maria and Court Entertainments.* Cambridge: Cambridge University Press, 1989.

Vickery, Amanda. "Golden Age to Separate Spheres? A Review of the Categories and Chronology of English Women's History." *Historical Journal* 36 (1993): 383–414.

Wahl, Elizabeth Susan. *Invisible Relations: Representations of Female Intimacy in the Age of Enlightenment.* Stanford, CA: Stanford University Press, 1999.

Wall, Wendy. *The Imprint of Gender: Authorship and Publication in the English Renaissance.* Ithaca, NY: Cornell University Press, 1993.

Wallingford, Katharine. "'Corinna,' Carlomaria, the *Book of Sports* and the Death of the Epithalamium on the Field of Genre." *George Herbert Journal* 14, nos. 1 and 2 (1990–91): 97–112.

Walls, Peter. Review of *Henry Lawes: Cavalier Songwriter,* by Ian Spink. *Music and Letters* 82 (2001): 298–301.

Watt, Tessa. *Cheap Print and Popular Piety, 1550–1640.* Cambridge: Cambridge University Press, 1991.

West, William N. "Thinking with the Body: Donne's 'Sappho to Philaenis.'" *Renaissance Papers* (1994): 67–83.

Wheatley, Christopher J. "'Your Fetter'd Muse': The Reception of Katherine Philips's *Pompey.*" *Restoration and Eighteenth-Century Theatre Research* 7, no. 2 (1992): 18–28.

Whitworth, Stephen. "The Name of the Ancients: Humanist Homoerotics and the Signs of Pastoral." Ph.D. diss., University of Michigan, 1997.

Wilcher, Robert. *The Writing of Royalism, 1628–1660.* New York: Cambridge University Press, 2001.

Willetts, Pamela J. *The Henry Lawes Manuscript.* London: Trustees of the British Museum, 1969.

Winkler, Amanda Eubanks. "Dangerous Performance: Cupid in Early Modern Pedagogical Masques." In *Gender and Song in Early Modern England,* edited by Leslie Dunn and Katherine Larson, 77–92. Aldershot: Ashgate, 2014.

———. "High School Musicals: Understanding Seventeenth-Century English Pedagogical Masques." Paper presented at the American Musicological Society Annual Meeting, Nov. 2011, San Francisco.

Winn, James Anderson. *The Pale of Words: Reflections on the Humanities and Performance.* New Haven, CT: Yale University Press, 1998.

———. *Unsuspected Eloquence: A History of the Relations between Poetry and Music.* New Haven, CT: Yale University Press, 1981.

Winship, Michael P. "Oxenbridge, John (1608–1674)." *Oxford Dictionary of National Biography.* Oxford University Press, 2004. Online edition, 2006. www.oxforddnb.com/index/101021048/John-Oxenbridge. Accessed Apr. 28, 2015.

Wiseman, Susan. "'Adam the Father of all Flesh': Porno-Political Rhetoric and Political Theory in and after the Civil War." *Prose Studies: History, Theory and Criticism* 14 (1991): 135–57.

———. "'Public,' 'Private,' 'Politics': Elizabeth Poole, the Duke of Monmouth, 'Political Thought' and 'Literary Evidence.'" *Women's Writing* 14, no. 2 (2007): 338–62.

———. "Unsilent Instruments and the Devil's Cushions: Authority in Seventeenth-Century Prophetic Discourse." In *New Feminist Discourses: Critical Essays on Theories and Texts,* edited by Isobel Armstrong, 176–96. London: Routledge, 1992.

Woudhuysen, H. R. "Writing-Tables and Table-Books." *Electronic British Library Journal* (2004), article 3. www.bl.uk/eblj/2004articles/pdf/rticle3.pdf. Accessed Jan. 28, 2015.

Wright, Gillian. *Producing Women's Poetry, 1600–1730: Text and Paratext, Manuscript and Print.* Cambridge: Cambridge University Press, 2013.

———. "Women Reading Epictetus." *Women's Writing* 14, no. 2 (2007): 321–37.

Young, Elizabeth. "Aphra Behn, Gender, and Pastoral." *SEL: Studies in English Literature, 1500–1900* 33, no. 3 (1993): 523–43.

Zaret, David. "Religion, Science, and Printing in the Public Spheres in Seventeenth-Century England." In *Habermas and the Public Sphere,* edited by Craig Calhoun, 212–35. Cambridge, MA: MIT Press, 1992.

Zwicker, Stephen N. *Lines of Authority: Politics and English Literary Culture, 1649–1689.* Ithaca, NY: Cornell University Press, 1993.

Contributors

LINDA PHYLLIS AUSTERN is associate professor of musicology at Northwestern University. Her articles and reviews have appeared in such journals as the *Journal of the American Musicological Society, Modern Philology, Music and Letters*, and *Renaissance Quarterly* as well as in a number of essay collections. Her books include *Music in English Children's Drama of the Later Renaissance; Music, Sensation and Sensuality* (editor); *Music of the Sirens* (coeditor with Inna Naroditskaya); and *Psalms in the Early Modern World* (coeditor with Kari Boyd McBride and David L. Orvis).

HARRIETTE ANDREADIS, professor emerita of English at Texas A&M University, is the author of several important articles on Katherine Philips as well as of *Sappho in Early Modern England: Female Same-Sex Literary Erotics, 1550–1714,* winner of the 2002 Roland H. Bainton Book Prize for Literature from the Sixteenth-Century Society and Conference. She is completing a volume of Philips's collected poetry, and her most recent project traces the early modern publishing and intellectual afterlife of the many subsequent editions of the 1680 Dryden/Tonson London edition of Ovid's *Heroides*.

CATHARINE GRAY is associate professor of English at the University of Illinois at Champaign-Urbana. She is the author of *Women Writers and Public Debate in Seventeenth-Century Britain* and coeditor with Erin Murphy of *Milton Now,* a collection of essays on

Milton marking the twenty-fifth anniversary of Mary Nyquist and Margaret Ferguson's *Re-membering Milton.* In addition to articles on seventeenth century women writers and politics published in *English Literary History* and *English Literary Renaissance,* she has published essays on military identity, the body politic, and royalist elegy. Her new book project, "Unmaking Britain: Poetry, Politics, and War in Seventeenth Century Britain," addresses the effects of the material realities of civil war on early modern poetic imaginings of gender identity and state formation.

Elizabeth H. Hageman, professor emerita of English at the University of New Hampshire, is textual editor of an edition of Richard Hyrde's 1529 translation of Juan Luis Vives's *Instruction of a Christen Woman* and author, twice with Andrea Sununu, of essays on manuscript and printed texts of Katherine Philips's poems and plays. Her current projects include, again with Andrea Sununu, a three-volume edition of Philips's writings and, with Jackson Campbell Boswell, a survey of seventeenth and eighteenth century references to Philips.

Elizabeth Hodgson is associate professor in the English Department at the University of British Columbia. Her published works include *Grief and Women Writers of the English Renaissance; Gender and the Sacred Self in John Donne;* and articles in *Milton Studies, SEL, MaRDiE, EMLS, Women's Writing,* and *Prose Studies* on the intersections between spiritual culture and gender history in Milton, Lanyer, Philips, Shakespeare, Chapman, Herbert, and others. She is currently editing a collection on Shakespeare and spectatorship.

Lorna Hutson is Berry Professor of English Literature at the University of St. Andrews, having also taught at the University of London and the University of California, Berkeley. Her books include *The Usurer's Daughter: Male Friendship and Fictions of Women in Sixteenth Century England* and *The Invention of Suspicion: Law and Mimesis in Shakespeare and Renaissance Drama,* which won the Roland H. Bainton prize in 2008. She is also the editor of *Feminism and Renaissance Studies.*

Paula Loscocco is professor of English at Lehman College of the City University of New York, where she teaches early modern and eighteenth century literature. She is the author of *Phillis Wheatley's Miltonic Poetics* and editor of *Katherine Philips (1631/32–1664): Printed Works 1651–1729*. She has published scholarly essays in *Renaissance Quarterly*, *Milton Studies*, and *Eighteenth Century* and has received grants from the National Endowment for the Humanities and teaching awards from Barnard and Lehman Colleges. She is currently working on an essay about Milton's and Philips's epithalamic poetics.

Christopher Orchard is professor of English at Indiana University of Pennsylvania. He specializes in Renaissance literature, specifically the literature of the 1640s and 1650s. His teaching interests include Marvell, Milton, early modern terrorism, the transatlantic literary review wars of the nineteenth century and post-9/11 literature. He has written articles on royalist translations, the influence of Milton on contemporary poetry, and a survey of the most seminal Renaissance works in the last 30 years. His latest book project is concerned with how writers in the civil war and Commonwealth period used tropes of marriage and divorce to explain political crises.

David L. Orvis is associate professor of English at Appalachian State University. He is coeditor, with Linda Phyllis Austern and Kari Boyd McBride, of *Psalms in the Early Modern World*. He has published articles in the *Journal of Homosexuality* and *Early Modern Culture* and contributed book chapters to *Shared Space: Reconsidering the Sacred and Profane in English Renaissance Literature*; *Performing Pedagogy in Early Modern England: Gender, Instruction, and Performance*; *Developments in the Histories of Sexualities: In Search of the Normal, 1600–1800*; *Magic, Marriage, and Midwifery: Eroticism in the Middle Ages and the Renaissance*; and the *Cambridge History of Gay and Lesbian Literature*. He is currently working on a book-length study tentatively titled *Shakespeare's Queer Marriages*.

Ryan Singh Paul is assistant professor of English at Texas A&M University–Kingsville. He specializes in Shakespeare, early modern poetry and drama, literary theory, and continental philosophy. He has published articles and book chapters on Middleton and Dekker's *The Roaring Girl,* Aemilia Lanyer's *Salve Deus Rex Judaeorum,* and the novel *Jasmine* by contemporary Indian-American novelist Bharati Mukherjee. His current projects include articles on political obfuscation in *Othello* and the temporality of sovereignty in *The Tempest* and the book of Revelation.

Amy Scott-Douglass is associate professor and director of graduate studies in English and humanities at Marymount University. She is the author of the "Theater" section of *Shakespeares after Shakespeare: An Encyclopedia of the Bard in Mass Media and Popular Culture* and *Shakespeare Inside: The Bard Behind Bars.* Her essays on women authors and on Shakespeare have appeared in *Pretexts; Shakespeare the Movie, Part II; Cavendish and Shakespeare: Interconnections; Borrowers and Lenders; "The Public's Open to Us All": Essays on Women and Performance in Eighteenth-Century England;* and *Weyward Macbeth: Non-Traditional Casting and the African-American Experience.*

Valerie Traub is the Frederick G. L. Huetwell Professor of English and Women's Studies at the University of Michigan. She is the author of *Desire and Anxiety: Circulations of Sexuality in Shakespearean Drama* and *The Renaissance of Lesbianism in Early Modern England.* She is also coeditor with David Halperin of *Gay Shame,* and with M. Lindsay Kaplan and Dympna Callaghan of *Feminist Readings of Early Modern Culture: Emerging Subjects.* Her latest book is *Thinking Sex with the Early Moderns.*

Index

absolutism, 17
agency, 26, 30; in marriage poems, 196–98, 203, 206–11
Agrippa von Nettesheim, Henry Cornelius, 219
Allen, Don Cameron, 321
amicitia tradition, 22–23, 38, 110–11, 155; Philips and, 248–49, 253–54, 268
amor impossibilis, 244, 249, 265, 277
Anderson, Penelope, 5, 42, 155, 245, 269–70; on betrayal in friendship, 110–11; *Friendship's Shadows* by, 22–23
Andreadis, Harriette, 12–15, 39, 184, 188, 270; on Donne's influence on Philips, 26, 58; on female friendships including and excluding men, 244–45; on Sapphic platonics, 254–55
Anglican churches, 48, 127, 144, 152; defacement of, 134–38, 141, 145; Philips as symbol of, 37, 129; Philips converting to, 37; reestablishment of, 134, 150–52
Anselment, Raymond, 49
"Antenor" (coterie name). *See* Philips, James
apologia genre, 75
An Appendix unto the Homily against Images in Churches (Gurnay), 134–35
Applegate, Joan, 29, 240, 332n95
Arcadia (Herbert), 133, 319–20
archipelagic literature and culture, 23–24, 41–42, 154
"Arion on a Dolphin, To his Majesty at his passage into England," 85, 120–21
"Articles of Friendship," 260
"Aubade" (Broumas), 308–09
Aubrey, John, 1–2, 87–88, 137–38
Aubrey, Mary ("Rosania"), 3–4, 45, 87, 313; as Elijah, 110–12; loss at separation from, 257–58; Lucasia and, 20, 110–11, 171, 383n37; Philips's early friendship with, 2, 48; Philips's poems addressed to or about, 6, 58, 109–11, 164, 255–56; Philips's poetry and, 52, 341n46; Philips's relationship with, 19, 383n37
Audley, John, 95
Austern, Linda, 38, 332n95
authorial voice, 25, 211
authors, 37, 125, 130–33, 147. *See also* poets; women writers
autobiographical code, 157
autograph manuscript, 33, 52–53

Bacon, Francis, 226, 228
Baines, Thomas, 280–81
Barash, Carol, 17–18, 41, 45, 260, 263–64, 383n37; on female friendship, 19–20; on *Poems*, 34, 129
Beal, Peter, 284, 333n103
Beckett, Isaac, 322
Behn, Aphra, 5, 28, 244, 292, 390n5
Berkenhead, Isaac, 47, 58, 343n59
Berkenhead, John ("Cratander"), 42–43, 45, 338n20, 343n57; autograph manuscript and, 52–53; Philips's verses for, 53–54, 341n47; political affiliations of, 51, 57–58
betrayal, in friendship, 22–23, 34, 42, 110–11
Bible, 94, 119; Daniel on heavenly throne room in, 106–07; Davidic

and Mosaic covenants in, 92, 100–03, 105–06, 108–09, 112–13, 117, 123; Elijah and Elisha in, 109–12; Orinda's prophecies and, 90–91, 93, 98–99; Philips using, 36, 37, 87–88, 100, 119–20, 122–23; and the psalms, 214–15
Blank, Paula, 163, 167, 174, 176, 251
bodies, 257, 273, 285, 354n17; in friendship, 281–82; music and, 217, 218, 228–29, 240; in same-sex intimacy, 279–80, 283; as signifier of male friendship, 268–69, 272, 274–75; in "To My excellent Lucasia," 180–81
Boyle, Ann, 4, 285–86
Boyle, Elizabeth, 4, 216, 221–23, 231
Boyle, Roger (Lord Broghill, Earl of Orrery), 4, 66, 80, 82–86, 127, 347n30
Bracebridge Hall (Irving), 312, 317–19, 395n12, 396n19
Brady, Andrea, 27, 188, 189
Bray, Alan, 14–15, 39, 278, 369n7; on civil society's effects of perceptions of friendship, 286, 288; *Homosexuality in Renaissance England* by, 244–45, 272–73; on wedded brotherhood of Finch and Baines, 280–81. *See also The Friend*
Brayman Hackel, Heidi, 319–21
Brereton, Andrew Jones, 320–21
Brief Lives (Aubrey), 87–88
Brooks, Cleanth, 321
Broumas, Olga, 39, 247, 307–09
Burton, Robert, 215, 220
Butler, Charles, 223, 237–38

Cartwright, William, 3, 17, 42–43, 56, 338n20; commendatory poems to, 46–47, 143–44; heroines of, 61–62; Philips and, 49, 51–53, 143. *See also Comedies, Tragi-Comedies, with Other Poems*
cathedrals, 136
Catherine of Braganza, 121–22
Cato, 315, 395n11
Catullus epithalamia, 369n8, 369n11, 371n35
Cavendish, Margaret, 4, 234, 249, 342n56, 385n10
Chalmers, Hero, 18–20, 42, 67, 108
Charles I, 58, 134, 139, 233; as absent in literature, 47, 52, 53, 260–61; characterizations of, 93, 94, 103–04; defacement of images of, 136–37, 145, 150; defeat of at Oxford, 46, 54; equated to Ahab, 94, 100; execution of, 17, 62–63, 94–96, 105–06, 120, 343n60; fleeing in disguise, 54, 136; Philips and, 54, 99
Charles II, 45, 149; characterizations of, 94–95, 117–18, 120–21; complexity of Philips's attitude toward, 22, 67, 93, 104–05; criticisms of, 65, 71–72, 79; Davenant offering advice to, 75, 77–78; desire for crown by, 65, 74; as divinely ordained, 109, 119; exile of, 17, 342n56; forces against, 62–63; as fugitive after Worcester, 68–69, 72, 74, 345n8; invasion of England by, 51, 345n8, 346n15; in "On the 3. of September, 1651," 68–69, 84; Philips's criticism of, 67–68, 81, 83–84; Philips's poem on coronation of, 117–19; Philips's poems as warnings for, 119–22; on religious tolerance, 151–52; return of from exile, 4, 18–20, 106, 151; support for, 70–71, 73, 76–78
Chernaik, Warren, 260, 284, 391n8
Christ, 100, 100–05, 107–08
Christianity, 282–83
civil society, 282, 286, 288
civil wars, English, 65, 72–73, 120, 296; attempts at healing after, 66, 149; competing loyalties in, 42, 382n30; effects of, 51, 72, 135; gender in, 16, 91; Philips's hope for resolution of, 89–90; seen as end-times, 91–92, 108
Clarke, Elizabeth, 25, 32
class, social, 61, 82, 194, 297, 392n13; virtue and, 75–76, 82
clemency, 22–23, 119
Clements, Henry J. B., 323
Clifford, Anne, 296–98
Clifford, Margaret (Countess of Cumberland), 296, 298
"Cloris Charmes Dissolved by Eudora" (Killigrew), 299
Closeted Writing and Lesbian and Gay Literature (Robinson), 14
Collection of Emblemes (Wither), 114, 115
"Come, my Lucasia, since we see," 238
Comedies, Tragi-Comedies, with Other Poems (Cartwright): commendatory poems in, 144–45; contributors to, 49–50, 338n18, 338n20; Oxford and, 46–47, 338n18, 338n20; Philips as only female author in, 3, 43, 143–44; Philips's poem in, 49–52, 144–45; royalists bonding through, 46–47, 67

Commission for the Propagation of the Gospel in Wales, 62–63, 340n40
community. *See* coterie, royalist
Compleat Gentleman, The (Peacham), 228–29
"Content, To my dearest Lucasia," 84
contract theory, of government, 119, 123, 155, 286
Convent of Pleasure, The, 249
Coolahan, Marie-Louise, 35, 41
Corneille. *See Pompey*
coronation, of Charles II, 117–19
coterie, royalist, 35, 108–09; as idealized community, 23, 58; Philips blurring differences among, 54, 57–58, 62; Philips praising, 53–57, 66, 141; poetic practices of, 32–34, 45, 52, 54–57, 60. *See also* Society of Friendship
Cotterell, Charles, 4, 270; Philips's correspondence with, 5, 15, 21, 189, 312, 321–22; Philips's relationship with, 33–34, 190, 379n17; *Poems* and, 126, 127; as "Poliarchus," 3, 379n17; unauthorized edition of *Poems* and, 30, 125, 130, 353n11
counterpublics, 44–45, 52, 63
country-house poems, 296, 391n9
"Country Life, A," 68
court culture, 155, 214, 291, 296, 299
Cowley, Abraham, 4, 84–85, 343n65; Philips's elegy by, 127, 359n83; Philips's poetic engagement with, 28–29; praise of for Philips, 133, 145–47, 185, 347n29
Crew, Clipseby, 196–98
criticism, literary: feminist, 6, 275–76; Philips's, 9, 35, 42, 153–54, 156–57; Philips's poetry marginalized by, 6–9; on Philips's royalism, 22, 67; on romantic female friendship, 10–11
Cromwell, Oliver, and Cromwellians, 69; ambitions of, 90, 344n71; James Philips and, 19, 44; Marvell on, 57, 76, 82, 342n54; royalists vs., 61, 159
Crouch, Nicholas, 52, 321
Cusick, Suzanne, 220

Daniel, biblical, 95–98, 106–07
Davenant, William, 66, 86, 347n30. *See also Gondibert;* advising on military campaigns, 75–78, 77–78; heroic virtue and, 36, 76; not admitting mistakes, 79–80; possibility of execution of, 78–79; virtue and, 75–76, 84
David, King, 105–06
Davidson, Henry, 144
Davies, John, 52, 341n46
Davis, Alex, 155
"De l'amitié" (Montaigne), 251–52
death, 68–69; Philips's, 4, 127, 130–31
defacement, 359n83; Parliament ordering, 134–38, 147; Philips condemning, 140, 144, 152; Philips's experience of, 138–39, 145, 152; publication of *Poems* equated to, 126–27, 129, 133; targets of, 135–36, 142, 145, 150
Defense of Poesy (Sidney), 75
Derby, Earl of, 73–74
Dering, Edward (Mary Harvey's husband, "Silvander"), 3, 48; and civil wars, 51, 340n41; masquerading as Orinda, 45, 55–56; Philips's poems and, 45, 341n46; Philips's verses for, 54–55, 341n47; in royalist coterie, 18, 49, 52–53, 57, 233–34; writing by, 3, 45, 52–53, 234
Dering, Mary Harvey. *See* Harvey, Mary
A Description of Cooke-ham (Lanyer), 296–98
desire, 20, 26; homoerotic, 252, 262–63; as illicit, 13, 39; lesbian, 9, 14, 45, 251; music and, 218, 223; in Philips's poetry, 9, 14–15, 45, 163–64
D'Ewes, Simonds, 138
"Dialogue between Lucasia and Orinda, A," 45
Dillon, Wentworth (Earl of Roscommon), 127
Discourse of the Nature, Offices, and Measures of Friendship with Rules of Conducting It, A (Taylor), 3, 14–15, 281–83
divine truth, 90, 99, 101, 105, 109
Donne, John, 32, 52, 132, 181, 314, 362n13; epithalamia by, 193–97, 204–06; friendship poems by, 58, 170–71, 173, 387n38; influence of on Philips, 26–28, 37, 58, 158, 249; love poems by, 153–54, 156, 161–64, 174; marriage of, 58–59, 343n61; Philips misusing poems by, 170–71, 173; Philips moving beyond works of, 26, 60, 158, 162, 166–67; Philips rewriting poetry of, 58, 60; Philips using poetry of, 153–54, 156, 161–64, 174; Sapphic rhetoric of, 11, 37, 158, 174–79, 182; and Walton, 157, 159–61, 186, 364n21
Duppa, Bishop, 56

Dubrow, Heather, 192, 194
Dugaw, Dianne, 29, 155
Dugdale, William, 142
Dungannon, Lord and Lady, 206–11, 207

Easton, Cecilia, 336n9, 362n14
education, Katherine's, 2, 48, 137, 215
egalitarianism, 20, 26, 60–62
Eikon Basilike (Charles I), 103–04, 136
Eikonoklastes (Milton), 94
"Elegie to the Lady Bedford" (Donne), 180–81
Elijah, 90–91, 93, 100, 109–12, 113, 122–23
Elisha, 109–13
Elmen, Paul, 31
"Emblem" (Broumas), 307–08
end-times, 94–96, 98, 103, 106–08, 113
England, 70; Charles II's invasion of, 77–78, 345n8, 346n15; Charles II's return to, 120–21; epithalamia tradition of, 192
"Ephelia," 298
epithalamia. *See* marriage poems
Epithalamion (Spenser), 343n64
"Epithalamion made at Lincolnes Inne" (Donne), 193–97, 202, 204–05
eroticism, 26, 250–51, 286, 299–300. *See also* homoeroticism
Evans, Robert C., 16–17, 21–22, 67–68, 97, 99, 363n17
Ezell, Margaret, 41, 52, 125

faces, 134, 147–49
Faderman, Lillian, 9–10, 326n16
Fairfax, Thomas, 145
Familiar Letters, 4–5
family, 253, 283, 286, 382n30
Fane, Mildmay, 48, 339n29
Fifth Monarchists, 95–98
Finch, Anne (Countess of Winchelsea), 298, 343n57
Finch, Francis ("Palemon"), 51, 56–57, 338n20, 342n48, 343n57; on friendship, 108, 114–16; Philips and, 45, 53, 114–16, 149; Philips's verses for, 143, 341n47; royalist writers and, 47, 52–53; writings by, 45, 52–54, 114–16
Finch, John, 280–81, 338n20
Fincham, Kenneth, 151
Finden, William, 322–23
Fineman, Joel, 250–51, 381n24, 381n25, 382n26
Flatman, Thomas, 127, 145–46
Fletcher, Miles, 132
folio production, 132, 149–50
Fowler, John (father), 1–2, 139
Foxe, John, 314
Fraser, Nancy, 44–45
Friedman, Susan Stanford, 303
"Friend, A" 165
Friend, The (Bray), 252–53, 277–79; and homosexuality, 274–75; Traub's review of, 268, 273; women omitted from, 15, 268, 272, 280; women's friendship in, 268–69
friendship, 68, 108, 183, 293; betrayal in, 22–23, 34, 42, 110–11; body as signifier of, 268–69, 272, 274–75; constancy of, 82–84; egalitarianism of, 20, 60; equated to Ark of the Covenant, 114, 116; eroticism and, 252–53, 298; ethics of, 3, 282–83; family and, 283, 286, 369n7, 382n30; Finch on, 53–54, 114–16, 143; and heroic virtue, 36, 42, 66; as marriage of souls, 281–82, 288, 295–96, 387n38; marriage vs., 164–65, 247–48, 260–62, 383n37; men's, 14, 16, 244–45, 251–53, 277, 288; men's vs. women's, 14–15, 268–69, 278–80; models of, 20, 22, 27, 110–11; perceptions of, 282, 286, 288; Philips's, 34–35, 154–55; Philips's idealization of, 7–8, 27, 36, 42, 84; in Philips's poetry, 5, 9; politics and, 5, 110–11, 270; public vs. private, 172; relation of to marriage, 59–60, 189, 254; romantic, 10–11; same-sex, 276–77, 283; women's capacity for, 253, 277, 283–84. *See also* friendship, women's; friendship poems
"Friendship," 174, 176, 179, 182
friendship, women's, 14, 20, 261; Charles II's return and, 18–19; chaste, 276–77; intensity of, 236, 238–39; lacking embodiment, 279–80; men in, 244–45; Philips's idealization of, 7–8; royalism and, 20, 154
"Friendship in Emblem, or the Seal. To my dearest Lucasia," 26, 27–28, 60, 113–14, 170–74, 180, 183, 261
friendship poems, 20, 58, 248; Donne's, 158, 170–71, 173; marriage poems compared to, 188–89; Philips's, 7–8, 17, 31, 157, 284; union in, 158, 169–70
"Friendship's Mystery, to my dearest Lucasia," 59–60, 82, 183; set to music, 29, 45, 235–36

Friendship's Shadows (Anderson), 22–23, 270

Gallagher, Catherine, 57, 342n56
Gell, Temperance, 324, 395n12
gender, 5, 16, 49, 116, 146; competition between, 28–29, 203–4; music and, 220, 227, 234; Philips's attitudes toward, 32, 190; in Philips's marriage poems, 190, 210–11; Philips's poetry and, 8–9, 44; in rhetoric, 157, 173–74, 177; royalism and, 61, 154, 337n13; women writers disguising, 57, 343n57; and women's vs. men's friendships, 14–15
gender roles, 20, 49, 234
Gentles, Ian J., 142
Goldberg, Jonathan, 273
Gondibert (Davenant), 36, 66, 75, 78–81
Gorboduc (Norton and Sackville), 133
Gosse, Edmund, 8
government, 119, 123, 155, 286
Gray, Catharine, 18, 21, 24, 108, 144, 154, 270; on Philips's royalism, 35–36, 67, 141
Greene, Frederick, 291
Greer, Germaine, 33
Gregg, W. W., 321
Guiney, Louise, 321
Gurnay, Edmund, 134–35

H. D. (Hilda Doolittle), 39, 247, 302–07, 393n26
Haddon Hall, 40, 312–19, 395n12
Hageman, Elizabeth, 34, 39–40, 333n103, 367n40
Haggar, Henry, 94
Hamessley, Lydia, 29, 184, 236, 239, 362n13
Hamilton, Duke, 70
Hammill, Graham, 20, 245, 270
Happier Eden, A (Dubrow), 192
harmony, 55, 104, 224, 226–28, 232
Harrison, Thomas, 70
Harvey, Mary, 3, 342n48; Lawes and, 215, 233–35; Philips and, 2, 48, 52; song composition by, 215, 234
Helgerson, Richard, 144
Henley, George (stepfather), 2
Henrietta Maria, Queen, 2–3, 17, 61; equated to Jezebel, 93–94, 100; poems written to, 46, 338n20
Herbert, George, 314–15
Herbert, Mary Sidney, 133, 234, 249–50, 355n26
heroic virtue, 82; friendship and, 36, 66; idealization of, 74–76; models of, 66, 83–86; Philips rejecting ideology of, 36, 42, 85; in Philips's poems, 53–57; in royalist culture, 53–57, 65–66, 154
Herrick, Robert, 193, 196–98, 233, 371n28, 371n30; marriage poems of, 37, 209
Herring, Michael, 138
Herringman, Henry, 31, 127, 353n9
Hewson, John, 81
Hill, Christopher, 94
Hirst, Derek, 159, 363n18
historicism, 246–47
Hobbes, Thomas, 76, 78, 84
Hobby, Elaine, 11, 26, 157, 188, 336n9
Hodgson, Elizabeth, 37
Holland, Philemon, 314
Holstun, James, 176–77
homoerotic laments, 155, 249, 265
homoeroticism, 155, 183, 246, 250, 344n74; coded, 189, 298, 307; Donne's, 167, 175–76, 181; female, 296, 298, 301–02, 307; marriage poems as displacement for, 187–88; pastoralism and, 256, 259, 293–94, 296, 301–02; Philips masking, 263–65, 362n14; Philips's, 59, 154, 175–76, 181; in Philips's poems, 158, 174, 238–39
homosexual identity, 272–73
homosexuality, 39, 272–75, 291. *See also* lesbianism
Homosexuality in Renaissance England (Bray), 244, 272–73
Horace, 312, 321
"How Prodigious Is My Fate," 216
Hughes, Ann, 16
Hunt, Richard, 138–39
Hutson, Lorna, 14–16, 38–39, 154–55, 189, 245, 269

iconolatry, 140–41, 143, 145–47, 150
Idylls (Theocritus), 292
innocence, 125, 130, 133; of female friendships, 12, 165–66, 244, 251, 259, 264; Philips claiming for love of women, 151, 182–83, 251, 261, 263–65
Interregnum, 16, 25, 91, 151, 296; as period of trial, 106, 119; Philips as writer of, 3, 21, 43; royalist culture in, 19, 45, 144; Society of Friendship in, 19, 108
Invisible Relations (Wahl), 12
"Invitation to the Countrey," 295–96

Ireland, 24, 41–42, 81, 254
"The Irish Greyhound," 24
Irving, Washington, 40, 312, 317–19, 396n14

Jackson, Virginia, 250, 381n23
Jacobs, Deborah, 32
Jane, Lady, 314
Jeffreys, John, 30, 126, 141, 340n33
Jewett, Sarah Orne, 321
Jones, Jenkin, 52, 62–63, 168–69, 341n46
Jonson, Ben, 132, 286–87
Jorgens, Elise Bickford, 237–38
Joseph, biblical, 119–20, 122

Keats, John, 5–6
Kerrigan, John, 23–24, 42
Kerrigan, William, 154, 156
Killigrew, Anne, 39, 247, 298–302
kinship, 253–54, 274–75, 369n7
Knight, Mary, 232–34, 343n57

La Boëtie, Étienne de, 251
"La grandeur d'esprit," 68
La mort de Pompée (Corneille). *See Pompey*
"L'accord du bien" ("The agreement of the good"), 21–22, 225
Lady Errant, The (Cartwright), 61–62
"L'amitié: To Mrs. M. Awbrey," 164, 259–60
Lanser, Susan, 245–47
Lanyer, Aemilia, 39, 88, 98–99, 247, 296–98
Laud, Archbishop, 90, 134–35, 137, 145, 151–52
Lawes, Henry, 3, 51, 232; compositions by, 233–34, 237–39; gatherings hosted by, 18, 233–34, 338n17; Mary Harvey and, 215, 234–35; Philips and, 45, 332n95; Philips praising, 55, 215, 229–33, 256–57; possibly called "Thrysis," 332n95; setting Philips's poems to music, 45, 213–14, 236, 238–41; setting poems to music, 29–30, 236–37, 338n20. *See also Second Book of Ayres and Dialogues*
lesbianism, 38, 255, 394n37; coded, 156, 307; cultural perceptions of, 185–86; discourses of, 176–78; history of, 12–13, 243, 276–77, 326n16; Philips and, 11, 15, 156; Philips's denial of, 184, 263; romantic friendship vs., 10–11
Leslie, David, 71
Letters from Orinda to Poliarchus, 5, 21, 312, 321–22
Life (Walton), 159–61
Lilley, Kate, 269, 284, 286, 328n23, 336n9
Limbert, Claudia, 44
Lintot, Bernard, 5, 322
Llewellyn, Mark, 27
Lochman, Daniel T., 269
Locke, John, 282
López, Maritere, 269
Loscocco, Paula, 5, 11, 26–27, 37, 188
loss, 244, 255–59, 297, 306–07, 390n4
love, 61, 175
Love, Christopher, 73
love poems, 249; Donne's, 153, 156, 161–67, 174; Philips's, 154, 156, 251, 260–61, 270
Lovett, Anne, 323
Low, Anthony, 162–63
Lowenstein, David, 96
Loxley, James, 136, 146, 189, 337n13
"Lucasia," 226
"Lucasia, Rosania, and Orinda parting at a Fountain, July 1663," 255–56
"Lucasia and Orinda parting with Pastora and Phillis at Ipswich," 316
"Lucasia" (coterie name). *See* Owen, Anne
Lupton, Christina, 319
lyric tradition, 249–50, 380n22, 381n23

Manners family, 317–18
manuscript collections, 46–47, 313; of Philips's poetry, 31–32, 52, 321, 341n46, 383n37
Marotti, Arthur, 32, 46–47, 343n61
marriage, 19, 61, 214–15, 254, 369n7. *See also* marriage poems; companionate, 261–62, 275–76; Donne's, 159–61, 343n61; economics of, 193, 195; female friendship and, 15, 246; as female vocation, 37, 59–60; and friendship, 59–60, 164–65, 189, 247–48, 254, 260–62, 284, 383n37; Philipses', 140, 163–69; functions of, 196, 200; Philips's ambivalence about, 38, 202–03, 205–06; Philips's indictments of, 90, 347n8; Philips's poems about, 141, 154, 156, 167–70, 189–90; power in, 20, 190, 199, 201, 203–05, 210; of souls, 280–81, 288; as union, 167–70; wedding services, 141, 371n33
marriage poems, 37, 169, 343n64, 370n15; and Catullus epithalamia,

369n8, 369n11, 371n35; conventions of, 188, 193–95, 198, 202–04, 206, 210–11; Donne and Herrick's, 158, 201–02, 204–05; friendship poems compared to, 188–89; and homoeroticism, 187–88; men's, 190–92, 203; Philips's, 158, 162, 180, 190, 198–211; sex in, 193–95; Stuart epithalamia, 192–98; tradition of, 191–92
"A Married State," 347n8
Marriott, Richard, 4, 30, 125–26, 130–32
Martha, Lady Gifford, 315
Marvell, Andrew, 43, 52, 56; on Cromwell, 76, 82; poems to Cromwell by, 57, 342n54
Mary, Queen of Scots, 314
mathematics, and music, 224–25
McBride, Kari Boyd, 98–99
McKnight, Laura Blair, 103–04
men: and female friendships, 244–45; friendships of, 14–16, 244–45, 251–53, 268–69, 272, 274–75, 277–80; and homosexuality, 272–73
Menges, Hilary, 34
Mermin, Dorothy, 131
Milgate, Wesley, 194
Milton, John, 88, 94, 98–99, 233
Minor Poets of the Caroline Period (Saintsbury), 6
Mintz, Susannah, 188
Miscellaneous Poems (Marvell), 43
monarchs, 94; divinity of, 95, 99–100, 103–06, 112–13, 122; equated to Christ, 100, 103–04; monuments to dead, 135–36; prophets and, 93, 109, 122–23; subjects and, 42, 159–60
monarchy: authority of, 19, 22–23, 123; England abolishing, 65; Philips as symbol of, 37, 129; Philips on, 21–22, 36, 92–93; restoration of, 119, 129, 134; royalists and, 63, 108
Montagu, Mary Aubrey. *See* Aubrey, Mary
Montaigne, Michel de, 251–53
Montrose, Louis Adrian, 291
monuments, funeral, 135–36, 141–43, 146, 150
Monumentum Regale, 47
Moody, Ellen, 31–32
More, Anne, 58–59
Morley, Thomas, 223–24
Moseley, Humphrey, 46–47
Moses, 113–14, 116–18. *See also* Bible, Davidic and Mosaic covenant in
Mulcaster, Richard, 218
Mulvihill, Maureen, 44
Musarum Oxoniensium Epibathpia Serenissimae, 338n20
muses, in Philips's marriage poems, 198, 201, 207–8
music: bodies and, 217–18, 228–29; conventions of, 238–39; and Mary Harvey's compositions, 215, 234; metaphors for, 224–25; nature and, 55, 229, 231–32; performance of, 218–20; Philips and, 38, 214–16; Philips as connoisseur of, 215–16, 221, 241; Philips's poems set to, 3, 29, 45, 213–14, 236, 238–41; physical and metaphysical, 227–31; poetry and, 216–17, 231, 241; power of, 55, 218, 233, 239–40; rationality and, 220, 226; in seduction, 220–23; song vs. instrumental, 219–20; speculative vs. practical, 223–24, 229; tuneful vs. declamatory songs, 237–39; women's participation in, 234–35
Muskerry, Lord, 81
"Mutuall Affection between *Orinda* and *Lucatia,*" 235–36

nature, 39, 256, 308, 394n37; female-female love and, 244, 249, 255, 259, 277; harmony of, 227–28; music and, 55, 229, 231–32
Neoplatonism, 27, 54–55
New Model Army, 142–43
No King but Jesus (Haggar), 94
Novarr, David, 194
"A Nuptiall Song, or Epitalamie, on Sir Clipseby Crew and His Lady" (Herrick), 193, 196–98

"Ode, upon the blessed restoration and returne of His Sacred Majesty, Charles the Second" (Cowley), 84–85
Ogilby, John, 71–72
"On Controversies in Religion," 88–90, 93, 134
"On Mr. Francis Finch [the excellent Palemon]," 114, 116
"On *Orinda's Poems*" (Cowley), 4
"On Rosania's Apostacy, and Lucasia's Friendship," 109–11
"On the 3. of September, 1651," 65, 67–69, 82, 84–85
"On the Death of an Infant," 240
"On the death of my first and dearest childe, Hector Philipps," 240
"On the Soft and Gentle Motions of Eudora" (Killgrew), 300–01

"On the Welsh Language," 24
Onley, W., 4–5
Orchard, Christopher, 42
Orchard, Richard, 36
"Orinda" (Philips's pseudonym), 3, 55–56, 250
"Orinda to Leonora," 319
"Orinda to Lucasia," 258–59
"Orinda to Lucasia parting," 170
"Orinda upon Little Hector," 29
Orvis, David, 36, 42
Osborne, Robin, 315
Overton, Robert, 52, 61, 344n70
Owen, Anne ("Lucasia"), 52, 141, 207, 379n17; end of friendship with, 170–71; Finch dedicating book to, 114, 341n47; and "Friendship in Emblem, or the Seal. To my dearest Lucasia," 26–28, 60, 113–14, 170–74, 261; harmony attributed to, 226–27; "Lucasia" as coterie name, 3, 61; Philips's friendship poems to, 58, 59–60, 82, 157, 174, 179–84; Philips's poems defending, 62–63, 227–28, 262–63, 341n46; Philips's poems on parting from, 170, 255–59, 316; Philips's poems to, 20, 29, 45, 84, 109–12, 179–83, 226, 229, 238, 256, 258; Philips's poems to set to music, 29, 45, 235–36, 257–58; Philips's relationship with, 15, 19, 26, 171, 254, 383n37; Rosania vs., 20, 110–11, 171, 383n37
Oxenbridge, Daniel (grandfather), 139
Oxenbridge, John (grandfather), 137
Oxenbridge, Katherine (mother), 1–2, 140
Oxford, 49, 340n36; Charles I fleeing, 54, 136; writers linked to, 338n18, 338n20
Oxford University, 46–47, 49, 52, 338n18

"Palemon." *See* Finch, Francis
Parliament, 57, 61, 338n18, 353n5; and campaign against Charles II, 69–70, 83; James Philips in, 2, 140; ordering defacement, 134–38, 147; persecution of royalists by, 48, 81, 345n8. *See also* Rump Parliament
Parliamentarians, 49, 139, 149
Parthenissa (Boyle), 66, 80–81, 83–84, 86
"Parting with a Friend," 170–71, 318
"Parting with Lucasia: A Song," 257–58
pastoralism, 39, 155, 249, 265, 291, 390n4; Anne Killigrew's, 298–301; conventions of, 292, 305–06, 390n5; eclogues of, 292, 389n1; as escapism, 293–96, 391n8; female, 259–60, 292, 296, 309, 390n5, 390n6, 394n37; H. D.'s, 302–07; homoeroticism and, 256, 296; Philips's, 39, 293–96; royalists' use as ideal, 16–18, 248
patronage, 285, 298
Paul, biblical, 100–03, 106, 108
Peacham, Henry, 228–29
Pearson, David, 312–13
Pecke, Samuel, 70, 81
Penington, Isaac, 135, 139
Perdita Project, 267, 271
Philips, Hector (son), 2, 29, 240
Philips, Katherine (daughter), 2
Philips, Frances (stepdaughter), 140, 141
Philips, Frances (stepsister), 140
Philips, James (husband, "Antenor"), 2, 340n36; "Antenor" as coterie name of, 3, 17, 90; Cromwell and, 19, 44; Jones's attack on, 168–69, 341n46; marriage of, 140, 167–70, 254; in new class of landowners, 60–61; politics of, 44, 49; sequestering estates, 51, 340n42; status of, 34, 48–49; suppressing royalist revolts, 73, 81; wife at odds with Parliamentarianism of, 49, 58; wife's poems to, 153–54, 161–67, 171–74, 179–80, 190
Phillips, Edward, 233
Phillipps, Richard (stepfather), 2, 139–40
"Philo-Philippa," 14, 127
Pindar, Penelope, 323–24
Pindaric ode, 28–29
platonism, of women's friendship, 9
Playford, John, 240
plays, Philips's, 215–16, 312. *See also* translations, Philips's
Poems (Donne), 132
Poems by Several Persons, 28–30
Poems by the Incomparable, Mrs. K. P. (unauthorized edition), 21, 333n98, 333n103; Philips's horror at, 34, 37, 125–26, 129, 353n11; readers' marks in, 320–21; reasons for quick suppression of, 30–31
Poems by the most deservedly Admired Mrs. Katherine Philips The Matchless Orinda (authorized edition), 4–6, 25, 128, 155; authenticity questioned, 30–31; commendatory verses in, 127–30, 149; manuscript copies of, 30–31; order of, 31–32, 122, 132, 150; Orinda's visions for Restoration in, 122; Philips's letter to Cotterell

reprinted in, 127, 130; Philips's portrait in, 127, 132–33; Philips's portraits in, 147–49, 148, 322–23; preface to, 127–33, 145–47, 184–86; publication of, 21, 126–27, 131; readers' marks in, 319–24; as response to Puritan iconoclasm, 147, 150; as restoration after defacement from unauthorized edition, 37, 129–30, 132–33, 149; unauthorized edition compared to, 30–31, 122, 127, 383n31
poetics: conventions of, 248; Sapphic, 154, 158, 174–78, 182, 186
poetics, Philips's, 2, 25, 27; and interactions with friendships, 34–35; Platonism vs. courtly love in, 255, 257; Sapphic, 154–55, 174–76, 179; sophistication of, 157
poetry, 35; authors' control over, 30, 33; circulation of, 33–34, 313; as dialogues, 32–34, 55–57; for elite audience, 75–76; Lawes setting to music, 29–30, 233, 236–37, 338n20; mottos inscribed on windows, 314–15; music and, 3, 216–17, 231, 241
poetry, Philips's, 134, 145, 336n7. *See also* friendship poems, Philips's; marriage poems, Philips's; *Poems;* in anthologies, 6, 155–56; audience for, 5–6, 52, 63; authorial voice of, 25, 211; books of, 4–5, 155, 320–24; criticisms of, 156, 284; depth and breadth of, 3, 35, 211, 312; evaluations of, 3, 5–6, 8–9, 157, 284–85; influence of coterie poetic practices on, 32–34; innovations/experimentation in, 9, 15, 16, 25; Interregnum vs. Restoration, 3, 19, 21; locations of extant copies of, 320–21; manuscript copies of, 4–5, 31–32, 52, 341n46; owners of extant copies of, 320–21; politics and, 36, 44, 53; rewriting of, 61, 344n70; seeking corrections to, 33–34; subjects left out of, 53, 57
poets, 78, 206, 216, 260; female, 43–44, 155, 292, 298; lesbian, 307, 394n37; male vs. female, 28–29, 203–04; and Philips as placeholder for male royalist, 8–9, 16, 51–52; royalist, 47–48, 52, 74–75, 141, 143–45, 363n18. *See also* women writers
"Poliarchus" (coterie name). *See* Cotterell, Charles
politics, 17, 24–25, 39, 82–83, 245; alternative, 44–45; complexity of Philips's, 67–68, 157, 363n17; friendship and, 5, 110–11, 270; gender and, 16, 269–70; Philips as active participant in, 25, 58, 336n9; and Philips as placeholder for male royalists, 8–9; Philips's complicated position in, 58, 67, 140, 382n30; in Philips's poetry, 5, 6, 31, 44; within royalist coterie, 35, 57–58; turmoil in, 260–61, 391n8; and women's political speech, 25–26, 32
Pompey (Philips's translation of *La mort de Pompée*), 33, 215–16; performance of, 4, 312; music to, 221–22; politics in, 22, 24, 119, 150; publication of, 4, 21
Powell, Amanda, 29, 155
Powell, Vavasor, 32, 62–63, 95–97, 341n46
précieux tradition, 27
préciosité, 17–18
Prescott, Sarah, 23–24, 42
Price, Bronwen, 26
Propagation Act, 48
prophecy, 112, 205; culture of female, 91–92; Daniel's, 95–98; and Elijah, 90–91, 10; eschatological, 95–98, 106–07, 113, 117; millenarian, 98, 107, 1130; Philips's, 98, 104, 107–08, 113–14, 123; and Philips's visions for Restoration, 117–19, 122
prophets, 93, 106, 109, 122–23
Protectorate, 19, 57
"Prothalamion" (Spenser), 196
Prynne, William, 220
public vs. private spheres, 20, 28, 44, 250, 270
publication: of Lawes's works, 234; Philips's compulsion to control, 353n11; of Philips's poetry, 6, 30–31; vs. circulatory manuscript culture, 3, 33–34
Pulteney, Jane, 196–98
Puritan Iconoclasm during the English Civil Wars (Spraggon), 136
Puritans, 59–60, 140, 214–15; anti-Laudianism of, 134–35; defacements by, 37, 135–36, 144, 359n83; iconoclasm of, 134–35, 141, 147–49, 150; Philips's background as, 1, 48, 137; Philips converting from, 37, 88; Philips's early devotion in, 137–38

Rankin, Deana, 41
Ravenscroft, Thomas, 216–17
readers' marks, 312–13, 319–24
rebellions, royalists', 49, 57, 73, 81

reconciliation, 19, 80, 86, 102–04
religion, 59, 89–90, 108; and Philips's devotion, 88, 137–38; tolerance in, 151–52. *See also* Anglican churches; Puritans
religious lyric, 25–26, 32
Renaissance of Lesbianism in Early Modern England, The (Traub), 12–13, 243–44, 264–65, 268–69, 276–77
Restoration, of Charles II, 4, 85, 122, 129; divine will and, 92, 119; effects on female friendship, 18–19; Philips's poetry and, 260–61, 344n70; *Poems* as metaphor for, 37, 150
Restoration period, 16, 21, 25, 149, 161
"A Retir'd Friendship. To Ardelia," 68, 183, 260, 293–95
Revard, Stella, 28
Rey, Michael, 280
rhetoric, 119, 153, 154, 157, 173–74, 177
Roberts, Josephine, 291
Roberts, Sasha, 25
Robinson, David M., 14
"Rosania" (coterie name). *See* Aubrey, Mary
Rosetti, Christina, 39, 247, 301–02
royalism/royalists, 122, 134, 142, 337n13; Charles II's defeat and, 65, 71–72, 346n28; community of, 17, 45, 48, 52–53, 108–09, 233–34; as covenanted people, 92, 100, 109, 112–13; equated with divine will, 36–37; as heroes in Philips's poems, 53–57; ideals of, 19–20, 35, 47–48, 53, 58, 80; James Philips and, 49, 81; leadership of, 76–77, 84; men blamed for loss of, 259–60; Oxford as lost ideal for, 46–47, 49; pastoral ideal of, 16–18; persecution of, 51, 71, 73–74, 345n8, 353n5; Philips identifying with, 2–3, 24, 48, 51–52, 144, 153–54; Philips seen as placeholder for male, 8–9, 16, 51; Philips speaking for, 21, 353n5; Philips's, 6, 60, 150, 156–57; Philips's contradictory position in, 17, 49, 67, 362n14, 363n17; Philips's disdain for, in battle of Worcester, 67, 83; Philips's qualified support for, 21–22, 36; poets as, 43–44, 46–48, 52, 127–29, 363n18; Puritan iconoclasm and, 136, 150; revolts of, 49, 57, 73, 81; self-image of, 63, 65–66, 105, 159; support for, 71, 73; values of, 60, 61, 85, 154, 159; vs. Cromwell, 61, 159; writers among, 46–47, 338n20, 343n60
Rump Parliament, 48
Russell, Anne, 42

Saintsbury, George, 6, 8, 31, 333n105
Salmon, Mrs., 2, 48, 137, 215
salons, 2–3, 17, 286–87
Sanchez, Melissa, 270, 385n10
Sandys, George, 218
"Sapho to Philaenis" (Donne), 153, 158, 174–75, 177–83
Sappho in Early Modern England (Andreadis), 12–13
Sappho/Sapphism, 247, 307; cultural perceptions of, 185–86; Donne's use of, 11, 37, 158, 174–79; H. D.'s use of, 302–03; Philips and, 184–86; Philips's use of, 180–81, 366n39
Savran, George, 93
Schudery, Madeleine de, 185–86
Schut, Rosalinde, 41
Scotland, 51, 69–71, 76–78
Scott-Baumann, Elizabeth, 25, 27–29, 188–89
Scott-Douglass, Amy, 36–37, 67
Second Book of Ayres and Dialogues (Lawes), 3, 53, 343n57; commendatory verses in, 232–34; Philips's dedicatory verse in, 215, 229–34; Philips's poems as songs in, 235–36
Sedgwick, Eve, 273
seduction, 220–23, 287
self, 250, 254–55
self-fashioning, 56–57, 91, 109
sex, 218, 245, 300, 343n65; as epistemological problem, 246–47; homo- and hetero-, 10–11, 59; in marriage poems, 193–95, 197, 206; in Philips's poetry, 6, 44, 244; Philips's use of imagery of, 262–64; signifying of, 247
sexual identity, 9, 245, 247
Shakespeare, William, 132; eroticism in, 250–51; homoerotics of, 381n25, 382n26; in lyric tradition, 249–50; stolen folios of, 149–50
Sharpe, Kevin, 149
Sheldon, Gilbert, 150–52
Sheppard, Samuel, 79
Shifflett, Andrew, 22, 119, 188, 363n17
Shipman, Thomas, 149
Shuttleton, David E., 149, 359n83
Sidney, Mary. *See* Herbert, Mary Sidney
Sidney, Philip, 52, 75, 216, 319–20, 355n26
"Silvander" (coterie name). *See* Dering, Edward

Skippon, Phillip (stepfather), 142–43
smallpox, 4, 131, 133, 147–49
Smith, Bruce, 291, 292
Smith, Nigel, 155–56, 363n18
Society of Friendship, 2, 17, 246, 254; as covenanted people, 108, 111, 113–14, 123; goals of, 19, 35, 248; membership of, 18, 35. *See also* coterie; royalism/royalists, community of
Solomon, Charles II compared to, 120–21
"Song: Sweetest love" (Donne), 179–80
"Song, to the Tune of *Sommes nous pas trop heureux*," 317
"Songs and Sonnets" (Donne), 188
Souers, Philip Webster, 7–8, 87, 382n30
souls, 227, 280–81, 288, 295–96, 387n38
Southey, Robert, 321
sovereignty, 22
Spenser, Edmund, 192–96, 198, 249–50
Spink, Ian, 236, 239
Spraggon, Julie, 136–37, 139, 151
St. John, Oliver, 137
St. Mary Woolchurch, 138–39
St. Paul's Cathedral, 142
St. Stephen's Coleman, 138–39
Stanley, Liz, 10–11
Stanton, Kamille Stone, 109
Stapylton, Robert, 68
Stiebel, Arlene, 58, 188
"Still Kissing the Rod?" (conference), 267–68, 270
Straznicky, Martha, 131
Stuarts, 137, 192–98
subjectivity, 7, 26, 245–46, 250, 381n24
subjectivity effect, 38, 245, 250, 287–88
"Submission," 134
"The Sun Rising" (Donne), 58
Sununu, Andrea, 34, 394n5
Surpassing the Love of Men (Faderman), 9–10
Sutch, Victor D., 151, 152
Suzuki, Mihoko, 24, 42
Swann, Marjorie, 197
Sylva sylvarum (Bacon), 228

Talbot, George, 314
Taylor, Jeremy, 285, 341n46; on friendships, 14–15, 108, 281–82, 288; Philips and, 3, 14–15, 52; on women's capacity for friendship, 283–84
Taylor, John, 284–85
Temple, Dorothy Osborne, 125–26, 315
Tenger, Zeynep, 33
Theatre of God's Judgments, The (Beard), 122
Theocritus, 292–93
Thomas, Patrick, 17–18, 104, 117, 144, 367n40; Philips's biography and, 4, 87–88; as Philips's editor, 30, 45
Thorn-Drury, George, 323
Tighe, Anne Lovett, 323–24
"To Antenor on a paper of mine wch J. Jones threatens to publish to his prejudice," 168–69, 341n46
"To his Grace Gilbert Lord Arch-Bishop of Canterbury," 126–27
"To Mr. Henry Lawes," 256–57
"To Mr. Henry Vaughan, Silurist, on his Poems," 116–17
"To Mrs. M. A. at Parting," 6, 257
"To Mrs. M. A. upon absence," 45
"To my dear Sister Mrs. C. P. on her nuptialls," 198, 202, 205–07
"To my dearest Antenor on his parting," 162–74, 179–80, 183
"To My excellent Lucasia, on our friendship," 157, 174, 179–84
"To my Lady Ann Boyle's saying that I look'd angrily on her," 285–86
"To my Lady Elizabeth Boyl, Singing—Since affairs of the State &c.," 316
"To My Lord and Lady Dungannon on their Marriage 11. May 1662," 198, 206–11
"To my Lord Biron's tune of—Adieu Phillis," 216
"To my Lucasia," 256, 258
"To my Lucasia, in defense of declared friendship," 228–29, 262–63
"To Regina Collier, on her cruelty to Philaster," 357n55
"To Sir Amorous La Foole," 287
"To the Countess of Thanet, upon her Marriage," 198–99
"To the Honoured Lady E. G.," 134
"To the Lady Mary Butler at her marriage with the Lord Cavendish, Octobr. 1662," 198, 200–01, 204–05
"To the much honoured Mr. Henry Lawes, On his Excellent Compositions in Musick," 215–16, 229
"To (the truly competent judge of Honour) Lucasia, upon a scandalous libel made by J. Jones," 62–63, 341n46
Tonson, Jacob, 4, 322
translations, Philips's, 4, 8, 42, 127
Traub, Valerie, 12–13, 38–39, 155, 189, 391n8; on history of lesbianism, 276–77; review of Bray's *The Friend*, 268, 273; on subjectivity effect,

287–88. *See also The Renaissance of Lesbianism in Early Modern England*
Trinity College folio, 397n27
Trolander, Paul, 33
Tudor, Elizabeth, 314
Tutin, J. R., 313, 321
Tyacke, Nicholas, 151
Tyrrell, James, 127, 146

Ulreich, John, 98–99
union, 27, 158, 277; beyond description, 174–75; in Donne's love poems vs. Philips's, 162–63; female, 37, 183; homoerotic, 175; marriage as, 159–61, 167–70, 174; in Philips's poems, 153–54, 161–62, 169–70, 174; and Philips's fear of disunion, 170–71, 173; privacy of, 162, 174; Sapphic-Platonic, 26, 180; through friendship, 42, 169–70
"Upon a Little Lady under the Discipline of an Excellent Person" (Killigrew), 298–300
"Upon Mr. Abraham Cowley's Retirement," 4, 322
"Upon Mrs. Philips her Poems" (Cowley), 185
"Upon the double murther of K. Charles," 32, 95–99, 122

"A Valediction: Forbidding Mourning" (Donne), 58, 343n61; Philips's poems compared to, 26–28, 179–81; Philips's use of, 153, 365n28
"A Valediction, Forbidding to Mourn" (Walton), 159–62, 166
Vaughan, Henry, 45, 116–17, 338n20; and other royalist writers, 52–53; Philips's verses for, 4, 53–55, 143, 341n47
Vaughan, Thomas, 63, 340n33, 340n40
Virgil, 292–93
virtue, 65, 75–76, 81–85

Wahl, Elizabeth Susan, 8, 12–13, 20, 263
Wales, 72; Philips's identification with, 23–24, 42; Philips's move to, 48, 139–40; royalists in, 49, 73–74
Wall, Wendy, 147
Walton, Izaak, 26–27, 37, 365n28; and Donne, 157, 159–61, 186, 364n21
war, 68, 84
"wedded" brotherhood, 274–75, 277, 280–81
wedding poems. *See* marriage poems
West, William, 177–78
Whitworth, Stephen Wayne, 291
Williams, Claire Byrony, 315, 395n12
Winniatt, Penelope Pindar, 323–24
Wiston Vault, 254
Wither, George, 114, 115
women, 60, 190, 268; equality of, 61–62; men vs., 259–60, 265; music and, 214–15, 220, 234–35; participation of in politics, 25–26, 269; Philips's love for, 45, 251; prophecy by, 91–92; repression of, 26, 49, 286–87; sexuality of, 9, 59; as subject of Philips's iconolatry, 141, 143. *See also* friendship, women's
women writers, 154, 271, 293, 370n15; devaluing of, 5, 343n57; in literary traditions, 155, 188–89; managing reputations, 31, 34; Philips's identity as, 24, 34; same-sex literary erotics of, 12–13. *See also* poets, female
Worcester, battle of, 65, 67–69, 71–72, 81–83, 343n59, 346n28
"The World," 134
Wright, Gillian, 5, 30, 33

York, Duchess of, 4, 355n26
Young, Elizabeth, 292, 390n5

Zwicker, Steven, 149